SOUTH ASIAN POLITICS
AND RELIGION

SOUTH ASIAN

POLITICS

AND RELIGION

EDITED BY

DONALD EUGENE SMITH

———————

PRINCETON, NEW JERSEY

PRINCETON UNIVERSITY PRESS

1966

TO A. WILLIAM LOOS

President

Council on Religion and

International Affairs

PREFACE

WHILE THE interaction of indigenous tradition and imported political institutions provides much of the subject matter for the study of contemporary South Asian politics, the problem of religion and politics has, until very recently, received little attention. When one considers the thousands of volumes which have been written on religion and politics or church-state relations in the West, the relative neglect of this subject in the South Asian context is striking. When one considers the fundamental role of religion or religious communalism in bringing about the present shape of South Asia—the partition of India and the creation of Pakistan—this neglect is all the more striking. Yet from the viewpoint of scholarly analysis, it is clear that South Asia offers unique opportunities for fruitful comparative studies, and that many intriguing subjects remain to be explored.

While in the West we are chiefly concerned with the major branches of Christianity, in South Asia we find a compact geographical region which is the meeting place of three major world religions. The majorities in the three most important South Asian countries, India, Pakistan and Ceylon, profess respectively Hinduism, Islam and Buddhism. The three countries share a common colonial background of British rule. The setting is thus near-perfect for a comparative study of the emerging relationships between religion and politics in these countries since independence.

This volume brings together the work of twenty-two scholars who have addressed themselves to various aspects of religion and politics in India, Pakistan and Ceylon. Indicative of the many facets of the problem is the fact that these scholars represent at least six disciplines: political science, history, anthropology, sociology, comparative law and comparative religion. Part One, "South Asia: Unity and Diversity," presents a comparative analysis of religio-political patterns in the three countries. Part Two, "India: The Politics of Religious Pluralism," emphasizes the rich diversity of Indian religious life and its political consequences, along with several studies concerned solely with Hinduism and politics. Part Three, "Pakistan: The Politics of Islamic Identity," is chiefly concerned with the political, ideological and legal problems which Pakistan has faced in attempting to define and construct an Islamic state in the mid-twentieth century. Part Four, "Ceylon: The Politics of Buddhist Resurgence," emphasizes the dramatic developments by which Buddhism has become deeply involved in the politics of the country.

Preface

The articles selected for inclusion in this book accurately reflect the real problems which are being faced in the three countries. Some significant parallels do exist, and may be seen in the chapters dealing with law, religious reform and communally oriented political parties. However, it would have been not only artificial but a serious distortion to force the material into a neat, preconceived, symmetrical scheme. Five of the chapters on India deal with the politics of religious minorities; the constitutional status of Hinduism is not an issue. The heart of the problem in Pakistan has been the struggle *within* the Muslim majority over the place of Islam in state and society. In Ceylon both the politics of competing religious communities and the politics of internal Buddhist reform have been prominent phenomena.

This book is the result of a three-year research project on religion and politics in South and Southeast Asia. This project, under my direction, was sponsored by the Council on Religion and International Affairs and financed by a grant from the Carnegie Corporation of New York. The Council on Religion and International Affairs is an inter-faith organization interested in stimulating serious discussion of the actual and potential relevance of the major world religions to international politics. The present research project is based on the recognition that a clearer picture of the role of religion in the internal politics of the emergent nations is necessary before coming to grips with the more elusive factors of foreign policy.

My two previous books, *India as a Secular State*, 1963, and *Religion and Politics in Burma*, 1965, were written in connection with this project. The final phase of the project was the organization of a seminar on religion and politics in South Asia. The five-day seminar was held in Colombo, Ceylon, in July 1964, with fifteen participants from India, Pakistan, Ceylon and the United States. This volume is the direct result of the Colombo seminar, although, unfortunately, not all of the authors were able to participate in person.

The contributors to this volume join the editor in expressing deep appreciation to Dr. A. William Loos, president of the Council on Religion and International Affairs, who first conceived the idea of the research project described above. It is most fitting that the book be dedicated to him with our warm regards. Grateful acknowledgment is hereby made to the Carnegie Corporation of New York for the generous research grant which made this project possible.

In a cooperative venture such as this there is of course much work which goes on behind the scenes. Sincere thanks are due to Mrs. Cathi Sabukewicz Caswell who did most of the secretarial work in preparation for the Colombo seminar. I also wish to express appreciation to my sister, Mrs. Ruth S. Reinhard, for her careful work in typing the manuscript for this book.

Chapter 18, by Khalid Bin Sayeed, appeared originally in a slightly different form in *The Middle East Journal*; chapter 20, by Sisir Gupta, was first published in *India Quarterly*. Grateful acknowledgment is hereby made to the publishers of these journals for permission to reprint the articles in this volume.

I wish to express deep appreciation to Professor Richard L. Park of the University of Michigan, who very kindly read most of the manuscript and offered many valuable criticisms and suggestions; many of the latter have found their way into this volume.

University of Pennsylvania   DONALD E. SMITH

CONTENTS

PREFACE   vii

Part I. SOUTH ASIA: UNITY AND DIVERSITY   1

     1. The Political Implications of Asian Religions   3
     DONALD E. SMITH

     2. Emerging Patterns of Religion and Politics   21
     DONALD E. SMITH

Part II. INDIA: THE POLITICS OF RELIGIOUS
PLURALISM   49

     3. Religion and Politics in a U.P. Constituency   51
     HAROLD A. GOULD

     4. The Jana Sangh: A Brief History   74
     CRAIG BAXTER

     5. The Effectiveness of Muslim Representation
in India   102
     THEODORE P. WRIGHT, JR.

     6. Indian Muslims and the Ideology of the
Secular State   138
     ZIYA-UL HASAN FARUQI

     7. Sikh Separatism in the Punjab   150
     BALDEV RAJ NAYAR

     8. Communal Interest Groups in Kerala   176
     V. K. S. NAYAR

     9. Buddhism and Politics in Maharashtra   191
     ELEANOR ZELLIOT

     10. Religion, Politics, and the DMK   213
     ROBERT L. HARDGRAVE, JR.

     11. The Concept of Change in Hindu, Socialist,
and Neo-Gandhian Thought   235
     JOAN V. BONDURANT AND MARGARET W. FISHER

     12. Religious Beliefs and Political Attitudes   249
     JOSEPH W. ELDER

xi

Contents

13. The Religious Aspects of Caste: A Legal View   277
    MARC GALANTER

14. The Reform of Hindu Religious Endowments   311
    J. DUNCAN M. DERRETT

Part III. PAKISTAN: THE POLITICS OF ISLAMIC
IDENTITY   337

15. Ideological Dilemmas in Pakistan's Political
    Culture   339
    WAYNE A. WILCOX

16. Pakistan and the Secular State   352
    FREELAND ABBOTT

17. The Ideology of Mawlana Mawdudi   371
    CHARLES J. ADAMS

18. Islam and National Integration in Pakistan   398
    KHALID BIN SAYEED

19. The Controversy over the Muslim Family Laws   414
    FAZLUR RAHMAN

20. Islam as a Factor in Pakistan's Foreign Policy   428
    SISIR GUPTA

Part IV. CEYLON: THE POLITICS OF BUDDHIST
RESURGENCE   451

21. The Sinhalese Buddhist Revolution   453
    DONALD E. SMITH

22. The Political Monks and Monastic Reform   489
    DONALD E. SMITH

23. Buddhism in Ceylon Politics, 1960-1965   510
    A. JEYARATNAM WILSON

24. Buddhist Reorganization in Ceylon   531
    C. D. S. SIRIWARDANE

INDEX   547

PART I
SOUTH ASIA:
UNITY AND DIVERSITY

CHAPTER 1

THE POLITICAL IMPLICATIONS
OF ASIAN RELIGIONS

DONALD E. SMITH

IN APPROACHING the subject of religion and politics in South Asia we find a situation of unusual complexity, with a richness of phenomena which at once intrigues and embarrasses. Studies of religion and politics in the West are concerned chiefly with the major branches of Christianity; in South Asia we find a compact geographical region which is the meeting place of three major world religions. The majorities in the three most important South Asian countries, India, Pakistan and Ceylon, profess respectively Hinduism, Islam and Buddhism.

One is impressed by the essential unity of South Asia in various important respects. Racially, linguistically, historically and to a considerable extent culturally, the region has a distinctive identity which cannot be readily merged with either Southeast Asia or Western Asia. At the same time there are strikingly different social values, institutions and patterns of behavior rooted in the three great religious traditions.

It is important to recognize that there are indeed *three* traditions. While Buddhism originated as a sectarian movement within Hinduism and accepted certain basic Hindu concepts with little modification, its social and political implications and manifestations have been very different. As we shall see, at several important points the differences between Buddhist Ceylon and Hindu India are fundamental. Hinduism and Islam share certain assumptions about the role of religion in society which find no parallel in Buddhist thought and practice.

This chapter is a brief analysis of the three Asian religions with respect to their major political implications—the concepts and institutions which predispose a society toward a certain pattern of relationships between religion and politics. There are five aspects of religion which are particularly relevant to our inquiry.[1]

First, the view of history taken by a religion, that is, whether human

Donald E. Smith is associate professor of political science at the University of Pennsylvania.
[1] This chapter is a revised form of material originally published in *India as a Secular State*, Princeton University Press, Princeton, 1963, pp. 24-40.

3

history is regarded as real and important, is a vital point. We may assume that a religion which regards history as unreal, or if real, ultimately unimportant, will be less concerned with securing or maintaining temporal power. On the other hand, a religion which regards the proper course of history as crucial, and central to its task in the world, is more likely to rely upon political power in order to influence history.

Second, we must consider the attitude of a religion toward other religious. Traditional attitudes of religious intolerance affect political behavior by reinforcing the tendency to use the political process for the exclusive benefit of one's own religious community.

Third, it will be important to note what capacity a given religion has demonstrated for effective ecclesiastical organization. A highly organized religious institution, like the Roman Catholic Church in the West, is in a position to confront the state and to make demands upon it. In general, the more highly organized the majority religion, the greater the degree of clerical involvement in politics.

Fourth, we must consider the historical traditions of separation or fusion of political and religious functions. Traditional concepts and practices which support the idea of a fusion of the two functions tend to increase a religion's involvement in politics.

Fifth, the extent to which a religion has tended to regulate social life will be a significant factor. All religions prescribe ritual, ceremonies, and festivals which are important to the social life of their peoples, but some go far beyond this to regulate virtually every aspect of society, as in the caste system or Muslim law. The stronger the tendency to regulate society, the greater the area of potential conflict between religious authority and the state.

We shall now proceed to examine the major religions of South Asia in the light of these five points. We shall necessarily have to deal in broad generalizations in attempting to discern the principal implications of each religion for our subject. There are exceptions to practically every generalization which will be made in the following pages. However, they are generalizations in which many scholars concur, and are presented as rough guides for the exploration of this field of inquiry.

HINDUISM: METAPHYSICAL TOLERANCE
AND SOCIAL RIGIDITY

The Hindu View of History

Hinduism provides a theory of cycles or recurring periods of creation and destruction. Each world system makes one complete cycle of creation and destruction, and this process has been repeating itself eternally. The present natural world of human experience was created out of the combination of matter and spirit by means of the action of *maya*, the illusory cosmic energy of Brahma the creator. The universal dissolution and destruction comes about when Brahma vanishes into himself. As S. J. Samartha puts it, "In the classical Hindu view history is not significant because it is swallowed up in the vastness of the cosmic process."[2]

Hindu thought holds that the essential self in man (*atman*, sometimes translated as soul) and the ultimate Reality are one. This doctrine, according to a Hindu writer, "emphasizes the fact that neither the empirical self nor the tangible phenomenal world, with which the empirical self seems to come into contact, possess any reality from the ultimate point of view."[3] Through original ignorance the essential self assumes individuality, and the permanence of the essential self is the basis for rebirth upon death. The law of cause and effect, *karma*, operates in such a way that one's lot in the succeeding life will be the moral consequence of deeds performed in this life. Liberation from the cycle of rebirths is reached by man's attaining complete realization of the nature of the self, namely, identity with the Supreme Being. The highest spiritual goal of the Hindu is escape from the cycle of history.

Hinduism regards human history as definitely a lower level of experience, for the essential self of man is never involved in the affairs of this world of phenomena. How does Hinduism reconcile this metaphysical position with its extremely detailed regulation of individual and social life? Chiefly by its teaching regarding the four ends of man. The expression of man's natural instincts (*kama*), material prosperity (*artha*), and the ethical life (*dharma*), all pertain to the lower, empirical life. Spiritual liberation (*moksha*) pertains to the higher level of reality, man's essential self.

Hinduism's concern with political institutions and the course of human history is thus at most a secondary concern. The ultimate philosophical and religious values of Hinduism do not require a

---

[2] S. J. Samartha, *The Hindu View of History: Classical and Modern*, Christian Institute for the Study of Religion and Society, Bangalore, 1959, p. 7.

[3] R. N. Dandekar, "The Role of Man in Hinduism," *The Religion of the Hindus*, ed. Kenneth W. Morgan, Ronald Press Company, New York, 1953, p. 121. This is not the only Hindu view on the subject. Some modern Hindu philosophers, most notably Dr. S. Radhakrishnan, are consciously reinterpreting the Hindu doctrines of *maya* and *karma* in order to give real meaning to the world and human history. This process of reinterpretation is well summarized in Samartha's pamphlet.

Hindu state, or any particular kind of political structure, for that matter. At this point the contrast with Islam is quite marked.

The Basis of Hindu Tolerance

The remarkable tolerance of Hinduism derives basically from the belief that Ultimate Reality or the Supreme Spirit is without name, form, personality or qualities. The particular name and attributes of any deity are regarded as limitations imposed on the Supreme Spirit by the weakness of man, who hungers for a god of love and mercy. The Vedic seer proclaimed, "Reality is one; sages speak of it in different ways." The doctrine of the chosen deity (*ishta-devata*) invites the worshipper to choose, from among all the gods conceived by man in the past, the one which best satisfies his spiritual longing. While this doctrine was originally applied to the numerous deities mentioned in the Hindu scriptures, there is no logical stopping-place, and the same tolerant attitude is taken toward other religions.

Hinduism thus holds that there are many ways, many paths which lead toward spiritual liberation. Historically it has convincingly demonstrated this belief. In addition to Jains and Buddhists, communities of Jews, Syrian Christians and Zoroastrians settled in India and lived there unmolested. Muslims lived peacefully in India for three hundred years before Islam came as a military force in the eleventh century A.D.

Hinduism, unlike Buddhism and Islam, is not a missionary religion, and the rejection of proselytism on principle is regarded by many Hindus as an important part of tolerance. While Hinduism has been characterized by tolerance in matters of religious faith and practice, Hindu communalism (discussed in the next chapter) has been as narrow and bigoted as any other kind of communalism. Hindu communalist attitudes are partly rooted in traditional social patterns of extreme group exclusiveness (caste) which in turn were sanctioned and supported by Hindu religious beliefs. A factor which may strengthen Hindu communalist tendencies is that Hinduism is an ethnic religion, the faith of one particular people, rather than an international missionary religion. India is the only home of the Hindus. As has been illustrated by Judaism in modern Israel, an ethnic religion may easily become closely identified with nationalism and national culture, to the decided disadvantage of the religious minorities.

Hindu Ecclesiastical Organization

What capacity for organization has Hinduism demonstrated? Has it succeeded in developing effective institutional means by which it can participate effectively in the political process? The answer to these questions is an almost unqualified negative. In the first place, there is no congregational worship in Hinduism such as is found in Christianity and Islam. In Christianity the parish church is a center of organized religious activity, and the basic unit of ecclesiastical organization. The lack of a clearly defined and trained Hindu clergy subject to the discipline of superiors is another point of weakness. The hereditary priesthood of the Brahmin caste long ago ceased to function effectively, and relatively few Brahmins today are priests by actual occupation. The clerical functions in Hinduism are performed by a wide variety of temple priests, pandits, astrologers, *sadhus* (holy men), swamis, *gurus* and so forth.

The Hindu "clergy" is thus not organized for an effective political role, nor do the *sadhus* and temple priests enjoy the general prestige which would make for success in politics. Many people in India, not only among the educated, regard them as ignorant men of questionable morals. They are tolerated but hardly revered. This is in marked contrast to the veneration shown the members of the monastic order in the Theravada Buddhist countries by all levels of society, from prime ministers down.

While members of the monastic order (Sangha) in Burma and Ceylon have made their political influence felt, and so have the Muslim clerical class (*ulama*) in Pakistan, the political expression of Hindu religion has only been through organizations of laymen. The Hindu Mahasabha, Jana Sangh and other communal political parties are the only groups which profess to speak for Hinduism on the Indian political scene.

Hinduism is divided into a vast variety of sects and sub-sects, although most of them could be classified as Vaishnava, Saiva or Sakta groups. A reformist group founded in the nineteenth century, the Arya Samaj, is controlled through a central authority with power to enforce discipline. The Radhaswami sect has a pontiff. The Ramakrishna Mission is organized along the same lines as an efficient religious denomination in the West. Certain Lingayat sub-sects have highly developed ecclesiastical organizations.[4] But most of the sects do not have such well-knit organizations, to say nothing of Hinduism as a whole.

Commenting on this lack of ecclesiastical organization a British scholar wrote: "Hence Hinduism has never prepared a body of canonical Scriptures or a Common Prayer Book; it has never held a General Council or Convention; never defined the relations of the laity and clergy; never regulated the canonization of saints or their

[4] *Mysore Gazetteer*, Government Press, Bangalore, 1927, vol. 1, p. 143.

worship; never established a single center of religious life, like Rome or Canterbury; never prescribed a course of training for its priests."[5] Furthermore, the writer added, Hinduism's failure to develop such institutions cannot be attributed to war, foreign domination, or any other external circumstance, but simply to the fact that "all such action is essentially opposed to its spirit and traditions." But Hinduism's failure at this point might well be a significant factor in certain aspects of India's modernization.

There is, however, a negative consideration also. Hinduism's lack of organization renders it largely incapable of effecting internal reforms, however badly they are needed. The state has thus been pressed into service as the agency of religious reform, and as we shall see, its efforts to legislate reforms of Hindu religious practice have created various problems. The same characteristic which precludes a major political role for Hinduism also encourages state interference in religion.

Religious and Political Functions

A clear-cut distinction was made in ancient Indian polity between the functions of priest and king. The Vedic king discharged no priestly functions; he performed no sacrifices on behalf of the nation, as was done in ancient Egypt and Greece. A conception of the two powers— the temporal and the spiritual—existed from earliest times, and was supported by a divinely ordained social order. The Brahmin embodied the spiritual authority, and he alone could perform the sacrifices and utter the sacred incantations. The Kshatriya caste provided the rulers and the warriors, although in course of time a few non-Kshatriya dynasties were founded. While the Brahmin stood at the top of the caste system, spiritually superior to the Kshatriya, his valid function was the priestly office only; his superior position gave him no direct authority in matters of government.

The Brahmin *purohita* or royal chaplain occupied a prominent place among the king's councillors during the Vedic age. His chief task was to counteract the magic of the enemy through the performance of the necessary rituals. The royal chaplain consecrated and blessed the war elephants and horses of the army before battle. Accompanying the king to the battlefield, he sought to ensure a victorious outcome by his prayers, sacrifices and incantations. The *purohita* also wielded considerable influence in some cases through his role as the king's *guru* or spiritual preceptor.

5 W. Crooke, "Hinduism," *Encyclopedia of Religion and Ethics*, ed. James Hastings, 1925, vol. 6, p. 712.

Donald E. Smith

The struggle between church and state, which occupies such a prominent place in early medieval European history, had a rather pale counterpart in ancient India. In the *Gautama Dharmasutra* (c. 500 B.C.) it is stated that the king's authority cannot touch the priests, since his prosperity depends on their support. Other texts warn that the gods will spurn the king's oblations if he fails to employ a qualified Brahmin priest. By bowing three times before the Brahmin at his coronation, the king accepts his subordinate position, and his success depends on continued recognition of this fact. Bitter curses are pronounced against rulers who confiscate the cows (i.e., wealth) of Brahmins.

As most of the texts were written by priests, only one side of the case was generally presented, and the Brahmin's claims were greatly exaggerated. The *purohita's* influence was greatest during the period when there was widespread faith in the Vedic sacrifices. These fell into disuse around the fourth century B.C., partly under the impact of Upanishadic, Jain and Buddhist thought. The available evidence does not point to a strong theocratic tendency in the polity of ancient India, despite the extreme claims made by the priests in the literature. There is little to suggest that the religious authority ever seriously attempted in practice to usurp the powers of the king.

The Regulation of Hindu Society

In contrast with its total lack of centralized ecclesiastical institutions, Hinduism has demonstrated a powerful capacity for the detailed ordering of social life through caste and Hindu law. Some reformist writers, such as K. M. Panikkar, have argued that Hindu social institutions have resulted from certain historical factors and "are in no way concerned with religion."[6] It is undoubtedly true that many Hindu social practices were non-religious in origin but were absorbed into the religious complex, rationalized by religious theories and enforced by religious sanctions. But the question of origin is of academic significance only. Most scholars would hold that if for a thousand years Hindus have regarded a particular social practice as part of their religion, it *is* a part of their religion.

Panikkar chose to deny recognition to the traditional Hindu understanding of the close relationship between religion and social institutions because his real concern is not with the past but the future. His deliberate attempt to separate the two aspects of Hindu life was intended to strengthen the cause of radical social reform.

[6] K. M. Panikkar, *Hindu Society at Cross Roads*, Asia Publishing House, Bombay, 1955, p. 49.

But the fact remains that many Hindus still accept the scriptural statement that the four original castes proceeded from the parts of the Creator's body, and that birth in a particular caste is governed by the inexorable law of *karma*.

Hinduism has prescribed detailed regulations which have in large measure determined the pattern of society. Caste is not a "system" in any coordinated sense, but is rather the all-pervasive principle on which social life has developed. The social regulations of Hinduism have not emanated from a single central authority (as we have seen, there is no such authority), but they have nonetheless been effective in providing a pattern of social organization.

BUDDHISM: SOCIAL FREEDOM AND
ECCLESIASTICAL POWER

Our brief discussion here will deal with Theravada Buddhism, the principal religion of Ceylon, Burma, Thailand, Cambodia and Laos. Buddhism as practiced in China, Korea and Japan is of the Mahayana school, and differs significantly from the Theravada in several points of doctrine and practice.

Theory of History

The Theravada Buddhist view of history must be examined from both the metaphysical and the practical points of view. As regards metaphysics, the Buddha insisted that all existence is impermanent, substanceless, and suffering. This fact is clear to the man of wisdom, even though others regard the phenomenal world as permanent reality. All existence is in a state of constant flux. All of life is a cycle of rebirths, and upon a man's death his consciousness flows on into another life. The law of *kamma*, cause and effect, operates inexorably to ensure that his rebirth will be the moral consequence of actions in the past life. The doctrine of *kamma* thus gives a moral significance to history, but the whole process perpetuates man's bondage. Freedom from the bondage of this cycle of birth, death and rebirth comes only by insight into the impermanent and substanceless nature of existence. This insight has the effect of uprooting attachment or desire. Being freed from desire and passion, one's actions no longer accumulate the potentiality of *kamma* which perpetuates the cycle of rebirth.

As in the case of Hinduism, the metaphysics of Buddhism seems to assert that the course of human history is not ultimately significant, based as it is on impermanent and substanceless existence. There is no particular goal toward which history is moving, and the most important thing that the individual can do is to extricate himself from history.

The Buddhist's practical view of history, however, contrasts markedly with that of the Hindu. Although history may ultimately be unreal, it is not without importance. Unlike Hinduism, Buddhism has a founder, a historical figure. It is important to the Buddhist that the Buddha lived in the sixth century B.C., that he is more than a shadowy mythological figure like Rama. Theravada countries use a calendar based on the Buddhist Era, beginning with the death of the Buddha (544 B.C.).

The Sangha, the monastic order founded by the Buddha, has maintained a historical continuity down through twenty-five centuries. This historical awareness is well expressed in the words of a Buddhist scholar: "If there had not been the Sangha, the Dhamma (doctrine) would have been a mere legend and tradition after the demise of the Buddha—it is the Sangha which has preserved not only the word of the Master, but also the unique spirit of the Noble Teaching since the Master's passing away."[7] Six Great Councils have been convened throughout the history of Buddhism, the first shortly after the Buddha's death and the sixth in 1954-1956 in Rangoon.

Buddhism came into existence at a time when India had a highly organized society. Primarily a new individualistic doctrine of salvation, early Buddhism had no political or social philosophy. Under the Buddhist emperor Ashoka, however, the whole context was transformed. As the "established church" of a vast empire, Buddhism suddenly acquired a definite stake in worldly concerns such as politics. All of this seems to indicate that, metaphysics notwithstanding, Theravada Buddhism is capable of developing an impressive concern for the course of human history.

Attitude toward Other Faiths

What degree of tolerance has Buddhism demonstrated throughout its long history? The attitude toward other religions is largely determined by the limited claims which the Buddhist makes for his own faith. Theravada Buddhism rejects the idea of revelation—it does not claim "to present through any form of divine revelation the whole truth of the absolute beginning and end of mankind's spiritual pilgrimage."[8] The Buddha himself *searched* and *discovered* the nature

---

[7] Maha Thera U Thittila, "The Fundamental Principles of Theravada Buddhism," *The Path of the Buddha*, ed. Kenneth W. Morgan, Ronald Press Company, New York, 1956, p. 75. For an excellent discussion of the theoretical basis of Buddhist historical consciousness, see B. G. Gokhale, "The Theravada Buddhist View of History," *Journal of the American Oriental Society*, 1965, vol. 85, no. 3.

[8] U Thittila, p. 71.

of the universe, and invited others to engage in this search for truth by rational inquiry. The searcher is instructed not to believe anything on the basis of tradition or authority, even the authority of the Master himself. He is invited to doubt the teaching until he is convinced of its truth through his own reflection and experience. This experimental approach to religious and philosophical truth has predisposed the Buddhist to assume an attitude of broad tolerance toward those who seek the truth by other paths.

While Buddhism is non-dogmatic and not based on any revelation of absolute truth, its adherents have nevertheless been extremely conscious of the uniqueness of their message. Buddhism has been a missionary religion ever since the Buddha sent out his followers to spread the Dhamma, a universal teaching which would bring enlightenment to all men. Buddhism differs significantly from Hinduism in this conviction that there is after all one known path to perfect enlightenment, and that the Buddha has discovered it. Within the Buddhist monastic order there has been a strong emphasis on the preservation of doctrinal purity, and rulers have from time to time intervened in order to suppress heretical elements in the Sangha, sometimes resorting to violent means. Buddhism is not as tolerant as Hinduism with the latter's constant emphasis on many ways, many paths.

Buddhism, nevertheless, has demonstrated a great practical tolerance of other faiths. From India it gradually spread over most of Southeast Asia and the Far East, but conversions took place only by persuasion. There is no record that force was ever used to obtain converts to Buddhism.[9] Furthermore, a liberal attitude was evidenced by the inclusion of many Hindu gods and goddesses in Buddhist ceremonies in the Theravada countries. In the Mahayana countries many indigenous deities have been accorded a place of honor within the system. Tolerance in Buddhism is not based on Hinduism's essential relativism as to the means of attaining salvation, but the path of the Buddha has never led to rigid exclusivism.

Buddhist Ecclesiastical Organization

The Sangha, or order of monks, is the institution founded by the Buddha to propagate the teaching. In most of the Theravada countries of the present day the Sangha is divided into two or three sects, but sectarian differences are very slight, reflecting historical origins and minor variations in practices. The Buddha promulgated detailed

[9] Hajime Nakamura, "Unity and Diversity in Buddhism," *The Path of the Buddha*, ed. Kenneth W. Morgan, p. 367.

rules governing life in the Sangha—the internal government of the order, admission to the order, ordination, the duties of the monks, etc. A senior monk is selected by the members of each monastery to head their organization and attend to the details of monastic life.

In pre-colonial Burma, the king appointed one of the senior abbots as a kind of archbishop of the Sangha, and he was assisted by district "bishops." "This system did not constitute a genuine ecclesiastical hierarchy, however, for the clergy over whom it presided was an aggregation of individual ascetics rather than an organized church community."[10] While the corporate life of the Sangha in modern Theravada countries is most impressive, the ecclesiastical organization is not one based on a hierarchy of authority by which decisions made at the top could be immediately passed down a chain of command. In some cases, however, the personality and informal spiritual authority of the leading elders of the Sangha is sufficient to achieve the same ends.

The most highly centralized organization of the Sangha is found in Thailand. There are two sects in Thailand, the Maha Nikaya (Great Sect) and the Dhammayuttika Nikaya (Sect of the followers of the Dhamma). Approximately 200,000 monks and novices belong to the former and 4,000 to the latter sect. The highest Buddhist dignitary of the kingdom is the Sangharaja (Ruler of the Sangha, or Supreme Patriarch) who is chosen by the heads of the two sects, approved by the ministry of education, and appointed by the king. The Sangharaja appoints a ten-man Council of Ecclesiastical Ministers headed by the Sangha Nayaka (corresponding to a cabinet and a prime minister). Under the Sangha Nayaka there are four boards, the board of ecclesiastical administration, the board of education, the board of propaganda, and the board of public works.

It might be thought a weakness that the basic unit of Buddhism's ecclesiastical organization is a monastic institution. However, the Buddhist *vihara* has traditionally been a center of social life, especially in the villages. It is not the secluded and inaccessible dwelling usually suggested by the word monastery in the West. Furthermore, in all of the Theravada countries except Ceylon, laymen frequently spend some time in the monasteries receiving instruction in the teaching, and then return to their secular occupations.

[10] John F. Cady, *A History of Modern Burma*, Cornell University Press, Ithaca, N.Y., 1958, p. 54. For a discussion of Sangha organization in Thailand, see Luang Suryabongse, "Buddhism in Thailand," *2500 Buddha Jayanti Souvenir*, ed. Ananda W. P. Guruge and K. G. Amaradasa, The Buddhist Council of Ceylon, Ministry of Local Government and Cultural Affairs, Colombo, 1956, p. 64. See also Prince Dhaninivat, Kromamun Bidyalabh, *A History of Buddhism in Siam*, The Asia Foundation, Bangkok, 1960, p. 40.

Political Implications

The Sangha, then, not only commands the reverence of the laity but is organized in such a way that it can effectively mobilize public opinion. If the leadership should desire a political role for the Sangha, there is no doubt of its ability to fulfil it, despite the Vinaya rules of monastic discipline which forbid a monk's involvement in mundane political affairs. The political potential of the Sangha in Ceylon and Burma has already been impressively demonstrated.[11] The Sangha can readily become a vigorous pressure group demanding for Buddhism the place traditionally accorded it by the state. Organizations of Buddhist laymen can also play an important role. The All-Ceylon Buddhist Congress, for example, with the support of prominent leaders of the Sangha, has had considerable influence in promoting the role of Buddhism in national life and in urging the government to do the same.

Religious and Political Functions

There has been relatively little fusion of religious and political functions in Theravada Buddhism, although the separation is not as clear-cut as in Hinduism where priest and king belonged to different castes. In a few cases, members of the royal families in Burma and Thailand gave up the yellow robe after many years in the Sangha in order to ascend the throne. While the same person could be monk and king, the two roles could never be accepted simultaneously. The renunciation of the world required of the monk was incompatible with the temporal wealth and power of kingship.

Certain political functions, however, were sometimes performed by monks. Leading members of the Sangha were occasionally sent on diplomatic missions by the king. Burmese monks were sent to Ceylon in the twelfth century to restore friendly relations between the two countries. In the thirteenth century a celebrated Burmese monk was sent to south China to sue for peace and offer humble submission to the invading Mongol armies. In 1826 King Bagyidaw even sent a monk to meet the invading British in the vain hope that they could be persuaded to withdraw.

In some ways the Sangha constituted a check on the king's absolute power in the traditional Buddhist state. Popular attitudes of reverence and veneration for the Sangha contrasted sharply with the universal

[11] See chapter 22, "The Political Monks and Monastic Reform," for a discussion of political monks in Ceylon. Buddhist monks played an important role in the 1960 election campaign in Burma, giving powerful support to U Nu who had promised to make Buddhism the state religion. See Donald E. Smith, *Religion and Politics in Burma*, Princeton, Princeton University Press, 1965. In Thailand the Sangha hierarchy is heavily dependent on government support, and government regulations have effectively kept the monks out of politics.

fear of government. The approval of the Sangha was therefore of some importance to the king in gaining a measure of popular support for his regime. Monks frequently served as advisers in the royal court. In Ceylon there were a few cases in which monks actually selected and supported princes for the throne contrary to the laws of succession, and in the tenth century the claim was even advanced that the Sangha *conferred* kingship.

Buddhism and Society

Our last consideration is the extent to which Theravada Buddhism has tended to regulate the general social life of its adherents. At this point an interesting comparison can be drawn between Hinduism and Buddhism. In Hinduism there has been very little over-all ecclesiastical organization, but extremely detailed regulation of ordinary social life through the caste system and Hindu law. In Buddhism the reverse is true—ecclesiastical organization is relatively well developed, as we have seen, but the regulation of ordinary social life is minimal. In this respect the Theravada Buddhist countries may bear some resemblance to modern western countries, where religion is highly organized institutionally but has relatively little connection with the pattern of social life.

Buddhism originated partly as a protest against the institution of caste, and has continued to pride itself on the absence of caste in the Theravada countries with the exception of Ceylon. There is no Buddhist law comparable to Hindu or Islamic law. The moral code to be followed by the Buddhist layman is a relatively simple one, centering in the Five Precepts—refraining from killing, stealing, unlawful sexual indulgence, wrong speech, and drinking liquor. As regards the prescription of ritual, "Indian Buddhism did not establish a system of ceremonies for family life comparable to those in Hinduism, nor have such ceremonies grown up in Theravada or Mahayana Buddhism."[12] Marriage ceremonies are performed by the elder men of the family, and are not regarded as religious ceremonies. Funerals and the tonsure ceremony performed upon male children, however, are religious ceremonies conducted by the monks.

ISLAM: DECISIVENESS OF HISTORY
AND ALL-PERVASIVE LAW

Islam's Approach to History

Professor Wilfred Cantwell Smith, in comparing the theories of history held by representatives of various faiths, arranges them in the following graded series: "the Hindu, for whom ultimately history

[12] Nakamura, p. 398.

is not significant; the Christian, for whom it is significant but not decisive; the Muslim, for whom it is decisive but not final; the Marxist, for whom it is all in all."[13] Hindu philosophy, as we have seen, relegates history to a lower metaphysical level, and ultimately regards it as unreal or at least not significant. Christianity regards itself as rooted in history, and as having as part of its mission the redemption of society as well as of individuals. But Christianity's consciousness of the failures and sinfulness of all human institutions prevents it from becoming totally absorbed in the present scene, and it looks beyond history for final redemption.

Islam cannot go as far as Marxism, for the Muslim (like the Christian) looks ultimately to God, and his endeavor to redeem history is derived from his faith in One beyond history. But it would be difficult to exaggerate the intensity with which Islam approaches its mission of establishing on earth a divinely revealed social order. Among the profoundest convictions held by the world of Islam are "that there is inherent in the structure of this world and its development a proper course, a right social shape; that the meaning of history lies in the degree to which these become actualized; and finally that they who understand the essential laws for these, and accept the responsibility involved, are entrusted with the task of executing that actualization, of guiding history to its inevitable and resplendent fulfillment."[14] In these vital respects, Islam approaches history with almost the total commitment of Marxism.

Attitude toward Other Faiths

Islam is a religion of revelation in the broad tradition of Judaism and Christianity. The Islamic teaching, in the words of H. A. R. Gibb, is that "in Muhammad the series of Apostles reached its culmination and that the Qur'an revealed through him is the final and unchangeable revelation of the Divine Will, abrogating all previous records of revelation."[15] The exclusivist claims of Islam have thus largely determined its attitude toward other faiths. These claims have made Islam an aggressively missionary religion.

The Qur'an deals with the question of religious toleration rather unevenly, with statements ranging from expressions of broad tolerance to extreme fanaticism. In one text (5:73), Jews, Christians and Sabians are included as inheritors of Paradise along with Muslims, provided

[13] Wilfred Cantwell Smith, *Islam in Modern History*, Princeton University Press, Princeton, 1957, p. 21.
[14] *Ibid.*, p. 26.
[15] H. A. R. Gibb, *Mohammedanism: An Historical Survey*, New American Library, New York, 1955, p. 12.

they believe in Allah and the last judgment and do good works.[16] In other passages they are classified together with pagans, and friendship with them is forbidden. In still other texts, Muslims are instructed to fight relentlessly against all other communities until they accept Islam or pay tribute. The system which was ultimately adopted was to tolerate the above three communities as "people of the book" (believers in a revealed scripture), but to disarm them and make them tributary. Strictly speaking, the very existence of other communities was forbidden.

The contacts of the West with Islam, from the time of the Crusades, have unfortunately resulted in the stereotype of the Muslim as bigoted and fanatical. There is much evidence to the contrary. Nevertheless, as we think of Islam in relation to our subject, we cannot avoid the conclusion that its general attitude toward other religions will continue to be a factor strengthening religious communalism in the politics of South Asia. The same is true of several Christian churches in the West, and goes far toward explaining the resistance to the separation of religion and politics in a number of countries despite the tremendous impact of secularizing forces.

Organization; Religious and Political Functions

When Muhammad and his followers moved to Medina in A.D. 622 he established an autonomous society, and it soon became clear that Islam was far more than a body of private religious beliefs. The Islamic community had most of the characteristics of a state, with its own system of government, laws, and institutions. This autonomous community was central in the very concept of Islam—its institutions were not mere appendages. Furthermore, it was a unitary society in which ecclesiastical and political functions merged together—in which, indeed, there was no significant distinction between religious and secular. "Muhammad ruled over his people as a divinely inspired and guided prophet. He led the public prayers; he acted as judge; he controlled the army."[17]

Upon his death a "successor" (*khalifah*, caliph) was chosen, who exercised similar authority. Successive caliphs delegated many of their powers to the *vizier* (prime minister), *diwans* (heads of administrative departments), the *imam* (leader of public prayers), and the corps of judges (*kadis*). But the power and prestige of the caliphate declined rapidly, and within the first century after Muhammad there was a

16 D. S. Margoliouth, "Muhammad," *Encyclopedia of Religion and Ethics*, ed. James Hastings, 1925, vol. 8, p. 877.

17 Duncan B. MacDonald, "Islamic Institutions," *Encyclopaedia Britannica*, 1956, vol. 12, p. 712.

growing cleavage between the religious and secular institutions of the Muslim community. The doctors of the Islamic law (*ulama*) refused to concede any spiritual authority to the caliphs. With the expansion of Islam and the inclusion of independent rulers within the faith, the state diverged more and more from the classical pattern. The Mongol invasions of the thirteenth century put an end to the historic caliphate of Baghdad. The Ottoman Empire later revived the institution (although in an unorthodox manner), and it continued until the Turkish Republic finally abolished the caliphate in 1924.

The *ulama* are in no sense priests; strictly speaking, Islam has no clergy, as any Muslim may lead a congregation in prayer. Nevertheless, the *ulama* early took on the characteristics of a clerical class, and "acquired precisely the same kind of social and religious authority and prestige as the clergy in the Christian communities."[18] The *ulama* continue to function in present-day Islam as legal and theological interpreters of the Qur'an and Tradition. However the *ulama* are in general poorly organized, and frequently disagree among themselves.

As we come to evaluate the organizational effectiveness of Islam, the evidence is mixed. In the past, tremendous concern for the organization of the community produced the caliphate of the classical period, which was truly theocratic in intent. The final elimination of this institution left the *ulama* as the sole authoritative spokesmen for Islam, unorganized as they were and are. One writer commented: "The complete absence of Muslim religious organization has (to non-Muslim observers) always appeared to be the missing backbone for all Muslim activity."[19] Islam has yet to develop institutions which can function in a coordinated way within a modern society.

The argument which has been advanced in these pages is that the lack of effective ecclesiastical organization is generally favorable to the separation of religion and politics. It seems clear, as one looks at the contemporary scene, that the religion of Islam, if it were well organized, could be a much more significant political force in Pakistan, Malaysia or Indonesia than it actually is. It is arguable, however, that had Islam, in the course of its history, developed a hierarchical ecclesiastical structure, the possibility of separation of religion and politics along western lines might have been enhanced.[20]

[18] Gibb, p. 77.

[19] C. A. O. Van Nieuwenhuijze, "Religious Freedom in Indonesia," *International Review of Missions*, 1951, vol. 40, p. 97.

[20] As Professor Joachim Wach pointed out: "Conflicts analogous to those between church and state in medieval Christianity could not arise in Islam because there never was anything like a distinct ecclesiastical body, to say nothing of a hierarchical constitution." Joachim Wach, *Sociology of Religion*, Kegan Paul,

THE POLITICAL IMPLICATIONS OF ASIAN RELIGIONS

	HINDUISM	BUDDHISM	ISLAM
1. *Theory of history.* Great concern with the course of history tends to increase a religion's involvement in politics.	History is metaphysically at a lower level of reality, and is ultimately not significant.	Metaphysically, similar to Hinduism. In practice, history is taken more seriously.	History is decisive. A certain pattern of life must be established on earth.
2. *Attitude toward other religions.* Attitudes of intolerance reinforce the tendency to use the political process for communal advantage.	Extremely tolerant philosophically, but pattern of group exclusiveness socially.	Missionary religion; generally tolerant philosophically and socially.	Theologically intolerant, and often so in practice.
3. *Capacity for ecclesiastical organization.* The more highly organized a religion, the greater its involvement in politics.	Practically no ecclesiastical organization.	Relatively well organized monastic order, the Sangha, but its connection with the laity is tenuous.	*Ulama* (doctors of the law) not effectively organized, but can be mobilized.
4. *Political and religious functions.* Tradition of fusion of these two functions tends to increase a religion's involvement in politics.	Two functions performed by separate castes.	Principle of renunciation of world—monks cannot rule.	Tradition of Muhammad and caliphs—fusion of temporal and spiritual authority.
5. *Tendency to regulate society.* The stronger this tendency, the greater the area of conflict between religious authority and the state.	Caste system, Hindu law.	No attempt to regulate society.	Islamic law—detailed regulation of society.

Regulation of Muslim Society

The minute regulation of ordinary social life has been accomplished by the Islamic law (*shari'ah*). This law is a total system of duties which fails to distinguish what modern jurisprudence would classify as religious, ethical and legal considerations. It includes all branches of civil and criminal law. The *shari'ah* was developed on the bases of the Qur'an, tradition, analogy and consensus.

As Islam spread beyond the Arabian Peninsula, it had to come to terms with the customary law of the new countries, which sometimes differed from the *shari'ah* in important respects. In modern times, statute law emanating from the sovereign introduced a further complication, so that two systems of courts have developed in almost every Muslim country, the one administering the *shari'ah* in private, religious and family affairs, and the other administering statute law. Despite these limitations, the *shari'ah* continues to exercise an extremely influential role in regulating the daily life of the Muslim.

* * *

This discussion of the political implications of Hinduism, Buddhism and Islam is summarized in the accompanying chart. It is clear that these three great religious traditions are very different in vital respects. In the following chapter we shall examine the patterns of their interaction with the politics of three South Asian countries.

Trench, Trubner and Company, Ltd., London, 1947, p. 310. It was *partly* the very conflicts between church and state in the West which led to the solution of separation.

CHAPTER 2

EMERGING PATTERNS OF RELIGION AND POLITICS

DONALD E. SMITH

AN ANALYSIS of the relationships between religion and politics in the West over the past one hundred years would have to take into account phenomena of great diversity and complexity. One large part of this subject would deal with church-state relations, the ways in which these two institutions have interacted. The various legal and constitutional relationships between church and state, and the changing boundaries of their respective jurisdictions, would have to be considered. In the past, conflicts have erupted over such issues as the church's claim to ultimate superiority over the temporal power, the state's attempts to control ecclesiastical affairs, and the demands of each that marriage law, education and other vital matters be recognized as within its exclusive jurisdiction. The structure of Roman Catholicism includes a state as well as a church, and the Vatican maintains normal diplomatic relations with a large number of other states.

But a consideration of church-state relations would not exhaust the subject. Religious loyalties would have to be examined as a factor in political behavior, especially in elections and the legislative process. Even churches which are not hierarchically structured have evolved means to translate their spiritual authority and social prestige into political influence. Church-oriented political parties and church-related pressure groups functioning in pluralist societies seek to protect their interests and to maximize the influence of their views.

Another important aspect would be the interaction of Christian social doctrine and modern ideologies: liberalism, democracy, socialism, communism and fascism. During this period the Roman Catholic Church has moved from a position of hostility toward liberalism and democracy to a policy of accommodation and then active support, partly in response to the threat of totalitarian communism. Various Christian socialist movements and new theological interpretations such as the social gospel have sought to make religion relevant to modern industrial society. These points serve merely to illustrate the many different kinds of relationships between religion and politics in the recent history of the West.

Turning now to South Asia, we are confronted by a compact

Donald E. Smith is associate professor of political science at the University of Pennsylvania.

geographical region which is the meeting place of three major world religions. In India the religion of the majority is Hinduism; in Pakistan it is Islam; in Ceylon it is Buddhism. From a comparative point of view it is important to remember that the three countries share a similar colonial background—all three were part of the British empire. British policies with respect to religion in undivided India and in Ceylon were not identical, but they did follow the same general lines. In terms of the basic policies inherited from British rule, then, the three new independent states shared a common legacy.

Religio-political developments in the three countries since independence have revealed similar patterns in some important respects and marked differences in others. We shall first examine four generalizations concerning religion and politics which appear to be valid for all three countries.

RELIGIOUS COMMUNALISM IN POLITICS

Religious pluralism is a basic characteristic not only of South Asia as a whole but of each of these three countries. In India the minorities include the Muslims, Christians, Sikhs, Buddhists and others. In Pakistan there are sizable numbers of Hindus, Christians and Buddhists. In Ceylon the largest minorities are the Hindus, Christians and Muslims.

What is the nature of these communities and how are they related to religion? First, religion provides each group with a focal point of identity and social solidarity, and large areas of its culture are intimately associated with religion. A member of the Muslim community may be an atheist, but the social institutions, personal laws, customs, traditions, history, art and literature which have helped to mold his individual and social existence have been closely related to Islam. Secondly, religious symbols represent group interests and group self-esteem. In undivided India hundreds of communal riots erupted over the killing of a cow by a Muslim or the passing of a noisy Hindu procession in front of a mosque. In 1963-1964 a chain reaction of very serious Hindu-Muslim riots in India and Pakistan followed the theft from a Muslim shrine in Kashmir of a hair revered as a relic of the Prophet Muhammad. Religious symbols continue to be emotionally powerful in unifying the group in the face of real or imagined threats from other groups, and are frequently used to disguise conflicts based on economic interests. The Sinhalese Buddhist who declares that Buddhism must be restored to its rightful place in Ceylon is saying, in part, that his community must enjoy unrivaled dominance in the fields of education and government service.

Donald E. Smith

As used in South Asia the term communalism means the tendency of the socio-religious group to attempt to maximize its economic, social and political strength at the expense of other groups. Powerful group loyalties in a pluralist society, functioning in the context of an economy of scarcity, lead almost inevitably to inter-group rivalry and conflict. In this respect, conflicts in which language or caste defines the group identity have many of the same manifestations as communalism based on religious differences. We are here concerned, however, only with the latter phenomenon.

Religious communalism is related to politics in several basic ways: (1) the legal recognition of communities as political units, (2) communal loyalties in political behavior, (3) communal political parties and pressure groups, and (4) the political problems of preventing or controlling communal violence. India, Pakistan and Ceylon have all faced problems involving these political manifestations of religious communalism.

To some extent communal tensions and conflicts have been a feature of social life in South Asia for hundreds of years. Under the old order there was, however, a basic pattern of peaceful coexistence among the various castes and communities, based on differing economic functions and segregated residential localities. The imposition of western political and administrative institutions on these societies provided new scope for the expression of communalism.

The new English-educated middle class which emerged was composed of members of all communities, although for various reasons these were not represented proportionately. In the competition for jobs and power, the small English-educated segment of each community (which socially had never been detached from it) sought and found support for its cause in the solidarity of the larger group. Appointments to government jobs could directly affect only a tiny minority of the members of each community, but the competition increasingly became a question of communal interest and prestige. Religion provided the different communities with their distinctive socio-cultural identities, but the substantive interests at stake frequently had little or nothing to do with religion as such.

The introduction of a system of elections to legislative bodies intensified the communal problem, despite the fact that the electorates were at first very small. Separate electorates for the Muslims were introduced in India in 1909 at the insistence of this minority that its interests could be adequately safeguarded only by this constitutional device which recognized a religious community as a separate political unit. This principle was extended to other communities in 1919 and 1935. Separate electorates, intended to protect the minorities from communal discrimination in elections, nourished the very spirit of separatism which lies at the heart of communalism. The system rigidified communal divisions in the political sphere precisely at a time when the processes of modernization in general were reducing their relevancy.

A related phase of the development of communalism in India was the organization of communal political parties, chiefly the Muslim League and the Hindu Mahasabha. These parties claimed to stand for the defense of the interests of their respective communities. The ideology of the Hindu Mahasabha was first expounded by V. D. Savarkar in the 1920's. According to his Hindu Rashtra theory, the Hindus were not a community but a nation; India's political advance could only proceed on the principle of Hindu nationality and Hindu nationalism. In 1940 the Muslim League accepted M. A. Jinnah's two-nation theory as its ideological basis; the Muslims and the Hindus were separate nations, and this theory provided the rationale for the demand for partition.

Since the attainment of independence in 1947 the government of India has made serious efforts to curb religious communalism in politics. In some areas these efforts have partially succeeded; in others they have failed conspicuously. In the Constituent Assembly the decision was made to abandon the separate electorates and reservation of seats in legislatures for the religious minorities. Leaders of the Muslim and Christian minorities took the lead in this decision, convinced that it would contribute to the evolution of a strong sense of common Indian citizenship unrelated to religion.[1] One of the important problems discussed in this book is the practical operation of the system of joint electorates. How many members of the minority communities get elected, and how effectively do they communicate the grievances of their communities and get action taken on them? This problem is considered with reference to the largest minority, the Muslims.[2]

The Indian government, the ruling Congress Party and the late Prime Minister Nehru have done much to establish the foundations of a secular state. Official and party policies have generally been sound. Other developments, however, have encouraged the growth of communalism in politics. Universal adult suffrage and regular elections have placed power in the hands of the illiterate masses who are still

[1] Donald E. Smith, *India as a Secular State*, Princeton University Press, Princeton, 1963, pp. 407-410.
[2] See chapter 5, "The Effectiveness of Muslim Representation."

highly susceptible to appeals to communal and caste loyalties. Considerations of caste and community are seldom absent in the selection of candidates, the formation of cabinets, and other aspects of the political process.

The great complexity of communal politics is the dominant theme of the section on India in this book. This section is titled "India: The Politics of Religious Pluralism," and emphasizes the regional and religious diversity in which the problem must be understood. In Faizabad constituency in Uttar Pradesh the problem revolves around long-standing Hindu-Muslim tensions, and the efforts of various politicians to exploit or neutralize these antipathies at the polls.[3] In the Punjab a Sikh communal political party, the Akali Dal, has led a vigorous movement for the creation of a Punjabi-speaking state in which the Sikhs would constitute the majority. This separatism is partly motivated by the fear that Sikh socio-religious distinctives will be absorbed in the sea of Hinduism unless Sikhism achieves its own concrete political identity.[4]

In Kerala the Christians constitute a sizable minority (22 per cent), and because of their long-standing leadership in the fields of education, business and the press have been able to exert considerable political influence.[5] In Maharashtra the Buddhists are a dynamic growing community (now over 7 per cent of the population) which has made a political impact through the Republican Party. With strong social solidarity and deliverable votes, the Buddhists already hold the balance of power in some constituencies.[6]

Communal political parties of the minorities include the Akali Dal in the Punjab and the Muslim League which has considerable strength in Kerala. A vigorous new Hindu-oriented party, the Jana Sangh, was founded in 1951 and quickly replaced the Hindu Mahasabha as the chief spokesman for Hindu interests in Indian politics.[7] While the Jana Sangh does not identify itself openly as a Hindu party and has accepted Muslims and Christians as members, organizationally it has been heavily dependent on a close link with the Rashtriya Swayamsevak Sangh (RSS), a group completely committed to the communalist Hindu Rashtra ideology. With the 1962 elections the Jana Sangh emerged as the largest opposition party in the legislative assemblies of Uttar Pradesh and Madhya Pradesh.

[3] See chapter 3, "Religion and Politics in a U.P. Constituency."
[4] See chapter 7, "Sikh Separatism in the Punjab."
[5] See chapter 8, "Communal Interest Groups in Kerala."
[6] See chapter 9, "Buddhism and Politics in Maharashtra."
[7] See chapter 4, "The Jana Sangh: A Brief History."

In Pakistan the political role of the minorities has been quite small. Virtually all of the Hindus and Sikhs in West Pakistan migrated to India at the time of partition; in East Pakistan, however, the Hindu minority is substantial, about 10,000,000. Pakistan was created in order to establish a state in which the Muslims would be in complete control. The basis for Pakistan was an ideology which identified socio-religious community with nationality—Jinnah's two-nation theory. Nevertheless, on the eve of partition Jinnah espoused the liberal view that Pakistan was to be one nation, that "in the course of time Hindus would cease to be Hindus and Muslims would cease to be Muslims, not in the religious sense, because that is the personal faith of each individual, but in the political sense as citizens of the state."[8]

The question of joint or separate electorates has been a matter of bitter controversy in Pakistan. In undivided India the Muslim League regarded separate electorates as the only adequate safeguard for the protection of the minorities. After the creation of Pakistan, with the Hindus now the minority, the Muslim League continued to insist on separate electorates. The Hindu leaders of the Pakistan National Congress continued to oppose separate electorates just as the Congress had done in undivided India. One Hindu leader argued: "We should, therefore, demand joint electorates without even as much as reservation of seats. It may be that for a long time Hindus may be out of the legislatures, out of the local self-government bodies, such as municipalities and local boards. But in the long run things will adjust themselves, and political parties will be formed on political issues, and as political consciousness grows, more and more progressive political and social values will prevail."[9]

The Muslim League feared that joint electorates would put the Hindus of East Pakistan in a position in which they could throw their weight behind opposition Muslim candidates and thus decide elections. The orthodox *ulama* rejected any arrangement which would merge the *kafir* (infidel) with the faithful in a common citizenship.[10] Joint electorates presupposed a theory of territorial nationalism which ignored Islam. The electoral law enacted in 1952 created separate electorates for Muslims, Caste Hindus, Scheduled Castes, Christians and Buddhists. The 1956 Constitution revealed the inability of the second Constituent Assembly to agree on the question, and simply

[8] Constituent Assembly of Pakistan, *Debates*, vol. 1, p. 20, August 11, 1947.

[9] Quoted in Keith Callard, *Pakistan: A Political Study*, Macmillan Company, New York, 1957, p. 241.

[10] *Report of the Court of Inquiry to Inquire into the Punjab Disturbances of 1953*, Superintendent of Government Printing, Lahore, 1954, pp. 212-214. See chapter 17, "The Ideology of Mawlana Mawdudi."

gave the National Assembly the power to determine whether joint or separate electorates should be adopted. The National Assembly, after consulting the provincial assemblies, adopted joint electorates for East Pakistan and separate electorates for West Pakistan. Six months later, in April 1957, the National Assembly voted to establish joint electorates in both wings of the country, and the issue continued to be hotly debated.

The Constitution was abrogated by the 1958 coup. The Constitution Commission in its 1961 report asserted that many of the caste Hindus had families in West Bengal and were under the influence of India. "In these circumstances, their demand for joint electorate seems clearly to be for some ulterior purpose other than the welfare of Pakistan." The commission concluded that "their demand was due to a desire to influence the elections against the ideology of Pakistan" and "until we can be reasonably certain that they have reconciled themselves to the continuance of Pakistan, it does not appear safe to have joint electorate. . . ."[11] Separate electorates were thus recommended for the protection of the majority. The 1962 Constitution promulgated by General Ayub Khan, however, provided for joint electorates. In the first elections under the new Constitution there were no non-Muslims elected to the National Assembly.

Joint electorates alone, without political parties committed to a relatively secular program and open to non-Muslims, obviously could not go far in promoting non-communal politics. Apart from the secular but predominantly Hindu Pakistan National Congress and the left-wing Ganatantri Dal, H. S. Suhrawardy's Awami League opened its membership to non-Muslims in 1955. The Muslim League was committed to the two-nation theory and excluded non-Muslims, and other parties found the emphasis on Islam a political necessity regardless of the personal inclinations of their leaders. The National Assembly elected under the new Constitution enacted the Political Parties Act of 1962 which appears to constitute a major obstacle to the development of secular parties. Clause 3 (1) states: "No political party shall be formed with the object of propagating any opinion, or acting in a manner, prejudicial to the Islamic ideology, or the integrity or security of Pakistan."

Hindu-Muslim communal violence has constituted a major law-and-order problem for both India and Pakistan, and has greatly complicated relations between the two states. In 1963-1964 large-scale communal riots occurred in both countries and minority migrations

[11] *Report of the Constitution Commission, 1961*, Government of Pakistan Press, Karachi, 1962, p. 76.

took place: Hindus and Christians from East Pakistan into India; Muslims from Assam, Tripura and West Bengal into East Pakistan. Both governments charged that the minorities were being pushed out with the connivance of local officials of the other government. The kind and extent of official involvement in communal upheavals is very difficult to determine objectively. However, census returns do indicate the broad picture of the respective minorities. According to the 1961 census figures of the two countries, over the decade the Hindu population of Pakistan remained about the same while the Muslim population of India rose 25 per cent.

In Ceylon, one of the dominant features of political life since independence has been the progressive communalization of politics.[12] While Ceylon had universal suffrage as early as 1931, for a generation politics was dominated by a westernized elite which found it unnecessary to resort to appeals to language, religion and culture, the factors which determined the masses' primary identity. In 1948 the Sinhalese Buddhist majority found itself in a markedly disadvantageous position in relation to the Tamils and the Christians in education, government services and the professions. S. W. R. D. Bandaranaike and his Sri Lanka Freedom Party (SLFP) came to power by appealing to the majority's strong sense of grievance.[13]

The most serious controversies in which religious (as distinguished from linguistic) communal identities have been uppermost have involved the Buddhists and the Roman Catholics. The Christians in Ceylon constitute 9 per cent of the population (7 per cent Roman Catholic, 2 per cent Protestant), the largest Christian community in proportion to total population in South Asia. Only in Ceylon did the Christians attain a powerful entrenched position in government services and the professions. Many members of the highly Anglicized elite were and are Christians, and most of the Buddhists who found their way into this class were educated in Christian institutions and considerably influenced by the high prestige of Christianity. Much of the Christians' success was attributable to their management of a large number of the Island's best educational institutions, which were heavily subsidized by government grants. Sinhalese Buddhist leaders asserted that the British government had favored the Christians as a matter of deliberate policy. In the Sinhalese Buddhist resurgence, most marked since 1956, the nationalization of aided schools became an important objective. This was achieved in 1960-1961.

12 This theme is elaborated in detail in W. Howard Wriggins, *Ceylon: Dilemmas of a New Nation*, Princeton University Press, Princeton, 1960.

13 See chapter 21, "The Sinhalese Buddhist Revolution," and chapter 23, "Buddhism in Ceylon Politics, 1960-1965."

Donald E. Smith

In Ceylon there have been strenuous efforts made to secure a system of quotas for the different communities in university admissions, scholarships and civil service appointments. In its 1962 report the National Education Commission held that the Buddhists had been systematically discriminated against in these areas. The report concluded: "With regard to the discrimination to which the majority of our people have been subjected under colonial rule and thereafter, we must understand that they have gone through this bitter experience simply because they have stuck to the religion which binds them to their native soil. Therefore, we recommend that the principle of quotas for Ceylon should be according to religion and not according to race."[14] The quotas recommended by the commission were: Buddhists—74 per cent, Hindus—10 per cent, Muslims—7 per cent, Catholics—7 per cent, and other Christians—2 per cent.

ECCLESIASTICAL ORGANIZATION AND GOVERNMENT

In the countries of South Asia, relations between government and the religious leadership tend to be informal, unstructured and sporadic. There is nothing comparable to the western phenomenon of sustained relations between state and church because the organizational cohesiveness and institutional continuity of religion in South Asia is so limited. Because Hinduism, Buddhism and Islam do not have highly organized ecclesiastical institutions, they are precluded from certain kinds of political involvement. Hinduism has the least organization and Buddhism the most; the differences between the two on this point are indeed very important. But even in the latter case the organizational development has not proceeded very far. The Sangha, or monastic order, is divided into several sects, with no supreme patriarch, and there is very little disciplinary authority which can be imposed on the individual monk outside of his own monastery.

An important point made later in this chapter is that religious functionaries in Ceylon and Pakistan have at times been quite powerful politically. But their power has not been based on a formal organization which has integrated the various elements of the religion. Thus, the monk Buddharakkhita built his own political organization, the United Monks Front, which could wage an effective election campaign and function as a powerful pressure group. Within the formal structure of the Ceylonese Sangha, however, Buddharakkhita was the presiding monk of a well-known temple and nothing more. The temple

[14] *Final Report of the National Education Commission, 1961*, sessional paper 17 of 1962, Government Press, Colombo, p. 153.

29

belongs to the Siam sect, and Buddharakkhita in theory acknowledged the spiritual authority of the Mahanayake, the head of his chapter of the sect residing in Kandy. The Mahanayake, in fact, had nothing to do with Buddharakkhita's rise to power.

The *ulama* (those learned in Islamic law) in Pakistan have on occasion been a significant political force. But their influence has been based on their general social prestige and membership in voluntary organizations such as the Jami'at-al-Ulama-i-Islam. Islam as such has no over-all organizational structure which the *ulama* could use in dealing with the government. The western phenomenon of sustained power struggles between church and state, each armed with its own weapons, has no real counterpart in South Asia. Religion in this region lacks the organizational means necessary to confront the state with a protracted challenge.[15]

In the traditional Hindu, Buddhist and Muslim societies of South Asia the relationship between religion and political authority was generally one of interdependence. Religious functionaries were expected to advise, support and help the king, and legitimate his temporal power through religious rites in the royal court. It was the duty of the king to promote religion—to build places of worship, to contribute to the maintenance of the clerical class, to use his power to enforce religious regulations relating to doctrine, ritual, or social observances. Since the disintegration of the traditional pattern under the impact of foreign rule, no internal organizational substitute has been found for the religious role of the king.

GOVERNMENT AND RELIGIOUS REFORM

In all three countries the state has assumed, or has had thrust upon it, the role of religious reformer. In this discussion, no value judgment of my own is implied by the use of the word "reform." We are here simply recording the fact that in India, Pakistan and Ceylon there is a considerable body of opinion which asserts that religion is in need of reform, either to restore it to its ancient purity or to make it compatible with modern values of rationality, equality, democracy, etc.

In marked contrast to the British colonial policy of religious neutrality, in pursuance of which the government declined to interfere with any religious practices except those of an extremely anti-social nature (e.g. *sati*, or widow-burning), the governments of the independent states are urgently required by public opinion to do something

[15] This problem is explored from a Buddhist point of view in chapter 24, "Buddhist Reorganization in Ceylon."

30

positive by way of religious reform. This is clearly the case in India and Ceylon; in Pakistan the initiative has come from a military government which sees Islam in its present state as an obstacle to the modernization of the country.

In the absence of effective ecclesiastical organizations, Hinduism, Buddhism and Islam cannot reform themselves. This necessary reformation can only be brought about by the state. Since the personnel of the governments concerned are now adherents of these respective faiths, there is no longer any reason for the state to decline this role.

It is ironic that India, the only country of the three which has committed itself to the ideal of a secular state, has engaged in the most extensive governmental intervention in religious matters in the interest of reform. Governmental intervention in religion in India has been both more far-reaching and more successful than in the other two countries. Of the three major faiths, Hinduism undoubtedly was most sorely in need of reform. Legislative measures have dealt with the social evils connected with caste, the codification and drastic alteration of Hindu personal law, various practices associated with temple worship such as animal sacrifices and temple prostitution, and the financial administration of Hindu temples.[16] The Hindu Religious Endowments Commission in its 1962 report made recommendations regarding such matters as: state legislation to regulate temple administration, the use of offerings made to temple deities, the establishment of institutes for the training of temple priests, the qualifications and scales of pay of these functionaries, and the appointment by temple authorities of religious teachers to deliver discourses to the Hindu public.[17]

In Ceylon, the Buddha Sasana Commission was appointed by the government in 1957 to deal with a wide range of problems concerning the internal discipline of the Sangha, the management of temple lands, and any other matter deemed necessary "for the purpose of according Buddhism its rightful place in Ceylon." In its report submitted in 1959 the commission recommended the creation of a Buddha Sasana Council, a Buddhist legislative body consisting of two chambers, one the chamber of the Sangha and the other composed of both clergy and laity. A second recommendation was the creation of a system of ecclesiastical courts to deal with cases in which monks were involved. Third, the commission proposed the creation of a new government department under a Commissioner of Temple Lands, which would take from the monks the management of such properties. Fourth, it was

[16] Smith, pp. 216-262. See chapter 14, "The Reform of Hindu Religious Endowments."

[17] *Report of the Hindu Religious Endowments Commission*, Ministry of Law, New Delhi, 1962, pp. 74, 172-174, 178.

recommended that each monk be required to carry an identification card, that restrictions be imposed on the appointment of monks to salaried positions and their participation in party politics.[18]

Opposition from some sections of the Sangha has thus far prevented any significant implementation of these recommendations. The government of Ceylon's failure is now clear, despite the long tradition of vigorous intervention by the Sinhalese kings to restore the doctrinal purity, orthodox ordination, discipline and hierarchical authority of the Sangha.[19] It is unfortunate that the Sangha today has sufficient prestige and political power to frustrate governmental attempts to reform it, but inadequate organization and leadership to reform itself.

In Pakistan, the government's efforts to reform religion were somewhat differently motivated. The reinterpretation of Islam was perceived as a vital national problem on which hinged the possibility of significant social, economic and educational progress. In an address to the *ulama* in 1959 General Ayub Khan spoke with considerable frankness. Ayub declared that Islam was originally a dynamic and progressive movement, but with the passage of time became dogmabound and static. "Gradually those who looked forward to progress and advancement came to be regarded as disbelievers and those who looked backward were considered devout Muslims. Every fresh advancement, every invention and every new educational system was suspected as a movement against Islam and that is why *fatwahs* were pronounced against the leaders of revolutionary movements among Muslims in almost every period of history. I invite you to examine objectively the sermons which are delivered these days at Friday prayers, and you will find that the majority of these sermons are critical of even the minor innovations of modern life merely because they are novel. This I consider a great disservice to Islam, that such a noble religion should be represented as inimical to progress."[20]

The Central Institute of Islamic Research was founded by the government of Pakistan in 1960. The government explained that the purpose of the institute was, first, "to define Islam in terms of its fundamentals in a rational and liberal manner and to emphasize, among others, the basic Islamic ideals of universal brotherhood, tolerance and social justice," and second, "to interpret the teachings of Islam

---

[18] *Buddha Sasana Commission Report*, sessional paper 18, Colombo, 1959, pp. 276-287.

[19] See chapter 22, "The Political Monks and Monastic Reform."

[20] Mohammad Ayub Khan, *Life and Religion*, Department of Advertising, Films and Publications, Government of Pakistan, Karachi, 1959, p. 3. This was a speech delivered at Darul Uloom Islamiya on May 3, 1959.

in such a way as to bring out its dynamic character in the context of the intellectual and scientific progress of the modern world."[21] The Institute has sought to establish the Islamic validity of the Muslim Family Laws Ordinance, the practice of birth control, the paying of interest in modern banking, and other practices condemned by traditionalist *ulama*. The institute has frequently come under attack by these same *ulama* because of its attempts to "modernize Islam."

While the Central Institute of Islamic Research was using the resources of scholarship to reinterpret Islam, the Bureau of National Reconstruction set up by Ayub Khan attempted a small program of indoctrination. Three-day seminars were held for the *ulama*, and two-month training seminars for *imams* (those in charge of mosques). Model *khutbas* (Friday sermons) were also prepared in Urdu and Bengali for the use of the *imams*.[22] In 1963, however, the Bureau of National Reconstruction went out of existence, and there was no other agency to perform these particular functions.

RELIGION AND IDEOLOGY

The dominant political ideologies of South Asia, nationalism, democracy and socialism, have been readily reconciled with the major religions, Hinduism, Buddhism and Islam. On the whole Marxism has been held to be incompatible with the religions of South Asia, although serious efforts have been made in Ceylon to demonstrate its compatibility with Buddhism.

Almost any highly elaborated system of thought, whether a political ideology or a set of religious doctrines, will have some assumptions or ideas in common with other systems of thought. A basic compatibility between two systems is established, consciously or unconsciously, by emphasizing these common assumptions or ideas and minimizing differences. In the absence of a recognized authority with power to set rigid limits to doctrinal compatibility, such as exists in the Roman Catholic Church, the process of mutual accommodation by reinterpretation can ordinarily go quite far.

In South Asia the imported western notions of nationalism, democracy and socialism have been accepted and assimilated by Hindus, Buddhists and Muslims with relatively little sense of conflict with the essential tenets of their religious faiths. While the western impact produced considerable secularization, the new interpretations

---

[21] *The Central Institute of Islamic Research*, published by the Institute, Karachi, n.d. (1963), p. 3.
[22] *Report of the Activities of the Bureau of National Reconstruction*, East Pakistan Government Press, Dacca, 1962, pp. 2-5, 36-37.

of Asian religion have sought to demonstrate that there was no need to abandon one's ancestral faith because it was quite compatible with modern values and ideologies.

One might think that Hinduism, to which the institution of caste is so closely linked, would be impossible to reconcile with democracy and socialism. Yet Dr. S. Radhakrishnan and others could point to the Hindu emphasis on individualism and freedom in the search for truth as an important value undergirding democracy. He found support for the idea of equality in the metaphysical assertion of Vedanta of the ultimate unity of all beings in the Absolute. If all individual souls are part of the same ultimate Reality, all are equal.[23] Hinduism, therefore, teaches equality, and caste has nothing to do with religion.

Gandhian thought gave rise to the remarkable Sarvodaya movement led by Vinoba Bhave, a kind of Hindu socialism aiming at a radical transformation of society by non-coercive means. Sarvodaya is the ideal social order, a casteless and classless society with equal opportunity for all; it is also a stateless society. Unlike the Marxists, however, the leaders of the Sarvodaya movement seek the withering away of the state by declining to use the machinery of state power to attain their immediate goals.[24]

The reinterpretation of Islam in the light of western values was seen most clearly in the writings of the Indian Muslim Amir Ali at the end of the nineteenth century. In his *Spirit of Islam* he sought to show that science, rationalism, liberalism and democracy were not only compatible with Islam but were clearly contained in the fundamental teachings of the Prophet.[25] The Islamic emphasis on equality was held to be a powerful assertion of democratic principle, and Islamic history was ransacked to discover democratic checks on the power of the caliphs. Such highly romanticized notions of Islam continue to be very much a part of the thinking of the present-day Pakistani intellectual.

In the encounter with modern socialism Muslim writers pointed to various aspects of Islam which rejected capitalist principles. The institution of *zakat* was an annual tax levied by the state on the wealthy and used to aid the needy. Islam prohibited the taking of interest on loans, thus preventing some of the evils associated with

[23] S. Radhakrishnan, *Religion and Society*, George Allen and Unwin Ltd., London, 1947, p. 42.

[24] See Chapter 11, "The Concept of Change in Hindu, Socialist and Neo-Gandhian Thought."

[25] Wilfred Cantwell Smith, *Modern Islam in India*, Minerva Book Shop, Lahore, 1947, pp. 49-54.

capitalism. The social order based on the teachings of the Prophet was described by some as Islamic socialism.[26] Muhammad Iqbal, the ideological founder of Pakistan, drew heavily on the Marxist analysis of the social evils of capitalism, and called for the nationalization of the means of production. Iqbal's socialism, however, was firmly rooted in the moral imperatives of theistic Islam.[27]

The reconciliation of Islam with Pakistani nationalism at first represented a difficult doctrinal problem. Islam was an international brotherhood, and required a loyalty far transcending territorial boundaries. For this reason many of the orthodox *ulama* during the period 1940-1947 rejected the partition proposal sponsored by the Muslim League politicians.[28] After the creation of Pakistan, however, many of the *ulama* held that Islam was inextricably tied up with Pakistani nationalism and indeed provided the only rationale for the existence of the new state.

Buddhism was found to contain elements which strongly supported democracy, including its rejection of authoritarianism, its emphasis on peaceful compromise (the Middle Way), and the ancient democratic procedures prescribed for Sangha assemblies. According to one Ceylonese writer: ". . . the Buddha himself was a staunch democrat. The Buddhist assemblies were fully democratic and had elaborate rules of procedure, election and debate. Scholars, among them British historians, have discovered in these assemblies of 2,500 years ago rudiments of the modern parliamentary system of government. An elected assembly, an embryo speaker, a chief whip, the moving of a resolution, use of ballot voting . . . strict adherence to the rules of a meeting and so forth are among the institutions that existed then."[29]

Socialism is not alien to the spirit of Buddhism, for the Sangha, the model Buddhist society, is one in which private property is non-existent. In this classless community every member is equal and all property is communally owned. The affinity of Buddhism to socialism extends even to Marxism. "Communism, in its orthodox theoretical form, is thus not at all inconsistent with the Communism of the original Sangha. . . . There are many Buddhists who are convinced that there is much more in common between Buddhism and Communism than between Buddhism and capitalism. The Buddhists,

---

[26] *Ibid.*, pp. 100-107.
[27] Khalifa Abdul Hakim, *Islam and Communism*, Institute of Islamic Culture, Lahore, 1962, pp. 111-130.
[28] Ziya-ul-Hasan Faruqi, *The Deoband School and the Demand for Pakistan*, Asia Publishing House, London, 1963, pp. 84-89, 124-126.
[29] D. C. Vijayavardhana, *The Revolt in the Temple*, Sinha Publications, Colombo, 1953, p. 595.

therefore, should avoid an indiscriminate condemnation of Communism, which would compel many, especially of the younger generation, to feel that they must choose between Buddhism and Communism."[30] Only in Ceylon have significant attempts been made to reconcile religion with Marxism; these efforts were intensified in June 1964 with the inclusion of three Marxist ministers in a government committed to the promotion of Buddhism.[31]

In the interaction of religion and political ideologies in South Asia briefly surveyed above, the new interpreters of religion have generally assumed the basic validity of the imported western ideas. In the process of reconciliation, the most important adjustments have been made in the Asian religions, not the western ideologies. In appealing to mass electorates, however, the politicians have had to start from the other end. Assuming the validity of traditional values, the effort has been made to secure the legitimation of political ideologies by associating them with religion.

* * *

The discussion thus far has dealt with four broad generalizations concerning the emerging patterns of religion and politics in South Asia. We have noted the prevalence of religious communalism in politics, the unstructured and sporadic relations between government and the religious leadership, the deep involvement of government in religious reform, and the serious efforts made to establish the compatibility of religion and modern poltical ideologies. These phenomena are important and common to India, Pakistan and Ceylon. We must now proceed to examine the patterns of diversity—the relationships between religion and politics which are found in only one or two of the three countries. There are five important points to be made here.

CASTE AND POLITICS

In independent India the religious aspects of caste have had significant political consequences; this is not true of either Ceylon or Pakistan. It is necessary to distinguish between the religious and social aspects of caste; only the former are relevant to this discussion of religion and politics. It is now recognized that caste is an important factor in political behavior in almost all parts of India. In the selection of candidates, bargaining over caste bloc votes, covert appeals to caste loyalties in elections, and factionalism within political parties,

[30] *Ibid.*, p. 597.
[31] See chapter 23, "Buddhism in Ceylon Politics, 1960-1965."

the factor of caste has frequently been prominent. Jayaprakash Narayan declared in 1960 that under the present system of elections, "caste has become the strongest party in India."[32]

For the most part, however, the castes which are involved in manipulating, or being manipulated in, the political process can be satisfactorily viewed simply as ascriptive social groups competing among themselves for economic and political advantages. For the most part, the religious aspect of caste is negligible.[33] This is also true of Ceylon, where caste is socially *and politically* important among Sinhalese Buddhists, but almost totally unrelated to religion.[34]

In India one sector of the broad problem of the role of caste in politics concerns explicitly religious aspects of caste, caste as an integral part of Hindu religion. In two political movements analyzed in this volume the revolt of lower caste groups entailed the complete rejection of Hinduism. In the Dravidian movement in Madras the attack on "Brahmin domination" involved the repudiation of all religious doctrines associated with the traditional priestly caste. E. V. Ramaswamy Naicker condemned all "superstitious beliefs" based on religion. "Just as more lies are needed to substantiate a falsehood, a horde of falsehoods like soul, heaven, hell, rebirth, fate, destiny have been coined to sustain the false philosophy of Hinduism."[35] The materialism and atheism of the movement have been moderated in recent years under the DMK in an effort to broaden its appeal in what is still a religious society. The political importance of the DMK can be gauged by the 1962 elections in which it won 50 out of 206 seats in the state legislative assembly.

The late B. R. Ambedkar rejected Gandhi's attempts to improve the status of untouchables within the framework of Hinduism. Ambedkar insisted that caste was a part of Hindu religion. "To ask people to give up caste is to ask them to go contrary to their fundamental religious notions."[36] In 1956 he led his followers in a mass conversion

[32] *Deccan Herald*, October 31, 1960. For a good summary of recent studies which emphasize this social aspect of caste in the political process see C. von Fürer-Haimendorf, "Caste and Politics in South Asia," in C. H. Philips, ed., *Politics and Society in India*, George Allen and Unwin Ltd., London, 1963.

[33] See chapter 13, "The Religious Aspects of Caste: A Legal View," in which Professor Galanter distinguishes three views of caste—sacral, sectarian and associational. See R. Kothari and R. Maru, "Caste and Secularism in India," *Journal of Asian Studies*, vol. 25, November 1965, for evidence that politics secularizes caste.

[34] See Michael M. Ames, "Magical-Animism and Buddhism: A Structural Analysis of the Sinhalese Religious System," *Journal of Asian Studies*, vol. 23, June 1964.

[35] Quoted in chapter 10, "Religion, Politics, and the DMK."

[36] B. R. Ambedkar, *Annihilation of Caste*, Bharat Bhushan Publishing Press, Bombay, 1937, p. 39.

to Buddhism, and shortly thereafter the Republican Party was formed and became the political vehicle of the Buddhists of Maharashtra. According to Eleanor Zelliot: "The figure of Dr. Ambedkar and what he stands for identifies the nature of both the Buddhist movement and the Republican Party: a push upward, independent of caste Hindu groups, toward modern, democratic and often material values, a movement that rejects traditional Hinduism but clings tightly to its Indian-ness."[37]

RELIGIOUS FUNCTIONARIES IN POLITICS

Religious functionaries, both individuals and organized groups, have assumed a significant political role in Pakistan and Ceylon; there is nothing comparable to this pattern in India.

Why is clerical participation in politics a negligible factor in India? Partly because in modern times there occurred a complete breakdown of the traditional system by which the Hindu priesthood functioned. The Brahmin caste still enjoys a great deal of social prestige and influence in most parts of India, but most members of the caste are not priests and in fact the traditional priestly functions of many Brahmin families were abandoned some generations ago.

The "clergy" in Hinduism is composed of a wide variety of religious functionaries including temple priests, *gurus* (personal spiritual preceptors), family priests, astrologers and *sadhus* (holy men). As emphasized earlier, there is no ecclesiastical organization which draws these diverse elements together. The Hindu Religious Endowments Commission reported in 1962 that most of the temple priests are either illiterate or semi-literate, that they do not know the meaning of the Sanskrit verses they intone in the ritual, and that they frequently extort money from the worshippers. A large number of ascetic holy men, *sadhus* or *sannyasis*, presumably engaged in the quest for spiritual liberation, wander from place to place living on alms. The Hindu clerical groups do not command much popular esteem, and are so unorganized that they would not be able to translate it into political influence if they did.

There is an interesting exception which proves the rule. In the 1962 elections a constituency in the Punjab elected to Parliament an accredited holy man, Swami Rameshwaranand, a member of the Jana Sangh. Swamiji took his seat in Parliament in the full apparel and insignia of the *sannyasi*, and follows the practice of intoning a Sanskrit hymn before making each speech.[38]

[37] See chapter 9, "Buddhism and Politics in Maharashtra."
[38] *The Hindu Weekly Review*, April 6, 1964.

Donald E. Smith

The Buddhist monastic order, the Sangha, was in origin closely related to the Hindu ascetic orders of *sannyasis*. In their present forms, however, the differences are striking. The Buddhist monk is not only respected but venerated, and devout laymen of the highest rank in society and government will kneel down in obeisance before him. The monastery is the basic unit of organization, and in some monasteries there are several hundred monks and novices living together as a well-ordered community. Clearly, the basic ingredients for political effectiveness are present in the Sangha.

One of the most remarkable Sinhalese political monks in recent times was the Reverend Mapitigama Buddharakkhita.[39] Buddharakkhita's involvement in politics began with a dispute over succession to the office of presiding monk of the famous Kelaniya temple near Colombo. The member of Parliament for Kelaniya, a prominent United National Party figure, supported his rival. After prolonged litigation Buddharakkhita won his case. Then, secure in his incumbency, he began to build his own political machine, and ultimately got the MP defeated.

Buddharakkhita came into national prominence in 1956 through an organization of Buddhist monks for political action, the Eksath Bhikkhu Peramuna (United Monks Front). There were over seventy-five regional monks' associations affiliated with the United Monks Front, all pledged to campaign vigorously to help elect the coalition headed by S. W. R. D. Bandaranaike's Sri Lanka Freedom Party (SLFP). The monks campaigned from door to door, addressed meetings and published campaign literature. Bandaranaike won an overwhelming victory, and with the new cabinet paid reverent homage at the Kelaniya temple.

The United Monks Front did not disband after the elections, but now applied pressure on Bandaranaike's cabinet to pay its political debts in terms of appointments and favorable policies. Buddharakkhita and another monk were also members of the SLFP central executive committee. On several occasions it was reported in the daily press that Buddharakkhita had outwitted and outmaneuvered Bandaranaike himself in the inner councils of the party. When the government failed to award a contract to a shipping company which Buddharakkhita, his brother and some friends had formed, the breach between the two men was complete. On September 25, 1959, the prime minister was assassinated by a monk, and Buddharakkhita was later

[39] See chapter 22, "The Political Monks and Monastic Reform."

convicted as one of the arch-conspirators. He is now serving a sentence of life imprisonment.

In Pakistan the political involvement of the *ulama*, those learned in Islamic law and theology, has been substantial. Although anyone can become an *alim* (singular of *ulama*) through the private study of Arabic, the Qur'an and Islamic jurisprudence, most of the *ulama* are the products of *madrassahs*, traditional schools devoted to the teaching of these subjects. These institutions are numerous in the eastern wing of the country and have proliferated at a remarkable rate since 1947. This educational system thus produces a large number of religious leaders without adequate opportunities for employment, but with high social prestige and considerable potential political influence. Much of the pressure for an Islamic state in Pakistan has as its source the yearnings of the *ulama* for a return to the kind of state and society in which their institution had a more prominent place. Tensions and conflicts between this traditional elite and the westernized politicians, civil servants and soldiers have been a frequent feature of Pakistani political life.

The *ulama* have functioned in politics at different levels and by various means. Mawlana Shabbir Ahmad Usmani was the leading *alim* of Pakistan during the first years after the creation of the state. He had played an important role in winning over many *ulama* to the Pakistan movement in 1945-1947, and had direct access to both M. A. Jinnah and Liaquat Ali Khan. There is no religious or social stigma attached to an *alim's* direct participation in party politics, and Mawlana Usmani was a Muslim League member of the Constituent Assembly. He was also president of the Jami'at-al-Ulama-i-Islam, an association of *ulama* formed in 1945 as an ally of the Muslim League. Another *ulama* group, the Jami'at-al-Ulama-i-Pakistan, was founded in 1948, and both groups have functioned as pressure groups. While the *ulama* have on occasion become involved in mass agitations, they have generally preferred to influence government by lobbying behind the scenes.[40]

The *ulama's* greatest impact came in the politics of constitution-making. It was the westernized politicians who had first raised slogans about the Islamic state, but the *ulama* pointed to their detailed knowledge of the sources of Islam and proceeded to define the Islamic state in their own terms. The Constituent Assembly set up a Board of Ta'limat-i-Islamia to advise it on all Islamic aspects of the consti-

[40] Leonard Binder, *Religion and Politics in Pakistan*, University of California Press, Berkeley, 1961, pp. 27-28, 30-31, 138.

tution. The first chairman of the board was Mawlana Usmani, and other prominent *ulama* were associated with it.

The board's views were very influential with the Basic Principles Committee, which in its 1952 report recommended: "No legislature should enact any law which is repugnant to the Holy Qur'an and the Sunnah." To determine the question of repugnancy, a permanent board of "not more than five persons well versed in Islamic laws"— *ulama*—would be appointed by the head of state. A bill could be re-passed by the legislature, however, over the *ulama's* finding of re-pugnancy.[41] The proposal for a board of *ulama* was later dropped, and the 1956 Constitution left the question of repugnancy up to the legislature itself. But the episode clearly revealed the actual and potential political significance of the *ulama*.

RELIGION AND LAW

In India and Pakistan legislation has produced far-reaching changes in personal laws based on religion. The state has thus expanded its jurisdiction at the expense of traditional Hinduism and Islam, over the vehement protests of the conservatives. In Ceylon this problem is non-existent, since there is no Buddhist law concerning marriage, divorce, inheritance, adoption, etc.

In independent India Hindu law has been codified and radically amended by legislative action. The Hindu Marriage Act of 1955, for example, confirmed the validity of all forms of inter-caste marriage (this had been established by special legislation in 1949). Before 1949, marriages between persons of different *varnas* (the four original castes) were strictly forbidden under Hindu law. The Hindu Marriage Act of 1955 made polygamy illegal despite the traditional religious sanctions which supported it. The act also made provision for divorce, which was completely foreign to Hindu law. Leaders of the conserva-tive Hindu parties in Parliament argued that marriage is one of the ten *sanskaras* or sacraments, necessary for the regeneration of men of the three highest *varnas*, and the only sacrament for women and Sudras. The leader of the Hindu Mahasabha made a fervent appeal to the Parliament: "Manu himself says that Vedic marriage is a *sanskara*. That is a solemn injunction. It is an inviolable union, an indissoluble union; it is an interminable union; it is an eternal fellow-ship. . . . In all humility . . . I appeal to all sections of the House, don't tamper with the Hindu sacramental marriage and introduce divorce into it."[42] The appeal was ignored.

[41] *Report of the Basic Principles Committee*, Government of Pakistan Press, Karachi, 1952, p. 4.
[42] *Lok Sabha Debates*, 1955, part 2, vol. 4, col. 6855.

Equally revolutionary changes were introduced by the Hindu Adoptions and Maintenance Act (e.g., the adoption of daughters as well as sons) and the Hindu Succession Act (e.g., the rights of a daughter as a simultaneous heir along with the son, widow, etc.). While all of these provisions were opposed by the orthodox as contrary to basic spiritual concepts underlying Hindu law, one decade later it is quite clear that the radical changes have been accepted. The forces of religious conservatism in Indian politics were no match for the Congress under Nehru's leadership, and while these forces are now stronger, it is most unlikely that their challenge to secularism and modernization will come at the point of law. The Indian government's objective of a uniform civil code which would apply to all citizens irrespective of religion will probably remain unrealized for a long time to come, primarily because of the objections of the Muslim minority.[43] But the steps already taken toward the secularization of law are unlikely to be reversed.

In Pakistan the problem has been considerably more difficult for successive governments to deal with.[44] In 1955 the government appointed a seven-member Commission on Marriage and Family Laws. Indicative of the government's modernist assumptions regarding Islamic law was the fact that the membership of the commission included three women and only one representative of the *ulama*, Mawlana Ihtisham-ul-Haq. In its report the commission rejected the traditional role of the *ulama* in the interpretation of law on the ground that Islam "recognizes no priests." "Some may be more learned in Muslim law than others, but that does not constitute them as a separate class; they are not vested with any special authority and enjoy no special privileges."[45]

The commission asserted that Islam is a progressive religion: "We have to go back to the original spirit of the Qur'an and the Sunnah and lay special emphasis on those trends in basic Islam that are conducive to healthy adaptations to our present circumstances."[46] The report recommended a number of far-reaching liberal reforms in Muslim family law, most of which were ultimately incorporated in the ordinance of 1961 discussed below. In a lengthy dissent the Mawlana bitterly condemned the effrontery of those who, ignorant of Arabic and Islamic jurisprudence, dared to propose western innovations in the name of Islam. "In Islam the provisions of the Holy

[43] See chapter 6, "Indian Muslims and the Ideology of the Secular State."
[44] See chapter 19, "The Controversy over the Muslim Family Laws."
[45] *Report of the Commission on Marriage and Family Laws, The Gazette of Pakistan, Extraordinary*, June 20, 1956, p. 1202.
[46] *Ibid.*, p. 1204.

Qur'an and the Sunnah, be they in the form of basic principles or individual laws, are authoritative and final for all occasions and for all epochs between the time of revelation and doomsday."[47]

Against a background of general political instability and the intense opposition of the *ulama*, successive civilian governments were unable to implement the report. It was only after the military coup of 1958 that decisive action was possible. In 1961 General Ayub Khan promulgated the Muslim Family Laws Ordinance.[48] One important provision is an elaborate procedure by which a man wishing to marry a second wife must first secure the approval of an Arbitration Council. Thus while polygamy (permitted by the Qur'an, to the extent of four wives) is not prohibited, it is definitely restricted and discouraged by the operation of the new law. Another major innovation was the regulation of the right of divorce, which was formerly exercised unilaterally by the man simply by repeating "I divorce thee" three times. Under the ordinance the formula must be repeated in three instalments, and the divorce must be approved by the Arbitration Council. The woman's right to divorce under certain circumstances is also recognized.

The problem of religion and law in Pakistan is of a very fundamental nature, and goes far beyond questions of marriage, divorce and inheritance. The most conservative *ulama*, living in their static universe, hold that the Islamic law found in the Qur'an and Sunnah is a perfect and complete code governing the whole range of human activity; legislation in the modern sense has no place in Islam, for the only valid function belongs to the jurist who must discover and apply the relevant rule.[49] This concept of law clearly challenges the very basis of the modern state.

RELIGION, LEGITIMACY, AND NATIONAL INTEGRATION

In Pakistan and Ceylon, the political system and governmental leadership have been closely associated with religion in order to secure their legitimacy and to promote national integration. In India, official policy has assumed that legitimacy and national integration can be achieved only through a secular state.

Ceylon gives no special constitutional recognition to the majority

[47] *The Gazette of Pakistan, Extraordinary*, August 30, 1956, p. 1567. For another detailed critical analysis see Khurshid Ahmad, ed., *Marriage Commission Report X-Rayed*, Chiragh-E-Rah Publications, Karachi, 1959.

[48] For the *ulama's* reaction see *Statement of 209 Ulama of Pakistan on Muslim Family Laws Ordinance, 1961*, Jama'at-i-Islami, Lahore, 1962.

[49] *Report of the Court of Inquiry*, pp. 211-212.

religion, but the essential thrust of governmental policy, especially from 1956 to 1965, has been to identify Sinhalese Buddhist religion and culture with Ceylonese nationality, and to forge a close link between Buddhism and the state. This can be seen in the frequent use of religious symbols by prime ministers and other officials, the extensive Buddha Jayanti celebrations (1954-1956) organized and financed by the government, the creation of two state-financed Buddhist universities based on traditional monastic institutions, and the numerous religious functions of the ministry of cultural affairs. A recent minister of cultural affairs wrote an article titled "Our Culture is based on Our Religion," and made it clear that the promotion of Ceylonese culture meant the promotion of Buddhism.[50] The official promotion of religion was an obvious path to political legitimacy, one in perfect keeping with the historical traditions of the Sinhalese kings. Furthermore, a renewed sense of Buddhist identity could draw together the western-educated and the more traditional elements of Sinhalese society, even if this necessarily entailed the alienation of the religious minorities.

Islam was so intimately associated with the events which led to the creation of Pakistan that no politician who aspired to significant power could afford to ignore its potent appeal. History also dictated that Pakistan would have to be declared an Islamic state, however that term were defined, for apart from Islam its claim to legitimacy would be in grave doubt. The facts of geography—East and West Pakistan separated by 1,000 miles of foreign territory—intensified the problem of national integration, and here again, Islam seemed to provide the answer. Religion was the one factor capable of holding the country together.[51]

During the first decade of Pakistan's existence the politicians fully exploited the name of Islam, but failed to provide the country with stable, constructive and effective leadership. After the 1958 coup the problems of legitimacy and national integration remained; sheer military force was not sufficient. Ayub Khan began to search for an *ideology* which would give a sense of unity and purpose to Pakistani society. In 1959 he wrote: "Such an ideology with us is obviously that of Islam. It was on that basis that we fought for and got Pakistan; but having got it, we failed to order our lives in accordance with it. The main reason is that we have failed to define that ideology in a

[50] See chapter 21, "The Sinhalese Buddhist Revolution."
[51] See chapter 15, "Ideological Dilemmas in Pakistan's Political Culture"; chapter 16, "The Secular State and Pakistan"; and chapter 18, "Islam and National Integration in Pakistan."

simple and understandable form. Also in our ignorance we began to regard the Islamic ideology as synonymous with bigotry and theocracy, and sub-consciously began to fight shy of it. The time has now come when we must get over this shyness. . . ."[52] While Ayub Khan would like to see a radically transformed Islam, he is now certain that Islam, however defined, is the only force which can create and sustain a sense of Pakistani nationality. The 1962 Constitution which he promulgated provided for an Advisory Council of Islamic Ideology. Pakistan, it is asserted, is an ideological state, and its ideology can only be Islam.

The pattern of religio-political developments in India has been strikingly different. While India's claim to being a secular state is weak at several points, this much is beyond dispute: official policy has not attempted to use Hinduism to establish political legitimacy or promote national integration. On the contrary, these are held to depend on the successful implementation of the ideal of a secular state.

RELIGION AND FOREIGN POLICY

In Pakistan religion has been a factor of some significance in the formulation of foreign policy; this has not been the case in India and Ceylon. Only in relations with Pakistan, with respect to minorities questions and the status of Kashmir, has the factor of religion been involved in Indian foreign policy to any appreciable extent. To be sure, efforts have been made to show that the policies of non-alignment pursued by India and Ceylon are supported by certain Hindu and Buddhist precepts and values. The late S. W. R. D. Bandaranaike interpreted non-alignment as the Middle Path prescribed by the Buddha. It is clear, however, that the vital roots of neutralism in South Asia are not to be found in traditional religion.

The creation of Pakistan was closely associated with a renewed sense of Islamic identity, and in the period 1947-1954, especially, a significant part of Pakistan's foreign policy was the search for friends and allies who could be attracted to the ideal of pan-Islamic unity.[53] The president of the Muslim League in 1949 visited a number of Middle Eastern countries to promote the idea of "Islamistan"—a group of contiguous Muslim countries which might be merged under the banner of Islam. Karachi became the venue for a number of Muslim gatherings such as the International Islamic Economic Conference of 1949. The 1956 Constitution directed: "The state shall en-

[52] Foreword to Javid Iqbal, *The Ideology of Pakistan and its Implementation*, Sh. Ghulam Ali and Sons, Lahore, 1959, pp. x-xi.

[53] See chapter 20, "Islam as a Factor in Pakistan's Foreign Policy."

EMERGING PATTERNS OF RELIGION AND POLITICS

	INDIA	PAKISTAN	CEYLON
1. *Religious communalism in politics.* Loyalty to socio-religious groups strongly influences political behavior.	Communal political parties of majority and minority religions. Communal factor strong in political behavior.	Communal ideology of two-nation theory. Debate over separate electorates. No strong secular political parties.	Gradual communalization of politics since 1948. Political use of grievances of majority community.
2. *Ecclesiastical organization and government.* Relations between government and religious leadership are unstructured and sporadic.	Hinduism almost completely unorganized, so government's relations with religious leadership are almost nonexistent.	Some influential *ulama*, but not well organized, and no recognized spokesmen for Islam as a whole.	Chief monks of leading sect of the Sangha have little to do with the government; relations sporadic.
3. *Government and religious reform.* Government has assumed the role of religious reformer.	Legislation reforming aspects of temple worship, temple administration, caste practices. Reforms recommended by Hindu Religious Endowments Commission.	Bureau of National Reconstruction held seminars for *ulama*, published sermons. Reinterpretation of Islam by Central Institute of Islamic Research.	Buddha Sasana Commission appointed by government recommended reorganization of Buddhism, regulation of the Sangha.
4. *Religion and ideology.* The dominant political ideologies have been readily reconciled with religion.	Democracy supported by Hindu metaphysical principles. Sarvodaya movement a kind of Hindu socialism.	Iqbal and others emphasize democratic values of Islam, and Islamic socialism. Islam prohibits interest, stresses ideal of equality.	Buddhist individualism and democratic procedures of ancient assemblies. Sangha has no private property, embryonic socialist society.

5. *Caste and politics.* Revolt of lower castes leads to political movements which reject the majority religion.	Mass conversion of untouchables to Buddhism and formation of Republican Party. DMK is anti-Brahmin and rejects Hinduism.		
6. *Religious functionaries in politics.* Individuals and groups among the clergy have significant political influence.		*Ulama* had a significant role in constitution-making. Associations of *ulama* have been effective pressure groups.	Individual monks and Sangha associations have wielded great power. Active in elections and agitations.
7. *Religion and law.* Modification by the state of marriage, divorce, and inheritance laws based on religion.	Hindu Marriage Act of 1955 prohibited polygamy, introduced divorce. Various other enactments in field of personal law.	Muslim Family Laws Ordinance of 1961 restricted polygamy and divorce by men, and confirmed women's right of divorce.	
8. *Religion, legitimacy, and national integration.* Use of religion by government to achieve legitimacy and promote national integration.		Emphasis on Islamic ideology as the basis for Pakistani nationality. State agency—Advisory Council of Islamic Ideology.	
9. *Religion and foreign policy.* Religion a significant factor in formulation of foreign policy.		Strong appeal of pan-Islamic aspirations. Serious efforts made to strengthen political ties with other Muslim countries.	Much use of Buddhist religious symbols by officials, promotion of Buddhism by ministry of cultural affairs, two Buddhist universities.

deavor to strengthen the bonds of unity among Muslim countries. . . ." In 1954, disillusioned with the Arab world in which Nasser's secular nationalism and neutralism (which had much in common with the ideas of Nehru) was in the ascendant, Pakistan turned to the West. Still, however, the emotional appeal of pan-Islam is potent, and official expression continues to be given to these aspirations.[54]

[54] The findings of this chapter are summarized in the accompanying chart.

PART II
INDIA: THE POLITICS OF
RELIGIOUS PLURALISM

CHAPTER 3

RELIGION AND POLITICS IN A U.P. CONSTITUENCY

HAROLD A. GOULD

In the 1962 general election, as in all previous elections, the communal parties were extremely active throughout the Republic of India.[1] We may define a communal party as one which exploits in some fashion the parochial sensibilities of any group in Indian society whose identity is determined not by economic interest or secular ideological criteria but by caste, religion or ethnolinguistic background. This essay proposes to deal with one such communal party, the Bharatiya Jana Sangh, in the context of Faizabad constituency politics where the party and its candidate came very close to unseating the Congress Party incumbent who had represented this area in the Uttar Pradesh legislative assembly since 1957.

We shall examine the place of the communal party in general in Indian politics today as a prelude to our consideration of the Jana Sangh and its standard-bearer, Guru Datt Singh, in Faizabad constituency. We shall also consider the historical and sociological contexts of politics in Faizabad. In this fashion, it is hoped that the complex events associated with the election and the lives of its participants, to be narrated presently, can be linked to more general processes at work in Indian society. Most important of all, we shall pay close attention to the manner in which a party that employs religious symbolism functions when confronted with the realistic possibility of gaining political power. How does its conduct differ from the so-called secular parties, if indeed it does, and to whom does such a party appeal? Who supports it at the polls and for what reasons?

COMMUNAL PARTIES AND MODERN INDIA

Several basic factors have contributed to the emergence of communalism as we have defined it. The most general of these has been

Harold A. Gould is associate professor of anthropology at the University of Pittsburgh.

[1] I wish to acknowledge the postdoctoral fellowships awarded by the National Institute of Mental Health which enabled me to do research in India from 1960 to 1962. I am also grateful to the University of Pittsburgh for the Mellon postdoctoral fellowship which enabled me to spend the academic year 1962-1963 analyzing and writing up field data.

the formation of the modern political state itself, a process which began in earnest in the early twentieth century, experienced its most rapid acceleration between the two world wars, and culminated in the establishment of full parliamentary democracy in 1947. This process was fundamental to the development of communalism because it meant the progressive channelization of collective aspirations and discontent into the action-forms characteristic of the modern state— political parties with mass-disseminated ideologies, legislative bodies that make laws and promulgate public policies, and universal adult franchise. Parochial interests rooted in caste, religious, and other subcultural systems inevitably manifest themselves in the forms that permit their meaningful articulation in modern society as do other types of group interest.

The nature of communal or parochial interests in India and their role in politics deserve some comments. Two factors are of special importance here. The first is the antipathy that developed between Hindus and Muslims as nationalism gained momentum; the second is the stress that the efforts to achieve the planned modernization of India has produced in almost every sphere of her social life. The former led increasingly to the outbreak of physical violence between the followers of India's two major religions, while the latter seemed, in the eyes of many, to pose a threat to the survival of religion and traditional society themselves as a consequence of the Congress Party's determination to build a secular state as rapidly as possible. Regarding the first factor, we may note Lambert's words: "The period 1924-1928 in many ways marks the watershed in communal relations in India and, during this period, the communal organizations sought to strengthen Hindu society against the Muslims and the Congress moderates. . . . Muslim attempts to conduct widespread proselytiza-tion among the Hindus made the organization of the Hindu commu-nity more imperative. The Hindu Mahasabha, although founded the same year as the Muslim League, only emerged as a party of all-India importance in these years. The Rashtriya Swayamsevak Sangh was formed in Nagpur to fight for Hindu interests in the riots that swept the city in 1924."[2]

Fear of the secular state by those who see themselves losing some-thing as a consequence of its establishment is an inevitable reaction by some in a rapidly changing society. Various writers have pointed out that the more rapidly industrialization takes place, the more

[2] Richard Lambert, "Hindu Communal Groups in Indian Politics," in Richard L. Park and Irene Tinker, eds., *Leadership and Political Institutions in India*, Princeton University Press, Princeton, 1960, p. 214.

serious the concomitant social and psychological dislocation, and the greater the degree of protest in a society. Just as the industrialization process comes to be managed by some group or groups in a society—in the case of India, the Congress Party with its ideological commitment to extensive secularization—so the protest its stresses generate will also come to be managed by someone. At the political level, opposition parties will supply this management and their ideological outlook and sources of recruitment will indicate the specific nature of the harm they believe the present regime is doing to the society.[3]

Since independence, Hindu-Muslim rivalry within the borders of the Republic of India has considerably abated. Resultantly, although the Hindu parties continue to warn of the danger emanating from Pakistan, and persistently impugn the loyalty of India's Muslim minority, they are less preoccupied with blocking rapprochement or accommodation with Muslims. The issue does not really exist any more in the form that it did during Gandhi's day. Protest has shifted its emphasis, therefore, to a preoccupation with the threat of a secular assault upon the traditional institutions that have sustained the status and the security of many Indians.[4] This preoccupation, I would submit, has grown and turned support toward communal parties in direct ratio to the occurrence of stress born of the attempt to industrialize Indian society. As managers of protest, the communal parties play up the solidarities, the securities, the privileged access to scarce resources which social structures like caste, religion and ethnolinguistic community have always afforded Indians and whose survival depends upon the retention of salient features of the traditional culture pattern. This is the common functional thread that runs through them all despite numerous variations that are observable in their philosophies, programs, and tactics. Communal parties manage the protest of those who see the dissolution of various particularistic aspects of the traditional social order as destructive of their personal chances for survival and prosperity.

FAIZABAD POLITICS: THE SETTING

We must turn now to the historical and sociological contexts of Faizabad politics. These are complex matters with which we can only deal in a cursory way; but even an examination of the bare

[3] For this conceptualization of the "management of protest" I am indebted to Professor Irving Sobel of Washington University, St. Louis.

[4] For a discussion of governmental policies of secularization in many areas of Indian life (law, education, culture, etc.) see Donald E. Smith, *India as a Secular State*, Princeton University Press, Princeton, 1963.

outlines will be helpful. The region began to acquire political importance of the kind relevant to modern history following the arrival of the Mughals under Babar in 1528. At that time, the only major community apparently was Ayodhya, a sacred city situated on the banks of the Ghagra River at the place where the God Rama is said to have led his courtly life.[5] Babar found a Hindu temple on what was supposed to be the actual spot where Rama was born. He had it destroyed and built in its place a mosque which came to be known as the Babar Mandir which stands to this day. We will presently have occasion to see how this edifice figured in Faizabad's communal politics.

Due to its importance to Hindu mythology, Ayodhya has always been a center of religious pilgrimage and other sacred activities. Its symbolic importance is attested by the fact that as the region gradually became a major province first of the Mughal Empire and later of the British it always bore names (Avadh under the former and Oudh under the latter) which were corruptions of the word Ayodhya.[6] The traditional princes of Oudh were known as Nawabs and in the period following Aurangzeb's death (1707) were its hereditary rulers. The second of the post-Mughal line was Safdar Jang who founded the city of Faizabad about eight miles to the northwest of Ayodhya by erecting a palace where there had previously been a hunting lodge.[7] From that time, the two communities of Faizabad and Ayodhya grew apace until by the second half of the nineteenth century they had become a more or less continuous urban complex. When this occurred, the British administration governing the region formally united them into a single chartered municipality which was called Faizabad-cum-Ayodhya. This occurred in 1869 making Faizabad-cum-Ayodhya, henceforth referred to simply as Faizabad, one of the oldest chartered muncipalities in India.

As a municipality, Faizabad was made responsible for the establishment and maintenance of basic facilities such as roads, water supply, electric power, health and sanitation facilities, etc., through its own municipal board consisting of eighteen members, fourteen of whom were elected and four of whom were nominated by the district com-

---

[5] See the Ramayana in any of its various versions (*e.g.*, Mazumdar, 1953). For a good account of Babar's career, see Stanley Lane-Poole, *Babar*, S. Chand and Co., Delhi, 1957.

[6] Under the British, Oudh was combined with Agra to form the United Provinces of Agra and Oudh, or simply U.P.

[7] Much of the information presented here concerning the history of Faizabad is taken from vol. 43 (Faizabad) of the *District Gazetteers of the United Provinces*, 1928. See especially chapters 3 and 5.

missioner. After independence in 1947, all board seats were made elective. This made the Faizabad municipal board and its chairmanship a key political plum to be sought by any group desirous of winning the provincial or national parliamentary seats whose constituency boundaries embrace the city.

Since 1952 when India's first general election was held, Faizabad constituency (for purposes of state legislative assembly representation) has been made up of the joint municipality of Faizabad-cum-Ayodhya, a small town (3,980 in 1951) named Bhadarsa ten miles south of the city, and 102 peasant villages.[8] In the 1951 census all the communities making up the constituency had a total population of 145,518; by 1961 the figure had grown to around 200,000.[9] Approximately 58 per cent of this number resided either in Faizabad city or Bhadarsa and so were classifiable as urban, while the remainder (42 per cent) were villagers and thus classifiable as rural. In the third general election, held in February of 1962, slightly more than 42,000 people cast votes for legislative assembly candidates running in the constituency.

Politics in modern Faizabad have naturally tended to reflect and correlate with basic economic, sociological and political patterns characteristic of Uttar Pradesh and the Indian nation as a whole. When the Congress Party of Gandhi and Nehru was fighting for independence from Great Britain during the inter-war years, nationalist agitation was widespread in Oudh. Because the old Mughal province was heavily rural and dominated by two especially pernicious categories of landlord (zamindars and taluqdars), this agitation in the main took the form of Congress Party workers providing leadership and ideological content to the spontaneous unrest of the ordinary peasantry and menials of the area.[10] The zamindars and taluqdars

[8] Through the kind assistance of Mr. Brij Nandan Prasad, principal, the Saraswati Inter-College, it was possible to obtain full data on all aspects of the Faizabad legislative assembly constituency both pertaining to voting behavior in 1957 and 1962 and to its geographic and demographic characteristics. The Congress Party incumbent, Mr. Madan Mohan Varma, also is to be thanked for the many ways in which his cooperation and help made all aspects of this study possible. Census data were employed in conjunction with the information supplied by Mr. Prasad and Mr. Varma. This was obtained from (a) *District Population Statistics, Uttar Pradesh*, No. 46—Faizabad (Census of India, 1951), (b) *District Census Handbook*, No. 46—Faizabad District (Census of India, 1951), (c) *A Handbook of the Provisional Population of Uttar Pradesh* (Census of India, 1961), and (d) *Revised Map of the Faizabad District, Seasons 1912 to 1916* (U.P. Government, May 1947).

[9] The estimate of 200,000 was made by obtaining the 1951 to 1961 growth rate for Tahsil Faizabad and applying it to the smaller legislative assembly constituency contained within it. This was necessitated by the fact that the provisional census figures for 1961 do not go below the Tahsil level.

[10] In his autobiography, Nehru described his work among peasant rioters at

of Oudh were essentially revenue farmers confirmed in their positions by British administrative fiat. Their claims to various gradations of nobility arose out of a desire, common in non-industrial societies, to convert purely economic statuses into traditionally legitimized statuses by genealogical means—*viz.*, by tracing lineal ancestries back to select figures in the old Mughal aristocracy (if Muslim), or (if Hindu) by asserting membership in an illustrious *gotra* or clan of a Brahmin or Rajput *jati* (caste). Thus, the nationalists simultaneously attacked the British regime as imperialists and the zamindars and taluqdars as the lackeys of the imperialists.

As the nationalist agitation bifurcated into Muslim and Hindu manifestations with the formation of the Muslim League, this schism too produced its consequences in Faizabad in the heightening of communal tensions. Muslims comprise about 15 per cent of the population of Faizabad constituency and 85 per cent of these reside in the two urban areas (the city and the town). Analysis of the 1891 census data[11] suggests that the proportions of Muslims and Hindus have remained relatively stable despite partition.

Besides the Hindu-Muslim schism in Faizabad, there are certain caste cleavages that deserve our attention. It has been noted that the old taluqdari and zamindari classes contained predominantly Muslims, Brahmins and Rajputs. In the pre-independence era, the upper socioeconomic stratum of most villages in Faizabad consisted of *jatis* of Brahmins and Rajputs. These Brahmin and Rajput *jatis* were extensions into the individual village communities of the landlord class both in fact (for many were kinsmen of the local rajas) and in principle (they reproduced the socio-economic system in microcosm).

Partabgarh and Rae Bareilly, both near Faizabad, and then noted: "A little later . . . Faizabad got its dose of widespread repression." The trouble had started when the servants of one zamindar had incited some peasants against another zamindar whom they disliked by telling the peasants that Gandhi wished them to undertake such an assault. Nehru went to the district, addressed the peasants, scolding them for committing violence in Gandhiji's name, and then asked those guilty of the deed to raise their hands, which several did in full view of the police. Then, in Nehru's words: "When I spoke to many of them privately later and heard their artless story of how they had been misled, I felt sorry for them and I began to regret having exposed these foolish and simple folk to long terms of imprisonment. But the people who suffered were not just two or three dozen. The chance was too good to be lost and full advantage of the occasion was taken to crush the agrarian movement in the district. Over a thousand arrests were made. . . ." Jawaharlal Nehru, *Autobiography*, Bodley Head, London, 1953, pp. 61-62.

11 Through the kindness of Professor Paul Brass of the University of Washington, I was able to obtain a photostatic copy of the *District Census Statistics, N.-W. Provinces and Oudh*, Faizabad (Census of India, 1891), which I have been able to use in conjunction with other census materials to assemble a picture of the region's social composition.

They dominated the villages politically and were the official liaison with the outside world in tax and police matters. They had the best land tenures and were in control of most of the best quality lands in the villages. They enjoyed the highest ritual status in the eyes of traditional Hinduism.

Beneath this elite stratum, and occupying an intermediate status in the rural social order, were two strata. One consisted of the cultivator *jatis,* whose members are often called the true *kisans* (farmers) because they specialize in the cultivation of the soil. Despite their being the most skillful farmers in the old order their average land-holdings were comparatively small and their tenures much inferior to those of the elite castes.[12] The principal *jatis* comprising this stratum in Faizabad were Ahir, Kurmi, Gujar and Murau. Numerically it accounted for the bulk of the population which means that under the zamindari system a major segment of the population consisted of skilled farmers whose well-being and social status were incommensurate with their technical capabilities.

The other stratum in the middle range was made up of the various artisan *jatis* such as carpenters (Barhai), iron workers (Lohar), goldsmiths (Sonar) and others who enjoyed a modest well-being. Their numbers were small and their economic position considerably more uncertain than those whose substance rested upon land, the most valuable commodity in agrarian society.

At the bottom of the rural hierarchy were the menial and untouchable *jatis* who had neither land nor socially valued skills and who were the veritable serfs of those who did. Chamars (leather workers) and Pasis (toddy tapers) were the principal defiled *castes* in Faizabad. Although smaller in number than the middle stratum, people of these menial-impure *jatis* were nevertheless extremely numerous and provided a vast reservoir of unskilled labor for both the big estates and the small-scale farmers.

The triumphant aftermath of the nationalist movement saw the initiation of planned economic development for India. This affected these strata differentially and thereby laid the foundations of some of the new political patterns that were emerging by the 1962 general election. One of the first reforms that followed independence in Uttar

[12] There were a large number of classifications of land holdings in U.P., but what most of them added up to was tenancy in which the cultivator never enjoyed full control of his land or its produce. A horde of intermediaries between the Raja and the cultivator claimed their share in both. Thus, the most enterprising farmers were deprived of the possibility of earning the capital that they above all others might be inclined to invest in improvements.

Pradesh was zamindari abolition.[13] This put an end to revenue farming, to the largest landholdings, and to the bewildering welter of land tenures which in themselves constituted a serious impediment to a modern agricultural system. In so doing, the act simultaneously abolished the economic foundations of the oligarchic political order which the numerically small, elite caste *jatis* had been able to maintain for centuries in the villages and the kingdoms into which the villages were incorporated. Especially the Rajputs, with their proud traditions of conquest and overlordship, were undermined and left in a state of disgruntled insecurity by the loss of their zamindari prerogatives. The Congress government became the chief target of their hatred because it had destroyed the system which had sustained their ancient hegemony.[14]

For the cultivator *jatis*, independence had precisely the opposite consequences. It meant a considerable improvement in their material and social lot. In the first place, independence brought economic planning which included heavy emphasis on the expansion of food production. The community development projects exemplified the new government's constructive approach to rural society, its major commitment of technical and economic resources to agriculture. Inevitably, those in the rural areas who practiced farming as their chief economic activity were destined to become the greatest beneficiaries of this commitment.

In Faizabad, the cultivator *jatis* got ownership rights in land through zamindari abolition and its concomitant reforms; they started to profit materially from their skills as food-growers; and they established contacts with community project workers who now resided in and near the villages and constituted a new locus of power and authority immune from the sanctions and controls of the traditional social order. This afforded them enough security and autonomy

13 The Zamindari Abolition and Land Reforms Bill was introduced in the state assembly in July 1949 and passed on January 16, 1951. Its opponents appealed to the Supreme Court which upheld the act on May 5, 1952.

14 In 1954, villagers south of Faizabad were telling the story of a village headman and ex-zamindar whose recent fate symbolized the new world that was dawning in rural India. This headman, a Rajput, accused two Koris (weavers) of having stolen from him while in his employ as landless laborers. After summoning them to his home, the Rajput ordered them to confess. When they persisted in their claim of being innocent, the Koris were taken to an outbuilding and beaten with *lathis* (bamboo staves) until they "confessed." Having gained their release, however, the two Koris hastened to the local police station and reported what had occurred. The Rajput headman was arrested on a charge of assault, tried in court, convicted, fined and given three months in jail. In the old days, what the zamindar did *was* the law; today it is *against* the law.

of action to enable them to offer a direct challenge to the old elite caste monopoly of power. Thus, Ahir and Kurmi *jati* members began to gain offices as headmen (pradhan) in villages and to obtain majorities on village councils (panchayats). Even members of menial-impure *jatis* began to obtain such power, especially in communities where there were large concentrations of them. These changes have been vividly described by Cohn: "In a generation's time, I think, the village will be in the hands of small peasant proprietors, with a floating group of landless workers counterbalanced by a modern industrial urban culture . . . paradoxically enough, India will develop a peasantry in the middle of the twentieth century such as we are familiar with in European history of the eighteenth and nineteenth centuries."[15]

Low caste *jatis* have gained less than the middle stratum from Congress rule in spite of the Scheduled Castes designation under which a number of special benefits and advantages have been channeled to them. They have made gains, however, and have been vocal and politically important wherever their numbers have been great enough. In certain parts of Faizabad constituency, Pasi (toddy tappers), Kori (cotton weavers) and Chamar (leather workers) *jatis* are well-organized and hold the balance of power in local power structures. This is not the rule, however. These *jatis* have been more inclined to support protest movements than have those of the middle stratum, according to data I have gathered, but protest movements ideologically to the left rather than to the right of Congress.

Faizabad municipal politics have tended to be dominated by men drawn from *jatis* of Kayasthas (scribes and accountants), Khatris (a Punjabi business caste), Banias (a merchant caste), Rajputs and Brahmins. Since the municipal board's inception, a Kayastha kin group and a Khatri kin group have been the chief rivals for its control; their local factional antagonism has in turn been linked to a provincial-level split in the Congress Party that follows somewhat similar caste lines.[16]

THE JANA SANGH AND THE 1962 ELECTION

Having provided a rough picture of the context of Faizabad politics, we are now ready to consider the Jana Sangh's role in the constituency election. Let us recall that the Jana Sangh was born of Hindu-Muslim

[15] Bernard S. Cohn, "Madhopur Revisited," *Economic Weekly*, special number, July 1959, p. 966.
[16] See Harold A. Gould, "Traditionalism and Modernism in U.P.: Faizabad Constituency," *Economic Weekly*, August 18, 1962, pp. 1345-1350.

conflict and of the Indian National Congress's efforts to direct India's destiny toward becoming a secular state. The Jana Sangh contends that it does not merely wish to retreat into the past or oppose the presence of Muslims or other minorities in India. It holds, on the contrary, that it will modernize and liberalize Indian society; this, however, will be done in a *Hindu spirit* rather than by programs and values "artificially imported" from abroad. "We have to be wary," asserts Dindayal Upadhyaya, a Jana Sangh spokesman, "while trying to be modern, lest westernism intrudes in the guise of modernism." The party "wants to preserve the age-old values of Bharatiya life, but does not desire to cling to customs and traditions which have lost their vitality or have degenerated." It works for "an inherent unity in our national life." India would be militarized, the Chinese ejected from her soil, and minorities made to realize that their allegiance to the motherland takes precedence over all others. "The Jana Sangh does not consider Muslims or Christians as a foreign element. They are part and parcel of this nation. However, due to some historical circumstances, they have imbibed some foreign traits. Their contribution in the fight for national emancipation has not been creditable. They have to be resurrected and rehabilitated. They can be both good Christians and Muslims and patriotic Indians. It requires decommunalizing our politics."[17]

The characterological roots of the Jana Sangh lie partly in the Rashtriya Swayamsevak Sangh, founded, as we saw, at Nagpur in 1924 in the heat of Hindu-Muslim rioting. The primary purpose of the RSS has been to recruit young men who can be imbued with a fanatical dedication to the aim of realizing a revitalized Hindu society. It is a non-political organization in the sense that it does not run candidates for office. Members are subjected to an ascetic discipline, are compelled to obey blindly the dictates of their leaders, and may never legitimately resign having once accepted membership. The moral development attained in the RSS is supposed to equip the member to participate positively in any aspect of life he subsequently enters. In politics, this means working in the ranks of, and rising to positions of power within, any party that holds promise of actualizing the Hindu values that the RSS espouses. Since the political party most ideologically compatible with these values is the Bharatiya Jana Sangh, its leadership is liberally saturated with the products of the RSS incubus. The RSS is, then, a training ground for managers of conservative Hindu protest.

[17] Dindayal Upadhyaya, "Jana Sangh," *Seminar*, January 1962.

One such manager is the man who was the Jana Sangh candidate for MLA (member of legislative assembly) in Faizabad in February 1962. The career of Guru Datt Singh in many ways illustrates the point that the management of protest becomes an alternate form of upward mobility for many of the effective people in the society who find no satisfactory niche for themselves among the managers of industrialization.[18] Although a Rajput, and thus of a caste that lost much through the commitment to modernize the country, Guru Datt is the member of a family that has encouraged higher education and entry into modern occupations. His father was a doctor; his eldest brother is a retired lawyer and the executive officer of the Azamgarh (U.P.) municipal board. He has a younger brother who is a doctor, another who is a professor, and another who is in government service. Guru Datt Singh is himself a university graduate; he retired in 1950 after 32 years as a gazetted officer of the Uttar Pradesh civil service. However, instead of identifying with the Congress Party during the course of his professional service, in the end he linked himself to the RSS and the Jana Sangh. The reasons Guru Datt gives for this are that he had always been "a man of God" who saw in Hinduism the true religious faith. However, he gradually became aware "that the very existence of Hinduism, and ultimately my own existence" were being threatened by his coreligionists who dominated the Congress Party. In other words, in his view, the Congress Party had embarked upon a program designed to secularize Indian society.

Although not a native of Faizabad, Guru Datt says he decided to settle there because, being a man of religion, he could live a life of peace and contemplation near the holy city of Ayodhya. His decision to take an active role in politics came, he contends, after retirement when he became convinced that he must help save India and Hinduism. He got himself elected president of the Faizabad district branch of the Jana Sangh and commenced running for various offices. In 1957 he ran for the Lok Sabha seat from Faizabad and lost. In 1959 he ran for the Faizabad municipal board and won. He was chosen municipal board chairman on that occasion. In 1962, as we shall see, he was narrowly defeated in his bid for the legislative assembly seat from Faizabad. Or put simply, the fame that Guru Datt Singh was able to garner in a few years as a manager of protest many times exceeded the recognition he had received during thirty-two years as an obscure provincial civil servant.

[18] See Irving Sobel, "The Labor Force in Industrial Development," a paper presented at Washington University, St. Louis, on March 4, 1957.

There is evidence that for Guru Datt Singh the gap between the desire for and attainment of recognition had been wide during most of his civil service career. The role he played in the Babar Mandir riots of 1949 is illustrative. During the last years of his government service, Guru Datt had been stationed in Faizabad as an assistant to the assistant commissioner for the Faizabad division,[19] a man named K. K. K. Nair. Nair was an outspoken Hindu communalist and a member of the RSS. It will be recalled that the Babar Mandir was built on the alleged site of Rama's birth in Ayodhya after Babar had conquered the region and annexed it to his growing realm. For centuries, therefore, the very location of the mosque had stood as a humiliating affront to the Hindu religion. In 1949, despite his official position, Nair was openly advocating the return to the Hindu community of the mosque built on the site of Rama's birth. Guru Datt was Nair's fervent supporter.

The incident began when a *murti*, or statue, of Rama suddenly appeared in the Babar Mandir. Word rapidly spread among the Hindus that the God Rama had returned to once more take possession of his birth site. Among the Muslims the word spread that the Hindus were planning to defile their mosque and deprive them of their place of worship. The riots that ensued were ugly and were quelled only with great effort by the police. Following the riots, litigation was initiated by both parties to the dispute and this continues to the present day.

The official investigation that ensued concluded that K. K. K. Nair's and Guru Datt Singh's roles in the incident were so flagrant that they must be invited to retire to private life. A reliable informant says that the two were indeed implicated in the affair as leaders of the Hindu militants who planted the statue in the mosque. But they grew frightened when the situation escalated into a communal riot and sought help from municipal officials in stopping what they had started. They had apparently neither foreseen nor deliberately sought the occurrence of violence. At any rate, it was his hunger for recognition and its consequences that had as much to do with Guru Datt's retirement as his hunger for religious retreat. And his decision to reside in Faizabad following retirement seems to have been motivated by the political prospects he foresaw for himself in the wake of the Babar Mandir tragedy. He now had a conservative Hindu following in Faizabad city and the surrounding countryside and could quickly

[19] Faizabad division is an administrative region consisting of six districts: Faizabad, Gonda, Bahraich, Sultanpur, Pratapgarh, and Bara Banki. Faizabad city is its headquarters.

acquire local leadership of the Jana Sangh, which was then being formed.

His subsequent career in Faizabad politics consistently followed the pattern he had set in the Babar Mandir days. After his unsuccessful bid for election to Parliament in 1957, Guru Datt was able, in 1959, to take advantage of the split in the U.P. Congress Party and win control of the Faizabad municipal board. There are, as already noted, two major factions in the U.P. Congress and their rivalries have seriously crippled the party for years. The intricacies of this factional struggle are outside the province of this essay, except to point out that almost every constituency in the state is effected by it. In Faizabad the local leadership of one of these factions is supplied by a Kayastha kin group while the other is led by a Khatri kin group. The Congressman who won the legislative assembly seat in 1957, Madan Mohan Varma, is the current Khatri leader and he is a loyal supporter of the C. B. Gupta faction in the provincial party. His antagonist is the Kayastha leader, Priyadatt Ram, who supports the other Congress faction which is led by a fellow Kayastha, S. M. Sampurnanand.

In order to assure his victory in the 1957 election, it is said, Madan Mohan Varma appealed to his factional rival, Priyadatt Ram, for a truce so that Congress could offer a unified front against the opposition. This was achieved and the two cooperated in the campaign with the result that Madan Mohan won 53 per cent of the vote. It was Priyadatt Ram's understanding that in return for the support he rendered to the Congress ticket, his own campaign to retain control of the Faizabad municipal board in 1959 (he was its chairman) would receive party backing. When he lost in this election to Guru Datt Singh and his Jana Sangh followers, Priyadatt Ram charged that he had been betrayed by Madan Mohan and the Gupta faction of Congress. He vowed that he would regain control of the municipal board in the end, and that in the meantime he would engineer the defeat of Madan Mohan.

Meanwhile, Guru Datt Singh was in control of the Faizabad municipal board as its chairman. Within a year, however, the board had been suspended by the U.P. government and Guru Datt was facing a hearing on charges of misconduct in office. The substance of the government's case was that the board had plunged the municipality into financial chaos. While piling up a municipal debt of 220,000 rupees, the board had voted on Jana Sangh initiative to *reduce* taxes. The specific charge against Guru Datt was that he was responsible for the misappropriation of 160,000 rupees. It seems the U.P. government had loaned this amount to Faizabad for the express purpose of improving drainage and sewage facilities in the city. Instead of employing the money for this purpose, however, Guru Datt authorized the expenditure of the entire amount on improvements in the holy city of Ayodhya whose population is but a small fraction of the entire municipality's. Both the municipal board and Guru Datt were still under suspension as the 1962 general election approached. Technically, of course, Guru Datt had resigned as municipal board chairman in order to run for the legislative assembly.

Once again, in these events, we see Guru Datt Singh as the implacable protest leader. He uses power to martyrize himself. He compels the punishment that enhances him in the eyes of the orthodox. Behavior that is irrational from the standpoint of political moderation is rational from the standpoint of one who would lead the enemies of political moderation.

There is another aspect of the behavior of a communal politician like Guru Datt Singh that makes him seem paradoxical. On one hand, he champions the application of the loftiest moral values to public life and chides his opponents for their contrasting worldliness; on the other hand, when he actually attains power his manner of using it does not distinguish him morally in any sense from those he superseded. In part this is probably because the possession of political power in a democratic state where a variety of interests simultaneously vie for expression imposes certain necessities upon the possessor. To survive, even the saintly must make deals and satisfy a diverse constituency in politics. Because they morally reject the system within which they are compelled to operate, both their self-assurance and technical comprehension are impaired at the point where they are faced with the responsibility for operating it. As Weiner says: "Those who resent the process of modernization are forced to use the political instruments created by the westernized. Orthodox Hindu communalists . . . increasingly use the accoutrements of western democracy—parties, parliaments, elections—to achieve their objectives. The Hindu-minded have lost much of their traditional authority and therefore find it necessary to accept the weapons of the more westernized elites."[20]

There is still another aspect of this paradox which Guru Datt symbolizes. His messianic dedication to Hindu spiritual values and his single-minded determination to actualize them in the political arena provide him with a focus for the mobilization of his energies that is probably only matched by the Communists. It is certainly not

[20] Myron Weiner, in Park and Tinker, p. 3.

matched by the ordinary moderate politican. Such dedication frequently provides the advantage which leads to political victory. However, the very vision of the morally pure society that can inspire
such fanatical zeal is incapable of realization in practice. Thus,
having attained power, the efforts of the Hindu communalist to
bring into being the society of his dreams is bound to lead to frustration, irrational and desperate acts, and ultimately to what will prove
to be self-destructive behavior. Each time Guru Datt through his
zealous labors has put himself in a position to wield real power, this
fundamental incapacity to translate vision into reality has revealed
itself and led to the most bizarre forms of behavior and, in the end,
to deposition. Would this incapacity be less likely to manifest itself
if the Jana Sangh should become powerful enough some day to rule
all India? It is a question which thoughtful Indians must frequently
ask themselves.

THE FAIZABAD VOTE: WHO SUPPORTS COMMUNALISM?

We saw that the schism in the U.P. Congress Party persuaded Guru
Datt Singh that his chances of capturing the assembly seat from
Faizabad were good. Opportunity seemed to be ripe as the election
drew close because it became ever more clear that Priyadatt Ram
would stand by his vow to oppose Madan Mohan Varma to the end.
In addition, there was evidence of a general trend of protest against
Congress throughout the province and, for that matter, throughout
the country. The stresses generated by a lagging rate of economic
growth, the seeming inertia and corruption of officialdom, the failure
to deal decisively with the Chinese border incursions, and creeping
inflation—all these were a combination of irritants causing a lot of
generalized grumbling and discontent. Some of this discontent resulted in support for the Jana Sangh argument that a revitalized
Hindu society was the best answer to India's current problems. The
explanation is that in periods of mounting stress personalistic solutions
have an inevitable appeal. Jana Sangh is communal in the sense that
it appeals strongly to parochial sensibilities: in other words, the
party endeavors to make people feel that their best hope for security
and prosperity lies in reliance upon a group whose identity is determined in personalistic terms.

Such an appeal is especially meaningful in India because even in
the best of times the necessities of life are in short supply, and because
castes, the ultimate in the particularistic social group, have for centuries been a dominant feature of her social organization. Indians

rather automatically think of security from harm and want in terms of being able to rely upon the personalistic ties that prevail between the members of one's caste or some comparable social group. And such groups, like the particularistic ties that sustain them, are legitimized by the traditional value system, by religion itself. The Jana Sangh aims its political propaganda at these personalistic needs and tendencies in the Indian population. By stressing the point that it works for a modern India rooted in the old Hindu traditions, it makes Hindus feel that they can have the best that the modern world has to offer while simultaneously forming "one caste" (*ek jat*) of co-religionists with particularistic claims on one another. They will homogenize themselves against the "other castes" who pose numerous dangers to the survival of Mother India (*Bharat Mata*)—the Muslims, the Christians, the Chinese, westernized Indians, etc.

Conditions in Faizabad constituency thus seemed ripe for a communalist offensive, and Guru Datt plunged into his candidacy. Priyadatt Ram was destined to give him a direct assist because, in his determination to destroy his Congress rival Madan Mohan, he too elected to exploit the mounting communalism for his own ends. A Muslim politician from Bhadarsa, Nasir Husain, had acquired a considerable local fame through his work in the Praja Socialist Party and his advocacy of cow protection, a Hindu cause. Husain had wanted to run for MLA on the PSP ticket in 1962 but had not been selected as the party candidate, with the result that he had become disgruntled and was searching for an outlet for his frustrations. Priyadatt Ram and Husain were friendly, so the former encouraged the latter to run for MLA as an independent. When Husain agreed, Priyadatt Ram felt he had taken a long step toward his goal of destroying Madan Mohan Varma.

Priyadatt's reasoning was that Nasir Husain's appeal as an independent would be largely communal. That is, Muslims would be tempted to vote for him thus denying many Muslim votes to the Congress ticket. Priyadatt's political instincts informed him that Jana Sangh sentiment had picked up since the last election, and he knew that Guru Datt Singh would actively endeavor to exploit this communalist sentiment, including Hindu antipathy for Muslims. The fanning of communalist passions by a party that looked strong enough to win would, Priyadatt Ram calculated, seriously frighten Faizabad's Muslims and thus send many of them running in panic to the protection of a candidate of their own religion.

Another factor which made Priyadatt Ram's strategy appear sound was the decision of the Communist Party to urge their followers to vote for Madan Mohan in the legislative assembly election. They too sensed a powerful Jana Sangh groundswell and felt the only way to head off a "reactionary" victory was by forming a popular front with the Congress, the sole party with a real chance to defeat the Jana Sangh. This Communist support was not inconsiderable. In 1957, their candidate polled 23 per cent of the urban and 15 per cent of the rural vote. Furthermore, there is evidence that a large proportion of the Communist vote in 1957 had come from the Muslim community, 80 per cent of whom are concentrated in some of the most crowded, impoverished *bastis* of Faizabad city. Thus, Priyadatt's maneuver held the promise of nullifying some of the potential effects of the Communists' alliance with the Congress Party at the very moment when the defection of many of Congress's conservative supporters to the Jana Sangh appeared inevitable.

Guru Datt Singh worked hard to exploit his seeming advantages. In public utterances, the Jana Sangh urged people to vote for their candidate if they wanted: (1) food taxes to be reduced, (2) a stop put to government meddling in private citizens' lives, (3) the restoration of the Faizabad municipal board's authority, (4) encouragement of the Faizabad businessmen, (5) an end to the Faizabad house tax, (6) an end to bribery, (7) the nation's frontiers successfully defended, (8) the preservation of traditional Hindu law, (9) religious places to be kept pure, and (10) a real opposition party in the country. Privately, the Jana Sangh spokesmen were intimating to all who would listen that all Muslims would be sent to Pakistan following a Jana Sangh victory at the polls. The elite castes in the villages were told that their lost prerogatives would be restored to them.

When the ballots were counted, both Guru Datt Singh and Priyadatt Ram had failed: the Congress candidate, Madan Mohan Varma, was reelected to his legislative assembly seat. However, communal politics had indeed made major gains in both Faizabad constituency and Uttar Pradesh generally. The managers of various forms of protest, in fact, had much reason to feel encouraged over their future prospects. Table 1 tells the story.

Congress was the biggest loser and the Jana Sangh the biggest gainer in the election. But other protest groups showed up well also. The Swatantra (Freedom) Party, which appeals to conservatism and unrest in the Indian business community, won 15 seats in its first try at the polls. The Communists increased their representation by more than 60 per cent, from 9 to 15 seats, indicating some movement away from both left and right wing moderation.

A U.P. Constituency

TABLE 1

Legislative Assembly Seats Won by Political
Parties in the 1957 and 1962 General
Elections in Uttar Pradesh[21]

Political Parties	No. of Legislative Assembly Seats		Net Changes
	1957	1962	
Congress Party	286	248	—38
Communist Party	9	14	5
Praja Socialist Party	44	38	—6
Swatantra Party	—	15	15[a]
Bharatiya Jana Sangh	17	48	31
Other Parties	} 74[b]	34[c]	} —9
Independents		31	
TOTAL	430	428	—2[d]

[a] Swatantra did not exist in 1957.

[b] No breakdown for two categories available except that one seat was won by the Ram Rajya Parishad.

[c] Socialists 24, Hindu Mahasabha 2, Republican Party 8.

[d] Poll countermanded in two constituencies in 1962: Bahraich South and Nagar (Basti District).

In keeping with the general provincial trend, the managers of protest in Faizabad constituency made significant gains. Madan Mohan Varma had received 53 per cent of the total vote in the 1957 election. In 1962, however, he did not win by an absolute majority; his share of the vote was under 47 per cent while Guru Datt's was 30 per cent. A summary of the vote distribution is contained in Table 2.

TABLE 2

Vote-Distribution by Parties in Faizabad Constituency
for 1957 and 1962, in Percentages

Political Parties	Rural		Urban		Total	
	1957	1962	1957	1962	1957	1962
Congress Party	54.6	53.4	52.3	41.1	53.2	46.7
Bharatiya Jana Sangh	21.4	27.0	16.9	33.3	19.0	30.2
Muslim Independent[a]	4.2	12.2	3.4	18.6	3.7	15.5
Communist Party[b]	15.3	—	22.4	—	19.3	—
Praja Socialist Party[c]	—	2.0	—	3.5	—	2.9
Other Parties	4.5	5.4	5.0	3.4	4.8	4.7

[a] Hashim was the Independent Muslim who ran in 1957.

[b] Did not run a candidate in 1962.

[c] Did not run a candidate in 1957.

[21] Source for this data is the *National Herald*, Lucknow, March 5, 1962.

Harold A. Gould

It is at once apparent that the most decisive changes in voting behavior occurred among the urban population. A mere 8 per cent separated Madan Mohan's vote from Guru Datt Singh's in Faizabad city. Support for the Jana Sangh had doubled there since 1957 and support for Nasir Husain, the Muslim independent, had increased more than five times. As Priyadatt had anticipated, the strong bid of the Jana Sangh did frighten Muslims into voting for a coreligionist. However, as the Communists had expected, enough of their followers swung over to the Congress Party to offset in part the latter's loss of conservative voters to the Jana Sangh.

Communalism was not as successful an issue in the villages although the Jana Sangh increased its share of the vote by about 6 per cent and Husain did 8 per cent better than the Muslim independent did in 1957. The Muslim increase meant little in absolute terms, however, because only 15 per cent of the Muslims in the constituency reside in villages. The increase in the Jana Sangh vote, all informants agreed, had come predominantly from elite castes, and especially Rajputs, to whom Guru Datt's supporters promised a return to the old order in which they had reigned supreme.

Space does not permit a detailed discussion of microscopic political patterns in the villages (a monograph on the subject is in preparation), but I possess data which shows that Jana Sangh support was heaviest in the western portions of the constituency where village headmanships were more often held by Rajputs than by representatives of any other caste. This evidence also suggests that both the so-called Scheduled Castes and the *kisan* castes, who have gained most economically and in improvement of status from rural development programs and who constitute a majority of the rural population, went heavily for Congress, though of course not exclusively. The Scheduled Castes had supported the Communists to some degree in 1957 and seemingly obeyed the Communist Party's request to support Congress this time. Thus, the managers of orthodox Hindu protest found their readiest response in the old ruling class that had lost the most through the rise of the secular democratic state. They found the least response among the emerging middle-class peasantry, who could perceive no advantage in restoring the social system in which they had languished as virtual serfs.

Close analysis of voting patterns in Faizabad city reveals the most about communally-inspired voting. It was there that Guru Datt Singh and Priyadatt Ram enjoyed their greatest personal prestige and power because both their political careers had been developed and had culminated in relation to the municipality rather than to the constituency at large. Consequently, it was there that their methods worked best. For whereas Madan Mohan Varma obtained 53 per cent of the rural vote, he won only 41 per cent in the city. Table 3 provides a breakdown of the vote in the polling stations of Faizabad-cum-Ayodhya together with an indication of their general social composition.

We see that in 1957 the Congress Party carried all of Faizabad's polling stations except one. In that one (Rath Haveli) the Communist candidate barely eked out a victory. In 1962, however, Madan Mohan could carry but eight of Faizabad's fourteen polling stations. Five of these six were lost to the Jana Sangh and the sixth went to Nasir Husain, the Muslim independent. Clearly, some profound changes had occurred in the municipality's political equilibrium.

All of the polling stations which Madan Mohan lost to Guru Datt Singh were areas where there were large Muslim minorities and large Caste Hindu majorities. This, in other words, was the condition most conducive to communal patterns of voting. It was here that Priyadatt Ram's strategy of encouraging the candidacy of a Muslim independent paid its richest dividends. And it was here that Guru Datt's Jana Sangh strategy of apotheosizing the old Hindu values got some decisive results. It is interesting to observe that those areas of Faizabad containing the largest proportions of Muslims had been the places where the Communists got their largest vote in 1957. Rath Haveli, the only station actually won by them, was the only one to give Nasir Husain a victory in 1962. This would appear to be a good indication that Muslim alienation is strong and very responsive to protest movements that stress either their religious minority status or their proletarian status. When the communal issue was dormant, they supported Communist protest; when the communal issue arose, they shifted their identification from a proletarian to a religious focus. In the former they were linked to Hindus who shared their economic lot; in the latter their Hindu linkages were severed.

Another fact emerging from the Faizabad city vote is that Jana Sangh propaganda does get a better response among Caste Hindus than among menial-impure Scheduled Caste Hindus. This is suggested by the outcome in Lal Bagh and Sahebganj stations. These are the only two stations, among those with heavy Muslim representation, that Madan Mohan carried for Congress. What is distinctive about them from the standpoint of social composition is that the proportion of Scheduled Castes there is somewhat higher. Defection from the Congress ticket by Caste Hindus and Muslims was in a

TABLE 3

Voting Behavior and Social Composition by Polling Stations in Faizabad City in 1957 and 1962 (in Percentages)

Polling Station	Vote for Political Parties*								Social Composition		
	CONGRESS		JANA SANGH		MUSLIM IND.		COMM.	PSP	Caste Hindus	Sched. Castes	Muslims
	1957	1962	1957	1962	1957	1962	1957	1962			
Cantonment	84.7	71.8	4.9	11.7	0.4	13.5	9.8	0.6	76.9	11.9	11.2
Civil Lines	76.9	62.0	11.7	26.6	0.5	7.2	9.7	1.3	83.7	4.6	11.7
Dal Mandi	48.2	30.8	21.3	40.9	3.2	25.2	23.6	1.7	70.0	2.7	25.2
Khandan Bazaar	49.5	33.8	24.8	40.5	2.3	21.7	21.1	1.9	63.7	3.9	32.4
Delhi Darwaza	51.6	35.3	21.4	35.8	1.6	23.8	23.5	2.9	64.0	2.5	31.5
Rekabganj	52.8	32.7	19.6	40.6	0.5	20.2	24.9	5.3	74.2	4.1	21.7
Haidarganj	46.3	33.7	16.0	37.6	1.1	26.3	34.7	1.1	62.8	1.2	36.0
Lal Bagh	36.0	36.9	27.7	31.9	2.7	24.8	29.9	1.9	63.0	10.3	26.9
Sahebganj	53.4	46.6	9.4	29.9	2.9	18.6	32.4	1.9	66.1	6.1	27.8
Rath Haveli	38.4	31.6	11.2	29.4	4.7	34.0	38.6	3.3	64.1	4.2	31.7
Ram Kot	63.2	58.2	5.0	19.4	11.8	8.0	8.9	7.8	83.3	3.3	18.4
Rai Ganj	58.2	45.4	13.9	33.5	9.9	4.9	11.8	4.6	86.6	6.1	7.3
Singer Ghat	50.3	41.6	22.0	35.9	2.2	4.0	14.5	7.8	96.7	2.3	1.0
Ayodhya	46.3	51.5	16.0	25.8	11.9	10.2	11.7	7.3	83.2	4.2	12.6

* Italicized figures indicate the winner of the polling station.

NOTE: This table was made possible by combining data obtained from two sources. Messrs. Brij Nandan Prasad and Madan Mohan Varma kindly supplied me with complete election results for the constituency by polling station and polling booth. From these figures I was able to compile my percentages. The election results were then matched with the data on social composition. This was possible through the use of demographic materials contained in the *District Population Statistics, Uttar Pradesh*, No. 46—Faizabad District (Census of India, 1951).

measure checkmated by the disinclination of these Scheduled Castes to vote for a party that implies it will revive untouchability (by making the temples "pure" once more) and restore to the old elite their oligarchic powers.

Where Muslim minorities were small, Caste Hindu defections were simply insufficient in themselves to carry the day for Guru Datt Singh and Priyadatt Ram. In all the polling stations where Caste Hindus amounted to more than 75 per cent of the population, Congress lost ground over 1957, to be sure, but by no means enough to make possible a Jana Sangh victory. Ironically, the only polling station in the city where Congress gained over 1957 was Ayodhya, the sacred city, where one might have expected Guru Datt to shine.

SUMMARY AND CONCLUSIONS

The career of Guru Datt Singh and the Jana Sangh in Faizabad appear to substantiate the thesis that in a society undergoing rapid change the stresses inevitably generated in the lives of various individuals and groups literally cry out for "management." The nature of the stress generated is naturally not the same for everyone, and so interpretations of its causes will vary. The Jana Sangh articulates the protest of those who believe that an industrialized society governed by secular values is an evil. Their approach is essentially religious and traditionalistic. They accuse the present leadership of destroying a past that is deemed sacred and of selling out the country to alien groups and ideologies.

Appeals of this sort are particularistic in nature. They seek to sharpen social identity based upon *community* so that Hindus can set themselves apart as Hindus from everyone else. Such a community may then be promised preferential access to scarce material and symbolic rewards on the ground that their moral superiority entitles them to such favoritism.

Guru Datt Singh's career also shows that the attempt to combine revivalistic religious protest with the practical exigencies of democratic politics is fraught with serious internal contradictions. While the communal politician is amply equipped by his fanatical dedication to a rather simplistic set of values to work tirelessly for the capture of political power, these same qualities ill equip him to exercise that power judiciously after its capture. Thus, Guru Datt Singh failed to keep the power that he had won because his fanaticism was an irrepressible feature of his political personality. This is a common trait of religiously-oriented parties that bears close watching in India and other Asian societies.

Priyadatt Ram's behavior demonstrates still another point. Communalism has a dozen uses in India where caste and religious endogamy make it a compelling reality, a fact of life. The avowedly secular politician who publicly disclaims any sympathy with communalism may nevertheless exploit it for his own ends. His professional and pragmatic inclinations make its exploitation an irresistible temptation, principles to the contrary notwithstanding. Thus, the pragmatism that is supposed to be a by-product of secular-oriented political systems frequently operates to perpetuate the very casteism and groupism that all secular political philosophies eschew.

The Faizabad election revealed both the advantages and the limitations of the communal approach in politics. We have seen that it does have the capacity to attract support from various discontented segments of society. It can evoke an equal and opposite communal reaction in some other group, as with the Muslims, and thus produce the kind of political atomization that is often disastrous to moderate parties whose success depends upon the possibility of securing a broad consensus. However, the example of the middle-range peasant *jatis* in the villages shows that people who are economically and socially secure, or who are at least optimistic about their chances for such security, are not particularly moved by the promise of a Hindu millennium. And the Scheduled Castes are not receptive to such promises, not because they are satisfied with the status quo but because their plight induces a quest for more radical rather than more conservative measures.

Finally, let us reiterate that in a developing, rapidly changing society like India, with her myriad problems, discontent and protest are inevitable and are destined at times to assume grave proportions. Communal parties thrive in such circumstances. As long as moderate parties like Congress can preserve their leadership of the society and their right to manage industrialization, these communal parties probably perform some useful functions as gauges of stress and releasers of protest in controlled ways. Where they gain the upper hand, however, they are dangerous because, as Guru Datt Singh's career illustrates, their programs are unrealizable and their practical failures lead to desperation, repression and violence.

CHAPTER 4

THE JANA SANGH:
A BRIEF HISTORY

CRAIG BAXTER

A LONG-TIME observer of the Indian political scene once described the founding of the Bharatiya Jana Sangh as the coming together of a political leader in need of an organization and an organization in need of a leader for the political aspects of its program. The leader was Dr. Shyama Prasad Mookerjee; the organization, the Rashtriya Swayamsevak Sangh (RSS).[1] Though this description is an over-simplification there is a large element of truth in it.

THE LEADER AND THE ORGANIZATION

Mookerjee had had a distinguished career both in the academic and political fields.[2] The son of a noted Bengali educationist, Sir Ashutosh Mookerjee, the younger Mookerjee became vice-chancellor of Calcutta University in 1934 at the age of thirty-three. He entered active politics shortly thereafter as a member of the Hindu Mahasabha at a time when the Mahasabha attracted a number of Bengali intellectual and professional men; another entrant at this time was Nirmal Chandra Chatterji.[3] In 1941 and 1942, Mookerjee was minister of finance in the Bengal cabinet headed by Fazlul Haq. After independence Mookerjee was one of several non-Congress politicians invited to join the Nehru cabinet; he was given the portfolio of industries and supply. Not unexpectedly the Bengali Mahasabhaite and the Congress prime minister had differences on many issues, and the breaking point came on the question of the treatment by Pakistan of the Hindu minority in East Bengal. Mookerjee favored a more vigorous reaction against Pakistan than the Nehru government was willing to accept. On April 19, 1950, Mookerjee resigned from the

Craig Baxter is a Foreign Service Officer who has held several posts in India; most recently he was political officer in New Delhi.
[1] Usually translated "National Volunteer Organization."
[2] The authorized biography is by Balraj Madhok, *Shyama Prasad Mookerjee*, Deepak Prakashan, Delhi, 1954. See also Myron Weiner, *Party Politics in India*, Princeton University Press, Princeton, 1957, pp. 187-190; and *Organiser*, December 24, 1951, p. 2.
[3] Chatterji, after leaving the Hindu Mahasabha, joined and left the Swatantra Party and is now an independent member of the Lok Sabha.

cabinet and joined the small group of oppositionists in the provisional Parliament; he was soon recognized as a leading spokesman for the opposition. Mookerjee had remained a member of the Hindu Maha-sabha while a cabinet minister although the party had been banned after the assassination of Gandhi. However, he tendered his resignation from the Mahasabha in December 1948, when his proposal to open its membership to non-Hindus was rejected.[4] Thus at the time of his resignation from the cabinet Mookerjee was not a member of any political party. His biographer calls this period of Mookerjee's career "the quest for a political platform."[5]

The RSS was founded in 1925 by Dr. Keshav Baliram Hedgewar in Nagpur.[6] During the period of Hedgewar's leadership the growth of the organization appears to have been slow, but the membership was highly disciplined; from among these early members have come most of the present leadership of the RSS and much of the leadership of the Jana Sangh. Hedgewar died in 1940 and was succeeded by the present *sarsanghchalak,* Madhav Sadashiv Golwalkar.[7] Under Gol-walkar the growth of the RSS was more rapid, particularly in the Hindi-speaking areas of India and in the Punjab. The "cultural and spiritual rebuilding of the Hindu community" was the purpose of the RSS. The RSS concept of the Hindu Rashtra (Hindu Nation) was based on that of the Hindu Mahasabha leader, V. D. Savarkar.[8] As to the place of non-Hindus in India, Golwalkar wrote: "The non-Hindu peoples in Hindustan must either adopt the Hindu culture and language, must learn to respect and hold in reverence Hindu religion, must entertain no idea but those of glorification of the Hindu race and culture, i.e., they must not only give up their attitude of intolerance and ungratefulness toward this land and its age-long traditions but must also cultivate the positive attitude of love and devotion instead—in a word they must cease to be foreigners, or may stay in the country, wholly subordinated to the Hindu nation, claim-

---

[4] The resignation was accepted by the Mahasabha on May 7, 1949. Indra Prakash, *A Review of the History and Work of the Hindu Mahasabha and the Hindu Sanghatan Movement,* Akhil Bharat Hindu Mahasabha, Delhi, 1952, p. 258. Also Madhok, *Mookerjee,* p. 50.

[5] Madhok, *Mookerjee,* p. 45.

[6] J. A. Curran, Jr., *Militant Hinduism in Indian Politics,* Institute of Pacific Relations, New York, 1951, and Anthony Elenjimittam, *Philosophy and Action of the R.S.S. for Hind Swaraj,* Laxmi Publications, Bombay, 1951.

[7] For a brief biography of Golwalkar see *Shri Guruji, the Man and His Mission,* Bharat Prakashan, New Delhi, 1956.

[8] For a discussion of the development of Hindu communalist ideology, see Donald E. Smith, *India as a Secular State,* Princeton University Press, Princeton, 1963, pp. 454-468.

ing nothing, deserving no privileges, far less any preferential treatment—not even citizen's rights."[9]

The RSS formally avoided political activities, but it "was non-political in only one sense: it did not take part in elections nor was it organized for electoral purposes."[10] It was not possible for the RSS to avoid, nor did it wish to avoid, a degree of involvement in the clashes between Hindus and Muslims in the years before independence, and RSS members played a large role in the riots at the time of partition in 1947. The RSS supported the freedom struggle, although its endorsement of the policies of the Congress was not without reservation. Individual RSS members probably lent political support to the Hindu Mahasabha to a much greater degree than to the Congress. In its opposition to the partition of Bharatvarsha the RSS declared Independence Day, August 15, 1947, a "day of mourning."

The assassination of Gandhi by Nathuram Godse, who had been associated with both the Mahasabha and the RSS, resulted in the banning of the RSS by the government of India. The government statement said: "The professed aims and objects of the Rashtriya Swayamsevak Sangh are to promote the physical, intellectual and moral well-being of the Hindus. . . . Government have, however, noticed with regret that in practice members of the Rashtriya Swayamsevak Sangh have not adhered to their professed ideals. . . . The objectionable and harmful activities of the Sangh have however continued unabated and the cult of violence sponsored and inspired by the activities of the Sangh have claimed many victims. The latest and most precious to fall was Gandhiji himself. . . ."[11] The ban was in effect from February 4, 1948, until July 11, 1949. The agreement with the government which resulted in the lifting of the ban included the renunciation of political activities by the RSS and the publication of a constitution for the organization.

This published constitution of the RSS describes the role of the organization as follows:

> The aims and objects of the Sangh are to weld together the diverse groups within the Hindu Samaj and to revitalize and rejuvenate the same on the basis of its Dharma and Sanskriti, that it may achieve an all-sided development of Bharatvarsha.[12]

[9] M. S. Golwalkar, *We, or Our Nationhood Defined*, Bharat Prakashan, Nagpur, 1947, pp. 55-56.

[10] Weiner, p. 182.

[11] *Justice on Trial*, Rashtreeya Swayamsevak Sangh, Bangalore, 1958, pp. 64-65. This pamphlet is a collection of documents concerning the ban on the RSS in 1948-1949.

[12] Article 3. The text is contained in *Organiser*, September 6, 1949.

Concerning political activities the constitution goes on to say:

(a) The Sangh believes in orderly evolution of the Society and adheres to peaceful and legitimate means for the realization of its ideals.

(b) In consonance with the cultural heritage of the Hindu Samaj, the Sangh has abiding faith in the fundamental principle of tolerance toward all faiths.

The Sangh as such has no politics and is devoted to purely cultural work. The individual Swayamsevaks, however, may join any political party, except such parties as believe in or resort to violent and secret methods to achieve their ends; persons owing allegiance to such parties or believing in such methods shall have no place in the Sangh.[13]

The constitution also provides:

He (i.e., a Swayamsevak) who is an office-bearer of a political party shall not be eligible as a candidate for election or as an appointee to any post [in the RSS] so long as he is such an office-bearer.[14]

In spite of the constitutional prohibition on political activity, articles appearing in *Organiser*, the semi-official organ of the RSS, and elsewhere suggested the entry of the RSS into politics. The *Organiser* resumed publication on August 22, 1949, and this issue contained the first of a series of articles entitled "The RSS and Politics" by C. Parmeshwaran.[15] Balraj Madhok, who was to take an important part in the formation of the Jana Sangh, wrote: "It is necessary that the Sangh must give the lead to the country in regard to the political and economic problems of the country. . . . Any organization of the people which fails to guide its component parts about the vital questions influencing their lives is bound to lose the force which keeps any organization alive."[16] *Organiser* editor K. R. Malkani wrote an article called "Programme for a New Political Party" and in the same issue the paper advertised a pamphlet edited by Mookerjee, largely written by Malkani, entitled "Principles for a New Political Party."[17]

Even before his resignation from the cabinet Mookerjee was viewed as the potential leader by many of those in the RSS who favored a greater political role for the organization. Vasant Rao Oke, the Delhi RSS chief, met with Mookerjee as early as 1949, and offered the then minister RSS support if he should decide to enter opposition

---

[13] Article 4.   [14] Article 10 (B) 1.
[15] *Organiser*, August 22, 1949.   [16] *Ibid.*, September 6, 1949, pp. 13-14.
[17] *Ibid.*, February 19, 1951, p. 4. Malkani's article is signed "Keval."

politics. To what extent Oke was exceeding his brief in making such an offer is subject to debate; down to the founding of the Jana Sangh and even after there were some in the RSS who opposed, or at least were lukewarm to, the entry of the RSS into politics. Following Mookerjee's resignation his reception by members of the RSS and the coverage of his activities in *Organiser* increased markedly. A group, largely composed of RSS members and sympathizers, gave Mookerjee a reception in Delhi on the evening of the day of his resignation from the cabinet. The group included Oke; Mauli Chandra Sharma, who was to succeed Mookerjee as Jana Sangh president; and Hans Raj Gupta, *sanghchalak* for Delhi. In the address presented to Mookerjee the meeting said: "The country . . . needs courageous leadership, and we the citizens of Delhi are confident that you will now give such lead to the country as will not be based on lack of hope, self-abnegation and abject appeasement of the enemy."[18]

By early 1951, the ingredients of the new political party had been brought together. Mookerjee had found the organization he needed to make his second entry into national politics. He had also gathered around himself some persons who were not directly associated with the RSS, though these held, almost without exception, views which were highly sympathetic to the RSS, and some were former members of the Hindu Mahasabha. While everyone in the RSS may not have been reconciled to the all but direct participation in party politics which was to follow, the abstainers appear to have been largely passive in their opposition. Golwalkar himself was perhaps not fully convinced and possibly saw the new party as a child which might outgrow its parent; in Ahmedabad on November 10, 1949, he said: "We have forgotten that politics is only a part and parcel of the comprehensive life. Life is higher and wider than politics. . . . To regard politics as all-comprehensive is to abandon the soul of Bharat."[19]

On April 8, 1951, Mookerjee in an address in Calcutta announced his intention to start a new party: "I have been out from the central cabinet for nearly a year. People from all parts of the country have been asking me as to what they should do. I have deeply thought over the matter. And in the course of the next few weeks I hope to give my considered opinion in the matter. One thing is clear. Congress policies are disintegrating the country. The need of the hour is a new all-Bharat political party, to give a new program, a new ideal to the country."[20] The "considered opinion" was delivered on May 5 when Mookerjee announced the formation of the "People's Party"; in Hindi

[18] *Ibid.*, April 24, 1950, p. 1.   [19] Quoted in Curran, p. 27.
[20] *Organiser*, April 16, 1951, p. 1.

the name was given as Bharatiya Jana Sangh. A conference held that day adopted a program, selected Mookerjee as provincial leader and invited groups with similar views in other provinces to associate with the new party. The program contained eight points: (1) united India, i.e., the reversal of partition; (2) "reciprocity instead of appeasement" in relations with Pakistan; (3) "a more realistic and independent attitude in matters of foreign policy consistent with Bharat's paramount self-interest"; (4) rehabilitation of refugees, with compensation from Pakistan; (5) increased industrial and agricultural production; (6) "maintenance and development of a common culture for the whole country based on 'Bharatiya Sanskriti and Maryada' "; (7) equal rights for all citizens and improvement of the "socially and economically backward classes"; and (8) a local issue, "the equitable re-adjustment of the boundaries of West Bengal."[21] The draft program is given in some detail as it clearly forms the basis of the major Jana Sangh policies which continue to the present.

The action in Bengal was followed shortly by the formation of a Bharatiya Jana Sangh for Punjab, PEPSU,[22] Himachal Pradesh and Delhi. In view of the continued importance of the Jana Sangh in Punjab as compared with the complete disintegration of the party in Bengal after Mookerjee's death, the Punjab activity was perhaps the more important. On May 27, 1951, a convention was held in Jullundur which resulted in the founding of the Punjab unit of the party. Among the persons participating in the convention were Balraj Bhalla, son of the noted Arya Samajist Mahatma Hansraj; Mauli Chandra Sharma, of Delhi, whose father had been a president of the Hindu Mahasabha; Bhai Mahavir, son of the Punjab revolutionary Bhai Parmanand; and Madhok, who became general secretary of the Punjab unit and whose political experience had already included participation with Prem Nath Dogra in the formation of the Jammu and Kashmir Praja Parishad.

The new group in Punjab followed the pattern of the Bengal group by making clear its direct opposition to the Congress; Bhalla told a meeting in Delhi in early June: "Our difference with the Congress, the Socialists and the Kripalanites and such others is one of principle and not of policy. . . . When the Socialists or Kripalanites abuse the government, their quarrel is not with Congress principles but with Nehru, who, they charge, has failed to translate them into practice. It is here we differ essentially, for we believe that it is in the vicious

21 *Ibid.*, May 7, 1951, pp. 8-9.
22 Patiala and East Punjab States Union.

principles of the Congress that the malaise of our country stands rooted."[23]

Sections of the still to be unified national party were formed in other states during the next few months. Mookerjee, Bhalla and Madhok traveled extensively to address provincial conventions. On September 2, Bhalla was in Lucknow and Madhok in Indore; the key Uttar Pradesh and Madhya Bharat units were formed on that date and both units predictably passed resolutions calling for a national convention. In Uttar Pradesh Raja Krishnapal Singh, now a Swatantra Party member of the Lok Sabha, became president, and Dindayal Upadhyaya became general secretary. Most of the other provinces soon had units. At times the Jana Sangh organizers seem to have been carried away with their own enthusiasm; many of the non-RSS founders of the party expected great success in the forthcoming general elections.[24]

The first national convention of the Bharatiya Jana Sangh was held in Delhi on October 21, 1951. Mookerjee was elected president of the national party; Sharma and Mahavir were named general secretaries. The convention set down guide-lines for an election manifesto which was to be written in detail by the working committee; it also provided that the provincial units of the party could add matters of local interest to the manifesto provided the proposals did not conflict with the national manifesto. The choice of candidates for the general election was largely left in the hands of the local units. This contrasts greatly with the rather strong central control of the party which exists today.

While the Delhi convention was in progress, RSS chief Golwalkar said in Madras: "In the coming general elections the RSS will not back the Hindu Mahasabha or any other party in particular. In the drama of elections we shall be mere spectators. The Swayamsevaks of the Sangh are free to vote as they please. All our efforts will be diverted into the constructive channels of character-building, infusing a sense of selfless service and teaching boundless patriotism. To create a well-knit organization for a homogeneous nation is our aim. This alone can free the nation from poverty and misery."[25] In reading this statement one could be led to believe that Golwalkar was totally unaware of the activities of many of his Swayamsevaks in founding a new political party at the very time he was speaking.

[23] *Organiser*, June 18, 1951, pp. 8-9. "Kripalanites" refers to the Kisan Mazdoor Praja Party led by Acharya J. B. Kripalani, a former president of the Congress.

[24] A number of these fell away after the election, and still more deserted after the death of Mookerjee.

[25] *Organiser*, October 29, 1951, p. 16. Much of this issue is devoted to the Delhi session.

Craig Baxter

The Jana Sangh was now in existence and its first task was to contest the general elections which were to begin in less than two months. A nationally known leader and the services of a disciplined organization were only part of the equipment needed. The RSS organization was a key to success but it was strong only in northern India; in southern and eastern India it was weak. In Maharashtra it suffered from its association in the public mind with the Chitpawan Brahmin community, a community which was the target of the anti-Brahmin movement in Maharashtra and which had been tarred with the label "assassins of Gandhi" when one of its members slew the Father of the Nation. Mookerjee's personal leadership was very effective in Bengal, but could not be counted on too heavily elsewhere.

The working committee issued the manifesto before the end of October.[26] The document stated the object of the Jana Sangh to be: "the rebuilding of Bharat on the basis of Bharatiya *Sanskriti* and *Maryada* as a political, social and economic democracy granting equality of opportunity and liberty to individuals so as to make her a prosperous, powerful and united nation, progressive, modern and enlightened, able to withstand the aggressive designs of others and to pull her weight in the council of nations for the establishment of world peace." The Jana Sangh thereby stated at its founding the policy which it has tried to follow ever since: the endorsement of the ideal of a modern society set in the background of the ancient culture of India. The blending of these two seemingly opposed concepts is a task which the Jana Sangh has set for itself.

The manifesto also set forth four "fundamentals" which would guide the party: one country, one nation, one culture and the rule of law. The actions which the Jana Sangh pledged to undertake were it returned to power by the electorate were classified under four headings: land policy, industrial policy, home policies and foreign policy. Under land policy the party proposed several steps to increase agricultural output, supported land reform with compensation, suggested steps toward cooperation among agriculturalists and pledged the prohibition of cow slaughter. The Jana Sangh "will encourage private enterprise" except in industries "especially catering to the essential defense needs of the country"; it also proposed the encouragement of small-scale industries and the decentralization of in-

26 The text is contained in *Organiser*, October 29, 1951, from which the quotations are taken.

dustry. Local government would be developed and strengthened but the concept of the "unitary state," which later became a major plank in the Jana Sangh platform, was not mentioned. Hindi was supported as the national language. The Jana Sangh stated its belief in equal rights but "minorities based on religion will not be recognized by this party." The Jana Sangh did not, and does not, recognize the partition of India into two states; therefore much of the foreign policy section of the manifesto was directed at Pakistan and particularly toward opposition to the alleged appeasement of Pakistan by the Nehru government. The Jana Sangh policy opposing a plebiscite in Kashmir and favoring the complete integration of the state into India was contained in the first manifesto and has continued to be the party policy.

The question of the Jana Sangh position toward minorities, particularly toward Muslims, was raised in the manifesto and has been raised regularly throughout the history of the party. The manifesto, as noted above, said that the party did not recognize religious minorities. A policy which the Jana Sangh has continued to maintain was stated by Sharma in Nagpur on October 29, 1951. He said there were Muslims in the Jana Sangh but added that the party "would not beg persons" of any religion to join simply to give the party a "national color."[27] Speaking in Agra on November 27, Golwalkar said: "The Congress cut the country in two. The Communists would cut it into ten. The sole aim of the RSS is to generate forces for the consolidation of the country from Kashmir to Kanyakumari. . . . Muslims are lying low in wait for trouble. It is yet too early to base our policies on the assumption of their loyalty. . . . I have the greatest regard for Jesus Christ. He was a great man. But Bharati Christians will have to mend their ways. Their subsidized attempt to impose their creed on poor Hindus is repugnant."[28] This statement of Golwalkar, which was no doubt accepted by most of the RSS membership including those active in the Jana Sangh, is more extreme in its condemnation of the Muslim and Christian minorities than any *official* statement of the Jana Sangh.

More typical of the formal Jana Sangh position is the comment made by "Free Thinker" in his discussion of Jana Sangh policies: "The Jana Sangh considers [Muslims] the flesh of our flesh, the blood of our blood. . . . The Jana Sangh invites them to accept our hand of brotherhood. It expects them to shed all those complexes which militate against this brotherhood. It looks forward to their disassociating foreign ways from the tenets of their religion. They are welcome to

[27] *Ibid.*, November 5, 1951, p. 12.
[28] *Ibid.*, December 3, 1951, p. 1.

worship the Islamic way. They are expected to *live* the Bharatiya way. . . . No other minority is a problem. It is a measure of the largeness of the Hindu heart that all minorities save one—and that too chiefly due to external forces—are as happy and at home as anybody else."[29] The Jana Sangh was attacked by its opponents in the 1951-1952 general elections as communal, and has been so attacked since. It has, however, never closed its membership to non-Hindus. In the 1962 election two of its assembly candidates were Muslims: one in Rajasthan was elected; another stood from Indore in Madhya Pradesh. The first president of the Madras unit was a Christian.

The selection of candidates and the organization of the campaign were other tasks facing the new party. The rush to choose candidates seems to have led to some hasty selections. This is suggested by a study of the candidates selected in the 1952 and the 1957 elections. Excluding Delhi and Himachal Pradesh which elected assemblies in 1952 but not in 1957, the Jana Sangh ran a total of 683 candidates for assembly seats in 1952. Thirty of these candidates were successful. In 1957, only twelve of the thirty successful candidates stood for reelection and less than 8 per cent of the 1952 candidates were renominated.[30] Disciplinary problems accounted for some of the dropouts, particularly in Rajasthan, where only three of the eight persons elected in 1952 stood on the Jana Sangh ticket for reelection in 1957.

The principal campaigner was Mookerjee himself. He spoke in many of the constituencies and made himself available outside Bengal almost as much as he worked in his home state. Old ties of friendship led Mookerjee to work for the election of Chatterji from Hooghly, Bengal, on the Hindu Mahasabha ticket. Several attempts were made to arrange an electoral alliance among the Mahasabha, the Ram Rajya Parishad and the Jana Sangh. Much has been made of the effects of the "failure to cooperate" among the three parties. In discussing the effects supporters of the principle of alliance make one basic assumption: that *all* of the votes received by the candidate of the withdrawing party could be transferred to the candidate of the party remaining in the contest. This assumption is of doubtful validity. If, however, this assumption is accepted the effect of the "failure to cooperate" seems to have been rather less than the protagonists of alliance would lead one to believe. In assembly seats, the Ram Rajya Parishad *might* have gained eight seats, the Mahasabha five and the Jana Sangh three in a total of 160 constituencies in which the parties faced each other.

[29] *Ibid.*, December 31, 1951, p. 5.
[30] This results from a district-by-district study of the candidates in 1952 and 1957.

In parliamentary seats the Parishad and the Jana Sangh *might* have won another seat each in the twenty-two constituencies in which the parties were in opposition. The points of greatest conflict were in the northern tier districts of Uttar Pradesh, in Madhya Bharat and Vindhya Pradesh, and in large areas of Rajasthan. With the exception of Rajasthan, the conflict remains a factor in the elections in these areas, although the Parishad and the Mahasabha have almost faded from the political scene.

In many ways the results of the first general elections (Table 1) were

TABLE 1

Jana Sangh 1952 Election Results

| | Parliamentary | | | | | Legislative Assembly | | | |
| | JANA SANGH | | | STATE | | JANA SANGH | | | Per |
Seats	Cont.	Won	LD		Seats	Cont.	Won	LD	cent
42	—	—	—	Andhra Pradesh	241	—	—	—	—
12	2	0	1	Assam	105	3	0	3	0.29
53	2	0	2	Bihar	318	44	0	42	1.15
22	—	—	—	Gujarat	160	4	0	3	0.10
17	—	—	—	Kerala	129	—	—	—	—
38	11	0	4	Madhya Pradesh	339	126	6	68	5.66
39	—	—	—	Madras	198	—	—	—	—
42	4	0	2	Maharashtra	299	36	0	32	1.29
25	4	0	4	Mysore	212	25	0	21	1.21
20	—	—	—	Orissa	140	—	—	—	—
23	12	0	11	Punjab	186	85	2	59	5.07
22	4	0	2	Rajasthan	189	65	11	35	6.34
86	41	0	23	Uttar Pradesh	430	210	2	153	6.44
36	6	2	0	West Bengal	250	85	9	60	5.31
4	3	0	0	Delhi	48	30	4	4	21.88
4	2	0	1	Himachal Pradesh	36	9	0	8	3.46
2	—	—	—	Manipur	—	—	—	—	—
2	2	0	2	Tripura	—	—	—	—	—
489	93	3	52	TOTAL	3283	722	34	528	2.76

a disappointment to the Jana Sangh which, like other opposition groups, thought the Congress would be badly hurt. Although the Congress was set back in some parts of India, the Jana Sangh was not the beneficiary. For purposes of comparison with the two succeeding general elections the parliamentary and assembly constituencies have been arranged according to the present alignment of the Indian states.[31]

[31] All election data in this article are taken from the respective official reports of the election commission. "Seats" indicates the total number of seats contested in the election; "Cont.," the number of seats contested by the Jana Sangh; "Won," the number of seats won by the Jana Sangh; "LD," the number of Jana Sangh candidates who lost their security deposits, i.e., failed to poll one-sixth of the vote;

Craig Baxter

Despite the disappointment engendered by over-optimism, the results were far from disastrous for so new a party. The Jana Sangh was
one of the five parties which achieved recognition from the election
commission as a "national party." The Jana Sangh polled 3.1 per cent
of the total national vote in parliamentary constituencies. Its share
of seats in the Lok Sabha was much lower, its three seats being only
0.6 per cent of the total. It had elected its leader, Mookerjee, by a
sizable majority. Mookerjee had aided Durga Charan Banerji to win
a large victory in Midnapur and the Mahasabhaite Chatterji to win
in Hooghly. The then little known Umashankar M. Trivedi gained
the other Jana Sangh seat in Chittorgarh, Rajasthan; Trivedi is now
the leader of the Jana Sangh group in the Lok Sabha. For the first
two years of the new Parliament the Jana Sangh also had one member
of the Rajya Sabha, Deva Prasad Ghosh of West Bengal.

Of the states as then constituted the Jana Sangh polled heaviest in
Madhya Bharat where it received 9.7 per cent of the votes cast and
won four assembly seats. Vindhya Pradesh was another area where
the Jana Sangh showed strength, winning two seats and polling 9.9
per cent of the votes. In Rajasthan the Jana Sangh won eight seats
and 5.9 per cent of the vote. Three seats were won in Ajmer. In
Uttar Pradesh the votes were rather evenly distributed throughout the
state. Punjab provided the greatest disappointment: out of 66 candidates for the assembly in Punjab and 23 in PEPSU, only two in
PEPSU were elected. It was Punjab proper and not PEPSU that had
provided the stimulus for the founding of the party. The secular but
faction-ridden Congress was faced by challenges from both the pro-
Hindu Jana Sangh and the communal Sikh Akali Dal; it seems these
two challenges canceled each other as the Congress won a large
victory.

PROBLEMS OF CONSOLIDATION AND LEADERSHIP

The first elections were over and the Jana Sangh had a clear indication of its areas of strength and weakness. It now set itself to
the task of growth and consolidation based on Mookerjee as parliamentary and national leader and the RSS as the spearhead of local
organization. The Jana Sangh would also attempt to bring the Hindu
Mahasabha and Ram Rajya Parishad into its fold.

The first step taken by Mookerjee was to consolidate his position
as leader of a section of the opposition in the Lok Sabha. In June

---

"Per cent," the percentage of all valid votes polled by the Jana Sangh candidates
in the election for the legislative assembly.

1952, the National Democratic Party was formed with 32 members drawn from the Jana Sangh, Hindu Mahasabha, Ganatantra Parishad, Akali Dal, Commonweal Party, Tamilnad Toilers Party and nine independents from South India. Among the more prominent members were Sardar Hukam Singh, then an Akali (now speaker of the Lok Sabha), Chatterji of the Hindu Mahasabha and A. Krishnaswamy Mudaliar of the Commonweal Party. The three members of the Ram Rajya Parishad did not join the group.

About the time the National Democratic Party was being together the Socialist Party and the Kisan Mazdoor Praja Party were working out the merger which resulted in the Praja Socialist Party. Each of the two non-communist groups in the opposition hoped to be able to line up the remaining splinter groups and independents. Mookerjee also hoped to transform the parliamentary coalition into a formal merger of conservative parties throughout India just as the Praja Socialist Party had resulted from the consolidation of democratic socialist forces. The parliamentary coalition linked conservatives from north and south India; had it resulted in merger the effect on the Jana Sangh would have been incalculable, for the Jana Sangh with its emphasis on Hindi remains today almost exclusively a party of the north. The inclusion of the Akalis, too, might have changed the course of Jana Sangh development in the Punjab where today it is considered to be a party of the Hindus, opposed to the Sikhs. The six members of the Rajya Sabha representing these parties also joined together.

The Jana Sangh held its annual session in Kanpur, December 29-31, 1952, and reelected Mookerjee president. A significant change in the national leadership was made when Dindayal Upadhyaya was appointed a general secretary to replace Mahavir. He has held this position ever since. The expansion of the party was a major point on the agenda. Representatives of the parties comprising the National Democratic Party were invited to attend the session. The president of the Ganatantra Parishad was reported to have agreed to merge his party into the Jana Sangh, but this did not materialize.[32] Resolutions were passed on the treatment of Hindus in East Bengal and the rehabilitation of refugees. Kashmir was another topic given much attention, as the questions of Pakistani occupation of part of the state, the role being played by Sheikh Abdullah and the internal political situation were discussed. The Praja Parishad of Kashmir sent representatives to the session; the Parishad's affiliation with the Jana Sangh was recognized.

[32] *Organiser*, January 5, 1953, p. 2.

The Praja Parishad had begun a *satyagraha* against the Abdullah regime. Support was given by the Jana Sangh, Hindu Mahasabha and Ram Rajya Parishad, each of which had sent demonstrators across the border into Jammu from Punjab. Mookerjee announced his intention to join the *satyagrahis*; Abdullah replied that the visit would be "inopportune." On May 8, 1953, Mookerjee left Delhi en route to Jammu. He refused to obtain a permit from the government of India, declaring: "Mr. Nehru has repeatedly declared that the accession of the state of Jammu and Kashmir to India has been hundred per cent complete. Yet it is strange to find that one cannot enter the state without a previous permit from the government of India. This permit is even granted to Communists who are playing their usual role in Jammu and Kashmir, but entry is barred to those who think or act in terms of Indian unity and nationhood. I do not think the government of India is entitled to prevent entry into any part of the Indian Union which according to Mr. Nehru includes Jammu and Kashmir."[33] Mookerjee asserted that as a member of Parliament he was entitled to travel anywhere within India to gather information. In the afternoon of May 11, Mookerjee and two companions crossed the Punjab-Jammu border and were arrested by the Kashmir police. They were taken to Srinagar Central Jail and later transferred to a cottage outside the city which served as a temporary sub-jail. The agitation continued in Jammu, Punjab and Delhi. A number of members of Parliament including Chatterji were among the estimated 10,000 arrested.[34] Prem Nath Dogra joined Mookerjee and his two companions in their cottage jail on June 19. Mookerjee's health began to fail and he was transferred to the hospital on June 22. In the early hours of June 23, 1953, Shyama Prasad Mookerjee died in Srinagar, Kashmir, a prisoner of the government led by Sheikh Abdullah. On August 8, Abdullah himself was out of office, arrested and replaced by Bakshi Ghulam Mohammed. The Praja Parishad *satyagraha* was terminated after Mookerjee's death.

The death of Mookerjee was a major setback for the Jana Sangh. It deprived the party of its national leader, and ended for all practical purposes the National Democratic Party coalition in Parliament. It led to the disruption of negotiations with other parties for a joint electoral front, particularly with the Hindu Mahasabha. And it brought to the fore the RSS—non-RSS struggle within the party which soon led to a split in the central leadership.

The merger negotiations with the Hindu Mahasabha began dur-

33 Madhok, *Mookerjee*, pp. 252-253.
34 *Organiser*, May 25, 1953, p. 1.

ing Mookerjee's lifetime and were carried on primarily with the then Mahasabha president, Chatterji. The factors favoring the merger were clear. Personally Mookerjee and Chatterji had a close and long-standing relationship. The political platforms of the two parties, while not precisely the same, were similar in many respects, and they had cooperated in the National Democratic Party. Chatterji, though less acceptable to the south Indian and Akali members of the group, was perhaps the most logical successor to Mookerjee as leader of the parliamentary group. The two parties, together with the Ram Rajya Parishad, had worked together in the Kashmir *satyagraha* movement.

The discussions, which at times included the Parishad, began shortly after the 1952 elections. After Mookerjee's death Chatterji continued to press for the merger, claiming it was one of Mookerjee's last wishes. It seems, however, that Chatterji was not able to carry the rank and file of the Mahasabha along with him and that some of the second-rank leadership opposed the president in the Mahasabha working committee. Jana Sangh president Mauli Chandra Sharma angered the Mahasabha when he told the press: "The Hindu Sabha is a communal body and welcomes princes, zamindars and other vested interests in its midst. Consequently the merger of the Sabha in the Jana Sangh is not possible . . . as long as the Hindu Sabha sticks to its communal policies."[35] To this Indra Prakash, editor of the semi-official organ of the Mahasabha, replied that indeed the Mahasabha is communal and it considers communalism "bliss."[36] The negotiations ended in December 1953 with considerable bitterness on both sides. Over the years, however, the Jana Sangh has gradually absorbed a number of former members of both the Mahasabha and the Parishad.

Sharma was promoted from his position as one of the general secretaries to succeed Mookerjee as president of the Jana Sangh, and was formally elected at the party session in Bombay in January 1954. Sharma was not as well known as Mookerjee and had difficulty holding in check the differences between the RSS and non-RSS factions. Sharma attempted to assert authority equal to that of Mookerjee; the RSS group, fearing a weakening of its position, also asserted itself, and a clash became inevitable. To outward appearances all seemed well within the leadership as late as the Indore session of the all-India committee of the party in August 1953. In November, however, Sharma went to the press with his grievances and accused the

35 *Ibid.*, November 30, 1953, pp. 8-9.
36 *Hindu Outlook*, August 30, 1953, p. 3, quoted in Weiner, p. 230. Weiner, chapter 10, discusses the merger attempt in some detail.

RSS of trying to take over the party. He resigned from the presidency on November 3. The working committee met on November 7, accepted Sharma's resignation, appointed Bapu Saheb Sohoni as acting president, and issued a statement which said in part: "In his statement Pandit Mauli Chandra Sharma has deemed it fit to drag in the name of RSS. His irrelevant reference to the RSS smacks of an anxiety to please certain quarters where the name of RSS is anathema. We hereby condemn this attempt of . . . Sharma to abuse the Jana Sangh forum to try to run down the RSS. The Jana Sangh looks upon all its members alike, and we strongly resent the attempt of . . . Sharma to artificially classify the party members on the basis of their affiliation with other organizations working in various fields and thus disrupt the harmony and homogeneity of the party."[37] With the departure of Sharma and some others who held views similar to his, the Jana Sangh organization came almost completely under the control of persons associated with the RSS. Since Sharma's exit, factionalism, a factor in other Indian political parties, has been all but non-existent in the Jana Sangh.

During the inter-election period the Jana Sangh was also occupied with by-elections, local elections and in Rajasthan a serious problem of indiscipline. In September 1953 the Jana Sangh directed its legislators to resign from the Samyukta Dal, a joint opposition front in the Rajasthan assembly. Only three obeyed the directive; the others were expelled from the party. In assembly by-elections the Jana Sangh recorded some strength in Delhi and Ajmer, but in the by-election for the Lok Sabha seat vacated by Mookerjee's death the Jana Sangh candidate forfeited his deposit and the seat was won by a Communist. In a Lok Sabha by-election in Lucknow in March 1955 Atal Behari Vajpayee made his election debut; he lost in a three-way contest but retained his deposit.

To succeed Sohoni as president the Jana Sangh elected Prem Nath Dogra, the president of the Praja Parishad. Dogra presided over the Jodhpur session in January 1955 at which the Kashmir issue provided one of the major topics of discussion. The party gave its endorsement to the Nehru foreign policy of neutrality and coexistence, but cautioned: "The policy of coexistence on the basis of *Panchshila* has much to commend it and is not new to Bharat. But it ignores the fact that countries which refuse to tolerate the very existence of different ideologies and thoughts within their own boundaries can have no genuine faith in coexistence with countries attached to dif-

[37] *Organiser*, November 15, 1954, p. 3.

ferent ideologies and political systems. Therefore Russia and China, if they have genuine faith in the principle of coexistence, must give up their principle and policy of spreading communism all over the world, must disband the Cominform and stop helping and assisting the communist parties in other countries."[38] The Jana Sangh has constantly emphasized its opposition to communism. This ideological bias has led the party frequently to assert its belief in a common tie with the western democracies, although specific policies of the West such as American arms aid to Pakistan have been roundly denounced.

Another subject which engaged Jana Sangh attention was the re-organization of the Indian states on a linguistic basis. The Jana Sangh had by now adopted the concept of a "unitary state," i.e., one without state governments and in which elected district governments would have increased local powers and would be responsible directly to Delhi. Thus from a theoretical point of view the party was not concerned with the arrangement of the states whose very existence the Jana Sangh opposed. Practical political considerations, however, made it essential to take a position on the issue. This was done at the Jaipur session in April 1956: "The Bharatiya Jana Sangh had accorded its general approval to the recommendations of the States Reorganization Committee with certain modifications. . . ."[39] The modifications included opposition to the suggested merger of Bengal and Bihar and the proposed split of Uttar Pradesh. For Punjab the party favored a merger of Punjab, PEPSU and Himachal Pradesh into a Maha-Punjab which would have a large Hindu majority. The Akali demand for a separate Punjabi-speaking state was of course strenuously opposed, an opposition demonstrated by the Jana Sangh's active participation in the 1957 *satyagraha* of the Hindi Raksha Samiti. The party suggested a "Washington status" for Delhi, with, however, an elected municipal council to direct purely local affairs. The Jana Sangh at first supported a bilingual Bombay state but when the 1957 elections were held the party became a constituent of the Samyukta Maharashtra Samiti and supported the Mahagujarat Janata Parishad, thereby placing itself firmly in the camp of those favoring a separation of the Gujarati- and Marathi-speaking areas.

1957 ELECTIONS AND PARTY REORGANIZATION

The Jana Sangh now prepared to contest the second general elections which were to be held in early 1957. On August 19, 1956, General Secretary Upadhyaya announced the Jana Sangh electoral policy: "Jana Sangh feels it desirable that multi-cornered fights in the next

[38] *Ibid.*, January 10, 1955, p. 3.   [39] *Ibid.*, April 30, 1956, p. 7.

election be avoided. For this purpose it would be prepared to enter into electoral adjustment with other parties. Even if such adjustment is not possible, we, on our part, have decided to set up candidates only in constituencies where Jana Sangh has already been effectively working."[40] Deva Prasad Ghosh, the president of the party, had stated in Calcutta that the Jana Sangh would not enter into alliance with the Congress, Communists or Praja Socialists. On the state level the Jana Sangh, Ram Rajya Parishad and Hindu Mahasabha again went through a period of discussions on electoral alliances but as in 1952 no alliance resulted.

At the annual session in Delhi, December 28-30, 1956, over which Ghosh presided, the election manifesto was adopted. The document was not greatly altered from that presented to the voters in 1952. The results of the election for the Jana Sangh are summarized in Table 2.

TABLE 2

Jana Sangh 1957 Election Results

Parliamentary JANA SANGH					Legislative Assembly JANA SANGH				
Seats	Cont.	Won	LD	STATE	Seats	Cont.	Won	LD	Per cent
43	1	0	0	Andhra Pradesh	301	8	0	8	0.11
12	—	—	—	Assam	108	—	—	—	—
53	2	0	1	Bihar	318	30	0	25	1.10
22	—	—	—	Gujarat	132	5	0	1	0.55
18	—	—	—	Kerala	126	—	—	—	—
36	21	0	6	Madhya Pradesh	288	124	10	70	9.89
41	—	—	—	Madras	205	—	—	—	—
44	7	2	1	Maharashtra	264	18	4	7	2.00
26	5	0	4	Mysore	208	20	0	5	1.37
20	—	—	—	Orissa	140	—	—	—	—
22	16	0	6	Punjab	154	64	9	39	8.60
22	7	0	0	Rajasthan	176	47	6	26	5.52
86	61	2	30	Uttar Pradesh	430	235	17	143	9.84
36	5	0	3	West Bengal	252	33	0	31	0.98
5	5	0	2	Delhi	—	—	—	—	—
4	—	—	—	Himachal Pradesh	—	—	—	—	—
2	—	—	—	Manipur	—	—	—	—	—
2	—	—	—	Tripura	—	—	—	—	—
494	130	4	54	TOTAL	3102	584	46	365	4.03

(The assembly totals for Andhra Pradesh include the 1955 elections in Andhra.)

In the elections for the Lok Sabha the Jana Sangh lost both of the seats it retained after the death of Mookerjee. Banerji did not stand

[40] *Ibid.*, August 27, 1956, p. 3.

91

for reelection; Trivedi changed constituencies and was defeated. The principal new entrant was the young (then 30) Atal Behari Vajpayee, who became leader of the four-man group. The two Lok Sabha seats from Maharashtra, as well as the four assembly seats, were not indicative of Jana Sangh strength but were the product of the alliance with the Samyukta Maharashtra Samiti. All of the Maharashtra seats were lost in 1962.

Madhya Pradesh became the strongest state for the Jana Sangh in terms of percentage of votes polled. The party built on its earlier strength in the former Madhya Bharat and Vindhya Pradesh areas and demonstrated some growth in the Mahakoshal area. In the other Hindi-speaking states, the party increased its share of the vote in Uttar Pradesh and Punjab, declined in Rajasthan and remained even in Bihar. Uttar Pradesh and Madhya Pradesh, by giving the Jana Sangh nearly one vote in ten, were marked as areas for expansion before the 1962 elections. In Punjab the Jana Sangh seems to have drawn almost exclusively on the urban Hindu population for its votes. The disciplinary difficulties in Rajasthan led to a setback there but the party leader Bhairon Singh was returned to the assembly.

The working committee met shortly after the results were announced. The following excerpts from the resolution passed by the committee are indicative of the party's reaction to the election: ". . . The committee feels that the Jana Sangh in spite of the odds against it, has registered a definite advance both in respect of votes polled and seats won. . . . In respect of state assemblies the election results in Uttar Pradesh, Madhya Pradesh, Rajasthan, Punjab and Bombay have been quite encouraging . . . Jana Sangh, however, has got a setback in West Bengal—where it has not been able to maintain the position it had secured in the last elections—as also in Bihar and Karnatak [Mysore] where Jana Sangh work had been going on for some time. . . . The committee feels deeply concerned over the important part played by casteism and communalism, particularly Muslim communalism, in the present elections. The party in power—and some opposition parties—deliberately worked up these feelings for temporary gain at the cost of wider national interests. Unless effective steps are taken to curb these forces, they would become a serious threat to national unity and undermine democracy itself. . . . The committee also decides to pay more attention to the eastern and southern regions in days to come."[41]

To give effect to the plans of the working committee for growth

[41] *Ibid.*, April 29, 1957, p. 3.

of the party and for greater activity in the south and east, the Jana Sangh made a change in the organizational structure of the party in 1958. A new tier of officials was placed between the central office and the state units. This level was made up of four "zonal secretaries." The persons appointed then have continued to hold the posts. Balraj Madhok was appointed for the north: Punjab, Delhi, Himachal Pradesh and Jammu and Kashmir. Nanasaheb Deshmukh oversees the east: Uttar Pradesh, Bihar, West Bengal and Assam. Sundar Singh Bhandari is in charge of the west: Rajasthan, Gujarat, Madhya Pradesh and (because it began as a branch of the Madhya Pradesh unit) Orissa. Jagannathanrao Joshi supervises the south: Maharashtra and the four southern states, Andhra Pradesh, Madras, Mysore and Kerala. In addition to the general secretary, Upadhyaya, two other secretaries are also posted in Delhi: Vajpayee is in charge of parliamentary work; Jagdish Prasad Mathur is in charge of the central office. All of these men are closely associated with the RSS. Another gesture toward expansion in the south was the holding of the December 1958 session at Bangalore. Ghosh, a Bengali, again presided.

The Jana Sangh, and the RSS, have branched out into other fields. The Bharatiya Mazdoor Sangh, a labor union, "follows similar policies" as the Jana Sangh though there is no official connection. The general secretary of the Mazdoor Sangh, D. B. Thengadi, was elected to the Rajya Sabha in 1964 as a Jana Sangh candidate. The Vidyarthi Parishad, a student group, similarly is ideologically close to the Jana Sangh but also has no official connection. The Parishad is particularly active in universities in northern India. The *Organiser*, an English language weekly published in Delhi, serves as the semi-official organ of both the Jana Sangh and the RSS. Its editor, K. R. Malkani, visited the United States in 1961-1962 on a Nieman grant to study at Harvard. During his absence the acting editor was L. K. Advani, who concurrently served as secretary of the Delhi unit of the Jana Sangh.

Yet again under the presidency of Ghosh the Jana Sangh held its annual session at Ambala, April 4-6, 1959. Kashmir and the rehabilitation of refugees again received attention but the location of the meeting led the party to focus on the Hindi Raksha Samiti agitation in the Punjab. In this the Jana Sangh was working with the Arya Samaj and the Hindu Mahasabha.

In the inter-election period the party was engaged in a series of by-elections, local elections and elections to upper houses. In 1958 the Jana Sangh returned to the Rajya Sabha after an absence of four years, when one of its members was elected from Uttar Pradesh. The party also placed members in the legislative councils in Bombay (Maharashtra after April 1960), Uttar Pradesh, Punjab and Andhra Pradesh. In by-elections to legislative assemblies the party about held its own in the five-year period. In the November 1957 civic elections in Uttar Pradesh the Jana Sangh made substantial gains and elected a Jana Sangh mayor in Lucknow. The Delhi municipal corporation elections in March 1958 provided an indication of the continued Jana Sangh strength in the capital. The Jana Sangh won 25 of 80 seats with 26.4 per cent of the vote; the Congress won 31 seats with 39.8 per cent of the vote.

Two parliamentary by-elections, one in June 1958 and the other in April 1961, were the highlights of the Jana Sangh electoral activity between the general elections. In June 1958 the Jana Sangh supported Prakash Vir Shastri in the by-election in Gurgaon, Punjab, which resulted from the death of Education Minister Maulana Abul Kalam Azad. The Congress nominated Mauli Chandra Sharma for the seat; the Jana Sangh relished the opportunity to oppose its former president. Shastri, a prominent young Arya Samajist, won the seat with 61.2 per cent of the vote. Sharma later was appointed a member of the Official Language Commission. In April 1961 a by-election was held for the New Delhi seat vacated by Sucheta Kripalani when she resigned from the Lok Sabha to accept a post in the Gupta ministry in Uttar Pradesh. The Jana Sangh nominated Balraj Madhok who had been defeated by Mrs. Kripalani in the 1957 general election. The Congress nominated Rana Jung Bahadur Singh; he had been elected to the Delhi legislative assembly in 1952 on the Jana Sangh ticket but disavowed his connection with the party as soon as the election was over. Four other candidates, including one from the Swatantra Party, also contested the election. Madhok won the seat with 46.1 per cent of the vote. His addition to Vajpayee in the Lok Sabha gave the Jana Sangh two prominent speakers in that body.

The birth of the Swatantra Party was viewed with some disfavor by the Jana Sangh. When the preliminary meeting of the Swatantra Party was held in Madras in June 1959 under the leadership of C. Rajagopalachari, the *Organiser* editorially "welcomed" the new party but wondered whether it would add or detract from the work of Jana Sangh and of conservative politics in general.[42] Writing just prior to the Madras meeting, but with knowledge of Rajagopalachari's plans, Madhok criticized the move to form a new party: "In the South Shri C. Rajagopalachari has been advocating for some time

[42] *Ibid.*, June 15, 1959, p. 1.

the formation of a new conservative party which may act as a brake on the Congress Party and work for preserving and conserving what is good in the traditional Indian way of life. . . . The economic program . . . and the role [of the new party] . . . do not seem to be much different from . . . the Bharatiya Jana Sangh. As such there is little scope or need for the creation of any such new party except that it will provide a new platform to the intellectual and economic aristocracy which is finding itself out of tune with the new rhyme of the ruling party but considers it below its dignity to join the ranks of the Jana Sangh. . . . The one good that such a party can and may do is to create a better understanding and appreciation for the Bharatiya Jana Sangh, which has already made its mark as a forward-looking and open-minded conservative party of India. The Jana Sangh circles, therefore, are indifferent about the formation of such a party though they would like all those who sincerely feel the need for it to study Bharatiya Jana Sangh more closely and objectively before plumping for a new party."[43] The Swatantra Party was formed in Bombay in August 1959 and the question of relations between the two parties has been a lively topic ever since.

Before the third general elections the Jana Sangh held two annual sessions and one "enlarged" meeting of the all-India committee. Pitamber Das of Uttar Pradesh presided over the Nagpur session in January 1960. A year later at Lucknow, A. Rama Rao of Andhra Pradesh presided. Both men were members of the legislative councils of their states; Pitamber Das continues to hold his seat in Uttar Pradesh. In November 1961 the all-India committee, supplemented by other delegates, met in Banaras under Rama Rao to decide the Jana Sangh 1962 electoral policy and platform.

In December 1961 the Jana Sangh gained the membership of Dr. Raghu Vira. A scholar specializing in Oriental languages, he had been a Congress member of the Constituent Assembly, and of the Rajya Sabha since 1952. He bitterly opposed the policies of Defense Minister V. K. Krishna Menon and when ordered by the Congress to explain his criticism Raghu Vira instead resigned from the Congress and joined the Jana Sangh. He ran in the Banaras Lok Sabha constituency in the 1962 elections and was defeated by the Congress incumbent. At the Bhopal session of the Jana Sangh in December 1962 Raghu Vira was elected president. While campaigning for the opposition candidates in parliamentary by-elections five months later he was killed in an automobile accident. Once again the Jana Sangh was deprived of its leader.

[43] Balraj Madhok, *Political Trends in India*, S. Chand, Delhi, 1959, pp. 142-144.

The Jana Sangh

SUBSTANTIAL GAINS IN 1962

The Jana Sangh decided to fight the 1962 general elections alone and to put up candidates wherever the party had an organizational unit. As a result the Jana Sangh contested more parliamentary and assembly seats than any party except the Congress. Although the party rejected "national alliances" it stated it would agree to "local adjustments" with other opposition parties except the Communists and the "communalists"; the latter term was specifically applied to the Muslim League, the Akali Dal and the Dravida Munnetra Kazhagam of Madras. Talks again were held with the Hindu Mahasabha and the Ram Rajya Parishad and again were to no avail. More important discussions were held with the Swatantra Party and in a few areas the parties managed to come to some agreement to avoid opposing each other, but these were few and scattered. The Jana Sangh, Praja Socialist Party and Swatantra Party worked together in support of the unsuccessful attempt by Acharya Kripalani to unseat Krishna Menon in the North Bombay constituency, and the Jana Sangh supported Socialist Party candidate Rammanohar Lohia against Jawaharlal Nehru in the Phulpur constituency.

All of the five Lok Sabha members elected on the Jana Sangh ticket were renominated. Sixteen others who were unsuccessful in 1957 were renominated in 1962. A number of 1957 parliamentary candidates ran for assembly seats in 1962; the reverse was also frequently true. Of the forty-six persons elected to the legislative assemblies on the party ticket in 1957, thirty were renominated and fifteen of these were reelected. Eight of the 1957 assembly winners were dropped as the result of disciplinary action; these were in Gonda and Mirzapur districts of Uttar Pradesh and Mahendragarh district in Punjab. Discussing the selection of candidates, Upadhyaya wrote: "In the selection of candidates preference has been given to party workers and to candidates who had earlier contested election on the Sangh ticket. All the sitting members are seeking re-election. Those who applied for Congress tickets and have been refused are not encouraged by the Sangh to enter the elections on its ticket. The Jana Sangh also does not believe in importing candidates from the outside and as a rule home constituencies have been allotted."[44]

The election manifesto adopted at the Banaras session repeated the policies of the party.[45] In the defense and foreign affairs sections China now equaled or surpassed Pakistan as the country seen as the chief

[44] Dindayal Upadhyaya, "Jana Sangh and the General Elections," in S. L. Poplai, ed., *1962 General Elections in India*, Allied Publishers, Bombay, 1962, p. 51.
[45] The text is contained in Poplai.

threat to India. Kashmir figured prominently as did the refugee problem. The Jana Sangh, like the Swatantra Party, came out squarely against cooperative farming: the Jana Sangh "considers cooperative farming detrimental to democracy." The attempt to combine ancient Indian culture with modern western ideas is perhaps best seen from the statement on education: ". . . evolve a new educational pattern which would blend our ancient *gurukul* modes with modern methods with their technical, vocational and scientific bias."

In the midst of the election campaign the Jana Sangh received an endorsement from Golwalkar: "At least that one party, we can expect will possess some content of idealism and integrity and be able to clean up the present-day foul political climate of the land to which all other parties have unfortunately fallen prey."[46]

The results of the election are summarized in Table 3. The Jana Sangh gains were substantial. In the Lok Sabha the party moved ahead of the Praja Socialist Party and became the third largest opposition group. There were, however, setbacks: all of the sitting mem-

TABLE 3

Jana Sangh 1962 Election Results

Parliamentary JANA SANGH					Legislative Assembly JANA SANGH				
Seats	Cont.	Won	LD	STATE	Seats	Cont.	Won	LD	Per cent
43	8	0	8	Andhra Pradesh	301	70	0	69	1.04
12	—	—	—	Assam	105	4	0	4	0.45
53	13	0	11	Bihar	318	75	3	61	2.77
22	5	0	5	Gujarat	154	26	0	23	1.33
18	4	0	4	Kerala	126	3	0	3	0.06
36	28	3	13	Madhya Pradesh	288	195	41	91	16.66
41	1	0	1	Madras	206	4	0	4	0.08
44	17	0	13	Maharashtra	264	127	0	100	5.00
26	7	0	6	Mysore	208	63	0	56	2.29
20	—	—	—	Orissa	140	—	—	—	—
22	17	3	10	Punjab	154	80	8	47	9.72
22	11	1	4	Rajasthan	176	94	15	55	9.15
86	74	7	33	Uttar Pradesh	430	377	49	192	16.46
36	4	0	4	West Bengal	252	25	0	24	0.45
5	5	0	0	Delhi	—	—	—	—	—
4	2	0	2	Himachal Pradesh	—	—	—	—	—
2	—	—	—	Manipur	—	—	—	—	-
2	—	—	—	Tripura	—	—	—	—	—
494	196	14	114	TOTAL	3122	1143	116	729	6.07

(Total includes Kerala mid-term assembly election of 1960.)

[46] *Organiser*, October 16, 1961, p. 5.

bers, including Vajpayee and Madhok, were defeated. Trivedi returned to the Lok Sabha and was selected leader of the group, but without the two principal spokesmen the party's performance in the Lok Sabha has not been commensurate with its numbers. Vajpayee was one of two Jana Sanghis elected to the Rajya Sabha in 1962; two more were added in 1964.

In the vote for state assemblies, the Jana Sangh increased its percentage of the total vote in every state except West Bengal. The party made token appearances in Assam and Madras as well as in the Kerala mid-term assembly elections in 1960; only Orissa has yet to see a Jana Sangh contest. The Jana Sangh became the official opposition party in both Madhya Pradesh and Uttar Pradesh. In the latter a key contest was won by Yaduvendra Dutta Dube, the Raja of Jaunpur, who defeated the state Finance Minister Hargovind Singh. In Madhya Pradesh Jana Sangh candidates defeated the chief minister, Kailash Nath Katju, and three deputy ministers. Bhairon Singh defeated Rajasthan Home Minister Ram Kishore Vyas. The party was encouraged by its first successes in Bihar, but in Punjab its expectations were unfulfilled. Though the percentage of the vote gained by Jana Sangh increased and three Lok Sabha candidates were elected, the party lost a seat in the assembly and saw the Sikh communal Akali Dal emerge as the principal opposition party.

One commentator on the election has written: "Madhya Pradesh, Rajasthan, Uttar Pradesh and Bihar are the four states where the Congress Party fared badly whereas the opposition parties, particularly the right-wing, did correspondingly well. . . . What does the attrition of Congress strength in this Hindi-speaking 'Prussia' of the Indian subcontinent tell us about the future structure of Indian politics?"[47] An independent weekly said: "The rise of the Jana Sangh, described as a 'communal party' by the prime minister among others, is as spectacular as that of the Swatantra Party. It is the Jana Sangh . . . that promises, because of its militant and disciplined character, a far greater opposition to the Congress in the years to come. One might or might not like this particular expression of opinion of the electorate but it is undoubtedly a force of great importance which needs quickly to be evaluated."[48] The *Hindustan Times* saw "the extension of the Jana Sangh's influence to the rural areas" as the "most significant development of this election in Uttar Pradesh."[49]

---

[47] Surinder Suri, *1962 Elections, a Political Analysis*, Sudha Publications, Delhi, 1962, p. 58.
[48] *Eastern Economist*, March 2, 1962.   [49] *Hindustan Times*, March 12, 1962.

The points suggested by these comments on the election should be examined briefly. First, the Jana Sangh made no substantial head-way outside the Hindi-speaking area. All of its parliamentary and assembly seats were won in the states of north India. Outside this area approximately 90 per cent of the Jana Sangh candidates lost their security deposits when they failed to poll one-sixth of the vote in their constituencies. Secondly, a study of the assembly constitu-encies in Uttar Pradesh shows that the Jana Sangh increased its share of the votes in rural areas, over 1957, at a much greater rate than it did in the urban areas, though both in rural and urban areas the share increased. Many observers had considered the Jana Sangh a party of the urban, middle-class Hindu. In Uttar Pradesh this seems to be changing, although in Punjab the party remains confined to the cities and dependent upon the votes of the urbanized Hindu population rather than the rural Sikhs. Thirdly, another theory held that the Jana Sangh would poll best in areas where the number of Muslims was substantial. A study of the districts in Uttar Pradesh shows that there is no apparent correlation between the percentage of Muslims and the percentage of votes received by the Jana Sangh.

Finally, there was the competition between the Jana Sangh and rival parties which had points in common with the Jana Sangh. In the 1962 elections the opposition of the Ram Rajya Parishad and Hindu Mahasabha continued, but the eclipse of these two parties made the rivalry of even less importance than in earlier elections. More important, both in the 1962 elections and for the future, is the competition between the Jana Sangh and the Swatantra Party. The two parties cost each other many seats, if the complete trans-ference of votes is accepted. Rajasthan, Uttar Pradesh, Bihar and Gujarat were the states in which the two parties faced each other most frequently.

There are pro- and anti-cooperation groups in both parties. Within the Swatantra Party it is believed that Rajagopalachari himself would favor some sort of understanding with the Jana Sangh as would the senior vice president, K. M. Munshi, Ganatantra Parishad leader P. K. Deo and much of the north Indian leadership. Opposing a Swatantra-Jana Sangh alliance are, among others, General Secretary M. R. Masani and Chairman N. G. Ranga. The pro-cooperation group in the Jana Sangh includes Madhok, Trivedi and others whose con-nections with the RSS are not all-encompassing; the late president, Raghu Vira, also favored an understanding. Less favorable toward an understanding with Swatantra and favoring a "go-it-alone" policy stand Upadhyaya, Deshmukh and some others who came to the Jana Sangh directly from full-time RSS work. Neither those for or against cooperation in either party seem to be so rigid in their views as to be unwilling to discuss plans for cooperation, but the "antis" appear to take the view that the other party must make all the concessions and should agree in effect to merge into the surviving party without condition. Examples of views which are unacceptable to the other party are Swatantra's stand for conciliation with Pakistan and Jana Sangh's demand for Hindi as the national language. It is upon such rocks that the talks on cooperation founder.

In a series of by-elections held in May 1963, Swatantra, Jana Sangh, the Socialist Party, and, in one constituency, the Praja Socialist Party cooperated to hand the Congress three losses in four contests. The by-elections brought into the Lok Sabha Kripalani, Masani and Lohia; the only loss was in Jaunpur, Uttar Pradesh, where Upadhyaya failed to retain a Jana Sangh seat. The support to the three victors by the Jana Sangh cadre in each of the constituencies is given a large share of the credit for the successes. The parties continued their cooperation long enough to support a Kripalani motion of no-confidence in the Nehru government, but it was not long before the moratorium on criticism of each other was ended and the intra-opposition feuding began anew.

PROSPECTS OF THE JANA SANGH

The Jana Sangh pictures its future as one of steady growth. In the short range of the 1967 elections, the party plans to run candidates in every state with the goal of entering the assembly of each state. From the present strength in Uttar Pradesh and Madhya Pradesh the party will make a determined bid for power in 1967. Elsewhere in the north the Jana Sangh aims to be the principal opposition in Punjab and Rajasthan and grow markedly in Bihar; in the last named state the disintegration of the state unit of the Swatantra Party might aid the Jana Sangh. Gujarat, Andhra Pradesh, Mysore and Maharashtra are secondary targets of the party, while the extreme south and the east are areas of doubtful results. Time is a commodity which the Jana Sangh feels is on its side; eventually, says the party, the country will turn to it and in the meantime steady work is what is necessary. The Jana Sangh believes that it will be the final, and successful, bastion against communism in India.

The Jana Sangh is not overly concerned with the charges of communalism leveled against it. Unlike the Hindu Mahasabha and the

RSS the party officially stands for "Bharatiya," i.e., Indian, and not "Hindu" culture; it has never officially supported "Hindu Raj." Also unlike the other two organizations, from one of which the Jana Sangh is politically descended and from the other draws much of its organizational strength, the Jana Sangh has never banned non-Hindus from membership. The differences in adjectives and in membership policy may be technical but they cannot be totally ignored, and have been stated in different terms deliberately. The lack of concern by the Jana Sangh is understandable in a country which is overwhelmingly Hindu.

The strength of the Jana Sangh lies in its almost unalterable determination to carry on with the program it has framed. This is being done with an organization which is second in numbers only to the Congress and which is often more youthful and dynamic than the Congress. On the other side are some of the policies of the party which hinder its growth outside the Hindi area. The party also lacks the flexibility which might add to its numbers and might lead to closer cooperation with other parties whose views do not differ widely from those of the Jana Sangh. After the 1962 elections *The Hindu* of Madras said: "If any clear outline is to be traced at all in this contradictory, and partly confusing, shift of electoral opinion in the various states, it must be sought primarily in a developing contest between the pragmatic socialism of the Congress . . . and the extremism of the Communists on the one side and on the other the progressive liberalism of the Swatantra and Jana Sangh with their emphasis on limits to the state's incursions in the economic field and greater realism in planning."[50] The resolution of the "developing contest" is yet to be seen.

[50] *The Hindu*, March 3, 1962.

CHAPTER 5

THE EFFECTIVENESS OF
MUSLIM REPRESENTATION
IN INDIA

THEODORE P. WRIGHT, JR.

IN A SECULAR democracy such as India is striving to be, the question of political representation for religious minorities as such is not supposed to arise.[1] Under India's 1950 Constitution citizens are represented, except for the temporary reservation of seats for the Scheduled Castes and Tribes, by legislators elected on the basis of geographical constituencies modeled after those of the older democracies. The western theory of representation assumes that delegates thus selected will serve all of their constituents impartially. Those of the latter who are nevertheless dissatisfied with their legislators will not be in a permanent minority, but will have recurrent opportunities to persuade a majority of their fellow voters to displace the incumbents. Since, however, a religious minority cannot mobilize a majority of voters short of the unlikely process of mass conversion, the assumptions of democratic theory must be called into question here. Religious minorities of considerable size continue to exist in India despite partition and, in the imperfect state of the country's secularity, to have some legitimate interests and grievances peculiar to themselves which may not be adequately voiced in the present system. The largest of these is the Muslim minority which still composes about 10 per cent of the population,[2] so this paper will be concerned entirely with their representation.

THE QUALITATIVE ASPECT OF REPRESENTATION

Recent writers on the subject of Muslim participation in Indian politics have dwelt mostly on its quantitative aspect. Both Donald E. Smith[3] and Sisir K. Gupta[4] have remarked that Muslims are not

Theodore P. Wright, Jr., is associate professor of political science at the Graduate School of Public Affairs, State University of New York, Albany.

[1] I wish to acknowledge the Fulbright grant which enabled me to do the research for this paper in India during the academic year 1963-1964.

[2] Census of India, *1961 Census—Religion*, Paper No. 1 of 1963, p. iv.

[3] Donald E. Smith, *India as a Secular State*, Princeton University Press, Princeton, N.J., 1963, p. 419.

[4] Sisir K. Gupta, "Moslems in Indian Politics, 1947-60," *India Quarterly*, 1962, vol. 18, p. 371.

to be found in the Parliament and state legislatures in the proportion
of their percentage of the population, although their position is better in the indirectly elected and politically weak upper houses. Gupta,
citing La Ponce, properly reminds us, however, that minority representation in legislative bodies and minority influence through electoral weight are not necessarily connected. A group's wishes may be
as well or better fulfilled by politicians of the majority community if
the outcome of closely contested elections is heavily dependent upon
the marginal effect of the minority's votes. Representatives of the
minority's own faith on the other hand may be discounted on the
ground of obvious partiality.[5] In fact, La Ponce warns[6] that the closer
minorities are to having a majority of seats, the more dangerous they
will appear from the dominant group's point of view with a consequent increase in the latter's cohesion in hostility.

Clearly then, the problem of minority representation has a qualita-
tive aspect which has been neglected. Who are the Muslim legislators
and ministers who are elected and what do they do to promote the
interests and redress the grievances of their coreligionists? In other
words, how effective is Muslim representation in India? This question
inevitably raises a normative one: does a Muslim in government have
the right to advance his own community in addition to his general
duties to his constituency and nation, or is such action incompatible
with democracy and the separation of religion and state?

As to who the Muslim legislators are, I have elsewhere concluded
a sociological analysis of 332 of them with the observation that those
elected since independence share many of the career characteristics of
the rest of the Indian political elite, and are therefore far from a
typical cross section of their own community.[7] I suggested that this
statistical "unrepresentativeness" was a common trait of all legislators
but that it might imply a danger of alienation for the minority elite
from its own group if a competing counterelite should come into

---

[5] E.g., in the Madras Legislative Council *Debates*, March 8, 1954, p. 170, Mohammed Raza Khan, speaking on the proposed U.S. arms aid to Pakistan, said "As a
Muslim I can say that Muslims have always supported the government on the
national issues. But it is likely that people say the Muslims are always accustomed
to talk like this. . . . My difficulty is that a question will be put to me (if I
don't), 'how is it that you kept quiet when such an important reference was made
by the chief minister?' "

[6] J. A. La Ponce, "The Protection of Minorities by the Electoral System,"
Western Political Quarterly, 1957, vol. 10, pp. 324, 338.

[7] Theodore P. Wright, Jr., "Muslim Legislators in India: Profile of a Minority
Elite," *Journal of Asian Studies*, 1964, vol. 23, pp. 253-267. 657 Muslims have been
members of state legislatures since independence.

existence and promise more radical solutions to the group's discontents.

Sociological description of parliamentarians does not, of course, automatically provide an infallible indicator of their legislative behavior, as Jean Meynaud has warned us.[8] Some of the most orthodox Muslims by education and association have been the most loyally silent of Congress MPs on "communal" issues.[9] Therefore the political activity of the legislators must itself be studied, a most difficult task in any country because of the well-known discrepancy between politicians' public pronouncements and their actual performance behind the scenes, but especially so for members of the minorities in a country where any sign of favor for one's own religion is branded as "communalism."

I have tried to get at the elusive truth by a combination of scanning legislative debates and interviewing some 53 past and present Muslim legislators, including nine ministers, to elicit their own conceptions of their roles in the political process.[10] With both these methods I have concentrated on Andhra Pradesh and Madras, the former because it contains the heart of the old Hyderabad State, a center of Muslim dominion and culture in the Deccan for several centuries[11] and therefore, like North India, a good laboratory in which to study the problems of adjustment of the once ruling religious minority; the latter, Madras, because it typifies the rest of the South where Muslims came peaceably as merchants and never ruled the Hindu majority for extended periods.

Up to this point, I have referred to the complaints of the Muslim minority as if they were a homogeneous package of demands supported equally by the whole community, but this in fact is far from the case. Rank and file Indian Muslims, like their political leaders, range all the way from the most fundamentalist followers of Islam to the most modernized Marxist lawyers whose connection with the religion is

[8] Jean Meynaud, "The Parliamentary Profession," *International Social Science Journal*, 1961, vol. 13, pp. 513-543.

[9] "Communal" is a pejorative term in Indian usage implying a desire to do harm to other groups. I use it only in the sense of "pertaining to the community." On "The Mounting Silence" of Muslim MPs, see *Siraat, the Fortnightly of Indian Minorities*, April 16, 1962, p. 7.

[10] Because most of these interviews were confidential, I am not listing them, or except in a few cases, citing specific interviews as sources. Suffice it to say that 12 each were in Andhra Pradesh and Madras, 9 in Maharashtra, 8 in Kerala, 5 in Uttar Pradesh, 4 in West Bengal, 2 in Mysore and 1 in Bihar. I wish to acknowledge here my debt to Alam Khundmeri of Hyderabad for interpreting at several interviews.

[11] See Wilfred Cantwell Smith, "Hyderabad: Muslim Tragedy," *Middle East Journal*, 1950, vol. 4, pp. 27-51.

exceedingly tenuous.[12] Their attitudes toward the usually posed issues differ accordingly, a source of great weakness in the community whenever it seeks to act in politics.

From a survey of demands made by Muslim spokesmen of various shades of opinion two lists can be derived: the essentially religious ones about which there is a great deal of disagreement among Muslims, and the political, social and economic demands on most of which some degree of consensus exists even if priorities differ. In enumerating them I make no judgment as to their basis in fact since their subjective reality is politically significant whatever the objective facts may be. The religious claims are:

1. Preservation of Muslim Personal Law[13] or at least its modification only by Muslims themselves and not by a secular Parliament with a heavy majority of Hindus.

2. Restoration of mosques, *idgahs*, *dargahs*, *madrassahs* and other religious structures which were seized or demolished in the troubles attending partition and the Hyderabad "Police Action," especially if they were desecrated by conversion into Hindu temples.[14] A related and continuing problem is that of encroachments on Muslim grave-yards. In Malabar the demand is for permission to build new mosques.

3. Compulsory religious instruction in Islam for Muslim children and the eradication of Hindu religious mythology and anti-Muslim historical references from state school textbooks.[15] Others would go further to require the elimination of Hindu rituals, music, dance and drama from state education and public ceremonies as offensive to Islam.

4. Censorship of publications repugnant to Muslim belief or sensibilities such as pictorial treatment of the Prophet Muhammad.[16]

5. Recognition of Muslim religious celebrations as holidays for Muslim civil servants and students.[17]

[12] However a Muslim MLC (Member of Legislative Council) in Madras pointed out "I may not be following the principles and tenets of my religion, but I am sure none of us will tolerate if anything is said against our religion." *Debates*, 1954, vol. 9, p. 651.

[13] Donald E. Smith, pp. 420-423.

[14] Hafiz Ali Bahadur Khan, a former Congressman subsequently in preventive detention, made a specialty of reporting such cases in his newspaper, *Minorities*.

[15] Examples are contained in a pamphlet by Dr. A. J. Faridi, MLC, UP, *Communal Riots and National Integration*, Lucknow, 1962.

[16] For instance, *Siraat*, October 1, 1963, vol. 4, No. 17, reports that the Maharashtra Muslim League demanded a ban on *Life* magazine of July 29, 1963, for portraying the Prophet.

[17] E.g., K. M. Seethi Saheb, MLA (Member of Legislative Assembly) in Madras Legislative Assembly *Debates*, July 10, 1952, p. 874.

6. Prohibition of alcoholic beverages.[18]
7. Prevention of the playing of music before mosques during prayers.[19]
8. No restrictions on the number of *hajis* (pilgrims) to Mecca.[20]
9. Cessation of governmental encouragement of birth control.[21]
10. Compulsory payment of *zakat* (tithes) by Muslims.
11. Election rather than appointment of Wakf (religious endowment) Boards and the use of wakf moneys only for the benefit of Muslims.[22]
12. Retention of the right of polygamy and its restoration to civil servants.
13. Preservation of purdah (veiling) for women, and at least some modesty in all women's attire.
14. Restoration of the right of cow slaughter to Muslims where now forbidden.[23]
15. Prohibition of interest-taking.

The non-religious demands include:
1. Security of person and property from communal riots; relief for their victims and the return of looted property and abducted women; impartial inquiries into the causes and responsibility for these disturbances; and collective fines on the guilty communities.
2. Preservation of the Urdu language (Arabic in Kerala) and script in education, in government documents such as bills, laws, legislative and Panchayat debates and agenda, notifications, regulations, petitions, applications, civil service examinations, court proceedings, electoral rolls and signboards in those states where an appreciable minority have Urdu as their mother tongue;[24] adequate Urdu programs on radio.
3. Representation for Muslims proportionate to their per cent of the population (or at least no discrimination against them) in legislatures,

[18] E.g., Salebhoy Abdul Kadar's pamphlet, *Draft Outline for an All-India Prohibition Scheme*, Bombay, 1963.
[19] This was the cause of a communal riot at Malegaon, Maharashtra as recently as September 1963. See *Siraat*, September 16, October 1, October 16, 1963 and *Link*, October 27, 1963.
[20] *Siraat*, January 1, 1964, vol. 5, p. 1.
[21] E.g., in *Radiance*, the organ of the Jama'at-i-Islami, August 18, October 6, December 29, 1963.
[22] *Siraat*, August 16, October 16, 1963.
[23] E.g., *The Hindu*, October 15, 1958, re Bangalore.
[24] *Petition to the President of India by the Anjuman Taraqqi Urdu Hind, February 15, 1954, under Article 347 of the Constitution of India*; also see Abul Hasan Ali Nadvi, *Muslims in India*, Academy of Islamic Research and Publication, Nadwat-ul-Ulema, Lucknow, 1960, chapter 9.

cabinets, government committees, courts, semi-governmental enterprises, civil service, Public Service Commissions, textbook committees, army and police, at all levels and with promotion on merit; no gerrymandering of districts with Muslim concentrations.[25]

4. Employment and economic opportunities for Muslim workers and businessmen in private commerce and industry through an end to discriminatory hiring practices,[26] aid to economically backward Muslims and to small-scale industries, and a fair share of government licenses and contracts.

5. Admissions to colleges, universities, technical institutes, medical and engineering schools more in proportion to their numbers in the population; "backward class" reservations for poor Muslims; an end to discrimination in interviews; maintenance of Aligarh Muslim University as a primarily Muslim institution.[27]

6. Restoration of falsely seized "evacuee" or "intending evacuee" properties, an end to the expulsion of Muslims long-domiciled on the Assam border as "Pakistani infiltrators" or illegal immigrants, free grant of passports to Indian Muslims and of visas to their relatives to come from Pakistan.

7. A correct census of Muslims and of Urdu-speakers.

8. Fair treatment of Urdu and English-language Muslim newspapers in licensing, allocation of newsprint and government advertising.

9. An end to corruption, caste favoritism and nepotism in government.

10. Preservation of historic Muslim monuments and documents; public commemoration of Muslim heroes of the nationalist movement.[28]

11. A fair share of civic amenities (roads, sewers, water, electricity) for heavily Muslim areas and special help for backward Muslim regions like Malabar.

12. A foreign policy of reconciliation with Pakistan, enmity to China and support of the Arab countries against Israel.

[25] It is commonly believed by Muslims that a secret circular from New Delhi to the state governments in the early years of independence excluded Muslims from the police and CID (Criminal Investigation Department).

[26] E.g., speech by Vice Chancellor Badruddin Tyabji of Aligarh Muslim University urging Indian businessmen to employ more Muslim graduates. *Siraat*, July 1, 1962, p. 9.

[27] *S.O.S. for Aligarh Muslim University*, by the Well-wishers, 1961?; see *Radiance*, September 15, October 27, 1963 re technical colleges admissions.

[28] The latter is designed to counter the charge that Muslims are potential traitors to India because they had no part in winning freedom. E.g., article in *Siraat*, January 1, 1964, on Mazhar-ul-Haq.

13. Government encouragement of Unani (Muslim medical) education and dispensaries.

14. Repeal of the Preventive Detention Act and cessation of censorship of mail, or at least the equal application of these to the RSS (Rashtriya Swayamsevak Sangh) and other anti-Muslim agitators.[29]

15. Fair compensation of ex-jagirdars and zamindars.

16. Full recognition of the legitimacy of Muslim political parties.

FACTORS RESTRICTING THE LEGISLATOR'S EFFECTIVENESS

The Muslim politician comes to the legislature predisposed in certain ways toward the foregoing issues by the manner of his nomination and election; he is not a free agent. The overwhelming fact is that since the 1950 Constitution replaced the old separate electorates and reserved seats for Muslims with joint electorates, all but a few legislators in Malabar, Murshidabad (West Bengal) and Kashmir have had to get elected from constituencies in which Muslims are a minority of the voters. Therefore they must take care lest too open an espousal of Muslim causes will antagonize the non-Muslim, primarily Hindu, voters. This was the intended effect of establishing joint electorates— to compel candidates to appeal to all groups. Yet the candidate has also been nominated usually *because* he is a Muslim; either to win important marginal votes from his coreligionists in a tight contest, or to satisfy party dictates from "the Centre" that a certain proportion of tickets be given to Muslims to prove the party's secular impartiality.[30] Which way he will lean in the face of these conflicting pressures may depend on whether, in American terms, he is a "Neuberger" or a "Javitz," i.e., whether the Muslim minority in his district is small or large.[31] One might expect that a "balanced slate" would be easier to achieve in India where there are no party primary elections to upset calculations as there are in America, but the process seems to work more effectively for Hindu castes than for the religious minorities. The cost of campaigning, which various informants estimated to be between fifteen and twenty-five thousand rupees, also inhibits

[29] *The Hindu*, December 21, 1957, p. 9; N. Sanjiva Reddi, chief minister of Andhra Pradesh, admitted in the assembly, July 2, 1958, that even the mail of legislators can be censored. *Debates*, 1958, vol. 16, no. 1, part I, p. 2.

[30] Gupta, pp. 369-370.

[31] The late Senator Neuberger was elected from Oregon, a state with a very small Jewish population; Senator Javitz of New York is from the state with the largest Jewish population. One might compare S. Mohammed Ismail, Congress MLA from Samalkot, AP with about a 1 per cent Muslim population, and M. Mohammed Ismail, Muslim League MP from Manjeri constituency in Kerala with a Muslim majority.

candidacy of the poor or leaves them beholden to those who pay their expenses.

In any case, nomination is increasingly no guarantee of election, even for a Congress Muslim, and he may be betrayed by disgruntled would-be candidates in his own party who defect to an opponent or run as independents.[32] If other parties run Muslim candidates for the same seats, the stage is set for a muted contest over which will do the most for the Muslim community. The operation, however, of something like Samuel Lubell's American "ethnic ladder" process for the benefit of the minority is hampered by specific laws against "communal appeals"[33] and by the lack of really effective two-party competition so far except in Kerala. As long as the Muslim politician has to depend on the generosity of the Congress Party rather than on its need for him, he cannot be a very useful spokesman for his people.

From the Muslim voter's point of view, the difficulty is the familiar one of how to hold the politician to his campaign promises. Although the parliamentary system theoretically provides more frequent chances to punish the delinquent office-holder at the polls than our presidential system of fixed elections does, in practice party discipline in the assemblies reinforced by the legislator's distaste for risking his seat have been sufficient to keep elections in India at their maximum five-year intervals.[34] As in Great Britain, by-elections may be a better

[32] For instance in the third general election the following Congress Muslims were defeated in Andhra Pradesh by independents: Mohammed Ibrahim (Mahbubnagar), Mohammed Dawar Hussain (Nizamabad), S. M. Rahmatullah (Cuddapah), Mirza Shukur Baig (Warangal) and Abdul Ghani Khan (Kurnool).

[33] Samuel Lubell in *The Future of American Politics*, Harper, New York, 1952, p. 77, argued that American ethnic minorities have risen up a ladderlike succession of political offices with the help of party competition for their votes. In August 1961, the Representation of the People Act of 1961 was amended to read: "Any person who in connection with an election under this act promotes or attempts to promote on grounds of religion, race, caste, community or language, feelings of enmity or hatred between different classes of the citizens of India shall be punishable with imprisonment. . . ." The act declares it a corrupt practice for a candidate to appeal for support in the name of religion, caste, community or race. Quite a number of elections have been set aside on these grounds. *The Hindu*, August 11, 1961, p. 1.

[34] Here again Kerala is an exception with special mid-term elections in Travancore-Cochin in 1954 and in the whole state in 1960. The successful operation of Lubell's "ethnic ladder" for the Muslims there as a result of tight party competition and frequent elections can be best demonstrated by a chart:

Muslims Elected by Each Party: (Travancore-Cochin and Malabar)

Year	Congress	Muslim League	Communists	Socialists	Totals
1952	1	4	2	1	8
1954	4	4	1	1	10

test of the voters' real feelings about individual candidates. The defeat of the Congress Muslim stalwart, Hafiz Mohammed Ibrahim, in the 1963 Amroha (U.P.) by-election was interpreted by some as a disavowal of Congress by the Muslims.[35] The important thing for the minority is not to let its votes come to be taken for granted by the party in power. This seems to have happened to some extent after the first two general elections in North India[36] where anti-Muslim Hindu communal parties like the Jana Sangh became increasingly the main alternative to Congress. Since its foundation in 1959, the more secular Swatantra Party appears to be more promising for the Muslims.[37]

In summary, then, the nomination and election processes work to put into the legislatures Muslims who are inclined to be docile and not to raise embarrassing issues too persistently lest they either not "get the ticket" next election or get shifted to less safe constituencies.

Once safely elected, what organizational and procedural imperatives affect the Muslim legislator's chances of being heard on communal matters? Here again the British parliamentary model is not conducive to an adequate hearing for minorities. A Syed Badrudduja or a Frank Anthony[38] may occasionally shake the Parliament with their eloquence on behalf of minorities, but the Congress Party steamroller invariably wins the votes so most of the real decisions are arrived at behind the scenes in cabinet and Congress Party meetings. Factional strife within the ruling party has apparently not given the minorities the leverage one might expect. Possibly individual Muslim Congressmen become too committed to particular factional group leaders for the sake of their own political survival to bargain

1957	3	7	2	1	13
1960	6	10	1	2	19
1965	3	11	4	1	19

This means that the Muslims have moved up steadily toward achieving the same proportion of seats in the Kerala assembly of 120 members as they have in the state's population (17.9 per cent).

[35] E.g., *Siraat*, July 16, 1963, p. 2, attributes the Congress defeat to Muslim dissatisfaction with the government's proposed interference with Muslim personal law, but of course many other factors were at work too.

[36] By contrast, several of my informants in Madras agreed that S. M. Abdul Majid was elevated to the state cabinet in 1962, the first Muslim there in 23 years, because Congress was losing Muslim votes to the DMK. See also *Link*, March 25, 1962.

[37] See Howard L. Erdman, "India's Swatantra Party," *Pacific Affairs*, Winter 1963-1964, pp. 397, 409.

[38] Syed Badrudduja's speech appeared in *Minorities*, June 16, 1962. Frank Anthony is the nominated MP for the Anglo-Indians. He spoke up for the West Bengal Muslims who suffered in the communal riots of January 1964.

on behalf of their constituents. For instance, I could find no evidence that the various maneuvers of T. O. Bava and A. A. Rahim in the kaleidoscopically shifting alignments of Kerala factions have advanced the cause of their community.

One procedural factor handicaps Muslims in some states considerably: the language of debate. The period since independence has witnessed, at the state level, the rapid decline of English in which the older generation of politicians was proficient. It was replaced after the states' reorganization of 1956 by regional languages, in which the Muslim may not be as well versed as his Hindu colleagues. In North India this takes the less crippling but nonetheless galling shape of Sanskritized Hindi written in Devanagari script. In the South it means the substitution of a quite dissimilar Dravidian tongue for English or Urdu.[39]

The problem is most acute in Andhra Pradesh. Urdu was the official language of the Nizam of Hyderabad's state, which was broken up along linguistic lines in 1956. The largest part, being a Telugu-speaking area, went to Andhra Pradesh, and Urdu-speaking Hyderabadis suddenly found themselves acutely disadvantaged. Most Muslim legislators were left unable to follow or participate meaningfully in debate. Time and again disputes would flare up over the translation of a supplementary question or of a minister's reply from Telugu into English or Urdu. A typical exchange in 1958 ran:[40]

> Sanjivayya: "Nobody can gainsay . . . that one or two people (here) do not know Telugu (but) this is a Telugu province and most of the people know only Telugu. So for the sake of two or three members out of 302, it is not fair that you should speak in English."
>
> Masuma Begum: "Sir, I had once requested that the honorable ministers answer questions in English to facilitate our asking supplementaries. The honorable speaker has said that this being a Telugu Desam (a) majority of the honorable members do not understand English. I only hope it is a broad-minded Telugu Desam and not a narrow-minded (one)."

On another occasion when Shah Jehan Begum spoke in Urdu, another MLA asked the speaker,[41] "Can we know what is going on, sir?" The latter replied:

[39] However the Kerala Muslims, called Moplahs, have Malayalam, the state language, as their mother tongue and most Madrasi Muslims know Tamil.
[40] Andhra Pradesh Legislative Assembly *Debates*, February 26, 1958, vol. 11, no. 1, pp. 13-15.
[41] *Ibid.*, April 18, 1957, vol. 2, no. 1, p. 18.

"You must enjoy (it). There are some members who do not know Telugu (too) and when we are talking Telugu are they not keeping quiet? You must be tolerant and enjoy the nice conversation. We must all bear this with patience, because it is going on and that lady member does not know Telugu. Therefore let the question be answered by the honorable minister."

Sanjiva Reddi: "I do not mind others enjoying it or keeping quiet, but at least the honorable speaker must know (what is being said) and there must be some method. . . ."

Speaker: "The difficulty is always this: here Urdu is the next (most) prominent language to Telugu and the speaker unfortunately does not know Urdu enough. I know only (how) to say 'bhaito' and 'javao.' Chief minister and speaker are both in the same boat. Somehow we must manage the whole business."

Most of the Muslim members in Andhra Pradesh claim to understand spoken Telugu but not how to speak it themselves or read it, and at that, they complain of the rapid dialect used in the assembly. Probably only those from coastal Andhra have a real comprehension of the majority's language.[42] The consequences for the other Muslims' effectiveness as legislators can readily be imagined.

SOURCES OF INFORMATION

How does the Muslim legislator hear about the grievances of his community? To an American the answer may seem absurdly obvious, flooded as he is by a surfeit of literature from interest group associations. But in a still partly pre-modern society with a heavy majority of illiterates the existence of organizations and techniques for aggregating, articulating and communicating the desires of constituents to their representatives cannot be taken for granted. As for the opposite direction of flow, no secretarial allowance is provided for the MLA and in any case few letters get answered. Face-to-face contact is therefore vital.

For the representative of an urban constituency, and a higher proportion of Indian Muslims than Hindus are city dwellers,[43] this means receiving individuals and delegations at his home or in MLA quarters. I sat a whole morning in the reception room of one

[42] S. Mohammed Ismail, MLA, says that Mohammed Tahseel, Rahmatullah, Shaikh Ghalib, Moula Sahib and himself speak Telugu fluently. Personal interview, June 25, 1964.
[43] Mohammed Halim Khan, "Muslims in India After 1947: A Study in Political Geography," unpublished doctoral dissertation, Clark University, 1958, pp. 79-80.

Hyderabad MLA and observed the steady stream of petitioners seeking his intervention with government.[44] From their extremely deferential, not to say servile approach to him, it was clear that the average voter has little conception of the legislator as a servant of the people, not their master. For this kind of "durbar" it would seem essential that the MLA live in his constituency. Yet India, following the British rather than the American rule, permits the election of non-residents of a constituency. This may be an admirable way to find seats for some cultivated, upper-class Muslims who could not get elected in their own neighborhoods or whom Congress wants to run in a poor Muslim ward, but it accentuates the risk of alienation between elector and elected referred to above. One estimable lady legislator who lives in the aristocratic section of Hyderbad admitted to me that she had never really seen the part of the city she was chosen to represent and in fact knew no one there before her nomination.

For resident and non-resident alike, it is important to show himself to his people at least once a week and listen to their problems even if he knows he can't do much for them. Since he is without a regular office except his home or shop, these consultations are apt to be rather casual and unrecorded, but then the Indian voter is used to a low level of formal organization in his daily life except in the overorganized bureaucracy whose red tape it is one of the legislator's functions to cut. The only MLA who kept a register of those who sought his help was M. M. Hashim of Hyderabad whose earlier military experience probably indoctrinated him in the need for orderly records.[45] However, the kind of personal petition conveyed in these ways is likely, as Hashim's opponents point out, to neglect the "bigger issues" affecting the whole Muslim community. The MLA from "the districts," i.e., the rural areas, must depend upon tours between sessions and occasional deputations.

The Urdu press is a replete if biased source of some complaints from the literate segment of the Muslim community, but it is limited by small circulation and therefore by excessive dependence upon government advertising,[46] in any case on government allocations of

[44] M. S. A. Majeed, a former MLA of Madras, told me that he is still approached by former constituents to intercede with his onetime colleagues. Personal interview, May 19, 1964.

[45] K. G. S. Haja Sheriff, MLA, Madras, a shipping magnate, has a business secretary who can handle his legislative correspondence but such cases are probably rare. Personal interview, May 20, 1964.

[46] In the Madras council, Subramaniam listed "circulation, *tone* and class of readers a particular government advertisement is intended to reach" as criteria for

scarce newsprint, and ultimately by the government's licensing power. The Hindu-owned English-language press is almost totally oblivious of the minority's activities and problems.[47] There are, as far as I could ascertain, only three Muslim-operated, English-language weeklies or fortnightlies in India: The Muslim League's *Siraat*, *Tarjuman* of Madras, and the Jama'at-i-Islami's *Radiance*. I saw copies of the last-named in Congress Muslim homes and had it recommended to me by men whose nationalist bona fides can hardly be questioned. Considering the disfavor with which the late prime minister regarded the Jama'at, this shows the desperate need for a sympathetic organ of Muslim opinion and news which can also reach the small but powerful layer of modern, educated, non-Muslim Indians in order to plead the Muslim case in terms of more general principles than the Urdu press must use. Muslims are incredulous when told that the most prestigious newspaper in the United States is Jewish-owned.

What organized Muslim interest groups can inform or bring pressure on legislators? Myron Weiner has observed that "compared with some other sections of (Indian) society . . . the poor and depressed . . . are relatively unorganized and inarticulate . . . (and therefore) have little access to administration and policy makers."[48] Evidently Muslims must be added to this category. It is revealing that Weiner mentions no Muslim organizations in his survey of "community associations." In North India the cause may be that much of the community's normal leadership has been drained off to Pakistan since 1947.

Few Muslim legislators could or would tell me of any regular organizations which approached them about issues. For instance in Kerala when the Communist government's education bill struck at private religious schools, it was the Christians and Nairs, not the Muslims, who had statewide organizations to resist. In fact, the Muslim MLA may have to go out himself and organize support for his own legislative positions as Mohammed Abdur Rahman of Malakpet in Hyderabad brought together the City Improvement Board Tenants'

---

choice of publication outlet and denied that the political views of a newspaper were taken into consideration. *Debates*, February 15, 1955, vol. 9, p. 815. See also the speech of Abdul Latif Farookhi, MLC and editor of *The Musalman*, charging that government advertisements for his paper were stopped after independence. *Ibid.*, March 28, 1952, vol. 7, p. 192.

47 An exception to this is *Link, Indian Newsmagazine*, a leftwing publication in New Delhi which has a number of Muslims on its board of directors.

48 Myron Weiner, *The Politics of Scarcity*, University of Chicago Press, Chicago, 1962, p. 16.

Association to defend their rights.[49] By contrast, the Hyderabad Ex-Armymen's Association and the Non-Gazetted Officers demonstrated their lobbying skill by the frequency with which their complaints were the subject of questions in the first Hyderabad assembly (1952-1957).

Another exception is in Madras, where the leather business has been practically a Muslim monopoly and is well represented by the Hides and Skins Merchants Association.[50] In fact, most of the Muslim legislators in Madras have been from this trade, so the interests of their industry figure prominently when they participate in debate. This situation resembles that in Britain, where interest groups gain representation by their members entering Parliament themselves instead of working through professional lobbyists as in the United States. Until 1957 the Hides and Skins Merchants enjoyed direct occupational seating on the Madras Municipal Corporation.[51]

Unions too are among the earliest modern type of association, but they are unlikely to agitate distinctively Muslim issues except in the rare cases where a significant number of the workers in a trade are Muslim, such as the beedi (cigar) workers, tanners, butchers, and in some areas, the weavers. For instance, in 1954 Syed Hasan (MLA, Hyderabad City) raised the question whether the Jami'at-i-Qureish (Muslim butchers) and the Momin Brotherhood (Muslim weavers) had made representations to include their communities among the approved list of "Backward Classes" of the state.[52] Most unions are too closely tied to the Congress, Communist or Socialist parties to lend themselves to communal purposes.

The preservation of the Urdu language is the only non-religious cause for which there is nationwide Muslim organization. The Anjuman-i-Taraqqi-Urdu and others have lobbied vigorously if not too successfully in Uttar Pradesh and Andhra Pradesh through both Muslim and Hindu legislators.[53] In the assembly debates of the latter state, a press communiqué of September 13, 1958, was quoted in

[49] Another case is Jehangir Kabir, MLA of West Bengal, an advocate who is general secretary of the Mariners' Union which is predominantly Muslim.

[50] These same businessmen have given financial support to another important organization, the Muslim Educational Association of South India, which has been more successful in founding and maintaining institutions of higher learning since independence than its counterparts in the north. The South Indian Chamber of Commerce was also originally largely Muslim in membership, but a Muslim merchant in Periamet told me that it has been swamped by Hindus.

[51] Madras Legislative Assembly *Debates*, November 1, 1957, vol. 6, p. 230.

[52] Hyderabad Legislative Assembly *Debates*, 1954, vol. 1, part I, p. 982.

[53] Note that the president of the Anjuman Tahafuz-i-Urdu of Hyderabad is M. Baga Reddy, MLA, *Siraat*, April 1, 1964.

extenso on the proper place of Urdu in the state.[54] The representations of the Anjuman were cited as the source of this announcement. The Urdu associations have the advantage that they constitute an entirely literate group and that many Muslim legislators, whatever their religious beliefs or party, have a sentimental bond to the language and are members. The high patronage it enjoys in Andhra Pradesh is indicated by the fact that Mir Ahmed Ali Khan, currently the only Muslim minister, is president of the Anjuman. Some Hindus will defend Urdu too, for instance the poet "Firaq Gorakhpuri" and Judge Anand Narain Mulla of Lucknow.[55]

Indian civil liberties organizations are weak or non-existent. A few Muslims several years ago joined with other minorities in Hyderabad and tried to create a body for the protection of constitutional rights,[56] but they lacked funds and above all the patronage of the kind of famous and idealistic majority community lawyers who add so much to the reputation of American equivalents like the American Civil Liberties Union.

Since religion in some form is the common denominator of all Muslims except those who are Communists, the community is better prepared to protect its essentially religious interests. Paradoxically, however, the religious associations appear to be no more successful than the non-religious ones. A glance at the two lists of issues does not establish a prima facie case for greater results for either. The cause for this may lie in my earlier hypothesis that there is a greater degree of consensus among Muslims on the "secular" demands. Even a rank unbeliever can agree on the importance of personal security, the preservation of Urdu and equal opportunity for Muslims in education and employment, whereas the stubborn defense of the *shari'ah*, while it has brought together such previously antagonistic orthodox organizations as the Jami'at-al-Ulama and the Jama'at-i-Islami[57] cannot help but antagonize the modernist Muslims who are most influential with the leaders of the Congress Party. Rumor has it, indeed, that it was several of the Congress Muslim MPs who initiated the

[54] Andhra Pradesh Legislative Assembly *Debates*, December 20, 1958, vol. 22, no. 6, p. 408, and interview with Habib-ur-Rahman, general secretary, Anjuman-Taraqqi-Urdu of Hyderabad, January 24, 1964.

[55] See his article "The Mistake of Hindi" in the *Indian Express*, reproduced in *Radiance*, December 1, 1963, vol. 1, no. 19, p. 4; for Judge Mulla see *The Hindu*, August 18, 1961.

[56] See "All-India Federal Association of Minorities, Constitution," established Hyderabad, October 13, 1957; "Federation is a Must for Indian Minorities" by B. Sham Sunder, 1961; and mimeographed proposal for a "Public Grievances Committee" by Khwaja M. Moinuddin, 1964.

[57] *Siraat*, August 16, 1963, vol. 4, no. 15, p. 2.

movement for reform of Muslim personal law in 1963. Partly too, the religious bodies are by their very traditionality ill-adapted to lobbying in a modern parliament. What legislator wants to quote a Jama'at-i-Islami report on unsecular state textbooks or on desecrated graveyards, however accurate they may be, when both the subject matter and the source will immediately brand him with the dread stigma of "communalist?" True, the Jami'at-al-Ulama has since its foundation in 1920 been close to Congress[58] and placed leading members in Parliament and cabinet, but the very closeness of the tie may have vitiated its influence on the ruling party. Some politicians assert that Congress lost respect for the *ulama* when they failed to carry the Muslim vote in the 1946 election. Also to some extent the religious associations have canceled each other out: Sunni vs. Shia, Jami'at vs. Jama'at, and in Hyderabad, Majlis Tamir-i-Millat vs. Majlis Ittihad-ul Muslimin.[59]

COMMUNICATING GRIEVANCES TO AUTHORITIES

Now that we have examined the Muslim legislator's sources of information about grievances, how does he channel them to the authorities or otherwise act to obtain redress? Naturally we find approaches by members of the party in power different from those favored by the opposition. The available techniques are mostly those provided in the parliamentary system anywhere: the introduction of bills and their amendment, the raising of issues in the question period, debate on the governor's address and the budget, "call attention" motions and motions of censure and adjournment, privilege motions and points of order. Or the legislative process may be bypassed by direct representations to "the concerned minister" or the chief minister.[60] If all these fail, there are always the appeal to New Delhi, recourse to the courts and, as a last resort, the various methods of agitation hallowed by the Gandhian tradition: *satyagraha* (non-violent non-

[58] For an explanation see Ziya-ul-Hasan Faruqi, *The Deoband School and the Demand for Pakistan*, Asia Publishing House, Bombay, 1963.

[59] The internecine feud between the last two named organizations over the former Majlis headquarters, Dar-us-Salam in Hyderabad, was reported in the *Indian Express* (Vijayawada edition) between April 10 and September 8, 1963.

[60] Before independence Muslims enjoyed a more than proportionate share of the higher civil service. These ICS men are said to have been an effective channel of informal representation for Muslims. At partition many opted for Pakistan and since then the number of Muslims recruited has dropped sharply to about half the Muslim percentage in the population. See the article by D. N. Rao and R. K. Trivedi, "Social and Economic Background of Direct Recruits to the IAS Since 1948," National Academy of Administration, Moosoorie. Muslim ICS officers who remained in India are said by their coreligionists to lean over backwards not to appear "communal."

cooperation), *hartal* (general strike), *morcha* (procession) and fast. Muslims are less inclined to the last-named, coercive group of methods, to the extent that they were not associated with the nationalist movement.

The Congress Muslim must, of course, eschew the more public forms of protest and is obliged by party discipline to work behind the scenes in legislature Congress Party meetings, or by taking deputations to his fellow Congressmen in the cabinet.[61] The low visibility of his actions leaves him vulnerable to charges by opposition Muslims that he "is only a front man" and doesn't do anything for the community. His reply is that as a member of the party in power, he alone can get results. A Congress MLA in Kerala said that he got petitions from Muslims in Malabar, outside his constituency, because there was only one Congress Muslim MLA from that region, a busy cabinet minister. Furthermore, the former was himself "thought to be in the good books of the ministry." A Hyderabad Congressman told of how he and two MPs had taken a deputation to the chief minister about the dismissal of forty Urdu-speaking clerks for not knowing English. The notice was rescinded the same day. He commented that "the cabinet is naturally more sympathetic to a quiet deputation than if it is subject to public embarrassment in question period." Some oppositionists even charge that fake cases are concocted so that bogus concessions can be made to Congress Muslims to enhance their popularity, but this accusation is unprovable and may be "sour grapes." Chief ministers do undoubtedly try to build up their Muslim ministers in the eyes of the Muslim voters by distributing some patronage and other benefits through them. For instance, Chief Minister Sen of West Bengal allotted money for the relief of Muslim students who lost their books in the January 1964 communal riots, and assigned S. M. Fazlur Rahman of his cabinet to distribute it.[62]

It seems clear from the nature of their situation that the Congress Muslims prefer to work on individual cases of injustice or hardship, on economic issues and practical errands for constituents rather than on group or religious grievances. As one MLA conceded, "Discussion within the (Congress) Party is on matters of common interest to the rulers and the majority community. It is the fate of the minority to

[61] An exception to the rule was A. A. Rasheed, Congress MLA in Madras (1957-1962), who became notorious for putting questions in the assembly, sometimes to the embarrassment of the Congress ministry, instead of working through the Congress legislature party. His queries were seldom "communal" and not always relevant, but they apparently nettled the leadership enough to cause him to be denied a seat in the council later. Personal interview, May 11, 1964.

[62] Personal interview, June 1, 1964.

follow the majority in most cases. If one were to take up minority interests, it would only cause a clash and the result would be harmful." In private some Congress Muslims will acknowledge that "the Muslim League is 100 per cent correct" but ask pragmatically, "what is the net result for Muslims? We must do work for the service of the minority by standing with Congress in order to solve problems more successfully, even if we are not thereby recognized as the community's leaders."

That this role of maintaining public silence or even playing spokesman for the cabinet to answer the opposition's charges must be frustrating to Congress Muslims is clear when they confide that now and then they will ask an oppositionist to place a supplementary question for them, or will go up to one afterwards in the lobby and congratulate him for raising a "communal" question in the assembly which they would not dare broach. A Mysore Congressman told me, "I left the assembly to devote myself to social work because the response to my questions there was so poor and to preserve my self-respect." Taunted by the opposition during a discussion of the January 1964 riots in Kashmir and West Bengal, N. Mohammed Anwar, Congress MP from Madras, burst forth with the sensational confession that "under the present system of joint electorate, Hindu society has no opportunity to get to know the real mind of the Muslim community because most of the Muslims whom they have adopted in the secular party have naturally gotten to be considered as show boys of the majority community. . . . (They are) those who by flattering the powers that be get into good positions to betray both the Hindu and Muslim communities instead of bringing relations closer together. . . . There is no political party of the Muslim community in this country excepting the Muslim League. . . ."[63]

As with all legislative intercessions with the bureaucracy on behalf of constituents, those by Muslim MLAs may reduce the rational efficiency of democratic government. A Congressman who "fixes" traffic tickets for poor rickshaw drivers, gets delinquent students out of trouble and into college, or obtains priority hospital admissions may be cutting through red tape or counteracting religious discrimination, but by the same token, he may be undermining the hard-won objectivity and morale of the civil service and encouraging them to even less edifying forms of favoritism. A most common favor done for constituents is the signing by MLAs of "nativity certificates" to obtain regional or "backward class" preferences in admissions in

[63] *The Hindu*, April 25, 1964, and personal interview, May 23, 1964. Anwar was a Muslim League MLA in 1946-1952.

Andhra Pradesh and Madras and "student good conduct certificates" for jobs in Kerala and Madras. Old age pension applications are also endorsed by MLAs.

The opposition Muslims are few in number but must be further subdivided into Marxists, members of Muslim parties, and Independents. All three are free to attack the government and in fact prefer to do so since their influence with the ministers is little and their main hope of winning concessions is by compelling action through public agitation.[64] It is they who raise the critical questions in the assemblies and councils. The differences among them lie in the subjects of their specialization. The Marxist is compelled by party discipline if not always by ideological conviction to emphasize economic problems; the man elected by an overtly Muslim political party inclines toward the specifically religious issues.

Here we must face the question of the compatibility of Islam and Communism: can a man be a Communist Party legislator and yet remain in any real sense a Muslim? Some twenty to twenty-five men and women with Muslim names have been elected to central parliament and state legislatures in India as Communists since independence. Muslims themselves are wary of too readily excluding a man from the fold. After all, there is no formal procedure of excommunication in Islam except among the Bohras. The more modernist Muslims who perform few if any of the required rituals assert that adherence to Islam is a matter of subjective self-definition. Even an Amir of the Jama'at-i-Islami said cautiously that he would hesitate to accept as Muslims only those who embraced wholeheartedly another ideology which clashes with Islam. On its side, the CPI (Communist Party of India) needs Muslims to "balance its ticket" with minority group members, and has supported some candidates whose hearts are still with their community at least on a few issues.[65]

In 1952, for example, when some of the Communist leaders were still in prison because of the Telengana uprising, the party through its front, the People's Democratic Front, backed seven Muslims for

[64] However, Ummer Koya, the Congress Muslim minister in Kerala says that Muslim Leaguers still approach him on matters like new Muslim schools and he acts upon their requests "when they are just" even though they are now in the opposition and he is "persona non grata with them." Personal interview, April 9, 1964.

[65] Unpublished paper on "Muslim Leadership: Problems and Prospects," delivered by Dr. Rasheeduddin Khan, Osmania University, at the International Political Science Association Round Table, Bombay, January 4-10, 1964, p. 13. In 1952 the Muslim League MLAs refused to join the Communist-led opposition in a vote of no-confidence against the Congress government of Madras on the grounds that they were atheists. *Debates*, 1952, vol. II, pp. 315, 374.

legislative assembly seats in Hyderabad of whom three were elected: Mohammed Abdur Rahman (Malakpet), Syed Akhtar Hasan (Jangaon) and Syed Hasan (Hyderabad City). Many Muslim voters probably voted PDF only to revenge themselves on the Congress which they held responsible for the so-called police action of 1948. The clash and estrangement from the Communist leadership which Abdur Rahman experienced illustrates the conflict of loyalties between the two faiths.

When the Congress ministry proposed a bill against cow slaughter, Abdur Rahman asked the PDF to oppose it on the ground that it interfered with the lives and offended the sentiments of Muslims.[66] The party leadership refused, arguing that it was not interested in religious matters. Despite this reaction, the MLA collected 12,000 signatures on a mass petition against the bill and submitted it to the speaker. After a week the bill was withdrawn. Next he demanded that feudal *mansab* grants, of which many poor Hyderabad Muslims were recipients, should not be abolished until the problem of their employment was dealt with. However the PDF was committed ideologically to the eradication of the remnants of feudalism first and would not agree to the condition. When Abdur Rahman threatened to quit the party and resign from the assembly, the party allowed him to move an amendment as a private member. The chief minister modified the bill to provide continued payments to the disabled, aged, minors and widows.

Other PDF members began to charge that their Muslim colleague was always raising only Muslim issues. An examination of the assembly debates for 1952-1957 shows that this was partly true. All three PDF-backed Muslims were among the most active members during question period. Abdur Rahman's inquiries concerned mostly the secular interests of the community: Unani dispensaries, CIB Housing (90 per cent Muslim tenants), civil service retrenchments and appointments of "non-Mulkis" (non-Hyderabadis) as well as the dismissal of Urdu-knowing teachers for failure to pass a Telugu examination.

Syed Hasan specialized in the supersession of largely Muslim senior civil servants by their Hindu subordinates, employment of Hyderabad ex-army men, cases of embezzlement and abuse of office, and obtaining "backward class" status for poor Muslims. He also dared to raise two distinctly religious questions: encroachments on Muslim graveyards (April 15, 1955) and obtaining Muslim holidays for civil serv-

[66] Personal interview, February 23, 1964.

ants (March 29, 1957). The last effort, Syed Hasan's swan song in the assembly, caused a hot exchange with the chief minister in which the MLA accused N. Sanjiva Reddi of trying to force Muslim employees to quit the public services by denying their basic religious rights under the Constitution. Syed Akhtar Hasan hewed closer to the Marxist line and specialized in questions about industry, employment and unions, albeit these concerned Muslims only indirectly because of the high rate of Muslim unemployment since the police action. Both Syed Hasan (June 30, 1952) and Abdur Rahman (September 5, 1955) chastised the government on the subject of communal riots.

The outcome of all these verbal fireworks was defeat for all three MLAs. Abdur Rahman was attacked in the PDF election board for "communalism," walked out and ran unsuccessfully as an independent against a Congress candidate whom the PDF chose not to oppose. In 1962 he swung to the right and accepted the Swatantra Party nomination with equal ill-success. Syed Hasan too lost the PDF endorsement and tried his luck as an independent, thereby contributing to the defeat also of the then-PDF lady candidate, Khatija Alam Khundmeri, by Mir Ahmed Ali Khan who is now the Muslim home minister of Andhra Pradesh. Syed Akhtar Hasan, on the other hand, got the PDF nomination again but lost to another Congress Muslim, Masuma Begum, probably because of the independent candidacy of a disgruntled PDF Hindu.

The orthodox Communists, Maqdum Mohiuddin and Mohammed Tahseel, do not say a word in the assembly which could be interpreted as showing any interest in the community into which they were born. In fact Maqdum urged the breakup of Hyderabad state, a change which reduced the Muslim minority from 12 per cent to 7 per cent of the population, and he does not defend Urdu although he is himself an Urdu poet. Tahseel is a frequent participant in question period but only in the interests of his rural Andhra constituency of Bhadrachalam. Whatever the results of his efforts, they certainly give the impression that he concentrates on keeping his fences well mended more than on pressing either distinctively Marxist or Muslim positions.

The only member of an out-and-out Muslim party to sit in the Hyderabad-Andhra Pradesh legislatures since the police action is Sultan Salahuddin Owaisi of the Majlis Ittihad-ul-Muslimin.[67] This

[67] Theodore P. Wright, Jr., "Revival of the Majlis Ittihad-ul-Muslimin of Hyderabad," *Muslim World*, 1963, vol. 53, no. 3, pp. 234-243.

party of which his father, Abdul Wahid Owaisi, is president, was the dominant force in Hyderabad politics under the leadership of Syed Kasim Rizvi in the year between Indian independence and the absorption of the Nizam's state into the Indian Union. It reappeared in 1957, won a startling success in the 1960 Hyderabad municipal elections, and nominated one MP and eight MLA candidates in the third general elections. Its only success then, however, was in the election of Owaisi to the legislative assembly. The program of the Majlis Ittihad-ul-Muslimin is frankly Muslim-oriented and contains most of the points on both our "religious" and "secular" lists of demands.

Although the younger Owaisi, who is also a municipal councillor, has to deal with the needs of individual constituents like the rest (pensions, admissions, certificates, jobs, etc.),[68] he is at a disadvantage in obtaining these compared to his colleagues because of his isolation in the assembly, the enmity of Congress towards his party, and linguistic limitations. The Urdu oratory of which he is proud is wasted on nine-tenths of the MLAs. In fact, he claims that the government discriminates against Majlis constituencies in its municipal appropriations to punish Muslim voters for their audacity in electing "communal" representatives.[69] His strong point therefore lies in his freedom to agitate what he regards as the really important Muslim issues about which both Congressmen and Communists must remain mute. Such topics as opposition to Muslim Personal Law reform, encroachments on Muslim graveyards, medical transplants from the dead to the living, and demolition of the Tarband mosque in an adjacent hamlet were ventilated in the assembly as never before.[70]

The Tarband case brought about a confrontation between Owaisi and his arch-rival, M. M. Hashim of Congress,[71] in November 1963,

[68] When I met him March 6, 1964, he was receiving a petition from some Muslim clerks who had lost their jobs in government fair price shops because of retrenchment.

[69] *Deccan Chronicle*, February 1, 6, 9, 13, 1964. Majlis members asked for much-needed improvements in the old city of Hyderabad instead of broadening of the Hussainsagar Tank Bund.

[70] Even opposition Muslims though may be diffident about arousing old quarrels about partition. Mohammed Raza Khan, MLC of Madras speaking on the Andhra State bill in 1953, said: "I do not like to talk much about this division business because some people may say 'you have supported a bigger division of the country; why do you preach homilies about partition now?'" Madras Legislative Council *Debates*, July 22, 1953, p. 177.

[71] Hashim, secretary of the Kashmir National Front, was defeated for the municipal council by Owaisi in 1960, bested a Majlis candidate in the 1962 MLA race and then backed a losing candidate, Imaduddin, against Owaisi in 1964.

which epitomized the opposite approaches to Muslim representation.[72] Owaisi, debating the governor's address earlier, had alleged that some city mosques were being pulled down with the help of bull-dozers. Hashim retorted that no such thing was done, at least not deliberately, and that he had already petitioned the authorities privately on the subject. The chief minister had assured him of redress. Hashim accused Owaisi of distorting his position in public speeches and calling him a *kafir* (infidel), a term calculated to arouse communal passions. Physical violence between the two men, both of military background, was narrowly averted and they tabled contradictory privilege motions against each other in the assembly.

When asked what use it was for a lone opposition deputy to raise issues likely only to antagonize the majority all the more, the Owaisis replied in terms of the need for "true and independent Muslim spokesmen" rather than of immediate efficacy. It is true that a small but vociferous minority can sometimes prod or shame an indifferent majority into remedial action on minority rights, although this is apt to be more effective when the appeal is to universal values shared by the majority. Some Muslims cling to the belief that "world public opinion" will pay heed, and bring pressure on the Indian government to ameliorate their condition. Then too, even if the outraged protest from within the country brings no response, it may have a cathartic value for the minority who want to hear their indignant sentiments voiced in the legislature regardless of consequences. If the Muslim assemblyman is neither an angry spokesman nor an efficient errand boy, he is likely to be defeated for reelection as is reputed to have happened to Dawar Hussain, Mirza Shukur Baig and Shahabuddin Ahmed in 1962.

Less embattled than Owaisi is the Muslim League's eleven-man delegation in the Kerala Assembly. They were elected in the 1960 special midterm election in the propitious circumstances of a Congress–PSP–Muslim League coalition. Although unrepresented in the Kerala cabinet, they were with the government until November 1961. Since then, even Congressmen will testify, they have played a constructive and relatively "non-communal" role in the assembly, stressing the regional interest of backward Malabar more than purely religious grievances.

I might conclude this section then by suggesting that there is a useful functional division of labor between the different types of

[72] *Deccan Chronicle*, December 10, 14, 1963.

minority legislators, and that Muslim representation is incomplete without some of each in all legislative bodies.

It seems appropriate to discuss the third type of Muslim opposition legislator, the independent, in conjunction with the legislative councils because the indirect system of selection to those bodies makes it easier for independents to get membership. We have already seen that the numerical position of Muslims in the upper houses of both Parliament and those state legislatures which have councils has tended to be more nearly proportionate to the Muslim population than it is in the directly elected lower houses. One reason may be that the Congress leadership has conscientiously sought to compensate here for its inability to get a sufficient quota of Muslims elected elsewhere. For instance Andhra Pradesh has 10 per cent Muslims in the upper house and only 2.5 per cent in the lower house, for a group which constitutes 7.55 per cent of the state population.[73] Without meaning to impugn the party's good intentions, however, it should be pointed out that the legislative councils are by far the less powerful of the two. One MLC (Member of Legislative Council) remarked acidly that "no bill has ever been introduced, amended, sent back for reconsideration or rejected by the council. It only gives its seal of approval." But this is not to say that individual council members are without influence. They do face special problems as spokesmen of minority opinion, but enjoy some other compensating advantages.

Their chief contrast to the MLAs is in their qualifications and constituencies. The provision for the government to nominate some MLCs from "arts and letters" and for others to be elected by the graduates constituency makes possible the membership of highly educated men like Professor Haroon Khan Sherwani and Mohammed Ataur Rahman, who either could not or would not win office in the popularly elected branch.[74] The graduates constituency has, of course, a highly selective electorate, campaigning is nonpartisan and the victorious candidate is in a good position to assert his independence as a critic of the government. The scattered distribution of the constituents all over the region makes it less easy for him to remedy individual injustices. Ataur Rahman has put questions in the council about discrimination in promotions against Urdu-speaking employees of the education department, about absorption of Hyderabad ex-armymen into civil service, and about provision of Urdu-medium schools. His opposition to prohibition ("I do not regard moderate

[73] Wright, "Revival of the Majlis," p. 235, and 1961 Census—Religion, *loc.cit.*
[74] Ataur Rahman ran sixth as an independent in the 1952 race for MP from Hyderabad City.

drinking as immoral") may well reflect the viewpoint of the university graduates, but illustrates the gap between the western-educated Muslim elite and the orthodox masses.

The real thorn in the flesh of the Congress government in Andhra Pradesh must have been the other independent, Professor Sherwani. This may seem surprising since, as a nominated member, he is completely at the mercy of the cabinet for a new term, but for an older man of some private means this is no consideration. The legislators' pay appears to us to be very low at some 200 rupees a month plus per diem, but for an uneducated man it is enough to make its retention important should he ever be tempted to criticize the government. It is to be hoped that government will take the long view and continue to nominate men of Sherwani's learning and strength of character.

Sherwani has far outdistanced all other Muslims in the council in his activity during question period. Reflecting his professional interests as an historian, he has specialized in the defense of Urdu through Urdu-medium schools, employment of Urdu-speakers in civil service, and having government bills and publications and Panchayat and Zilla Parishad proceedings translated into Urdu. He also pleads for the preservation of historic monuments and documents from the period of Muslim rule, and for the maintenance of educational standards. In addition to these more secular demands, he did evince religious sensitivity by chiding the law minister about the training of Muslim jail prisoners to sing *bhajans*, Hindu religious songs which are repugnant to Islam because they invoke deities other than Allah. Other MLCs who are themselves seldom heard in debate doubt the efficacy of Sherwani's witty and slightly condescending sallies against the cabinet members. But in some situations it is better to exasperate than to be ignored. Few may be listening to him in the council, but if an issue creates a commotion in the press, action may result.

Finally, we must consider what one might call the "sympathetic Hindu" as a spokesman for Muslims. Needless to say, many Muslims are nominally represented in legislatures and Parliament by non-Muslims. They may feel no hesitation about approaching these men of different religion for assistance regarding some matters, just as the Muslim legislators claim that their Hindu constituents come to them. In both situations it probably helps if legislator and constituent are of the same party, although the democratic ethic requires every politician to say that he serves all his people regardless of political allegiance. One may surmise, on the other hand, that the more religious the matter a voter wants to bring up, the more doubtful he will be of addressing himself to a man of different faith, and the more he will prefer to seek out his own. The almost unanimous testimony of the Muslim legislators that they receive petitions from Muslims outside their constituencies testifies to this proposition.

Nevertheless, it is not to be ruled out that a politician of a different religion, particularly the majority religion, will, as I suggested at the beginning of the paper, sometimes be as useful if not more so than a fellow Muslim because his secular bona fides cannot be questioned as easily. Practically any Muslim knowledgeable about politics can readily name a few Hindus, from the late prime minister down to municipal councillors, who at least would give Muslims and Muslim causes a fair hearing and at best might have sentimental leanings toward various aspects of Indian culture to which Muslims have made major contributions such as Urdu poetry, music or architecture which would predispose them favorably toward individual Muslims. Of course some non-Muslims may favor individual friends but be prejudiced on group matters.

In Andhra Pradesh the most frequently mentioned sympathetic Hindus are Gopala Reddi, P. V. G. Raju, Subba Reddi and Narsing Rao. In Madras, C. Rajagopalachari and Kamaraj Nadar. On the negative side of the ledger, the most anti-Muslim minister is said to have been Phoolchand Gandhi who caused the dismissal of hundreds of Urdu-speaking school teachers in the early 1950's for not passing a Telugu examination for the study of which they had been given inadequate facilities. A reading of the assembly debates quickly reveals that some Telengana Hindus have advocated the cause of Urdu because it is in reality their mother tongue and they and some of their educated constituents have suffered almost as much as the Hyderabad Muslims by the introduction of Telugu as the state language.[75] Other apparently pro-Muslim Hindus are Communists eager to use any stick to beat the government.

Surprisingly, many Muslims now regard the Telugu-speaking Andhras from former Madras state as less prejudiced than the Telengana and especially the Marathwada (now in Maharashtra) Brahmins who formerly dominated Congress and among whom the Hindu revivalist Arya Samaj made deeper inroads. In Madras, of which coastal Andhra

[75] Rasheeduddin Khan, in "Electoral Behavior in the City of Hyderabad," *Journal of the Osmania University*, March 1964, vol. 2, p. 15, cites the example of Dr. Raj Bahadur Gour, a Communist candidate of the Kayastha caste which provided clerical staff, teachers and professionals in the Nizam's state.

was a part until 1953, the principal communal movement was anti-Brahmin, so the Reddi caste politicians who have taken over the Andhra Pradesh Congress and government since 1956 can look with some detachment on the problems of the Muslim minority. If they exclude Muslims from government it is more a result of nepotism in favor of caste fellows than of active malice toward the other religion. However, one Muslim suggested to me half humorously that a natural alliance for his people would be with the displaced Brahmin elite.

THE ROLE OF MUSLIM MINISTERS

Potentially far more powerful than the legislator is the Muslim who becomes a member of a state or central cabinet. As in the British system, Indian law-making and policy is largely in the hands of the executive, which reduces the parliamentary role to the rubber-stamping of bills and providing a public sounding board for the opposition.

Since independence, nine Muslims have been members of the Union ministry[76] and some fifty-four have sat in state cabinets or been deputy ministers. All but one (T. A. Majid of the Communist cabinet in Kerala in 1957-1959) have been Congressmen. Are they just "window-dressing" as so many of their disgruntled coreligionists charge, or do they represent their community as spokesmen and redressers of grievances? If and to the extent that the latter is true, again we must ask as we did of the legislators, is it proper in a secular democracy for a cabinet minister to work for the interests of part of the citizenry rather than the whole?

It is no secret that cabinet posts are much sought after in Indian politics for the power, prestige, perquisites, patronage and pelf that go with them. Perhaps there are also a few dedicated men and women who seek high office for the sake of national service and many more who rationalize their power drive in these terms. What kind of Muslim survives the bitter, cutthroat competition and reaches the top? In the first place, they are not necessarily all of unimpeachable nationalist background as one might expect. At least four are former Muslim Leaguers who have been accorded places in state ministries as part of the attempt by Congress to absorb the League's voters. Other non-Congressmen were appointed in princely states like Hyderabad and Mysore where neither Congress nor League was as well organized as in British India. One might surmise that these men

[76] Mawlana Abul Kalam Azad, Rafi Ahmed Kidwai, Humayun Kabir, Hafiz Mohammed Ibrahim, Mohammedali Currim Chagla, ministers; and Abid Ali Jaferbhay, Shah Nawaz Khan, Dr. Syed Mahmud and Ahmed Mohiuddin, deputy ministers.

must be extra cautious lest they draw upon themselves the reproach "And where were you during the nationalist struggle?" There are indications on the other hand that some senior and indubitably nationalist Muslims like Dr. Syed Mahmud of Bihar and Mohammed Yasin Nuri of Bombay have been frozen out of office for attempting too vociferously to defend the legitimate interests of the minority.[77]

Disappointed office-seekers will charge that only those Muslims are taken into cabinets who "have no tongue" and are not fighters. Perhaps a fairer judgment would be that while a Muslim minister is appointed *because* he is a Muslim, once he is in office he cannot act *only* as a Muslim, but must take a national perspective. Credit should be given here to the Muslim minister who is so genuinely secular in his beliefs that he consciously rebuffs petitions for help on "communal" issues, thinking that in the long run it would be better for Muslims to seek aid from Hindus through non-communal organizations.

This, however, is no excuse for the hypocrisy of promising during election campaigns in Muslim-populated constituencies to help fellow Muslims and then refusing to do so once safely in office. The appearance of doubledealing can be due to the necessary secrecy of the minister's efforts on their behalf which, if exposed, would end his usefulness. He is, after all, usually only one in a ministry of from ten to twenty non-Muslims with little room to maneuver because he is bound by the rule of cabinet solidarity known as collective responsibility. If we could read the cabinet minutes, we might see a different story. None, let it be noted however, has had the courage to risk his career by resigning on a clear-cut "communal" question. Whatever the truth of the matter, the fact remains that many Muslims are dissatisfied with the poor results obtained by "their representatives." Certainly the pre-ministerial careers of the Andhra Pradesh cabinet members in the assembly question period exhibit a propensity towards caution.[78]

Can women speak for a minority known for its anti-feminist bias? While thirty-two Muslim women have sat in legislatures since inde-

[77] Both spoke critically of the Muslim situation at the All-India Muslim Convention in New Delhi in June 1961. See "Presidential Address by Dr. Syed Mahmud, June 10, 1961." Surinder Suri in *1962 Elections, a Political Analysis*, New Delhi, 1962, p. 79, quotes from the *Statesman* of January 2, 1962, the charge that Fakhruddin Ali Ahmed of Assam, a longtime loyal Congressman with a mass following in the state, "is not the state's chief minister just because he is a Muslim . . . (which) provides a sad commentary on the secular nature of our country."

[78] One MLA claims that a later Muslim minister farmed out his tough questions and grievances to others. On the other hand, the *Deccan Chronicle* of April 26, 1962, reports his inspecting a Muslim graveyard to assess complaints of desecration.

pendence, only one, Masuma Begum of Andhra Pradesh, has attained cabinet rank. Her previous career as a social worker and her record in the assembly demonstrated greater interest in women and Harijans than in Muslims. Since the first three Muslim cabinet members in Hyderabad–Andhra Pradesh were all Shi'as, the Sunnis, who constitute the large majority of Muslims in the province, agitated unsuccessfully for an additional Muslim in the cabinet, male and Sunni. In 1962 Masuma Begum was defeated for reelection, not so much as a woman, though her successful opponent, Owaisi, was candidate of the religiously conservative Majlis Ittihad-ul-Muslimin, but as a Shi'a. The Sunni Congressmen withheld their support, thus enabling Mir Ahmed Ali Khan, a fellow Sunni, to achieve ministership.[79]

The issue most likely to place educated Muslim women at odds with the men is the reform of Muslim personal law. Men claim that the *shari'ah* rules concerning divorce, dowry and inheritance do not disadvantage Muslim women substantially compared to their western sisters, but the vehement stand which one lady legislator in Bombay took in favor of reform in discussing it with me shows that those emancipated from purdah think otherwise. Thus on some issues a woman MLA would not reflect the prevailing attitudes and values of the Muslim community as a whole.

A word should be said about the role of Congress factions in choosing Muslims for office. Increasingly Congress ministers are selected because of caste affiliation or personal following.[80] Since Muslims do not share caste with Hindus they must depend all the more on the latter. Mehdi Nawaz Jung is said to have been squeezed out of the Andhra Pradesh cabinet because he didn't belong to either Congress faction and Jehangir Kabir of West Bengal has probably been denied office because he is not in Atulya Ghosh's dominant faction. A personal follower is probably not in a very good position to make requests of his leader for his community unless he can point to a large potential loss of votes if a particular *cause célèbre* is not solved satisfactorily. In day-to-day contacts, the sycophancy of the "yes-man" is more rewarding. Factional politics, as we have noted above, does not seem to be as beneficial to minorities as genuine party competition.

Besides factional affiliation, an aspirant for a ministry may be considered on the basis of his regional origin within the state as part of a geographic balance in the cabinet. Thus in Mysore, three Muslim deputy ministers, the late Jukaku Shamsuddin, Maqsood Ali Khan

---

79 Rasheeduddin Khan, p. 18.

80 See Marcus F. Franda, "The Organizational Development of India's Congress Party," *Pacific Affairs*, Fall 1962, vol. 35, 248-260.

and H. R. Abdul Gaffar, have represented former Bombay, former Hyderabad and the old Mysore parts of the state respectively. In Kerala when the coalition ministry was formed in 1960, one reason that A. A. Rahim of Quilon, a former Travancore-Cochin minister, was passed over in favor of his junior, P. P. Ummer Koya, was that the latter came from Malabar and the large Muslim minority of that region had to have a place without bringing in the Muslim League. Ummer Koya was the only Congress Muslim MLA who met the specifications.

A Muslim minister can represent his community in a number of different ways. Simply by holding office he is a symbol of minority participation in politics, which gives confidence to his people regardless of what he actually can do for them. When the Naik cabinet was constituted in Maharashtra in late 1963 without a Muslim member to replace the outgoing minister, Salebhoy Abdul Kadar, an outcry arose from Muslim organizations which by February 1964, obliged the chief minister to appoint Dr. Rafiq Zakaria as minister of urban development and wakf.[81] The insistent demands of the Muslims of Kerala and West Bengal for the appointment of one of their numbers to the state high courts is a similar case of symbolic representation.

In the work of his own portfolio, the minister may not be in a position to serve Muslim interests even if he wants to. As a former minister complained to me, "My post entailed work with Harijans, tribals and backward classes so how could I help caste Hindus or Muslims except through personal donations?" A number of Muslims have held the post of minister of public works, which must carry with it some job and contract patronage. A few others have held the post of home minister, which touches on the vital question of personal security but does not always include the law and order section.

The only post which solely concerns Muslims is the ministry of Wakf or Islamic religious endowments. The minister appoints the eleven Wakf Board members. Opponents of the party in power charge that this and supplementary appropriations are a source of Congress patronage to buy out potentially dissident Muslims and to create showpieces to help elect them. People of this opinion demand that the board be elected by the whole Muslim community. A former president of the Board in Andhra Pradesh pointed out, however,

---

[81] *Times of India*, February 13, 1964. S. M. Abdul Majid, Congress minister in Madras, also admits that Muslim organizations made representations to obtain a Muslim member in the state cabinet in 1962. Personal interview, June 4, 1964. One of them must have been the South Indian Muslim Convention, a Congress affiliate. Interview with C. A. Mohammed Ibrahim, its president, June 6, 1964.

that the Central Wakf Act sets some strict limitations to cabinet control by laying down requirements for membership: Sunni and Shi'a representation in the ratio of their endowments, a number versed in Islamic law, a *mutawalli* who has endowed a Wakf, an MP, an MLA and an MLC. Furthermore, once nominated for their five-year terms, they cannot be removed except for cause.[82] He concluded that the board is a practically autonomous body. Past scandals over misappropriation of Wakf moneys also justify government's auditing control.

Outside the minister's own portfolio his power to intercede on behalf of a fellow Muslim depends upon his personal influence with the "concerned minister" or the chief minister. Opponents say that S. M. Abdul Majid, minister for municipal administration of Madras since 1962, will give a sympathetic hearing to petitions but can't do anything about them. For instance, when the Madras municipal election campaign of 1964 was, perhaps inadvertently, scheduled to occur during Ramadan, the Muslim month of fasting, protests were lodged by the Muslim League with the minister[83] but he was not able to obtain a change of date from his chief minister, Bhaktavatsalam. One of the three Mysore deputy ministers, the late Jukaku Shamsuddin, said that Muslims would either channel their grievances through one of the three depending upon what region the case came from, or would write directly to the appropriate department, sending a copy to him. The same informant remarked that few bills considered by the cabinet as a whole affected Muslim interests directly, and prejudicial administrative actions would be the subject of individual consultation with other ministers.

There was complete lack of agreement among my informants on whether the cabinet would turn to a minority member to sound out Muslim reaction on proposed measures. Even if they do, it may be a fair accusation that he is so often unrepresentative in the sense of atypical or even isolated from the community that his opinion on such subjects is not valid. A good example, already referred to, is the abortive proposal in the spring of 1963 to reform the *shari'ah*. It was apparently broached first by a group of modernist Congress Muslim MPs but then met with such a storm of protest from orthodox organizations that Vice President Zakir Hussain had to get the central cabinet to retreat and surrender the problem to a committee of the *ulama*.[84] The fiasco need never have happened if the cabinet had

---

[82] Shahabuddin Ahmed, ex-mayor of Hyderabad, ex-MLA, was recently removed for unexcused absence from three meetings.

[83] *Siraat*, December 16, 1963, p. 1.

[84] *Ibid.*, July 16, 1963, p. 1; *Radiance*, August 11, 1963, p. 2.

consulted more representative Muslim leaders first. The Muslim minister may be so determinedly "anti-communalist" that if his opinion is sought, e.g., on the proposed detention of an opposition Muslim, he may be "more Catholic than the Pope" in urging drastic action. Another former office-holder criticized this stance, maintaining that "it is the duty of a Muslim minister to help if he is the representative of Muslims," and added, "why are they afraid to admit that they are?"

Can a minority minister appeal to New Delhi to overrule an adverse state cabinet decision? Scattered evidence would seem to indicate not unless there has been a clear invasion of union jurisdiction by the state. The repeated failure of Urdu associations to protect their language from the adverse policies of the Uttar Pradesh government bears witness to the powerlessness of both the Muslim state ministers (assuming that some are interested) and the Muslims in New Delhi to counteract the policy of a determined Hindu majority. On the other hand, a visiting dignitary from the center may be helpful in securing action on an individual case of injustice. For instance, it is said that Sadiq Ali, secretary of the All-India Congress Committee, got a notice rescinded in short order which dismissed some 3,000 *naqarnavises* (legal clerks) of Hyderabad who knew neither English nor Telugu but had long seniority of service in the courts. If the state cabinet Muslim is also the bearer of high office in the Pradesh Congress Committee, it may facilitate such contacts and interventions, but the chances are that to have obtained an inside position he must have been so cautious or so "secular" that he would be unlikely to use his power. There is always some aspiring careerist waiting to take over his job if he slips up and displays any "anti-national attitudes."

STRENGTHENING THE MUSLIM POSITION

There are limits to the kinds and amounts of group conflict which a political system, especially a new one, can tolerate without risking disintegration or foreign conquest. The maintenance of those understood limits to political competition are dependent upon the achievement of a "fair" distribution of benefits, the creation of common symbols of allegiance which do not offend the religious sensibilities of minorities, the discovery of a national enemy which unites rather than divides, and a modicum of legitimate force.

How these prerequisites are to be achieved in a multi-religious state without necessitating the complete assimilation of the minorities has been a problem which has plagued Europe too since the Reformation. The western solution is said to be the separation of church and state, but that, one suspects, has really been possible because of the erosion of all religion by modern science.[85] Where religion has revived or quasi-religions like Nazism and Communism have appeared, tolerance has quickly faded.

The modern crust of Indian leadership, both Hindu and Muslim, would clearly prefer the rapid growth of those economic and social forces which progressively circumscribe the role of religion in life and therefore in politics. But in the meantime, during the transition, even they must admit that the religious minorities have legitimate grievances, that is, they suffer violations of their acknowledged constitutional rights at the hands of the less secularized members of the majority both inside and outside of government. Wherever such a sense of injustice exists, there is the basis for separate political organization and action and a demand for effective representation.

If the Muslim demand for more effective representation is real and constitutional as has been the import of this paper, how can it be achieved? The older minority leaders outside Congress still think in terms of a return to reserved seats and separate electorates for legislative bodies such as they enjoyed in 1909-1950, or some other device like proportional representation or the Lebanese system.[86] All these, I contend, are futile and unrealistic. They would only reduce governmental stability, a change not always a boon to minorities, without altering essentially the minority's position as a minority.

To an American several possible courses of action suggest themselves in the light of the experience of our racial, ethnic and religious minorities. First and foremost, the Congress Party monopoly on governing must be broken. It has no doubt been vital to India to have a strong national ruling party with firm control of Parliament and state legislatures in the first period after independence. But if India is to graduate to a full-fledged democracy, it must sooner or later undergo the experience of alternation of party in power. This is necessary not only because otherwise the "outs" will become increasingly desperate and irresponsible and the "ins" increasingly corrupt and complacent, but also because the Indian National Congress has yet to recognize the real right-to-exist and fitness-to-rule of its opponents and therefore the inevitability of a rotation of power in democracy. Minority rights are not as well safeguarded by the paternalistic concern or intraparty feuds of a single party as they are by interparty competition.

[85] Donald E. Smith, p. 14.
[86] Jacob M. Landau, "Elections in Lebanon," *Western Political Quarterly*, 1961, vol. 14, pp. 120-147.

Secondly, Muslims need to make more alliances with other minority groups and parties. A promising example of this policy occurred in 1962 when a number of Muslims in western Uttar Pradesh joined the Republican Party, the former Scheduled Castes Federation of Dr. Ambedkar, and helped to elect an MP and several MLAs of their own religion.[87] Harijans and Muslims do share some grievances against Congress and caste Hindus but a broader alliance is inhibited by social distance, by some conflicts of economic interest, and by the ease with which Congress can buy off the Harijans with reserved seats and other patronage at the disposal of the party in power. In 1964 the Muslim League of Madras forged a coalition with the Tamil nationalist DMK party and the Swatantra Party which increased its representation in the municipal councils of the state.[88] The Swatantra ought to be able to attract more Muslim small businessmen who stand to lose from the socializing policies of all the other parties.

Thirdly, there is a crying need for an aggressive all-India civil liberties organization made up of noted members of all communities through which minorities can press for their legal rights without being discounted as purely self-interested. The demand for redress of grievances, I would stress again, must be stated in universalist terms which will appeal to the consciences of educated members of the majority and the ruling class.

Fourthly, Muslims would benefit from the acceptance by Indians of a broader conception of what is "political." They draw too sharp a distinction between political parties on the one hand, narrowly conceived as organizations which nominate candidates for election, and social welfare associations on the other hand, which are supposed to be pure and free of "politics." If Indians could come to accept, as Americans have, the legitimacy of organized pressure groups and their right to lobby in the legislatures and administration, minority groups like Muslims could better promote their interests. Otherwise they face the twin pitfalls of engaging in hopeless electoral contests or of retreating to the powerless irrelevancy of "social, religious, economic and educational" activities. Pressure group politics is admittedly more difficult in India than the United States because individual parliamentary votes can almost never be swayed by extraparty considerations, but that is simply a challenge to direct pressures

[87] That this combination has worried the Congress government is apparent from the arrest of the Republican MP, Muzaffar Hussain Kachochvi, and the attempt to unseat one of the MLAs, Professor Abdul Baseer Khan of Aligarh, *Times of India*, March 7, 1964, and *Hindustan Times*, January 2, 1964.

[88] *Siraat*, March 16, 1964, p. 2.

at earlier stages of the legislative process as big business has apparently succeeded in doing.[89]

Fifthly, the Muslim minority badly needs an English language press with a national circulation among the elite. Too often Muslims write their protests for Urdu publications which do not reach beyond their own community. *Siraat* and *Radiance* have made a good beginning but no one interested in broad news coverage would yet consider dropping the *Times of India, Hindu* or *Statesman* for one of these weeklies. A Muslim press could watch and badger Muslim legislators, publicizing their speeches and votes.

This leads to the sixth point, the need to improve the community's economic strength by encouraging more young men to enter business. This proposal may sound like putting the cart before the horse, since greater political representation is often demanded for the very purpose of increasing employment of Muslims in civil service and to obtain more government licenses and loans for business. But one perspicacious Muslim businessman in Malabar stated that his people would do better to forego politics like the Parsis or the Brahmins of Madras and concentrate on making money. The record of the Jewish minority in the United States proves the success of this path. The Muslims of Southern and Western India have always been more business-minded than those of the North and Hyderabad because they had no dynastic patronage upon which to rely, which leads one to regard their political future as more promising. Once a minority community has money, it can do many more things in politics including behind-the-scenes financing and manipulation of majority community politicians.

Lastly, Muslims ought to decide which of the distinctive elements of their culture and religion are essential, and which are peripheral and need not be defended against the assimilative pressures of the majority. A noted Muslim lawyer of Bombay told me that he did not think the Urdu language could be preserved in the long run since study in Urdu medium disadvantaged Muslim youth in the competition for jobs. He argued that the great religious and poetic works could be translated, as they were earlier from Arabic and Persian to Urdu itself.[90] The experience of the Malayalam-speaking Moplahs of Kerala would seem to bear this out. The insistence, on the other hand, on complete secularity of state school textbooks and instruction

[89] Weiner, *The Politics of Scarcity*, chapter 5.
[90] Along the same lines see Danial Latifi, *Language and Script: A New Proposal*, reprinted from the *Monthly Statistical Commentary on Indian Economic Conditions*, vol. 5, no. 5 of the Indian Institute of Public Opinion.

would seem to be vital and more easily defensible in modern terms.

In general it would seem wise and more promising of success for Muslims to press for those rights which they share with other citizens than for those which isolate them and simply exasperate the majority without thereby winning them allies. Decisions as to which causes to fight for and which to surrender are bound to cause some agonizing soul-searching among Muslims, but it is vitally important that they conserve their strength to contest the truly crucial issues.

CHAPTER 6

INDIAN MUSLIMS AND THE IDEOLOGY OF THE SECULAR STATE

ZIYA-UL HASAN FARUQI

IT IS APPROPRIATE to begin this paper with an extract from the presidential address of Mawlana Abul Kalam Azad (1888-1958) delivered at the Ramgarh session of the Indian National Congress in 1940. At that critical moment of modern Indian history he declared: "I am a Musalman and I am proud that I am a Musalman. I have inherited the glorious traditions of thirteen centuries of Islam. I am not prepared to see an iota of this perish. The teachings of Islam, its history and traditions, its art and sciences, and all that can be epitomized as Islamic culture is my treasure; and it is my bounden duty to protect and preserve it. As a Muslim in a particular religious and cultural sphere I possess an individuality on which no encroachment is acceptable. Yet, with all this, I have another feeling, too, and this feeling is the creation of the realities of my life. Islam is in no way opposed to this. It is, as a matter of fact, a guide on this path. I feel with pride that I am Indian. I am an element of the indivisible United Indian Nation, an inalienable element without which the image of its greatness remains incomplete; and, in no circumstances, can I give up this position."[1] Many Muslims, intoxicated at that time with the idea of a separate homeland, ridiculed this powerful assertion of Indian nationality. Until August 14, 1947, they followed the Muslim League leadership in the hope that the creation of Pakistan would provide a solution to all of their problems. The partition, however, solved no problems for the forty million Muslims who remained in India.

Many of the problems faced by Indian Muslims today are shared with other citizens of free India struggling to reconstruct herself. There are, however, problems peculiarly their own and closely inter-

Ziya-ul Hasan Faruqi is principal of Jamia College, Jamia Millia Islamia, New Delhi.

[1] Mawlana A. Azad, *Khutbat-i-Azad*, edited by Shorish Kashmiri, 3rd ed., Lahore, 1944, pp. 38-39. The Mawlana delivered the address only three days before the historic resolution to partition the country was passed by the general session of the All-India Muslim League at Lahore (March 23, 1940).

woven with the developments that led to the partition. This paper is concerned with the diverse Muslim reactions to the ideal of a secular democracy as adumbrated in the Constitution of India, their misgivings about the attitude of the majority community, and the positive contribution they could make toward strengthening secular democratic trends.

ISLAMIC OR SECULAR IDEALS: THE STATE

Indian Muslims in the early 1940's dreamed of the establishment of an Islamic state. The ideal was perfectly in harmony with the neo-Islam of which Iqbal (1876-1938), the poet-philosopher, was the chief exponent.[2] Now the Indian Muslims have to adjust themselves intellectually and spiritually to the concept of a secular state in which non-Muslims form the vast majority.

For the Muslims, as for other religious communities which affirm the sovereignty of God in all aspects of life, the idea of the secular state involves a theological question, and there are groups in the Indian Muslim community which have viewed it from this angle. They find the concept of secularism foreign to the very fundamentals of Islam. The Jama'at-i-Islami, though it has accepted secularism as a matter of expediency, makes no secret of the fact that it regards the secular state as a negation of the religious attitude, implying that God and His guidance should be relegated to the private sphere of an individual's life, and all other spheres, cultural, educational, political and economic, should be independent of His influence. In the context of contemporary needs, the Jama'at considers that there is hardly any justification for the continued retention of such a concept of secularism. The following extract represents the official stand of the Jama'at on secularism: "In propagating a religious ideal in a country which is avowedly secular, the Jama'at is not contravening any accepted article of the Indian Constitution. Secularism is a state policy which implies that there should be no discrimination or partiality on the basis of religious minority. But if beyond this *utilitarian expediency* some people have the deeper philosophical connotations in mind, we beg to differ. These philosophical connota-

---

[2] Note the following remark made by Iqbal in his presidential address to the All-India Muslim Conference in 1932: "Patriotism is a perfectly natural virtue and has a place in the moral life of man. Yet that which really matters is a man's faith, his culture, his historical tradition. These are the things which, in my eyes, are worth living for and dying for, and not the piece of earth with which the spirit of man happens to be temporarily associated." *Speeches and Statements of Iqbal*, compiled by Shamloo, Al-Manar Academy, Lahore, 1948, p. 38.

tions are essentially western in origin, and carry a spirit and a history which are totally foreign to our temper and needs."[3]

There is no doubt that this is a fundamental question. It is the crux of the problem in so far as the religious-minded Muslims are concerned. In general, the Indian Muslims are prepared only to tolerate the idea of secularism; they are not ideologically equipped to support it actively and to strengthen its bases. When India framed her new Constitution based on the principles of democracy, secularism and a welfare state, there were Muslims who interpreted the situation as nothing new to Islam, and pointed to the concept of *mu'ahadah*, mutual contract, such as the one concluded by the Prophet of Islam between the Muslims and the Jews of Medina. They acclaimed the Constitution as a covenant between the Muslims and the non-Muslims of India to establish a secular state.[4] Such a covenant, then, is permissible in Islam. But is such a covenant theologically ordained? Is it not possible to interpret it in terms of "utilitarian expediency"? Is it not questionable to press the analogy too closely? Nationalist Muslim leaders vigorously affirm this theory of the covenant, but there are lingering doubts; the explanation has bypassed the main body of classical Islamic political thought.

In the early years after the promulgation of the Constitution, when the Indian leaders, both Muslims and non-Muslims, emphasized in their speeches its secular character, the Urdu papers translated the word "secular" as *ghayr mazhabi* and *la dini*. *Ghayr mazhabi* means something contrary to religious commandments and *la dini* is irreligious or atheistic. Almost all the Urdu papers, *Al-jamiyat, Da'wat, Madina, Azad Hind* and others used these terms. The common man was very easily led to conclude that the Indian state was against religion. It is, however, gratifying to see that the Urdu papers have started to transliterate the word "secular," but still sometimes they use the words "secular" and *ghayr mazhabi* in the same paragraph. This mistranslation created a great deal of misunderstanding.[5] Then

---

[3] *Introducing the Jamaat-e-Islami Hind*, Publications Bureau, Jamaat-e-Islami Hind, Rampur, 1960, p. 24. (Italics added.) Also see the resolution passed on secularism by the Advisory Committee of Jama'at-i-Islami in April 1961.

[4] Wilfred C. Smith, *Islam in Modern History*, Princeton University Press, Princeton, 1957, pp. 284-285. This is still the official position of the Jami'at-al-Ulama-i-Hind. Dr. Syed Mahmud, who can be said to represent the western-educated nationalist Muslims, is of the same opinion. Note his statement published in *Madina* (Bijnore) March 5, 1964, in which he exhorts the Muslims to greater involvement and urges them to consider themselves as co-partners in the government, a status accorded them by the Constitution.

[5] More or less the same thing happened in Turkey. Lewis writes: ". . . more important than the out-and-out positivists were those who preached the separation

were heard Congress slogans such as "socialist pattern of society" which, in turn, reminded the Muslims of Karl Marx and the atheistic societies of the Soviet Union and China. They were already well aware of Jawaharlal Nehru's agnosticism. All this, together with the challenges of modernity and the educational and language policies of certain state governments, led them to think that their religion and culture were in danger, and encouraged them to seek security by isolating themselves from the mainstream of Indian life.

As hinted before, the idea of a secular state is foreign to Muslim political thought. The controversy that raged between the Azhari *ulama* and the modernists in Egypt in connection with the publication of 'Ali 'Abdur-Raziq's book, *al-Islam wa Usul al-Hukm* (Cairo, 1925) illustrated the intensity of the ideological conflict. In this book the author, deriving much from the political ideas of modern European thinkers, departed radically from the medieval Muslim conception of state and government.[6] The thesis propounded by him may be questioned on several points. But the point is that any deviation from accepted norms could not be tolerated by the *ulama*.

The *ulama* are, fortunately or unfortunately, the leaders of the Muslim community. They are intellectually unequipped to discuss secularism, socialism, or democracy on an academic level; and if any of them talks about these ideas, he does so in a particular frame of reference which is predominantly religious. Secularism has a history behind it; it is a modern concept based on certain theories about the nature of the state and law. To become an active supporter of secularism means to understand the historical forces which have led to such theories and accept the logical consequences of their application to practical problems. It is unfortunate that no one, not even a western-educated Muslim, has made any attempt to deal with the subject coherently and exhaustively. No one has explained that the fundamental constituents of modern culture are totally different from what the Muslims have inherited from their *aslaf*,[7] and that,

---

of religion and the state—the forerunners of the laicism of the Republic. The most notable was the ideologist of Turkism, Ziya Gokalp. It was perhaps unfortunate that, to render the unfamiliar French term *laique*, he should have used the word *la-dini*, which could mean irreligious. In the opinion of a well-qualified Turkish observer, the resulting confusion between laicism and irreligion 'did much to lead the Muslim clergy, with the Shaykh al-Islam at their head, into a hostile attitude.' " Bernard Lewis, *The Emergence of Modern Turkey*, Oxford University Press, London, 1961, pp. 396-397.

[6] C. C. Adams, *Islam and Modernism in Egypt*, Oxford University Press, London, 1933, pp. 261-267.

[7] To Muslim orthodoxy *aslaf* are those who championed the cause of orthodox Islam against the influences of Greek philosophy and *ajami* ideas. Ibn-i-Rushd,

in order to serve larger national and world purposes, they have to comprehend and assimilate all this so that it is not in conflict but harmoniously blended with their own cultural and religious heritage.

Among western-educated Muslim intellectuals, serious efforts are being made to establish the position that, besides orthodoxy, there are trends and traditions which are equally an integral part of the Islamic heritage. These intellectuals emphasize the scientific attitude which Muslim thinkers like Ibn-i-Rushd (1126-1198) and Ibn-i-Khaldun (1332-1406) possessed and through which they contributed to the richness of the world culture. They hold that, excepting the earliest years of Islamic history, the dominant feature of the Muslim state was mundane and secular. This feature was the product of the realities of life, and the generality of the Muslim masses accepted it. Even the majority of the *ulama* supported the secular organization of the Muslim state; and the most conscientious and pious among them, instead of opposing the state, kept themselves strictly aloof from court life and the activities of the state. This attitude of the *ulama* was based on the idea that a stable political system, whatever its nature, was better than a state of anarchy.

The Indian Muslims in general, like others, are under the impression that the Muslim states right from the Ummayyids to the Indian Mughals and Turkish Ottomans were the custodians of the *shari'ah* which, in turn, dominated all aspects of Muslim life. For many it would be totally unacceptable, even heretical, to state that the *shari'ah* was never operative as a common social and moral code. One of the urgent tasks of the Muslim intellectual is to disseminate a more accurate notion of the character of past Muslim societies, shorn of all romanticism. Writing about the Indian Muslim society of the mid-fourteenth century Professor M. Mujeeb of Jamia Millia Islamia, New Delhi, pointed out: "In political and administrative matters, the decrees or commands of the sultan had overriding authority. The *shari'ah* and the laws of the sultans differed in the matter of punishments, the sultans disregarding altogether the penal code of the *shari'ah*. The appointment of a *shaikh-ul-Islam* and a *muhtasib* or superintendent of public morals was no more than a formal acknowledgement of the existence in theory of a common code of behavior. The commandments of the *shari'ah* could never be enforced. Drinking could never be prohibited or prevented or sexual indulgence controlled. The laws regarding commercial transactions could not be applied, because trade and commerce were largely in the hands of

---

Ibn-i-Khaldun, Ibn-i-Sina (980-1037) and others like them are not counted among the *aslaf*.

non-Muslims. Even in the very important field of the law of inherit-ance, the converted professional classes and tribes could not be forced to follow the *shari'ah* rather than their custom. Apostasy and heresy were sometimes punished; mainly they seem to have been left unchallenged. It was only in questions of theology that the existence of a *shari'ah* became apparent, and theology was of interest to the *ulama*. The realities of social life lead one inevitably to the conclusion that for the generality of the Muslims the *shari'ah* was only an object of reverence, not a body of law that was, or could be, enforced."[8]

There is thus the vital task of reinterpretation of the Muslim herit-age which is being carried on by Muslim intellectuals concerned with modernizing the outlook of their brethren. But there are other fac-tors also upon which, to a large extent, the success of secularism in India depends. The Muslims, if they zealously adopt secularism, will undoubtedly make a positive contribution towards the realization of secular ideals. It is, however, the non-Muslim majority which will decide the issue finally. It is the majority, which, by a just and benevolent attitude toward the minority, makes it confident about its future and provides a real assurance that its rights will be safe-guarded. The Indian Muslims are a minority the bulk of which car-ries with it the stigma of having supported the demand for Pakistan. This is a complex situation. The majority community does not seem to want to forget the past; and it cannot do so until there is a radical change in the policies of Pakistan toward India. Till then the Indian Muslims will not be trusted. They will continue to feel "rejected, mistrusted, and afraid."[9] Besides, there is ample ground for their mistrust of the majority community. No doubt the secular and democratic Constitution of India has granted to the Muslims all the freedoms that it has given to other communities, and there are people in the government as well as outside who are deeply committed to seeing these freedoms and rights translated into action. Yet, it seems they have little control over the trends, particularly in the Hindi-speaking areas, which lead in a different direction.

The Muslims are totally dissatisfied with the educational policies of some of the state governments; they have, as a matter of fact, become apprehensive. The booklets published by the Dini Ta'limi Kaunsil (Council for Religious Education) and Dini Ta'limi Bord (Board for Religious Education), the statements given by their spokes-men, and the editorial comments of respectable journals like *Ma'arif* (Darul-Masannifin, Azamgarh) and *Burhan* (Nadwat-ul-Musannifin,

---

8 M. Mujeeb, *Indian Muslims*, London, 1965.
9 Smith, p. 265.

Delhi), all indicate the extent of the anxiety, fear and suspicion with which the Indian Muslims contemplate their religious and cultural future. They are reminded of the British rule when the administration of education was impartial and non-religious, and did not represent any particular faith or culture.[10] Unfortunately, in free India, they conclude, at least in some states, the Muslims are face to face with a different situation. Now they find "a system of education and a course of study . . . that teach a creed which is opposed to the basic concepts of Islam, which cut across the fundamental doctrines of Divine Unity and Apostleship, preach openly pantheistic and polytheistic beliefs and force the Muslim children to learn the mythology of another religious community after believing in which no Muslim can remain a Muslim by any stretch of the imagination."[11] Undoubtedly, this is a grave situation, and it mars the prospects of success for secularism in India. The Muslims have reason to suspect that the majority community is not honest in its profession of secular ideals and the state itself is lax in safeguarding their cultural rights as guaranteed in the Constitution.

The Muslims have become so suspicious that they reacted strongly against the recent amendment in the Wakf Act of 1954, and agitated vehemently against the intention of the government to appoint a committee to explore the possibility of making some changes in the Muslim personal law. The apprehension that the Muslim wakfs (endowments) were surreptitiously being given a secular character was, as a matter of fact, baseless. The apprehension was, however, present, and was strengthened by the statement of a responsible minister in the Lok Sabha. The amendment, which gave cause for much public criticism and was denounced as an interference with the basic principles of Islam, concerned the definition of the term "beneficiary."

Formerly "beneficiary" meant: "a person or object for whose benefit a wakf is created and includes religious, pious and charitable objects and any other objects of public utility *established for the benefit of the Muslim community*." Now the amendment deletes the italicized words and substitutes the phrase *"sanctioned by the Muslim Law."*[12] The implication is that institutions which serve the public such as schools, colleges and dispensaries, from which non-Muslims, according to the general Muslim law, are not excluded as beneficiaries, but

[10] Abul Hasan Ali Nadvi, *Education or Cultural Aggression in Free India?* Anjuman-I-Taaleemaat-I-Deen, Lucknow, 1960, p. 22.

[11] Abul Hasan Ali Nadvi, *Khutbah-i-Sadarat*, Istet Dini Talimi Kanfarans (State Religious Education Conference), Lucknow, June 1961.

[12] Manzoor Alam, "The Wakf (Amendment) Bill, 1964," *Radiance*, Delhi, June 7, 1964.

which could not be registered as wakfs under the previous act, now fall within its ambit. This brings all the wakfs under the control and administration of the state boards and provides a further check on the possibility of misappropriation and misuse of the wakfs as such.

The amendment, to the present writer, is an act of wisdom and in perfect accord with the general Muslim law. It affects only that provision of the act which is related to "objects of public utility." Other provisions in regard to the wishes of the Wakif (creator of the endowment), the purposes of the wakf and the proper utilization of the income from wakfs, have been left untouched. Thus the sanctity of the Muslim law has not been violated. Yet, the strong reactions expressed by the Muslims represent the degree of apprehension and suspicion that the attitude of the majority community, in general, has created among them. They also represent the obstinacy of the Muslim mind in regard to any steps that a Parliament with a non-Muslim majority might intend to take in legislating on Muslim affairs. It is also noteworthy that the amendment was opposed by the ignorant and sentimentalist section of the Muslim population and by the people who had some vested interest in the present administration of the wakfs. And ignorance, sentimentalism and vested interests, whether Muslim or non-Muslim and at any place in the world, have been a great hindrance in the way of progress.

ISLAMIC OR SECULAR IDEALS: THE LAW

The question of making changes in the Muslim personal law is a much more serious thing, for here the Qur'an and the Sunnah are involved. The Indian Constitution, democratic and secular in nature, directs: "The state shall endeavor to secure for the citizens a uniform civil code throughout the territory of India."[13] Mr. Durga Das Basu in his learned commentary states: "The object of this article is to introduce a uniform personal law for the purpose of national consolidation. It proceeds on the assumption that there is no necessary connection between religion and personal law in a civilized society."[14] This is a legal, political and religious problem of a very delicate nature, and the Indian government has been very cautious in approaching it. Toward the end of 1962, however, a few western-educated Muslims suggested to the government that it appoint a committee to explore the possibility of making some changes in the Mus-

[13] Article 44.
[14] Durga Das Basu, *Commentary on the Constitution of India*, vol. 2, 4th ed., S. C. Sarkar and Sons, Calcutta, 1962, p. 315.

lim personal law. Almost at the same time Mr. Samadani, a Muslim member of the Maharashtra legislature, moved an unofficial bill to prohibit polygamy which is permissible in Islam.[15] Muslims throughout India interpreted these moves as interference in their religious affairs, and warned the government of the serious consequences to which these might lead.[16]

Dr. Zakir Hussain, the vice-president of India, was perturbed by the countrywide protest of the Muslims against the appointment of the proposed committee, and in July 1963 convened a meeting of representative Muslim leaders of almost all shades of opinion. The meeting unanimously advised the government to give up the idea of appointing such a committee and leave the matter to the Muslims themselves.[17] The result was that the law minister in the government of India, Mr. Asoke K. Sen, made an announcement in Parliament to the effect that "in so far as the minorities are concerned, proposals to enact any reform in their personal law should come from their own side. This is not the policy of the Indian government to take initiative in such matters of minority communities."[18]

This is the story in brief, but this is not the end of the matter since the question may be raised again at any time. The Directive Principles of State Policy in the Constitution include article 44 which commits the state to the objective of a uniform civil code. The freedom of religion guaranteed under the Fundamental Rights does not prevent the state from making "any law regulating or restricting any economic, financial, political or other secular activity which may be associated with religious practice" (article 25). Now it is the Muslim community itself which has to decide whether there is need to review the Muslim code with an eye to reform, or regard it as perfect, complete and unchangeable. Protests and agitations can succeed in postponing the matter for a short while, but this is no solution. The Parliament of India, the sovereign legislative body, may at any time take a bold step and amend the Muslim law, and there are well-meaning educated Muslims who would support it. It was, perhaps, the correct assessment of this situation that impelled Mawlana Saeed Ahmad Akbarabadi, dean of the faculty of theology at Aligarh Uni-

[15] The Jami'at-al-Ulama-i-Hind, in its general session at Meerut in June 1963, passed a resolution condemning Mr. Samadani for his "irresponsible move" and declaring that no member of any legislature has a right to take the initiative in suggesting a change in the Muslim personal law without obtaining the sanction of the *ulama*.

[16] *Nida-i-Millat*, Lucknow, June 28, 1963.

[17] *Ibid.*, July 12, 1963.

[18] *Qaumi Awaz*, August 21, 1963, quoted by Atiqur-Rahman in *Nida-i-Millat*, February 7, 1964, p. 7.

versity and editor of the monthly *Burhan*, to ask the *ulama* to realize the urgency of the matter and themselves take the initiative to suggest reforms that are not in contradiction with the Qur'an and the Sunnah. Otherwise there may come a time when the government, without consulting the *ulama*, might enact such laws as would constitute downright interference with the *shari'ah*.[19]

No section of the Muslim intelligentsia, excepting perhaps the Barelwi school which has been reactionary and opposed to all reforms, is against a thorough review of the Muslim personal law as it exists today.[20] But there are sharp differences of opinion regarding the competent authority to make such a review and suggest reforms, and the extent of the reforms. The present education minister of India, Mr. M. C. Chagla, may be said to represent the secularist-modernist section of the Muslim educated class. His thesis is that, apart from matters which strictly concern personal belief and the practice of that belief, there is hardly anything in the life of the individual which does not have an impact on society and the state. He asserts that as India is a secular state, there should be no objection on the part of members of any particular community to laws being made for the common good. Since this secular state has already concerned itself with economic and political matters which affect the life of every Indian citizen there is no reason why the individual should be left to himself in matters that concern personal law. He points out that laws and judgments have already considerably modified and are still modifying Muslim personal law. It is therefore not correct to hold that this personal law is sacrosanct and that no interference with it can be allowed. His opinion is that personal law should not be interfered with where it concerns the individual's personal faith, but Parliament has the right to decide what is good for the people as a whole.[21] This approach is rejected outright by the other sections of the Muslim intelligentsia. They are not prepared to leave the matter with the exclusive authority of the Indian Parliament. Rightly or wrongly, they consider it against the very principles of secularism and democracy that legislatures should act independently in matters of religious importance.[22]

Among the *ulama*, who are considered to be the custodians of the

[19] Saeed Ahmad Akbarabadi, "Nazarat," *Burhan*, Delhi, August 1963, p. 69.
[20] Ziya-ul Hasan Faruqi, *The Deoband School and the Demand for Pakistan*, Asia Publishing House, Bombay, 1963, pp. 127-128.
[21] *Jami'ah*, Delhi, February 1964, pp. 62-63.
[22] *Ma'arif*, Azamgarh, February 1964, pp. 83-84.

shari'ah and to whom the Indian Muslims generally look for guidance in religious matters, there is a sizable group which seems to have awakened to the situation and have given serious thought to the problem. The establishment of the Majlis-i-Tahqiqat-i-shara'iyah at the Darul-Ulum Nadwatul-Ulama, Lucknow, in September 1963 was a manifestation of the anxiety of the *ulama* representing different associations and institutions to understand the challenges of modernity and examine the validity of a number of accepted propositions relating to Muslim jurisprudence in the light of the present situation.[23] But the scope of this Majlis is vague and the procedure adopted complicated. Its terms of reference being limited, it does not say anything about advising the government in matters of reforms in the personal law. My impression is that, in spite of the anxiety shown at the time of the proposal to appoint an official committee, the *ulama* took up the problem half-heartedly, and as far as I know, nothing substantial has thus far been done by the Majlis. This reluctant attitude is not confined to this particular question. The *ulama* generally are incapable of taking any positive steps to reconstruct Muslim society. And yet, it is the *ulama* who are the leaders and wield authority with the masses.

Mawlana Saeed Ahmad Akbarabadi is perhaps the only *alim* whose approach is bold, realistic and clear. But, because of these very characteristics, his opinions do not carry much weight among other influential *ulama*. In the symposium on "Changes in Muslim Personal Law" which was held on the occasion of the twenty-sixth session of the International Congress of Orientalists in Delhi, he spoke with great frankness. He distinguished between two aspects of Islam—*din* and *shari'ah*. While the *din* is immutable, the *shari'ah* has been constantly changing. Mawlana Akbarabadi quoted an opinion of Imam Abu Yusuf to the effect that one who is not familiar with the times is not competent to judge matters of the *shari'ah*. He also distinguished between various types of injunctions. Where the injunctions of the Qur'an were explicit, they could not be changed. But there were others not based on explicit injunctions which could be changed in the common interest. For instance, polygamy could be checked, controlled, or abolished if it was felt to be in the common interest. Such action would not be inconsistent with the Qur'an or the Sunnah and the door of *ijtihad* or interpretation is not closed. He concluded by saying that only a body of Muslim jurists would be competent to

23 *Burhan*, November 1963, pp. 258-259.

effect changes in Muslim personal law. Such a body of jurists could act under the guidance of the ministry of law.[24]

I consider the approach of Mawlana Akbarabadi as sound and practicable; it provides a solution and can meet the exigencies of the time. Moreover, there is ample scope for reform in the existing Hanafi law in India. Legislation relating to personal laws in Egypt has been kept within the limits of the Qur'an and the Sunnah by considering the rules of all four schools of Sunni Islam and those of Shi'i jurisprudence. The result is that Egyptian reforms relating to personal law are reasonable and meet the requirements of the modern age. Yet, the question remains: are the Indian Muslims psychologically prepared to permit the Indian Parliament to help them in enacting reforms in their personal law? I personally think that it is possible if the majority community succeeds in convincing them that it really believes in democracy and secularism, and is earnest in giving due protection to their genuine cultural and religious rights. Even then the initiative to introduce necessary changes in the personal law of the Muslims must be taken by the Muslims themselves; and they should do it immediately and with all seriousness of purpose. For this will certainly strengthen the forces of secularism in the country.

The above discussion has emphasized two main points concerning the Muslims and Hindus of India. First, the Muslims need to understand that secularism as adopted in India is not atheistic in nature and does not imply any negation or rejection of religion. It is a secularism based on democratic traditions and liberal thought and is not only tolerant toward religion but grants to all full freedom of religious faith and practice. They should also realize that in a country like India it is only this brand of secularism which can provide safeguards for their cultural and religious freedom and can give strength to their status as a religious minority. It is, therefore, in their own interest to support the secular ideal envisaged in the Constitution with sincerity and ardor. Second, in addition to any change in the Muslim attitude, it is the attitude of the majority community upon which, to a great extent, the success of secularism in India depends. Thus Muslims and non-Muslims are urgently required to cooperate in promoting that national integration which is essential to the building of a modern India.

[24] "Daily Bulletin" of the XXVI Session of the International Congress of Orientalists, Delhi, January 9, 1964, p. 10.

CHAPTER 7

SIKH SEPARATISM
IN THE PUNJAB

BALDEV RAJ NAYAR

ONE OF THE SEPARATIST movements that has achieved great prominence
and publicity in India since independence has been that mounted
in behalf of the religious community of the Sikhs by the political
party known as the Shiromani Akali Dal. It is common to refer to
this movement as a Sikh separatist movement, but whether the claims
and activities of the Akali Dal do, indeed, command the support of
the total Sikh community is a matter for empirical investigation and
not of peremptory judgment. This is not to assert that the claims
of the Akali Dal are unconnected with certain developments within
the Sikh religion and the Sikh community; it shall be precisely the
burden of this paper that they are intimately connected. However,
there is need for circumspection in implicating the total Sikh community in the activities of the Akali Dal.

What the Akali Dal demands is the redemarcation of the boundaries
of the state of Punjab, on the northwestern borders of India, in order
to form a smaller state called *Punjabi Suba*, or Punjabi-speaking
province. Ostensibly, in recent years, the demand has been made in
the name of Punjabi language, that is, for the creation of a state
whose boundaries correspond to the linguistic boundaries of the
Punjabi language. However, Akali leaders in innumerable explicit
statements on the subject and by their activities have left no doubt
of their real objective—the creation of a state in which the Sikhs
as a religious community would become the dominant political power
as a result of changing the population proportions in favor of that
community. Although initially such a state is asked for within the
present federal structure of India, several Akali leaders have given
pointed expression to greater political ambitions. In fact, before 1956,
the Akali Dal's own constitution explicitly stated that the "Shiromani
Akali Dal stands for the creation of an environment in which the
Sikh national expression finds its full satisfaction,"[1] an aim more
vividly stated in the Punjabi version by the use of the expressive term
desh-kaal, whose literal meaning is "country and era." In the past,

Baldev Raj Nayar is assistant professor of political science at McGill University.
[1] Quoted in speech of Amar Singh Ambalvi, in *The Sikh Students' Bulletin*,
January-February, 1958, p. 7.

the Akali leaders have interpreted this aim to mean the creation of a sovereign Sikh state.

THE LEGACY OF PARTITION

That the Akali Dal should aspire for a territorial arrangement in which the Sikhs as a religious community exercise political power is nothing new in that organization's history. Since the 1930's the Akali Dal, joined at times by other spokesmen in behalf of the Sikh community, has advocated a rearrangement of the boundaries of the Punjab in such a way as to give the Sikh community the determining voice in the political affairs of the Punjab, and also the creation of a sovereign Sikh state. Toward this end, before the partition, several schemes for Azad Punjab and Sikhistan were formulated by Akali leaders. Whatever the virtue of these schemes and whatever the strength of sentiment among the Sikhs for them, the demographic situation of the Punjab stood as an irresistible rock against the achievement of Akali objectives. Before the partition in 1947, the Muslims were concentrated in the western districts of the Punjab, where they formed over 60 per cent of the population. Similarly, the Hindus formed over 60 per cent of the population in the eastern districts. In the central districts were concentrated the Sikhs, but they did not form anywhere near a majority; the population here was about equally divided among the Hindus, Muslims and Sikhs. Although the British were sympathetic to the demands of the Akali Dal, they too were faced with the compulsions of this demographic situation. Sir Stafford Cripps explained the issue thus to the British Parliament in July 1946: "The difficulty arises, not from anyone's underestimate of the importance of the Sikh community, but from the inescapable geographical facts of the situation . . . it will be seen that what they demand is some special treatment analogous to that given to the Muslims. The Sikhs, however, are a much smaller community, five and one-half as against ninety millions, and, moreover, are not geographically situated so that any area as yet devised—I do not put it out of possibility that one may be devised in the future—can be carved out in which they would find themselves in a majority."[2]

In order to overcome the obstacles that it thus faced in the achievement of its objectives, the Akali Dal also entered into negotiations with leaders of the Muslim League. Such negotiations were a source of irritation to the Congress leaders and in April 1946 Nehru accused

[2] Statement of Sir Stafford Cripps in British Parliament, in Maurice Gwyer and A. Appadorai, *Speeches and Documents on the Indian Constitution 1921-47*, Oxford University Press, Bombay, 1960, vol. 2, pp. 638-639.

Master Tara Singh, the top Akali leader, of "sitting at one and the same time on about fifteen stools."[3] The negotiations between Akali and League leaders appear to have been mediated through several British officers in the government of India. In his book on the communal disturbances in the Punjab in 1947, Moon writes in some detail of his own role as a "go-between" and also that of Major Billy Short.[4] Moon found, however, that the Muslim League was unwilling to make any concessions to the Sikhs. Having been unable to secure a special position for the Sikh community from the Muslim League, the Akali Dal reconciled itself to the partition of the Punjab, with the Muslim majority districts going to Pakistan and the non-Muslim majority districts to India. This meant the division of the Sikh community into two somewhat equal halves in India and Pakistan.

The partition of the Punjab, however, was not a peaceful one. It was followed by mass rioting and murder, and resulted in the migration of about twelve million people—the entire Hindu and Sikh population moving from West Pakistan to India, and similarly almost the entire Muslim population from East Punjab (now part of India) to Pakistan. This mass migration could be easily explained by the element of fear, considering the mass rioting at the time and the relations among the different religious communities in the years preceding partition, but Moon argues that in the case of the Sikhs, a more rational objective was behind the mass migration. He states: "This factor was none other than the determination of the Akali leaders to ensure the survival of the Sikhs as a compact, coherent, undivided community. . . . The migratory movements that were thus set going became, no doubt, largely spontaneous and instinctive, the natural product of fear and danger, but there lay behind, as the original source of the initial impulse, this rational motivation. To grasp this is to grasp an important clue to the understanding of these events. The determination of the Sikhs to preserve their cohesion was the root cause of the violent exchange of population which took place. . . ."[5]

Whatever the causes, the Sikh population became heavily concentrated, as a result of the mass migration, in the northwestern districts of the Punjab in independent India. Most of these northwestern districts now became Sikh-majority districts, whereas the southeastern

[3] *The Times of India*, April 8, 1946.

[4] Penderel Moon, *Divide and Quit*, University of California Press, Berkeley, 1962, p. 43; see also Durlab Singh, *Sikh Leadership*, Sikh Literature Distributors, Delhi, 1950, p. 18.

[5] Moon, pp. 279-280; see also Alan Campbell-Johnson, *Mission with Mountbatten*, Robert Hale Ltd., London, 1951, pp. 66, 149, 174-175, 188, 191, 204, 357.

districts and the northern hill districts continued to be Hindu-majority. In the area which has come to be called the Punjabi-speaking region of the Punjab, which forms the core of the demand for Punjabi Suba, the Sikhs form now about 55 per cent of the approximately twelve million population, while they are less than 10 per cent in the remaining about nine million population in the so-called Hindi-speaking region. Some Hindu leaders allege that this concentration of the Sikhs in the northwestern districts, bordering on Pakistan, was a deliberate design on the part of Akali leaders. They point out that at the time of the resettlement of refugees the two most important portfolios in the Punjab ministry—home affairs and rehabilitation— were headed by Sikh leaders who had been prominent in Akali politics before the partition.[6] Part of the reason for this concentration may perhaps have also been the official policy of the Punjab government to resettle refugees, in so far as possible, in their ancestral districts from which they had originally migrated to West Punjab (Pakistan). In any case, the concentration of the Sikhs in these districts eliminated the major block to the earlier demand for a sovereign Sikh state—the absence of a geographically compact Sikh-majority area.

As it turned out, the Punjab had hardly recovered from the shock of murder and mass migration when the demand for a Sikh-majority province began to be made. In February 1948, Master Tara Singh announced that "we want to have a province where we can safeguard our culture and our tradition."[7] He went on to say that "we have a culture different from the Hindus, our culture is Gurmukhi culture, and our literature is also in Gurmukhi script."[8] On the point whether this was a communal demand, he stated: "I want the right of self-determination for the Panth in matters religious, social and political. If to ask for the existence of the Panth is communalism, then I am a communalist."[9]

It was clear, however, that so soon after the partition of the country, with the grave consequences that followed in its wake, no strictly communal demand could be acceptable to the nationalist leadership that had now assumed power. Equally clear was the fact that any plan to create a Sikh-majority province or state would be

[6] From an interview with a Hindu leader in Jullundur.

[7] The demand seems to have been made even earlier, as Mountbatten's press attaché noted on September 23, 1947, that "already the solution which has been mooted of creating a new Indian province of Sikhistan fails to measure up to Sikh demands," Campbell-Johnson, p. 205.

[8] *The Tribune*, February 26, 1948, quoted in Satya Mehta, "Partition of the Punjab," unpublished Ph.D. dissertation, University of Delhi, 1959, pp. 476-477.

[9] *The Statesman*, February 29, 1948.

met with determined opposition from those Hindus and Harijans, both Hindu and Sikh, who were likely to be included in such a state. Either because of these considerations or because of a newly-found genuine commitment to the principle of linguistic demarcation of provincial boundaries—a principle which had become highly important by then in Indian politics—the Akali Dal began to demand at this time a Punjabi Suba, excluding the allegedly Hindi-speaking but Hindu-majority areas and including the so-called Punjabi-speaking areas—producing inadvertently or otherwise a state in which the overwhelming majority of the Sikh population would be included.

In spite of the shift to the linguistic argument, Akali leaders also stressed that Punjabi Suba would be favorable to the Sikh religion and culture, and would relieve the Sikhs from the dominance of the Hindus. In an article on the subject, Master Tara Singh stated that what he wanted was a state where the Sikhs would be in the majority so that they could escape from Hindu dominance in the legislature. He did not care very much what name might be given to the state; however, a Punjabi-speaking state would amount to precisely this kind of a state.[10] It is statements such as these by the top leaders of the Akali Dal that have made it impossible to divest the demand of Punjabi Suba of its communal associations and implications. In addition, it should be noted that to the Sikh masses the demand was frankly presented in the name of the Sikh religion and as one that would secure the rule of the Sikhs.

One cannot help but note the impressive refrain in the speeches, interviews, and published material of Akali leaders and sympathizers that the Sikhs as a religious community should hold political power in a definite territorial area. Granted this aspiration for political power by the Akali Dal on behalf of the Sikh community, it remains to inquire as to what the basic impulses are behind this aspiration. Why is it so essential for the Akali Dal to acquire a territorial unit in which the Sikhs as a community should exercise political power? Here three factors seem important: (1) the nature of the Sikh community as interpreted by Akali leaders and intellectuals; (2) the fear about the possible disintegration of the community resulting from religious unorthodoxy; and (3) a sense of grievance over alleged discrimination against the Sikh community.[11]

[10] Master Tara Singh, "Punjabi Suba," reprinted as chapter x in Gurcharan Singh, *Sikh Kya Chahtey Hain? (What Do the Sikhs Want?)*, New India Publications, Delhi [1950] p. 122.

[11] For an analysis of Sikh politics which deals with these issues, see Donald E. Smith, *India as a Secular State*, Princeton University Press, Princeton, 1963, pp. 438-453.

Baldev Raj Nayar

THE NATURE OF THE SIKH COMMUNITY

Under the impact of Islam, new schools of thought developed among the Hindus both through the assimilation of certain Islamic ideas, such as the belief in a single God and recognition of the equality of man, and through the resurrection of older ideas with the object of reforming Hinduism so as to meet more effectively the Islamic challenge. One of these new schools of thought was that of Sikhism started by Guru Nanak (A.D. 1465-1539), the first Guru (spiritual teacher) of the Sikhs. He was succeeded by nine more Gurus over a period of about two centuries. All ten Gurus came from the Kshatriya caste of the Hindus. The followers of Sikhism almost all came from among the Hindus, with the overwhelming majority from the Jat peasantry belonging to the then Sudra caste of the Hindus in the central Punjab. The Jat Sikhs later acquired political power and became the elite caste among the Sikhs.

Authorities differ as to the influence that worked to create the Sikh religion. Some hold that Sikhism represents a mixture of Hinduism and Islam.[12] Others say that while Sikhism was a synthesis of Hinduism and Islam, "in its general system of belief it was closer to Islam than Hinduism."[13] Another authority dismisses the idea that Sikhism is a synthesis, and asserts that "although precipitated by Islam, Sikhism owes nothing to that religion. It is, on the other hand, a phase of Hindu religious revival and has in consequence, retained all essential features of real Hinduism."[14] Still another authority, the burden of whose work is the insistence that Sikhism is a "new way of life," distinct from Hinduism and Islam but "aiming at the final synthesis and convergence of both these religious and cultural streams into itself,"[15] nonetheless admits that Sikhism accepts Hinduism's "basic philosophic concepts though these concepts are, in some respects, interpreted differently and evaluated otherwise, than in the various cults of Hinduism. Viewed thus, Sikhism is essentially and basically a Hindu religion."[16] Although the philosophical foundations of Sikhism have been a matter of dispute, until the end of the nineteenth century much social contact existed between Hindus and

[12] Charles Eliot, *Hinduism and Buddhism: An Historical Sketch*, Routledge and Kegan Paul Ltd., London, 1921, vol. 2, pp. 262-273.
[13] Khushwant Singh, *The Sikhs*, George Allen and Unwin Ltd., London, 1953, p. 45.
[14] Gokul Chand Narang, *Transformation of Sikhism*, New Book Society of India, New Delhi, 1960, pp. 254-255.
[15] Kapur Singh, *Parasharprasna*, Hind Publishers Ltd., Jullundur, 1959, pp. 8 and 31.
[16] *Ibid.*, p. 19.

Sikhs. Intermarriage took place between members of the two communities; often in the same family, members belonged to the two different faiths.

In Sikhism there is belief in the unity of God,[17] though some authors say that the God of Guru Nanak's conception is pantheistic rather than monotheistic.[18] God is equated with truth, and is endowed with the attributes of "omnipresence, omniscience, formlessness, timelessness, and the power to destroy (evil)."[19] The Sikhs believe in the ten Gurus, but there is no belief in divine incarnation. There is no idol worship, but extreme respect is given the *Adi Granth*, the sacred book of the Sikhs. The equality of man is emphasized; the caste system is attacked though Sikhism has been unable to get rid of it.

The most important aspect of Sikhism is not its religious ideas but its social constitution. Initially, the Sikhs were a quiet, pietistic group, but later became extremely militant in reaction to the repressive policies pursued by several of the successors of the tolerant Mughal emperor Akbar. The Sikh struggle against the Muslims was epitomized in the last of the ten Gurus, Guru Gobind Singh (1666-1708), who gave the Sikhs a thoroughgoing military organization, transformed a religious group into a military society to challenge the might of the Mughal Empire, sanctified the use of the sword, and convinced the Sikhs that victory was on their side in this crusade because "the Sikh Khalsa shall rule and its enemies will be scattered."

Guru Gobind Singh laid down a baptismal ceremony for all Sikhs, and required them all to wear on their persons the five distinguishing "K's" as the mark of every true Sikh: (1) the *Kesh*, or unshorn hair; (2) the *Kacchha*, or short drawers; (3) the *Kara*, or iron bangle; (4) the *Kirpan*, or steel dagger; and (5) the *Kanga*, or comb.[20] Those who went through the baptism and wore the five K's became members of the order of the *Khalsa* (the "pure," the "elect," the "chosen") and recognized Guru Gobind Singh and his wife as their parents. All male members of this order assumed the last name of Singh. Through these actions Guru Gobind Singh tried to create a community distinct from other groups. Finally, Guru Gobind Singh proclaimed that the line of the Gurus would end with him, and that thereafter the visible body of the Guru would be present in their

[17] Khushwant Singh, p. 34.
[18] Narang, p. 258.
[19] Khushwant Singh, p. 35.
[20] Both utilitarian and metaphysical reasons have been given by authors for the adoption of these symbols by Guru Gobind Singh. See Khushwant Singh, p. 31, and Kapur Singh, pp. 137-154.

book, the *Adi Granth*, and in the *Panth* or the organized Sikh community.

The new militancy, along with the elaboration of its outward forms and symbols, made for a certain differentiation within the Sikh community. At first, there were the followers of the tolerant and pacifist doctrines propounded by Guru Nanak. These followers considered themselves Sikhs and were faithful to the tenets of the first Guru. Except for their beliefs in the doctrines of Guru Nanak, however, they could not be distinguished physically and socially from the Hindus, with whom they often intermarried and had close social relationships. Many of these Sikhs became members of the order of the Khalsa, established by the tenth Guru, and started wearing the five distinguishing K's; they were now not only Sikhs but Singhs. These Sikhs are known as *Keshadhari* Sikhs, who consider themselves to be the more genuine Sikhs and the term Sikh in practice seems to apply exclusively to them. Members of the other group, who do not wear the five symbols, are known as *Sahajdhari* Sikhs (the slow adopters). The distinction between these two types of Sikhs continues even today.

The tenth Guru left behind a tradition of undying hostility toward the Muslim rulers. A long struggle between the Sikhs and the Muslims ensued. In the mid-eighteenth century the Sikhs became a sovereign power, with several Sikh chiefs ruling over different parts of the Punjab. At the beginning of the nineteenth century, Maharaja Ranjit Singh subdued several of the other Sikh chiefs and brought the northwest of India under his monarchical rule. After his death, however, the Sikh kingdom became unstable and was finally annexed by the British in 1849.

Such in brief is the history of the Sikhs up to the British conquest. Now, it is claimed that the Sikh community is a separate political entity. This assertion is in answer to the Hindu assumption that the Sikhs are but a part of the Hindu community, just like the Jains, the Arya Samajists and several other sects. Many Hindus maintain that all the ten Sikh Gurus were Hindus, who followed Hindu customs and rites in their actual lives. They criticize the view that Guru Nanak intended to start a new religion.[21] They say that the ten

---

[21] See Tara Chand, *Billa Shuba Naveen Sikh Hindu Nahin (Undoubtedly the New Sikhs Are Not Hindus)*, Sat Sangh Kutiya, Kotarkhana, n.d.; Tara Chand, *Sikh Mat Ke Dharam Pustak (The Religious Scriptures of Sikhism)*, Punjab National Press, Delhi, n.d.; and Alakh Dhari, *Case for United Punjab*, Abha Printing Press, Ambala Cantt, 1956, pp. 60-65. See also Eliot, vol. 2, pp. 267-268, who says that Guru Nanak "did not at first claim to teach from many other religious bodies who reprobated caste and idolatry"; and Khushwant Singh, p. 183, who says: "There is little evidence to support the belief that Guru Nanak planned the founding of a new community synthesizing Hinduism and Islam. He simply planned to reform Hinduism."

Gurus made no radical departure from Hinduism but only reformed it in certain respects. The creation of the Khalsa Panth by Guru Gobind Singh is taken to be the development of an armed wing for the protection of Hinduism and not the creation of a separate religion.

Sikh leaders and writers who contest the claim that the Sikhs are a part of the Hindu community, however, are agreed upon one point —at the time of the arrival of the British in the Punjab, the Hindu and Sikh communities were very close to each other and were considered as kith and kin. They attribute this to a number of historical causes, but do not dispute the fact that the differences between the Hindus and Sikhs were slight. As one Sikh writer points out, "they worshipped the same old gods and indulged in the same old superstitious practices from which their Gurus had so heroically worked to extricate them. Their baptism and five symbols became a mere anomaly."[22] Whether any different state of affairs, in fact, ever existed earlier remains a matter of controversy.

However, after the British conquest, several reform movements arose in Sikhism. One of the more important of these was the Singh Sabha movement in the last quarter of the nineteenth century. The purpose of this movement was "to study the original sources of Sikhism, and to restore it to its pristine purity."[23] The process of reform took the shape of "dehinduizing" the Sikhs, since, it is remarked, "the only trouble with Sikhism at that time was that its doctrines and institutions had been completely Hinduized."[24] Associations known as Singh Sabhas were opened in various parts of the Punjab to further the objectives of the movement. The main business of these associations was to hold weekly meetings where "lectures were delivered against Hindus and their institutions, or debates were held to controvert the attacks of the Arya Samajists."[25] A new literature was developed emphasizing the distinctive character of Sikhism, including the work known as *Ham Hindu Nahin* (We Are Not Hindus) by Bhai Kahan Singh, which "did more to dehinduize the Sikhs than anything else."[26]

As part of the reform movement, new rites and ceremonies, different from previous Hindu ones, were instituted for the Sikhs. The reformers also opened Sikh schools which provided not only education but "also served as strongholds of Sikhism wherever they were established."[27] The spread of education brought political consciousness

---

[22] Teja Singh, *Sikhism: Its Ideals and Institutions*, Lahore Book Shop, Lahore, 1938, p. 97.
[23] Teja Singh, *Essays in Sikhism*, Sikh University Press, Lahore, 1944, p. 119.
[24] *Ibid.*, p. 130.   [25] *Ibid.*, p. 141.   [26] *Ibid.*, p. 136.   [27] *Ibid.*, p. 142.

among the Sikhs and, together with the particular doctrines disseminated by the Singh Sabha movement, led to demands for the recognition of the Sikhs as a separate community in politics and in law, and for the grant of rights and privileges to them on that basis.

It is believed in some quarters that the British for their part encouraged separatist tendencies among the Sikhs. It was but natural that the British should look favorably upon any Sikh attempt to assert their separate entity, since the Sikhs had helped the British quell the Indian mutiny in 1857 and thus saved the British empire in India. The growing nationalism in India in the latter part of the nineteenth century also made it a political necessity for the British "that as many elements as possible should be segregated from the general body of Hindus who were responsible for the agitation for political reform in India."[28] Significantly the fundamental rules of the Singh Sabha associations required that no discussion of an anti-government nature should take place at Sabha meetings.[29] Some hold that the Singh Sabha movement would have developed an anti-Hindu character in any case, because any reform of Sikhism could take place only through eliminating Hindu influences.[30] Others believe that the movement itself and its anti-Hindu form took place as a result of the anti-Sikh propaganda by certain sections of the Hindu community, notably the Arya Samaj.[31]

At any rate, the British themselves before long began drawing a distinction between Hindus and Sikhs for official purposes. As one British observer stated in connection with census operations, "at former enumerations village Sikhs in their ignorance generally recorded themselves as Hindus, as indeed they virtually were. With the experience gained by time, a sharp line of demarcation has now been drawn between Sikhs and Hindus."[32] Evidently, the British authorities took upon themselves the task of determining what a person's religious classification should be. They, however, went further and provided preferential treatment for Sikhs. In listing the reasons influential in strengthening the power of the Sikh community, the Punjab census report of 1891 mentioned, among other things, "the marked preference shown for Sikhs in many branches of government service."[33] This preference was especially noticeable in military

---

[28] *Ibid.*, p. 129.   [29] *Ibid.*, p. 132.   [30] *Ibid.*, p. 130.

[31] Khushwant Singh, p. 98; and Hukam Singh, "Sikh Character and the SGPC Election," *The Spokesman*, vol. 9, no. 30 (Annual Number, 1959), p. 27.

[32] M. Macauliffe, *A Lecture on the Sikh Religion and Its Advantages to the State*, Government Central Printing Office, Simla [1903], pp. 27-28.

[33] Quoted in India, Census Commissioner, *Census of India, 1931*, Civil & Military Gazette Press, Lahore, 1933, vol. 17, part 1, p. 305.

recruitment. Although the Sikhs were less than 2 per cent of the Indian population, their proportion in the army at times went up to as high as 33 per cent. The premium on recruitment of Sikhs to the army helped in the conversion of many Hindus to Sikhism.

In the case of the Sikhs, the British government even made an exception to its traditional policy of religious neutrality. It made the baptismal ceremony a condition for enlistment of Sikhs to the army, because the Sikh regiments would then be able to serve as important agencies for the encouragement and promotion of Sikhism."[34] Sikh soldiers were further required to keep the five symbols of Sikhism. The British believed that "the orthodoxy of a Sikh means loyalty to his sovereign" and that the British government would benefit from "a rigid belief in Sikhism and faith in their Gurus" by the members of the Sikh community.[35] Even outside the military sphere, the British government tried to preserve Sikh traditions. Positions in legislative and in government offices reserved for the Sikh community were allocated to those who adhered to Sikh forms and symbols.[36]

All these measures and privileges were greatly appreciated by the Sikhs. "This friendship," comments a Sikh scholar, "put some heart again into Sikhs, and they began to enlist themselves in the British army, where they could keep their baptismal forms intact."[37] As friendship developed between the British government and the Sikh community, so did friction between the Hindus and Sikhs; at any rate, "the Hindu-Sikh schism in its active form dates from the British annexation of the Punjab."[38] On the intellectual plane, the gulf between the two communities widened, some Hindu leaders allege, as a result of the biased works on Sikh religion and history by British writers like Macauliffe.

Whatever the role of the British during the Singh Sabha movement, the next event, which further strained relations between Hindus and Sikhs, brought the Sikh community into conflict with the British government. Known as the Gurdwara Reform movement or the Akali movement, it superseded the Singh Sabha movement, especially in the political sphere. At the end of World War I, certain sections of the Sikh community felt that radical changes in Sikh rites and ceremonies could be brought about only through a change in the management of Sikh shrines which were at the time and had been

[34] Remarks by the Lieutenant Governor, in Macauliffe, *A Lecture on the Sikh Religion*, pp. 28-29.
[35] *Ibid.*, p. 26.
[36] Khushwant Singh, "Struggle for the Gurdwaras," *The Statesman*, June 18, 1959.
[37] Teja Singh, *Sikhism*, p. 97.
[38] Khushwant Singh, p. 184.

for generations, by and large, under the control of Sahajdhari, and not Keshadhari, priests. The leaders of the Akali movement attempted to oust these priests and bring the management of the gurdwaras under the popular control of the Sikh community. In the attempt to forcibly evict the priests, the Akali volunteers came into conflict with the British government which felt that it was its duty to protect the right of property and to maintain law and order.

This struggle against the priests and the British government lasted for about five years and developed into a mass movement which spread into the rural areas. In its anti-government aspect, the Akali movement did receive sympathy and support from nationalist leaders of India. In so far as the Punjab was concerned, however, it created a further gulf between the Hindu and Sikh communities, since it meant not only the removal of priests who served as a bridge between the two communities, but also the breaking of Hindu idols and elimination of Hindu elements in worship at Sikh shrines.[39]

The doctrine which is held to be the basic motive force behind the various reform movements in Sikhism and is presented as having a strong hold on the Sikh mind today—at least among those belonging to or sympathizing with the Akali Dal—is that the Sikhs are a separate political entity. According to this doctrine, Sikhism is not a religion like other religions. By religion others understand a relationship between the individual and God, whereas the Sikh religion concerns itself with the whole activity of man in the context of this world.[40] Religion and politics are said to be combined in Sikhism. The sixth Guru wore the two swords of *miri* (worldly power) and *piri* (religious authority). The *Akal Takht* (the throne of the Immortal One) in the city of Amritsar is the highest seat of both religious and political authority for the Sikhs.[41] Guru Gobind Singh made the Panth supreme in matters both religious and political.[42] According to Master Tara Singh, the Panth is a political organization which has been founded upon religion.[43]

It is further maintained that participation in politics, with the Sikh community acting as a single political group and as a single group alone, is imperative for the existence of the Sikh religion. Without

[39] Vasdev Verma, "Hindu Sikh Ekta" (Hindu Sikh Unity), *Pratap* (Jullundur), December 31, 1961.

[40] Teja Singh, "Religion and Politics," *The Spokesman*, June 25, 1956, pp. 11-12.

[41] Harbans Singh, "Future of Sikhs' Central Political Organization," *The Statesman*, April 4, 1948.

[42] *Ibid.*

[43] Master Tara Singh, *Charhdi Kala: Present Sikh Politics No. 2*, Panthic Tract Society, Amritsar, n.d., p. 46.

political organization and participation in politics, the Sikh religion cannot survive. It was precisely for this reason, it is said, that Guru Gobind Singh established the Panth; other than organizing the Sikhs into a political community, he made no change in the Sikh religion as formulated by Guru Nanak. If the Sikhs were to give up political activity as a community and, as a result, their political organization, the entire Sikh community would be scattered.[44]

Not only is political activity and organization considered essential for the protection of Sikh religion and the prevention of its disintegration, but some hold that participation in politics by the Sikhs as a community is built into Sikh religious ideology. The Panth was created, it is indicated, "for the avowed purpose of facilitating the emergence of the global Fraternity."[45] Being dedicated to this cause, political activity is inherent in the Panth, "and it is in this context that the litany which is repeated in every Sikh congregation, throughout the World, every morning and evening, to the effect that, 'The Khalsa shall rule and none shall defy them' is to be understood and appreciated. The Order of the Khalsa, as divorced from political activity, and not dedicated to the achievement of political ends, aiming at the eventual establishment of universal equalitarian global Fraternity, has no intelligible connotation."[46] Further, it is argued that the Sikh religion requires the Sikh to combine in himself both wisdom and power, in equal measure; hence, the compulsion to obtain "control of the commercial and industrial machine which is the State today, and control of the organized military power, which was the State always."[47] Expressing the same thought in a different way, Master Tara Singh has said that the "Khalsa Panth will either be a ruler or a rebel. It has no third role to play."[48]

Loyalty to the political organization of the Panth has furthermore to be a complete one on the part of Sikhs. A Sikh individual cannot owe loyalty to any other political organization "without violating his loyalty to the first—the Khalsa Panth—of which he is a member as soon as he is born."[49] As Master Tara Singh has said, "I am a Sikh

[44] *Ibid.*, pp. 3-46. In a foreword to a book by Sarup Singh, *The Forgotten Panth*, The Sikh Religious Book Society, Amritsar, 1945, Master Tara Singh says, "there is not the least doubt that the Sikh religion can live only as long as the Panth exists as an organized entity."

[45] Kapur Singh, p. 40. Kapur Singh has been an advisor of the Akali Dal, and in 1962 was elected to Parliament on the Akali ticket. He is a former member of the Indian Civil Service.

[46] *Ibid.*, p. 41.   [47] *Ibid.*, p. 42.

[48] *The Hindusthan Standard*, July 4, 1958. Since then, Master Tara Singh has expressed these sentiments in a signed article in his newspaper *Prabhat*.

[49] Sarup Singh, p. 20. Sarup Singh was an active and prominent leader of the

first and last," and also that nationalism "has a place but in a corner."[50] The Panth, as a whole, may conceivably enter into coalitions with other political organizations "for some common purpose on the basis of honor and equality." However, "a member of the Panth cannot become, over its head, a member of some other body, e.g., the Indian National Congress, without violating his loyalty to the Panth, for their spheres clash—the Panth itself being a religious-cum-political organization of the Sikhs."[51]

From the Panth as an exclusive political organization, with its membership coeval with and confined to the Sikh religious community, the analysis is carried one step further to convert the Panth into a nation. It is proclaimed that "the Khalsa Panth was, based as it was on the common ideology of the Sikh religion, a nation."[52] It is emphasized that the ideology of the Khalsa Panth brings a transformation in its converts, welds them together in "a kinship which transcends distance, territory, caste, social barriers and even race,"[53] and through this process of conversion the Sikhs have become a nation.

The basic doctrine of the Akali Dal has thus been that religion and politics are inextricably combined in Sikhism and that the Sikhs are a separate political community. It is in the light of this doctrine that the demand for a separate sovereign Sikh state before the partition in 1947 is understandable. Even now the exposition of this doctrine at times goes hand in hand with the demand for Punjabi Suba on a linguistic basis. This is evidenced, among other things, in one of the pamphlets—widely distributed at Akali conferences—supporting the demand for the establishment of Punjabi Suba, prepared in 1960 by the legal adviser of the Akali Dal.[54] In the second chapter on "The Theopolitical Status of the Golden Temple," the author tries to establish firmly that (1) "there is no ultimate dichotomy in the true Sikh doctrine between this world and the next, the secular and the religious, the political and the spiritual,"[55] and (2) the metalegal constitution of the Sikhs prescribes that "they must be approached and dealt with at state level as a collective group and entity"[56] and "not by atomizing them into individual citizens."[57]

Akali Dal until 1961 when he was expelled from the organization on account of differences with Master Tara Singh. He also served as vice-president of the Akali Dal.

[50] *The Hindusthan Standard*, March 30, 1959.

[51] Sarup Singh, p. 20.   [52] *Ibid.*, p. 10.   [53] *Ibid.*

[54] Gurnam Singh, *A Unilingual Punjabi State and the Sikh Unrest*, Super Press, New Delhi, 1960. Gurnam Singh was elected in 1962 to the Punjab Vidhan Sabha on the Akali ticket and then became leader of the Akali party in the legislature.

[55] *Ibid.*, pp. 12-13.   [56] *Ibid.*, p. 11.   [57] *Ibid.*, p. 17.

However, this ideological position of the Akali leaders not unexpectedly raises serious doubts in the minds of the Hindus who would be included in the Punjabi Suba as to the nature of the proposed state. The advocates of Punjabi Suba hold that it will be a political unit not unlike any other state organized on a linguistic basis in India, and charge that the Hindus display a narrow communal mentality in opposing a demand which is in accord with nationally recognized principles. But the advocates of the Punjabi Suba are also the ones that maintain that the Panth must act as a united group in politics. As a consequence, the Hindus feel that in a state where one religious community acts as a united group and does not even allow its members the freedom, as individuals, to join other political groups, there could be only one result if such a religious community were politically powerful—the imposition of its rule, as a religious-cum-political community, over other religious communities. Whether such a state is in accordance with the letter and spirit of the Constitution or not may be debatable. But the doctrinal basis of the Akali Dal provides a clue to the determined opposition of the Hindus in the Punjab—granting for the moment that the demand is tenable on a linguistic basis—to the formation of Punjabi Suba.

THE THREAT OF RELIGIOUS UNORTHODOXY

The second factor which "forms the main motive, but not the argument for the demand of Punjabi Suba," is the growth of religious unorthodoxy among the Sikhs today.[58] The impact of the scientific age and the industrial revolution upon religious and spiritual values, in general, has often been commented upon. Sikh authors, too, have attempted to evaluate the impact of these factors specifically on Sikhism. They have noted that there is a questioning among the Sikh youth about the values of Sikh religion as a result of contact with western science and thought. Along with the element of doubt about religious values, there is noted also the decline in the observance of Sikh rites and ceremonies.[59]

It would seem that the impact of the modern scientific and industrial age on Sikhism is no different from that on other religious systems. The question then arises as to why Akali leaders feel so intensely concerned about religious unorthodoxy and seek a political solution

[58] From an interview with an influential intellectual of the Akali Dal. See also Khushwant Singh, *The Statesman*, June 18, 1959; and Khushwant Singh, *The Sikhs*, pp. 184-185.

[59] Kartar Singh, *Rekindling of the Sikh Heart*, Lahore Book Shop, Lahore, 1945, p. 29. See also Ratan Singh, *The Revolt of the Sikh Youth*, Modern Publications, Lahore [1943].

for it. The answer lies in the fact that the impact, in so far as Sikhism is involved, becomes dramatically visible because if unorthodoxy proceeds far enough it involves the cutting or complete removal of hair from head and face, contrary to the strict injunction of the tenth Guru. Akali leaders further feel that once the process of unorthodoxy sets in for individuals it culminates in their absorption in the Hindu community, and fear that eventually it must mean the assimilation of the Sikhs into Hinduism. Such a prospect must, indeed, seem dreadful to a set of leaders who over the years have advocated the separation of Sikhs from the Hindu community.

The basis for this assimilation is alleged by some to be the close social and cultural relations between Hindus and Sikhs,[60] and by others that, apart from the outer forms and symbols, there is nothing to distinguish Sikhism from the reformed sections of Hinduism.[61] Consequently, if one gives up the forms and symbols the sole defense against absorption into Hinduism is eliminated.[62] Khushwant Singh traces the process of absorption into Hinduism as a gradual development from one generation to another. The trimming of facial hair in one generation is followed by shaving and cutting of hair on the head in the next generation, and so on. He sums up the process of assimilation in four successive stages: (1) orthodox Sikh; (2) unorthodox Sikh; (3) Sahajdhari Sikh; and (4) Hindu.[63] According to some authorities, the process of unorthodoxy among Sikhs seems to be well advanced.

Although the presence of a certain degree of unorthodoxy among the Sikhs can be easily verified by observation, there is no empirical evidence as to whether it represents (1) a relapse from an earlier state of orthodoxy in the observance of Sikh forms and symbols, or (2) a continuing phenomenon of which the leaders have recently become more acutely aware, or (3) a combination of both. If it is the second point, then the present concern over unorthodoxy may essentially represent unfinished business from earlier reform movements aiming at separating the Sikhs from the Hindu community. At any

[60] In one interview, Master Tara Singh said that the need of an independent political organization for the Sikhs was "very great because they have so close social and cultural relations with the Hindus that the Sikhs can be easily absorbed." *The Tribune*, July 6, 1956.

[61] The remarks of one author concerning Sahajdhari Sikhs are significant in this regard; he says that "there is no such thing as a Sahajdhari Sikh. For all practical purposes he is a Hindu believing in Sikhism." Khushwant Singh, "Future of the Sikhs," *The Spokesman*, January 3, 1952, p. 4.

[62] "The dividing line between Sikhs and Hindus is the external appearance of the Sikh." Khushwant Singh, *The Sikhs*, p. 180.

[63] *Ibid.*

rate, one of the most impressive demographic aspects of the Punjab has not, indeed, been the absorption of Sikhs by any other community, but the tremendous growth in Sikh population.[64] The rate of population growth of the Sikh community has been far higher than that of any other community in the Punjab.

Nonetheless, whatever unorthodoxy exists is galling to the Akali leadership, and a solution for the problem is sought through the establishment of Punjabi Suba. Among the many statements of Master Tara Singh on the subject is an interview given the editor of a New Delhi newspaper in May 1961 in which the relationship between unorthodoxy and Punjabi Suba was elaborated: "During a long talk we had last Saturday, Master Tara Singh made no secret of his motives in asking for a Punjabi Suba. The Sikhs as a distinctive community, he emphasized, must be preserved, and they could be preserved only in a 'homeland' of their own. Left in their present position, he asserted, the Sikhs would be gradually 'absorbed' by the majority community—this he must avoid, at least in his own lifetime. His clear thesis is: The Sikhs with their exterior symbols of distinction can last as a separate community only if they enjoy power and can extend patronage for the continuance of the symbols."[65] The important Sikh weekly, *The Spokesman*, asserted in 1955 that: "The Sikhs felt like orphans everywhere and hence the apostasies. This is why too many Sikhs fear their extinction. This is why the Sikhs seek to be equals of the Hindus in political power. They can think of no other way to escape from extinction, except the demarcation of a Punjabi Suba, wherein the Sikhs would be about 45 per cent."[66]

Apart from their chief objection to the establishment of any state on a communal basis, the Hindus in the Punjab question how unorthodoxy among the Sikhs means absorption into Hinduism unless—they remark with a feeling of self-satisfaction—the two are the same to begin with. If the latter is true, the Hindus feel, then it knocks out the case for an independent political entity of the Sikhs so carefully built and sustained over the past century. How fragile the claim of the Sikhs to nationhood is in reality, they point out. However, they absolve themselves of any responsibility for unorthodoxy in Sikhism; they challenge the Sikhs to point out any activities of the Hindus to encourage Sikh absorption into Hinduism, though they

[64] Kingsley Davis, *The Population of India and Pakistan*, Princeton University Press, Princeton, 1951, p. 182.

[65] Prem Bhatia, "Prospect and Retrospect: Alternatives Before Akalis," *The Times of India*, May 16, 1961.

[66] "To Be or Not To Be," *The Spokesman*, October 5, 1955, p. 4.

feel such activities would be justified in view of the Sikh community's own record of proselytization. Nonetheless, they believe that Sikh symbols, like the Hindu symbols of the sacred thread and tuft of hair on the head, will not last either, because there is no scientific reason for their retention.[67]

The refrain in Akali arguments is that Punjabi Suba is essential to stem the unorthodoxy. However, there is no clue provided as to the specific way in which the proposed Suba would deal with the problem of unorthodoxy. Would laws be passed in the Punjabi Suba to prohibit the trimming and shaving of beards?[68] How would this be consistent with the secular nature of the Indian Constitution? If laws prohibiting unorthodoxy are impossible to enact under the Constitution, would Sikhism be made attractive in the Punjabi Suba through preferences in government patronage as Master Tara Singh seems to suggest? Would this be any more consistent with the Constitution, which prohibits discrimination between citizens on the basis of religion? If these measures are not feasible under the Constitution, is it logical to assume that pressure may be exerted later to change the very basis of the constitutional framework? Can the Punjabi Suba then really be potentially a state like any other state in India, as Akali leaders sometimes maintain? If unorthodoxy cannot be stopped in the Punjabi Suba, would a sovereign Sikh state then be demanded? Under such conditions, how is the Hindu community going to be persuaded to agree to the formation of such a Suba? In fact, it is precisely such questions, inherent in the logic of the demand, that make for such a vigorous denunciation by Hindus and Harijans in the Punjab of any concessions toward the formation of Punjabi Suba.[69]

The third main factor which seems to form the basis of the demand for a separate Punjabi-speaking state is a certain sense of grievance among the leaders and rank and file of the Akali Dal that there is discrimination against the Sikh community.[70] It is felt

[67] An effort to support the wearing of unshorn hair on a scientific basis is the work of Chanda Singh, *The Hair and Health*, Human Hair Research Institute, Kot Kapura, 1956.

[68] One author comments that "in the Sikh state the Sikhs would not only be free of Hindus and Hindu influences, but the Sikh youth would also be persuaded (if necessary compelled) to continue observing the forms and symbols of the faith." Khushwant Singh, *The Sikhs*, pp. 184-185.

[69] Virendra, "Punjabi Suba or a Sikh State: A Rejoinder," *The Spokesman*, July 31, 1961, p. 11.

[70] "It is only the Akalis who protest against discriminations (largely imaginary) practiced against Sikhs in the services and interference in their religious affairs." Khushwant Singh, *The Statesman*, June 18, 1959.

that only if there is a state in which the Sikhs are in an influential political position can an effective end be put to this discrimination, and justice assured for the Sikh community.

Initially, the charge of discrimination was made with respect to public employment: recruitment, promotion and treatment of Sikhs in the services. Apart from the general allegation of discrimination, however, the leaders of the Akali Dal have preferred not to make any specific charge against the government. For its part, the government has expressed its readiness to investigate any complaint of discrimination against the Sikh community as such and not mere personal grievances of employees. In 1961, the government of India established a commission to determine whether there was any discrimination against the Sikh community. The Akali Dal, for reasons of its own, failed to provide any evidence before the commission. The finding of the commission, however, was that there was no basis for any allegation of discrimination on the part of the government against the Sikh community.

It has been asserted, on the contrary, that the Sikh community has been enjoying privileges and opportunities far out of proportion to its numbers. It is said that though they are less than 2 per cent of the Indian population, they constitute about 20 per cent of the Indian army, have double their proportionate share in the Indian administrative services, and that in the Punjab their share in the services, as also in the legislature, the cabinet, and the Congress Party organization, is higher than their proportion in the population. In fact, the demand has been mounting on behalf of the Hindu community in the Punjab that a commission should investigate discrimination against the Hindus.

The Akali Dal has also made charges about government interference in the religious affairs of the Sikhs, but has not presented any concrete evidence on the subject. The allegation of discrimination has also been made in another area. After the implementation of the Indian Constitution, the Akali Dal launched an agitation against the government for not extending the same privileges for Harijans belonging to the Sikh community as had been given to those of the Hindu community. The government first argued that since Sikhism does not recognize caste, the demand was not justified, but it allowed the concession in respect of four major castes among the Sikhs as part of a political settlement with the representatives of the Sikh community. Finally, faced with an agitation, the government decided to grant the same privileges for all Harijans in the Punjab, irrespective of whether they were Hindus or Sikhs.

Another alleged grievance against the Congress Party and the government is that before independence certain pledges were made to the Sikh community which the Congress Party subsequently failed to honor. Consequently, it is said that the Sikhs cannot put any trust in paper promises of the Congress but would like an area in which their own political influence will count.[71] However, Congress leaders maintain that there are no outstanding commitments to the Sikh community. In regard to the pledge in 1929 that the Congress would not agree to a constitution which was not acceptable to the Sikhs, the Congress leaders say that the partition settlement was made with the full concurrence of the Sikh leaders, and that the present Constitution was enacted with the support of the elected Sikh representatives. As for any promises alleged to have been made in 1946, before the partition, Congress leaders have denied any commitments.[72]

While the charge of discrimination still continues to be made against the government, the content of the allegation has undergone a change over the years. Initially, discrimination was alleged in relation to Sikh representation in the public services, but now it is held to mean that the denial of Punjabi Suba itself is a discrimination against the Sikhs as a community. It is contended that had Hindus been in a majority in the proposed Punjabi Suba, the demand would have been granted without any question, but simply because the Punjabi Suba would reduce the majority of the Hindus, the government refuses to concede it. And the Akali Dal demands that this discrimination be ended because it implies distrust of the Sikh community and also because the dominance of the "communal-minded" Hindus is unbearable to the Sikhs.

THE SHIROMANI AKALI DAL

The political organization which has propagated the particular doctrines discussed above and has worked for the achievement of political objectives that flow therefrom—specifically, the objective of Punjabi Suba—is the Shiromani Akali Dal. The origins of this organization go back to the days of the Gurdwara Reform movement in the 1920's. At the time, thousands of Sikhs came forward as volunteers to oppose the government and occupy the gurdwaras (Sikh temples) and "a semi-military organization called the 'Akali dal' (the Akali army)

---

[71] "No arrangement that reduces the Sikhs to an impotent minority could be acceptable to the Sikhs. No paper safeguards could protect an ineffective minority. Either the Sikhs must live as equals or accept virtual extinction." "Punjab's Tangled Skein," editorial, *The Spokesman*, February 6, 1956, p. 3.

[72] See the speech of Sardar Patel, in India (Dominion), Constituent Assembly, *Debates: Official Report*, 1949, vol. 10, p. 247.

was formed."[73] The history of the organization has been coeval with the political life of its supreme leader, Master Tara Singh, who "has been bestriding the Sikh political world like a colossus" for the last third of a century.[74] Indeed, one of the most striking features of Akali politics since 1930 has been the "perpetual leadership" of Master Tara Singh, who has managed to retain it through skillful control of the party treasury and press, and through the employment of political workers. However, since 1962 his leadership has been actively and effectively challenged by Sant Fateh Singh, who has even established a rival party organization.

The headquarters of the Akali Dal are located within the precincts of the Golden Temple at Amritsar, "the Mecca of the Sikhs."[75] Membership in the Akali Dal is open only to Sikhs. Any Sikh adult of over eighteen years of age can become a member on payment of a nominal fee, provided he is not an apostate and does not belong to another organization whose aims are opposed to the Panth or the Akali Dal, or one that has been declared by the Akali Dal as anti-Panthic.[76] At the head of the Akali Dal is a president, formally elected by a general body consisting of about 400 delegates from the district branches. Since 1930 the president has been either Master Tara Singh himself, one of his protégés, or a party leader loyal to him. Funds for the party come from Sikh big businessmen in Delhi, Bombay, Calcutta, and Kanpur. However, the single most important resource is the income from the gurdwaras which results from Akali control of the Shiromani Gurdwara Parbandhak Committee (committee for the management of gurdwaras). This committee, with its large funds and vast patronage, contributes substantially to the basic strength of the Akali Dal.

The objective of the Akali Dal is "the protection of the Panth."[77] More specifically, the Akali Dal seeks to work for "the protection of Sikh rights and ensuring the Sikhs' continued existence as an independent entity."[78] In actual practice, however, the Akali Dal not only stands for the protection of the Panth but equates itself with it.[79] It is in the context of this equation of the Akali Dal with the Panth

[73] Khushwant Singh, *The Sikhs*, p. 109.
[74] Khushwant Singh, *The Statesman*, June 18, 1959.
[75] Gurnam Singh, p. 9.
[76] Shiromani Akali Dal, *Shiromani Akali Dal Di Bantar De Niyam (Constitution of the Shiromani Akali Dal)*, Amritsar, 1961, pp. 3-4.
[77] See the statement of Master Tara Singh in *Prabhat*, quoted in *The Tribune*, August 2, 1958.
[78] *Ibid.* See also clause 1 of *Shiromani Akali Dal Di Bantar De Niyam*, p. 3.
[79] See Master Tara Singh, *Charhdi Kala*, pp. 8-9.

that it becomes intelligible why all those who oppose the Akali Dal are not only considered anti-Akali but are immediately labeled as "traitors" to the Panth. Outside of the Communist parties, there is perhaps no other political party in the world which employs with greater frequency the term "traitor" than does the Akali Dal, especially its leader Master Tara Singh. However, it is individuals who must act for organizations, and in the end the identification of the Akali Dal with the Panth has meant the identification of the Panth with the personal leadership of Master Tara Singh himself.

In its struggle for the achievement of Punjabi Suba, the Akali Dal has access to large and significant financial and organizational resources. There is no denying also that it can mobilize an extensive segment of the Sikh population in support of its demand. The important question then is, how does the Akali Dal utilize these important resources in the pursuit of its objective, and what are the various methods and techniques employed? Three political strategies emerge as important in a consideration of Akali activities: (1) constitutional, (2) infiltrational, and (3) agitational.

The constitutional strategy involves the use of methods which are within the framework of the existing constitutionally guaranteed rights, do not violate any laws, and are employed in the open view of the public. The methods under the constitutional strategy cover a wide range. At the governmental level, the Akali Dal may submit memoranda and petitions to government officials, including commissions of inquiry, outlining the alleged grievances of the Sikh community and urging acceptance of Akali demands. As a further step, Akali leaders may wait in deputation upon the president of India, the prime minister, the home minister, or the president of the Congress party, to convince them of the necessity and justness of Akali demands. In regard to the substantive demands of the Akali Dal, the submission of memoranda and petitions and waiting in deputation may usually be preparatory to the launching of an agitation.

At the public level, the Akali Dal arranges large meetings and conferences where speeches denunciatory of the government and the Congress leaders and other groups are delivered, and resolutions are passed setting forth the alleged grievances of the Sikhs as well as the demands of the Akali Dal. The Akali Dal may further hold mass rallies and long disciplined marches of Sikhs stretching over several miles in order to protest against government policies and to convince Congress leaders of tremendous popular support. At the level of the mass media, the Akali appeals are directed through newspapers in the Indian languages.

The Akali Dal also participates in parliamentary activity not only to use the legislature as a forum for the propagation of its demands but also, if possible, to gain a share in political power. It endeavors to send to the legislature, in the periodical elections, as large a bloc of Akali representatives as possible in order to influence the governmental process. The last general elections in which the Akali Dal participated were in 1962, and these provided a test of its claim that a majority of the population supports its demand for Punjabi Suba. The Akali Dal formed several alliances with other political parties to obtain the most favorable outcome, but the election results devastatingly repudiated the Akali claim that a majority of the population favored its demand for Punjabi Suba. Of the 89 seats in the Punjabi-speaking region, the Akali Dal won only 19, and secured only 19.8 per cent of the total vote polled. In the Punjab as a whole, the Akali Dal obtained only 11.7 per cent of the vote, with no seats outside the Punjabi-speaking region. The verdict of the elections in 1962, however, has not deterred the Akali Dal from persisting in its demand for Punjabi Suba.

Pursued in relation to the state government in the Punjab, the infiltrational strategy involves the merger into the Congress Party, which controls the government, of the well-knit group of Akali members in the legislature, in order to work for such objectives as the Akali Dal may direct. On a sheer political basis, the strategy must obviously seem a highly rational one for the Akali Dal, since its representatives are not only a minority in the total membership of the Punjab legislature but also in the group of Sikh representatives in the legislature, and therefore do not have a chance of forming an alternative government on the basis of a program that is confined solely to the Sikh community. In order to gain political power for the implementation of its goals, the next best alternative would appear to be an alliance with the party in power, the Congress Party. However, since that party proclaims itself to be a secular body and ideally disinclined to align itself with a party which it considers communal, Akali members from time to time have joined the Congress Party as a group in an attempt to gain political concessions or to consolidate concessions already obtained through agitational pressure. Twice since independence Akali leaders in the legislature have merged in the Congress Party and become a part of the government—in 1948 and again in 1956. While such leaders worked for concessions and privileges for the Sikh community from within the government, other Akali leaders on the outside, particularly Master Tara Singh, vehemently criticized the government, pressed for Akali claims and threatened mass agitations.

The agitational strategy is the most dramatic of the strategies employed by the Akali Dal, and involves the launching of a series of agitations or, in the more expressive term used by the Akalis, *morchas*. A *morcha* literally means an entrenchment, but while the Akalis do entrench themselves firmly inside the gurdwaras, which police normally do not enter, they also engage the government in a direct confrontation, organized and directed from within the gurdwaras, through the sending out of quasi-military, though not necessarily violent, formations which deliberately violate the law in an attempt to fill the jails. The purpose of the *morchas* is to overwhelm the government by inducting into the agitation thousands of volunteers ready to court imprisonment, thus forcing all government activity to concentrate on coping with the agitation. Such situations contain a high potential for the imminent breakdown of law and order, and thus coerce the government into making concessions. The main objective here, then, is to intimidate the government through a contest of will and strength into making concessions which the Akali Dal has found it difficult to achieve through constitutional methods.

A successful agitation launched by the Akali Dal is usually followed by a process of bargaining with the government, in the background of which may be an Akali threat to revive the agitation. A political settlement may result from the negotiations, and perhaps even an Akali-Congress coalition may be formed. To the extent that the government seems to make political concessions in response to agitations, it seems equally rational for Akali leaders to pursue the agitational strategy for the achievement of their demands. The nature of concessions accepted by the Akali Dal is interesting in that while the agitations are launched in the name of a secular principle, the concessions obtained are always for the satisfaction of a single religious group.

Of the several agitations launched by the Akali Dal, two are most outstanding. One is the Punjabi Suba Slogan Agitation of 1955. According to Akali figures, some 12,000 Sikhs courted arrest in the *morcha*. When finally the government made a conciliatory gesture to bring the agitation to an end, the Akalis interpreted this as a "victory" for their cause. The ensuing negotiations resulted in the merger of the Akali Dal into the Congress party, and the acceptance of several Akali claims. The other agitation, known as the Punjabi Suba Agitation of 1960-1961, was even more spectacular. According to government accounts, some 26,000 Akalis were arrested; the Akali Dal places the number at 57,000. However, the government this time refused to give in. One of the top Akali leaders, Sant Fateh Singh, went on a fast-unto-death but had to break it in order to enter into negotiations with the government. Following the failure of these negotiations, Master Tara Singh started a fast-unto-death, but the government still refused to make any concessions. He then broke his fast at the end of 48 days, when the government merely decided to appoint a commission to investigate any alleged grievances of the Sikhs.

Undoubtedly the Akali Dal has met with considerable success in its various activities, but the results of the general elections have effectively demonstrated its complete failure to secure even 20 per cent support of the population, not only in the Punjab as a whole but even in what it considers the "pure" Punjabi-speaking areas. Assuming that the Sikhs constitute at least 50 per cent of the population of the Punjabi-speaking region, then the conclusion is obvious: the Akali Dal does not even have the support of 40 per cent of the Sikh population, despite its public claims of being the sole representative of the Sikh community.

Despite this lack of popular support among the population in the Punjabi-speaking region for the Akali demand, it speaks highly for the skills and resources of its leadership and organization that the Akali Dal has been able to secure substantial political concessions toward its demand for Punjabi Suba through the agitational and infiltrational strategies. Each political concession has been a further step toward the formation of Punjabi Suba. And the concessions have been many and far-reaching: the "parity formula," the "Sachar formula," the "services formula," and the "regional formula." But every time the Akali Dal has obtained a concession and has arrived at a political settlement with the government—a settlement which the government has presumed to be final—the Akali Dal has immediately moved on to the next step after consolidating the earlier concessions. The Akali Dal has seemed to act on the principle that what it has obtained is its by right, but what it wants further is certainly negotiable, though all of it may not be given in one round. The most dramatic illustration of this phenomenon came in 1957 when Master Tara Singh reactivated the Akali Dal in politics, revived the demand for Punjabi Suba and put up candidates against the Congress Party, soon after the organization under his leadership had accepted the regional formula and had undertaken to refrain from politics as part of a political compromise that permitted the Akalis to join the Congress Party *en masse*. It seems that at this point the Indian government and the Congress Party realized that the Akali Dal was playing for higher stakes, and that the settlements negotiated earlier were only intermediate points toward its ultimate goal of *desh-kaal*. It is precisely this realization that explains why the Indian government in 1960-1961, after making concessions in one form or another up to that time, finally adopted a firm policy toward the Akali Dal. As Lord Birdwood had said on one occasion in relation to the demand of Punjabi Suba, "Mr. Nehru had not taken office to preside over the liquidation of the Indian Union."[80]

Has the Akali Dal exhausted the various strategies that it is capable of employing? Perhaps a policy of violence may seem an alternative, but the Sikhs do not suffer, relative to other segments of society, from any disability and have too much at stake in the existing social and political order to risk giving support to such a policy. Moreover, unless the Congress leadership loses its nerve, the powers of the government are so great that no policy of violence can possibly succeed under normal circumstances. On the other hand, it is obvious that the Akali leadership is too committed to the demand for Punjabi Suba to give it up, as the threats of self-immolation on the part of several Akali leaders in the latter half of 1965 so vividly testify.[81]

[80] Lord Birdwood, *The Hindustan Times*, December 26, 1954.

[81] EDITOR'S NOTE: On March 9, 1966 the Congress Working Committee adopted a resolution directing the government to carve out of the existing Punjab a state in which Punjabi would be the official language. A leading newspaper commented editorially: "In the hands of Master Tara Singh the demand had grown steadily from a simple extension of the linguistic principle on which states in the rest of the country had been reorganized to a claim for a 'self-determined' status for the Sikhs. It is a tribute to the patriotism and political courage of Sant Fateh Singh that he wrenched the demand firmly out of its communal integument and presented it as nothing more or less than a claim for parity of status for Punjabi with the other major languages of the country which had been given a territorial basis. In this form, the demand was clearly one which all Punjabi-speaking communities in the state could support. That in fact only one community has supported it does not make it less valid." *Hindustan Times*, March 11, 1966.

CHAPTER 8

COMMUNAL INTEREST GROUPS IN KERALA

V. K. S. NAYAR

RELIGIOUS AND CASTE-CENTERED interest groups exercise a greater influence on state politics in India than pressure groups based on class or occupation. Caste continues to be the basis of social organization so far as the Hindus are concerned, and the larger caste groups tend to play a leading part in state and local politics due to their numerical strength. Each of the numerically important castes or communities tends to develop a political sub-culture of its own based on the values, attitudes and aspirations of its elite. Religious and caste-centered interest groups generally find it advantageous to operate through established political parties formed on a secular national basis.

This chapter is concerned with three communal interest groups in Kerala: the NSS (Nair Service Society) representing the Nair caste, the SNDP (Sree Narayana Dharma Paripalana Yogam—Society for the Protection of the Dharma of Shree Narayana) representing the Ezhava caste, and the Syrian Christians organized into Catholic and non-Catholic churches. The Christians are a very important minority, comprising one-fifth of the population of the state. While the NSS and SNDP are community associations devoted to social reform and education, the Syrian Christian churches are mainly religious bodies though they run a number of educational institutions. As it is more difficult to analyze the political attitudes of the churches it is proposed to analyze the economic and social interests of the Syrian Christians as a community and to show how these interests influence political behavior.

THE NAIRS AND THE NSS

The Nairs formed the military caste of Kerala for several centuries, but are now mainly a community of landholders. Until 1925 the Nairs were governed in their laws of inheritance and family organization by the matrilineal system which was the distinctive feature of Kerala social organization. Scholars differ as to the origins of matriarchy in Kerala. According to some it is a survival from the Indus Valley and Dravidian civilizations, while others believe that the

V. K. S. Nayar is professor and head of the department of politics at the University of Kerala.

system was introduced among the Nairs for military reasons and spread to other communities. With the exception of the Brahmins all the Hindu castes in Kerala including the princely families followed the matrilineal system. Under the system the matrilineal joint family was organized in a hierarchical pattern, all authority being concentrated in the eldest male member. Men and women had an equal share in the property held in trust by the joint family, and women therefore did not depend on marriage for economic support. The system led to the formation of large landed estates held by the joint families and cultivated by tenants belonging mainly to the Christian and Ezhava communities. The income which each member earned went into a common pool, and it was felt that to a great extent the system limited individual initiative and enterprise.

The NSS was formed in 1914 with two objectives: to change the matrilineal system of inheritance which was considered reactionary and blocking the community's progress, and to start a few high schools so that the community would be in a position to compete with the Syrian Christians who had a number of high schools and even colleges managed by the churches. The founder of the NSS was Mannath Padmanabhan who still guides its activities today at the age of eighty-seven.[1] The NSS soon became a political force in the princely state of Travancore, and the village units were active in elections to the state legislature. The NSS newspaper *The Service*, published from the capital, played a leading role in the politics of Travancore state up to 1931 under its editor N. K. Krishna Pillai.[2] *The Service* supported the Congress in the struggle for freedom at the all-India level. However, so far as local politics was concerned *The Service* was against the administration of the state by Brahmin prime ministers appointed by the maharaja, and sought to have "Brahmin rule" replaced by the rule of non-Brahmin communities. The agitation for social reforms led to the passing of the Nair Act of 1925 which replaced the matrilineal system of inheritance with a patrilineal system.[3]

[1] Mannath Padmanabhan published the first volume of his autobiography (in Malayalam) a few years ago; a biography has also been published. As a young man Padmanabhan was a teacher, and later became a lawyer in magistrates' courts. He gave up his practice and founded the NSS in 1914. Since then he has served as general secretary and president of the NSS. He guides the policies of the NSS today even though not holding any formal office. Though he has traveled all over India, Malaya and Europe he does not know English or any foreign language. He is one of the most powerful orators in the Malayalam language.

[2] N. K. Krishna Pillai (1889-1954) was editor of *The Service*, published in Trivandrum until 1931. He was head of the village organization wing of the NSS from 1943 to 1946, and associate editor of the *Malayala Manorama* from 1947 to 1954. He was also a well-known novelist in Malayalam.

[3] The passing of the Nair Act was a revolutionary measure affecting the social

By about 1932 the NSS had to give up its anti-Brahmin policy due to a new alignment of communal forces in Travancore. This was the formation of a new organization called the Joint Political Congress consisting of Syrian Christians, Ezhavas and Muslims. The leadership of this group was provided by the Syrian Christians who did not like the increased political prominence of the Nairs. The leaders of the Joint Political Congress were T. M. Verghese, a Syrian Christian who became a minister in Congress governments, C. Kesavan, an Ezhava who later became a Congress chief minister, and P. K. Kunju, a Muslim who became a minister in the PSP government.[4] The Joint Political Congress favored reservation of seats in the legislature and appointments to the civil service on the basis of the population strength of each community. The acceptance of these demands by the state government led to the reduction of Nair strength in the legislature as well as in the civil service.[5]

The Joint Political Congress fought the elections of the Travancore legislature in 1936 and won a substantial number of elected seats, reducing the Nairs to a minority. The leaders of the Joint Political Congress came to the conclusion that they would get direct power only by a system of responsible government. The Indian National Congress was then setting up state congresses to agitate for responsible government in the princely states, and the Joint Political Congress thereupon merged with the Travancore State Congress. The State Congress had several Nairs in the organization including its president Pattom Thanu Pillai.

The NSS decided to oppose the State Congress, as the latter was considered to be a political party dominated by the Syrian Christians. A counter-organization, the National Congress, was organized by NSS leaders with the blessing of the government. Though the NSS op-

---

structure of Kerala. It was passed in the teeth of fierce opposition by the conservative sections of society. See P. K. Parameswaran Nair, *Sahityapanchanan*, Kottayam, 1958, pp. 356-374, for a detailed description of the controversy over the Nair Bill.

[4] T. M. Verghese, a Syrian Christian leader belonging to the non-Catholic Mar Thoma Church, has played a leading part in Kerala politics. He was speaker of the legislative assembly and held ministerial office several times. C. Kesavan was chief minister from 1951 to 1952. His autobiography, *Jeevita Samaram*, Trivandrum, 1958, gives a picture of the Ezhava community. P. K. Kunju, who was at one time a member of the Congress, was leader of the PSP in the Kerala legislature which was dissolved in 1964.

[5] Under the Travancore Legislative Reforms Act of 1932, a bicameral legislature was constituted in Travancore State. The prime minister (dewan) appointed by the maharaja was president (ex-officio) of both houses of the legislature. In the legislative assembly of 72 members, 48 were elected, 12 were ex-officio and 12 were nominated. Thus the government could get a majority if it had the support of 13 out of 48 elected members.

posed the State Congress and kept out of the struggle for responsible government, it decided to join forces with the State Congress in 1947, a few months before independence. This was a calculated political move, as the NSS leadership thought that with the dawn of Indian independence the Congress would be in power in the state. Mannath Padmanabhan, the NSS leader, led the struggle against the Travancore state government and courted imprisonment.

The NSS began to play an important independent political role in 1948. Its policy was directed toward: (1) furthering the interests of the organization and in particular its educational activities (2) defending the interests of upper caste Hindus, including Brahmins who are linked to Nairs by the system of inter-caste marriages (3) defending the interests of Nairs as a politically dominant caste (4) safeguarding the interests of Hindus in general. In matters of economic policy the NSS championed the interests of land-owning classes against those of tenants. It supported state industrial enterprises, as privately owned industries were mainly in the hands of non-Nairs. The political effectiveness of the NSS has derived in large part from its organizational strength at the village level. Though the activities of the NSS are spread all over Kerala, its voting strength is concentrated in three districts where it has a large number of village units.

The resignation of the Pattom Thanu Pillai ministry in 1948 after seven months in office brought the NSS leadership into an open clash with the Congress organization.[6] Though Pattom Thanu Pillai was succeeded as chief minister by another Nair, T. K. Narayana Pillai, the NSS continued to pursue an anti-Congress policy. The T. K. Narayana Pillai ministry tried to conciliate the two leading Hindu community associations by appointing Mannath Padmanabhan, the NSS leader, to the chairmanship of the board for managing Hindu temples in the state, and R. Sankar, the SNDP leader, to membership on the board. However, this tactic failed to achieve its purpose and for a brief time the two community associations joined hands in the Hindu Maha Mandal, a Hindu political party formed to fight the "Christian domination" of the state by the Congress. The fall of the

[6] Pattom Thanu Pillai was president of the Travancore State Congress from 1937 to 1948, suffering imprisonment several times in the course of the struggle for independence. He became prime minister of Travancore in March 1948 and resigned his office as well as the presidency of the State Congress in October 1948, as the result of a signature campaign against him. He was chief minister in the PSP government of 1954-1955. He became chief minister in 1960 in the Congress-PSP coalition government. He was appointed governor of the Punjab in 1962 and transferred as governor of Andhra Pradesh in 1964.

T. K. Narayana Pillai cabinet was mainly due to lack of support from the NSS and from Hindu public opinion.[7]

The NSS supported the Congress in the election held in 1954. This election did not give the Congress a majority, however, and the party had to support a minority PSP (Praja Socialist Party) government led by Pattom Thanu Pillai, which was defeated by a vote of no-confidence in 1955. A Congress government was then formed by Panambilli Govinda Menon, another Nair, but it soon lost the confidence of the NSS leadership, and its defeat in the legislature on a no-confidence motion was engineered by supporters of the NSS. This was followed by a period of President's rule, the formation of the linguistic state of Kerala in 1956, and the general election of 1957 which brought the Communists to power. The NSS was very lukewarm in its support of the Congress in that election. The Communists won due to the fact that the Nair vote was divided among the Congress, the PSP and the Communists. Many village units of the NSS openly supported Communist candidates who happened to be Nairs.

The formation of the Communist government was, in a sense, welcomed by the NSS, but there was some apprehension as the NSS was not sure about the extent of the influence it could exert on the new government. The Communists were determined to sponsor land reforms which would hit the landowning class of the Nairs in particular. On the other hand, the Communist government was welcomed because the Syrian Christians had practically no influence over the government and were not in a position to exert any pressure. The Communists tried to win over the NSS by naming its president as chairman of the state board for administering Hindu temples; on the other hand they proceeded with their land reform bill, refusing to accommodate the demands of the NSS. The Communists also introduced an education bill providing for state control of privately managed schools, including schools managed by the Catholic Church. The leadership of the Communist Party felt that this bill would be popular with the Nairs as it would strike a solid blow at the Church. However, the Communist policy of dividing the Nairs and Christians did not work. The immediate issue which infuriated the NSS leader Mannath Padmanabhan was the refusal of the government to permit the NSS to start an engineering college at Palghat.

[7] T. K. Narayana Pillai became chief minister in October 1948 following the resignation of the Pattom Thanu Pillai ministry. The T. K. Narayana Pillai ministry resigned in 1951 due to differences of opinion in the cabinet. Narayana Pillai enjoyed the backing of Syrian Christians and the powerful Syrian Christian daily the *Malayala Manorama* while he was chief minister, but he did not have the support of the NSS.

Permission was given to a local committee which ultimately was unable to raise the money required.

Mannath Padmanabhan suddenly decided to join forces with the Christians in an agitation over the education bill. He decided to attack the bill as this was the only way in which he could find common cause with the Christians. The real grievance of the NSS was that it could exercise no influence over Communist policies. Congress policy had always been pragmatic and open to compromise; the Communists were determined to push forward their legislative program without attempting any compromise with religious or caste interest groups.

The "liberation struggle" launched by Mannath Padmanabhan with the support of Christian school managers was soon joined by the Congress, the Praja Socialist Party and the Revolutionary Socialist Party. The struggle had the desired effect of forcing a reluctant central government to dismiss the Communist ministry by proclaiming President's rule.[8] The success of the liberation struggle established the fact that a government could not function in Kerala if it incurred the active hostility of the leading communal interest groups. It also revealed that the leadership of interest groups was much more vigorous and in touch with public opinion than was the leadership of the political parties. Mannath Padmanabhan lifted himself from the position of the leader of a community association to the status of a national figure by his successful fight against the Communist government.

The attempt of the NSS to get a large number of its nominees accepted as Congress Party candidates in the election that followed did not succeed,[9] but the NSS succeeded in installing Pattom Thanu Pillai, the PSP leader, as chief minister. A former president of the NSS was appointed as a minister in the new coalition government, and when he died he was replaced by a director of the NSS. However it must be emphasized that these two ministers, though representing the NSS, were not the personal nominees of Mannath Padmanabhan. The NSS exerted an influence over the policies of the

[8] President's rule was declared in Kerala by a proclamation of the president on July 31, 1959. This proclamation suspended the council of ministers and the state legislature.

[9] A general election was held in Kerala in February 1960. In the election the Communists were defeated by a coalition of the Congress, the PSP, and the Muslim League. A coalition government of the Congress and the PSP was formed after the election. Though the PSP was a very small party, its leader, Pattom Thanu Pillai, was made chief minister in view of his age and position in public life. Nair public opinion expressed through the NSS had great influence in making him chief minister in preference to the Congress leader R. Sankar, an Ezhava.

new government. The new land reforms bill passed by the Kerala legislature gave some protection to the small landholders, the bulk of whom are Nairs or other high caste Hindus.

With the replacement of Pattom Thanu Pillai, a Nair, as chief minister by R. Sankar, an Ezhava, the NSS drew closer to the Catholic group in the Congress led by a minister, P. T. Chacko. Chacko was forced to resign from the cabinet by Sankar, and the death of Chacko a few months after his resignation led to an open breach between the Chacko group and Sankar. The Sankar government was overthrown in September 1964, as the result of the passing of a no-confidence motion by the legislature which was supported by fifteen members of the Congress Party. It is an open secret that the NSS leader Mannath Padmanabhan was principally responsible for engineering the fall of the Sankar government. Six out of the fifteen Congress legislators who voted against Sankar were Nairs belonging to the NSS group. The fall of the Sankar government proved that the NSS can pull down a government which is not amenable to its influence. Mannath Padmanabhan then played a leading role in supporting the new party of the Congress dissidents called the Kerala Congress. In the elections of March 1965 the Kerala Congress won 24 seats while the official Congress won 36.

THE EZHAVAS AND THE SNDP

The second most important community association in Kerala is the Sree Narayana Dharma Paripalana Yogam (SNDP) founded in 1902, much earlier than the NSS.[10] The SNDP also started as a social reform organization promoting the uplift of the Hindu caste of the Ezhavas. While the Nairs were a landowning caste the Ezhavas were either tenants, landless laborers or toddy tappers. The Ezhavas were classified as an *avarna* caste and were denied admission to Hindu temples. As untouchables, they were not admitted to government schools or appointed to the civil service even if considered eligible on other grounds. The founder of the SNDP was Sree Narayana Guru, a saint belonging to the Ezhava community, who preached the gospel of "One Caste, One Religion, One God." The SNDP was in no sense capable of functioning as a political pressure group during its early decades. It worked in collaboration with the NSS which favored throwing Hindu temples open to all castes.

SNDP leaders took an active part in the Joint Political Congress

[10] For accounts of the origin of the SNDP see: P. K. Balakrishnan, ed., *Narayana Guru*, Cochin, 1954; P. K. Madhavan, *T. K. Madhavan*, Quilon, 1936; C. Kesavan, *Jeevita Samaram*, Kottayam, 1958.

formed under Syrian Christian leadership. The Congress championed the demands of the Ezhavas for communal representation in the civil service and the legislature. However, the concession of these demands by government and the throwing open of Hindu temples to all castes in 1937 satisfied practically all the SNDP demands. As a result of this the SNDP leadership left the State Congress and came closer to the NSS. In the 1940's the leadership of the SNDP felt that the proper role of the organization was to influence the government in power rather than to struggle for a change in the system of government. This was basically the stand of the NSS also. Like the NSS, the SNDP concentrated on building up village units as well as starting schools and colleges; it also collaborated with the NSS leadership in the National Congress formed to oppose the State Congress.

The SNDP followed a policy of working with the NSS even after independence. The leaders of both organizations were nominated to the board for the management of Hindu temples by the Congress government with a view to placating the two interest groups. As was mentioned above, a joint front of the NSS and the SNDP known as the Hindu Maha Mandal was formed to resist the "Christian domination" of the Congress. Like the NSS, the SNDP drew closer to the Congress by about 1952, when the Communists began to pose a strong challenge to the Congress. A former leader of the SNDP was chief minister of the state in 1951-1952, the first Ezhava to achieve this eminence. The SNDP leader R. Sankar was prominent in the Congress organization, though he failed to get elected to the legislature as the bulk of the Ezhavas voted for the Communist Party. While the SNDP's links with the Congress were approved by the small Ezhava middle class, the vast majority of the caste consisting of tenants, landless laborers, factory workers and toddy tappers continued to support the Communist Party in elections.

The formation of a Communist government in 1957 gave the SNDP leadership the opportunity to play a leading political role which had been denied to it before. R. Sankar was elected president of the Kerala State Congress Committee. A man of considerable organizing ability, he was able to give new life to the Congress Party. The SNDP leadership thus came to be closely identified with the Congress leadership in the state, and was active in the "liberation struggle" against the Communists led by Mannath Padmanabhan. R. Sankar, as president of the Congress organization, worked hard in the election that followed the dismissal of the Communist government. He was himself elected from a constituency in the north of Kerala though he came from the southern part of the state. It was clear that the bulk of the

Ezhavas voted for the Communist Party in the election.[11] However, the leadership of R. Sankar resulted in a large proportion of the Ezhava middle-class vote going to the Congress–PSP–Muslim League coalition. Sankar was elected leader of the Congress Party and became deputy chief minister in the new coalition government headed by Pattom Thanu Pillai. In 1962 Sankar became chief minister in the Congress government that was formed after the resignation of Pattom Thanu Pillai. In 1964 the Sankar cabinet was forced to resign due to the passing of a no-confidence motion in the legislature, but Sankar continued to be the effective leader of the SNDP even after his resignation.

In spite of the political eminence which the leader of the SNDP achieved the organization is less effective as a pressure group than the NSS. The SNDP represents the Ezhava middle class which is numerically small and less influential than the Nair middle class, and the vast majority of the Ezhavas have favored the Communist Party. The gulf between the Ezhava middle class and the Ezhava working class is greater than that between the Nair classes. The NSS organization also has a much broader geographical base than that of the SNDP.

THE SYRIAN CHRISTIAN CHURCHES

The Christians formed one-third of the population in the princely states of Travancore and Cochin. However, in the enlarged state of Kerala the Christians represent 21 per cent of the total population, and 75 per cent of these are Syrian Christians. The Syrian Christians are a very old community, as Christianity in Kerala is said to date from the arrival of St. Thomas, one of the apostles of Christ, on the Kerala coast. The members of the church in Kerala came to be called Syrian Christians as they followed a Syrian liturgy and used prayers and scriptures written in Syriac.[12] The name Syrian Christian as used in popular parlance indicates the members of the Jacobite, Mar Thoma, and Syrian Catholic churches using the Syrian liturgy. A Syrian colony was established in A.D. 345 by an Armenian, Thomas of Cana, in the northern region of Kerala. The Knanaya Syrian Christians of today claim descent from Thomas of Cana and his band

[11] In a study of the 1960 general election by the present writer (in press), a survey of voting intention in nine constituencies (selected from each of the nine districts of Kerala) revealed that 57 per cent of the Ezhava sample favored the Communists as against 10 per cent of the Christian sample and 15 per cent of the Nair sample.

[12] *The Census of India 1941*, vol. 25, pp. 133-141, deals with the Christians in Kerala. More details are available in the *Manorama Yearbook*, 1964, published in Malayalam.

of colonists, and the Catholic Knanites have a separate bishop of their own. A large section of the Syrian Christians came to be known as Jacobites, as they came under the church of Antioch which was re-organized by Jacob Baradaeus.

With the arrival of the Portuguese in the Kerala coast in 1498, attempts were made to make the Kerala Christians accept the authority of Rome. A Latin Christian Church consisting of Christians con-verted to the Catholic faith was founded in 1557 and placed under the newly created bishopric of Cochin. At the Synod of Udayamperur, Archbishop Menzies of Goa compelled all the Syrian Christians to acknowledge the supremacy of the Pope, and subscribe to the Latin doctrines and rituals. With the decline of the Portuguese power the Jacobites met at Koonen Cross in Cochin in 1653 and renounced their allegiance to Rome. Attempts were made to persuade the Jacobites to accept Catholicism and a Syrian Catholic bishop was consecrated in 1657. Thus Syrian Christians who remained in communion with Rome came to be popularly known as Syro-Romans or Syrian Catholics.

The Jacobites themselves split into two groups by the twentieth century, those recognizing the authority of the Catholicos of the East residing in Kerala, and the others owing allegiance to the Patriarch of Antioch. A civil suit between the two groups which started in 1913 was finally decided in 1958 in favor of the Catholicos, after which the Patriarch of Antioch recognized his authority. Today all the Jacobites recognize the Patriarch of Antioch as well as the Catholicos of the East.

The Mar Thoma Church owes its existence to a reform movement in the Jacobite church in the nineteenth century as the result of the influence of Protestant missionaries. The Church became separate in the middle of the nineteenth century and has five bishops headed by a senior bishop. The members of the Mar Thoma Church believe that they are the real followers of the church established by St. Thomas. There is also a Chaldean or Nestorian church which claims to date from the arrival of St. Thomas. This church, which is under the Patriarch of the East, has a following of about 15,000 persons and is under a bishop. A small section of the Syrian Christians belong to the Anglican church, which has since merged into the Church of South India consisting of a number of Protestant denominations.

The Roman Catholics in Kerala are divided into two broad groups, the Syrian Catholics and the Latin Catholics. The Syrian Christians use Syriac for religious rites while the Latin Catholics use Latin. Apart from this there are ethnic or caste differences as the Syrian

Catholics consider themselves as Syrian Christians belonging to the same caste group as the Jacobites and Mar Thomites. The Latin Christians are supposed to consist of converts from different castes including a large proportion of lower castes. The Syrian Christians claim that they are partly descendants of Syrian colonists who came with St. Thomas and partly of high caste Hindus who embraced the Christian faith at that time. The Syrian Catholics have a separate hierarchy of bishops headed by the archbishop of Changanaserry. There is also a separate Syrian Catholic church following Antiochan rites headed by the archbishop of Trivandrum. This church was formed by Jacobites who left the Jacobite church by about 1930. The Latin Catholics are under seven bishops headed by the archbishop of Varapuzha.

The Syrian Christians are the leading business community in Kerala as well as the leading farming community. Most of the rubber, tea, coffee, pepper and cardamom plantations are owned by Syrian Christians. However, the community also includes a class of tenants engaged in cultivating the lands of the Nairs and other caste Hindu landlords. Syrian Christians run most of the schools and colleges in the state and are naturally opposed to extensive state control of the schools.

As the bulk of the Christians in Kerala are Syrian Christians and as they form a separate ethnic or caste group, we shall analyze the political attitudes of this community organized into several churches, Catholic and non-Catholic. The political pressure exercised by the Syrian Christians is not through community associations like the NSS or the SNDP, but rather through their church hierarchy and through newspapers controlled by the churches or by members of the community.

Malayala Manorama, one of the two papers enjoying the largest circulation in Kerala, is controlled by a Jacobite family. This family has played a leading part in the affairs of the Jacobite church and in the civil suit which dragged on for half a century between the two wings of the church. The Catholicos of the East who died a few years ago was a relative of the family which controls the *Malayala Manorama*. The *Kerala Bhushanam* is controlled by a Syrian Christian family belonging to the Anglican church, and the *Kerala Dhwani* by a Syrian Christian family associated with the Protestant Brother Mission. To a certain extent the management of this paper may be said to be in the hands of the Mission.

The dailies owned by Catholics are five in number, the *Deepika*, the *Malabar Mail*, the *Thozhilali*, the *Kerala Prakasam* and the

Kerala Times. The first four dailies are controlled by Syrian Catholics and the last by Latin Catholics. The *Deepika,* one of the oldest dailies in Kerala is controlled by the Carmelite Order, the *Malabar Mail* by the Syrian Christian archbishop of Ernakulam, the *Thozhilali* by Father Vadakkan, a Catholic priest and leader of the Catholic anti-Communist front in Kerala, and the *Kerala Times* by the Latin Catholic archbishop of Varapuzha. The *Kerala Prakasam* is controlled by a labor leader, Mathai Manjooran, and is the only Catholic newspaper not directly or indirectly controlled by the Church.

The Syrian Christians welcomed British rule in India as rule by a Christian power and did not sympathize very much with the freedom struggle in the 1920's. They followed, like the NSS, an anti-Brahmin policy directed against the Brahmin prime ministers of Travancore. However, the growth of the NSS brought the Syrian Christians into a clash with the Nairs in the 1930's. Syrian Christian leaders took the initiative in organizing a Joint Political Congress for the purpose of fighting Nair "dominance." The merger of the Joint Political Congress into the State Congress brought the Syrian Christians into the freedom struggle and the Indian National Congress, which was a revolution in the political outlook and attitudes of the community. The Syrian Christian leadership became convinced that they could exert pressure on government only within a democratic setup.

In the postindependence period the Syrian Christians tended to support the Congress very strongly, though the PSP also had a few supporters. The resignation of Pattom Thanu Pillai as prime minister in 1948 was welcomed by Syrian Christian newspapers and leaders. The government of T. K. Narayana Pillai, which succeeded the Thanu Pillai government, was backed by Syrian Christian newspapers as they felt that the new government would be more responsive to pressure from Syrian Christian groups. In 1952, the support extended by the Syrian Christians led to the election of A. J. John, a Syrian Catholic, as party leader and his appointment as chief minister. In the contest for the leadership John defeated Panambally Govinda Menon, a Nair, by a narrow margin. The Syrian Christians did not have much influence in the PSP ministry of Pattom Thanu Pillai during 1954-1955 or the Communist government of 1957-1959. It was during the period of Communist rule that the Syrian Christians demonstrated their strength as an interest group, and the community as a whole participated vigorously in the successful "liberation struggle."

As the main issue behind this struggle was the Communist government's education bill it will be useful to examine the attitude of the

Christian churches in Kerala toward the educational question. The Christian churches, both Catholic and non-Catholic, have long managed a large number of schools and colleges. The Catholic Church, in particular, has staunchly resisted attempts by the state to encroach on the freedom of the Church to run these schools as they like. In Kerala, as elsewhere in India, government policy has been to give grants to privately managed schools which conform to the conditions prescribed by the state. As elementary schools charged no fees and as high schools levied only nominal fees, teachers in privately managed schools were paid out of state grants.

In 1945, the government of the state of Travancore proposed to take over the management of elementary schools as it was decided to introduce compulsory elementary education. In the voting in the legislature on the issue four Christian members voted in favor, while eight voted against it and three were neutral.[13] The Catholic bishop of Changanaserry, Mar James Kalacherry, issued a pastoral letter which attacked the government decision in strong terms. He declared that if the "primary rights of the individual are affected to the slightest extent, as a result of the socialistic policy of government, nature will grow angry with the government, rouse up all the forces under the sun and wipe out from the face of the earth the unjust authors of nationalization." The government, headed by the appointed prime minister Sir C. P. Ramaswamy Iyer, a Brahmin, threatened the bishop with dire consequences if he did not withdraw the letter. The letter was not withdrawn and the government was forced to make its peace with the Catholic Church by exempting schools controlled by the church from nationalization. The Catholic bishops also opposed strongly the attempt made by the Congress minister of education, Panambally Govinda Menon, to pay the salaries of private school teachers directly from the state treasury instead of disbursing block grants to the managers of schools. The scheme had therefore to be given up.

The Communist government which came into power in 1957 with a narrow majority in the legislature introduced a comprehensive education bill which was passed by the legislature in the teeth of opposition from the Catholic as well as the Jacobite and Mar Thomite churches.[14] The education bill provided for the payment of salaries

[13] See the Pamphlet by Joseph Thaliath, *Truth about the Travancore Educational Policy*, Trivandrum, 1945, which gives the history of the controversy over the educational policy of the government from the Catholic point of view and quotes the bishop's pastoral letter. Thaliath had formerly been chief justice of Travancore.

[14] A defense of the Communist government's educational policy and a strong attack on the Catholic opposition is given in a pamphlet in Malayalam, *The*

to teachers directly from the treasury, gave security of tenure for teachers, and provided that teachers should be appointed from a list prepared by the state civil service commission. The last clause provoked the strongest opposition, as it interfered with the right of Catholic managers to appoint Catholics as teachers. It was felt that the state civil service commission would appoint atheists and Communists as teachers in schools managed by the church. The first to attack the education bill was the Catholic corporate management of schools. A large procession was organized in Trivandrum, the capital of the state.

The "liberation struggle" against the Communist government which began in 1959 was officially started by the Kerala Private School Managers Association, a body controlled by the Catholic managers though it included managers belonging to other Christian groups as well as Hindus.[15] This struggle was led by Mannath Padmanabhan, the leader of the NSS, who had originally welcomed the education bill. The Catholic, Jacobite and Mar Thomite bishops openly supported the struggle. Soon the political parties, the Congress, the PSP, the Muslim League and the RSP joined the agitation. They demanded the ouster of the Communist government, on the basis not of the education bill, but of the "unconstitutional acts" committed by the government. While the leadership of Mannath Padmanabhan was responsible for launching the liberation struggle, the Christian churches and in particular organizations like the All-Kerala Catholic Congress played a very important role in the agitation, which was ultimately successful.

In the general election of 1960 the Christian bishops, in pastoral letters, directed their followers not to support the Communists. A coalition government consisting of the Congress and the PSP was formed after the election. Of the cabinet of eleven members, two were Christians, one a Syrian Catholic and the other a Jacobite. The strong man of the cabinet was P. T. Chacko who held the vital portfolio of law and order. As we have seen, Chacko was forced to resign from the cabinet in 1964 by chief minister Sankar. The death of Chacko, a few months later, led to a split in the Congress, and the formation of the Kerala Congress.

Agitation over the Educational Question and the Facts behind it, 1959, by Joseph Mundassery, himself a Syrian Catholic and the Communist government's minister of education, who introduced the controversial education bill.

15 See *Kerala Turning Red*, Calicut, 1958, a supplement issued by the weekly *Prakasam* (edited by a Catholic, Rev. Hormice), for the full text of the memorials addressed to the governor of Kerala by the Kerala Private School Managers and to the chief minister of Kerala by the Kerala Christian Education Action Committee.

The Kerala Congress is backed by powerful sections of the Syrian Christian community as well as by the NSS. Most of the Catholic dailies as well as two non-Catholic dailies supported the Kerala Congress. However, the leading Jacobite daily, the *Malayala Manorama*, supported the official Congress organization in the state. Thus, for the first time, sizeable sections of the Syrian Christian community came forward to oppose the Congress in Kerala. The creation of a political party completely controlled by interest groups, the Catholic Church and the NSS, is also a new development in Kerala politics. In the elections held in March 1965 the Kerala Congress won 24 seats in a house of 133 members, making it the third largest party in the legislature. The majority of the members of the Kerala Congress returned to the legislature were Christians, of whom most were Catholics.

As a pressure group the Syrian Christian community has had to operate under certain disadvantages. They have not been able to function under the leadership of a single community association like the NSS or the SNDP. The Catholic and non-Catholic groups have not always seen eye to eye, and no Christian political leader has ever enjoyed the support of all sections of the Christian community. Finally, the Christian bishops, despite their extensive ecclesiastical power, have not been able to participate in day-to-day politics in the way the leaders of the Hindu community associations have done.

CONCLUSIONS

A study of the political role of the NSS, the SNDP and the Syrian Christian churches in Kerala reveals that very often the leadership of these communal interest groups has been able to dictate to the formal leadership of political parties. It would be impossible to conceive of a Congress cabinet without representatives of the NSS, the SNDP and the Syrian Catholics. Governments which have failed to accommodate communal interest groups like the Congress government of Panambally Govinda Menon (1955-1956) and the Communist government (1957-1959) have been overthrown. The fall of the Sankar cabinet in September 1964 was due to the opposition of two interest groups, the NSS and the Syrian Catholics, who felt that Chief Minister Sankar was not sufficiently responsive to the demands of their groups. It is clear that one of the major factors contributing to governmental instability in the state has been the ability of communal interest groups to overthrow cabinets which have been found unresponsive. The fear of such a fate has, in turn, tended to make governmental leadership conservative in its policies.

CHAPTER 9

BUDDHISM AND POLITICS
IN MAHARASHTRA

ELEANOR ZELLIOT

IN THE PERIOD between the 1951 and the 1961 census, the number of Buddhists in India jumped 1,670.71 per cent. There are now 3,250,227 Indian Buddhists, a census figure which is probably minimal.[1] Of this number, 2,789,501 are in Maharashtra, where only 2,487 Buddhists were counted in 1951. The Buddhist community in that state now is five times as large as the Christian community, almost as large as the Muslim, and accounts for 7.05 per cent of the total population. This rather staggering conversion figure is the work of one man, Dr. B. R. Ambedkar, and has taken place largely within his caste, the Mahars, a Maharashtrian Scheduled Caste.[2]

The initial conversion ceremony was held on October 14, 1956, in Nagpur. Dr. Ambedkar took *diksha* at the hands of the oldest Buddhist monk in India and then administered simple conversion rites to a crowd estimated at 300,000 to 600,000 people. Conversion spread rapidly at first, more slowly later, chiefly in the area that is now Maharashtra, but also in Madhya Pradesh (113,365 Buddhists in 1961 in contrast to 2,991 ten years earlier), Punjab (14,857 in contrast to 1,660), Uttar Pradesh (12,893 in contrast to 3,221). The areas in which there were mass conversions correspond, with the exception of

Eleanor Zelliot is an instructor in history at the University of Minnesota.

[1] *Census of India, Paper No. 1 of 1963, 1961 Census—Religion*, New Delhi, 1963. The figures are minimal because some Scheduled Caste members who have participated in a conversion ceremony still list themselves as Hindus in order to claim government benefits reserved for Scheduled Castes. The Buddhists themselves claim that the census figures are not accurate because census takers prefer to minimize the extent of the conversion. The figures in the first and second paragraphs are all from this census paper.

[2] A note on nomenclature: four terms are used to describe the same group: Untouchable, Depressed Class, Scheduled Caste, Harijan. The word Untouchable is used freely among the Untouchables themselves. Those Untouchables who are influenced by Gandhi's organization, the Harijan Seva Sangh, and most caste Hindus use the term Harijan (people of God). Its use by an Untouchable indicates that he is of Congress, not one of Dr. Ambedkar's followers. Depressed Class was the term used widely until Scheduled Castes came into currency in 1935, according to the schedule prepared under the Government of India Act. The term neo-Buddhists, generally used for the converts, is unacceptable to them. They now call themselves, simply, Buddhists.

Madras,[3] to those areas in which Dr. Ambedkar and his political party, the Scheduled Castes Federation, had some direct influence.

Conversion to another religion as a way to escape the disabilities of untouchability in Hinduism is not a new idea in Indian history. Islam and Christianity grew in large part by the conversion of lower caste peoples. The differences between the 1956 conversion to Buddhism and the earlier movements are that (1) the Buddhist conversion involves the greater part of one entire caste; (2) the Untouchables have not joined an established larger body, as in the case of Islam or Christianity, but are themselves building a new religious organization, retaining much of their social structure, caste loyalty and old leadership; (3) the conversion has taken place among a people who were already involved in an independent political party, in opposition to Congress.[4]

Now, ten years after the initial mass conversion, it is too soon to judge whether or not the acceptance of a new religion by Untouchables can secure a higher status for them. What can be recorded is the relationship of that conversion to their previous struggle for equality with higher castes, and the relationship of the conversion to their political life. This paper will deal with these questions largely from the standpoint of the involvement of the Mahars.

The Buddhist conversion has touched, according to the census figures, less than 1 per cent of India's population, about 5 per cent of the Scheduled Castes. About 75 per cent of the Mahars, a number of Jatavas (a Chamar caste in Uttar Pradesh who came strongly under Ambedkar's influence) and pockets of Scheduled Castes in Gujarat, Punjab, Rajasthan, Mysore and Madhya Pradesh have declared themselves Buddhists. Generally speaking, Buddhist conversion has occurred among castes which have some history of a struggle for rights independent of Congress and caste Hindu organizations. Most Scheduled Caste communities, including Maharashtrian Scheduled Castes other than the Mahars, remain acknowledged Hindus and generally support the Congress Party.

At the moment, only Buddhists in Maharashtra, placed in the

---

[3] Madras has some history of lingering Buddhist influence. N. Shivraj, president of the Scheduled Castes Federation and later the Republican Party, called himself a Buddhist, as did his father. Nevertheless, there has been no conversion movement in the Madras area.

[4] The Independent Labor Party, founded by Dr. Ambedkar in 1936, became the Scheduled Castes Federation in 1942, and that group in turn took the name, the Republican Party, in 1957. The leadership and the program, allowing for time change and the loss of caste Hindu supporters of Dr. Ambedkar in Bombay when the party took on a direct Scheduled Caste relationship in 1942, has remained much the same.

Eleanor Zelliot

Backward Classes category in 1961, retain the rights given to the Scheduled Castes previously in matters of education and economic benefits. Elsewhere, and in all matters relating to the central government, a Scheduled Caste convert to Buddhism loses his privileges. How many Scheduled Caste individuals think of themselves as Buddhists but retain their Scheduled Caste status out of economic necessity is impossible to judge.[5] A recent *satyagraha* (December 1964-January 1965) organized by the Republican Party and involving, it is claimed 300,000 volunteers, mostly in Maharashtra, Uttar Pradesh and Punjab, stressed as one of its demands the retention of Scheduled Caste privileges in education and government positions by converts to Buddhism. Assurances by Prime Minister Lal Bahadur Shastri that the demands would be considered brought the *satyagraha* to an end. Whether the valued rights of educational scholarships and a percentage of reserved places in all government offices will actually be given Buddhists, and what difference this will make in the numbers who declare themselves converted, remains to be seen.

AMBEDKAR THE REBEL

The key figure in the Buddhist conversion movement and in the political history of the Mahars is Dr. Bhimrao Ramji Ambedkar, a Mahar who was born in 1891 and who died on December 6, 1956, two months after the initial conversion ceremony. Catalyst of aggressive forces within the Mahar community already pushing upward, innovator of new techniques for rising, and symbol of achievement for many Untouchables outside the Mahar caste as well as within, Dr. Ambedkar, ten years after his death, still dominates both the conversion movement and the political activities of the Republican Party. The history of the movement and of the party can be written only in terms of his life.

Prior to Ambedkar's first public statement on the political rights of the Depressed Classes in 1919, the Mahars' attempts to raise their social and economic status were made through claims to recognition of worth within the Hindu religion, and use of British-created economic opportunities. Four of the best-known Mahar leaders in the pre-Ambedkar era illustrate the use of both paths. Gopal Swami Yagavkar, a saint whose *samadhi* (grave) is still venerated by Mahars

[5] Scheduled Caste privileges include some economic aid in housing and small industry, scholarships at both state and central government level at all stages of education, reservation of 12½ per cent of all posts in government service. For a discussion of the effect of conversion on Scheduled Caste privileges see Donald E. Smith, *India as a Secular State*, Princeton University Press, Princeton, 1963, pp. 322-326.

and caste Hindus as well, was a paymaster in the British army. Gopal Baba Walangkar, also a soldier in the British army, wrote an essay showing that the Vedas did not support untouchability.[6] Kisan Fagoji Bansode, from the Vidharba region, collected the songs of Chokhamela, the Mahar saint in the Pandapur pantheon, wrote Chokhamela's biography, and joined the Prarthana Samaj.[7] Shivram Janba Kamble, a butler in a British club in Poona, directed an unsuccessful *satyagraha* at Parvati, Poona's holy hill.

Shivram Janba Kamble was the chief author of a petition written in 1910 which pled for the reestablishment of Mahar enlistment in the army. The document, which seems to have been ignored by the British government, illustrates both the consciousness of low position and the aspirations of the Mahar of that time: "We, the Mahar inhabitants of India, residing in the Bombay Presidency, have experienced the vitalizing influence of the general awakening of our Indian people, and long to participate in the new privileges which have been granted by our illustrious Emperor. . . . We do not aspire to high political privileges and positions, since we are not educationally qualified for them, but humbly seek employment in the lowest grades of the public service, in the ranks of police sepoys and soldiers in the Indian army. . . . We have been excluded from the military service entirely, for reasons unknown to us. . . . If the other castes of the Hindus should object to our enlistment in the same regiments with them . . . we would request that separate regiments of our people might be created, or separate companies of our people might be attached to Muhammadan regiments. . . . The kindly touch of the Christian religion elevates the Mahar at once and forever socially as well as politically, and shall not the magic power of British law and British justice produce the same effect upon us, even as followers of our own ancestral faith?"[8]

Eight years later, more "new privileges" were to come to the Indian people as the British raj attempted to broaden the representative base of its power. The opportunity to testify to the Southborough (Fran-

[6] Gopal Baba Walangkar also made some effort to deny Brahmin superiority. He formed a group of Mahar *joshis* to perform the astrological services that normally were the prerogative of the Brahmin *joshi*. The fixing of the proper astrological time for ceremonies was the only service generally performed for the Mahar by the Brahmin priest. It is said that Dr. Ambedkar greatly admired Walangkar for his independent spirit.

[7] Kisan Fagoji Bansode is the only one of the group without a British connection. Although attracted to Ambedkar, he remained attached to Hinduism and was critical of the announcement of conversion in 1935.

[8] The full document is quoted in H. N. Navalkar, *The Life of Shivram Janba Kamble and Brief History of the Poona Parvati Satyagraha*, S. J. Kamble, Poona, 1930, pp. 142-157.

chise) Committee, which prepared a report to be used in the Montagu-Chelmsford reforms, coincided with the arrival on the scene of a Mahar who was well educated enough to "aspire to high political privileges." Dr. Ambedkar, himself from a Mahar army family and the second high school graduate among the Mahars, had returned in 1917 from three years of education in America (M.A., Ph.D., Columbia University), and one year in England, made possible by the liberal Gaikwad of Baroda as part of his program of educating the lower castes. One of two Untouchable witnesses, the other also a Mahar,[9] Dr. Ambedkar used the opportunity to outline a complete franchise system for Bombay Presidency. But his main plea was for direct representation of the Depressed Classes in the Bombay legislative council in proportion to their population, through their own electorate separate from that of the caste Hindus. His testimony gave a gloomy picture of the state of the Untouchable in 1919: "Socio-religious disabilities have dehumanized the untouchable. . . . The untouchables are so socialized as never to complain of their low estate. . . . The exact description of the treatment cannot be attempted. The word untouchable is an epitome of their ills and sufferings. Not only has untouchability arrested the growth of their personality but it comes in the way of their material well-being. It has also deprived them of certain civil rights. . . . The principal modes of acquiring wealth are trade, industry or service. The untouchables can engage in none of these because of their untouchability. . . . In the whole Bombay Presidency there [are] one B.A. [himself] and six or seven matriculates among the depressed classes."[10]

In Ambedkar's testimony were various elements which were to recur again and again throughout his career; some of these bear a relationship to the final conversion to Buddhism. He emphasized: the need of the Untouchable for self-respect; the reality of the division between caste Hindu and Depressed Class, which had to be acknowledged if any justice was to be done; the belief that the Brahmin's "deep ingrained ethnocentrism has prevented a reconstruction of Hindu society and stood in the way of a revision of vested rights for the common good"; distrust of the Congress as a group composed of social conservatives; the representation of Untouchables by Untouchables, for caste Hindus, however sympathetic, could not properly represent their wants and grievances; the need for political power and political

[9] G. A. Gavai of Amravati, who reported to the committee from Central Provinces and Berar.

[10] *Evidence taken before The Reforms Committee (Franchise)*, vol. 2, Government of India, Calcutta, 1919, pp. 729-739.

education for the Depressed Class. Ambedkar appeared before the Southborough Committee in the hope that the coming transfer of some power to popular assemblies would include direct representation of the Depressed Classes so that "the hardships and disabilities entailed by the social system should not be reproduced and perpetuated in political institutions." His plea was ignored by the Southborough Committee, which in its final report gave one nominated seat (Ambedkar had asked for nine elected seats) to the Depressed Classes in the Bombay Presidency. But Ambedkar was to continue to use every opportunity which presented itself to attempt to secure political power for the Depressed Classes.

Another trip to England, financed by the Gaikwad of Baroda and also the Maharajah of Kolhapur, an active figure in the Non-Brahmin movement, gave Ambedkar the additional qualifications of barrister-at-law and M.Sc. and D.Sc. (economics) from the London School of Economics and Political Science. After his second return, he gave some attention to the process of improving the Untouchables' status by the traditional means of emulating the religious practices of the higher castes, but there was ambivalence in his attitude toward Hinduism. In an early editorial in *Mooknayak* (The Voice of the Dumb), his first newspaper which was started in 1920, he wrote: "We are not yet ready to give an answer to the question of whether the Untouchables should have a temple of their own or attempt to enter the Hindu temple."[11] On a few occasions, Ambedkar made some attempt to enter, physically or symbolically, the Hindu temple. The right to participate in the public Ganpati festival was secured; on at least one occasion, Ambedkar and his followers donned the sacred thread symbolizing rebirth worn by the three higher castes; an abortive attempt to enter the temple at Amravati was followed in 1930 by a large-scale *satyagraha* at the Kalaram temple in Nasik.

Even the Nasik *satyagraha* may have been more of a social device than a battle for religious rights, for in 1934 Ambedkar himself wrote to the Nasik leader, Bhaurao Gaikwad, that the proposed renewal of the attempt (still unsuccessful) to gain entrance to the temple should be stopped altogether. "I did not launch the temple entry movement because I wanted the Depressed Classes to become worshippers of idols which they were prevented from worshipping or because I believed that temple entry would make them equal members in and an integral part of Hindu society. So far as this aspect of the case is

[11] Cangdeo Bhavanrao Khairmode, *Dr. Bhimrao Ramji Ambedkar*, vol. 1, Yeshwantrao Ambedkar, Bombay, 1952, p. 266 (Marathi). This sentence, and other translations from the Marathi, were made with the help of D. R. Maheshkar and Mrs. Y. B. Damle.

concerned, I would advise the Depressed Classes to insist upon a complete overhauling of Hindu society and Hindu theology before they consent to become an integral part of Hindu society. I started temple entry *satyagraha* only because I felt that that was the best way of energizing the Depressed Classes and making them conscious of their position. As I believe I have achieved that, therefore I have no more use for temple entry. I want the Depressed Classes to concentrate their energy and resources on politics and education."[12]

But if he did not stress the need for the Untouchables to become "an integral part of Hinduism," Ambedkar did insist that Untouchables should look and act like the highest of caste Hindus. In his newspapers and at innumerable conferences he enjoined: stop the traditional Mahar work of dragging the dead cattle out of the village and the practice of eating carrion; dress well; don't drink; don't beg alms; get education and send your children to school; be self-respecting. In 1942 when recalling the progress made during twenty years of work, Ambedkar's references were not only to political gains but also to the process of self-purification of those practices which "justified" the untouchability of the Untouchable. The Scheduled Caste man, he declared, has stopped eating dead animals, observing meaningless Hindu customs, and now had the privilege of sending representatives to the legislature.[13] On another occasion in the same year he congratulated his audience on its political awareness (75,000 people had attended the public meeting), good progress in education, and entry into the police and the army. However, "the greatest progress that we have made is to be found among our woman folk. Here you see in this conference these 20 to 25 thousand women present. See their dress, observe their manners, mark their speech. Can any one say that they are Untouchable women?"[14]

While the process of purifying and modernizing was going on within the caste, Ambedkar had further opportunities to bring Untouchable grievances and demands before the British government. The emphasis on the Depressed Class as a separate element in Indian society was intensified, and Ambedkar increasingly urged constitutional arrangements which would accentuate this separateness. The demand for joint electorates with adult franchise before the Simon Commission in 1928 gave way to insistence on separate electorates at

[12] A typed copy of the letter dated March 3, 1934, in English, is in the Khairmode files at the University of Bombay Library.

[13] *Times of India*, April 27, 1942, reporting Dr. Ambedkar's speech on the occasion of his fiftieth birthday.

[14] *Report of Depressed Class Conferences, Nagpur Sessions*, G. T. Meshram, Nagpur, 1942, pp. 28-29.

the Round Table Conference in 1930, probably in the light of the Muslim minority's demands. Ambedkar argued that the Depressed Classes "must be regarded as a distinct and independent minority. . . . We cannot be deemed part of the Hindu community."[15] This was later softened, however, to a plea for the Depressed Classes to be called "Protestant Hindus" or "non-caste Hindus."[16]

For Dr. Ambedkar, the selection of two Depressed Class members (Rao Bahadur R. Srinivasan from Madras and himself) as delegates to the first Round Table Conference in 1930 was in itself recognition of the right of the Depressed Classes to be considered a separate element on the Indian political scene, and he felt the conference acknowledged that as a fact. At the second Round Table Conference in 1931, however, Mahatma Gandhi was also present, representing Congress and speaking strongly against the idea of the Untouchables as a separate entity in Indian society. In Gandhi's mind, separate electorates might allow Dr. Ambedkar himself to "mount to power and position but nothing good will accrue to the 'Untouchables.' "[17]

The conflict at the Round Table Conference over who represented the Untouchables and whether they were or were not a separate group was heightened a year later when the Communal Award was announced. In an attempt to meet both the requirements of Dr. Ambedkar and Mr. Gandhi, the British government announced that Depressed Class members were to have a double vote: one in the general electorate, the other in a special electorate only for Depressed Class voters. Gandhi, confined in the Yeravda Jail in Poona, went on a fast[18] to protest this decision on the grounds that it would be harmful for the Depressed Classes and would vivisect and disrupt Hinduism, would serve neither as penance for caste Hindus nor as a remedy for the degradation the Depressed Classes had groaned under for centuries.[19] Gandhi claimed the Depressed Classes question was predominantly a religious matter. Ambedkar regarded political power as vital for the Untouchables' progress; direct election of Depressed

---

[15] *Indian Statutory Commission*, vol. 16, "Selections from Memoranda and Oral Evidence by Non-officials (Part I)," London, 1930, p. 54.

[16] "Supplementary Memorandum on the Claims of the Depressed Classes for Special Representation, submitted to the Round Table Conference by Dr. Bhimrao R. Ambedkar and Rao Bahadur R. Srinivasan," November 4, 1931. quoted in B. R. Ambedkar, *What Congress and Gandhi Have Done to the Untouchables*, Thacker & Co., Ltd., Bombay, pp. 315-317.

[17] Quoted in *ibid.*, p. 71.

[18] *The Epic Fast* is the title of Pyarelal's book (Navajivan, Ahmedabad, 1932) describing Gandhi's 1932 Yeravda Jail fast against the principle of separate electorates.

[19] Gandhi's letter to Sir S. Hoare, March 11, 1932, quoted in *ibid.*, pp. 99-103.

Class members to legislatures, without the possibility of caste Hindu votes determining the outcome, was essential. He had by that time no interest and little faith in the Depressed Classes' full assimilation into Hinduism.

Gandhi's fast unto death against separate electorates placed his life in Ambedkar's hands. Ambedkar agreed to the Poona Pact, capitulating on the matter of separate electorates at the price of an increased number of reserved seats for Untouchables in legislative bodies, and Gandhi gave up his fast.

The conflict with Gandhi had been foreshadowed in a speech given by Ambedkar in Nagpur in 1920 in which he criticized V. R. Shinde, organizer of the pioneering Depressed Class Mission and a Maratha by caste, for suggesting that the representatives of the Untouchables should be selected by the members of the legislative council, not by government or by Untouchable institutions. Dr. Ambedkar's objection was that the caste Hindu could not know the mind of the Untouchable; caste Hindu organizations for the uplift of the Depressed Classes should be opposed.[20]

Ambedkar considered Gandhi an enemy of the Untouchables from the time of the Round Table Conference until Gandhi's death in 1948. The conflict between the two men can be defined in several ways: Ambedkar's insistence on the *rights* of the Depressed Classes versus Gandhi's stress upon the *duty* of the caste Hindus to do penance; Ambedkar's complete rejection of caste versus Gandhi's defense of *chaturvarna* (the idealized four-caste system with no untouchability) as necessary to Hinduism; Ambedkar's rational, democratic liberalism versus Gandhi's appeals to traditional modes of thought; and the inevitable clash between the aggressive demands of a minority group leader and the slower, broader-based and somewhat paternalistic extension of rights by the majority group reformer.

Ambedkar was critical of the British government in India, but he was of the school which demanded social reforms before political reforms, and he preferred British raj to a "Hindu raj" in which the Untouchables would not have established rights. A few years after the Poona Pact he took two steps, one religious and one political, which underlined his position as the leader of a group independent of Hinduism and independent of Congress. Criticism of Hinduism became flat rejection in 1935 at a conference at Yeola (near Nasik), when Ambedkar stated: "I was born in the Hindu religion; but I

[20] Dhananjay Keer, *Dr. Ambedkar, Life and Mission*, Popular Prakashan, Bombay, second ed., 1962, pp. 42-43.

will not die in the Hindu religion."[21] A conference of Mahars called the next year in Bombay resolved to leave Hinduism, to stop participating in worship and festivals. The reaction to this announcement among Mahars beyond reach of the conference is hard to judge; certainly any attempt to stress religious practices as a way toward higher social status was abandoned. But it is doubtful that disbelief in the efficacy of prayers and vows to the Hindu gods suddenly descended, and such Hindu rituals as were used for weddings and other ceremonies undoubtedly continued. The reaction to the announcement among caste Hindus was vigorous and almost totally critical. The reaction of other religions was to offer hospitality to Dr. Ambedkar and the Depressed Classes without question. Muslims, Sikhs and Buddhists sought him out; Christians, not convinced of the appropriateness of mass conversion, expressed great interest but at a little distance.

The conversion announcement was made without reference to any religion. Dr. Ambedkar seemed to incline toward Sikhism, explaining later that "conversion to Islam or Christianity would denationalize the Depressed Classes."[22] But after several interchanges with the Sikhs, including the building of a college in Bombay by Sikhs as earnest of good will toward the Scheduled Castes, Dr. Ambedkar let the issue of conversion lapse, probably because he suspected that the reserved seats won for the Depressed Classes might be sacrificed by entrance into Sikhism. In 1946, when Dr. Ambedkar was asked by a Christian minister why he did not embrace Christianity rather than Islam, which was the strongest rumor of that time, he said that it was not easy to uproot humanity. The Untouchables were willing to stay where they were provided they had political safeguards, and there was no agreement among them as to where to go.[23]

In 1936, the same year the Mahar conference resolved to abandon Hinduism, Dr. Ambedkar founded the Independent Labor Party to fight Congress in the elections to be held in 1937. The Independent Labor Party issued a platform quite broad in scope, mildly socialistic, with only incidental mention of the Depressed Classes. One section urged legislation to prevent social reformers from being outcasted by the orthodox and to penalize terrorism or boycott used to prevent

[21] Shankarrao Kharat, *Asprishyanca Muktisangram* (The Battle of the Untouchables for Freedom), published by De. Shri Joshi and M. D. Lokhande, Poona, n.d. (Marathi), p. 204.

[22] *Times of India,* July 24, 1936, quoted in Keer, p. 278.

[23] *Jai Bheem,* December 25, 1946, Madras. Typed copy in the files of Nanak Chand Rattu, New Delhi. The interview, originally in the *Globe,* was with the Rev. Gordon Livingston.

individuals or classes from exercising their rights. Another plank was the demand for facilities for higher education and foreign education for communities which were educationally backward. A third asked for modernization of *vatan,* the village system that gave payment in kind for traditional services from its village servants, which Ambedkar considered detrimental to the progress of the Mahars. A few caste Hindus were influential in the party, and its general program was to rectify the injustices suffered by any underprivileged group. In the 1937 elections, the Independent Labor Party scored considerable success, winning 16 of the 18 seats it contested, including 3 general seats and 10 reserved seats out of 15 in the Bombay state legislature, and 3 reserved seats in the Central Provinces and Berar.

In 1942, along with increasing pressure for separate electorates, Ambedkar turned the Independent Labor Party into the Scheduled Caste Federation, making a direct appeal to the Scheduled Castes to win power through unity. A large meeting at Nagpur brought together delegates from Bombay, the Central Provinces and Berar (who were for the most part Mahars), and also from Madras, Bengal, Punjab and the United Provinces. The first article of the new party's constitution read: "The object of the All-India Scheduled Castes Federation is the attainment by the Scheduled Castes of a status as a distinct and separate element in the national life of India and to obtain them their political, economic and social rights to which they are entitled by reason of their needs, their numbers and their importance."[24]

This would have been the strategic time, with many Congressmen in jail, for the development of a strong all-India organization that might have welded the Scheduled Castes into the force Ambedkar dreamed of. But Ambedkar was labor member of the Viceroy's executive council and hampered by that official post from large-scale political activity. His own temperament also prevented him from using the war years to build his organization, as M. A. Jinnah did with the Muslim League. A biographer, Dhananjay Keer, wrote in what seems an accurate judgment: "Ambedkar did not try to organize his political party on modern lines. He had no taste for individual organization. There were no regular annual conferences or general meetings of the organizations with which he was connected. Where and when he sat was the venue of conference and the time for decision. . . . When he wanted his people to assemble under his banner, he simply gave them a clarion call and the organization sprang up like the crop in the rainy season. In the summer there would be nothing in the

[24] *Constitution of the All-India Scheduled Castes Federation,* printed in *Report of Depressed Class Conferences,* G. T. Meshram, Nagpur, 1942.

field, the banner resting in his study corner and the people at home."[25]

Resolutions, petitions, memorandums, large-scale *satyagraha* at provincial legislatures in Poona, Nagpur, Kanpur and Lucknow, and a flying visit to England in 1946, all failed to bring British recognition of what Ambedkar felt were the rights of the Scheduled Castes to a separate electorate. Independence in 1947 brought partition and with it the end of the question of separate electorates for the Muslims, and for the Scheduled Castes too. And with independence came the surprising and gracious gesture, in view of his outspoken criticism of Congress, Gandhi and Nehru, of Ambedkar's appointment to the Constitution drafting committee, then to the committee chairmanship and to Nehru's first cabinet as law minister.

The proposed "Constitution of the United States of India" which Ambedkar published in *States and Minorities* in March 1947, before his appointment, is quite different from the actual draft Constitution he defended before the Constituent Assembly in November 1948. Gone is the provision for agriculture as a state industry, which Ambedkar regarded as the only solution to the problems of the Scheduled Castes, the great majority of whom were agricultural laborers.[26] Gone also were the provisions for separate electorates and separate villages for Scheduled Castes. Similar in both documents are anti-untouchability clauses, an officer to look after "minority affairs," representation of Scheduled Castes in legislature and the services, and special governmental responsibility for the education of the Scheduled Castes. The Constitution, of course, is the reflection of the thinking of Congress leaders of the time, not a product of Ambedkar's mind only. Actually, his main contributions to the Constitution may have been more in the general fields of stressing centralized government and a unitary judiciary, plus his skill in guiding the draft Constitution through the Constituent Assembly.

Ambedkar became known as the draftsman or author of the Constitution, but his efforts to get the Hindu Code Bill as a whole through Parliament, an achievement he desired even more, failed. He resigned in 1951, chiefly over the failure of the cabinet to support the bill. Out of the cabinet, Ambedkar faced two election defeats and increased illness in the final years of his life. But the last two public

[25] Keer, p. 477.

[26] Dr. Ambedkar did make such a proposal to the drafting committee, but dropped it when it received little support. G. A. Austin, "Tryst With Destiny: The Indian Constituent Assembly and the Framing of the Indian Constitution," thesis submitted for the Ph.D. degree, Oxford University, St. Anthony's College. I am grateful to Mr. Austin for some of my ideas about Dr. Ambedkar and the Constitution, although he is not responsible for my interpretation.

acts of his life, the Buddhist conversion and the founding of the Republican Party, are not symptoms of failure or renewed expressions of separatism.

The conversion to Buddhism in October 1956, which came just before Dr. Ambedkar's death, was the result of personal conviction as well as a conscious effort to lay down a way his people could follow after his death. Dr. Ambedkar's own path to Buddhism cannot be entirely correlated with his political life. His interest began when a Bombay teacher, K. A. Keluskar, gave him a copy of the life of Buddha in 1908, on the occasion of his passing his matriculation examination, an incident which is part of the religious lore of the Buddhists today. Some time in the 1920's he corresponded with Maharshi Shinde, the Maratha reformer of whom he was very critical on other points, about Shinde's interest in Buddhism.[27]

In 1934 the house he had built in the predominantly Brahmin Hindu Colony in Dadar, Bombay, was named Rajgriha, after the ancient city of the Buddhist kings. The first of the colleges established by his People's Education Society, which began in 1946 in hutments in Bombay, was called Siddharth, one of the names of the Buddha. In 1948 he republished *The Essence of Buddhism*, first published in 1908, and noted in the introduction that the author, Laksman Narasu, had battled not only against caste but also against British high-handedness. And in the same year he published his own book, *The Untouchables*, with its thesis that the Untouchables had been Buddhists, degraded and banished from the villages because they had held fast to their Buddhism when others returned to Brahminism. As early as 1951 he urged his followers to convert to Buddhism, and that year he began writing the "Bible," *The Buddha and His Dhamma*, a secular, rational, social interpretation of Buddhism, which he felt was needed to bring Buddhism to the masses.

The conversion actually came twenty-one years after the initial announcement that the Scheduled Castes should leave Hinduism. It has been called a political stunt by many, but it makes little political sense except as a unifying force for the Mahars, who probably would have remained cohesive in any case, or as a corollary to the Republican Party then being formed, an effort to weld the Scheduled Castes, Scheduled Tribes and Backward Classes into a powerful political

27 Principal M. P. Mangudkar of Shri Shahu Mandir Mahavidyalaya, Poona, reports seeing these letters among the Shinde papers. Principal Mangudkar's discussion of Dr. Ambedkar's pragmatic philosophy has been of great help to me.

group. It is fairly certain that most of Dr. Ambedkar's political lieutenants were against conversion, thinking that it might result in the loss of hard-won rights to reserved seats and reserved government jobs and serve no positive political purpose. But Dr. Ambedkar's leadership of the Scheduled Caste Federation and of the Mahars was unchallengeable, and the day of conversion found the political leaders as well as the masses of ordinary folk, mostly Mahars, dressed in white and assembled in Nagpur, ready to become Buddhists.

There seem to have been two main purposes for the conversion in the mind of Dr. Ambedkar: (1) the rejection of Hinduism and in consequence the status of untouchability; (2) the establishment of a religion which would serve as a bulwark against communism and to which all India could eventually turn. The first purpose is illustrated by the stories of his ill-treatment as an Untouchable which Dr. Ambedkar related during the *diksha* speech, and by the references to Hindu practices in six of the twenty-two oaths used during the ceremony. The oaths, in Marathi, are used at each conversion ceremony. They proclaim belief in the Buddhist way, but also such statements as: "I will not regard Brahma, Vishnu and Mahesh as Gods nor will I worship them"; and "I embrace today the Buddha Dhamma discarding the Hindu Religion which is detrimental to the emancipation of human beings and which believes in inequality and regards human beings other than the Brahmins as low-born."[28]

The second purpose is illustrated by an address on "Buddha and Karl Marx" delivered by Ambedkar at the World Fellowship of Buddhists meetings at Katmandu shortly after his conversion. In this address he regarded Buddhism as a substitute for Communism: "If we all become one-tenth as enlightened as the Buddha was, we can bring about the same result by the methods of love, of justice and good will."[29] As early as 1950, Dr. Ambedkar wrote in the *Maha Bodhi Journal*: "Some of those who believe that only the acceptance of the gospel of Buddha can save the Hindus are filled with sorrow because they do not see much prospect of the return or revival of Buddhism. I do not share this pessimism."[30] He felt that not only all the suppressed and the downtrodden but also all those who felt there was something wrong with Hinduism would turn to Buddhism, much as

[28] The Twenty-two Oaths are printed in English in a leaflet entitled *Dhamma Deeksha*, published by the Buddhist Society of India, Ambedkar Bhavan, New Delhi.
[29] The speech, given November 20, 1956, at the fourth conference of the World Fellowship of Buddhists at Katmandu, has been published in a pamphlet, *Buddha and Karl Marx*, M. D. Panchbhai, Nagpur.
[30] *The Maha Bodhi*, vol. 58, April-May 1950.

the masses in the Roman Empire had turned to Christianity for "mental and moral relief." At the time of conversion, he told his people that they must be honorable, respectable, responsible Buddhists, and if they could accomplish this, "We will save our country."[31]

The first of these purposes seems, from the standpoint of those who converted, well served. The conversion was accompanied by the throwing out of the Hindu gods from the Maharwada, the Mahar quarter of the village, sometimes quite unceremoniously and with obvious intent to defy the caste Hindus, in other places immersed in rivers or tanks or buried more courteously. The palanquin of the village goddess, usually kept by the Mahars, was given over to the keeping of the caste Hindus. Along with the break with Hindu religion went an intensification of the process of abandoning ritual duties or work traditionally given the Mahar as part of his service to the village. The conversion encouraged the Mahars to make the last break with any village duty that defined their low position and this action, more than actual conversion, brought some reprisals from caste Hindus. Even now, newspaper reports tell almost monthly of violence in some village where Mahars (or Buddhists) refuse to do village sanitation work, refuse to carry petromax lamps on their heads for weddings, or refuse to do road work without cash payment in advance.

The conversion seems also to have been successful in removing from the Mahar himself any vestige of a feeling of inferiority. Buddhists often say that they experienced a sudden sense of release, a psychological freedom. A Brahmin teacher who was at Siddharth College in 1956 reported that his Buddhist (formerly Mahar) students not only threw out their gods and goddesses but also were noticeably filled with a new spirit of self-confidence. A sociologist who spent several months in 1962 surveying the situation of Untouchables in villages stated: "The Buddhists are still in a gallant mood. They haven't cooled down yet."[32]

The conversion continues the "purifying process" that has been part of the movement all along, a "Pali-ization" rather than a "Sanskritization" of practices, to use the Buddhist equivalent for M. N. Srinivas' useful word for the emulation of high caste practices.[33] A

---

[31] From the Marathi speech of Dr. Ambedkar on October 14, 1956 in Nagpur, as published in *Prabuddh Bharat*, October 27, 1956.

[32] Dr. M. G. Kulkarni of the Gokhale Institute of Politics and Economics, Poona, has made available to me his reports on surveys of villages in Buldana and Nasik districts in 1962. I have quoted only his personal remark, but his detailed knowledge of the village situation has added to my understanding of present conditions.

[33] The term was first used by Dr. Srinivas in *Religion and Society among the*

Buddhism and Politics in Maharashtra

part of the conversion ceremony, and of any Buddhist occasion, is the taking of the Panch Sila in Pali—five moral affirmations which announce the intent to avoid doing harm to any living being, to refrain from taking what is not given, to refrain from sexual misconduct, to refrain from wrong speech, and to refrain from intoxicating liquor and drugs. The vow to refrain from alcohol is particularly important in the Indian context. The Buddhists themselves and some observers (not all) say that there has been a decrease in drinking among the converts. Community pressure is not infrequently used to bring an indulging Buddhist into line. Since the conversion there have also been increased efforts to secure education, particularly in the villages, this again an intensification of a process of awakening that can be traced back to 1890 in some areas.[34]

The social significance of Buddhism is that it has become the culmination of the process begun years before of denying the doctrine of untouchability, attempting to remove any low caste characteristics that separated the Untouchables from caste Hindus, and cutting any ritual or economic ties that reinforced the low position of the Untouchable. The adoption of the name "Buddhist" is not an escape for the Untouchable; it is now a synonym for Mahar or Untouchable. But it gives the Mahar a sense of freedom, of progress, of change from Hinduism without a lessening of his Indian-ness. While the Buddhist today claims Buddhist tradition and Buddhist history as his heritage, he rejects any implication that Buddhism is part of Hinduism.

The Buddhist is also caught in a situation in which he rejects the idea of his untouchability in converting, and yet does not reject the benefits conferred upon him by government, which he feels Dr. Ambedkar won for him and which are recompense for the ill-treatment of the Untouchable. Some Buddhists would prefer to cut all

---

Coorgs of South India, Oxford, 1952, p. 30, and is detailed in "A Note on Sanskritization and Westernization," first published in the *Journal of Asian Studies* and now reprinted in *Caste in Modern India*, Asia Publishing House, Bombay, 1962.

[34] Since the Buddhists are no longer counted as Scheduled Caste, no figures on their literacy are available. *The Census of India, 1961*, vol. 10, Maharashtra, Part V-A, "Scheduled Castes and Scheduled Tribes in Maharashtra—Tables," Delhi, 1964, does give figures on literacy and education for those who registered themselves Mahars. The Mahar literacy rate in 1961 was 15.69 per cent, compared to 29.82 per cent as a general figure for Maharashtra, and was considerably lower than that for the Chambhars, another Scheduled Caste group primarily found in cities. However, among those Scheduled Caste individuals who have matriculated or gone on for higher education, the Mahars predominate. It is a general belief in Maharashtra that the Mahars' (and Buddhists') eagerness for education surpasses that of all but the highest castes.

links, helpful and unhelpful, with their former status; most do not see why they should lose benefits which attempt to correct former injustice, economic and educational, because they themselves reject social injustice by conversion. Many have hopes that the problem will be resolved for their children, who will be "true Buddhists" without caste.

THE REPUBLICAN PARTY

Plans for the Republican Party, and the name indicates Ambedkar's hope for a broader base than the Scheduled Castes, were not completely formulated before his death. Correspondence with Rammanohar Lohia of the Socialist Party, and letters written to P. K. Atre and S. M. Joshi, leaders of the Maharashtra opposition to Congress, just before his death (but not mailed), are evidence of a hope for some new sort of alliance. Although he gave permission in the fall of 1956 for the Scheduled Caste Federation to join the Samyukta Maharashtra Samiti, a group of all opposition parties which successfully pressed for a Marathi-speaking Maharashtra as a separate state, he made no long-range plans for the operation of a new allied party. When the manifesto of the Republican Party appeared, after his death, it expressed interest in cooperating with the organizations of the Backward Classes and the Scheduled Tribes, which it considered lacking in political consciousness. It also expressed hope for the emergence of an all-India party in opposition to Congress, of which it could be a unit, but no more specific foundation for a new force was laid.

In Maharashtra, Republican Party members are Buddhists;[35] Buddhists are Republicans. The number of Congress Buddhists can be counted on the fingers of one hand. Ostensibly, the leaders of the Republican Party are the leaders of the Buddhist movement. But there is another group of religious leaders who are apart from politics. The writers of the dozens of pamphlets on Buddhist ceremonies and doctrine, the pilgrims to Bodh Gaya and Sarnath, the young men who learn enough Pali to lead *wandana* (prayer) and conduct wedding, naming and funeral ceremonies, the thinkers, the worriers, are

[35] The Buddhist who wishes to contest a reserved seat must register himself as a Mahar. A recent Supreme Court decision deprived D. P. Meshram of Nagpur of his seat in the Maharashtra legislative assembly on the grounds that his activities in the Buddhist religion proved him a Buddhist, and as such not eligible for the reserved seat. The decision was generally approved by Buddhists, since it underwrote their conviction that they are no longer Hindus. The Republican Party's inability to win a majority of the reserved seats from Congress candidates, in any case, has caused them to ask for non-renewal of reservations on the state and national level in legislative bodies.

usually a-political. There is an effort to create a new religious culture that is unrelated to the political field.

Dr. Ambedkar's hope that the Republican Party would be a more broadly based political group than the Scheduled Castes Federation has not been fulfilled. In the 1962 election, the Republican Party captured 3 seats in the Maharashtra legislative assembly (in contrast to 19 during the Samyukta Maharashtra Samiti period), 8 seats in the Uttar Pradesh assembly (due to a Republican-Muslim alliance that is probably temporary), and 3 seats in the Lok Sabha from Uttar Pradesh. It lost the 5 state assembly seats it had won in 1957 in Punjab, and Lok Sabha seats it had formerly held from Madras, Mysore, Gujarat and Maharashtra.

In Maharashtra, the same factor that accounts for the strength of the party (it claims to be second in strength, after Congress) imposes corresponding limitations. The solid bedrock support of the Mahars or Buddhists provides a powerful base, and in certain favorable situations (railroad towns, mill towns, areas where the Buddhists are 15 per cent or more) a significant number of elected places in local governing bodies have gone to the party. But the support is limited by the number of Buddhists, since the identification of the party with the Buddhists defines its constituency. Historically, the Republican Party and its predecessor, the Scheduled Caste Federation, have been related in one way or another with almost every other political group on either the national or local scene—an inevitable consequence of being too small to stand alone and too united to be of no consequence. What direction the party will go now to gain electoral strength is unrelated to the fact of the Buddhist conversion.

Because of its program, the natural alliance for the Republicans would be a socialist party. But the Socialist Party-Scheduled Caste Federation alliance of the first general elections in 1952 was not an entirely happy experience. The Federation felt it had not received promised support. In the Bhandara by-election in 1954, Socialist Ashok Mehta was elected to the general seat; his running mate, Dr. Ambedkar, lost the reserved seat. For their part, the Socialists felt that the Mahars could be counted on to vote for Mahars, but not necessarily other party-endorsed candidates. Some Socialists were unhappy about the party's outspoken criticism of Gandhi and Nehru; some felt uncomfortable with the social status of the Federation's members. A recent invitation from the Samyukta Socialist Party to the Republican Party to join its alliance was turned down on the grounds that the Socialists were concerned only with economic matters and the problems of the Scheduled Castes and Buddhists demanded action on more than one front.

The Scheduled Caste Federation joined forces with the Communists only once, in the Samyukta Maharashtra Samiti,[36] along with every other opposition party in Maharashtra. There is an assumption among Buddhists and some political observers that the natural political direction of the Untouchables is toward communism. Windmiller and Overstreet note the small number of Untouchables (three) among the 139 delegates to the Communist Party of India Congress in 1943, and add: "It is interesting to note the number of Untouchables was so small, for this oppressed class would seem to be a rich source of recruits for the party."[37] The Buddhists themselves often say that except for Dr. Ambedkar, who was always critical of the Communist Party, and for the Buddhist conversion, the Mahars would be Communists.

The theory that the Untouchable would inevitably be drawn to communism is not substantiated by the American counterpart of the Indian situation; few Negroes have found the Communist Party an acceptable home. In India, support for the Communists comes from Untouchable castes only in Andhra and Kerala. In other states they are by and large Congress or Republican. The attraction of communism for middle-class unemployed youth is not found to any significant degree among the Mahars or Buddhists. The educated Buddhist at the moment finds unemployment no problem because his numbers are not yet great enough to fill the reserved government jobs available to him, and hence he is not as subject to the frustration of unemployment or as open to radical theories. Added to this is the fact that all Ambedkar's influence was on the side of parliamentary democracy. He was never attracted to communism, either in his years abroad or in India. The Communist Party in Bombay was for him "a bunch of Brahmin boys."[38]

For Ambedkar, and for many Republican leaders, theoretical communism is synonymous with economic justice. In his last speech on Buddhism, given in 1956 at Katmandu, Dr. Ambedkar said that Buddhism contained all of communism's economic and egalitarian bene-

[36] The Communists' hope that perhaps the Samiti had "laid the basis of healing the great split between the democratic movement and the Untouchable masses, led by the late Dr. Ambedkar," has remained unfulfilled. Quoted from B. T. Ranadive, "Maharashtra Election Review," *New Age*, July 1957, p. 15, by Selig Harrison, *India, The Most Dangerous Decades*, Oxford University Press, Madras, pp. 192-193.

[37] Gene D. Overstreet and Marshall Windmiller, *Communism in India*, University of California Press, Berkeley, 1959, p. 358.

[38] From an interview with Dr. Ambedkar quoted in Harrison, p. 191.

fits without communism's violent methods. If the push for education produces Buddhists ready for white-collar jobs in such numbers that reservations no longer provide for them, or if the Communists find a way to organize the vast depressed army of agricultural laborers, the Buddhists may become more interested, or the Republican Party itself may find reason for common cause.

The most effective political alliance of the Buddhists today is with the Muslims in Uttar Pradesh. Three of eight Republican Party MLAs are Muslims; one of three MPs. Although that grouping has brought election results, it is limited to U.P. There is some cooperation and understanding between Buddhists and Muslims in daily life. The Buddhists do not feel in economic or social competition with the Muslims, do not feel that the Muslims regard them as Untouchables. In cities and small towns, the Muslim localities often neighbor those of the Buddhists. Buddhist functions may be held in Muslim institutions more easily than in caste Hindu buildings. Dr. Ambedkar understood the mind of the Muslim minority well enough to produce the prophetic *Thoughts on Pakistan* in 1940, a book which delineated all the reasons why the Muslims were part of India and should not want a separate state, but declared that the mental attitude of nationhood was stronger than race, language or habits, and that therefore Pakistan was inevitable. However, many Buddhists today do not differ from the normal caste Hindu feeling about Pakistan or Kashmir, and many hold the same stereotype of the Muslim as a militant person whose first loyalty is outside India. It does not seem likely that localized political cooperation in some parts of U.P. and in a few Maharashtrian cities will spread.

Temporary alliances with conservative parties such as the Jana Sangh in local elections are not unknown, but the primarily high caste constituency and conservative economic platform of the Jana Sangh, plus Dr. Ambedkar's warning against right-wing parties, makes extensive cooperation unlikely. Thirty years of anti-Congress teaching would make it difficult for the Republican Party to cooperate closely with Congress, although there have been a few arrangements made at high levels for voting support. Rumors persist that this, or that, leader, or indeed the whole party, will go over to Congress. But at this time, any leader transferring his allegiance from the Republican Party to Congress loses the support of his own people in gaining a reserved seat or a cabinet post.

In addition to the problem of limited constituency and unsatisfactory alliances, the Republican Party is troubled by a split which occurred in 1959 ostensibly over the issue of communism (continued alliance with the Samiti, in which the Communists were very active), but more probably over the question of leadership. Republicans in Maharashtra are still divided into two hostile groups, although the power of the new faction is waning. A recent split in Bombay adds a third faction in that area. There is, in spite of the general unity and cohesion of the Buddhists, much quarreling over leadership and much local factionalism. Both the split and the leadership rivalry reflect the fact that the party has had no one clear leader since the death of Dr. Ambedkar; his long-time associate, Bhaurao Gaikwad of Nasik, comes the nearest and commands general respect, but not total obedience. A number of Buddhists remark on the political situation with considerable bitterness: "Each man is a little Ambedkar." "It is like brothers quarreling over their inheritance."

Two other factors affect the leadership of the party. One is the almost irresistible temptation to a man from a low economic status to make secure his new-found position at the expense of a larger ideal, an affliction that hampered the effectiveness of the Justice Party at an earlier date in South India. The other is the fact that the way up for a Buddhist or a Scheduled Caste man is through government service. Positions in private industry, teaching posts in secondary school or college, or a small business of his own, are either very difficult for the Buddhist to secure or of less economic advantage than a government post. This governmental path upward effectively removes most of the educated, concerned Buddhists from direct political activity.

One effect of both the Buddhist conversion and the work of the Republican Party has been to link those who have progressed economically and socially with those still backward, thus limiting the tendency of those in the upper strata to cut themselves off from their past and to form a new urban caste, neither high nor Untouchable.[39] Although many Mahars do "pass," the sense of identity and pride in the community is still strong, giving the whole caste a feeling of moving upward as individuals within the group improve their position or gain recognition for worth.

LEADER, RELIGION, POLITICAL PARTY

The figure of Dr. Ambedkar, dominating both Buddhism and the Republican Party, is the key to the direction of both movements. The respect accorded him borders on devotion, both for village Buddhists and for the educated. Not only is there a photograph or painting of

[39] Harold R. Isaacs has described this situation in terms of the educated ex-Untouchables who "do not quite get *nowhere*, but neither do they get *somewhere*." See *India's Ex-Untouchables*, John Day Co., New York, 1965.

Dr. Ambedkar in almost every home and at every meeting, both religious and political, but his very name has become a symbol. The Indian nationalist cry, *Jai Hind*, has been transformed into *Jai Bhim* (For *Bhim*rao Ramji Ambedkar), with *Jai Buddh* added at religious occasions. On Buddhist invitations the traditional Hindu salutation *Saprem Namaskar* becomes *Saprem Jai Bhim*. Occasionally in political meetings the term *Bhim Raj* will be used to replace the Hindu term for the ideal government, *Ram Raj*. A great body of songs has grown up with Ambedkar's life and teachings as their theme, and singing parties in many areas celebrate the lives of Ambedkar and Lord Buddha.

The devotion to Dr. Ambedkar would seem to assume the nature of a cult, except that its entire direction is to lead the Buddhist into the westernized, educated, secular world. The photographs of Dr. Ambedkar more often than not show him in a blue pin-stripe business suit surrounded by books, and even those pictures which portray him as a Bodhisatva in a yellow robe look somehow very western. Often pictures showing him with the late President Prasad or the late Prime Minister Nehru are prized, as if to say: "We too share in the leadership of our country." The recent Republican Party *satyagraha* included, along with demands for land, slum clearance, justice to the Untouchable and implementation of the Minimum Wages Act, a demand for a portrait of Dr. B. R. Ambedkar, "The Father of the Indian Constitution," to be placed in the central hall of Parliament. In his delineation of the values established by the advanced castes and adopted by low castes in the hope of raising their status, Richard Lambert adds a new idea to the usual list of cleanliness, literacy, economic or political power—the value of sharing in and contributing to the mainstream of cultural accomplishment.[40] It is largely through Dr. Ambedkar as a national figure that the Buddhists claim this achievement.

The figure of Dr. Ambedkar and what he stands for identifies the nature of both the Buddhist movement and the Republican Party: a push upward, independent of caste Hindu groups, toward modern, democratic and often material values, a movement that rejects traditional Hinduism but clings tightly to its Indian-ness. Those groups which have joined the movement have a sense of self-respect, a feeling of unity, an ambition for higher social and economic status, and a political awareness which may yet aid significantly in the solution of India's age-old problem of untouchability.

[40] R. D. Lambert, "Untouchability as a Social Problem: Theory and Research," *Sociological Bulletin*, Bombay, March 1958, vol. 7, no. 1.

CHAPTER 10

RELIGION, POLITICS, AND THE DMK

ROBERT L. HARDGRAVE, JR.

In 1962, in India's third general elections, the Dravida Munnetra Kazagham emerged as the strongest opposition ever to challenge the entrenched Congress Party in Madras state. Although the party was denounced as atheistic and anti-Brahmin, the DMK by-passed the question of religion to campaign on the issues of bread-and-butter politics. Its election manifesto reflected an immediate economic concern which all but forgot the aspiration for a separate and independent Dravidasthan, the issue which once had been the driving force of the Dravidian movement. As the aspirations of Tamil nationalism were accommodated by the non-Brahmin Congress ministry of Kamaraj Nadar, the Dravidian movement increasingly abandoned the vitriolic attacks on Puranic Hinduism, the desecration of sacred images, and the defamation of Brahmins which had characterized its earlier history. In the process of the Tamilization of politics in Madras, the issue of Dravidasthan became a symbol of a growing specificity of regional demands against the central government on the part of the DMK and began to recede as a realistic goal in the minds of even the most nationalistic Tamilians.[1]

NON-BRAHMIN SELF-ASSERTION

The roots of the Dravidian movement lie fundamentally in the conflict which came to manifest itself between the Brahmin and the non-Brahmin in Tamilnad. Numbering little more than 2 per cent of the population, the Brahmins of South India retained an exclusiveness of caste orthodoxy which set them far apart from the castes below them in the ritual hierarchy. Often combining religious authority with economic power derived from land ownership, the Brahmin further separated himself from the lower castes and increased his control over them. In the modern period, the Brahmin community, as the indigenous element of high ascriptive status, was the first to respond to westernization. The literary tradition of the Brahmin gave

Robert L. Hardgrave, Jr. is assistant professor of government at Oberlin College.
[1] See Robert L. Hardgrave, Jr., *The Dravidian Movement*, Popular Prakashan, Bombay, 1965.

him the initial advantage in Western education; with a command of English, he entered the colonial administration and gained a new criterion of status in addition to the old, together with new political and economic advantages—further widening the gap between the elite and the mass.

Without education, economic power, or political influence, the non-Brahmin of Tamilnad felt the yoke of oppression and exploitation. Among the urban non-Brahmin classes, however, there gradually emerged a counter-elite of those politically articulate and highly educated members of the communities of lesser ritual status and power. In reaction to the incipient nationalist movement, represented by nineteenth-century Hindu revivalism, for example, which would increase and fortify the position of the Brahmin caste, the non-Brahmins of Madras presidency sought alliance with the colonial regime, believing that foreign rule would protect their position and in some way neutralize the power differences within the population.

In pursuit of these aims, the South Indian Liberal Federation was founded in August 1917. Seeking to uplift the position of the non-Brahmin community, the Justice Party, as it was commonly called, bitterly attacked caste, condemning it as a tool of Brahmin oppression. "It is the Aryans who have introduced this birth distinction, which they have elaborated into the system of Varnashrama Dharma with its concomitant evils. It was that civilization which brought about illiteracy in the country, the pedestal on which is erected the exclusive oligarchy of Brahmins. . . . Every successive attempt to put down the Brahminical tyranny ended in failure, so much so that the Brahminical influence grew stronger and stronger, with the result that they elaborated the present system of untouchableness and pollution. Thanks to the British government the times have changed, our Brahmin friends have given up their pious occupations and turned to worldliness. The great veneration in which the people held them for their piety, learning and austerity of life is now dying out, the great disillusionment has begun, and this is the most opportune moment for the social reformer to knock down all barriers of caste and uplift the Depressed Classes."[2]

If the Justice Party was anti-Brahmin, it was not anti-Hindu. Eugene F. Irschick, in describing the early Justice Party policy toward Hinduism, has suggested that the party's leaders were "essentially orthodox" religiously. The Tamil leadership in the party was vested

[2] Sir P. T. Chetty, Address, Non-Brahmin Confederation, December 28, 1917, published in: T. Varadarajulu Naidu, *The Justice Movement: 1917*, Justice Printing Works, Madras, 1932.

largely in the land-owning Vellala community. These leaders were, for the most part, socially conservative Saiva Siddhantins who presented their sect as an alternative to more Brahminical Hinduism. They did not, however, dispense with the Brahmin's priestly services. Irschick notes, nevertheless, that while atheism played virtually no role in the Justice Party, there lay within it the germ of anti-Hinduism which was later to find fertile ground in the Self-Respect Movement of Ramaswamy Naicker.[3]

With the victory of the Justice Party in the 1920 elections after the Montagu-Chelmsford Reforms, anti-Brahminism rode high on a tide of reforms directed toward the betterment of the non-Brahmin majority of Madras. The reforms included the establishment of quotas based on caste and religion for civil service posts, ensuring the rights of non-Brahmins in seeking government office. The party retained its elite character, however, and the growing popularity of the Congress in Madras brought the Justice Party to defeat at the hands of the Swarajists in 1926. In 1937, the Congress formally accepted the reins of power in Madras, after securing assurances against the misuse of the discretionary power held by the governor. C. Rajagopalachari formed the first Congress ministry.

The Justice Party defeat reflected the growing nationalist movement throughout India. The party was riddled with factionalism and discontent, and large numbers of disappointed claimants had drifted into the Congress fold. The Justice reforms had been highly communal in character, reinforcing caste rigidity, the very tyranny they sought to destroy. The Congress issued bitter attacks on the Justice Party for its communal orientation, accusing it of engendering and thriving upon caste conflict. The Congress appealed to the Gandhian spirit of unity and took full advantage of the power of Gandhi's charismatic personality. The Congress called the Justice Party an agent of British imperialism, and the long history of intimacy between the Non-Brahmin movement and the British Raj was cited. The Justice Party countered feebly with cries for Swaraj. They declared Justice opposition to the "Three B's"—the British, the Brahmin, and the Bania—but their long association with the government was too much to overcome.[4] The party had strangled itself on the rope it had woven: support for the British Raj had brought it to power, but

<hr>

[3] For an incisive analysis of the early Justice Party see: Eugene F. Irschick, "Politics and Social Conflict in South India: the Non-Brahmin Movement and Tamil Separatism, 1916 to 1929," Ph.D. dissertation, University of Chicago, 1964.

[4] Interview with T. A. V. Nathan, Madras, October 17, 1960. Nathan was editor of *The Justice* from 1929 until 1938.

with the impact of national self-consciousness and aspiration for Swaraj, its elitist character and imperial connections brought it defeat.

THE GREAT SAGE AND THE DK

As the Justice Party began to decline, there emerged one of the most dynamic and colorful political leaders South India has ever produced. E. V. Ramaswamy Naicker, known as Periyar, Great Sage, was born in 1879 in Erode of a respectable middle-class family of artisans. He married at the age of thirteen, but after six years, he became a *sannyasi*, traveling as a religious mendicant over the whole of India. In his visits to pilgrim centers, he gained an intimate knowledge of the evils of popular Hinduism. Disgusted with what he saw as exploitation of the masses by the Brahmin priest, Naicker abandoned the role of a holy man. Returning to Erode, he soon became involved in local politics. His opposition to caste regulations condemned him in the eyes of the high caste communities, and as an advocate of the rights of women, he defied his orthodox kinsmen by encouraging his young niece to remarry after she had lost her husband early in marriage. Naicker, outcasted by his own people, had gained the confidence of the non-Brahmin community of Erode and was soon elected chairman of the municipality.[5]

Although an ardent opponent of Brahmin power, Naicker was drawn toward the Congress rather than the Justice Party. Joining the non-cooperation movement in 1920, he campaigned vigorously for prohibition and khadi and served two terms of imprisonment. Elected secretary of the Tamilnad Congress Committee, he soon antagonized the Brahmin leadership of the Congress in Madras through his *satyagraha* at Vaikom for the opening of temples to Harijans. Naicker's protest against caste discrimination in an orphanage operated under Congress auspices and his advocacy of reserved seats for non-Brahmins won little favor with the leadership of the provincial Congress committee.[6] In 1922, Naicker narrowly defeated his Brahmin opponent for the presidency of the Tamilnad Congress Committee, but before he could take office another prominent Brahmin leader moved a successful vote of no-confidence.[7]

Naicker bolted the Congress and attacked it as a tool of Brahmin

[5] P. D. Devanandan, *The Dravida Kazagham: a Revolt Against Brahminism*, Christian Institute for the Study of Religion and Society, Bangalore, 1960, p. 5.
[6] *Ibid.*, pp. 5-6.
[7] "The Congress is a Brahmin Dominated Organization—Views of an Experienced Person," *Objectives of the Dravida Kazagham*, Dravida Kazagham, Madras, 1949, p. 36, cited in Selig Harrison, *India: the Most Dangerous Decades*, Princeton University Press, Princeton, 1960, p. 122.

domination. In 1925, he organized the Self-Respect Movement, designed as a Dravidian uplift, seeking to expose the Brahmin tyranny and the deceptive methods by which they controlled all spheres of Hindu life. Naicker publicly ridiculed the Puranas as fairy tales, not only imaginary and irrational, but grossly immoral as well. Influenced in his religious thinking by Robert Ingersoll, much of whose work he had translated into Tamil, Naicker—still bitter from his experiences as a *sannyasi*—attacked religion as the instrument of Brahminical control. He carried on active propaganda in an attempt to rid the people of Puranic Hinduism and wean them away from the religious ceremonies requiring the priestly service of the Brahmin. He denounced caste observances, child marriage, and enforced widowhood. Attacking the laws of Manu, he described them as the basis of the entire Hindu social fabric of caste, not only essentially but "totally inhuman." The laws, Naicker indicated, were designed to secure the supremacy of the Brahmin and to ensure his unquestioned authority. In order to propagate these views, he founded a Tamil journal, *Kudiarasu* (People's Government), which was soon followed by others of a similar nature, *Puratche* (Revolt), *Pakutharivu* (Discernment), and *Viduthalai* (Liberty).[8]

Naicker returned from a trip to the Soviet Union in 1931, more firmly convinced that materialism was the answer to India's problems, and openly advocated mass revolution and the overthrow of the government. His extremism was tempered somewhat by imprisonment for sedition in 1933-1934, and upon his release he indicated a willingness to join one of the major parties on a conditional basis. Formulating a fourteen-point program, he presented it to both the Congress and the Justice Party. It was wholly unacceptable to Congress, but the Justice Party, then rapidly going downhill, gave the nod.[9] Under the Congress ministry of Rajagopalachari in 1937, Hindi was introduced to the South as a compulsory subject in schools. Tamil patriots, taking this as an affront to Tamil culture and its rich literary tradition, reacted with violent protest, and Naicker, ready to exploit the opportunity, waved the black flags of rebellion in his first anti-Hindi campaign. The agitation against the imposition of Hindi brought Naicker to the fore and inflamed the non-Brahmins against the ministry. The campaign, which brought about the death of two agitators through police retaliation, forced the government to change Hindi from a required to an optional subject in schools.[10] The fol-

[8] Devanandan, pp. 6-8.
[9] Interview with E. V. K. Sampath, New Delhi, December 10, 1960.
[10] Devanandan, p. 9.

lowing year, 1938, while in jail for his anti-Hindi agitation, Naicker was elected president of the Justice Party.[11]

Naicker saw the imposition of Hindi as a subjugation of the Tamil people which could only be avoided through the creation of a Dravidian State. In the Justice Party Convention in December 1938, it was resolved that Tamilnad should be made a separate state, loyal to the British Raj and "directly under the Secretary of State for India."[12] This demand soon became the fundamental issue of the Justice movement, giving a new lease on life to what had been a dying party.

In 1939, Naicker organized the Dravidia Nadu Conference for the advocacy of a separate and independent Dravidasthan. The demand was reiterated the following year in response to the Muslim League's Lahore resolution demanding the establishment of Pakistan.[13] Naicker gave full support to the scheme for Pakistan and tried to enlist League support for the creation of Dravidasthan.[14] The basic presupposition of the movement toward a separate state was that the Dravidian non-Brahmin peoples (Tamil, Telugu, Kannada and Malayalam) are of a racial stock and culture which distinguishes them from the Aryan Brahmin.

The Justice Party was reorganized in 1944, under the guidance of Naicker, as the Dravida Kazagham or Dravidian Federation, and, at its Salem conference, took on the character of a highly militant mass organization. Naicker, who in the 1930's had visited the Axis countries as well as the Soviet Union, declared that "members of the Kazagham should wear black shirts whenever possible, as a symbol of the present day down-trodden condition of the Dravidians."[15] Many of the more conservative Justice Party members, such as P. T. Rajan, left the movement, retaining the old Justice Party label for their new and virtually insignificant organization.

At the 1945 conference at Tiruchirapalli, the Dravida Kazagham adopted a constitution and took as its symbol a black flag with a red circle in the center, the black representing the mourning for the subjected Dravidian peoples, the red for the hope of Dravidasthan. The organization of the party was to be based on units in each village, taluq and district. The object of the DK was proclaimed to be the

[11] B. S. Baliga, *Tanjore District Handbook*, Government Press, Madras, 1957, p. 113.

[12] Devanandan, pp. 9-10.

[13] G. S. Seshadri, "The Dravida Kazagham in Madras," *Indian Affairs Record*, vol. 3, no. 1, February 1957.

[14] Baliga, p. 117.

[15] "Aims and Constitution of the Dravida Kazagham," *Our Aim*, Dravida Kazagham, Madras, 1950, cited in Harrison, p. 123.

achievement of a sovereign independent Dravidian republic, federal in nature and made up of four units corresponding to the linguistic divisions, each with residuary power and autonomy of internal administration.[16] It would be a "casteless society," an egalitarian Dravida Nadu to which the depressed and downtrodden could pledge allegiance. The party proclaimed its opposition to the British Raj, and Naicker called upon DK members to renounce all titles conferred by the British and to resign all offices connected with the National War Front.[17] This action greatly enhanced the prestige of the movement, on both provincial and national levels. The DK could no longer be considered a handmaid of the British, as had the Justice Party from its very inception.

In 1947, as the time approached for the transfer of power from the British Raj to an independent India, communal strife permeated the subcontinent. The decision for a separate Muslim state of Pakistan had spread bitterness and dissatisfaction in both Muslim and Hindu society, and within Hindu society itself the divisive tendencies of regional nationalism were asserting themselves to the detriment of Indian unity. On the eve of independence, Naicker called upon the Dravidian peoples of South India "to guard against a transfer of power from the British to the Aryans."[18] Fearing Brahmin dominance under Aryan "imperialism," Naicker called for the formation of Dravidasthan, enjoining his followers to sign a pledge of support for complete separation from the Indian Union.

In the Dravida Kazagham, as in the Self-Respect Movement, one of Naicker's basic objectives was to remove all "superstitious belief" based upon religion or tradition. In speaking of the concept of the soul, the Periyar declared that it "is a piece of protective false imagination to protect another false imaginary religion. Just as more lies are needed to substantiate a falsehood, a horde of falsehoods like Soul, Heaven, Hell, Rebirth, Fate, Destiny have been coined to sustain the false philosophy of Hinduism. Man is born, bred, functions according to his body structure and dies. After his death his body is destroyed. This is what we see of man personally and what is the philosophical explanation for the rest except to call them as a matter of guess, fiction, bluff and superstition."[19]

---

[16] T. S. Thiruvengadam, *The Dravidian Movement: a Retrospect*, n.n., Madras, 1955.

[17] J. R. Chandran and M. M. Thomas, *Political Outlook in India Today*, Committee for Literature on Social Concerns, Bangalore, 1956, p. 122.

[18] *The Hindu*, February 11, 1946.

[19] E. V. Ramaswamy Naicker, *Philosophy*, Karnatak Dravidian Association Publications, Bangalore, 1959, p. 24.

Reinforcing the materialist philosophy, no member of the DK was allowed to wear the sectarian marks of faith on his forehead. Members were urged to boycott the use of Brahmin priests in ceremonies. Naicker campaigned vigorously for widow remarriage and inter-caste marriage. The "reform" marriage rites of the DK, dispensing with the priest and Hindu ritual, gained relatively wide acceptance among the non-Brahmins of Tamilnad. The couple to be married is seated and one of the guests, without consideration of caste, is selected to preside over the function. To seal the ties of marriage, he requests the couple to exchange garlands, and in some cases, the man ties a *tali*, a simple gold wedding symbol, around the bride's neck.[20]

The ceremonies and rites of passage at which Brahmins officiated were despised by the Dravida Kazagham, and the Hindu religion was denounced as an opiate by which the Brahmins had dulled the masses so that they might be controlled. Both God and religion, according to Naicker, are but fictions designed to guide man in the life contrary to nature, the life in civil society. "So God and religion are not only essential for the preservation of rich, poor, high caste, divinity, etc., but also to function effectively the machinery of King, law and punishment. If people can be induced to have belief in God and Religion the former can bind them where the King fails while the latter may be used in place of law whenever an occasion demands [sic]."[21]

Atheism became virtually a cult among Kazagham members. "A Hindu in the present concept may be a Dravidian, but a Dravidian in the real sense of the term cannot and shall not be a Hindu."[22] Kazagham members were urged to destroy the images of sacred Hindu deities such as Rama and Ganesa, and the Sanskrit epics were distorted to serve the political ends of the Dravida Kazagham. The most conspicuous perversion was that of the Ramayana. In the Sanskrit version, the hero, Rama, is pitted against the villainous king of Ceylon, Ravana. Naicker transposes the hero and villain roles, however, and concludes that "Rama and Sita are despicable characters,

---

[20] *Sunday Times*, Madras, September 25, 1960. Lloyd Rudolph reports that "in 1953, such a marriage, contracted under the auspices of the *Purchit Maruppu Sangham* or Anti-Brahminical Priest Association, was declared illegal by the Madras High Court. Subsequently the Special Marriages Act validated such marriages among others if the participants registered according to the provisions of the Act." "Urban Life and Populist Radicalism: Dravidian Politics in Madras," *Journal of Asian Studies*, 1961, vol. 20, p. 289.

[21] Naicker, *Philosophy*, p. 15.

[22] A. S. Venu, *Dravidasthan*, Kalai Menram, Madras, 1954, p. 13, cited in Harrison, p. 127.

not worthy of imitation or admiration even by the lowest of the fourth-rate humans." Ravana, on the other hand, is depicted as a Dravidian of "excellent character." In the preface to Naicker's "True Reading" of the Ramayana, he states that "the veneration of the story any longer in Tamil Nad is injurious and ignominious to the self-respect of the community and of the country."[23] Naicker called for the eradication of all Aryan cultural influences. "As after the achievement of so-called independence the statues of whites and their names to the places were removed and Indian names were given to them instead, the Aryan Gods and significance (sic) that defile the respect and the feelings of Tamils should be razed out. Every Tamilian in whose veins the pure Dravidian blood runs should deem it his duty to fulfill this vow."[24]

The Ramayana and other plays were staged by DK dramatic groups throughout Tamilnad in order to attract popular support to the movement for Dravidasthan. The presentation of plays, however, was only one part of the "cultural offensive." It was very much a part of a larger Tamil renaissance which witnessed the revival of literary classics, a movement in "new writing," and a de-Sanskritization of the Tamil language. Out of the resurgence of literary effort came a concern for the purity of Tamil. It was estimated that in 1900, nearly 50 per cent of the words in written Tamil were influenced by Sanskrit. Fifty years later, its influence had been reduced to only 20 per cent.[25] While many prominent Tamil scholars and leaders of the cultural renaissance had no connection with the Dravida Kazagham, the party nevertheless exerted a tremendous influence over the flowering of Tamil literature in the twentieth century. Indeed, it was through its literary efforts that the DK found support in non-Brahmin academic centers, such as Annamalai University; its vice chancellor, Dr. S. G. Manavala Ramanujan, was an ardent supporter of Naicker.[26]

Young people, attracted to the Kazagham by powerful speakers and forceful writers, were encouraged to contribute to the cultural growth of Tamilnad. The glories of the Tamil kingdoms were hailed as peaks in the cultural history of India, and the antiquity of Dravidian civilization was pushed further back into the past with the aid of English scholars such as Robert Caldwell. The culture of the ancient Aryans was belittled as barbarian in comparison to the splendor and richness

[23] E. V. Ramaswamy Naicker, *The Ramayana: a True Reading*, Rationalist Publications, Madras, 1959, pp. iii-iv.
[24] *Ibid.*, p. iv.
[25] Interview with A. C. Chettiar, Professor of Tamil, University of Madras, October 13, 1960.
[26] Devanandan, pp. 11-12. *The Hindu*, September 20, 1960.

of Dravidian tradition and Tamil culture. The past was resurrected and given a reality on very little evidence.

The Dravida Kazagham, even though its attacks upon Puranic religion aimed at the heart of the tradition of Brahmin and non-Brahmin alike, was instrumental in bringing the people of Tamilnad to an awareness of themselves as a community. DK organizational units, in every district and taluq in Madras, brought the message of Tamil nationality to the masses. Through plays presented in even the most isolated villages, through voluminous literature and inflammatory speeches, the movement was able to create a heightened self-consciousness of Tamil group identity. In so doing, it served to preserve the community and at the same time actually brought it into being as a nationality. The organization served as a means for social mobility on the part of individual leaders, both in the community and in the larger political arena, but the most important development was that the Dravidian movement encouraged the community to raise its status as a whole through political activity.

PARTY REVOLT AND THE DMK

The Dravida Kazagham, in spite of its appeals to the masses, retained a quasi-military organization and a basically elite character, but a challenge to the virtually deified position of Naicker arose within the ranks of the party to form a "progressive" wing. This wing, upholding the principles of democratic party organization, was continually frustrated by Naicker's intransigence, and broke with the DK in 1949 to form a separate party, the Dravida Munnetra Kazagham. Through its elaborate organization, its broadened financial support, and its conferences and campaigns, the new party sought mass membership as the base for political power.

The vitality of the Dravida Kazagham had attracted many outstanding young men, of whom one of the most talented was C. N. Annadurai. Born in Conjeevaram in 1908, he took an M.A. degree in economics from Pachiappa College in Madras, but abandoned further studies in favor of a career in journalism. Joining the Justice Party in 1935, Annadurai became an ardent supporter of the anti-Hindi movement and participated in Naicker's 1938 campaign. Upon the formation of the Dravida Kazagham in 1944. Annadurai became one of Naicker's chief lieutenants.[27]

At the time of partition, Naicker tried to secure the help of Jinnah, so that Dravidasthan might be formed simultaneously with Pakistan.

27 Devanandan, pp. 10-11.

Jinnah refused assistance, and the British ignored the Dravidian agitations. Outraged at the British "betrayal" of the Dravidian peoples in turning the bureaucracy over to the Brahmin oligarchy, Naicker boycotted the independence day celebrations.[28] He refused to honor the national flag, just as he later refused to recognize the Indian Constitution, seeing it only as a tool of Brahmin tyranny.

Annadurai, however, saw national independence as the accomplishment of all India, not merely the Aryan North. Naicker refused to listen, just as he ignored Annadurai's repeated demands for democratization of leadership within the party. Naicker had no faith in democracy, either in the organization or in the Dravidasthan he visualized; consequently, in the 1948 DK conference, Annadurai led a walkout in protest against Naicker's political autocracy. Naicker utilized the conference to condemn the "renegades," but, alarmed at the possibility of a split, he attempted a compromise by appointing Annadurai as president of a conference held later that same year. He refused, however, to give in to Annadurai's demands for a democratic party organization.[29]

Naicker's popularity suffered a disastrous blow in 1949, when, at the age of seventy-two, he married a twenty-eight-year-old girl who had been an active member of the party. He announced that he had no confidence in his lieutenants, and so he was marrying a girl in whom he had full trust, who would lead the party after his death.[30] On the pretext that the marriage was contrary to the avowed social objectives of the Kazagham, which included the elimination of the practice of unequal marriage, Annadurai seceded from the party to form the Dravida Munnetra Kazagham, the Dravidian Progressive Federation.[31] The original leaders of the DMK included E. V. K. Sampath, who, as he was Naicker's nephew, abandoned a considerable inheritance by leaving the DK.

In reaction to the structure of the DK, Annadurai sought to weld the DMK into an effective mass political organization. The party constitution establishes the basic structural unit as the ward committee in the cities and the village committee in rural areas, each requiring a minimum of twenty-five members. Starting with a handful in the year of the party's formation, these branches had grown to an estimated 3,000 by 1960. Above these units lay the taluq and district committees and the Tamilnad general council.[32] The principal

[28] *Ibid.*, p. 15.
[29] Interview with E. V. K. Sampath, New Delhi, December 10, 1960.
[30] *Ibid.*   [31] Harrison, p. 123.
[32] Interview with E. V. K. Sampath, Madras, October 20, 1960.

source of party funds is a 50 naya paisa membership fee (about 10 cents) for two years, and admission charges for district and special conferences held during the year. The charges cover a wide range and are scaled according to the member's ability to pay.[33]

The conferences often attract as many as 200,000 people, drawn by the spellbinding oratory of Annadurai and by the popular Tamil film stars who glamorize the party functions. Annadurai, as well as other members of the party, is intimately connected with the film industry in Madras as a writer, director and producer, and many of the films produced are open propaganda. Many film artists have been drawn into the movement through their desire to increase their own popularity by association with the DMK. Others, however, such as Shivaji Ganesan, found that, at the height of fame, association with the DMK became a serious liability.

The DMK membership has grown yearly at accelerating rates, to the estimated 175,000 in 1960.[34] Annadurai, though a member of the upper Mudaliar caste, oriented his movement toward the urban lower classes, the proletariat, lower middle classes and students. He appealed, not so much to the prosperous non-Brahmin communities of his own caste or to the Vellala landowners or industrialists who had been the foundation of Naicker's power, but rather to the masses, the lower castes of the Nadar, Maravar and Adi-Dravida untouchables.[35] The party constituency, largely in the age range of twenty to forty, is drawn mainly from the middle classes, especially workers, petty officials, small traders, urban unemployed, and students, while the leadership is concentrated primarily among writers and journalists who utilize communications media as the catapult to political power. While DMK support has been virtually limited to urban centers and immediately adjacent areas, it has, with expanding communication, begun to make inroads into the villages of interior and southern Madras.

The leadership of the DMK manipulated the non-rational symbols of the community in such a way as to expand the base of membership and to win increasing support at the polls. Using the symbols of common culture within Tamilnad, harking back to the glories of the Dravidian past, and dwelling upon the social oppression suffered by the non-Brahmin at the hand of the Brahmin, the Bania and the Aryan North, the party attempted to mold the masses into a self-

33 *Ibid.* Phillips Talbot, "Raising a Cry for Secession," *India*, Report PT-9-'57, American Universities Field Staff, New York, 1957, p. 8.
34 *Sunday Times*, September 18, 1960.
35 Harrison, p. 123.

conscious community, where before there had been only the most narrowly-defined primary associations. Through its broadly-based and hierarchically structured organization, its series of anti-Hindi agitations, its propaganda and political campaigns, the DMK has sought power through the exploitation of the symbolic paraphernalia of language and nationality. The party, however, backed quietly away from the attacks Naicker leveled at the Hindu religion; although its leaders had been schooled in the DK's militant atheism, their anti-religious fervor gave way to the more secular calculations of electoral politics.

In the first general elections of 1951-1952, the Congress Party in Madras captured 133 of the 190 seats in the legislative assembly. Neither the Dravida Kazagham nor the Dravida Munnetra Kazagham contested the elections. The DMK supported independent candidates and two opposition parties, the Tamilnad Toilers' Party and the Commonweal Party, both of which represented the Vanniyar caste, a lower agricultural caste concentrated in northern Madras. While supporting opposition candidates to Congress, Annadurai announced that the DMK was "genuinely communist" in its ideals, but that it could not support Communist candidates until the CPI signed a pledge of support for Dravidasthan.[36] Naicker's DK, on the other hand, extended support to the CPI on the basis that "my enemy's enemy is my friend," but the alliance was short-lived. Naicker accused the CPI of treachery. "The Communists have their office at a foreign place, Bombay or Delhi, and they are just as interested in exploiting our country as any of the other foreign-controlled parties. Besides, most of the Communist leaders are Brahmins."[37]

Though the elections yielded no great victories for the Dravidian movement, they marked the beginning of a series of separate agitations by both the DK and the DMK against "northern imperialism." The imposition of Hindi was opposed with mass picketing and the burning of Hindi books. The Five Year Plans were denounced for discrimination against the South. The DK extended its attacks to include such instruments and symbols of "Aryan oppression" as the Indian Constitution, the national flag, pictures of Gandhi, and sacred Hindu relics and images. These demonstrations were often accompanied by violence directed against the Brahmin community, and numerous outrages resulted in the jailing of DK members. Nehru decried these agitations as indicative of the party's "tribal mentality."[38]

The DMK demonstrations were more moderate than those of

[36] Interview with E. V. K. Sampath, New Delhi, December 10, 1960.
[37] Quoted in Harrison, pp. 185-186.
[38] Chandran and Thomas, pp. 123-124.

Naicker's storm troopers. DMK agitation began with the Three Fronts Campaign of 1953. The first front was organized to register the protest of the Dravidian people against the increasing economic oppression of the North. The front was symbolically focused upon the village of Kallakudi in Tiruchirapalli district, where Dalmia, a North Indian industrialist, had established a cement factory and had persuaded authorities to rename it "Dalmiapuram." The DMK proposed to restore the original name to the village. The second front was directed against the "Delhi Sultanate": to demonstrate Dravidian national honor, all trains were to be stopped from dawn to dusk on the 15th of July. The third front, and by far the most important, was directed against the proposed caste-based education policy of Chief Minister C. Rajagopalachari, which would require children to be schooled in the occupations of their parents. The chief minister's residence was to be picketed in protest.[39]

Annadurai, Sampath, Natarajan, Nedunchezhian and Mathislagan —the DMK's "big five"—were jailed as a preventive measure, but on the appointed day the Three Fronts offensive was made. In Kallakudi and Tuticorin the police opened fire, killing six youths, and altogether more than 6,000 demonstrators were arrested during the day's agitation.[40]

The significance of the campaign lies not so much in the number arrested as in its effect upon C. R.'s Congress ministry. His educational scheme to perpetuate duty according to caste (*varnashrama dharma*) was opposed not only by the DMK, but also by large numbers of Congressmen. Taking advantage of the bitter agitation against the bill and the widespread support for the campaign, these Congressmen, rather than exploring the possibilities for compromise in persuading C. R. to drop the unpopular measure, took the opportunity to get rid of him.[41]

The president of the Tamilnad Congress Committee, K. Kamaraj Nadar—long termed the "king-maker"—took over the reins of power from Rajagopalachari. An astute politician of lower caste, Kamaraj immediately began to consolidate his position as chief minister. Though only forty-nine years of age, he was already a heroic figure, "a *sannyasi* in white clothes." A member of the Congress since 1920, he embodies Gandhian self-sacrifice—as a bachelor, in his constructive work for the party, and in his six jail sentences, with a total imprisonment of more than 3,000 days.[42] Unlike C. R. and much of the

39 *Sunday Times*, July 17, 1960.   40 *Ibid.*
41 V. P. Raman, "Politics in Madras," *Quest*, December 1957-January 1958, p. 16.
42 *The Hindu*, March 15, 1962.

Brahmin leadership in the Madras Congress Party, Kamaraj is a man of the people. He speaks only Tamil and his powerful political machine is rooted in traditional loyalties and primordial identifications. Indeed Kamaraj represents, perhaps more clearly than anyone in India, the growing trend in state leadership toward a regionalization and parochialization of politics. Kamaraj is the political "broker" who is able to operate effectively at the local level, within the structures of village factionalism, caste and communal identification, and at the same time can function within the essentially modern political context of parliamentary democracy.

Kamaraj, of low caste and humble peasant origins, shrewdly realized that if the Congress Party in Tamilnad was to retain power, it would have to accommodate traditional loyalties. Aware of the growing sense of nationality and "Dravidianism" among the people of the Tamil country, Kamaraj appealed to Tamil patriotism, and included no Brahmins in the cabinet. Soon after he came to power he had to face a by-election, and made a bid for the support of Ramaswamy Naicker.[43] The DK leader, who had carried on bitter anti-Hindi campaigns in 1952 and 1953 against the Congress government, extended his full support to the new ministry and, out of deference to Kamaraj, declared that no agitations would be staged in 1954.

In 1955, however, in response to the central government's moves toward the establishment of Hindi as the national language, Naicker appealed to members of the DK to burn the national flag. Although Naicker emphasized that the action was not to weaken Kamaraj, the chief minister condemned the proposed agitation and succeeded in persuading the aged Periyar to abandon the flag-burning.[44] The criticism had hardly died down when Naicker started on another campaign, this time against the Constitution, which he called "illegal": it had been framed before the introduction of the adult franchise and the people of Tamilnad had had no voice in it.[45] This campaign was tabled in favor of another, however, the aim of which was to burn pictures of Rama, who symbolized Sanskritic Brahmin domination over the peoples of Tamilnad.[46] At this point the government took action, and placed Naicker, together with 1,000 DK agitators, under preventive detention.[47]

In the period that followed, Naicker continued his yearly campaigns

---

[43] Raman, p. 17.
[44] *The Hindu*, July 13, 22, 24, 28 and 30, 1955; August 13, 1955.
[45] *Ibid.*, July 31, 1955.   [46] *Ibid.*, August 1, 1956.
[47] *Ibid.*, August 2, 1956.

against Northern "imperialism" and Brahmin domination, still maintaining his support for the Congress ministry of Kamaraj Nadar. In 1957, he began a series of vicious speeches directed against the Brahmin community, reportedly inviting his followers to assault and kill Brahmins and to set fire to *agraharams* (Brahmin localities). Upon his arrest, Naicker stated, "In my 40 years of public life, I have not done the slightest injury to anyone. I want to get things done in a peaceful way without resorting to violence. . . . Probably it is my fault in not having done anything of that kind that makes Brahmins do all kinds of false and mischievous propaganda."[48]

During the abortive campaigns which followed the 1951-1952 elections, it became increasingly evident that the Dravida Kazagham was moving away from its advocacy of a South Indian Dravidian state to that of a purely Tamil-speaking state of Tamilnad. Fearing submersion of the Tamils in the Dravidian whole, Naicker opposed the formation of a South Indian state, warning that Dakshina Pradesh would be "a life and death matter for Tamilians."[49] With the reorganization of states in 1956, Naicker abandoned his goal of Dravidasthan.

DRAVIDIAN ACCOMMODATION WITH HINDUISM

When Ramaswamy Naicker supported Kamaraj's Congress ministry, the Dravida Munnetra Kazagham soon became the vanguard of the Dravidian movement. In the years immediately following the split in the Kazagham, the two parties, the DK and the DMK, had often demonstrated striking similarity in aims and action, but in spite of a unity of purpose—the creation of Dravidasthan—major differences emerged. The formation of the Kamaraj government in 1954 was the turning point for both parties and the beginning of a major transition

[48] *Hindu Weekly Review*, November 11, 1957. The "facts" of Naicker's speech have never been properly documented, but a DK proverb, chalked on walls throughout Tamilnad at that time, proclaimed: "When you meet a Brahmin and a snake, kill the Brahmin first." Lloyd Rudolph, in his "Urban Life and Populist Radicalism: Dravidian Politics in Madras," pp. 286-287, reports that at a public meeting in March 1957 Naicker claimed that Brahmin C. Rajagopalachari resigned his chief ministership because of his "threat of violent direct action using the knife." *Indian Express*, March 5, 1957. When a DK member actually tried to carry out Naicker's injunction three years later, the leader completely repudiated the idea. *Link*, April 24, 1960. After the incident, Naicker expressed his abhorrence of violence as a means of settling political differences, and Annadurai, leader of the DMK, condemned the attempt with the "utmost disgust." Rajagopalachari, as leader of the new Swatantra Party, paid tribute to Naicker on his eighty-second birthday. *Link*, October 30, 1960. "Such," Rudolph suggests, "are the miracles wrought by the strength of the Dravidian appeal in Madras politics."
[49] *The Hindu*, February 2, 1956.

within the Dravidian movement. The DK abandoned its aim of a Dravidian state in favor of Tamilnad and pledged its support to a Congress non-Brahmin chief minister. The new government, while it did not abandon the secular unity of the Indian Constitution, took on a new regional image of Tamil nationalism. By undercutting the growing power of the Dravidian appeal through a process of accommodation, and by revitalizing the stagnating party organization, Kamaraj had given the Congress in Madras a new face.

The DMK, having failed to contest the 1951-1952 elections, sought access to the political system outside the democratic framework through mass demonstrations and agitation. While the party used these campaigns as a means of augmenting its organizational strength and of winning mass support, agitation was also directed toward influencing public policy, as in its campaign against the imposition of Hindi on the South. The increasingly Tamilian character of the Congress ministry of Kamaraj, however, robbed the DMK of its claim to represent Tamil nationalism in Madras politics. Fighting for survival, the DMK, while still waving the symbolic banner of Dravidasthan, gradually began to formulate demands representing a specificity of interest, together with a basic acceptance of constitutional procedures. Extra-democratic agitations on the part of the DMK became a part of the larger aspect of lobbying and parliamentary participation. Annadurai denounced the DK's flag-burnings and its desecration of sacred images.

With the approach of the 1957 elections, the DMK became increasingly concerned with basic economic issues and the plight of the industrially deprived South. The fundamental problem for the party, however, was the "Brahmin-Bania" domination of business and industry in Madras. "Almost all banks in the South are controlled by Marwari . . . northern classes," declared a prominent leader of the DMK. "They are slowly buying up the textile industries and more than 90 per cent of export-import trade is in their hands. The government plants under the plans have even been put in the hands of North Indians. Except for textiles, every economic activity is dominated by Northern elements, even the big plantations which were formerly in the hands of Europeans."[50]

The DMK charged that the Marwaris were "the power behind the throne" in New Delhi and that they wanted to keep the South as their own private economic reserve. They attacked the Five Year Plans as an instrument of Bania tyranny, a scheme to industrialize

[50] Interview with E. V. K. Sampath, Madras, October 20, 1960.

the North while leaving the South open to exploitation by Marwari financiers. "The benighted South has simply passed from British hands to still worse Marwari tyranny."[51]

As the Marwari came to be blamed for almost all the woes of the Dravidian people, the DMK desisted from attack upon the Brahmin community, condemning instead the caste mentality of "Brahminism." The DMK leader, Sampath, declared: "It cannot be disputed that India has been for centuries a hotbed of superstition and evil social practices in the name of religion. . . . (But) sometimes the Brahmin and the Brahminism got confused. Many had fallen victims to the temptation that with the extermination of the Brahmin caste, the evil influences of Brahminism, the base of casteism and Hindu superstition would be got rid of, unaware of the fact that there are many Brahmins who have freed themselves from the bad influences of Brahminism and there are many more non-Brahmins who are completely under the spell of Brahminism."[52]

Anti-Brahminism had, nevertheless, left its social scars upon the Brahmin community. The Brahmins of Tamilnad increasingly came to feel discriminated against, if not persecuted. With reservation of seats for "backward" communities in government and universities, the Brahmin was often denied the position commensurate with his ability and training. The development within the community of new forms of devotional Hinduism was in part a defensive response to this somewhat hostile environment. Milton Singer, in describing the devotional movement of the Radha-Krishna *bhajans* of Madras City, suggests that "the Dravidian movement for linguistic regionalism with its championing of Tamil against Sanskrit, Telugu, Hindi, and other Indian languages; of non-Brahmins against Brahmins; and of 'rationalism' against 'superstition,' drives the orthodox Hindu, and particularly the Smarta Brahmin, to a defense of his religion, his culture, and his caste."[53]

The defense of Hindu religion, however, necessitated new patterns of inter-caste association. According to Singer: "No doubt some of these interfaith activities are a common defensive measure against the trend of increasingly secular legislation and, particularly in Madras State, against the outspoken and sometimes violent anti-Brahmin, anti-Hindu attacks sponsored by two regional political parties, the Dravidian Federation and the Dravidian Progressive

[51] A. S. Venu, *Dravidasthan*, p. 34, cited in Harrison, p. 131.
[52] *Sunday Times*, September 25, 1960.
[53] Milton Singer, "The Radha-Krishna *Bhajans* of Madras City," *History of Religions*, 1963, vol. 2, p. 226.

Federation. It is the Smarta Brahmins, however, who have been the first to see these trends as a danger to Hinduism and to respond by joining and organizing movements that cross sect, and even caste, lines."[54] Indeed, the development of this kind of devotional Hinduism has tended to make caste irrelevant, at least in this limited context. "Caste differences are minimized by inviting non-Brahmins to *bhajans,* by feeding the poor and even untouchables on the occasion of the marriage *bhajans,* and by the salutations and prostrations of the devotees to one another irrespective of caste. Many participants say that 'there is no caste in the world of devotion' and that they 'forget their caste differences in the *bhajan.*' "[55]

In the 1956 Tiruchi Conference, the DMK decided to contest the forthcoming elections and issued a manifesto embodying a socialist image. The party called for the abolition of Northern domination over the South and for the fullest exploitation of natural resources in Madras. Dravidasthan, the symbol of Tamil nationalist aspiration, was at the most a side issue, for the manifesto implicitly accepted the existing constitutional order.

The final results of the election brought the Congress, supported by the Dravida Kazagham, a resounding victory, but the DMK had established itself as the second most powerful party in Madras, wining fifteen seats in the assembly and 14.6 per cent of the vote. In addition, the DMK won two Lok Sabha seats, one going to Sampath. DMK support, however, was basically limited to the urban areas of northern Madras state. Its seats were won only in Madras City and in North and South Arcot, areas with a comparatively high degree of communications exposure. The DMK made no inroads into the rural-based stronghold of the Congress in the districts of central and southern Madras, including Tanjore district, the locus of DK strength.

After its successes in the general elections, the DMK, aware of its urban strength, planned a major offensive to capture control of the Madras city corporation, and in the municipal elections held in the spring of 1959 the party made a dramatic show of power which shook Congress complacency. In electoral alliance with the Communist Party, the DMK won control of three of the five largest city governments in Madras state.

The DMK's electoral success, however, was clouded by growing dissatisfaction with party leadership on the part of some elements within the movement. Sampath denounced Annadurai as a "dictator"

[54] *Ibid.,* p. 210. [55] *Ibid.,* p. 212.

in the style of Naicker. In response to Annadurai's negotiations with the DMK's former arch enemy, C. Rajagopalachari, for the formation of an electoral alliance between the DMK and the newly-formed Swatantra Party, Sampath bolted the party to form the Tamil Nationalist Party, taking the left wing of the DMK with him. In spite of Sampath's militancy, however, all but the most dedicated stalwarts slipped quietly back into the ranks of the DMK. The promise of political office held the aspiring candidate in the grip of the party, and the DMK's increasing concern with specific economic demands was far too attractive to be abandoned by the party's past supporters. The strength of the DMK remained such that all the opposition parties in Madras sought some sort of electoral arrangement with it, in order to benefit by association with the Dravidian movement.

The 1962 DMK election manifesto, drafted by Annadurai, declared that its long-range goal was the creation of a Dravidian "Socialist" Federation, but that in the meantime the DMK would place an immediate program before the people. The manifesto reflected, as in 1957, an increased concern with economic issues—and, even though the demands were far from realistic, it played a significant part in the orientation of the DMK's campaign. The fact that the manifesto received elaborate consideration testifies to the growing concern for a broader social base for the party. Dravidasthan, as an electoral issue, was shelved in favor of a concerntration on the problem of rising prices in Madras—a bread-and-butter question of immediate concern to every voter.[56] The DMK never raised the Hindu religion as an issue, and curried favor with the Brahmins, rather than attacking them. Indeed, the DMK made a concerted attempt to win support from the Brahmin community. DMK membership lay open to Brahmins, and, although few joined the movement, one of the DMK leaders, V. P. Raman, is a Brahmin.

The thrust of the DMK's expanding social base, however, was directed at the areas of central and southern Madras state. Relying on the cinema as the most effective instrument of communication and the popularity of the film stars as its greatest drawing card, the DMK staged rallies throughout the state, emphasizing the issue of rising prices.

On the other side, Naicker became the self-appointed wheelhorse, and of the Congress campaign, and nominated Kamaraj as his heir-apparent. "I am old, I may not live very long. After I am gone Kamaraj

[56] *The Hindu*, February 4, 1962; February 6, 1962.

will safeguard the interests of the Tamils. He is my heir."[57] The eighty-five-year-old Periyar called on the people of Tamilnad to vote for all Congress candidates, be they donkeys or Brahmins. "Ultimately it is Kamaraj who counts—not others, candidates or even voters who are anyway unfit to judge what is right and good for them. Take my word, vote Congress and you will be well. If you don't the ingenious Rajaji riding the DMK horse, will trample you all without mercy!"[58]

In January 1962, Naicker called a conference of the DK to endorse the Kamaraj ministry. Abandoning his love of austerity, he sanctioned Rs. 5,000 for decorating the dais of the conference and provided food for over 2,000 delegates upon the payment of a modest charge. In a procession which included representatives of the Congress, the PSP, and the Tamil Nationalists, Naicker rode in the resplendent grandeur of a horse-drawn chariot, covered with garlands.[59]

During his vigorous speeches for Congress, Naicker eased the severity of his attacks upon Brahmins and his condemnations of Hinduism, but the criticism nonetheless aroused by the Periyar's campaign impelled Kamaraj to disclaim any formal association with the DK. "If any Congressmen have supported Mr. E. V. Ramaswamy Naicker, presented him with garland, etc., they have done so in their own individual capacity."[60] Kamaraj still, however, fully exploited the popularity of Naicker and identified himself with Tamil nationalist aspiration. In February, the chief minister introduced a bill changing the name of Madras to "Tamilnad" for inter-state communication, and he advocated that Madurai become the capital of Tamilnad. Harking back to the days of the Pandyan kings, he said that Madurai had "nurtured" Tamil language, culture, and political life.[61]

There was little question that the Congress Party would be returned to power with a substantial majority of seats, but the results of the 1962 elections revealed the emergence of the DMK as a force far more formidable than the Congress had ever anticipated. Capturing seven seats in the Lok Sabha and fifty seats in the legislative assembly, the DMK became the strongest opposition ever to challenge the Congress government in Madras. Yet, at the height of its power, the movement for Dravidasthan was virtually dead. It had been transformed, under the impact of social mobilization and accommoda-

[57] *Link*, May 28, 1961.
[58] *Ibid.*, November 26, 1961.
[59] *Ibid.*, January 14, 1962.
[60] *The Hindu*, February 19, 1962.
[61] *Ibid.*, August 18, 1961.

tion by the government, from a secessionist movement based on the glories of a resurrected past and a vague and impossible hope for the future, to a political party representing an increasing specificity of interests and a germinal acceptance of basic democratic electoral and parliamentary values and practices. Secularized by the aspirations for political office, the Dravidian movement had made its truce with Hinduism.

CHAPTER 11

THE CONCEPT OF CHANGE IN HINDU, SOCIALIST, AND NEO-GANDHIAN THOUGHT

JOAN V. BONDURANT AND MARGARET W. FISHER

RELIGION, PHILOSOPHY, AND POLITICS are closely interwoven in every area of high culture. The manner in which each complex pattern bears upon the others can perhaps best be understood through an inquiry into questions about social and political change. What does change mean in a given culture? This is, in large part, a question about the conceptual frame. Where lies the competition for men's allegiances as they are confronted with the rapid tempo of change characteristic of our day? This is, initially, a question about pre-disposition. The need to comprehend the underlying considerations expressed in ethic-principles and idea systems is the more compelling in India where philosophical patterns significantly different from those of the West have conditioned thought and belief over several millennia. We find here a unique interaction of theories of change. This interaction issues in forms of political leadership and political action which can be illuminated by a comparative inquiry addressed to concepts—and precepts—of change.

The ethical system of the Hindus was traditionally threefold and in each of its aspects the individual's duty was the central consideration. The most prominent code of Hindu duties binds the individual through a set of obligations consequent upon his birth within a given social group—obligations relative both to the group in question and to the successive stages in his own life.[1] There is also a code of specific duties, binding upon all individuals as members of a specific group in their ritual obligations toward all others as members of their particular groups.[2] The third type of duty enjoins the individual to seek self-perfection.[3] This is a duty of the individual in his tran-

Joan V. Bondurant and Margaret W. Fisher are lecturers in the department of political science and associate research political scientists at the Institute of International Studies, University of California, Berkeley.

[1] *Varnashrama dharma.*   [2] *Sadharana dharma.*

[3] *Cittasuddhi.* See the discussion by Sushil Kumar Maitra in his *Ethics of the Hindus*, Calcutta University Press, Calcutta, 1925.

scendental relation to the Ultimate. As compared with western systems of ethics, Hindu philosophy, for all its complexity and elaboration, is poorly developed in just that aspect where one individual is related to another without primary reference to the group, or to put it in other words, in that area where ethics goes beyond ritual and where value is defined in terms of the interaction of individuals. The strengthening of this poorly developed facet of Indian social philosophy was among Gandhi's most fundamental contributions. He generated an ethical concern in a manner which defined right action not in terms of withdrawal in pursuit of self-perfection, but in the individual's concern for and involvement with the welfare of all others, without regard to the ritual restrictions imposed by caste and creed. The Gandhian technique of action—so significant a part of the nationalist politics of India—was based upon an ethic-principle which, in turn, represented a shift in Indian thought, and at least in western eyes, an advance.

Gandhian innovations not only marked a new departure in Indian political thought, but the philosophy of action which underlay the national political movement embodies precepts which were fashioned in the course of dramatic change. Once the goal of political independence was achieved, the dynamic process was channeled in other directions. A new government, charged with tasks of development and committed to extensive change, deliberated on policy and process. Basic to the government's actions, as also to the efforts of the political opposition, are attitudes and assumptions which, whether given expression or allowed to remain implicit, condition and direct the political decisions of the day. What can be said of these underlying attitudes and assumptions? Indians, with reason, generally take pride in having been able to establish a secular, parliamentary democracy, but the major cultural milieu is necessarily provided by Hinduism, albeit a Hinduism influenced through historical contact with Islam and Christianity, and modified more recently by the Gandhian experience. With few exceptions,[4] competing ideologies have tended to present themselves in the outward garb of "socialism," although the inner content ranges from Hindu nationalism through Congress empiricism to the several non-Marxist and Marxist variants. Of par-

---

[4] The Swatantra Party, and to some extent the Jana Sangh as well, displayed opposition to "socialism" in manifestoes issued in conjunction with the 1962 elections. Both parties, however, went on record in favor of state planning and advocated state ownership of heavy industry, railroads, and other service industries. See S. L. Poplai, ed., *1962 General Elections in India*, Allied Publishers Private Limited, New Delhi, 1962, pp. 51-66, 130-168.

ticular pertinence to our analysis is an indigenous form of socialism, the neo-Gandhian philosophy called Sarvodaya.[5]

To treat of Hinduism, socialism, and Sarvodaya (neo-Gandhism) in so brief a compass requires the telescoping of extended philosophies and a rigorous selectivity in the abstracting of concepts. If, however, we boldly relate our inquiry to an elucidation of problems besetting a representative government attempting to modernize a complex, largely traditional society possessing a high culture, there can perhaps be no more promising and certainly no more direct approach than to examine the competing theories of change which ineluctably condition political action. For the course and culmination of development, the progressive or regressive potential, the determined regularities or indeterminate essentials—these and other components which enter into propositions about the direction, quality, capacity, and instruments of change condition not only thought about the individual's role and purpose in his universe, but also those considerations which issue in social arrangements and the instruments of influence.

Delimitation of the scope of the discussion does not of itself, admittedly, remove the pitfalls inherent in dealing with doctrines as all-embracing as the religious and philosophical traditions of the Hindus, as unsystematized as the social philosophy of Sarvodaya, as amorphous as non-Marxian socialism, and as controversial as Marxian socialism. Nevertheless, the underlying assumptions about change can be brought together in a way which, although partial, can still be said to be representative. With Hinduism it is necessary to speak of cosmology, but we shall see how assumptions drawn from their cosmological context affect the Indian view of social change.

Directly related to assumptions about change, and in some respects more accessible to analysis, are the several approaches to the relationship of ends and means. Each of the philosophies considered has a different view of this relationship. The manner in which each understands the ends-means nexus conditions political forms and styles, and bears directly upon the respective quality and role of acceptable leadership.

The accompanying chart presents, in outline, major concepts relating to change: its course through time, its objective, its trend, and process. The discussion which follows compares the Hindu, Marxist, Socialist, and Neo-Gandhian approaches to the problem of change

[5] For further discussion of Sarvodaya and the Congress Party's "socialist pattern," see Margaret W. Fisher and Joan V. Bondurant, *Indian Approaches to a Socialist Society*, Indian Press Digests Monograph Series, number 2, University of California, Berkeley, 1956.

and contrasts the manner in which developmental assumptions condition these four patterns of thought.

THE COURSE OF CHANGE THROUGH TIME

All orthodox schools of Hindu philosophy are in general agreement about the cyclical course of change. The universe is viewed as passing through cycles, each cycle consisting successively of perfection, decline, deterioration, and dissolution. Following the dissolution of a world-cycle is a period of quiescence, after which a new cycle—precisely like the earlier one—is created, only to degenerate, in its turn, to the point of dissolution. The concept is one of a cycle of cycles, without beginning or end. The process of change is similar in all cycles, and man has no capacity to affect it; he can only escape it. For the human soul is reborn endlessly in successive bodies until it wins release from the incessant round of rebirth. The discovery and practice of the means for liberation is the goal of all orthodox Hindu religious and philosophic systems.[6]

Modern theories of social change in the West have been preponderantly unilinear in direction. The comparative (historical) method which dominated social thought in the nineteenth century aimed at the recovery of change through time, and posited a series of stages through which every society necessarily passed. Marx's departures differed in objective and in the determinants of process: having adopted the method of his day, he claimed to have found that the determining elements lay in modes of production. But for Marx, as with the dominating nineteenth-century theories of change, civilization progresses through stages towards a specified end, with no suggestion of return or of reversal.

Implicit in democratic socialist thought is a progressive, unilinear trend. Freedom from historical determinism in the several non-Marxian theories of socialism which developed in the West, and in socialist thought as it has been adapted in India has, however, precluded any commitment to a given direction, or course of change through time.

The contemporary movement carrying the name Sarvodaya[7] reflects

[6] The heterodox Carvaka materialist school is an obvious exception, of mainly historical interest. See Surendranath Das Gupta, *A History of Indian Philosophy*, vol. 3, Cambridge University Press, Cambridge, 1940, pp. 512-550. For a discussion of fundamental points of agreement common to all orthodox Hindu philosophic systems, see *ibid.*, vol. 1, 1922, pp. 71-77.

[7] The word "Sarvodaya" (literally, "uplift of all") was coined by Gandhi and given as the title to his translation into Gujarati of John Ruskin's *Unto This Last*.

CONCEPTS OF CHANGE: HINDU, SOCIALIST, AND NEO-GANDHIAN

| | HINDUISM | SOCIALISM | | SARVODAYA |
		MARXIST	DEMOCRATIC	
Course of Change through Time	*Cosmological:* Cyclical Deterministic	Unilinear Deterministic	*Historical:* Non-deterministic	*Cosmological:* Modified Cyclical Non-deterministic *Personal:* Non-deterministic
Objective of Change	Individual perfection	Societal perfection = communism	Societal welfare (rising aspirations, receding goals)	Individual perfection within societal context
Trend of Change	*Cosmological:* Repetitive *Personal:* Erratically progressive	Progressive Inevitable	Progressive	(Unformulated)
Process of Change	*Cosmological:* Devolutionary *Personal:* Retributive	Evolutionary (with economic and social determinants) Revolutionary (to consummate change)	Environmentalist (through economic and social institutions)	(Unformulated)

principles which were basic to Gandhi's contribution, but in some aspects departs from Gandhian thought. Sarvodaya is free from historical determinism, and again, as in non-Marxian socialism, a limited linear progression is suggested.

Propositions relating to the course of change through time are clearly stated in the several philosophies of Hinduism. Indian Marxists, to the extent that they remain attached to Hinduism, are confronted with a conflict between the unilinear concept upon which Marxist theory proceeds, and the cyclical pattern presented in Hindu cosmology. When the further questions are raised about the respective objectives and qualities of change, the conflict becomes more serious in that it then bears directly upon the effecting of social and political change.

Neither the democratic socialist nor the Sarvodayite is directly in conflict with the grand design of Hindu tradition. The conflict begins to arise at the point where the objective of change is concerned.

THE OBJECTIVE OF CHANGE

In Hinduism the great space-time cycles provide the backdrop for the multitude of individual souls who continue to take on successive life forms until they achieve liberation—*moksha*. In this philosophy the objective of each human being is to strive towards a transcendent state of union with the Absolute. From one point of view this transcendence is to be achieved by conscious self-denying efforts to liberate the Self from its ties to worldly desires and actions, and from another, to be affirmed by consciously engaging the self in a pursuit of true knowledge to the point of full awareness of an identity between the Self and the Absolute which had always existed and remained only to be realized. The objective for the individual is autological[8]—the knowledge and mastery of self, and the ultimate realization that, as the *Gita* states it:

[8] Coomaraswamy comments on the quality of Brahmanical autology, that it is "no more pessimistic than optimistic, but only more authoritative than any other science of which the truth does not depend on our wishes. It is no more pessimistic to recognize that whatever is alien to Self is a distress, than it is optimistic to recognize that where there is no 'other' there is literally nothing to be feared. That our Outer Man is 'another' appears in the expression 'I cannot trust myself.' What has been called the 'natural optimism' of the Upanishads is their affirmation that our consciousness of being, although invalid as an awareness of being So-and-so, is valid absolutely, and their doctrine that the Gnosis of the Immanent Deity, our Inner Man can be realized *now*: 'That *art* thou!'" Ananda K. Coomaraswamy, *Hinduism and Buddhism*, Philosophical Library, New York, n.d., p. 18.

J. V. Bondurant and M. W. Fisher

I am the same to all beings,
  No one is hateful or dear to Me;
But those who revere Me with devotion,
  They are in Me and I too am in them.[9]

The objectives of change as expressed in the political philosophies of socialism are in contrast to the highly individualistic objective of Hinduism. In Marxist thought, the objective is communism: that stage of social development which is conceived to follow socialism and to be characterized by an economy of abundance, a disappearance of class warfare, and the elimination of repressive force as represented by the state. With the attainment of this ideal, the operative principle in society, as Marx envisaged it, was to be "from each according to his capacity, to each according to his need."

Non-Marxian socialism seeks to establish a form of political economy in which economic security is guaranteed to all, as a prerequisite to social fulfillment. Democratic socialism does not share with Marxist thought an historical determinism. Implicit in most schools, however, is a rising aspiration level. In contradistinction to Marxist subordination of present to distant goals, democratic socialism though longing for an ideal social arrangement displays little need to *define* ultimate goals in its preoccupation with mechanism, social manipulation, and evolutionary process for the attainment of interim objectives.

Sarvodaya shares with socialist thought the ideal of social fulfillment, but economic prosperity has, at most, no more than secondary value. Sarvodaya does seek the establishment of minimal economic satisfactions; for ultimate goals or fundamental objectives, however, fulfillment is spiritual, and in this emphasis, it shares much with Hinduism. Where Sarvodaya differs from the classical statement of Hinduism, it constitutes a social philosophy for which the ideal is spiritual consummation through social action and within a social medium.

The objective of change thus differs substantially among the several approaches examined. Hinduism, in so far as human change is considered, is highly individualistic in purport. Sarvodaya shares with all schools of socialism a central social element. For Marxism, social relationships are determinants of change, and the ultimate objective is stated in terms of a social and political condition. Democratic socialism emphasizes social relationships and a social, as well as an

9 *The Bhagavad Gita*, tr. and interpreted by Franklin Edgerton, Part I: Text and Translation, The Harvard Oriental Series, vol. 38, Harvard University Press, Cambridge, 1944, p. 95.

economic, ideal, but does not make any given set of social relationships a necessary determinant of the course or direction of change.

Sarvodaya, on the one hand, shares with socialism the ideal of social fulfillment and, on the other, draws from Hinduism the ideal of spiritual fulfillment. The manner in which Sarvodaya makes available to the individual a path upon which the individual may enter towards the end of his own spiritual fulfillment reflects the Gandhian tradition, albeit with some change of emphasis. Of the three elements conditioning the character of the objective of change—economic, social, and spiritual—the economic, in its strictest sense, carries the least weight. Nevertheless, the magnitude of the challenge presented by Indian poverty has led the proponents of Sarvodaya to occupy themselves prominently with such economic activities as Bhoodan, gramdan, and other allied "dan" (gift) movements.

THE TREND AND PROCESS OF CHANGE

The Hindu view of the universe takes, as destined, the complex cycles through which each world-system must pass in eternal repetition. Within each world-system, successive ages reflect the character of their position in the cosmic time scheme. *Satya Yuga*, or *Krita Yuga*, is the earliest, golden age of truth; deterioration culminates in *Kali Yuga*, a dark age dominated by the lowly and the incompetent.

The significance of Hinduism's cosmological determinism is remote for the individual who views himself in the more limited setting of a social being in a phenomenal world. The guiding principle for every Hindu is *dharma*. Within the context of change, *dharma* enjoins a way of life which will prevent regression from the highest standard of character and conduct previously reached. *Dharma* is also the law governing man's relationships within his society and his relationship to divine power—*dharma* is religion in the broadest sense. The individual is presented with a perspective on his own place and duty through the specific dharmic system known as *varnashrama*, whereby his caste and biological age group determine his obligations within society.

It is important not to overlook the flexibility provided in the Hindu system as it bears upon the Hindu view about the trend of change: only cosmologically is the process regular and determined, for in the history of an individual soul, much rests with achievement. Just as self-realization may be a brief or a vastly protracted process, so too, in the *varnashramadharma*, the individual may telescope the progression and enter, even as a young man, upon the life of a *sannyasi*—a holy man devoted to religious pursuits. He may do so, that is, providing that he is prepared to conduct himself in accordance with the requirements of a disciplined life removed from conventional relationships. This accepted departure from the normal progression was further modified in the Gandhian tradition to allow for a direct approach to the individual's involvement in social reform and in politics.

The related concepts of *karma* and *moksha*, upon which all orthodox Indian philosophical systems are in fundamental agreement, reflect the developmental assumptions operating in Hinduism. *Moksha*, which signifies salvation in the sense of the liberation of the Self from the chain of successive death and rebirth, is a timeless, changeless state, characterized by a blissful awareness of identity with the Absolute. Prior to this release, the Self moves from death to new life through the operation of the law of *karma*. Although the several Hindu systems may differ as to the evaluation to be placed on various actions, they are in agreement in acceptance of the following: "Whatever action is done by an individual leaves behind it some sort of potency which has the power to ordain for him joy or sorrow in the future according as it is good or bad. When the fruits of the action are such that they cannot be enjoyed in the present life or in a human life, the individual has to take another birth as a man or any other being in order to suffer them."[10] The effects of evil actions—however these may be defined—may take more than one such lifetime to counteract. Hindu metaphysics establishes the perfectibility of the individual; its cosmological propositions sustain the eternal repetition of the creation and dissolution of world systems.

The concern of Hinduism with the social relationships of the individual is marked and specific, but is a concern on the lower, empirical level which has meaning only as a transitory phase from which man is ultimately to be liberated. His development is conditioned by moral laws and expressed in societal terms, but his capacity for development is inherent and ultimate.

The advance of the individual towards his ultimate salvation is in no case considered to be a necessarily orderly or regular movement, because the individual, through his own accomplishments, is to determine the rate and the order of his advance (or regression). Even though one can speak of stages of development in Hinduism, the course of change for any given individual as he strives to perfect himself is likely to be erratic in character.

[10] Das Gupta, vol. 1, p. 71.

The Concept of Change

There is no place for the erratic in theoretical Marxism. Marx built his dialectical materialism upon the assumptions about change which were common to his day: change is natural, progressive, inevitable; and laws governing change can be discovered. Marx's contribution to a theory of social change lay in his supplying economic determinants. Marxism, as developed by Lenin, added the revolutionary concepts which seemed to provide a remedy to the slow and gradual process assumed by scholars of the nineteenth century, who had employed evolutionary theories to design the comparative (historical) method. As for the trend of change, Marx reflected the conditioning assumption of his time: change is progressive.

The dialectical materialism of Marxism depends upon developmental concepts. The radical character of social change and its universality results from a process of transformation based upon the principle of inherent opposing factors which force an internal movement issuing in a new synthesis. All things must, then, be investigated in terms of their histories, and the rate and direction of change is significant.

The social philosophy of Marxism is centrally historical materialism. Society passes through stages in the course of a complex evolution, and changes are influenced primarily by economic factors. Material forces of production and economic relations are the significant aspects of influence. Development is evolutionary with the most advanced stage postulated as a classless society characterized by productive employment and societal welfare.

The historical materialism of Marxism is inherently deterministic. Principles of materialist dialectics are first inferred from, and then applied to, human society. The stages through which society necessarily passes are determined by the changes taking place in its economic base—changes in the forces of production, including technology, and changes in economic relations, including systems of ownership and distribution. Social institutions are believed to have emerged in their successive forms as a result of basic economic changes. Law, government, and other social institutions (as well as philosophy and the arts) constitute a superstructure which changes in response to variations in economic relations brought about by conflicts of interest in respect to productive forces. Causal action is traced both ways between base and superstructure, but the general direction of social evolution is irrevocably established.[11] For a Marxist, society is ripe

[11] In a letter to Annekov, about 1846, Marx wrote: "Are men free to choose this or that social form? Not in the least. Take any particular stage in the development of the productive forces of man and you will find a corresponding

for revolution when inherent contradictions have become acute and the next phase in the long-term evolutionary process is ready for delivery.

Non-Marxian socialists have not designed a systematic theory treating of the movement of change. They reject determinism and rely upon the rational use of social institutions as instruments through which change may be brought about. The implication in all socialist thought is that the history of mankind is, or at the very least, can be, progressive. The historical inevitability characteristic of Marxist thought finds no place in democratic socialism. There is, however, an expectation that progressive change will follow upon the establishment of successive socialist institutional forms and procedures.

For some non-Marxian socialists, revolution is a process of growth. Proudhon viewed revolution as a permanent force. "Just as the notion of light is eternal and innate in mankind," he wrote, in 1858, "so, too, is the Revolution innate and eternal."[12] Proudhon's struggle against authority is replaced in democratic socialism with the reliance upon legislative forms and process and a gradualism which characterizes contemporary schools of socialist thought.

The social end to which democratic socialists look forward is similar to the final condition envisaged by Marxists, wherein economic security and the welfare of all is established. They agree that social ownership of the means of production will secure ends. However, just as they provide no deterministic philosophy to make progress inevitable, neither do they view change in terms of necessary stages of evolution. Socialists, other than Marxists, neither supply nor depend upon developmental assumptions. Implicit in their theoretical framework of the environmental conditioning of the individual, is the idea that man's circumstance is meliorable.[13]

---

form of trade and consumption. Take definite stages in the development of production, trade, consumption, and you have a corresponding form of social constitution, a definite organization of family, race or classes, in a word a corresponding form of civil society. Take such a civil society, and you have a definite political situation, which is only the official expression of civil society. It remains to add that men are not free masters of their forces of production—the foundation of their whole history—because these forces are acquired, are the product of previous activity. . . ." J. Hampden Jackson, *Marx, Proudhon and European Socialism*, Collier Books, New York, 1962, p. 56.

[12] *De la Justice dans la Revolution et dans l'Eglise*, quoted in Henri De Lubac, *The Un-Marxian Socialist: A Study of Proudhon*, tr. R. E. Scantlebury, Sheed & Ward, New York, 1948, p. 169.

[13] One Indian socialist, in a modification of the traditional socialist position, has referred to environmentalism as a "vice." Rammanohar Lohia, in an address in 1952, described the task ahead as the elaboration of a system in which it

The Concept of Change

Except for the rudimentary notion that man's condition can be improved, developmental assumptions are no necessary part of Sarvodaya. The appeal which proponents of Sarvodaya make to their fellow Indians is highly colored by uniquely Hindu metaphor. Implied in this appeal is the emphasis laid by Hinduism on the perfectibility of the individual. There is no rejection, outright, of the Hindu cosmological view of cyclical change. But in the current phase of this cycle, mankind is thought to be doomed to endure social and societal deterioration for hundreds of thousands of years yet to come. Such a belief is incompatible with efforts to effect substantial social and societal improvement. Sarvodaya's emphasis departs from that of Hinduism in the attention given to social values, and in this it follows the lead of Gandhi who had resolved an inherent conflict through a transformation of values.[14]

Vinoba's approach has been to declare, on his own authority, that the age of degeneration (*Kali Yuga*) has come to an end, and he has appealed for help in reestablishing *Satya Yuga* ("Age of Truth"). Vinoba, like Gandhi before him, believes that man is not impotent to effect change. Whatever difference in style of leadership and mode of thought can be distinguished between Gandhi and the neo-Gandhians (and between one contemporary Sarvodaya leader and another), Sarvodaya shares the characteristic Gandhian effort to reformulate norms and to transvaluate precepts. Perhaps the most dramatic innovations have been introduced in the realms of caste considerations. Contemporary Sarvodaya proponents, following the Gandhian lead, substitute universal social values for the restricted loyalties familiar to orthodox Hindus, eliminating social disability and special privilege in the interest of equality of opportunity and welfare of all. The orthodox assertion of degenerating time cycles is also set aside. Sarvodaya's concern for the individual *in his social context* attaches little significance to the notion of trend in change. The neo-Gandhian approach is, however, reminiscent of pre-Marxian schools of socialism, reflecting principles of association and mutualism and sharing a moral emphasis.

would not only be possible for the individual to be good, but also "necessary for him to be so." He criticized earlier socialist doctrine where "the environment alone mattered, where changes in law and in government and administration were sufficient to make the individual good." *Marx, Gandhi and Socialism,* Nava Hind Publications, Hyderabad, India, 1963, p. 136. This is one of several points of rapprochement with Gandhians, and represents a departure from traditional socialist theory.

[14] See Joan V. Bondurant, "Traditional Polity and the Dynamics of Change in India," *Human Organization,* Spring 1963, vol. 22, no. 1.

To summarize, determinism is central to Marxist social thought and characteristic of Hindu cosmology: change is believed inevitable in both. Social institutions, in Marxist thought, are conditioned and determined by inherent processes. Individual betterment depends upon and follows societal change; the stages through which society necessarily passes determine the all-important environment which conditions the individual. The individual who discovers and cooperates with the inherent laws of change is thought to alter the speed with which the objective can be attained.

The focus of change in Hinduism is the individual, with social arrangements serving to regulate and to promote the individual's efforts to realize his oneness with ultimate reality. *Dharma* provides a moral law and serves as a guide to the individual in his choice of how to advance towards his personal goal. In the Gandhian tradition which underlies Sarvodaya, the manner in which the individual understands his own *dharma* is an interrelated social concern: the individual's conduct in his society bears directly upon his own progress, but in a manner quite different from the orthodox Hindu view of an individual bound to his group by an irrevocable moral law and a rigid set of burdensome social conventions. Sarvodaya departs from Hinduism in the quality of social consciousness and social action required of the individual. Every member of society, in the broadest possible context, acquires merit through engaging in service to others. Conversely, the capacity of many individuals to participate in mutually supportive activities conditions the form of polity and the extent to which coercive procedures may be eliminated.

For socialists, social institutions condition and determine the welfare of the individual. The nineteenth-century western commitment to inevitable progress, though not uncongenial to democratic socialists, is for them neither a theoretical construct nor a necessary postulate. The humanistic approach of democratic socialism finds a place in Sarvodaya at several, but not all, levels. Within a given world system (i.e., in an historical, rather than a cosmological context), the course, objective, and trend of change appear open to the influence of man. This potential for influencing social change is significant not only for an individual engaged in his own advance toward ultimate goals, but also for the character and function of political leadership. It is clear from the significant variation in the underlying assumptions of these four approaches that developmental concepts condition the manner in which the purpose of political institutions is viewed and the direction in which political forms are oriented.

The Concept of Change

The significance of change in the modern world is in little danger of being underestimated. Scholarly literature and policy papers alike are replete with considerations in which change is central. Whether the consideration is that of inducing controlled change, or of discovering how things have come to be as they are, a prior requirement is an understanding of the matrix and the context. Change is neither to be set over against stability, nor to be understood as antithetical to tradition. Dynamic processes at work in India include extraordinary views of and unique approaches to change. Failure to take them into account will not only blind the observer to the potential of approaches as yet quite novel to the rest of the world, but also blunt his comprehension of the unusually complex tasks of development and modernization facing India.

CHAPTER 12

RELIGIOUS BELIEFS AND POLITICAL ATTITUDES

JOSEPH W. ELDER

IN HIS BOOK *On the Theory of Social Change*[1] Everett E. Hagen examines factors that enable a traditional society to become one in which economic growth is occurring. According to his definition, a traditional society is one in which the ways of behavior "continue with little change from generation to generation."[2] Traditional societies can differ in many other respects. Some are small tribal groups; others are loosely connected communities; others are large empires. Furthermore, the same society can shift from traditional to non-traditional and then become traditional again at some later point in its history. However, Hagen suggests that, despite many differences, when societies are traditional, they are characterized typically by particular forms of social organization. "Behavior is governed by custom, not law. The social structure is hierarchical. The individual's position in the society is normally inherited rather than achieved. And . . . economic productivity is low."[3] Furthermore, the members of traditional society tend to share certain attitudes in common, attitudes that contribute to maintaining traditionalism: "The image of the world of the simple folk and elite classes alike includes a perception of uncontrollable forces around them that restrict and dominate their lives. . . . The lines of dependence extend upward to the spiritual powers, to whom the members of the society appeal for protection against the physical forces. . . . Each individual finds his place in the authoritarian hierarchy of human relationships . . . the simple folk find satisfaction in both submissiveness and domination; their personalities as well as those of the elite are authoritarian. . . . In these societies, except for struggles within the class of the elite itself, class relationships are fixed. Since the lower classes are of essence inferior, of course there is no way in which they can merit eliteness."[4]

Hagen suggests that the traditional "image of the world" described above constitutes what is in fact a coherent whole. However, as one ex-

Joseph W. Elder is associate professor of sociology at the University of Wisconsin.
[1] Dorsey Press, Homewood, Illinois, 1962.
[2] *Ibid.*, p. 55.   [3] *Ibid.*, pp. 55-56.
[4] *Ibid.*, pp. 83-84.

amines this "image," one discovers that it is made up of conceptually separate parts.

1. Empirical fatalism (the belief that empirical phenomena occur for no knowable reason, and they cannot be controlled). Hagen: "The image of the world . . . includes a perception of uncontrollable forces around them that restrict and dominate their lives."

2. Theological fatalism (the belief that God or some moral order controls man's destiny). Hagen: "The lines of dependence extend upward to the spiritual powers, to whom the members of the society appeal for protection against the physical forces. . . ."

3. Political authoritarianism (a preference for hierarchical structure with orders from above and obedience from below). Hagen: "Each individual finds his place in the authoritarian hierarchy of human relationships."

4. Personality authoritarianism (personalities that view the world as a threatening and dangerous place, project guilt and hostility outward, and find gratification in dominance-submissive relationships). Hagen: ". . . the simple folk find satisfaction in both submissiveness and domination; their personalities as well as those of the elite are authoritarian."

5. Social fatalism (the belief that one's general social position in life is fixed and one cannot or could not have done anything to change it). Hagen: ". . . class relationships are fixed . . . there is no way in which [the lower classes] can merit eliteness."

Given the above conceptually separate parts of Hagen's traditional "image of the world," one can ask the question: To what extent do these parts actually correlate with one another? If they are part and parcel of a traditional "image of the world," it might be expected that as one attitude changes the others will also change. The purpose of this paper is to find out whether, in one situation where data are available, this is actually the case.

The research upon which this study is based was conducted in India in 1963. With the help of teams of interviewers using a carefully pretested interview schedule, I gathered over 2,500 interviews, half of them in Lucknow and its environs in the northern Hindustani-speaking state of Uttar Pradesh, and half of them in Madurai and its environs in the southern Tamil-speaking state of Madras. My sampling units were intact nuclear families (fathers and mothers alive and in residence) with eleven-year-old boys. In both North and South India I drew systematic samples of approximately 100 families from a city, 100 families from a town, and 100 families from villages. Among them were illiterates as well as college graduates, Muslims, Sikhs, and Christians as well as Hindus, professional beggars and landless laborers as well as high-level government administrators. From all of them the interviewers asked the same set of questions tapping a wide range of attitudes. Among these attitudes were a number closely related to different parts of Hagen's traditional "image of the world." These attitudes, and the specific questions tapping them, were as follows.

1. Empirical fatalism (the belief that empirical phenomena occur for no knowable reason, and they cannot be controlled). *Question*: One learned man says, "Most things that happen like disease and poverty are caused by fate. As it is written, so must it happen." Another learned man says, "There are other reasons besides fate for why these things happen. If we can discover the reasons, we can change what will happen." Which of these learned men do you think is correct?

Those answering the first man ("Caused by Fate") were considered empirically fatalistic; those answering the second man ("Caused by Discoverable Reason") were considered empirically non-fatalistic.

2. Theological fatalism (the belief that God or some moral order controls man's destiny). *Question*: One man says, "One must work hard in order to have better results." A second man says, "One must work hard, but the results are in God's hands." A third man says, "One need not work hard, because the results are in God's hands." Which of these three men do you think is correct?

Those answering the second or third man ("Results in God's Hands") were considered theologically fatalistic; those answering the first man ("Results from Work") were considered theologically non-fatalistic.

3. Political authoritarianism (a preference for hierarchical structure with orders from above and obedience from below). *Question*: One man says, "Our country needs a strong leader who will take over the government and make everybody obey him." Another man says, "Our country needs leaders who have been chosen by the people and who will act in accordance with the people's wishes." Which of these men do you think is correct?

Those answering the first man ("Pro-Dictatorship") were considered politically authoritarian; those answering the second man ("Pro-Democracy") were considered politically non-authoritarian.

4. Personality authoritarianism (personalities that view the world as a threatening and dangerous place, project guilt and hostility out-

ward, and find gratification in dominance-submissive relationships).

To tap this attitude, I used a modified form of the "F-Scale" described by T. W. Adorno, et al. in *The Authoritarian Personality*,[5] especially chapters four through seven. The following statements were read, and the respondent stated whether he felt each was true or false. *Questions*: An insult to one's honor should always be punished. Human nature being what it is, there will always be wars and conflicts. People can be divided into two classes, the strong and the weak. It is not good to think too much. A great many things can be predicted by astrology. There are so many evil people nowadays that it is dangerous to go out alone. Nowadays courts don't give as severe punishments to law-breakers as they ought to.

Those agreeing to six or seven of the statements were considered "High Authoritarian"; those agreeing to five of the statements were considered "Medium Authoritarian"; those agreeing to four or less of the statements were considered "Low Authoritarian."

5. Social fatalism (the belief that one's general social position in life is fixed and one cannot or could not have done anything to change it). From the eleven-year-old boys I asked: *Question*: If you had sufficient money from your family or from the government, up to what level would you like to study? From the fathers and mothers I asked: *Question*: If you had had the opportunity, would you have liked to study further? (If the answer were "Yes," I asked:) Up to what class would you have liked to study?

Of the five parts comprising Hagen's traditional "image of the world," three (empirical fatalism, theological fatalism, and personality authoritarianism) are essentially "perspectives," with no direct implications for how people accepting those beliefs should behave. The other two parts (political authoritarianism and social fatalism) are more "action oriented." They imply that persons holding those views endorse certain types of political structures or personal career goals.

For purposes of analysis, we shall first see the extent to which the three "perspectives" beliefs actually co-vary with one another, then we shall examine what other factors co-vary with these beliefs, and finally we shall turn to an analysis of those factors that co-vary with the "action-oriented" beliefs.

Hagen tested his propositions about traditionalism and economic development with evidence from England, Japan, Colombia, Burma and the Sioux. He did not, however, work with data from India. In his own words: "The situation in India has seemed to me too complex

[5] Harper and Brothers, New York, 1950.

to lend itself to analysis in terms of the analytic model presented in this volume."[6]

India's history may well be too complex for a clear test of Hagen's propositions. Furthermore, India today is undergoing sufficient change so that Hagen might consider it no longer to be a traditional society. Nevertheless, perhaps India's complexity and her current changes permit a closer analysis of the component elements of the traditional "image of the world" than would be possible in some more homogeneous and traditional society.

THE ASSOCIATION OF TRADITIONAL "PERSPECTIVES"

If there are intrinsic links between the three "perspectives" pertaining to the traditional "image of the world," it would be expected that those who held one of the traditional "perspectives" would be more likely to hold another of the traditional "perspectives." Tables 1, 2 and 3 show to what extent this was the case.

TABLE 1

There Is No Significant Association between
Empirical Fatalism and Theological Fatalism
(Sons, Mothers, Fathers)

	Empirical Fatalism	
	"Caused by Fate"	"Caused by Discoverable Reason"
Theological Fatalism		
"Results in God's hands"	57%	56%
"Results from work"	43%	44%
	100%	100%
	n=1375	n=984

NOTE: The no association pattern remains the same when broken down by Sons, Mothers, and Fathers and broken down further into educated and uneducated.

As is apparent from the tables, empirical fatalism, theological fatalism and personality authoritarianism are virtually independent of each other. Only one of the five tables shows any significant degree of association (Table 3b), and this is in the *reverse* direction from that suggested in Hagen's description of the traditional "images of the world," i.e., in South India those with *lower* personality authoritar-

[6] Hagen, pp. 427-428.

ianism have a *higher* degree of theological fatalism. In short, the fact that a person holds a traditional view in one of these "perspectives" does not appear to influence whether or not he holds a traditional view in another "perspective."

OTHER VARIABLES RELATED TO
TRADITIONAL "PERSPECTIVES"

If these "perspectives" are not associated with each other, are they associated with any other factors? We turn now to a separate analysis of each of the three "perspectives."

TABLE 2

There Is No Significant Association between
Empirical Fatalism and Personality Authoritarianism
2a (Uneducated Mothers and Fathers)

	Empirical Fatalism	
	"Caused by Fate"	"Caused by Discoverable Reason"
Personality Authoritarianism		
High and Medium Authoritarian	60%	62%
Low Authoritarian	40%	38%
	100%	100%
	n=602	n=195

2b (Educated Mothers and Fathers)

	Empirical Fatalism	
	"Caused by Fate"	"Caused by Discoverable Reason"
Personality Authoritarianism		
High and Medium Authoritarian	36%	38%
Low Authoritarian	64%	62%
	100%	100%
	n=343	n=421

NOTE: Both personality authoritarianism and empirical fatalism are so strongly associated with education that I analyzed the uneducated (those with no schooling) separately from the educated (those with one or more years of schooling). The field pre-test showed that the eleven-year-old Sons could not understand the modified version of the "F-Scale"; so the scale was dropped from their interviews. The association pattern remains as above when broken down by Mothers and Fathers and broken down further into North India and South India.

254

TABLE 3a

In North India There Is No Significant
Association between Theological Fatalism
and Personality Authoritarianism

	Theological Fatalism	
	"Results in God's Hands"	"Results from Work"
Personality Authoritarianism		
High and Medium Authoritarian	63%	62%
Low Authoritarian	37%	38%
	100%	100%
	n=616	n=236

TABLE 3b

In South India Low Theological Fatalism Is Associated
with High Personality Authoritarianism

	Theological Fatalism	
	"Results in God's Hands"	"Results from Work"
Personality Authoritarianism		
High and Medium Authoritarian	28%	36%
Low Authoritarian	72%	64%
	100%	100%
	n=325	n=383

chi^2 = 4.5
sig. 0.05

NOTE: Theological fatalism is so strongly associated with region of India (North vs. South) that I analyzed North Indians separately from South India. In both 3a and 3b, the association pattern remains as above when broken down further by Mothers and Fathers.

Empirical Fatalism

Empirical fatalism is the belief that empirical phenomena occur for no knowable reason and they cannot be controlled.

One factor that is markedly associated with empirical fatalism is education (see Table 4).

Inasmuch as one of the main processes carried on in Indian schools today is describing and explaining empirical phenomena, it is not surprising that the more a group is exposed to such explanations, the

TABLE 4

As Education Increases,
Empirical Fatalism Decreases

	Amount of Education		
	None	Primary	Higher
Empirical Fatalism			
"Caused by Fate"	72%	53%	31%
"Caused by Discoverable Reason"	28%	47%	69%
	100%	100%	100%
	n=904	n=1063	n=383

$chi^2 = 218.7$
sig. 0.001

NOTE: The cutting points for schooling in the sample of Sons are: "None" = 0 or 1 year of schooling; "Primary" = 2 to 6 years of schooling; "Higher" = 7 to 9 years of schooling. The cutting points for schooling for Fathers and Mothers are: "None" = 0 years of schooling; "Primary" = less than 5 years of school; "Higher" = more than 5 years of school. The association patterns remain as above when broken down by Sons, Mothers, and Fathers.

less likely that group is to accept "fate" as a satisfactory explanation for why things happen.

A second factor that is associated with empirical fatalism is religious affiliation. My evidence suggests that Hindus are the most empirically fatalistic, followed by the Muslims, and then the Christians and Sikhs (see Table 5).

Why is it that Hindus are more empirically fatalistic than Muslims, Christians or Sikhs? Perhaps some clues lie in the doctrines of these various religions. Except for such branches as the *Carvaka* school of Hindu philosophy, there is a theme running through Hinduism that stresses the relative importance of the spiritual world, the relative unimportance of the physical world, and the usefulness of intuition as a means of acquiring knowledge. It may be this subtle Hindu denigration of the physical world that leads more Hindus to conclude that "as it is written, so must it happen."

In this regard, Islam, Sikhism and Christianity are willing to make considerable concessions to the physical world, to justify the search for physical causality, and even to express the desirability of controlling the physical world. Perhaps the more empiricist orientation of the Muslims is an offshoot of the Islamic doctrine of evangelism and the remaking of the world according to the teachings of the Qur'an. The empiricist orientation of the Christians might stem

TABLE 5

Empirical Fatalism Is Most Prevalent
among Hindus, Less among Muslims, and
Least among Christians and Sikhs

	Hindus	*Muslims*	*Christians and Sikhs*
Empirical Fatalism			
"Caused by Fate"	60%	53%	40%
"Caused by Discoverable Reason"	40%	47%	60%
	100%	100%	100%
	n=1835	n=451	n=72

chi² = 16.9
sig. 0.001

NOTE: Aside from the Christians and Sikhs, whose numbers become too small when subdivided, the association pattern remains as above when broken down into Sons, Mothers, and Fathers and broken down further between North India and South India and educated and uneducated, with a few exceptions. There is virtually no difference in degree of empirical fatalism between North Indian Hindu and Muslim Mothers, and there is an actual reversal of the above association pattern among North Indian educated Sons and South Indian uneducated Sons.

from their evangelistic and missionary-minded orientation as well, while the empirical orientation of the Sikhs has been a theme in their martial and now mechanical tradition.

Theological Fatalism

Theological fatalism is the belief that God or some moral order controls man's destiny.

The factor that appears to be most markedly associated with theological fatalism is region within India (see Table 6).

In terms of the general impression one gets while traveling and living in both North and South India, the above findings make sense. The Tamils of Madras state appear less overawed by God's power than do the Hindustani-speakers of the Gangetic plain. Why this should be the case is difficult to explain.

One contributing factor to greater theological fatalism occurring in North India might be the nature of the Hindu gods and centers in the north as opposed to the south. In North India, formal or classical Hinduism holds sway, with teachings from the epics or Puranas, dominance of Brahmin priests over religious matters, etc. The pilgrimage centers and sacred cities are described in the ancient Sanskrit texts.

257

TABLE 6

Theological Fatalism Is More Prevalent
in North India Than in South India

	North India	South India
Theological Fatalism		
"Results in God's Hands"	69%	43%
"Results from Work"	31%	57%
	100%	100%
	n=1280	n=1070

chi² = 132.0
sig. 0.001

NOTE: Pattern of distribution remains the same when broken down into Sons, Mothers, and Fathers, and when broken down further into Hindus and Muslims and educated and uneducated.

In South India the relations between worshippers and deities are more individualistic and varied. There are many different gods that hold sway over particular hills, groves of trees, fields and shrines. In the south, unlike the north, there are gods of castes, families, and lineages. Rarely are these gods clearly worked into the classical Hindu pantheon. Where efforts have been made through legend to unite the indigenous gods of South India with the classical gods of North India, the fit has usually been less than satisfactory. The Brahmins in the large, urban temples of the south may try to retain links between what people actually worship and what people are supposed to worship according to classical texts. However, much of the religious activity of South India goes on without the formal assistance of Brahmins and relates to gods of family and locality—more informal sorts of gods than the ones in the classical pantheon.

A second factor that appears to be associated with theological fatalism is religious affiliation (see Table 7).

Why do the Muslims, Christians and Sikhs, more frequently than the Hindus, subscribe to the view that God is the determiner of the outcome of actions? Here again the answer might be in the formal doctrine of the religion itself. However, as far as the relative importance of God determining actions' results and those actions determining their own results, religious systems typically make statements supporting both sides. Comparing Islam, Christianity and Hinduism, for example, there are close parallels between the Gita's teaching that man must act according to his duty, but the results of those

Joseph W. Elder

TABLE 7

Theological Fatalism Is More Prevalent among Muslims,
Christians and Sikhs Than among Hindus

Theological Fatalism	Muslims	Christians and Sikhs	Hindus
"Results in God's Hands"	69%	65%	54%
"Results from Work"	31%	35%	46%
	100%	100%	100%
	n=452	n=71	n=1827

Differences between Muslims and Hindus
chi² = 32.6
sig. 0.001

NOTE: Aside from Christians and Sikhs, whose numbers become too small when subdivided, the association pattern remains as above when broken down into Sons, Mothers, and Fathers and when broken down further into North and South and educated and uneducated.

actions are in God's hands, the Islamic concepts of *kismat* or *mukaddar,* and the view that Allah moves according to His infinite wisdom and mercy in ways inscrutable and often mysterious to man, and the Christian belief that somehow "all things work together for good to them that love God."

There are also close parallels in the somewhat different view in Hinduism that ultimately through the mechanism of *karma* every sin a man commits is punished and every virtue he performs is rewarded, and the Islamic and Christian eschatology in which every man will be lifted to heaven or condemned to hell on the basis of the acts he has performed and the beliefs he has held.

In short, it would be difficult to make a strong case for one of these religions being clearer than the others in its doctrine—either that God determines the results of actions or that actions determine their own results. Within all three religions one finds, on one hand, expressions that the outcomes of actions are controlled by God, and on the other hand that man is responsible and accountable for his own actions.

Given as it were a roughly similar range of doctrines within these religions, the question remains why do the Muslims, Christians and Sikhs select the doctrine "Results in God's Hands" more frequently than do the Hindus?

One answer suggests itself. Each of these theologically more fatalistic groups is a religious minority surrounded by the Hindu majority.

259

Religion and Political Attitudes

Possibly the members of a religious minority group are generally more aware of religious matters and more self-conscious about their theological beliefs than are members of the large, majority society. One way to test this proposition might be to ask the same questions of Hindus and Muslims in Pakistan, where the majority-minority relationships are reversed. Unhappily, however, I have no comparable data from Pakistan.

A third factor that appears to be associated with theological fatalism is education, but the picture is somewhat complicated. Within the Hindu majority group, an increase in education is accompanied by a decrease in theological fatalism (see Table 8).

TABLE 8

Among Hindus, as Education Increases,
Theological Fatalism Decreases

	Uneducated Hindus	Educated Hindus
Theological Fatalism		
"Results in God's Hands"	59%	49%
"Results from Work"	41%	51%
	100%	100%
	n=964	n=870

chi^2 = 16.8
sig. 0.001

NOTE: The association pattern remains as above when broken down into Sons, Mothers, and Fathers and when broken down further into North India and South India, with a few exceptions. There is virtually no difference in degree of theological fatalism among North Indian Mothers, and there is an actual reversal of the above associations among the South Indian Sons.

When one contrasts the Hindu picture with the picture for the Muslims, for example, one sees that education appears to have no noticeable effect on the theological fatalism of the Muslims (see Table 9).

In short, it appears that minority-group status is a more important factor in shaping one's theological fatalism than is education. However, among members of a religious majority group, where perhaps one's own sense of identity is not so clearly aligned with the survival of the identity of one's religious group, education does appear to reduce somewhat one's acceptance of theological fatalism.

TABLE 9

Among Muslims, as Education Increases,
Theological Fatalism Remains Unchanged

	Uneducated Muslims	*Educated Muslims*
Theological Fatalism		
"Results in God's Hands"	69%	69%
"Results from Work"	31%	31%
	100%	100%
	n=217	n=235

NOTE: There is no significant pattern of association when one breaks the Muslims down into Sons, Mothers, and Fathers and then into North India and South India.

Personality Authoritarianism

Personality authoritarianism refers to personalities that view the world as a threatening and dangerous place, project guilt and hostility outward, and find gratification in dominance-submissive relationships.

Two factors are most markedly associated with personality authoritarianism. The first of these is family type (see Table 10).

TABLE 10

Authoritarian Personalities Are More Prevalent
in Distant-Marriage Kin Groups Than in
Close-Marriage Kin Groups

	Distant Marriage	*Close Marriage*
Personality Authoritarianism		
High Authoritarian	33%	14%
Medium Authoritarian	35%	24%
Low Authoritarian	32%	62%
	100%	100%
	n=606	n=905

chi^2 = 138.4
sig. 0.001

NOTE: Pattern of association remains the same when broken down into Mothers and Fathers (Sons did not answer the "F-Scale" items), and when further broken down into "Educated" and "Uneducated."

Religion and Political Attitudes

A considerable body of literature already exists dealing with the question of what an authoritarian personality is and what social experiences contribute to its development.[7] One proposition is that home atmospheres that are characterized by "lack of love, and a general atmosphere of tension and aggression . . ." will generate authoritarianism.[8] In light of this proposition, our discovery of an association between a family type and authoritarian personality suggests that the Distant-Marriage kin group in India may generate a greater "atmosphere of tension and aggression" than the Close-Marriage kin group. To determine the plausibility of this proposition, we shall have to take a closer look at the family and marriage systems in India.

Throughout India the overwhelming majority of marriages are still parentally arranged, and the overwhelming majority of marriages—even among Muslims—are still within the appropriate caste group. To this extent there are basic similarities between all the family structures included in my sample. However, beneath the similarities lie marked differences:

1. *North Indian (U.P.) Hindus* (Distant Marriages). The generally quoted rule for marriages among the Hindus of U.P. is that one must not arrange a union with someone who is removed by less than seven degrees from the father or five degrees from the mother. Marriages with persons more closely related are considered incestuous. As a rule, the social-distance regulations are compounded by geographical-distance regulations, for example, it is generally forbidden for a bride and groom to come from the same village.[9] This means that as a girl approaches marriageable age, her parents must search among more or less strangers for a suitable match. When one is found, typically there ensue protracted negotiations over dowry, with each family trying to enhance its relative status at the expense of the other. After the wedding, typically the daughter leaves her own native place

---

[7] See for example R. Nevitt Sanford, "Genetic Aspects of the Authoritarian Personality: Case Studies of Two Contrasting Individuals," in T. W. Adorno, et al., pp. 787-816. In the same volume see Else Frenkel-Brunswik's discussion, pp. 482-486. Also see R. Christie and M. Jahoda, eds., *Studies in the Scope and Method of the "Authoritarian Personality,"* Free Press, Glencoe, Ill., 1954; Chapman and Campbell, "The Effect of Acquiescence Response Set Upon the Relationships Among the F Scale, Ethnocentrism, and Intelligence," *Sociometry*, June 1959, pp. 153-161; and Seymour M. Lipset, *Political Man, the Social Bases of Politics,* Doubleday, Garden City, New York, 1960, especially chapter 4, "Working-Class Authoritarianism."

[8] Lipset, p. 120.

[9] For a more complete discussion of marriage practices in North India, see Irawati Karve, *Kinship Organisation in India,* Deccan College Monograph Series, no. 11, Poona, 1953, pp. 93-136.

and goes to live in her husband's home. There she is surrounded by relative strangers. Frequently her meaningful contacts are reduced to her husband, her mother-in-law, her husband's sisters, and her husband's brothers' wives. Until after she has produced a living child, the new bride is considered a tentative member of the groom's family. If, after a number of years, she proves barren, it is often the custom for her husband to marry some other wife who may prove more fertile. In such cases, the first wife may be retained as something of a family servant, or she may be sent back to her father's house.

The unhappiness of the new bride in her husband's home and the tense relationships she has with those around her have been captured in numerous folk stories and songs.[10] Like other popular accounts, there are undoubtedly exaggerations; nonetheless, the pictures they paint are that of a lonely and unhappy wife, far from the home and village in which she was raised, surrounded by strangers, some of whom can be harsh, and considered little better than a family-provided mistress by her husband and a not very competent servant by her mother-in-law. If she is mistreated, there is little she can do, since her father and brothers are far away, and the channels of communication may even be effectively sealed.

The birth of a child gives the bride a higher position in her new home. However, the intrigue and jockeying for status continue. Younger brides marry into the village, and *they* must be supervised and put in their places, otherwise they may endanger the status of her husband's family. In short, the very structure of the marriage arrangement is one that generates continuing tension.

2. *South Indian (Madras State) Hindus* (Close Marriages). In certain respects the Tamil marriage arrangements in South India are the opposite of those in U.P. Where the U.P. system requires that brides and bridegrooms be sought for in the homes of strangers, the Tamil system requires that, as far as possible, marriages be arranged within a fairly tight family circle. In fact, the preferred marriages are with one's elder sister's daughter or one's father's sister's daughter, though actually most marriages are not within this tight a circle. But they are generally arranged within the broad range of cross-cousins.

The upshot of this is that where the North Indian marriage system spreads and scatters, the South Indian system draws together and reunites. According to Dr. Karve, the result of this is: "A man

10 For examples of words to some of these songs, see Oscar Lewis, *Village Life in Northern India*, University of Illinois Press, Urbana, Illinois, 1958, chapter 5, "The Marriage Cycle."

does not bring a stranger as a bride to his home, a woman is not thrown among complete strangers on her marriage. Marriage strengthens existing bonds. The emphasis is on knitting families closer together and narrowing the circle of the kin group. . . . The distinction between the father's house and the father-in-law's house is not as sharp as in the north. The distinction between "daughters" and the "brides or wives" is not as deep as in the north . . . [a girl's] husband is either her uncle or her cross-cousin and his mother is either her own grandmother or her aunt. Neither is she separated for long periods from her parents' house."[11]

3. *Indian Muslims* (Close Marriages). The Muslims in India can be divided into two major groups, the *Ashraf* ("honorable") Muslims, including divisions such as the Sayyads, Shaikhs and Pathans, who trace their origin to such foreign lands as Afghanistan or Arabia, and the other Muslims who trace their origin to indigeneous Muslim converts and who often retain their formerly-Hindu caste names. From the very beginning there has been relatively little recognized intermarriage between the *Ashraf* Muslims and the converted Muslims. Furthermore, both groups are subdivided into two religious sects, the Sunni and the Shi'a; these in turn generally do not intermarry. Even within these clan, caste and religious faction categories, there are often more specific kin groups called *Bradari* or *Bhaiband* that comprise the restricted circle within which marriages generally take place. In rare cases the endogamous circle becomes so narrow that it includes only one kinship group.[12] Within the narrow kinship group, Quranic law permits not only cross-cousin marriage but also parallel-cousin marriage. To this extent, Islamic incest regulations are less stringent than South Indian Hindu regulations. However, Islamic law does not permit a man's marrying his niece; whereas South Indian custom does; so it would be difficult to maintain that one system is more "liberal" than the other.[13]

Despite specific points on which the Muslim and the Tamil Hindu rules of marriage differ, both systems work in the same way to knit together already existing kin groups. Just as the Tamil form of marriage provides protection for the new bride and a retention of familiar ties with relatives, so the Islamic system throughout India provides

[11] Karve, p. 229.

[12] For further details regarding Muslim marriage, see Ghaus Ansari, *Muslim Caste in Uttar Pradesh*, Ethnographic and Folk Culture Society, Lucknow, 1960, chapter 6, "Caste and Social Organisation."

[13] For a discussion of the classical Islamic rules regarding marriage, see Reuben Levy, *The Social Structure of Islam*, Cambridge University Press, Cambridge, 1963, chapter 2, "The Status of Women in Islam."

the same kind of protection and retention of the familiar for its new brides. The transition from daughter to wife is structured so as to maintain considerable continuity.

Assuming that authoritarian personalities are a product of homes characterized by a "general atmosphere of tension and aggression," we would expect to find a higher level of authoritarianism among the North Indian Hindus than among the South Indian Hindus or any of the Muslims. The analysis has led us back to our starting point, for this is the observation that led to the inquiry as to differential family structure.

This association between personality structure and family types raises an interesting question: do highly authoritarian personalities reflect an *early childhood* exposure to tension and aggression, or do they reflect *current* exposure to tension and aggression? Fundamental though such a question might be from the perspective of personality theory, our data are not sufficiently refined to provide an answer, since the personalities being measured had been exposed to the relative strains of their family system during childhood and were, at the time of the interview, still exposed to the strains as adults.

A second factor that is associated with personality authoritarianism is education (see Table 11).

The importance of literacy in changing a person's outlook has been discussed in a variety of sources. For example, Daniel Lerner has written: "Literacy is the basic skill that underlies the whole modern-

TABLE 11

Authoritarian Personalities Are More Prevalent
among the Uneducated Than among the Educated

	Uneducated Hindus and Muslims	Educated Hindus and Muslims
Personality Authoritarianism		
High Authoritarian	27%	16%
Medium Authoritarian	34%	22%
Low Authoritarian	39%	62%
	100%	100%
	n=789	n=717

chi² = 75.2
sig. 0.001

NOTE: Pattern of association remains the same when broken down by Mothers and Fathers and broken down further by Muslims and Hindus.

izing sequence."[14] And Lucian Pye has stated, ". . . early schooling and first experiences with the written word can . . . be a crucial factor shaping the outlook of people. . . ."[15] Clinical evidence was provided in the initial work by Adorno on the authoritarian personality showing a negative correlation between education and ethnocentrism, and a positive correlation between ethnocentrism and authoritarianism.[16] Combining our data from India with other available data, there appears to be evidence of significant links between education and authoritarian personalities as a general principle.

So far we have discussed three of the five component parts of Hagen's traditional "image of the world"—A. Empirical fatalism, B. Theological fatalism, and C. Personality authoritarianism. We first discovered that there are no significant positive associations between these three parts of the traditional "image of the world." Our search for other possible associated variables yielded the following:

Traditional "Perspective"	Variables with Which It Is Associated
A. Empirical fatalism	a. Amount of education
	b. Religious affiliation
B. Theological fatalism	a. Amount of education (majority group only)
	b. Religious affiliation
	c. Region within India
C. Personality authoritarianism	a. Amount of education
	b. Type of kin group

We now turn to the two more "action-oriented" parts of Hagen's traditional "view of the world"—political authoritarianism and social fatalism.

VARIABLES ASSOCIATED WITH
TRADITIONAL "ACTION-ORIENTED" BELIEFS

Political Authoritarianism

Political authoritarianism refers to a preference for hierarchical structure with orders from above and obedience from below.

---

[14] *The Passing of Traditional Society*, Free Press, Glencoe, Ill., 1958, p. 64.

[15] *Communications and Political Development*, Princeton University Press, Princeton, 1963, pp. 150-151.

[16] Daniel J. Levinson, "Ethnocentrism in Relation to Intelligence and Education," in Adorno, et al., pp. 280-288, and R. Nevitt Sanford, et al., "The Measurement of Implicit Antidemocratic Trends," *ibid.*, pp. 262-279.

Two factors that are markedly associated with political authoritarianism are family position and region within India (see Table 12).

TABLE 12

Political Authoritarianism Is Strongest
among South Indian Sons and Mothers

		North India	
	Sons	*Mothers*	*Fathers*
Political Authoritarianism			
"Pro-Dictatorship"	25%	29%	22%
"Pro-Democracy"	75%	71%	78%
	100%	100%	100%
	n=431	n=433	n=403
		South India	
	Sons	*Mothers*	*Fathers*
Political Authoritarianism			
"Pro-Dictatorship"	56%	54%	25%
"Pro-Democracy"	44%	46%	75%
	100%	100%	100%
	n=364	n=360	n=345

$chi^2 = 81.3$
sig. 0.001

NOTE: The South Indian Sons' and Mothers' pattern of association remains constant when broken down into educated and uneducated. The South Indian Fathers' pattern of association is skewed by education, with relatively more of the educated Fathers approving of democracy and relatively more of the uneducated approving of dictatorship.

Why is it that the South Indians are more pro-dictatorship than the North Indians, and why is it that among the South Indians, the Sons, Mothers, and uneducated Fathers are the ones who most prefer a dictatorship? Perhaps one way to try to answer these questions is to examine the recent political history of Madras state to see in what ways it differs from that of U.P.

In Madras state as early as 1922 the anti-Brahmin Justice Party waged an ideological battle against the Brahmins and the Congress Party, maintaining that South India had almost as much to fear from North Indians as she had to fear from the British. In 1945 E. V. Ramaswamy Naicker, leader of the Justice Party, decided to found a more militant mass organization, the Dravida Kazagham. Prior to independence in 1947, Naicker warned his fellow Tamils, "We must guard against a transference of power from the British to the Aryans."[17] Two years after independence a portion of the Dravida Kazagham split off under the vigorous leadership of C. N. Annadurai to establish the Dravida Munnetra Kazagham or DMK. Today the DMK is the popular protest movement in South India, and its emotional and political center is frequently the city of Madurai (where the urban part of the South Indian survey was conducted). Pictures of Annadurai and Tamil-championing film stars hung in many of the homes in which we conducted interviews, and the red and black flag of the DMK fluttered from countless tree tops and electric light posts. Party reading rooms, public rallies, parades, and political posters are elements of the everyday life of Madurai.

In addition to criticizing Brahmin "domination" and the North Indian attempts to "force" Hindi on the South, the DMK has championed a broad spectrum of religious, educational and social causes including (1) a renaissance of Tamil language and culture, (2) the spread of literacy, (3) self-respect marriages not employing Brahmin priests, (4) the destruction of idols, (5) the abolition of caste and color distinctions, (6) eradication of superstitions, (7) and the adoption of rationalism and science.

In U.P. in North India, on the other hand, there is no popular party making the broad-spectrum demands for change that the DMK is making in the south. Even in the capital city of Lucknow, mass political activities emerge primarily at election time and then subside until the next election. There are not the same number of dramatic issues being raised again and again; there are no charismatic figures like Annadurai or movie stars championing the cause of widespread ideological modernization or denouncing the threats to the continuation of one's mother tongue or one's literary tradition. In the 1962 elections the platforms of the major U.P. political parties—the Jana Sangh, Praja Socialists, Lohia Socialists, and Congress—differed only in minor detail. As a matter of fact, the platforms were of such little significance to the electorate as well as the campaigners that it was difficult to find any copies of the platform—even at party headquarters. In short, in contrast to Madras state, with its frequent mass rallies and its broad spectrum of issues included in political platforms, especially that of the DMK, the level of activity and the spectrum of issues handled by U.P. political parties were limited and unexciting.

17 *The Hindu*, February 11, 1946, quoted by Selig S. Harrison, *India: The Most Dangerous Decades*, Princeton University Press, Princeton, 1960, footnote p. 123. See chapter 10, "Religion, Politics, and the DMK."

Joseph W. Elder

Possibly the very breadth of issues defined as "political" in south India helped generate the pro-dictatorship sentiments. Evidence for this possibility may be seen in the fact that a type of authoritarian crystallization had taken place in South India; whereas there was no evidence for such a crystallization in the north. For example, in the south, personality authoritarianism is associated with political authoritarianism; whereas in the north there was no such association (see Table 13).

TABLE 13

In South India There Is an Association between
Political Authoritarianism and Personality
Authoritarianism; in North India There Is
No Such Association

| | North India (Mothers, Fathers) | |
	"Pro-Dictatorship"	"Pro-Democracy"
Personality Authoritarianism		
High Authoritarian	31%	30%
Medium Authoritarian	28%	34%
Low Authoritarian	41%	36%
	100%	100%
	n=231	n=611
	South India (Mothers, Fathers)	
	"Pro-Dictatorship"	"Pro-Democracy"
Personality Authoritarianism		
High Authoritarian	17%	7%
Medium Authoritarian	29%	16%
Low Authoritarian	54%	76%
	100%	99%
	n=283	n=420

$chi^2 = 37.3$
sig. 0.001

NOTE: The pattern of association remains constant when broken down into Mothers and Fathers.

In the same way South India shows a polarization of theological fatalism and political authoritarianism, while there is no such polarization in North India (see Table 14).

This crystallizing of some of Hagen's traditional "world views" in South India to form a cluster around the dimension of political authoritarianism suggests a possible generalization:

269

TABLE 14

In South India There Is an Association between
Political Authoritarianism and Theological
Fatalism; in North India There Is
No Such Association

| | North India (Sons, Mothers, Fathers) | |
	"Pro-Dictatorship"	"Pro-Democracy"
Theological Fatalism		
"Results in God's Hands"	67%	70%
"Results from Work"	33%	30%
	100%	100%
	n=332	n=933
	South India (Sons, Mothers, Fathers)	
	"Pro-Dictatorship"	"Pro-Democracy"
Theological Fatalism		
"Results in God's Hands"	47%	39%
"Results from Work"	53%	61%
	100%	100%
	n=488	n=580

chi^2 = 6.1
sig. 0.02

NOTE: The pattern of association remains constant when broken down into Sons, Mothers, and Fathers.

In India, and perhaps in other nations too, as the breadth of the issues defined as "political" increases, the degree of authoritarian crystallization also increases, with people whose general world view is authoritarian adopting political authoritarianism as well.

One final point may be worth mentioning before we leave political authoritarianism. Although when we divided the South Indian population into educated and uneducated, we failed to produce any association with pro-dictatorship sentiments, a further refinement of categories produced such an association. Primary school seems to have little effect on pro-dictatorship sentiments. However, Mothers who have attended high school subscribe less to pro-dictatorship sentiments than do other Mothers (see Table 15).

Given the nature of this association among the Mothers, it is interesting to speculate why there is no such association between high school education and pro-democracy sentiments among the Fathers.

Joseph W. Elder

TABLE 15

Among South Indian Mothers, There Is an
Association between Pro-Dictatorship
Sentiments and No High School Education

| | South India (Mothers) | |
	"Pro-Dictatorship"	"Pro-Democracy"
Primary Education or Less	95%	89%
High School Education or More	5%	11%
	100%	100%
	n=195	n=164

chi² = 4.4
sig. 0.05

NOTE: Among North Indian Mothers this same association holds, with the high school educated showing less preference for dictatorship. However, this association does not hold among either North Indian or South Indian Fathers.

Perhaps the Fathers have so much out-of-school exposure to political information that their formal schooling has a less significant effect on their political ideologies. The Mothers, with their more restricted political worlds, may be more markedly affected by the political information they acquire during their high school education.

If our earlier proposition is correct, i.e., that as the breadth of the spectrum of issues defined as "political" increases, the degree of authoritarian crystallization also increases, then we can now proceed one step further and suggest that in a society with such broad-spectrum political issues (as in South India), those in possession of less political information are the ones most likely to support dictatorship. In our study this means the Sons and Mothers; among the Mothers it means those with less than high school education.

Social Fatalism

Social fatalism refers to the belief that one's general social position in life is fixed and one cannot or could not have done anything to change it.

I was curious to see if empirical fatalism or theological fatalism were closely associated with social fatalism and social mobility aspirations. After trying as many combinations as I could, my conclusion came as something of a surprise. Neither empirical fatalism nor theological fatalism are noticeably associated with social fatalism.

Once this had been established, I started hunting elsewhere for possible variables associated with social fatalism. It did not take me

long to discover where these variables lay. As in the United States
and Britain, the dramatic variables appear to be those having to do
with social status. Thus, the higher the Father's occupation, the higher
the Son's educational aspirations (see Table 16).

The same two factors that influence the Sons' mobility aspirations,
i.e. occupational position and caste or religious status, also seem to

TABLE 16

The Higher the Father's Occupation, the
Higher the Son's Educational Aspirations

	Father Unskilled	Father Skilled or Owner	Father White Collar, Managerial, Professional
Son Aspires High School or Less	42%	19%	11%
Son Aspires More Than High School	58%	81%	89%
	100%	100%	100%
	n=353	n=159	n=96

chi² = 47.3
sig. 0.001

NOTE: The association pattern remains as above when broken down by North
and South India.

TABLE 17

High-Caste and Minority-Group Sons Aspire
to More Education Than Low-Caste Sons

	Scheduled Castes	Middle Castes	Muslims	"Twice-Born" Castes	Christians and Sikhs
Son Aspires High School or Less	51%	27%	18%	11%	8%
Son Aspires More Than High School	49%	73%	82%	89%	92%
	100%	100%	100%	100%	100%
	n=170	n=263	n=148	n=185	n=24

chi² = 82.1
sig. 0.001

NOTE: The association pattern remains as above when broken down by North
and South India, and when broken down further by education, i.e. 4 years or
less = "uneducated," 5 years or more = "educated."

have the greatest influence on the retroactive mobility aspirations of the Fathers (see Tables 18, 19).

TABLE 18

Higher Occupation Fathers Wish They Could Have
Studied Further Than Lower Occupation Fathers

	Unskilled	Skilled or Owner	White Collar Managerial Professional
Would Have Studied Primary School or Less	56%	33%	29%
Would Have Studied High School or College	35%	45%	34%
Would Have Studied Post-College	9%	22%	37%
	100% n=372	100% n=170	100% n=198

chi^2 = 75.4
sig. 0.001

NOTE: The association pattern remains as above when broken down by North and South India.

TABLE 19

High-Caste and Minority-Group Fathers Wish They
Could Have Studied Further Than Low-Caste Fathers

	Scheduled Castes	Middle Castes	Muslims	"Twice-Born" Castes	Christians and Sikhs
Would Have Studied Primary School or Less	62%	46%	35%	33%	13%
Would Have Studied High School or College	30%	47%	34%	30%	42%
Would Have Studied Post-College	8%	7%	31%	38%	46%
	100% n=167	100% n=257	100% n=140	101% n=165	101% n=24

chi^2 = 118.2
sig. 0.001

NOTE: The association pattern remains as above when broken down by North and South India, and when broken down further by education, i.e., no schooling = "uneducated," some schooling = "educated," with the exception of the South Indian "educated," where there is virtually no difference between the castes and religious groups.

In short, those who "have" appear to be the most eager to "continue having." Also, those who are marginal but deny the legitimacy of their marginality (such as the Christians, Sikhs and Muslims) appear to be equally keen to "have" or to "have more." It is clear that there can be several variables unrelated to the traditional "world view" of Hagen that can produce the same phenomenon of upward social mobility.

We have now discussed the last two of the five component parts of Hagen's traditional "image of the world," political authoritarianism and social fatalism. Our search for possible associations has yielded the following results:

Traditional "Action-Oriented" Belief	*Variables with Which It Is Associated*
A. Political authoritarianism	a. Region within India
	b. Family member (S. India)
	c. Personal authoritarianism (S. India)
	d. Theological fatalism (S. India)
	e. Amount of education (Mothers)
B. Social fatalism	a. Occupational status
	b. Caste or religious affiliation

CONCLUSIONS

The purpose of this paper was to examine the question: To what extent do the various parts of Hagen's traditional "image of the world" actually correlate with one another, and to what extent do they change independently of each other?

Our major finding is that in the sections of India in which I conducted my research these attitudes are independent of one another. The fact that a person is "traditional" in one dimension provides no evidence that he is "traditional" in one of the other dimensions.

The only exception to this general unrelatedness of parts concerns political authoritarianism. Within the unique circumstances pertaining in South India, political authoritarianism, personality authoritarianism and theological fatalism are significantly associated. The fact that these associations do not exist in North India suggests that the links discovered between the three parts of Hagen's "image of the world" are the result of special circumstances rather than the result of some intrinsic bond extending between the three.

To the initial question about the extent to which the various parts of Hagen's traditional "image of the world" actually associate with each other, we can reply that they associate very little. To the initial question about the extent to which the various parts can change independently of each other, we can reply that they can and they do.

A second major finding of this study is that the variable most affecting change from "traditional" to "non-traditional" images of the world is education. Increasing education is associated with decreasing empirical fatalism, decreasing theological fatalism (among the members of the majority religious group), and decreasing personality authoritarianism. Likewise, to the extent that education corresponds with higher occupational status, increasing education is associated with decreasing social fatalism. Even though the various parts of Hagen's traditional "image of the world" may not influence each other, many of them are markedly influenced by the same common variable—education.

A third major finding is that the two areas in which the effects of education seem least certain and most dependent on other variables are the areas of theological fatalism and political authoritarianism. As far as political authoritarianism is concerned, education appears to make little difference in whether the respondents are pro-dictatorship or pro-democracy. In the total sample there are roughly equal percentages of educated pro-dictators and uneducated pro-dictators. It is only after a highly politicized milieu has come into existence (as is the case in South India) that any noticeable associations appear between greater education and less political authoritarianism. At the same time other variables such as theological fatalism and personality authoritarianism also begin to be associated with political authoritarianism.

As far as theological fatalism is concerned, education appears to influence only to a small extent the theological fatalism of the *majority* religious group. *Minority* religious groups, regardless of amount of education, appear to retain a constant level of theological fatalism—with an equal proportion of educated and uneducated subscribing to the view that the outcome of actions are in God's hands.

The relative invulnerability of political authoritarianism to education might serve as a warning to any who may feel that education automatically establishes a basis for a democratic form of government. Obviously there are specific attitudes that need to be generated for such a basis to be established. Literacy as such is not enough.

The relative invulnerability of theological fatalism to education might provide reassurance to those who fear that a people or a nation loses its identity after the introduction of mass literacy campaigns. The evidence presented here suggests that even fairly drastic changes in attitudes regarding, for example, physical causality, do not necessarily change a person's theology or his belief that ultimately the outcome of his actions are in God's hands.

What we have here is a small cross-section of a large society undergoing marked economic, political and social changes, yet at the same time managing to maintain certain ties with its past beliefs. The types of "perspectives" and "action-oriented" beliefs suggested by Hagen in his traditional "view of the world" enable us to obtain a close view of the simultaneous processes of continuity and change.

CHAPTER 13

THE RELIGIOUS ASPECTS OF CASTE: A LEGAL VIEW

MARC GALANTER

IT IS WELL KNOWN that the Indian Constitution envisages a new order both as to the place of caste in Indian life and the role of law in regulating it. However, in spite of much talk about a "casteless" society, the Constitution is quite unclear about the position of the caste group in Indian life. There is a clear commitment to eliminate inequality of status and invidious treatment and to have a society in which government takes minimal account of ascriptive ties. Beyond this the treatment of caste is undetailed and in some respects unclear. In this paper, I shall attempt to elucidate some features of the relation between caste and law by considering the religious aspects of caste and their treatment by courts and government since Indian independence.

Both western and Indian writers reveal some hesitation and vacillation over whether or not to characterize castes as "religious" groups. To many writers caste groups are the very units of Hinduism; to others they are "purely social" with only an accidental attachment to Hinduism.[1] Much of this confusion derives from different views of "religion." I shall not attempt any reconciliation of these views; instead I shall look at the way the legal system has dealt with caste as a religious grouping. This is of historical importance, for there is evidence that the legal system is a powerful disseminator of images about the nature of groups in society and may affect their self-image and the image others have of them.[2] Also, it is of some practical importance in a legal system in which there are on the one hand restrictions on the power of castes, on governmental recognition of caste, on claims that can be made in the name of caste standing and where the government is committed to abolish certain undesirable

Marc Galanter is assistant professor in the social sciences at the University of Chicago.

[1] See, e.g., K. M. Panikkar, *Hindu Society at Cross-Roads*, Asia Publishing House, Bombay, 1955.

[2] E.g., William McCormack suggests that the notion of a unitary Lingayat group with a single distinctive culture appeared as a result of the application of the Anglo-Hindu law and British judicial administration, "Lingayats as a Sect," *Journal of the Royal Anthropological Institute*, 1963, vol. 93, part I, pp. 59-71.

features of caste;[3] and yet on the other hand religious groupings enjoy certain constitutional protections and the government is committed to allow them free play within broad limits.[4] Which way a caste group is characterized by the law may, then, be of crucial importance. And to the extent that these legal notions influence behavior, the legal characterization of the caste group may be an influential factor in the reformulation and reorganization of Hindusim taking place in India.

In order to describe the judicial conceptualization of the caste group, I propose to use three models: these models represent different ways of visualizing caste groups and their mutual relations. We shall find all of them employed by judges in dealing with concrete issues. Often the judicial response to an issue may employ more than one of these models or approaches. However, I believe these models are helpful in pointing to very different ways of visualizing the caste group; and these differences prove useful in describing recent changes in the legal view of caste. The first model sees the caste group as a component in an overarching sacral order of Hindu society. Hindu society is seen as a differentiated but integrated order in which the different parts may enjoy different rights, duties, privileges and disabilities; these are determined by the position of the caste group in relation to the whole. We may call this the *sacral* view of caste. In contrast to this is what we might call the *sectarian* view which sees the caste as an isolable religious community distinguished from others by idiosyncratic doctrine, ritual or culture.[5] It is a self-contained religious unit, disassociated from any larger religious order. The rights and duties of the group and its members follow from its own characteristics, not from its place in a larger order. Where the *sacral* view visualizes castes as occupying the various rooms, shrines, courtyards and outbuildings of the great labyrinth temple of Hinduism (to each of which is attached special prerogatives and disabilities), the *sectarian* view visualizes castes as a series of separate chapels under independent management. In the sacral view, the rights and duties of a caste can be determined by its relation to the whole (or at least to its surroundings); in the sectarian view, they can be described by

3 See Constitution of India, Arts. 15 (1), 15 (2), 16 (2), 17, 29.

4 See Constitution of India, Arts. 25, 26, 29, 30.

5 In employing the term "sectarian" it is necessary to resist both the connotation that such groups have been "cut off" from some larger body and the implication that such groups are associated with a distinctive and precise doctrine.

reference to its own internal order. It is the difference between a ward in a great and dense city and in a small town.

There is yet a third view of caste which lies beyond both the sacral and the sectarian. For want of a better term we might call it the *associational* view of caste. Here, the caste is seen as a body of persons with internal autonomy and rule-making powers, but characterized neither by a fixed place in some larger religious order nor by distinctive and idiosyncratic religious beliefs or practices. It is a kind of association with its own principles of affiliation and its own internal order. These may be in some respects like those of a corporation, a club, a dissenting church (in English law), or some other voluntary association, but they make the caste a form of association *sui generis*. The nature of the tie is not characterized conclusively by religious fellowship. The bonds of association may include religious ones, but the religious tie is only one among a constellation of affinities— economic, educational, occupational, associational. Like the sacral view of the caste group, the associational view avoids characterization in terms of specific religious characteristics. Like the sectarian view it does not identify the caste by its standing in a differentiated religious order of society. The sacral view regards the caste group in terms of its relation to the larger body of Hinduism; the sectarian view sees it in terms of its own religious distinctiveness; finally the associational view defines caste in terms of its associational bonds. These may include religious features along with others, but the religious ones are not conclusive in identifying or characterizing the group.[6]

During the latter part of the British period all three views of caste can be found in judicial pronouncements. I submit that by and large the sacral view prevailed as an integrating principle to organize and inspire the judicial view of castes as the component units of Hindu

[6] The organization of these models may be schematized as in the following chart.

		Characterization of group in terms of its position in the larger society	
		−	+
Conclusiveness of religious factors in characterizing the group	+	Sectarian View	Sacral View
	−	Associational View	

The empty box represents a fourth possibility—that view which sees the caste group in terms of its position in the wider society but not exclusively in terms of religious criteria. The use of caste in selecting "backward classes" strikes me as an instance of the use of this fourth model which I call the "organic" view; however, I have made no attempt to distinguish it in the body of this paper.

society. It is my contention that the Constitution and post-independence developments must be read as rejecting the sacral view and emphasizing in its stead the sectarian and associational views of caste groups, and that the courts have in good part responded by dismantling the sacral view and replacing it with the others. The rest of this paper will try to suggest this process and some of its possible implications and consequences.

In order to trace the changing judicial conceptualization of caste, I would like to take several kinds of cases in which caste comes before the courts and see how its religious aspects are treated. The matters I have chosen are (1) the administration of "personal law"; (2) the recognition of claims for precedence and for the imposition of disabilities; (3) the recognition of castes as autonomous self-governing groups. After briefly suggesting the judicial characterization of caste that prevailed in each of these fields in the latter days of British rule[7] in India, I shall attempt to trace developments since independence to show the emerging judicial view of the religious aspects of caste.[8]

THE OLD REGIME

Personal Law

The Hindu law applied by the courts in matters of "personal law"[9] did not address itself to the multitude of caste groups, but recognized

[7] By this I refer to the period since the founding of the modern legal system, which can be dated about 1860.

[8] The developments described here are at the higher and more authoritative levels of the legal system. In describing the development and application of doctrine by legislatures and higher courts, it is not intended to imply any one-to-one correspondence between the pronouncements of these higher authorities and the day-to-day operations of magistrates, officials, and lawyers, and much less the lay public. In the long run, however, the higher courts' pronouncements are uniquely influential; first, by disseminating influential "official" conceptions of caste which have an impact on the caste system; and second, by deflecting behavior toward conformity with the doctrines they promulgate.

[9] Under the legal system which the British established in India, all persons were subject to the same law in criminal, civil and commercial matters. However, a group of matters that might roughly be described as "family law"—marriage and divorce, adoption, joint family, guardianship, minority, legitimacy, inheritance and succession, and religious endowments—were set aside and left subject to the laws of the various religious communities. The applicable law in these fields was "personal" rather than territorial. In these family and religious matters, Hindus were ruled by *dharmasastra*—not by the ancient texts as such, but by the texts as interpreted by the commentators accepted in the locality. This was to be modified by prevailing custom since the doctrine that "clear proof of usage will outweigh the written text of the law" was early accepted as part of the Hindu law. However the application of stringent common law requirements for proving a valid custom made it difficult to prove variation from the rules of the lawbooks and had the effect, it appears, of extending the rules of the classical lawbooks to sections of

only the four *varnas* (and occasionally the intermediate classes of classical legal theory).[10] This law contained a number of instances in which different rules were to be applied to members of different *varnas*—in most cases one rule for the three twice-born *varnas* and a different rule for the Sudras. The most notable of these differences were in the law of succession, the law of adoption and the law of marriage.[11] With limited exceptions, marriages and adoptions involving members of different *varnas* were not valid at all. In order to apply these rules which differed according to *varna*, it was necessary for the courts to determine which castes and individuals were included within which *varna*. The assignment of standing in the four-*varna* system to actual castes presented an opportunity, often taken advantage of, for eliciting legal recognition of the ceremonial status of the group and certification of its claims for higher status.

The courts developed several kinds of tests to determine the *varna* standing of particular castes. One was the listing of certain diagnostic customs: e.g., admission of illegitimate sons to commensality and marriage within the group, the prevalence of second marriages for widows, marked the group as *Sudras*.[12] Another line of cases developed an alternative approach to testing the *varna* standing of a caste group by its own consciousness of its status and by the acceptance of this self-estimate by other castes in the locality.[13] These tests involve reliance on the widespread conventional notions of purity and pollution; they emphasize orthodox and prestigious practice rather than refinements of doctrine or ritual.[14] These notions of differential purity

---

the population which had previously been strangers to them. The British period then was marked by an attrition of local customary law at the expense of the written and refined law of the texts. See my paper "Hindu Law and the Development of the Modern Indian Legal System" in David Wilson, ed., *Political Institutions in Underdeveloped Countries*, forthcoming.

[10] The judicial treatment of the relation between *varna* and caste was plagued by confusion, engendered in part by the use of "caste" to refer both to the four great classes or *varnas* into which Hindu society is theoretically divided by the Sanskrit lawbooks and to the multitude of existing endogamous groups or *jatis*. In the sequel, unless the context indicates otherwise, caste is used only in the latter sense.

[11] These differences are concisely summarized by J. D. M. Derrett, "Statutory Amendments of the Personal Law of the Hindus since Indian Independence," *American Journal of Comparative Law*, 380, 83-85 (1958).

[12] See, e.g., *Gopal v. Hanmant*, I.L.R. 3 Bom. 273 (1879).

[13] See, e.g., *Subrao v. Radha*, I.L.R. 52 Bom. 497 (1928).

[14] Mere performance of ceremonies associated with higher castes will not elevate lower classes to that station, though "where caste is doubtful, the performance of Vedic or Puranic ritual may be important evidence as to caste. . . ." *Maharajah of Kolhapur v. Sundaram Ayyar*, A.I.R. 1925 Mad. 497 at 553.

The Religious Aspects of Caste

are used to assign castes to their proper *varna*. It is assumed that the castes are components of the *varnas* which in turn comprise Hinduism. It is assumed that all groups within Hinduism are subsumed under one or another *varna*. Although there are some instances of judicial departures from the symmetry of this scheme,[15] generally the picture of Hinduism found in the administration of personal law is one which regards caste and *varna* as co-extensive with Hinduism. Castes, therefore, have certain religious characteristics; they occupy their respective places in the sacral order of ranks which embraces all groups within Hinduism. Positions in this order could be assigned by certain widely-shared notions about the relative standing implied by certain practices.

Precedence and Disabilities

Prior to British rule, some Indian regimes had actively enforced the privileges and disabilities of various caste groups. Indeed such enforcement of the caste order is urged by Hindu legal tradition as the prime duty of the Hindu king. During the latter part of the British period the prerogatives and dignities of castes received only limited support by active governmental sanctions. This limited support was undertaken on the basis of upholding customary rights, but these rights were often conceptualized in terms of the religious characteristics of caste groups.

With respect to the use of religious premises, caste groups did enjoy the support of the courts in upholding their claims for preference and exclusiveness. Courts granted injunctions to restrain members of particular castes from entering temples—even ones that were publicly supported and dedicated to the entire Hindu community.[16] Damages were awarded for purificatory ceremonies necessitated by the pollution caused by the presence of lower castes; such pollution was

[15] Thus it is possible to have *varna* standing without belonging to a caste group. *Sunder Devi v. Jheboo Lal* A.I.R. 1957 All. 215 (convert to Hinduism); *Upoma Kuchain v. Bholaram* I.L.R. 15 Cal. 708 (1888), (daughter of outcaste); cf. *Ratansi v. Administrator General*, A.I.R. 1928 Mad. 1279 (convert to Hinduism). For some purposes at least, Hindu caste groups may fall outside of or below the four *varnas*. *Sankaralinga Nadan v. Raja Rajeswara Dorai*, 35 I.A. 176 (1908). Possibly one can be a Hindu without caste or *varna*. See *Ratansi v. Administrator General, supra*. Caste and *varna* may apply to persons who are not strictly Hindus, *Inder Singh v. Sadhan Singh*, I.L.R. (1944), 1 Cal. 233 (Sikh Brahmins). For some purposes caste groups have been recognized which neither have *varna* nor are Hindu in any sense. *Abdul Kadir v. Dharma* I.L.R. 20 Bom. 190 (1895). Again members of the same caste may hold different *varna* statuses. *Subrao v. Radha, supra*.

[16] *Anandrav Bhikaji Phadke v. Shankar Daji Charya*, I.L.R. 7 Bom. 323 (1883); *Sankaralinga Nadan v. Raja Rajeswara Dorai*, 35 I.A.C. 176 (1908); *Chathunni v. Appukuttan*, A.I.R. 1945 Mad. 232.

actionable as a trespass to the person of the higher caste worshippers.[17] It was a criminal offense for a member of an excluded caste knowingly to pollute a temple by his presence.[18] These rights to exclusiveness were vindicated by the courts not only where the interlopers were "untouchables," but also against such "touchables" as Palshe Brahmins and Lingayats, whose presence in the particular temple was polluting.

In these cases the courts were giving effect to the notion of an overarching, differentiated Hindu ritual order in which the various castes were assigned, by text or by custom, certain prerogatives and disabilities to be measured by concepts of *varna*, of pollution and required ceremonial distance. Thus, in *Anandrav Bhikaji Phadke v. Shankar Daji Charya* the court upheld the right of Chitpavan Brahmins to exclude Palshe Brahmins from worshipping at a temple, on the ground that such an exclusive right "is one which the courts must guard, as otherwise all high-caste Hindus would hold their sanctuaries and perform their worship, only so far as those of the lower castes chose to allow them."[19]

In 1908 the Privy Council upheld the exclusion of Shanars from a temple and granted damages for its purification after a careful scrutiny of their social standing. Finding "their position in general social estimation appears to have been just above that of Pallas, Pariahs, and Chucklies (who are on all hands regarded as unclean and prohibited from the use of Hindu temples) and below that of the Vellalas, Maravars, and other cultivating castes usually classed as Sudras, and admittedly free to worship in the Hindu temples," the Council concluded that the presence of Shanars was repugnant to the "religious principles of the Hindu worship of Shiva" as well as to the sentiments and customs of the caste Hindu worshippers.[20] As late as 1945, Nair users of a public temple were granted damages for pollution for the purificatory ceremonies necessitated by Ezhavas bathing in tanks.[21] Untouchable Mahars who entered the enclosure of a village idol were convicted on the ground that "where custom . . . ordains that an untouchable, whose very touch is in the opinion of devout Hindus pollution, should not enter the enclosure surrounding the shrine of any Hindu god," such entry is a defilement in violation of Section 295 of the Penal Code.[22]

---

[17] See cases cited, note 16 *supra.* Cf. *S. K. Wodeyar v. Ganapati*, A.I.R. 1935 Bom. 371, where damages were awarded although the parties agreed there should be no finding on the question of pollution.

[18] *Atmaram v. King-Emperor*, A.I.R. 1924 Nag. 121.

[19] 7 Bom. 323 at 222.   [20] 35 I.A.C. 176 at 182.

[21] A.I.R. 1945 Mad. 232.

[22] A.I.R. 1924 Nag. 121.

The Religious Aspects of Caste

While Hinduism is seen as a unified order, it is also seen as differentiated. Religious obligations and prerogatives for groups differ according to their standing in this whole. Where Brahmins tore the sacred thread from the neck of an Ahir who had lately taken to wearing it, the court ruled that since he was a Sudra, the wearing of it was not "part of his religion" vis-à-vis other Hindus. To them it was an assertion of a claim to higher rank. Therefore the injury was not to his religious susceptibilities—an offense—but only to his dignity.[23] Had it been torn by non-Hindus, it might have been an insult to his religion itself.

In these cases the courts clearly express their notion of a rank ordering of all Hindu groups in a scheme of articulated prerogatives and disabilities. One looks to the position of the caste in the whole—its position on the scale relative to the other groups—to find what are its rights. This approach did not always work to the disadvantage of the excluded class. In *Gopala v. Subramania,* members of the Elaivaniyar community obtained a declaration of their right to enter the outer hall of the temple and an injunction restraining other worshippers from ejecting them. The court declared that each group enjoyed a prima facie right to enter that part of the temple assigned his caste (i.e., *varna*) by the *Agamas* (texts on use of temples), that these texts authorized the entry of Sudras in this part of the temple, and that the plaintiffs were "at least Sudras." Their right could only be overcome by proof of a custom of exclusion.[24] Similarly where Moothans were convicted for defiling a temple by entering the part open to "non-Brahmins" the court reversed the conviction on the ground that Moothans are Sudras, no lower or more polluting than the Nairs who were allowed to enter the temple.[25]

Again we see the notion of a single articulated Hindu community in which there are authoritative opinions (supplied by custom and accepted texts) which determine the respective rights of its component groups. The effect of this conception of the Hindu order is revealed clearly in the case of *Michael Pillai v. Barthe.* Here a group of Roman Catholic Pillais and Mudalis sued for an injunction to require the bishop of Trichinopoly to reerect a wall separating their part of the church from that entered by "low caste Christians" and to declare plaintiffs' exclusive right to perform services at the altar. The court characterized the claim as one for "a right of freedom from contact

[23] *Sheo Shankar v. Emperor,* A.I.R. 1940 Oudh 348.
[24] A.I.R. 1914 Mad. 363.
[25] *Kutti Chami Moothan v. Rama Pattar,* A.I.R. 1919 Mad. 755.

which can have but one origin . . . that of pollution,[26] but refused to recognize pollution as either a spiritual or a temporal injury among Christians. Nor could Christians constitute "castes" with rights based on their respective purity. Not being Hindus, plaintiffs "cannot . . . invoke the authority of accepted sacerdotal texts for perpetuating the distinction between touchables and untouchables during a particular life solely by reason of birth."[27] Having placed themselves by conversion outside the sacral order of Hinduism, caste groupings are not invested with those rights which follow only upon their occupying a place in that order.

Exclusionary practices did not enjoy the same judicial support in regard to "secular" public facilities such as schools, wells and roads. The courts declared that no right could be maintained to exclude other castes or sects from the use of streets and roads.[28] The situation is more complicated regarding the use of water-sources. The Lahore court held other users had no right to prevent Chamars from drawing water from a public well,[29] but other courts conceded that a right to exclude might be upheld if a custom of exclusive use by higher castes could be proved. However, such customs were difficult to prove. In *Marriappa v. Vaithilinga,* Shanars obtained an order allowing them to use a large tank on the ground that no custom of exclusion was proved. (A right of exclusion was upheld in regard to one well in the dispute where such a custom was proved.) The interesting thing for our purpose is that even in denying the exclusionary claims of the higher groups, the courts reveal an implicit view of an integrated Hindu community with graded rights. The absence of a custom of exclusion from the large tank, as distinguished from the well, is indicated by textual passages to the effect that precautions for impurity may be less intense in a body of water of this size.[30] Again, in *N. D. Vaidya v. B. R. Ambedkar,* the court found it unproven that there was any long-standing custom of exclusion. Textual provisions indicating that no elaborate precautions against pollution are required in a tank of that size rendered it "doubtful whether any attempt would have been made to secure exclusive use of the water until such time as the tank came to be surrounded by the houses of caste Hindus."[31]

In dealing with exclusionary rights the courts tried to confine themselves to claims involving civil or property rights, as opposed to

[26] A.I.R. 1917 Mad. 431 at 433.   [27] *Ibid.,* at 442.
[28] E.g., *Sadogopachariar v. Rama Rao.* I.L.R. 26 Mad. 376, aff'd 35 I.A. 93.
[29] *Kazan Chand v. Emperor,* A.I.R. 1926 Lah. 683.
[30] 1913 M.W.N. 247.   [31] A.I.R. 1938 Bom. 146 at 148.

mere claims for standing or social acceptance. Thus the courts refused to penalize such defiance of customary disabilities as failure to dismount from a wedding palanquin or failure to concede another caste an exclusive right to ceremonial deference.[32] The prevailing notion was that social and religious matters did not give rise to legal rights unless the right was the sort of thing that could be possessed and made use of. Thus we find gradation from the temple cases, where there was ready enforcement of exclusionary rights, to watersources, where it seems enforcement might be forthcoming if difficult technical requirements were met, to customs in no way connected with the use of specific property, where there was no enforcement at all.[33] Where government intervened, it upheld custom, but this custom was evaluated and rationalized by the courts in terms of notions of ceremonial purity and pollution—existing in different degrees among different groups of Hindus.[34]

Caste Autonomy[35]

Castes were early recognized as juridical entities with the right to sue and be sued, to sue on behalf of their members, to acquire, hold and manage property. More importantly for our purpose here, the caste was recognized as a group having the power to make rules for itself and to constitute tribunals to enforce these rules. While caste power was limited by confining jurisdiction over many matters (e.g., criminal law or the validity of a marriage) to the official courts, on most matters the caste could make, modify and revoke its rules. The

[32] *Jasnani v. Emperor*, A.I.R. 1936 All. 534; *Govinda Amrita v. Emperor*, A.I.R. 1942 Nag. 45.

[33] While there was no support for these usages at the high court level, there is evidence of widespread local acquiescence in and enforcement of such practices. See, e.g., the actions of the local officials described in *Kazan Chand v. Emperor*, A.I.R. 1926 Lah. 683; A.I.R. 1927 Lah. 430; *Jasnani v. Emperor, supra.* note 32; *Govinda Amrita v. Emperor, supra.* note 32.

[34] However, these prescriptive rights and disabilities received their greatest governmental support not from direct judicial enforcement but from the recognition of caste autonomy—i.e., from the refusal of the courts to interfere with the right of caste groups to apply sanctions against those who defined these usages. Members of the caste could be outcasted and outsiders could be boycotted for violations of customary usage.

[35] For detailed analysis and references in the area of caste autonomy, see L. T. Kikani, *Caste in Courts*, Rajkot, 1912; "Caste Customs, Caste Questions and Jurisdiction of Courts," *Hindu Law Journal*, vol. 1 (Journal Section), pp. 32ff. (1918-1919). The only legislation directly impinging on caste autonomy was the Caste Disabilities Removal Act (Act XXI of 1850, also known as the Freedom of Religion Act) which provided that there was to be no forfeiture of civil or property rights "by reason of renouncing, or, having been excluded from the communion of, any religion, or being deprived of caste. . . ."

majority, or the established authorities within the caste, could not be overruled by the civil courts on these "caste questions." Caste questions were said to include all matters affecting the internal autonomy and social relations of a caste. The right to have a fellow caste member accept one's food, gifts, or invitations; the right to receive invitations from him; the right to have precedence in leading one's bullock in a procession—in all of these cases of dignity, acceptance or precedence within the caste, the civil courts would not entertain a suit. Again, claims to leadership of a caste, claims to a caste-office, claims to enjoy privileges and honors by virtue of such office, and claims to officiate as priest, were held to be caste questions. Even if the dispute resulted in the expulsion of one person or faction, the courts would take no cognizance in such cases. Publication of a sentence of excommunication to other caste members was privileged—i.e., immune from a claim for defamation—so long as it was not more extensive than necessary to effect the purpose of informing the caste.

But the courts were willing to take jurisdiction where they found that the claim was not merely for social acceptance or dignities, but involved enforceable civil or property rights—these included rights in caste property, the right to offices with pecuniary emoluments and the right to reputation. Even here, the courts were wary about the extent of intervention and set up standards that emphasized procedural rather than substantive supervision. The courts would entertain claims only: (1) that the decision of a caste tribunal had not been arrived at *bona fide*; (2) that the decision was taken under a mistaken belief; (3) that the decision was actually contrary to the rules or usage of the caste; or, (4) that it was contrary to natural justice. The latter was the most important of these rules—violations of natural justice included omission of proper notice to the accused and the denial of an opportunity to be heard and to defend himself.

Here we have a judicial view of caste more congenial to our sectarian or associational models than to the sacral model. Castes are seen as independent bodies with their own internal order and the rights and duties of individual members follow from this order. This order is not determined by the position of the caste in an overarching order of Hindu society. Although analogies are sometimes drawn from such associations as clubs,[36] corporations, partnerships or dissenting churches, the courts never subsume the caste group under any of these. It is a group *sui generis*.[37] Although some courts speak of the caste

[36] See *Appaya v. Padappa*, I.L.R. 23 Bom. 112.

[37] "The Hindu caste is an unique aggregation so wholly unknown to the English law that English decisions, concerning English corporations and partnerships tend

as a voluntary organization in the sense that one can leave it, it is generally conceded that "the caste is a social combination, the members of which are enlisted by birth, not by enrollment."[38]

Is the caste group a "religious body?" We have seen that the courts refused to take cognizance of suits for mere "religious honors" or to enforce obligations they regarded as purely religious. The caste group was recognized as a proper forum for settling these religious questions. The caste is recognized as a corporate body with the right to promulgate and enforce its own religious doctrine, ritual and leadership.[39] But it cannot be conclusively characterized by its religious attributes. "The caste is not a religious body, though its usages, like all other Hindu usages, are based upon religious feelings. In religious matters, strictly so called, the members of the caste are governed by their religious preceptors. In social matters they lay down their own laws."[40]

Thus the caste unit is not solely religious in its concerns and nature. It is mixed—partly civil and partly religious.[41] Or as a Madras court summed it up, "a caste is a combination of a number of persons governed by a body of usages which differentiate them from others. The usages may refer to social or religious observances, to drink, food, ceremonies, pollution, occupation, or marriage." That is, a caste is not wholly or solely to be characterized by religion, either in doctrine or practice.[42] Castes are autonomous units with internal government and characterized partly by religious and partly by non-religious usages. Unlike the personal law[43] and the cases involving precedence and disabilities where castes were allocated differential religious honor because of their place in the wider Hindu scheme, here the castes are treated as autonomous and self-sufficient entities whose order proceeds from internal organs.

This detachment from the context of the wider Hindu society comes out clearly in the treatment of non-Hindu groups under the heading of caste autonomy. Here we find that the autonomous caste group is

---

rather to confusion than to guidance upon matters relating to caste." *Jethabhai Narsey v. Chapsey Kooverji* 34 Bom. 467.

38 *Raghunath v. Javardhan* 15 Bom. 599 at 611.

39 See, e.g., *Devchand Totaram v. Ghaneshyam* A.I.R. 1935 Bom. 361 (jurisdiction of caste includes outcasting of members for adherence to sub-sect said to be outside Vedic religion).

40 *Raghunath v. Javardhan, supra.* note 38, at 611.

41 *Haroon v. Haji Adam,* 11 Bom. L.R. 1267.

42 *Muthuswami v. Masilamani,* I.L.R. 33 Mad. 342 (1909).

43 The personal law inclined away from the sacral view toward a view more like that found in the caste autonomy area in the recognition of castes as units whose customs, where proven, would serve to vary the law of the textbooks.

recognized not only among Hindus but also among Muslims, Parsis, Jews, Sikhs, Jains and Christians.[44] In this context caste groups are not subsumed under the *varnas*; they are treated as a special kind of group. Where the rights and powers claimed by a caste derive from a place in a larger Hindu order they are not recognized in non-Hindu groups. But where they derive from internal order, customary and deliberative, of the group as an autonomous entity, they are recognized among all religions.

THE NEW DISPENSATION

The Constitution sets forth a general program for the reconstruction of Indian society.[45] In spite of its length, it is not detailed in its treatment of the institution of caste and of the existing group structure of Indian society. But it clearly sets out to secure to individuals equality of status and opportunity,[46] to abolish invidious distinctions among groups,[47] to protect the integrity of a variety of groups— religious, linguistic and cultural,[48] to give free play to voluntary associations,[49] the widest freedom of association to the individual,[50] and generally the widest personal freedom consonant with the public good.[51] Without pursuing all of these in detail, it is clear that the following general principles are consistently in evidence: (1) a commitment to the replacement of ascribed status by voluntary affiliations; (2) an emphasis on the integrity and autonomy of groups within society; (3) a withdrawal of governmental recognition of rank ordering among groups.

In order to see how the new constitutional scheme has affected the judicial view of the religious aspects of caste, we shall trace recent developments in the areas previously discussed and in some new problem areas that have emerged since independence.

[44] See, e.g., *Abdul Kadir v. Dharma*, 20 Bom. 190 (1895) where the court observed that "caste" comprised "any well-defined native community governed for certain internal purposes by its own rules and regulations," and was thus not confined to Hindus.

[45] This new dispensation did not arrive on the scene suddenly. It represents the culmination of more than half a century of increasing anti-caste sentiment among reformers, the gradual acceptance by politicians of the need for reform of caste, a variety of provincial anti-disabilities and temple-entry legislation, and the growing conviction that caste is inimical to democracy and progress and should play a restricted role in the new India.

[46] Preamble, Articles 14-18, 23, 46.

[47] Articles 14-17, 25-30.

[48] Articles 25-30, 347, 350A, 350B.

[49] Articles 19(1)c, 25, 26, 30.

[50] *Ibid.*

[51] See generally, Parts III and IV of the Constitution.

The Religious Aspects of Caste

Personal Law

The Constitution contains a commitment to replace the system of separate personal laws with a "uniform civil code."[52] In spite of its strictures against discrimination on the ground of religion, the Constitution has been interpreted to permit the continuing application of their respective personal laws to Hindus and Muslims. The continuing validity of disparate rules of personal law and the power of the state to create new rules applicable to particular communities has been upheld.[53] Within the Hindu law itself, the constitutional ban on caste discrimination has not been read as abolishing differences in personal law between Hindus of different castes. Although legal enforcement of disabilities against lower castes was sometimes rationalized in *varna* terms, the use of *varna* distinctions in the personal law is not included within the constitutional abolition of untouchability.[54] However, the Hindu Code Acts[55] of 1955-1956 have largely abandoned the shastric basis of Hindu law and established a more or less uniform law for Hindus of all regions and castes. The new law creates the hitherto unknown capacity to marry and adopt across *varna* lines and, with a few minor exceptions, eliminates all of the distinctions along *varna* lines embodied in the old law.[56] *Varna* has virtually been eliminated as an operative legal concept—although for the present the courts still have to apply it to transactions covered by the older law. In addition the new legislation severely curtails the opportunities for invoking caste custom in order to vary the generally applicable Hindu law.

Precedence and Disabilities

The Preamble to the Constitution resolves "to secure to all of its citizens . . . EQUALITY of status and opportunity." Accordingly, it confers on all its citizens a fundamental right to be free of discrimina-

---

[52] Article 44.

[53] *State of Bombay v. Narasu Appa Mali*, A.I.R. 1952 Bom. 84.

[54] The assignment of a community to a *varna* has been held not to constitute a deprivation of rights to equality before the law, nor is it religious discrimination. *Sangannagonda v. Kallangonda*, A.I.R. 1960 Mys. 147. The classification of the offspring of a Sudra and his Brahmin concubine as a *chandala*, the lowest of untouchables in the traditional scheme, did not strike the court as unconstitutional in *Bachubhai v. Bai Dhanlaxmi*, A.I.R. 1961 Guj. 141.

[55] I.e., the Hindu Marriage Act of 1955, the Hindu Succession Act of 1956, the Hindu Minority and Guardianship Act of 1956 and the Hindu Adoptions and Maintenance Act of 1956.

[56] Derrett, note 11, suggests that the only instances in which *varna* might continue to have effect are succession to *sannyasis* and determination of the maximum age for adoption.

tion by the state on the ground of caste. But the Constitution does not only forbid caste discrimination by the government; it goes on to outlaw invidious treatment on the basis of caste by private citizens as well. Art. 15 (2) prohibits discrimination by private persons in regard to use of facilities and accommodations open to the public such as wells, tanks, shops and restaurants.[57] Art. 17 provides that "Untouchability" is abolished and its practice in any form is forbidden. The enforcement of any disability arising out of "Untouchability" shall be an offense punishable in accordance with law. The guarantee of freedom of religion is explicitly qualified to permit temple-entry legislation.[58] Under these provisions, there is no longer any governmental power to make discriminations among citizens on caste lines.[59] Nor may government enforce any customary right to exclude certain castes from a public facility.[60]

The Untouchability Offenses Act of 1955 outlaws the imposition of disabilities "on grounds of untouchability" in regard to, *inter alia*, entrance and worship at temples, access to shops and restaurants, the practice of occupations and trades, use of water sources, places of public resort and accommodation, public conveyances, hospitals, educational institutions, construction and occupation of residential premises, holding of religious ceremonies and processions, and use of jewelry and finery. Enforcement of disabilities is made a crime, punishable by fine or imprisonment, and the power of civil courts to recognize any custom, usage, or right which would result in the enforcement of any disability is withdrawn.

In order to gauge the scope of Art. 17 and this legislation, it is necessary to determine the meaning of "untouchability." Although it is yet unclear in detail, judicial construction so far gives us some

[57] See also Arts. 28 (3) and 29 (2) which forbid discrimination in private educational institutions.

[58] Art. 25 (2)b. When the Constitution was enacted, customary exclusion of lower castes from temples and secular facilities, previously recognized and to some extent enforceable at law, had been transformed into statutory offenses throughout most of India. For a survey of this provincial legislation and its continuing efficacy, see my article, "Caste Disabilities and Indian Federalism," *Journal of the Indian Law Institute*, 1961, vol. 3, pp. 205-234.

[59] See, e.g., *State of Madras v. Champakam Dorairjan* [1951] S.C.J. 313; *Sanghar Umar v. State*, A.I.R. 1952 Saur. 124. Caste cannot be recognized for electoral purposes. The Constitution rules out electorates according to caste for Parliament and state legislatures. Art. 325. Communal electorates in local bodies are unconstitutional. *Nain Sukh Das v. State of U.P.*, A.I.R. 1953 S.C. 384; nor can caste be used as a criterion in delimiting territorial constituencies (by excluding from a ward "houses of Rajputs in the east of the village"). *Bhopal Singh v. State*, A.I.R. 1958 Raj. 41.

[60] *Aramugha Konar v. Narayana Asari*, A.I.R. 1958 Mad. 282.

guide-lines. Apparently the "untouchability" forbidden by the Constitution does not include every instance in which one person is treated as ritually unclean and polluting. It does not include such temporary and expiable states of uncleanliness as that suffered by women in childbirth, mourners, etc.[61] Nor does it include that "untouchability" which follows upon expulsion or excommunication from caste.[62] It is confined to that untouchability ascribed by birth rather than attained in life. Further, it does not include every instance in which one is treated as untouchable in certain respects because of a difference in religion or membership in a different or lower caste. It includes, in the words of the first court to pass on the issue explicitly, only those practices directed against "those regarded as 'untouchables' in the course of historic development"—i.e., those relegated "beyond the place of the caste system on grounds of birth in a particular class."[63] Thus it would not include practices based on avoidance due to a difference of religion or caste, except in so far as the caste was traditionally considered "untouchable" and "outside the pale of the caste system." Thus disabilities imposed, e.g., by one group of Brahmins on other Brahmins, by Brahmins on non-Brahmins, by "right-hand" on "left-hand" castes would all fall outside the prohibition of Article 17.

The meaning of untouchability then is to be determined by reference to those who have traditionally been considered "untouchables." But it is no easier to define untouchables than it is to define "untouchability." "Beyond the pale of the caste system" is a misleading and unworkable formulation. Even the lowest castes are within the system of reciprocal rights and duties; their disabilities and prerogatives are articulated to those of other castes. Presumably the Mysore court means, by this phrase, outside the four *varnas* of the classical lawbooks. In reference to their customary rights, untouchables have sometimes, particularly in southern India, been referred to as a fifth *varna*, below the *Sudras*.[64] But in other places they were regarded as *Sudras*.[65] For purposes of personal law, the courts have never attempted to distinguish untouchables from *Sudras*; all Hindus

---

[61] *Devarajiah v. Padmanna*, A.I.R. 1958 Mys. 84.

[62] *Hadibandhu v. Banamali*, A.I.R. 1960 Or. 33; cf. *Saifuddin Saheb v. State of Bombay*, A.I.R. 1962 S.C. 853.

[63] *Devarajiah v. Padmanna*, note 61, at 85.

[64] See, e.g., *Sankaralinga Nadan v. Raja Rajeshwari Dorai*, 35 I.A.C. 176 (1908).

[65] See, e.g., *Atmaram v. King-Emperor*, A.I.R. 1924 Nag. 121.

other than the twice-born have been lumped together as *Sudras*.[66]
Even where untouchables are popularly regarded as *Sudras*, they cannot be equated with them since there are non-untouchable groups
which belong to this category. Thus, the tests used for distinguishing
Sudras from the twice-born, cannot be used as a satisfactory measure
of untouchability. Thus although the abolition of untouchability
amounts to a kind of negative recognition of the sacral order of
Hinduism, it is not likely that the jurisprudence recognizing that
order will find new employment for the purpose of identifying "untouchables." In attempting to identify untouchable groups for the
purpose of giving them benefits and preferences the government has
not tried to apply general criteria, but has adopted the device of com-
piling lists of castes in each locality.[67]

Thus the "untouchability" forbidden by law is confined to discriminations against certain not readily defined classes of persons.
It includes not every discrimination against them, but only those
imposed because of their position in the caste system. The provisions
making untouchability an offense attempt to distinguish between those
disabilities and exclusions imposed on grounds of caste position and
those which derive from religious and sectarian difference. Crucial
sections of the Untouchability Offenses Act are qualified to make
an offense only the exclusion of untouchables from places "open to
other persons professing the same religion or belonging to the same
religious denomination or section thereof."[68] Thus the scope of the
rights conferred on untouchables by the act depends on the meaning
of the phrases "the same religion" and "the same religious denomination or section thereof." To the extent that caste distinctions are con-

[66] See, e.g., *Muthuswami v. Masilamani*, I.L.R., 33 Mad. 342 (1909): *Maharajah of
Kolhapur v. Sundaram Aiyar*, A.I.R. 1925 Mad. 497, 521.

[67] Such lists derive from earlier attempts (in the 1930's) to find a single set of
criteria to measure "untouchability." These included such tests as whether the
caste in question was "polluting" or "debarred" from public facilities—which may
admit of no equivocal answer—and whether they were served by "clean" Brahmins
—which has only a local and comparative reference. All attempts to set up tests
based on the assumption that "untouchables" are set off by some uniform and
distinctive pattern of practices proved inadequate to isolate the groups which local
administrators felt deserving of inclusion. Additional criteria of poverty and
illiteracy had to be added. The government lists then give little guide to the
meaning of untouchability. There is no adequate inclusive list of all groups considered untouchable or any single set of criteria for identifying them. For a discussion of the problem of identifying the "untouchables," see Lelah Dushkin, "The
Backward Classes," in *The Economic Weekly* for Oct. 28, Nov. 4, and Nov. 18, 1961
and her "The Policy of the Indian National Congress Toward the Depressed
Classes," unpublished M.A. thesis, University of Pennsylvania, 1957.

[68] Sec. 3 (1).

ceived of as religious or denominational differences, the rights of untouchables are limited. Thus exclusion of untouchables by Jains is not forbidden, in so far as it is on the ground that they are non-Jains rather than because of their caste.[69] In spite of some attempt by the lawmakers to minimize such distinctions,[70] courts have (on solid textual grounds) been reluctant to read the act as obviating these distinctions. In *State of Kerala v. Venkiteswara Prabhu*,[71] untouchables were prevented from entering the Nalambalam of a temple belonging to the Gowda Saraswat Brahmin community. Since only members of this community ordinarily entered this part of the temple, the court held that exclusion of untouchables was not an offense since they did not belong to the same "denomination or section thereof." The acceptance by the court of denominational lines within Hinduism as limiting the operation of the temple-entry provisions may produce some unanticipated results. For the "religion" and "denomination" qualifiers also appear in other provisions of the Untouchability Offenses Act.[72] Thus judicial solicitude for the sectarian prerogatives of groups within Hinduism may severely limit the rights granted by some of the central provisions of the act.

Since untouchability has been interpreted to include only discriminations against untouchables, the legislation against it has not touched discriminations against other classes of Hindus. The anomalous situation that it is an offense to exclude untouchables from temples, but classes of touchable Hindus may be excluded with impunity, has led several states to enact supplementary legislation. A Bombay act, for example, makes it an offense to prevent "Hindus of any class or sect from entering or worshipping at a temple to the same extent and in the same manner as any other class or section of Hindus."[73] These laws extend protection to non-untouchables and they also overcome the sectarian and denominational limitations

[69] *Ibid.; State v. Puranchand*, A.I.R. 1958 M.P. 352.

[70] See the "Explanation" attached to Sec. 3 of the Untouchability Offenses Act.

[71] A.I.R. 1961 Ker. 55.

[72] The qualification appears in the provisions relating to: use of utensils and other articles kept in restaurants, hotels, etc.; use of wells, water-sources, bathing ghats, cremation grounds; the use of "places used for a public or charitable purpose"; the enjoyment of benefits of a charitable trust; and the use of dharmasalas, sarais and musafirkhanas. Sections 4 (ii), 4 (iv), 4 (v), 4 (vi), 4 (ix). Strangely enough it does not appear in Sec. 4 (x) regarding "the observance of any . . . religious custom, usage or ceremony or taking part in any religious procession." Thus untouchables seem to have access to the religious processions of Hindu denominations and sects, but not to their wells, etc.

[73] Bombay Hindu Places of Public Worship (Entry Authorization) Act, 1956. Cf. United Provinces Temple Entry (Declaration of Rights) Act, 1956.

which the courts have found in the Untouchability Offenses Act. It remains to be seen whether these limitations represent a constitutional restriction and to what extent the state is constitutionally obliged to recognize these sectarian distinctions.

The attack on discrimination is only one side of the attempt to remove the disabilities of the lower castes. For the purpose of securing equality, the government is authorized to depart from indifference to caste in order to favor untouchables, tribals, and backward classes. These provisions for "protective discrimination" are the only exceptions to the constitutional ban on the use of communal criteria by government. The Constitution authorizes government to provide special benefits and preferences to previously disadvantaged sections of the population. Reserved posts in government, reserved seats in legislatures,[74] reserved places in public education and an array of preferences and welfare measures have been made available to the Scheduled Castes and, to a lesser extent, to the "backward classes."

With membership in these groups a qualification for preferment of various kinds, it is not surprising that disputes have arisen concerning such membership. In order to qualify for preferences, one must be a member of the listed caste. In *Chatturbhuj Vithaldas Jasani v. Moreshwar Pareshram,* the Supreme Court decided that a Mahar who had joined the Mahanubhava Panth, a Hindu sect which repudiated the multiplicity of gods and the caste system, remained a Mahar and was thus eligible to stand for a reserved seat in the legislature. The court arrived at this conclusion on the ground that he had continued to identify himself as a Mahar and had retained full acceptance by the Mahar community. The court concluded that "conversion to this sect imports little beyond an intellectual acceptance of certain ideological tenets and does not alter the convert's caste status."[75] Thus the court saw no distinctive religious content in membership in the caste; its bonds are "social and political ties." "If the individual . . . desires and intends to retain his old social and political ties" and if the old order is tolerant of the new faith and does not expel the convert, the conversion does not affect his caste membership.[76] However, the court recognized that there is a religious dimension to caste affiliation as well; it is not only his own choice that must be taken into account "but also the views of the body whose

---

[74] As originally enacted, the Constitution provided reserved seats in Parliament and the state legislatures for the Scheduled Castes and the Scheduled Tribes for a ten-year period. This has been extended for another ten-year period by the Constitution (Eighth Amendment) Act, 1959.

[75] [1954] S.C.R. 817 at 840.

[76] *Ibid.*, at 839.

religious tenets he has renounced because here the right [to stand for a reserved seat] is a right of the old body, the right conferred upon it as a special privilege to send a member of its own fold to Parliament."[77] So here we see the court treating the caste group as primarily bound by "social and political ties" but also as having "religious tenets." In this case, the latter are given no effect.[78]

Recently the same question came before the Madras High Court in the case of *Shyamsunder v. Shankar Deo*,[79] where the question was whether the candidate had lost his membership in the Samgar caste by joining the Arya Samaj, a Hindu sect which rejects idolatry and ascription of caste by birth. The court said there would be no deprivation of caste unless there was either expulsion by the old caste or intentional abandonment or renunciation by the convert. Since there was no evidence of expulsion or ostracism by the old caste, the question was whether there had been a break from the old order "so complete and final that . . . he no longer regarded himself as a member of the Samgar caste."[80] Here the court felt this was refuted not only by his activities, but by his testimony that he believed in idols and in texts repudiated by the Samajists. Again, while religious criteria played a secondary role in defining membership in caste, the court, like the *Jasani* court, conceived of the caste as having some body of religious tenets. One might remain a member while repudiating them, but adhering to them was evidence that one regarded oneself a member. In these cases the caste fits what we have called the associational model of the caste. It is a group characterized by a constellation of social and political ties; it has "religious tenets" though adherence to them is not an indispensable requisite for membership so long as the other ties are not severed.

In *V. V. Giri v. D. Suri Dora* the question before the Supreme Court was whether a candidate had lost his membership in the Moka Dora tribe by becoming a Kshatriya. The candidate was born a Moka Dora and his family had described itself as such in all documents from 1885 to 1923. Since that time they had described themselves as Kshatriyas. There was evidence that the family had adopted Kshatriya customs, celebrated marriages in Kshatriya style, was connected by marriage to Kshatriya families, employed Brahmin priests

[77] *Ibid.*, at 839.
[78] Perhaps "religious tenets" are mentioned here only because the court used as authority the case of *Abraham v. Abraham*, 9 M.I.A. 199 (1863), which involved conversion from one religion to another with retention of personal law.
[79] A.I.R. 1960 Mys. 27.
[80] *Ibid.*, at 32.

and wore the sacred thread in the manner of Kshatriyas.[81] His election was challenged on the ground that he was no longer a Moka Dora and was therefore ineligible to stand for a seat reserved for Scheduled Tribes. The Supreme Court solved the question by deciding that he had not in fact become a Kshatriya because "the caste status of a person in this context would necessarily have to be determined in the light of the recognition received by him from the members of the caste in which he seeks entry." Finding no evidence of such recognition, the court said that "unilateral acts cannot be easily taken to prove that the claim for the higher status . . . is established."[82] This recognition test is essentially a variant on the reputation test for the *varna* standing of caste groups. It is notable that it completely excludes any religious test of Kshatriyahood. One judge (J. L. Kapur), dissenting, vigorously rejected the majority notion that caste is determined in the first instance by birth and can only be varied (at least upward) by recognition of his claims by members of the group to which he aspired. He put forward a theory that caste rank varies as a consequence of the *gunas, karma* and *subhavana* and is dependent on actions; he found that the candidate had "by his actions raised himself to the position of a Kshatriya. . . ."[83] The majority did not accept this but did regard the *varna* order as hierarchic. It was a hierarchy determined by mutual social acceptance rather than by possession of traits indicative of religious capacity or attainments.

The provisions for "protective discrimination" extend not only to untouchables but to "other socially and economically backward classes." Although the Constitution refers to backward *classes*, caste groups have commonly been the units selected as backward. Increasing criticism within and without the government and the increasing willingness of the courts to subject preferences for backward classes to close scrutiny have caused a trend away from caste in favor of non-communal economic and educational criteria. It is constitutionally

---

[81] A.I.R. 1959 S.C. 1318. Apparently the candidate's family was one of a number of families of Mokasadars or large landholders who, according to the Election Tribunal, "would not like to be called Moka Doras but considered themselves Kshatriyas." XV E.L.R. 1 at 38 (1957). The tribunal found that the candidate had ". . . totally given up feeling himself to be a member of the Moka Dora tribe and considers himself a Kshatriya." For a comparison of the divergent approaches of the Election Tribunal, the High Court and the Supreme Court in this case, see my article, "The Problem of Group Membership: Some Reflections on the Judicial View of Indian Society," *Journal of the Indian Law Institute*, 1962, vol. 4, pp. 331-358 at 337-339.

[82] A.I.R. 1959 S.C. at 1327.

[83] *Ibid.*, at 1331.

permissible for the state to use castes or communities as the units it designates as backward,[84] but the Supreme Court struck down a scheme for reservations in colleges for backward classes on the ground that they were selected primarily on the basis of caste—i.e., the groups were chosen on the basis of their ritual and social standing. The Supreme Court is willing to permit recognition of the caste as a group of persons associated with a given level of resources, attainment and opportunities. But the state cannot rely exclusively on "the test of caste," i.e., it cannot select the caste solely by its rank or standing in the religious and social order. Here again we find willingness to recognize caste in our associational model, but not in the sacral one.

We have seen that so long as they are dealing with caste within Hinduism, whether it is the precedence or rights of a caste or membership in it, the courts have been unwilling to describe and rationalize these differences in terms of the sacral model of caste. They assign only a minor role to the religious content of caste and avoid invoking the idea of an overarching sacral order in which all castes are hierarchically arranged. The use of their "untouchability" as the criterion for selecting the Scheduled Castes implies a kind of reverse recognition of the Hindu ritual order. However, it is clear that such recognition cannot be extended to the selection of the "backward classes." The only instance so far in which we have seen implicit reference to a hierarchical ordering is in the case of the tribals. In the Moka Dora case, the Kshatriya status was denied on grounds that implied such a hierarchy, even though it had no specially religious content.

However, when we move to questions which concern persons and groups outside "Hinduism" we find that the religious content of caste reemerges.

The "Hindu" Component of Caste

The Constitution forbids religious discrimination on the part of the state[85] and guarantees freedom of religion.[86] The courts have been vigilant in invalidating governmental measures framed along religious lines.[87] Nevertheless, in some instances religion has been

---

[84] *Balaji v. State of Mysore*, A.I.R. 1963 S.C. 649; *Ramakrishna Singh v. State of Mysore*, A.I.R. 1960 Mys. 338.

[85] Arts. 15, 16.

[86] Arts. 25, 26, 30.

[87] *State of Rajasthan v. Pratap Singh*, A.I.R. 1960 S.C. 1208; *Nain Sukh Das v. State of U.P.*, A.I.R. 1953 S.C. 384; *State of Jammu and Kashmir v. Jagar Nath*, A.I.R. 1958 J & K 14.

made a qualification for preferential treatment. The president's order specifying Scheduled Castes provided that "no person professing a religion different from Hinduism shall be deemed a member of a Scheduled Caste."[88] Who is a Hindu? What is the role of caste in deciding who is a Hindu? What is the role of Hinduism in determining membership in a caste group?

The legal definition of Hinduism, developed for the purpose of applying appropriate personal law, was neither a measure of religious belief nor a description of social behavior as much as a civil status describing everyone subjected to the application of "Hindu law" in the areas reserved for personal law.[89] Heterodox practice, lack of belief, active support of non-Hindu religious groups,[90] expulsion by a group within Hinduism[91]—none of these removed one from the Hindu category, which included all who did not openly renounce it or explicitly accept a hostile religion. The individual could venture as far as he wished over any doctrinal or behavioral borders; the gates would not shut behind him if he did not explicitly adhere to another communion.[92] In *Chandrasekhara Mudaliar v. Kulandaivelu Mu-*

[88] Constitution (Scheduled Caste) Order, 1950, para. 3. Cf. the Government of India (Scheduled Caste) Order, 1950, para. 3, which provided that "No Indian Christian shall be deemed a member of a Scheduled Caste." The Constitution (Scheduled Tribes) Order, 1950, contains no analogous provision.

[89] Or, more accurately, all who would be subject to Hindu law in the absence of proved special custom or of a contingency such as marriage under the Special Marriage Act (III of 1872).

[90] *Bhagwan Koer v. Bose*, 30 I.A. 249 (1903). A similar latitudinarianism may be observed in the tests for whether a tribe is sufficiently Hinduized to attract the application of Hindu law. Orthodoxy is unnecessary; it is sufficient that the tribe acknowledge themselves as Hindus and adopt some Hindu social usages, notwithstanding retention of non-Hindu usages. *Chungu Manjhi v. Bhabani Majhan*, A.I.R. 1946 Pat. 218.

[91] *Ratansi D. Morarji v. Admr. General of Madras*, A.I.R. 1928 Mad. 1279, 1283.

[92] No proof of formal abandonment of his new religion is necessary for the convert to effect a successful reconversion to Hinduism. While a mere declaration is not sufficient to restore him to Hinduism, acceptance by a Hindu community with whatever formalities it deems proper—even none at all—is sufficient. *Durgaprasada Rao v. Irulappa Konar*, A.I.R. 1934 Mad. 630. However, cf. *Marthamma v. Munuswami*, A.I.R. 1951 Mad. 888, 890, where the primary test is the "intention" of the reconvert; the court says "the religious persuasion of a man now-a-days depends on his 'subjective preference' for any religion."

For purposes of at least certain preferences, reconverts to Hinduism who were born in Scheduled Castes are deemed members of the Scheduled Castes. But those born in another religion (e.g., whose fathers were converts) are not treated as members of Scheduled Castes "whatever may be their original family connections." *Report of the Commissioner for Scheduled Castes and Scheduled Tribes*, 1953, p. 132. In the personal law cases, acceptance by the community was a measure of one's success in reentering Hinduism; here, Hindu birth is a pre-condition of gaining membership in the community.

daliar[93] the Supreme Court had to decide on the validity of a consent to adoption by a sapinda who disavowed belief in the religious efficacy of adoption, in Hindu rituals and scriptures, in the existence of *atma*, and salvation. But the court found that "the fact that he does not believe in such things does not make him any the less a Hindu. . . . He was born a Hindu and continues to be one until he takes to another religion. . . . [W]hatever may be his personal predilections or views on Hindu religion and its rituals. . . ."[94]

In the post-constitutional cases involving preferences the same broad conception of Hinduism has been carried over from the area of personal law. To "profess" Hinduism merely means to be a Hindu by birth or conversion. Unorthodoxy or lack of personal belief in its tenets does not mean lack of profession for this purpose.[95] In effect the test seems to amount to a willingness to refrain from calling oneself something else. Thus where the election to a reserved seat of an active supporter of Dr. Ambedkar's neo-Buddhist movement was challenged on the ground that he was not a Hindu, the court found that "it has to be established that the person concerned has publicly entered a religion different from the Hindu . . . religion." Mere declarations falling short of this would not be sufficient.[96] The candidate had supported the movement for mass conversion by serving on the reception committee, editing a newspaper supporting the movement and attending a rally where an oath, "I abandon the Hindu religion and accept the Buddha religion" was administered by Dr. Ambedkar. When those who wished to convert were asked to stand, the candidate stood. But there was no evidence that he did in fact take the oath; the court held that in the absence of evidence of such a declaration, he remained a Hindu.[97]

Converts to Christianity and Islam are, of course, non-Hindus.[98] Although Buddhists, Sikhs and Jains are treated as Hindus for some purposes, they are considered non-Hindus for purposes of preferences.[99]

[93] A.I.R. 1963 S.C. 185.   [94] *Ibid.*, at 200.

[95] *Michael v. Venkataswaran*, A.I.R. 1952 Mad. 474.

[96] *Karwadi v. Shambharkar*, A.I.R. 1958 Bom. 296, 297.

[97] *Ibid.*, at 299. The vagaries of the declaration test are illustrated in *Rattan Singh v. Devinder Singh*, VII E.L.R. 234 (1953), XI E.L.R. 67 (1955), where the candidate had at various times described himself as a Mazhabi Sikh, a Harijan Hindu, a Balmiki, and a Balmiki Hindu.

[98] *Michael v. Venkataswaran*, note 95. But Hindu personal law has sometimes been applied to Christians (see, e.g., *Abraham v. Abraham*, note 78) and to Muslims (until the passage of the Muslim Personal Law [Shariat] Application Act [XXXVI of 1937]).

[99] These groups are Hindu for purposes of personal law. But their separateness

Sikhs were excluded from the Scheduled Castes and are now mentioned separately from Hindus.[100] Neo-Buddhists lose their right to preferences. "As Buddhism is different from the Hindu religion, any person belonging to a Scheduled Caste ceases to be so if he changes his religion. He is not, therefore, entitled to the facilities provided under the Constitution specifically for the Scheduled Castes."[101] The central government, recognizing that conversion itself is unlikely to improve the condition of the converts, has recommended that the state governments accord the neo-Buddhists the concessions available to the Backward Classes. Such preferences, less in scope and in quantity than those for Scheduled Castes, have been granted in some cases.[102] Persistent efforts by neo-Buddhists to be treated as members of Scheduled Castes have proved unavailing.[103]

The "Hinduism" test for recipients of preferences has been challenged as an infringement of the ban on religious discrimination by the state. The judicial response to this challenge presents a problem of characterizing the relation of the caste group to Hinduism.

In *S. Gurmukh Singh v. Union of India*[104] a Bawaria Sikh protested his exclusion from the Scheduled Castes in which the president had included Hindu Bawarias. The court conceded that Scheduled Castes were to be designated on the basis of their backwardness. But, finding that the Constitution vested in the president the entire power to make such determinations, the court refused to review his order by considering whether the Sikh Bawarias were in fact sufficiently backward to be included. In this situation, it was conceded that these non-Hindus either constitute or are members of a caste group; what

---

has been recognized in other contexts. E.g., Jains are not Hindus for purposes of temple-entry legislation. *State v. Puranchand*, A.I.R. 1958 M.P. 352; *Devarajiah v. Padmanna*, A.I.R. 1958 Mys. 84.

[100] *Gurmukh Singh v. Union of India*, A.I.R. 1952 Pun. 143; *Rattan Singh v. Devinder Singh*, note 97. Sikh members of four of the thirty-four Scheduled Castes listed for the Punjab were included in the Scheduled Castes. See Constitution (Scheduled Castes) Order, 1950, sec. 3 and cases cited *supra*.

[101] *Report of the Commissioner of Scheduled Castes and Scheduled Tribes, 1957-1958*, vol. 1, p. 25. This ruling is based squarely on the "Hinduism" requirement of the president's order. See the statement of Pandit Pant, *Times of India*, August 21, 1957.

[102] *Report of the Commissioner of Scheduled Castes and Scheduled Tribes, 1957-1958*, vol. 1, p. 25, vol. 2, p. 60. While some states have included neo-Buddhists within backward classes, others have continued to treat them like Scheduled Castes for some purposes and still others have withdrawn all preferential treatment.

[103] A bill to this effect was defeated in the Lok Sabha. *New York Times*, August 30, 1961.

[104] A.I.R. 1952 Pun. 143.

was decided was that the president's exclusion of that group (or part of the group) was unreviewable.[105]

In *Michael v. Venkataswaran*[106] the religious requirement was upheld against a Paraiyan convert to Christianity who wished to stand for a reserved seat. Even if there are cases in which both the convert and his caste-fellows consider him as still a member of the caste, the court found, "the general rule, is [that] conversion operates as an expulsion from the caste . . . a convert ceases to have any caste."[107] The presidential order, according to the court, proceeds on this assumption and takes note of a few exceptions. The court declined to sit in judgment on the president's determination that similar exceptional conditions do not prevail in other instances. Thus the presidential order was upheld not because of an absence of judicial power to review it but of its accuracy in the general run of cases.

In *In re Thomas*[108] another bench of the Madras Court considered a convert case which did not involve the presidential order. The Madras government had extended school-fee concessions to converts from Scheduled Castes "provided . . . that the conversion was of the . . . student or of his parent. . . ." A Christian student whose grandfather had converted could not, it was held, complain of discrimination since converts did not belong to the Harijan community. By conversion they had "ceased to belong to any caste because the Christian religion does not recognize a system of castes."[109] The concessions to recent converts were merely an indulgence and the state could determine the extent of this indulgence.

The theory that acceptance of a non-Hindu religion operates as loss of caste reflects the continued force of the sacral view of caste.

[105] The unreviewability of the presidential order would seem open to question in the light of subsequent cases which have firmly established judicial power to review the standards used by government to designate the recipients of preferential treatment. *Balaji v. State of Mysore*, A.I.R. 1963 Mys. 649. There is no indication in the Constitution that executive action, even in pursuance of expressly granted and exclusive constitutional powers, is immune from judicial review for conformity with constitutional guarantees of fundamental rights. The position in the Gurmukh Singh case must be seen as one of judicial restraint rather than judicial powerlessness. See Art. 12. The restraint there expressed seems out of line with later judicial assertiveness in this area.

[106] See note 95.

[107] *Ibid.*, at 478.

[108] A.I.R. 1953 Mad. 21.

[109] *Ibid.*, at 22. The exclusion of neo-Buddhists from the preferences for Scheduled Castes has been similarly justified by the notion that "Buddhism [does] not recognize castes." Statement of B. N. Datar in Rajya Sabha, August 26, 1957. Reported in *Times of India*, August 27, 1957.

The question arises in two kinds of factual situations: first, those involving a caste group or a section of a caste made up of members who are non-Hindus; second, those involving an individual convert. In the first type, there is little dispute that such persons as, e.g., the Sikh Bawarias in the *Gurmukh Singh* case, are in fact, members of a caste in the associational or sectarian sense of caste encountered in the law regarding "caste autonomy." The existence of such caste groups among non-Hindus in India is well known and has long been recognized by the judiciary.[110] To refuse to recognize caste membership among such non-Hindu groups implies that the "caste" of which the court is speaking is not caste in the sense of a body of persons bound by social ties, but caste in the sense of a body which occupies a place in the ritual order of Hinduism.

In the case of individual converts, the question facing the court would seem to be whether the individual convert's acceptance of Christianity, Islam or Buddhism evidences a loss of membership in the caste group to which he belonged at the time of the conversion. This can be treated as a question of fact, to be answered by evidence about his observable interactions with other members of the group. This was the approach taken in the cases dealing with conversions to sects within Hinduism.[111] In at least some cases of conversion outside Hinduism there is evidence that the convert continues to regard himself and to be regarded by others as a member of the old caste.[112] However in dealing with these conversions to religions outside Hinduism the courts have forsaken this empirical approach and have treated the conversion as depriving him of his membership as a matter of law. This conclusion derives not from the facts of the individual case but from a view of castes as the components in the sacral order of Hinduism. When that overarching scheme is abandoned, so is caste membership.

[110] Cf. *Report of the Backward Classes Commission*, vol. 1, pp. 28-30.
[111] A similar empirical approach is found in dealing with conversions among Scheduled Tribes. *Gadipalli Paroyya v. Goyina Rajaryya*, XII E.L.R. 83 (1956).
[112] The reports are replete with cases in which converts have lived so indistinguishably with their caste-fellows that the courts retrospectively infer a tacit reconversion without either formal abjuration of the new religion or formal expiation and readmittance to Hinduism. *Durgaprasda Rao v. Sundarsauaswaram*, A.I.R. 1940 Mad. 513; *Gurusami Nadar v. Krulappa Knoar*, A.I.R. 1934 Mad. 630; *Venkatramayya v. Seshayya*, A.I.R. 1942 Mad. 193. The "indulgence" extended by the state in the Thomas case, note 108, seems to reflect an awareness that recent converts, if not effective members of their old castes, are at least subject to similar disabilities. And cf. *Muthuswami Mudaliar v. Masilamani*, I.L.R. 33 Mad. 342 (1909) where Christian wives were accepted as members of a Hindu caste.

The Religious Aspects of Caste

Caste Autonomy

Notwithstanding the common rhetoric about the casteless society, the Constitution is quite unclear about the position of the caste group in Indian life. While there are guarantees to preserve the integrity of religious and linguistic groups,[113] there are none for the caste group—it would not seem to enjoy any constitutional protection as such. This silence may represent an anticipation that caste will wither away and have no important place in the new India. Or it may represent an implicit ratification of the old policy of non-interference.

Apart from explicit restrictions on caste discrimination, there is a tendency to discourage any arrangements which promote the coherence and integrity of the caste group as such. Thus, for example, the Supreme Court recently struck down (as unreasonable restrictions on property rights) laws providing for pre-emption on the basis of vicinage. The court held that the real purpose of these laws was to promote communal neighborhoods, a purpose which could have no force as public policy since the desire to promote such exclusiveness could no longer be considered reasonable.[114] There is a desire to minimize the impact of caste groupings in public life. The government has discouraged the use of caste as identification on official documents, and appeals to caste loyalty in electoral campaigning are forbidden.[115]

What is left of caste autonomy? What remains of the prerogatives previously enjoyed by the caste group? The caste retains the right to own and manage property and to sue in court. Section 9 of the Civil Procedure Code, with its bar on judicial cognizance of "caste questions" is still in force. Courts still refuse to entertain suits involving caste questions (e.g., fitness of an officer to manage property),[116] and castes retain their disciplinary powers over their members (e.g., the courts refused to declare invalid the assessment of a fine for an alleged breach of caste rules).[117] The caste retains its power of excommunication. It is still a good defense to a criminal action for defamation to assert the privilege of communicating news of an excommunication to one's caste fellows.[118] Yet these powers are subject to some restriction—the Untouchability Offenses Act makes inroads by outlawing any disciplinary action directed to enforcement of untouchability.

[113] Arts. 25-30, 350A, 350B.
[114] *Bhau Ram v. Baij Nath*, A.I.R. 1962 S.C. 1476.
[115] Representation of the People Act, Sec. 123.
[116] *Kanji Gagji v. Ghikha Ganda*, A.I.R. 1955 N.U.C. 986.
[117] *Bharwad Kama v. Bai Mina*, A.I.R. 1953 Saur. 133.
[118] *Panduram v. Biswambar*, A.I.R. 1958 Or. 259.

The Representation of the People Act forbids the use of caste disciplinary machinery for political purposes.

In one sense the autonomy of the caste group is enhanced by the constitutional provisions. One of the basic themes of the Constitution is to eliminate caste as a relevant factor in the relationship of government to the individual—as subject, voter, or employee. The Constitution enshrines as fundamental law that government must regulate individuals directly and not through the medium of the communal group. The individual is responsible for his own conduct and cannot, by virtue of his membership in a caste, be held accountable for the conduct of others. Thus the imposition of severe police restrictions on specified castes in certain villages, on grounds of their proclivity to crime, was struck down as unconstitutional since the regulation depended on caste membership rather than individual propensity.[119] Similarly, the Supreme Court held unconstitutional a punitive levy on a communal basis since there were some law-abiding citizens in the penalized communities.[120] Thus it would appear that regulative or penal measures directed at certain castes are beyond the power of government; a caste, then, enjoys a new protection from regulation directed at it as a corporate whole.

The autonomy of the caste group is also affected by the provisions of the Constitution which guarantee the prerogatives of religious groups. Art. 26 guarantees to every "religious denomination or section thereof" the right to establish and maintain religious and charitable institutions, to own and administer property and to "manage its own affairs in matters of religion." It is in the application of these denominational rights that we can see the courts viewing castes in our sectarian model.

In *Sri Venkataramana Devaru v. State of Mysore* the government sought to apply the Madras Temple Entry Act to a temple which the trustees claimed was exempt as a denominational temple belonging to the Gowda Saraswat Brahmin community. The government contended that the temple was "only a communal and not a denominational temple" unless it could be established that there were "religious tenets and beliefs special to the community. . . ."[121] Finding that members of the community brought their own idols to the temple, that they recognized the authority of the head of a particular Math, and that others were excluded from certain ceremonies, the Supreme Court concluded that they were indeed a "religious denomination."

---

[119] *Sanghar Umar Ranmal v. State*, A.I.R. 1952 Saur. 124.
[120] *State of Rajasthan v. Pratap Singh*, A.I.R. 1960 S.C. 1208.
[121] 1958 (1) Mad. L.J. 109 at 114.

A denomination's right to manage its own affairs in matters of religion included not only matters of doctrine and belief but also practices regarded by the community as part of its religion—including the restriction of participation in religious services. However the court found that the temple-entry rights granted by Art. 25 included such denominational temples and overrode the denomination's rights to exclude untouchables completely. Nevertheless the denomination's rights are not entirely without effect. The court held that the denomination's rights may be recognized where "what is left to the public is something substantial and not merely the husk of it." Since the other occasions of worship were sufficiently numerous to make the public's rights substantial, the court was willing to recognize the right of the denomination to exclude all non-members during special ceremonies and on special occasions.

Thus we find that the caste's assertion of its denominational character enables it to enjoy certain prerogatives. But this view of the caste is of a sect or denomination; their claim rests not on their position in the Hindu order, but on their distinctiveness.

In a recent and important case the Supreme Court held that the power to excommunicate for infractions of religious discipline is part of the constitutional right of a religious denomination to manage its own affairs in matters of religion.[122] The case, involving excommunication from a Muslim religious sect, held unconstitutional a Bombay act making excommunication a criminal offense. This does not imply a similar protection for caste groups as such; it would presumably protect only those that can qualify as religious denominations. It probably would not protect excommunication that was merely social and was not intended "to preserve the essentials of religion." Even if the excommunication were a matter of religious discipline, it would probably not be constitutionally protected if the breach of discipline involved failure to observe untouchability or if its purpose were political.

Once a caste is recognized as a religious denomination, then as a religious group it is presumably a "minority . . . based on religion" and as such enjoys a constitutional right under Art. 30 (1) "to establish and administer educational institutions of [its] choice." Art. 30 (2) provides that in granting aid to educational institutions the state shall not "discriminate against any educational institution on the ground that it is under the management of a minority, whether based

[122] *Saifuddin Saheb v. State of Bombay*, A.I.R. 1962 S.C. 853.

on religion or language." (On the other hand, once it receives state aid it cannot discriminate on caste lines in admissions).[123]

To the extent that its religious (or other) distinctiveness can be construed as giving it a "distinct . . . culture of its own" the caste group may merit the protection afforded by Art. 29 (1) which provides that "Any section of . . . citizens . . . having a distinct language, script, or culture of its own shall have a right to conserve the same." Art. 29 (1) has rarely been considered by the courts independently; usually it has been mentioned in the context of the assertion of rights under Art. 30 (1). Apparently every religious denomination could qualify as a cultural group. Their right to "conserve" their culture clearly includes the right to transmit this culture. In the Bombay Education Society case "the right to impart instruction in their own institutions to children of their own community in their own language" was referred to as the "greater part of the contents of Art. 29." Recently the Supreme Court has indicated that this right extends to political action to preserve the distinctive characteristics of the group.[124] The potential protections of Articles 29 and 30 have been greatly enhanced by several recent Supreme Court cases which refer to these rights as "absolute"[125]—in contrast to most fundamental rights which are subject to "reasonable restrictions" in the interests of the public.

Presumably, then, any group that can characterize itself as either "a minority based upon religion" or a "section of citizens with a distinct . . . culture" may qualify for a wide range of protections. The characterization of the caste group by the sectarian model puts it in the constitutionally privileged status of a religious denomination. Once so characterized the group enjoys, to some extent at least, constitutional protection not only in its right to control its religious premises, but also to excommunicate dissidents, to maintain educational institutions free from governmental regulation which is not in *its* interest, and to "conserve" its distinctive culture by political means. Of course this applies only to those castes which could qualify as "religious denominations or sections thereof." However it seems unlikely that any government could allow these privileges to some castes and not others; and in any event it seems probable that all castes could

123 Art. 29 (2).
124 *Jagdev Singh v. Pratap Singh,* A.I.R. 1965 S.C. 183.
125 *Rev. Sidhrajbhai Sabbaj v. State of Gujerat,* A.I.R. 1963 S.C. 540; *Jagdev Singh v. Pratap Singh, supra* note 124. Cf. the less stringent views in *In re Kerala Education Bill,* A.I.R. 1958 S.C. 956; *Dipendra Nath v. State of Bihar,* A.I.R. 1962 Pat. 101, 108; *Arya Pratinidhi Sabha v. State of Bihar,* A.I.R. 1958 Pat. 359.

produce enough distinctive ritual or doctrine to qualify as denominations. This view of caste would seem to present difficulties to those proponents of the casteless society who advocate prohibition of communal charities and educational institutions.[126]

New Models for Old

Before suggesting some of the implications of this new dispensation, let us summarize briefly the way in which castes have been characterized by the law since independence. There has been no refusal to recognize the claims of caste; nor, once it is recognized, is it treated as a strictly non-religious grouping. Caste is still recognized and so is its religious character. However this character is visualized in a new way.

Since independence, the sacral view has been drastically impaired. In the personal law, *varna* distinctions (and with them the necessity of determining the *varna* standing of caste groups) have been eliminated—at least for the future, although these matters persist for a time. In the area of precedence and disabilities, there has been a withdrawal of all support for precedence based on ritual standing— provisions against caste discrimination, the abolition of untouchability, temple-entry laws. The government has now reversed its previous policy by intervening to prevent the imposition of disabilities and to give preferential treatment to those at the bottom of the socio-religious order. In administering these preferences, the courts have avoided giving recognition to this sacral view, at least when dealing with transactions with Hinduism, although the shadow or mirror of it appears in the definition of untouchables and it appears in an attenuated form in a few instances involving non-Hindus.

Even where the sacral order remains implicit, the religious content remains relatively diffuse and indefinite. But in other post-independence developments we see caste given a more positive religious treatment. A different image of the caste group is found alongside the remnant of the older one. This view sees the caste group as a religious unit, denomination or sect distinguished by its own idiosyncratic cult, doctrine and ritual. This we found in the cases involving temple-entry and in the protection of denominational rights.

Finally, there is the associational model which sees the caste as

126 See, e.g., Shriman Narayan, "Socialist Pattern and Social Revolution" in Myron Weiner, ed., *Developing India*, University of Chicago, 1961, vol. 2, p. 75; Irawati Karve, *Hindu Society—An Interpretation*, Poona, 1961, p. 154 ("Contributions to funds intended to benefit castes or communal groups should be stopped by law").

an association characterized by a complex of features (including but not exclusively religious ones). We find this view strengthened since independence. The area of caste autonomy where it previously prevailed is largely unimpaired and in some respects enhanced. It remains in a minor way in the personal law area. It prevails in the area of preferences where it is the economic, occupational and educational aspects of the caste group that are stressed. It has been accepted in the cases involving group membership, at least within Hinduism.

We can, in short, say that there has been a decline in the use of the sacral model and an increasing reliance on the sectarian and associational models to characterize the religious aspects of caste groups. We may think of the courts during the British period as conceiving of castes primarily as graded components in the sacral order of Hinduism and secondarily as autonomous associations. In administering the law, they were sensitive to vertical differences between castes (expressed in *varna* distinctions and pollution) as well as horizontal differences (expressed in sectarian distinctiveness and in caste autonomy). The Constitution now forbids them to give recognition and support to the vertical, hierarchical distinctions; but other constitutional provisions (guarantees to religious denominations and of the integrity of groups) enjoin the courts to recognize and support the horizontal distinctions. The Constitution can be read as the "disestablishment" of the sacral view of caste—the courts can give no recognition to the integrative hierarchical principle; yet it recognizes the religious claims of the component parts. Claims based on the sacral order are foreclosed (in personal law reform, temple-entry, abolition of untouchability, de-recognition of exclusionary rights), but claims based on sectarian distinctiveness or group autonomy are not. The British system worked the attrition of "the tangled networks of medieval Indian civilization"[127] by substituting unified radial or pyramidal networks of cultural communication (among them the court system). While the new dispensation continues this unification in some respects, the disestablishment of the predominant organizing model of cultural unity may give new vitality to lesser traditions and new scope for innovation.

But the substitution in large measure of the sectarian for the sacral view of caste may leave unsatisfied two groups: those who would have the state refuse to recognize any connection between caste and religion

[127] McKim Marriott, "Changing Channels of Cultural Transmission in Indian Civilization" in Verne F. Ray, ed., *Intermediate Societies, Social Mobility and Communication: Proceedings of the 1959 Annual Spring Meeting of the American Ethnological Society*, p. 72.

and those who would have the state promote a unified monolithic Hindu society.

Does India's secularism require that the sectarian view of caste be avoided? Government is forbidden to confer recognition of hierarchic superiority; does the Constitution similarly withhold a mandate to recognize claims of religious distinctiveness of caste groups? A refusal to recognize such claims would perhaps be gratifying to those whose refined notions of Hinduism detach it entirely from caste practices. But if such a distinction is made by many educated Indians, it should be acknowledged that large numbers of people regard their caste practices as imbued with religious values. So long as such a condition prevails, the sectarian view of caste protects them from the imposition of a view of "religion" alien to them. Similarly the withdrawal of official recognition and support for the sacral order of Hinduism may be offensive to some of those who see it as divinely ordained and appropriate for a Hindu state. Yet recognition of the sacral order encounters the same objection of imposing a view which might violate the understanding of many groups.

On the whole, the present arrangement seems a fair middle course. It implements freedom of religion and the integrity and autonomy of the group by permitting the group to choose the distinctive traits that it wishes to emphasize in characterizing itself. It avoids government promulgation of an official over-all view of the Hindu social order with which component groups may not agree. Thus the law's combined use of the associational and sectarian models of the caste group is compatible with the constitutional commitments to voluntarism, withdrawal of recognition of the rank ordering of groups and respect for the integrity of groups within the society. In most respects, the present legal view of the religious aspects of caste strikes a balance which combines the commitment to a far-reaching transformation of the social order with the commitment to permit the widest range of freedom in the present. Remnants of the sacral view persist and in some cases raise serious constitutional questions of religious discrimination and freedom of religion which have as yet received no definitive answer. One expects that before long the courts will address themselves to these questions and will employ views of caste that are compatible with voluntarism and pluralism.[128]

---

[128] Two recent Supreme Court cases have important bearings on the matters discussed here but were received too late for inclusion. They are: *Chitralekha v. State of Mysore*, A.I.R. 1964 S.C. 1823 (on the use of caste criteria in selecting backward classes); *Punjabrao v. D. P. Mershram*, III *Maharashtra Law Journal* 162 (1965) (on the exclusion of Buddhists from the Scheduled Castes).

CHAPTER 14

THE REFORM OF HINDU
RELIGIOUS ENDOWMENTS

J. DUNCAN M. DERRETT

THE INDIAN CONSTITUTION protects individual freedom of conscience
and religious liberty, and, within certain stated limits, freedom for
religious denominations to manage their own affairs. India is a multi-
religious state tending towards a secular state, though how far she, or
at any rate the Hindus among her citizens, really wish for a truly
secular state has been doubted. When the question is asked whether
religious endowments should be reformed—a question which implies
that objectionable or socially disapproved practices or institutions
might be restricted or abolished—a counter-question at once emerges:
how far any projected reform would be consistent with the fundamental freedoms guaranteed by the Constitution. It is not impossible
that the Constitution should be amended to make way for reform, but
everyone is agreed that every possible attempt should be made to
effectuate desired reforms within the bounds laid down by the existing
Constitution.

The freedoms which are involved in this discussion are the freedom
of religious communities or denominations to manage their own
affairs,[1] including their institutions' properties, and that of all persons to acquire and enjoy property.[2] As we shall see, the freedom of
property intrudes substantially into all discussions of the freedom of
religion, more than one might expect. Art. 31 (1) of the Constitution

J. Duncan M. Derrett is professor of oriental laws at the University of London.
[1] Art. 26: "Subject to public order, morality and health, every religious denomination or any section thereof shall have the right (a) to establish and maintain
institutions for religious and charitable purposes; (b) to manage its own affairs in
matters of religion; (c) to own and acquire moveable and immoveable property;
and (d) to administer such property in accordance with law." This does not
of course make a community or denomination owner of an endowment, the
property of which vests (at present) in an idol or a mahant. The Supreme Court
clearly distinguishes between management in matters of religion (i.e., ceremonies,
etc.) and management of assets, funds—the latter can be vested in overseers who
are government servants and can be appointed as a result of political patronage.

[2] Art. 19 (1) (f) is subject to the proviso that the state may make a law imposing
reasonable restrictions on the exercise of the right in the interests of the general
public. The notion that the "general public" has an interest in public endowments is rapidly growing. For the meaning of the constitutional provisions see
D. D. Basu, *Commentary on the Constitution of India*, 4th edn., Calcutta, 1962.

reads: "No person shall be deprived of his property save by authority of law." In all discussions there is some vagueness as to whether non-Indian conceptions of freedom of property or freedom of religion have any place in preparations for the reform of religious institutions.

Reforms in the field of religious endowments in India have affected several religions. Statutes confined to Hindu institutions exist,[3] but others provide for regulation, control, and supervision of institutions of a public character belonging to all religious communities.[4] This paper will be confined to the problems of the Hindus, with as much reference to other communities as is helpful or conventional.

THE NATURE OF THE PROBLEM

Many religious endowments have received accessions of wealth, after their original creation, by donations and conveyances of land, or of rights to some source of profit, or by gifts from members of the public. In theory the Indian Parliament, or indeed any state legislature, could interfere with such vested rights, could even terminate the existence of a religious endowment, wind up its assets and distribute them, provided that the step was legal and constitutional.[5] The courts also clearly have the power to wind up and distribute the assets of a religious group. Neither of these powers, however, need be considered for practical purposes. What the legislatures have done, amidst endless controversy, and what the courts unquestionably have the jurisdiction to do, is to exercise control over the manner in which the properties of religious endowments are enjoyed and utilized. Our problem is whether they are using this power effectively, and if not what modifications are required and which of them are practicable within the framework of the present Constitution.

It is obvious that there is a broad practical distinction between public and private endowments. The distinction itself is technical, and highly involved problems constantly arise as to whether a particular

[3] Bihar Hindu Religious Trusts Act, 1950; Orissa Hindu Religious Endowments Act, 1951; Travancore-Cochin Hindu Religious Institution Act, 1950; Madras Hindu Religious and Charitable Endowments Act, 1959.

[4] Bombay Public Trusts Act, 1950; Madhya Pradesh Public Trusts Act, 1951; Rajasthan Public Trusts Act, 1959. The Religious Trusts Bill, 1960, purports to be a general provision for all communities. In fact it was drafted so as to apply only to Hindu endowments. All the acts and the bill referred to above are printed in the appendix to B. K. Mukherjea, *Hindu Law of Religious and Charitable Trust*, 2d edn., T. L. Venkatarama Aiyar, Calcutta, 1962.

[5] See *Mahant Narayan Dessjivaru v. State of Andhra*, A.I.R. (All India Reporter) 1959 An. P. 471. An example is the Shri Badrinath Temple Act, 1939.

temple is public or private.[6] In the field of public trusts members of
the public can at any rate ventilate their suspicions about the honesty
and correctness of the management. They may be disappointed in that
the machinery of the law may not enable them to commence proceedings for the appointment of new trustees, for the appointment of a
receiver, for the framing of a scheme, and other such remedies as the
court in its ordinary jurisdiction may provide.[7] But at least they can
instil fear into the managing trustees, and that is something. Under
statutes affecting public trusts there is usually a method by which
members of the public interested in the endowment may draw the
attention of government-appointed officials to some problem which
is worrying them, and set wheels in motion.[8] In the field of private
trusts, however, the number of persons concerned may be relatively
small. As we shall see, these are, since recent developments in the personal law of the Hindus, less likely than they used to be to be members of a single family in close touch with the actual managers. Concern about mismanagement is likely to be less widespread and virulent,
if not less sharp. So far the Indian legislatures have not attempted
to investigate needs for reform in the field of private trusts, under
the impression (doubtless) that the existing machinery was adequate.

It must be a part of any such study as this one to inquire into the
validity of this convenient distinction between public and private
trusts, and to see whether a comprehensive solution is not needed
which will take care of the problem fundamentally. The amounts of
money or extents of land involved have nothing to do with the
matter. A set of stones may be a public temple within a particular
statute,[9] and may have two fields endowed for its upkeep and the
performance of worship; on the other hand the "private" deity of a
wealthy Bengali or Bihari family may "own" numerous large farms.
The stones may own no jewelry; the deity might own enough orna-
ments and valuable clothing to set many an impoverished family in
the same village on its feet economically.

Another aspect of the problem is how far religious endowments
may be validly created. Whatever may have happened in the past,

[6] E.g., *Narayan Bhagwantrao v. Gopal Vinayak*, A.I.R. 1960 S.C. 100; *Deoki
Nandan v. Murlidhar*, A.I.R. 1957 S.C. 133.
[7] The consent of the advocate general (a political-administrative, and not a
judicial, act) may be refused, as in *Raju v. Adv.-Gen.*, 1962 Mad. 722. (References
in this style are to the Indian Law Reports series, by High Courts; S.C.R. refers
to the Supreme Court series of the same publication.)
[8] See, e.g., Bombay Public Trusts Act, 1950, s. 50.
[9] *Comm., Hindu Rel. End., Madras v. Narasimham*, A.I.R. 1939 Mad. 134.

are people now at liberty to start, on their own initiative and without consent of the legislature, a religious endowment with its individual rules, purposes, and method of descent of the right of managership? Certainly the Hindu Succession Act, 1956, has interfered somewhat with any such freedom, perhaps by accident, but in any case not insignificantly. For the rest, the court's jurisdiction to determine over what trusts it will exercise its powers of regulation, in other words, its jurisdiction to determine what is a valid religious trust is a power of some considerable value. Society, through the court, determines within some limits what can validly be set up as a charitable endowment, and what cannot. This power has in recent times been exercised with distinct socio-political overtones.

How can the state prevent the creation of a religious trust; how can it control the exercise of the managers' powers; how can it secure that the capital and income of the endowed properties are used in the public interest; how can it enable improperly alienated properties to be recovered; and how can it satisfy the religious urges of the public? Some curious and unexpected facts emerge from even a cursory study. We are fortunate in that we have available to us expressions of opinion, as well as expressions of law, by judges and others who understand the desires of the public—both their ancient and traditional attitudes and the modern cosmopolitan approach—and who can express in intelligible terms the inconsistencies and anomalies which arise daily.

WHAT IS A RELIGIOUS ENDOWMENT?

A religious endowment is, by definition, an endowment for a religious purpose. The court will not recognize or give effect to a trust for a purpose which is nominally but not actually religious (unless it is truly a charitable purpose), or which is nominally religious but which cannot be so deemed from the point of view of any religion known and practiced by any considerable group of people in India. That a practice is superstitious will not prevent its being religious, if it conforms to that requirement and is an essential and integral part of the religion. But the court is inclined to the view that some practices are of *so* peculiar or even purely superstitious a nature as to cease to be in any legal sense religious,[10] and this delicate distinction can be real enough to enable the court to cut down a trust, which someone has created by deed or will or otherwise, on the ground that

10 Dicta of Gajendragadkar, J., at *Durgah Comm., Ajmer v. Syed Hussain Ali*, A.I.R. 1961, S.C. 1402, 1415 (see Mukherjea, p. xii; also per Sinha, C. J., at A.I.R. 1962 S.C. 864-5).

its purposes are not religious.[11] What is religious, apart from this proviso, is to be determined according to the beliefs and practices of the community itself.[12] The process of law does not always enable the best evidence to be available for this purpose, and here it would be an advantage if the attorney general or the advocate general of the state concerned had the duty to prepare and carry a brief on behalf of the public on the subject of the beliefs and practices of the community.

Meanwhile, here is scope for the introduction of socio-political ideas into a purely legal, objective discussion. The question may arise, is this practice religious and is it thus protected, e.g., by the Constitution? Is a trust created by bequest for this purpose a valid Hindu religious trust? Let us suppose that the trust is for the provision of sacrifice of buffaloes in a state where such sacrifices have been prohibited. The court will certainly declare this no religious trust, and void. Let us suppose that it is a bequest for pouring oil on stones. To oil stones may or may not be capable of being established as a religious practice by a group or community. If the oral evidence is inconclusive an attempt may be made to support the practice by reference to works of authority, in Sanskrit or any other Indian language. Supposing that no evidence is forthcoming from any authoritative religious book which justifies the practice it is open to the learned judges to say that no self-respecting Hindu will worship stones or mythical (or historical) persons commemorated by them, that such practices are not countenanced by the Vedas or Shastras or other sacred literatures of orthodox Hindus, and that the bequest is void. In one case where the building of tombs or commemorative structures (*samadhis*) for deceased Hindus other than *sannyasis* was in question the courts held that the practice of erecting such structures and worshipping there was not countenanced by Hinduism,[13] even though it seems there was evidence that the community had been in the habit of doing this for a long time.[14] The court's jurisdiction to determine what is religious assumes curious proportions when we understand that the judges' concept of Hinduism is formed in school and college and through the private reading of neo-Hindu literature, and that the gap between the actual habits of the general public and the outlook of the intelligentsia is notoriously wide.

Unfortunately, though the negative power of the court is sub-

11 See *Rangrao v. Gopal* (1957) 60 Bom. L.R. 675.
12 *Jamshedji C. Tarachand v. Soonabai* (1907) 33 Bom. 123.
13 *Saraswathi Ammal v. Rajagopal Ammal*, A.I.R. 1953 S.C. 491, 495.
14 *Ravanna Koovanna v. Vana Pana*, A.I.R. 1962 Mad. 500.

stantial, an equal positive power is lacking. Where a testator leaves money for the creation of a trust for purposes which he evidently thinks religious but which are too vague in the eye of the law the court cannot frame a scheme for carrying out his intentions.[15] Unless the testator uses the appropriate form no trust is valid as a religious trust, though his intention was evidently religious.

Let us assume, however, that the endowment is either so old that its religious character cannot be doubted, or that the court could raise no objection to its validity. What are the broad categories of these endowments? First and most important come the *private* temples; next, though of more recent origin and significance, the trusts for the payment of charitable donations to the poor, or to Brahmins or monks, and for the performance of *sraddhas* at special places or otherwise, and for the expenses of pilgrimage; one would mention next the grant or bequest to a public temple, whether to install an idol[16] (now very rare) or to further endow an existing idol; thereafter come the creation (now very rare) of *mathas* (orthodox colleges, hereafter called mutts),[17] or the further endowment of such; and finally the creation or further endowment of institutions which are neither temples nor mutts[18] but are individual institutions for worship or religious exercises or charitable activities, such as public feeding, under their own constitutions.[19]

In all these connections, what is the religious motive behind the gift? This is a complicated subject, but fundamental to our study. The state affects to be indifferent to religion and religions, but it plainly is not indifferent to the misuse of public, and, as we have seen, to a lesser extent private funds in the name of religion. The state is against swindles. But whether the public is so is open to question. The distinction between the state and the public is at first sight unexpected, but it is readily appreciated by students of India who are accustomed to officials' and government servants' having one opinion and outlook officially, and quite another personally. Parliament may therefore enact, and the courts pass decrees, upon the assumption that

---

[15] The rule in *Runchordas v. Parvatibai* (1899) 26 I.A. 71 (I.A. indicates the Indian Appeals series of the English *Law Reports*), followed in, e.g., *Mohanlal v. Habibullah*, A.I.R. 1963 Pat. 430, is no longer good law in Maharashtra and Gujarat in view of the Bombay Act cited above, s. 10.

[16] *Bhupati Nath Smrititirtha v. Ram Lal Maitra* (1910) 37 Cal. 129 (Full Bench).

[17] For the nature of mutts see Mukherjea, p. 25; for their origins see *ibid.*, pp. 309-310.

[18] *V. Mariyappa v. B. K. Puttaramayya*, A.I.R. 1958 Mys. 93.

[19] *N. Ramaswami Mudaliar v. S. A. Aiyasami Chettiar*, A.I.R. 1960 Mad. 467; *Gajanan Maharaj Sansthan v. Ramrao*, A.I.R. 1954 Nag. 212.

an opinion is true and inescapable which the majority of the population (and by no means chiefly the less educated) cannot accept.

Orthodox Hinduism can perhaps supply the key. It is fundamental to orthodox Hindu belief, which does not differ from traditional Hinduism, that self-sacrifice earns merit.[20] In a supersensory sense, in a transcendental content, the generosity as a matter of duty (*dharma*, righteousness) which one has shown during one's life will earn in a subsequent life either a better caste or a more happy existence or both, but in any event progression towards *moksha*, release from the circle of birth, death and rebirth which it is axiomatic that the living individual desires to escape. Gifts to Brahmins, gifts to other holy men, gifts to idols, gifts for animals, gifts, failing these, to the poor or to any human being, have their merit, and some texts would rank gifts in an order of priority according to the fitness of the *patra* or recipient.[21] It is clear that giving, followed by acceptance by or for the use of the donee, is the valuable and important element, provided that the gift is with the intention of earning merit and not for any other purpose. Since Christianity has exerted enormous influence in molding the outlook and vocabulary of educated Indians and since Christianity does not regard giving as directly conducing to merit in the same sense as does Hinduism, influential Hindus of today have difficulty in seeing why mere giving should be religious, and beneficial in a public sense, without regard to the economic effects of the giving.

It follows from the emphasis on the gift (a) that the givers, by and large, are not much concerned with what happens to the object given after the gift has taken effect, and (b) the modern Indian intelligentsia, influenced by western concepts, fail to understand how this lack of interest can serve as an excuse for peculation, embezzlement, or maladministration. The very concept of peculation of endowed funds could not, as we shall see, arise in this form in the traditional mind; and though maladministration could certainly be conceived of, it would be applicable, if at all, within a much narrower field. To explain this requires a further definition of the religious gift.

The concept of worship of a deity in Hinduism differs very considerably from that of Christianity, though with the emergence of the concept of *bhakti* and doctrines commonly attributed to the

---

[20] P. V. Kane, *History of Dharmasastra*, Poona, 1941, vol. 2, pp. 836-847. K. V. Rangaswami Aiyangar, ed., Laksmidhara, *Krtyakalpataru*, vol. 5, *Danakanda*, Baroda, 1941, introd., pp. 60-62.

[21] Kane, p. 115.

Bhagavad Gita and associated works the gap between the two concepts appreciably narrowed. Avoiding technicality and adhering to broad usage it would be true to say that the Hindu deity can be worshipped by personal service (like a human friend), and the concept of worshipping a deity (*devata*) and that of serving a friend are hardly different in nature, while service of a revered teacher or other prestigious fellow-human, such as a *sannyasi* or king, would fall somewhere between the two, though well within the narrow circle which comprehends all these manifestations of personal devotion. Worship (*puja*) can take the form of offerings, whether of flowers,[22] song, or actual "service" to the idol if there is one, and there usually is in all the contexts with which we are concerned. If one can worship by offering flowers, naturally more costly offerings are possible, from coins to acres of land. As soon as it was possible to visualize a deity the idea of worship brought within the bounds of possibility a religious endowment.

The regular appearance of idols brought the details into prominence. The idol has his house, his attendants, his hours of audience, his repose.[23] He has his consort or consorts, other idols, and these have their own establishments. Payment for the buildings and their upkeep, the idol's meals and entertainment, baths, clothing and so forth, must be found somewhere. The attendants, cooks, reciters of prayers, all must have some means of livelihood. The idol requires, from this point of view, an establishment, and lastly a business manager.[24] The more famous the deity the more important the idol and its shrine, the greater the number of visitors. The notion of vows and thank offerings naturally arises. The idol accumulates wealth, and this has somehow to be invested or deployed. Though the actual cost of the god's "meals" may amount to no more than Rs. 5 a day, dedications and offerings may bring in a yearly income of some Rs. 5,000.[25] What is to happen to this accumulation? The business manager, to whom the law gives the general name shebait, must manage it.[26] In whose interest? The idol's. Can the interest of the idol differ from that of the shebait? Naturally,

22 *Thakur Mukundji Maharaj v. Goswami Persotam*, 1956 1 All. 421.

23 *Ram Brahma v. Kedar*, 36 C.L.J. 478, 483, quoted by Mukherjea, p. 141.

24 For a medieval establishment (contrasted with the establishments itemized in the *Report* cited below) see Derrett, *Bulletin of the School of Oriental and African Studies*, 1957, vol. 19, pp. 162-166.

25 For the size of the endowments and their annual incomes see *Report of the Hindu Religious Endowments Commission*, Government of India, Ministry of Law, New Delhi, 1962, pp. xiv, xvi, xix.

26 For the legal status of the shebait see Mukherjea, p. 183; Derrett, *Introduction to Modern Hindu Law*, Oxford University Press, Bombay, 1963, paras. 780-802.

though if a shebait or even *de facto* manager pursues his own interests vigorously this by no means necessarily operates against the welfare imputed to the deity by the law,[27] but that brings us to the thorny question of the legal personality of the Hindu *devata*.

Perhaps no subject has aroused more doubt and confusion.[28] The pronouncements of the courts have been accepted as self-evident truths[29] more with a sense of relief than of positive satisfaction. The theory is that the idol owns the offerings, and that the idol owns the endowment, but that the idol's interests are voiced by the shebait alone, and the right to manage and spend the property lies with the shebait alone. However, if the legal procedure is commenced sufficiently soon, the shebait may be removed for certain kinds of misconduct, and certain of his transactions may be upset, provided they are held to be, in the eye of the law, otherwise than for the idol's legal necessity or benefit.[30] This attitude fully represents the notions of the man in the street. Curiously, it conflicts most completely with orthodox Hindu juridical theory.

The notion that the idol, who cannot speak or vindicate his rights otherwise than through some representative or next friend, is the legal owner, that it has a legal personality and that therefore a trespasser can possess adversely to it and acquire title by mere lapse of time,[31] fits fairly closely with the popular belief that the gifts please the deity, that the deity can accept them, and that the fruit of such gifts is the merit of the donor. The practical difficulty with this view is that the shebait has no title in the offerings, which he would accept only as the idol's manager, and therefore his transactions with regard to them could be upset (in the Hindu system after any lapse of time) and his prerogatives (and therefore incentive to develop the cult) would be at an end.

If one thing is certain it is that making a personal profit out of possessing an idol is as old as the Vedic age, and perfectly legitimate.

[27] *Sapta Koteshwar . . . Trust v. Ramchandra*, A.I.R. 1956 Bom. 615.

[28] G. D. Sontheimer, "Religious Endowments in India: the Juristic Personality of Hindu Deities," *Zeits. f. vergl. Rechsw.*, 1964, vol. 67, pp. 45-100.

[29] Especially by opponents of reform. After a careful review of the case-law the Hindu Religious Endowments Commission repeatedly emphasized the inadequacy and unpropitious tendencies of the existing legal rules, and, in some respects, the inadequacy of the state statutes on these accounts.

[30] Mukherjea, pp. 256-259; Derrett, *Introduction to Modern Hindu Law*, para. 795. The leading case law is that the shebait can in any case alienate without legal necessity for the duration of his own "incumbency." The state statutes aim to prevent the creation of such rights even for that period.

[31] *Gossamee v. Rumanlolljee* (1889) 16 I.A. 137. The position is in some states modified by statute.

A man should be able to make a living out of possessing ancestral charms and potions; why not out of an idol which could perform miracles? A class of Brahmins despised to this day is the class which attends upon idols. Now to be an attendant upon an idol is no sinecure. To know the proper ceremonies—in the case of the larger and more famous temples this might be a considerable achievement—and to act faithfully as intermediary between the idol and the visiting public; to conduct "services," especially the seasonal festivities, and to be a receptacle of tradition and myth relating to the shrine and its pious founders and patrons would hardly be regarded as a useless or amateurish occupation. But the traditional contempt of the temple-Brahmin stems not from his having taken less willingly to western-type education, but from the ancient recognition that he lives parasitically on the offerings to the idol. He exploits the idol for his own gain. There was not the least social or legal or even moral objection to this, but Hinduism favored a devotional attitude and less of the *quid pro quo* attitude which the populace obviously favored and still favors. And a Brahmin who was dependent upon the populace in this fashion was, though not a whit less a Brahmin, a second-class Brahmin.[32]

Accordingly the *mimamsa* system of Indian philosophy, which the jurists preferred to follow rather than the philosophy of Shankaracarya, declared that idols could not own anything.[33] They could not accept, for they could form no intention, and there was no question of any fruit coming to the donor from the acceptance of his gift. The gift therefore did not vest in the deity at all, but the shebaits, or other receiving ministrants accepting the gift, constituted it a fund which was available to them according to custom. It was the duty of the king to protect and supervise such foundations (though this was not stressed), and property "belonging" to idols was property which in the old system could never be acquired by adverse possession.[34] This convenient system, which allowed the shebaits to enjoy the assets without liability to charges of sacrilege, has the advantage that the shebaits could not be disciplined by the king except for flagrant maladministration, or excessive diversions of the funds from the idol's service to their own uses. And in a roundabout fash-

[32] For categories of Brahmins see Kane, pp. 130-134. For the low status of temple Brahmins see *ibid.*, pp. 109-110. Even Manu (III. 152) looks down on the *devalaka*.

[33] S. C. Bagchi, *Juristic Personality of the Hindu Deities*, Calcutta, 1933; A. S. Nataraja Ayyar, "Juristic Personality of Deities in Hindu Law," *Vyavahara Nirnaya*, University of Delhi, 1954, vol. 3, 1954, pp. 106-177; G. D. Sontheimer, cited above.

[34] Kane, 1946, vol. 3, pp. 327-328 (citing Katyayana, 330). The king's duty is dealt with by Kane, vol. 2, pp. 911-912.

ion this fits the popular outlook and the modern Anglo-Hindu (as contrasted with the recent statutory) legal position.

Religion therefore did not require that the funds donated should be applied in any particular way. Donations were made to, or for, the deity or his needs; the donation was made into the hand of the Brahmin and what he did with it was a matter which could be governed by custom. That the public fully expected him to enjoy it himself, in part or even substantially, is shown by a little rather obvious reflection. The first charge on the endowment is for the idol's meals. These are prepared, one will suppose, to the taste of those who will eventually eat them, namely those entitled to eat the idol's "leavings," his attendants. After being offered to the idol the food is at the disposal of the staff. Alternatively offerings of food, etc., made to the deity may be distributed *in natura* or in the form of ash to worshippers or persons "honored" by such participation in the idol's effects. It is inconceivable that the ministrants, shebaits or others should not have been recognized from the earliest times as substantial beneficiaries from the endowment. This recognition by no means hindered votaries' gifts to the *dharmakarta* or shebait himself. When the latter claimed the property as his own the courts have declared him to be merely the manager, the title really being in the endowment,[35] but the outcome might not be so very different in practical terms.

When the temple has to be repaired the shebait will expect some commission. After worship and repairs and other necessaries have been paid for, the shebait has always had the cash at his disposal, and the decision to whom to let the land on lease, and upon what terms has rested entirely with the shebait. The jurisdiction of a court to set aside an improper alienation of land is important, but it rather confirms than weakens the general picture of the shebait's freedom. How this freedom is abused (according to the intelligentsia) we shall see later. Ancient concern on this subject is evidenced by the terms of the Munirabad stone inscription of A.D. 1088 in which detailed information is given as to the employment of any surplus of temple funds after the expenses of worship and repairs have been met. But even there nothing was said about offerings obtained by the shebaits from casual worshippers.

The religious reason for the donations and for the maintenance of idols as recipients of offerings was the desire for merit. That

[35] *Nanduri Yogananda v. Sri Agetheswaraswamivaru*, A.I.R. 1960 S.C. 622. Contrast *Jogendra Nath Das v. Charan Das*, A.I.R. 1958 Or. 160.

desire was completely unaffected by the dishonesty of shebaits, and indeed it may be asked whether the appropriations and peculations of shebaits were ever regarded as dishonest in the modern sense of that word. Even if the shebait was a man of evil reputation, provided he did not go too far, his right of management would remain vested in him. The Hindu religion by no means required that the capital and income should be spent on the idol's needs, and on these only. Nor was there any means of limiting the accumulation of donations and capital in this type of mortmain. The result was the proliferation of priests, ministrants, clerks, accountants, managers, stewards, and other hangers-on.

A similar disregard for the relation which real service bears to reward is to be observed in connection with the *pandas*, guides at the places of pilgrimage. *Pandas* and other *gurus* have a hereditary clientele and charge fees for their services to generations of rustic innocents in search of spiritual gratification or merely of a holiday with pious overtones. These professional people are nowadays regarded by the intelligentsia with a distaste which is out of touch with their real hold on the public at large. A large income is obtained in the name of religion by people who can offer spiritual service of a kind. But can this be said of the temple shebaits in contrast to *pandas*? The shebait could be said to offer nothing of any value except the opportunity to make an offering to the idol (i.e. substantially to himself).

This is what annoys the western-educated Hindu. In his view priests should be like priests of other religions, i.e. not merely recipients of offerings, the somewhat inhuman and unresponsive counterpart to the charitable spirit upon which they live, but rather persons of learning and prestige, of moral quality and stature, pastors, capable of giving spiritual guidance and consolation. The idea constantly arises that this is really what temple-priests and shebaits are, though they show every appearance of being the reverse—often being ignorant, proud, ill-mannered and generally indifferent to everything except the opportunity of obtaining offerings. At public functions where some religious ceremony plays a role the modern Hindu obliges temple-priests or managers to "officiate" by making a distribution of *prasada* from the idol.[36] This cannot by any means take the place of common prayer and religious devotion, which in any event is evidenced at

[36] See record of proceedings in celebration of the centenary of the Madras High Court at I.L.R. 1962 Mad., i: "the trustees of the Devasthanams . . . associated themselves with the religious function with all the paraphernalia of temple music and spectacular procession and paid temple honors to the judges and other important members of the bar in their own distinctive style."

Hindu functions in a different spirit and by different means without any reference to temples or to the religious endowment. It is this modern feeling that Hindu temples should somehow resemble churches that is responsible for the current urge to reform and refashion the whole system of temple-worship. Reform movements have been going on within Hinduism in many directions and for relatively long periods; but the attack on the institutions of the public temple and the mutt, as these existed in the first few decades of the century, is a special phenomenon which attempts to modernize the oldest features of Hindu religion, and so combine the traditional and the most advanced.

ABUSES UNDER THE PRESENT SETUP

The idea that priests should be like clergymen, and that temples should be like churches is of course one which few Hindus will accept after reflection. Insensibly the influence of the West has made itself felt, chiefly when caste and economic considerations sharpened the point of the discussion. Hindus have long tolerated *sannyasis* who were unchaste and corrupt—in fact, tolerance for corruption in immediate association with divine institutions is one of Hinduism's most remarkable features. The picture of the unedifying and selfish individual masquerading as a religious leader is so familiar to the Hindu (it has been a reality since Kautilya, perhaps 2,250 years ago)[37] that a program of turning him into a benevolent spiritual leader in fact as well as in theory has little actuality. This is because the mahant, the "incumbent" of a mutt, although more like a spiritual leader than a temple-priest or a shebait (who may have in fact no religious knowledge or interests whatever), is far more of a social and even an economic figure than a spiritual one.

Naturally the range of personalities is wide. The choice of mahant will seldom lie with persons who are themselves qualified in any spiritual or scholarly sense. A reputation for adherence to tradition, a charismatic personality, a person apt to attract and keep adherents to the sect in question, and one who can keep discipline (including regular payments of "presents") without giving rise to splinter-sects or wholesale defections, such a one will be chosen by any of the methods whereby mahants obtain appointment.[38] In the course of the many bitter and unedifying squabbles which have gone through the courts

[37] Kaut. I, 11.
[38] *Ramprapanna Ramanuj Das v. Sudarsan*, A.I.R. 1961 Or. 137; *Somar Puri v. Shyam Narain Gir*, A.I.R. 1954 Pat. 586; *Tulasiram Das v. Ramprasanna Das*, A.I.R. 1956 Or. 41. Derrett, *Introduction to Modern Hindu Law*, paras. 815-818.

regarding appointments to headships of mutts three main types of appointing-machinery have emerged as a matter of custom. In none of them is there a method of selection which requires scholarship, religious knowledge, the ability to teach. The next mahant is often the favorite disciple, often the son of the previous mahant. Sometimes other mahants appoint the new "incumbent." One has heard of appointment being in the gift of people who advertise in the newspapers.[39] In the cases where the mutt is really a money-lending institution a good business head would be a qualification.[40] On the other side of the coin we do in fact find learned and able personalities in the key positions among mahants, particularly at the famous mutts of South India where the reigning Shankaracarya will often keep discipline among the members of his sect upon a truly moral footing, excommunicating persons guilty of irregularities, giving advice on social and spiritual questions,[41] exhorting the public to beware of sinful conduct,[42] and in many cases contributing to moral development and scholarship by publications. But this is by no means typical.

This being the position with mahants who are the head and heart of the religious endowment, little is to be expected of temples, which are a grave problem to the modern cosmopolitan Hindu. No spiritual guidance is forthcoming from most temples, and the squabbles between the priests and the shebaits, and their dealings with the endowment properties cause much grief. The scandal of the temple-prostitutes is barely out of the way[43] when attention falls upon the completely non-religious behavior of shebaits who sell the temples[44]

[39] *Surendra v. Dandiswami*, A.I.R. 1953 Cal. 687.

[40] *Mahant Ganeshgir Gosai v. Fatehchand Bania* (1934) 31 Nag. L.R. 282, 289. Mutts are often money-lending or business institutions because in the early British period sects with reputations and solidarity alone could attract and invest capital in the really prosperous trade throughout the peninsula. See Bernard S. Cohn, "The Role of Gosains in the Economy of Eighteenth and Nineteenth Century Upper India," *Indian Economic, Social and Historical Review*, 1964, vol. 1, no. 4, pp. 1-8.

[41] As in the case of *Madhavrao Raghavendra v. Raghavendrarao* 1946 Bom. 375, where the mahant's opinion was overruled by the court.

[42] *The Hindu* of Madras frequently prints extensive reports of edifying pronouncements by the Shankaracharyas.

[43] Bombay Devadasis Protection Act, 1934; Bombay Devadasis Protection (Extension) Act, 1957; Madras Devadasis (Prevention of Dedication) Act, 1947; Madras Devadasis (Prevention of Dedication) (Andhra Amendment) Act, 1956. The Madras statute relative to religious endowments provides for the enfranchising of land dedicated for the maintenance of devadasis. The institution of the devadasis as an actuality is not extinct.

[44] See note 22 above.

and even the idols,[45] and pawn and sell their rights as shebaits,[46] or on priests who sell their "turns of worship"[47] and other curiosities the existence of which is explained only in terms of the traditional Hindu approach to the question of who owns dedicated property and its proceeds.

The way in which these non-clerical "clerics" hold on to their wealth is not unnatural, but scandalizes the modernized Hindu. A great temple which has received the wealth of generations of princes as well as the widows' mites of centuries is ruled by a potentate who claims, if need be, that the temple is his private property.[48] The *pandas* are the chief offenders in this respect. The intelligentsia which has had to pass examinations to obtain positions of power cannot stomach these exponents of puranic lore who show pilgrims around shrines, insist upon receiving personal fees as if they were charitable donations[49] or even for the purposes of the idols, and then share out the proceeds in a peculiar type of partnership.[50] Over the centuries shrines have multiplied, myths have been invented, tall stories embellished in order that the credulous and superstitious might cross the palms of these professional touts with silver.[51] Squabbles between groups of *pandas* and between *pandas* and shebaits (when the former were taking more of the offerings than the latter liked) are evidenced from centuries ago to our own day.[52]

Meanwhile shebaits themselves have in the past been heard to argue that the idol is the deity and receives, through them, offerings from the faithful; furthermore, once those offerings have been received,

---

[45] In *Sree Sree Iswar Lakshi Durga v. Surendra* (1941) 45 C.W.N. 665 it was said obiter that an alienation of the idol would be void. Cf. *Radhakrishna v. Radharamana*, A.I.R. 1949 Or. 1.

[46] *Bameswar v. Anath*, A.I.R. 1951 Cal. 490: *Prayag v. Govindacharlu*, A.I.R. 1935 Mad. 220; *Bhagaban v. Narayana*, A.I.R. 1946 Pat. 27, and references there cited.

[47] *Hemanta K. Mukherjee v. Prafulla K. Bhattacharjee*, A.I.R. 1957 Cal. 685; *Jogesh v. Sree Sree Dhakeswari* (1941) 45 C.W.N. 809 (strong case). For an invalid sale to a divided agnatic relation see *Narayanan Seshacharyulu v. N. Venkatacharyulu*, A.I.R. 1957 A.P. 876.

[48] *Tilkayat Shri Govindlalji v. State of Rajasthan*, A.I.R. 1963 S.C. 1638 reversing *Tilkayat v. State*, A.I.R. 1962 Raj. 196. The *Report* criticizes this tendency at pp. 40-41. Scandals connected with the Tilkayat are also alluded to in the *Report*.

[49] *Guru Estate v. Comm., I.T., Bihar and Orissa*, A.I.R. 1963 S.C. 1452.

[50] Last document quoted by N. Patnaik, "Administration of Jagannath Temple in the 18th century," *Man in India*, 1963, vol. 43, pp. 214-217.

[51] One explanation for the proliferation of miraculous legends regarding places of pilgrimage, and the excessive multiplication of shrines to be visited within each, is the interest of guides, who have had a lien on the content of puranic and connected lore related to such places and their spiritual importance.

[52] *Nar Hari Shastri v. Shri Badrinath Temple Committee* 1954 1 All. 42 (S.C.).

the assets belong entirely to the shebaits themselves and need not be accounted for to anyone.[53] The courts in repelling this contention were quite unable to provide any real check upon the expenditure of temple property, should the influential members of the caste or others interested in the shrine make a bargain with the shebaits. Nowadays the courts are very outspoken about the contrast between the spiritual pretentions of these functionaries when receiving offerings and their very businesslike attitude to their own financial interests once the offerings have been obtained.[54] Yet there has been no attempt to explain, much less to resolve, the anomaly that now exists between the traditional attitude toward gifts for religion and the modern belief that religious endowments exist for the spiritual benefit of the worshippers.[55]

As evidence of this anomaly we find recent cases in which the view is aired that the endowment exists not for the benefit of the idol (the ancient and "correct" view historically), nor (one need hardly say) for the benefit of priests, *pandas* and shebaits, but for the good of the worshipping public. These dicta, which have a juridical significance, completely overlook the fact that worship in the traditional Hindu sense is different from worship in a modern cosmopolitan sense with its strong Christian connotations. The church with its facilities for "worship" offers quite different amenities and fulfils quite a different function from the temple in which the idol condescends to receive visitors, who are expected to bring offerings with them, like subjects presenting themselves before a maharaja. Whatever is amiss with "unreformed" temples, few Hindus can be excluded from interest in them and agitation is a by-product (perhaps an intended by-product?) of temple-entry statutes.[56]

The word "abuse" therefore will have a different meaning to the traditionally-minded and to the modern observer. To the traditional

---

[53] *Manohar Ganesh v. Lakhmiram* (1888) 12 Bom. 247. Tergiversations of judges are revealed in Mukherjea, pp. 228-231. At *Girijanund v. Sailajanund* (1896) 23 Cal. 645 the head priest claimed exclusive right to all the offerings of the idol (Baidyanath temple). In *Rama Rao v. Board of Commissioners, H.R.E.,* A.I.R. 1965 S.C. 231 the *archakas* demanded not less than a half of all offerings.

[54] *Guru Estate,* cited above.

[55] *Deoki Nandan v. Murlidhar,* A.I.R. 1957 S.C. 133. *Upendra v. Anath* 1951 1 Cal. 665, 672: "The image is . . . a compendious expression of the pious purpose."

[56] Madras Temple Entry Authorization Act, 1951 (construed in *Sri Venkataramana Devaru v. State of Mysore* [1957] 21 S.C.J. 382, 1958 S.C.R. 895—a masterpiece of compromise); Bombay Harijan Temple Entry Act, 1947, amended in Bombay Hindu Places of Public Worship (Entry Authorization) Act, 1956 in response to *Bhaichand Tarachand Gandhi v. State of Bombay* (1951) 54 Bom. L.R. 69.

Hindu the shebaits or mahants are guilty of abuses if they give away the endowment's lands to relatives, deprive the idol of worship and neglect worshippers and the amenities which these expect according to custom, live grossly immoral lives, e.g., consorting with widows[57] (it was not necessarily sinful to consort with dancing-girls) or otherwise flagrantly break caste rules under the shelter of their financial power. To the contemporary intelligentsia the scope of abuse is much wider. It is necessarily somewhat difficult to establish, since the power wielded by mahants and by shebaits of the greater temples is enormous—these functionaries are quite the equal of political patrons in ability to distribute favors, contracts and the like, so that witnesses and documents are not readily forthcoming and hearsay and rumor have to do service for more reliable accusations. Yet the Hindu Religious Endowments Commission (1960-1962) had the following abuses to report: neglect of temples and mutts, alienating property to favored parties without real regard for the needs of the endowment, favoring dependents and nominees out of the endowment's funds, treating the endowment property as their own exclusive property,[58] endeavoring to convert it into such an estate as shall pass to their heirs, sexual irregularities, marriage in the case of mahants who are by custom required to be celibate, various irregularities, malpractices, and failures in the conduct of the trusts (pp. 382-389 of the *Report*). Another abuse to which the Report draws attention is the employment at ridiculously low wages of the actual *pujaris* or persons charged with the details of worship of the idol, who are therefore uneducated people in many cases, and driven by their situation into the mercenary attitude which is so much to be deplored. The shebaits may have the administration of hundreds of thousands of rupees, while the actual ministrants are paid Rs. 50 a month.

MEANS OF CONTROLLING TRUSTEES

The modern outlook has its positive as well as its negative side. The desire for reform of Hindu religious endowments operates for the improvement of the amenities of the temples, trying to make them more accessible to more people, to improve the standard of learning of their ministrants, to make the lives of their staffs more edifying,

[57] *Annual Report of Epigraphy*, Madras, 1909, no. 125 of 1908 (about A.D. 1291).
[58] The Raja of Puri actually contended that the vast temple of Jagannatha was his private property, though in fact the court was unable to find that he had any beneficial right in the temple properties, and was, until the statute of 1955 regulating the endowment, the administrator or supervisor of the trust, which then suffered under multiple "abuses." *Raja Bira Kishore Deb v. State of Orissa*, A.I.R. 1964 S.C. 1501 (1964) 2 S.C.J. 682.

to turn the idle endowment funds (where these still survive) to educational and charitable uses for the benefit of the Hindu community or for India at large. But this could not be achieved without a positive structure of administration and supervision, operating not merely by threats but by constructive advice and cooperation with the temple authorities. It was not enough to leave the initiative in the hands of members of the public, who might be intimidated by the mahants or shebaits and their associates in peculation; the power of inspection of accounts was given to a public official. At the same time that the legal machinery, to correct abuses and to enable misappropriated property to be recovered, was being made more efficient, new machinery was created in some states to enable the properties of endowments to be preserved, in certain circumstances to be gathered in, and to be spent on worthwhile undertakings.[59]

The states worked independently and by a process of trial and error. Boards of religious endowments were set up and their powers increased and modified as time and experience suggested. The legislative schemes were subjected at every turn to well-financed and relentless opposition. The temple and mutt officials did not want their accounts (which were often very faulty or at times non-existent) to be open to audit; they did not want to be told what they could do with the money; they did not want to have their alienations of land, for example, void for want of some government official's sanction. That the actual temple precincts should be invaded by persons who were not even of the right caste seemed almost sacrilegious. Opposition to reform on the twin grounds of breach of the freedom of religion and the freedom of property was intense.[60] At long last a situation has been reached where the state laws can operate within the Constitution, but in the course of this development painful gaps have been found in the defenses which the law, as it stands, has been unable to fill, and the report alluded to above seeks to suggest what is needed.

The old methods of control were strictly negative. Under the Civil Procedure Code persons interested in the trust could apply to the advocate general for permission to sue for the removal of the trus-

[59] Madras H. R. and C. Endowments Act, 1959, s. 66 (appropriation of endowments), s. 97 (Common Good Gunf). This is not a feature common to all statutes on the subject, nor of the bill of 1960. The commission believed that poor temples should be assisted by rich temples out of their surplus (pp. 75-89). It is curious that respectable and highly educated witnesses objected to temple funds being spent on hospitals and orphanages (p. 79).

[60] *Ratilal Panachand Gandhi v. State of Bombay* (1954) 56 Bom. L.R. 1184 (S.C.).

J. Duncan M. Derrett

tees, for the appointment of a receiver, for the appointment of other trustees, for the framing of a scheme, and incidental reliefs.[61] Where a mahant or shebait had been alienating property, particularly land, improperly, i.e. without legal necessity or benefit to the idol, the next mahant or other shebaits or, where shebaits were in collusion with the alienees, members of the public interested in the endowment, could sue for the setting aside of the transaction.[62] The law of limitation would operate to perfect the alienees' titles in course of time. Thus large sums of endowment funds have gone into secular use beyond hope of recall. The new methods placed the responsibility for looking after the endowments in the hands of a public body, which might charge fees (to be paid out of the endowments) for its services, and which would seek to eliminate malpractices and foster worthwhile employment of the funds. It has been objected that propaganda for Hinduism has resulted,[63] which may be an abuse in a secular state; also that the officials of the board can fall into errors similar in kind to those of the shebaits and mahants,[64] but the truth of this has not actually been established.

The main gaps lay in the solid legal protection of the "incumbents." The shebait, as temple manager, had obtained through the development of Anglo-Hindu law a definite right of property in his shebaiti, or right to be shebait.[65] This is not surprising since the courts have somewhat naively admitted that the shebait has a right to utilize at his discretion (i.e. for his personal purposes) the surplus after the needs of the idol have been met, and it is entirely in his discretion what these needs may amount to.[66] The courts have sometimes denied that he has a right of property in the idol's property,[67] but

[61] S. 92. To be repealed when the bill becomes law, when the protection of public trusts would lie with the commissioner, whose jurisdiction and procedure are set out in the bill.

[62] *Vikrama Das Mahant v. Daulat Ram Asthana*, A.I.R. 1956 S.C. 382; Mukherjea, pp. 240-241, 248, 250. Derrett, *Introduction to Modern Hindu Law*, para. 798. For mutts see *ibid.*, para. 822.

[63] Donald E. Smith, *India as a Secular State*, Princeton University Press, Princeton, 1963, p. 253. The commissioners did not regard this as a defect.

[64] *Report*, p. 368 (allegations).

[65] *Angurbala v. Debabrata* 1957 S.C.R. 1125, 1132-1134; *Janki v. Koshalvanandan*, A.I.R. 1961 Pat. 293. The office of *archaka* (though the *archaka* is the shebait's servant: *Sree Kalimata Thakurani v. Jibandhan*, A.I.R. 1962 S.C. 1330) is also heritable and partible property: *Ramanujacharyulu v. Panduranghacharyulu*, A.I.R. 1957 A.P. 272.

[66] *Kumaraswami v. Lakshamana* (1930) 53 Mad. 608; Mukherjea, p. 230. Note, however, a trenchant dictum of Mukherjea, J., at *Jogesh v. Sree Sree Dhakeswari* (1941) 45 C.W.N. 809, 816a.

[67] *Govinda v. Shyama* (1940) 44 C.W.N. 1004, 1008.

this denial is for the moral welfare of the public, a façade, and does not truly represent the actual position. In the surplus to which we have alluded the shebaits actually exercise rights of property except where by special statute their disposal has been made subject to schemes supervised by others. At the same time the courts have emphasized that the shebaits are like trustees in that they manage what is not their own property: i.e. to the extent that the idol's needs are ubiquitously to be met from any part of the funds, they manage them all for the idol. The shebait cannot therefore alienate in his own name and for his own purposes legally, and the burden of proof that the alienation was for the idol's purposes lies on the alienee.[68] But of course if the next shebait and the next mahant were party to the transaction or intended to pursue the same or similar schemes it would not be practicable to upset the faulty gift, lease or sale. Leases in perpetuity at nominal rents are often heard of.

Naturally, when the statutes enabled a board to direct the manner in which temples' funds should be administered and applied, shebaits complained that this was a violation of their right of property. To this the eventual answer was[69] that the shebaits managed on behalf of the idols and could not complain if the statutes required them to render accounts and otherwise provided for the proper administration of the idol's assets. The shebait's right of property in his office was not touched, but it was rendered to a large degree infructuous in the case of public trusts. The effect this had on the economic and socio-political power of shebaits can be imagined. Their power passed into the hands of the members of the board, who might or might not be both disposed and able to use it.

The position with regard to the mahants was different. The courts had compared them with the *sajjadanashin* of the Islamic shrine;[70] both functionaries were occupied with collecting and preserving offerings to a holy place, and had the exclusive right to employ and dispose of these. These functionaries seemed to resemble in some ways a corporator sole; yet on the other hand their exclusive right to represent the endowment did not amount to ownership of it and they were more like trustees.[71] However, trustees or not, the properties were vested in them in the eye of the law, subject to a limited

[68] Derrett, *Introduction to Modern Hindu Law*, para. 795.
[69] *Ratilal*, cited above was distinguished in *Sudhindra*, cited below.
[70] *Durgah Committee, Ajmer v. Syed Hussain Ali*, A.I.R. 1961 S.C. 1402 and references there given.
[71] Mukherjea, pp. 312-315; *Vidyavaruthi v. Balusami* (1921) 48 I.A. 302; *Mahant Kesho Das v. Amar Dasji* (1934) 14 Pat. 379.

power of disposal for the legal necessity of the shrine or mutt or its benefit.[72] Consequently the right of property of a mahant was in law more pervasive than that of a shebait, and the mahant's ability to resist interference by the statutory board turned out to be as strong as his financial capacity to litigate the question. At present the state statutes which would direct the mahant how to apply funds surplus to the requirements of the mutt have been held to be to that extent unconstitutional.[73] No doubt case-law under the pre-statutory system held that the mahant enjoyed the surplus strictly as trustee for the purposes of the mutt and to be used in accordance with the customs of the mutt,[74] but this too was a façade, a pretense, attempting to squeeze the medieval mahant into contemporary ecclesiastical garments, and no one treated it seriously. The mahant was still allowed to receive presents in his *personal* capacity—which seems scandalous in a *sannyasi* who has abandoned the world—and these might be of substantial value.[75] The mahant, with his great social and even political influence, therefore remained a focus of resistance to reform.

The Hindu Religious Endowments Commission reported a large number of needed improvements in the law. Positively, the system of control of religious endowments should be put on a national basis with a parliamentary statute.[76] The powers of the commissioners should be increased. On the positive side, again, a system of recruitment and training of *pujaris* should be envisaged, so that they might become a sort of "clergy."[77] The whole thing should be made much more respectable. Charitable and educational enterprises (one hopes in cooperation with existing governmental and traditional institutions) ought to be further fostered and encouraged. The dead hand should not be allowed to keep good money out of circulation. Chief of all the proposals was that the right of property of trustees should be abolished.[78] Extreme language is used to justify the consequent amend-

---

[72] Derrett, *Introduction to Modern Hindu Law*, para. 820.

[73] *Sudhindra Thirtha Swamiar v. Comm., H.R.C.E.*, A.I.R. 1956 Mad. 491, in the Supreme Court at A.I.R. 1963 S.C. 966; relying on *Comm. H.R.E. v. Sri Lakshmindra Thirtha Swamiar, Shirur*, A.I.R. 1954 S.C. 282. See also *Sri Jagannath Ramanuj Das v. State of Orissa*, A.I.R. 1954 S.C. 400; *Sri Sadasib Prakash Brahmacari v. State of Orissa* 1956 19 S.C.J. 397; *Mahant Moti Das v. S. P. Sahi*, A.I.R. 1959 S.C. 942.

[74] *Arunachellam v. Venkatachalapathi* (1919) 46 I.A. 204; *Comm., H.R.E. v. Lakshmindra*, A.I.R. 1954 S.C. 282.

[75] *Laxmi Narasingha Swami Mahaprabhu v. Patta Sahuani*, A.I.R. 1957 Or. 86. See Sri P. Kameswara Rau at pp. 196-197 of the *Report*.

[76] *Report*, pp. 172-173.

[77] *Ibid.*, pp. 174-175.

[78] *Ibid.*, pp. 173, 194. See S. C. Bhat, "A Note on the Report of the Hindu Religious Endowments Commission," A.I.R. 1964 Journal 98-99.

ment of the Constitution, without which, it is said,[79] institutions will be spoiled irreparably, since at present people assume trusteeships for ulterior motives. Shebaits and mahants alike should be cut down to a full trustee status, with no right to dispose of any part of the assets at their own will and pleasure. The right of their nominees and favorites to retain endowment lands simply because complaints were not pursued in time should be abolished; the law of limitation should be amended accordingly.[80] Part at least of this last recommendation had been achieved in some state statutes,[81] and the new Limitation Act appears to make some small improvements in the same direction.[82]

Now that the notion has been fairly well ventilated that endowments exist for the spiritual welfare of the public, now that large sections of the public have access to some if not all parts of most temples for most of the relevant times of day, and now that shebaits and mahants are supposed to be pillars of society in more than a traditional sense, it follows that the public is prepared to watch the modern temple-manager and mahant being shorn of his ancient privileges and perquisites. It is not beyond possibility that temple staffs and mutt staffs will become government servants with fixed salaries, that offerings will be fixed by regulation, and that the visitor to the temple or mutt will have his money's worth. The persons occupied in temples may long retain their low social status, although this may improve if salaries are raised and qualifications are expected from entrants to the profession. On the other hand, once the economic power of the mahants is ended with their discretion to apply their funds, interest in appointments to mahantships is likely to flag. But if the salaries of mahants are fixed by government regulation at a reasonable figure competition will remain, and we shall find these posts occupied by doctors of philosophy, doctors of oriental learning, and the like. The splendor of the old type of mahant will give way to the status of the director of a research institute, much as some maharajas have changed their style and aims with the times. A suggestion made in some quarters[83] that each trust should be the subject

[79] Sri P. Kameswara Rau at p. 201 of the *Report*. At A.I.R. 1954 Jou. 91-94 Sri R. N. Sarkar (a well-known writer on Hindu law) already argued that the shebait's and mahant's right of property in their endowments under the current law was incorrect and that the cases had been wrongly decided.

[80] *Report*, chapter 10; p. 182.   [81] Madras Act of 1959, s. 109.

[82] The new Art. 96 of the Lim. Act, 1963, is advantageous as it abolishes the highly prejudicial rule in *Venkateswara Sarma v. S. N. Venkatesa Ayyar* 1941 Mad. 599 (F.B.), construing Art. 134B of the old act.

[83] S. R. Baj, "Juristic Personality of an Idol in the Hindu Legal Philosophy," *Jaipur Law Journal*, 1963, vol. 3, pp. 229-236. The article supports the commission's general approach and attacks the current legal theory.

of a separate statute has the merit of acknowledging the success of the very numerous statutes that exist,[84] but it is hardly as practical a solution as that recommended by the commission.

THE FAMILY IDOL

It will have been noticed that the *pandas* have not been mentioned. The commission did consider that *pandas* should be regularized, and their fees settled,[85] but no attempt to interfere with the family business aspect of being a *panda* was suggested. It was felt that guides are needed at holy places, and if these could be persuaded to abandon the outlook of the tout, so much the better. Great success was claimed for the Madras legislation in abating the nuisance of *pandas*.[86] But the terms of the commission's appointment precluded their concern with institutions other than the temple and mutt, and other public trusts. Private trusts remain entirely unaffected by the legislation, old and new,[87] and no recommendations have so far been made regarding their future. The members of the commission were lawyers with no affiliation with the Congress Party as such. They approached their task in a non-political spirit. But it is the tacit political implications of the business which explain why private trusts were immune from their scope of reference and equally from the overt scope of their recommendations.

It is extraordinary that this topic has been neglected. Since shebaiti is property it passes on death to heirs and is partible, though as we have seen it ought not to be alienable according to the law administered by the courts. Now that property passes, on intestacy, to a large group of heirs, some of them cognates along with agnates, females as well as males,[88] shebaiti is necessarily split among relatives many of whom have no interest in the idols. The significance of this strikes one only when it is realized that no alienation by one shebait without the concurrence of the others is legally valid.[89] Further, the courts have now denied the obviously attractive theory that if no one objects the family which has an endowed idol can break the trust, throw the idol in the river and secularize or enfranchise

---

[84] E.g., Shri Jagannath Temple Act, 1954 (Orissa Act 11 of 1955).

[85] *Report*, p. 177.

[86] *Report*, p. 248, note by Sri Shankar Saran.

[87] The results can be disturbing: *Mahant Ram Saroop Dassji v. S. P. Sahi*, A.I.R. 1959 S.C. 951.

[88] Hindu Succession Act, 1956, ss. 8, 15. Intestate succession is compulsory (see note 92 below). The commissioners inquired whether the Hindu Succession Act should not be applied to mahants as well.

[89] Mukherjea, pp. 231-232.

the property.[90] The genesis of this idea requires no explanation, since Hindu family religious trusts were invented as a development of the original religious endowment much on the pattern of the Islamic *wakf*, so that property might remain in the family immune from creditors and rapacious tax-gatherers, and free for enjoyment among descendants and others irrespective of a once customarily harsh law of succession.[91] Thus when one realizes, in addition, that testamentary dispositions of shebaiti inconsistent with the intestate law of succession are not allowed,[92] the crisis which has developed in the world of religious endowments by virtue of the Hindu Succession Act can be imagined. The subject cried out for thought on more than one ground.

But the shebait of the family idols wields no political patronage, and whatever difficulties can be created in the realm of transfer of land, and the like, by manipulations with the property of *devatas* (called "debutter property"), the influence obtained through managership of a family trust is slight. Malpractices and irregularities, which occur in this field as regularly as in the public field, pass without question. How is this? Because after all the motive behind the family trust was to give discretion to the shebait for the time being, and without it the position would not be worth having.

Yet, if the subject were viewed from the point of view of strict religion, of the religious benefit of the worshippers, certain reforms would suggest themselves in the family field as readily as in the public one. Family trusts are at least as numerous, and in sum their properties cannot be any less valuable. Land reforms have not hit debutter properties equally in all states; and debutter income is not accessible to income tax. One would suppose that shebaits of any religious foundation ought to be capable of being rendered accountable whether the foundation were public or private. The spiritual objects upon which the commission lay stress[93] apply no less urgently here than

[90] *Sukumar Bose v. Abani Kumar Haldar*, A.I.R. 1956 Cal. 308.

[91] Derrett, *Introduction to Modern Hindu Law*, para. 787.

[92] *Sm. Raikishori Dassi v. Off. Trustee of W. Bengal*, A.I.R. 1960 Cal. 235.

[93] The root idea (see p. 193) of (all) temples and mutts is that the divine entity is the primary object of resort and worship and offerings must be devoted to the propagation of the ideas which originated each foundation. This is a novel approach, evolved partly from a consideration of the case-law, partly from questioning experts and others, and partly from the commissioners' own reflection. Mutts were originally founded to assist in the propagation of ideas, but there is no historical evidence that idols were consecrated or temples founded for this purpose in pre-British times. Treading carefully between the toes of the powerful and possibly vindictive mahants and high priests, the commissioners, anxiously seeking to preserve to them all their honors and ceremonial rights, hasten to add that

there—and legislation actually to prevent excessive dedications to private idols would not be impossible, especially if the bogus "private" temple were redefined as "public." Perhaps the difficulties in administering such a scheme are too great. On the other hand, the spirit which works for the development and reform of the public institution works also for the decay and neglect of the private. How, again, is this? Surely religion is more meaningful in the home? Fewer Hindus worship in temples than worship in their own homes. Yet the cosmopolitan intelligentsia, who desire that temples should in some manner become respectable and approximate unobtrusively to churches or cathedrals, are at the same time people who have given up keeping an ancestral shrine and no longer perform daily worship of family idols. To them the family idol is a charming anachronism, and the fact that the institution was kept afloat chiefly by economic motives does nothing to endear it to them. If the family trusts gradually break up through neglect, if the assets gradually become secularized, if no more property is dedicated to family idols, they will not care. The misuse of power by the trustees of public institutions is one thing, the decay of private institutions is altogether another. Religion inspired both, but the considerations that inspired the movements for reform in the 1960's are not religious ones.

The reader will ask, but what of the private religious foundation other than the family temple? This is altogether outside the schemes for reform, though it has not escaped the critical eye of the educated observer. An enterprising fake ascetic spreads a rumor that an idol in his possession has miraculous powers. He admits the public to worship it and collects the offerings. In no time a building is erected, the institution goes from strength to strength, and the tales of miracles lengthen. This is recognized by lawyers and the educated public alike as a business indistinguishable from a money-lender's business or a cycle-shop.[94] Private enterprise and initiative, within the criminal law, are not to be interfered with, and it is not surprising that, as we have seen, respectable mahants, threatened with legal pressure, have claimed that they were successful operators of what were essentially private enterprises. If the enterprise were so successful that the "incumbent" were able to operate as a political boss the outlook might change, but no evidence of this is so far forthcoming.

---

personal gifts to selected holy men in their individual capacities should lie quite outside the reorganization and regulation which is proposed.

[94] *V. Mahadeva v. Comm.*, *H.R.E. Board* 1956 Mad. 624, 631-632. Derrett, *Introduction to Modern Hindu Law*, para. 804.

CONCLUSION

Some readers may have been reminded of the Reformation in England. Had the church in England remained indifferent to wealth, i.e. had it refused to accept offerings beyond a fixed maximum, it could quite possibly have retained the affections of the state. It was its emergence as an independent power, able to threaten and influence the course of policy at all levels, which laid it open to control and ultimately to a break with the past. The need to reform religion operated as an excuse to tamper with the institution of which non-ecclesiastics were jealous. Necessary reforms in the purely religious sphere were neglected when the main object had been achieved. Hinduism cannot offer an exact parallel, though there are further similarities which we need not pursue here. The lack of an established church and a hierarchy, the lack of dogma and creed, make it very much easier to adjust and temporize and meet emergencies as they arise. Yet, as we have seen, some concept of religion as a reality, which demands some standards from a religious trust's purpose, and which demands some rectitude in the ministers of the endowments of a public character, is now making itself felt; and it is taken for granted that a particular view of what Hindus and Hinduism demand can justify an onslaught on the endowments which suits, in fact, selective social, economic, and political ends.

PART III
PAKISTAN: THE POLITICS OF
ISLAMIC IDENTITY

CHAPTER 15

IDEOLOGICAL DILEMMAS IN PAKISTAN'S POLITICAL CULTURE

WAYNE A. WILCOX

FEW COUNTRIES in the world offer as many paradoxes in their history and development as does Pakistan. In its creation religion played a key role and yet successive governments have followed secularist aims. Party platforms and public oratory have been dominated by religious slogans but policy has followed a course little different from that of other underdeveloped countries in the region. New institutions and procedures were created to magnify the voice of religious leadership but the residual *apparat* of British colonial rule is unchallenged in its dominance. Exemplifying the paradoxes of a state sometimes thought to be a medieval theocracy is its president, Field Marshal Mohammad Ayub Khan, himself a highly westernized, Sandhurst-trained military modernist. It is small wonder that Pakistan baffles friends, foes and neutrals alike, and that the spiritual dimension of its public life is elusive.

Many westerners find it difficult to understand the role of religion in politics; this phenomenon in our own history now seems remote in time and foreign in concept. In the mid-twentieth century even secular ideologies seem to be out of vogue in the industrial and affluent cultures. But it is not solely the foreigner's lack of empathy that inhibits understanding, for even within Pakistan there is a lively controversy concerning the fundamentals of Pakistan's unique ideology. And on the urban surface, at least, Islam as a political program has left indistinct markings.

THE ORIGINS OF THE POLITICAL GOSPEL

In traditional India religion was not unlike faiths elsewhere in a peasant culture. Dogma, fatalism and piety were themes interwoven in a rural milieu. Religious epics and festivals leavened mundane hardships with drama and romance; religious teachings underscored the values and ideals of the better parts of life; philosophy comforted

Wayne A. Wilcox is assistant professor of government and research associate in the Institute of War and Peace Studies at Columbia University.

339

men and women in their sorrow. Religious leaders in rural India were cast in these roles, warning their followers that the path was narrow, the perils many and salvation sure only to the faithful.

New to nineteenth century India were new forms of religion arising from urban social change, a cultural renaissance and the involvement and commitment characterizing nationalism.[1] One need not allude in detail to the facets of the Hindu and Muslim revivals to note that new social leadership in changing India found the need for a "modernized" and generalized faith capable of carrying a political valence, and that such a faith developed.

As social change came to affect an ever larger public, first and primarily in the cities, the contradictions between traditional religion and the new forms became more pronounced. The separate religious revivals of Hindus and Muslims became more important when both faiths became politicized, Islam in the Khilafat movement and Hinduism in Tilak's radical politics and Gandhi's tactics. Despite a programmatic unity between the Indian National Congress and Muslim political leadership after the first World War, political religion was a dangerous development threatening future Indian unity. As Jawaharlal Nehru wrote: "The insistence on orthodox religion as the heart of the national movement and the proclamation of the supposed spiritual superiority of the ancient Hindu civilization to modern 'Western civilization' (what modern psychologists would no doubt term a compensatory delusion), inevitably retarded and weakened the real advance of the national movement and of political consciousness, while the emphasis on Hinduism must bear a share of responsibility for the alienation of wide sections of Moslem opinion from the national movement."[2]

As early as the founding of the Indian National Congress in 1885, some Muslims leaders were apprehensive of any movement which represented majority, i.e., Hindu, interests and which argued for representative government on the British model. By 1906 the Muslims had organized a political party to look after their interests at the court of the Viceroy, and had secured a separate system of electorates in the Government of India Act, 1909. When the partition of Ben-

[1] For detailed studies of the phenomena, see: N. S. Bose, *The Indian Awakening and Bengal*, K. L. Mukhopadhyaya, Calcutta, 1960; Ziya-ul-Hasan Faruqi, *The Deoband School and the Demand for Pakistan*, Asia Publishing House, Bombay, 1963; Khalid Bin Sayeed, *Pakistan: The Formative Phase*, Pakistan Publishing House, Karachi, 1960; and Hafeez Malik, *Moslem Nationalism in India and Pakistan*, Public Affairs Press, Washington, 1963.

[2] Quoted in A. R. Desai, *Social Background of Indian Nationalism*, Popular Book Depot, Bombay, 1959, 3rd ed., p. 306.

gal[3] was reversed, the Muslims became apprehensive that new and hostile forces within the Congress would not be countered by British firmness. During the war there was a general moratorium on communal clashes, and in the postwar period the Congress was able to bring the more orthodox sections of Muslim opinion into a broad, anti-British struggle. After the allies had withdrawn from Ataturk's new Turkey and the Turks had themselves eliminated the Caliph, the politically sensitized Muslims turned back to Indian affairs.

In the inter-war period, Indian Islam was characterized by deep social cleavages and multiple political visions. There were secular nationalists who believed that religion had no place in modern politics, and that political parties were a function of group interests. A second group agreed that Islam should not serve as the focus for a political party because such a development would inhibit Islam's fulfillment as a proselytizing faith in India.

Other points of view emphasized the problems of the Indian Muslims in a potentially Hindu-majority state. In the light of the doctrine of *Dar-ul Islam* and *Dar-ul Harb*[4] and the existence of certain militant Hindu parties, many Muslim leaders feared that their community was under a strong threat of state-sponsored "conversion, absorption and assimilation." Even those Muslims who felt that this was a remote possibility were concerned about the future of Indo-Muslim culture. Since 1900 there had been a struggle between Hindi and Urdu enthusiasts in North India, a struggle which would in a democratic system end in the defeat of Urdu and an end to the heritage of the Mughals.

To these clusters of attitudes could be added many more. There was some appeal, obviously, for a system which provided separate and generous treatment of Muslims in jobs, seats in universities and in government employment. Inasmuch as the Muslims had been late in accepting the skills of British Indian civilization, their immediate competitors were not the British, but the Hindus with a generation's head start.

These various reactions to the probable future of a Hindu-dominated India might have held less terror for the Muslims if they had been involved in the new system. As Nirad Chaudhuri has written:

[3] The presidency of Bengal was divided by Lord Curzon into two provinces, one of which was a Muslim majority area. The justification was administrative, the response was political.

[4] Literally the world of Islam and the world of War, the two theoretical possibilities in orthodox doctrine. Muslims are enjoined to ensure that political authority manifests and protects Islamic values.

"Thus the new Indian culture of the nineteenth century built a perimeter of its own and put specifically Muslim influences and aspirations beyond the pale. In relation to it the Muslims stood outside as an external proletariat, and if the Muslims wanted to come into its world, they could come only after giving up all their Islamic values and traditions."[5]

The British Indian culture, the ideal of democratic government resting on the rule of the majority, and even the xenophobic qualities of Indian nationalism lacked the assimilative force so marked elsewhere among the new nations. In India, nationalism strengthened the so-called traditional residues which, because of their origins and their history, became hostile. This was especially true as politics lost its elitist and moderate base in the Indian cities and as electoral politics made it necessary to reach the rural populace.

It seems clear that 1937 was the turning point, for in that year the competitive play of politics pitted a weak Muslim League against a vigorous Congress Party throughout India. The electoral results—a landslide victory for the Congress—and the absence of *noblesse oblige* on the part of the victors[6] presented Muslim leaders with a grim choice. They could either surrender to the overwhelming might of the broad, liberal and centrist Congress coalition on Congress terms, or they could radicalize their own party and appeal. The former was an alternative which lacked dignity and self-respect, but the latter was equally difficult because it implied turning from the ideals of modern society back to Islamic origins.

To understand why the Muslim leadership found its heritage politically distasteful is to understand the impact of British rule and development in India.[7] Western culture and techniques were so obviously superior and appealing to the new urban classes that they became converts. British rule allowed a considerable degree of social mobility in which a new and dominant middle class, created and employed by the British rulers, replaced the traditional aristocracy.

[5] Nirad C. Chaudhuri, *The Autobiography of an Unknown Indian*, Macmillan Company, London, 1951, p. 231. His section on the origins of "Hindu-Muslim Enmity" is convincing, see pp. 229-237.

[6] For a detailed discussion, see Maulana Abul Kalam Azad, *India Wins Freedom*, Longmans Green, New York, 1960, and Choudhury Khaliquzzaman, *Pathway to Pakistan*, Longmans Pakistan Branch, Lahore, 1961, pp. 152-155.

[7] I have discussed this point at much greater length in "Political Development in India; A Case Study," *Annals*, March 1965. President Ayub Khan wrote in 1959 that "in our ignorance we began to regard Islamic ideology as synonymous with bigotry and theocracy, and subconsciously began to fight shy of it." See the foreword to *The Ideology of Pakistan and Its Implementation*, by Javid Iqbal, Sh. Ghulam Ali and Sons, Lahore, 1959.

Western education, the industrial ethic, the intellectual life of Oxford, Cambridge and London—all of these were part of the modern India. Rarely was the modern Muslim leader as comfortable in Persian and Arabic as he was in English and with the classics of the West.

But politics dictated that the Muslims develop a strong and united voice in the protection of their own interests, however differently those interests might be seen, and hence politics dictated the utilization of the one bond of the Indian Muslims, their common religion.

THE TACTICAL DEVELOPMENT OF THE POLITICAL GOSPEL

As Mohammad Ali Jinnah, leader of the Muslim League, viewed the debacle of the 1937 elections, he was forced to admit that in no province was the Muslim League in actual control. The critical provinces were Bengal and Punjab because they were the largest Muslim-majority provinces. The North-West Frontier province, Kashmir state and Sind were also important. Therefore, the Muslim League's program had to provide for the capture of the Muslim-majority provinces despite the fact that in 1937 all of them fell to other parties.

It is clear that political leadership in the provinces was, if not actively hostile to "national" leadership, at least concerned with maintaining the widest range of policy choices. Each government in a Muslim-majority province had to conclude working agreements with the non-Muslims because in no province other than Sind and the Frontier were the Muslims much more than 50 per cent. Any radical program in the provinces would tend to destroy legislative coalitions, and the divisions among Muslim politicians would then prove fatal to ministerial stability, as was demonstrated in the case of Sind. Mr. Jinnah's all-India vision meant very little to successful working politicians in the provinces.

Given the broad need for Muslim unity seen by leaders from provinces where the Muslims were a minority, and the reluctance of politicians in Muslim-majority provinces to narrow their coalition base, the "national" leadership had only one choice—to replace provincial leadership. The only strong issue which the Muslim League could mobilize was religion; moreover, it was an issue which could not be preempted by local leaders because of their coalition partners in provincial politics.

While it may be true, as Edward Shils suggests, that "the gestation, birth and continuing life of the new states of Asia and Africa, through all of their vicissitudes, are in large measure the work of intellectuals,"[8] it would be more correct in the case of Pakistan to suggest that the birth of the state was the work of politicians who may have used intellectuals. It was primarily the interplay between provincial and "national" political leadership before independence which accounted for the heavy emphasis on religion and ideology in the struggle for Pakistan.

The tactical development of Islam as a political platform followed Mr. Jinnah's assessment of the Muslim future in an independent India. As Gandhi had demonstrated, one of the few channels of communication which exist between the cities and the countryside in India is religion. By manipulating religious symbols and awakening the peasantry to politics in the name of religion, the Muslim League was able to mobilize the Muslim masses and at the same time undercut the urban-based Muslim coalition parties (except in Punjab where the reverse held true). It was also possible to bring the lower middle class of the cities into opposition to the aristocracy or the urban upper classes dominating Muslim politics in a given area. In every sense, therefore, the Muslim League was following a revolutionary policy of mobilizing strength by politicizing religion.

In the course of the struggle, *which was actually between alternative Muslim elites rather than between Muslims and Hindus*, League-sponsored policies forced the hand of Muslim provincial leadership. The "direct action" campaigns in Bengal and Punjab destroyed the coalitions of H. S. Suhrawardy and Khizr Hyat Khan. In their stead, Mawlana Akram Khan and Khwaja Nazimuddin in Bengal, and the Khan of Mamdot in Punjab were empowered with the writ of the national Muslim League. These campaigns between the Muslim elites were fought in the streets of Lahore and Calcutta between Hindus and Muslims, thereby fostering the militant Muslim quality of the League appeal.

In mobilizing religion for political ends, the League leadership managed to consolidate power over the Muslim-majority provinces despite its extra-local origins, but in the process it stimulated the growth of strong forces antagonistic to the social *weltanschauung* of the national leaders, and exaggerated the importance of the local political-religious elite which was an incipient counter-force to the inherited British-trained bureaucracy. The inherent significance of Pakistan as an expression of Islam, however, remains undiminished.

[8] "The Intellectuals in the Political Development of the New States," *World Politics*, April 1960, vol. 12, pp. 329-330.

Wayne A. Wilcox

In the words of Wilfred C. Smith: "Within the confusion of Islamic modernism, and alongside the hesitancy of much of Islam's contemporary self-statement, the emergence and development of Pakistan stand out, as dramatic, and creative, self-disclosure."[9]

FROM SEPARATISM TO STATE-BUILDING

Pakistan, divided into two widely separated parts of nearly equal population, came into existence in mid-August, 1947, but its existence was precarious from the start. The very haste with which Pakistan was created became the first and great determinant of its subsequent policies. Its leaders had to build a state to accompany a curiously defined nation, one which had to exclude a major part of the Indian Muslims still resident in independent India.

The new government of Pakistan clearly wanted peace in which to build from the ground up, and it wanted an end to the religious wars which its tactics had, at least in part, ignited. As an initial example of good will, the new Constituent Assembly of Pakistan elected as its temporary chairman and first leader a Hindu from the Scheduled Castes. Later, upon Mr. Jinnah's election as president of the Constituent Assembly, he called attention to the need for national unity. "If you change your past and work together in a spirit that everyone of you, no matter to what community he belongs, no matter what relations he had with you in the past, no matter what is his color, caste or creed, is first, second and last a citizen of this state with equal rights, privileges and obligations, there will be no end to the progress you will make."[10]

Despite this plea and the favored treatment given many prominent Hindus in the country, the spirit of the violent fanaticism engulfing the Punjab in war was pervasive. Just as politicized religion had made Pakistan possible, so too did it make possible the holocaust of the late summer, 1947. When it was over, Pakistan stood scorched and nearly dead, both the victim and the product of what a medieval European would have called a religious "fury."

Credit for Pakistan's continuing existence must be given to the civil servants and soldiers who managed to safeguard and then to develop what little governmental framework existed in the areas which had suddenly become an independent country. The vast masses of peasants, 85 per cent of the population, were generally not highly

[9] Wilfred Cantwell Smith, *Pakistan as an Islamic State*, Sh. Muhammad Ashraf, Lahore, 1951, p. 3.
[10] Address to the Constituent Assembly of Pakistan, *Debates*, 1947, vol. 1, pp. 13-14.

dependent upon a well-developed administrative machine, and could therefore continue to live without reference to the violence and dislocation. It was the cities which suffered, which received the refugees and were the scene of the expulsion of the minorities.

Because the violence was associated with religious passion, and because the real needs of Pakistan were for a functioning state, the spirit of government policy in the first few years of independence was mundane and secular. Law and order was important, and its guardians were given wide latitude in erecting the institutions of civil government. In the developing war for Kashmir, the army also had to be developed to safeguard Pakistan's tenuous territorial integrity. The magnitude of these achievements has not been fully realized.

FROM STATE-BUILDING TO NATION-BUILDING

With the prime energies of Pakistan's leadership committed to the development of the state apparatus, largely on the basis of the British Indian model, politics were practically ignored. In the first few years, no serious mention was made of the need for implementation of Islamic forms of government or legislation.

The task of writing a constitution for the country, however, brought politics to a fever pitch. The very success of the efforts to develop a viable government allowed latitude in the debate on national priorities, a latitude further encouraged by a healthy economic situation arising from good harvests and the Korean War boom in prices of raw materials.

The first problem faced by Pakistan's politicians was the death, within less than two years, of *Quaid-i-Azam* Mohammad Ali Jinnah. Jinnah's role went far beyond his formal power, or even his position as fully accepted leader of the entire country. Jinnah was the man who held the balance in domestic politics, and once he was no longer at the helm, the balance was questioned.

Leadership fell to his lieutenant from the United Provinces, Liaquat Ali Khan. While Liaquat's principles were commendable, his failure to move to the post of governor general was perhaps fatal. Real power in Pakistan was within the establishment of civil and military forces, and the governor general exercised important functions concerning them. Political leadership on the floor of the house was not Liaquat's forte, nor could it be, since increasingly the real power lay with the large provinces comprising Pakistan. Jinnah had recognized that national leadership was possible only by mobilizing competitive political elites from an invulnerable position. Liaquat did not. By staying on the floor and trying to build a national constitutional consensus, to ensure continuing central control of the major provinces and to manage the government, he attempted too much. His assassination in 1951 signaled the end of the dominance of the refugees in the central government, and the rise to importance of the provincial political leaders.

The second problem faced by Pakistan's politicians after independence was their management of the legacy of Islam. It is undeniable that the common basis for the popular acceptance of Pakistani nationalism was religion, and that this ideological theme constituted the primary link between the urban elites and the rural masses. If the leaders of the Muslim League were to continue to resist the onslaught of their provincial rivals, they had to continue to make Islam a real factor in politics, and to preempt it as the state ideology of their party. As a later president of Pakistan put it: "[Pakistani nationalism was] based more on an idea than any territorial definition. Till then, ideologically we were Muslims, territorially we happened to be Indians and parochially we were a conglomeration of at least eleven smaller provincial loyalties. But when Pakistan emerged as a reality, we . . . were faced with the task of transforming all our traditional, territorial and political loyalties into one great loyalty for the new state of Pakistan."[11]

This was a unique problem. Pakistan's nationalism lacked almost all of the generally accepted attributes of nationalism such as a common language, a common past, a common territory under foreign rule, common customs or common class interests.

THE PROBLEM OF NATIONAL IDENTITY

Pakistan's leaders, even before the creation of the state, had an ambiguous vision of their own role and future. On the one hand, their religious community was both a past glory and a present need; on the other, their vision of the future was one defined by modern western society. A prominent Pakistani politician could argue: "The spirit of Pakistan is Islam or if you prefer it, Muslim. That spirit has to be preserved. You can only cherish and safeguard it if . . . vehicles for the operation of the *millat* [nation] within the *qaum* [state] are afforded and preserved."[12] On the other hand, however, very few of Pakistan's leaders saw the state goals as anything other than

---

[11] Field Marshal Mohammad Ayub Khan, "Pakistan Perspective," *Foreign Affairs*, July 1960, vol. 38, p. 549.
[12] Mian Mumtaz Daultana, Constituent Assembly of Pakistan, *Debates*, October 10, 1956.

social, political and economic. They were not intent upon re-creating seventh century Arabia in Pakistan, nor were they intent upon converting the world to Islam. Indeed, it was precisely because they would do neither that they were abused by the religious leadership. Many men identified the good life with one corresponding to religious ideals, but they proposed to create conditions favorable to the realization of the ideal, not to legislate the ideal itself. The terrestrial heaven was, in any case, the business of the planning commission and not of councils of religious leaders.

Political leadership in Pakistan also was made aware of the severe limitations of state policy. They had seen the privation and destruction accompanying a breakdown of law and order, and they were naturally apprehensive about a subsequent crisis. While they understood Islam's equalitarian themes, they were practical men who knew that the nation's only early hope was in private investment, investment which was beginning to flow into manufacturing operations. While they appreciated the desire for a speedy return to social harmony based on Quranic principles, they daily faced the conflicts which seemed best parried by western institutions and practices.

Since Pakistan was a poor state, exporting to earn foreign exchange, its government had to keep an orientation which would allow development. Urban leaders conducted business in English, and kept up with *The Economist* and *Time* because London and New York were as important to Pakistan's future as were Lahore and Dacca. This position of weakness and vulnerability in the world inhibited Pakistan's government from sponsoring changes which would have aligned the state more closely with other Muslim states. Prime Minister Suhrawardy once tersely rejected a pact between Middle East countries and Pakistan by remarking, "zero plus zero equals zero."

While it is true that the environmental constraints in Pakistan militated against governmental changes which would have reflected Islamic values, these constraints were not obvious to most Pakistanis. The press and increasingly the legislatures of the country were forums for an undisguised disenchantment with "secularist" government. The new political parties of importance throughout the country employed religious symbols to call the government into question, and to attack its legislation.

The more fundamental problem, however, was the nature of national identity. If Pakistan was to be merely a secular, development-minded state, why was its creation necessary? India was following precisely the same policy. For millions of people who knew they were

Muslim but did not know how their faith related to their nation, there was a feeling of frustration or a lack of national identification. This was the more important because the same masses were intensely conscious of being part of a regional, provincial or linguistic culture which might or might not be considered complementary to a broader loyalty.

Government officials understood that modern society has a pattern and logic in its operation quite as comprehensive and profound as those of traditional religious society and that industrialization was not simply a bag of tricks, to be borrowed for building dams and jet planes, and then put away when it challenged traditional religious values. But there seemed to be no way in which to capture the fervor of a largely religious nationalism and meld it with the new forms of modernizing society. The task was made more difficult when local politicians seized the religious issue to further their own interests, and when provincial leaders began substituting regional and linguistic loyalties for national ones. These dilemmas, culminating in governmental instability, were among the contributory factors in the coup d'état of October 1958, which spelled an end to parliamentary democracy in Pakistan.

MILITARY GOVERNMENT AND THE NATIONAL IDEOLOGY

The military regime, in reality a coalition between the army and the civil administration, attempted to end "a great deal of loose groping which infected our politics and our intellect alike."[13] It was, more particularly, the re-creation of an environment not unlike that of the first years of the country. The government was free to conduct its business with a minimum of political interference, and its business was essentially providing a climate for economic and administrative development. The army stood behind the police to enforce domestic law and order, and threats to civil administration were not tolerated.

Politically, President Ayub Khan's position was similar to that of Mohammad Ali Jinnah, who stood as the titular and *de facto* head of the state and government. President Ayub Khan's power was possible because he could manipulate alternative provincial leaders, much as could the early Muslim League politicians. Like Jinnah, the new governor of the country could establish the precise meaning of Islam in politics because he could dominate the public dialogue. But, again like Jinnah, President Ayub Khan has not been able to still the opposition to his modernist version of a socially reformist Islam,

[13] Mohammad Ayub Khan, p. 547.

even though he has been able to arrest his critics, and deny them a public forum.

President Ayub Khan has increasingly seen Islam not as religious doctrine, but as the historic product of the Muslims in India. His speeches and concern with Iqbal and Sir Syed Ahmad Khan mark an attempt to limit the perimeters of Islam to a recognized *corpus* of specific writings and doctrine. He has also established institutions for the interpretation of contested aspects of Islam, has let it be known that he is the follower of a *pir* and has been a patron in the establishment of an Islamic University at Bahawalpur. Despite his early stand against the nomenclature of the state, he has accepted "The Islamic Republic of Pakistan" and has named the new capital Islamabad.

The metamorphosis of President Ayub Khan from a chief ruling by martial law to his more recent role of constitutional near-monarch has been marked by increasing attention to Islam. It is clear that no popular figure can govern in Pakistan without reference to the religious faith which links leaders and masses, and which acts as a foil to provincial and parochial loyalties. Islam is probably overrated as a factor holding East Pakistan to the national union, but it is not overrated as a rallying ground for all the people of the country.

IDEOLOGICAL COMMITMENT AND PURPOSIVE POLICY

Ideologies, in this age of democratic politics, have become crucial in the new states, with their need for concepts of legitimacy and popular sovereignty after decolonization. As change disrupts old societies and as the austerities of national savings and investment plans are implemented, peoples need discipline and a spirit of self-sacrifice. They need a vision with which they can identify their course through history toward the unclear future. As President Ayub Khan has argued, ". . . [man] has a great yearning for an ideology for which he will lay down his life and sacrifice all more readily than anything else."[14]

In Pakistan Islam was a factor determining the primary political loyalties of the Muslims under British rule. It established, on the basis of the past and of the value system held in common, a cause worth great human sacrifice. Those who suffered for the new Muslim state, and those who identified with Islam as a cluster of values and directions in human society, wanted Pakistan to embody those values as social realities.

[14] In the foreword to Javid Iqbal, p. x.

The government of Pakistan was staffed with western-educated and western-oriented men who saw purposive public policy in technical terms. The task was to maximize the efficiency of production and administration, to attract capital investment and maintain civil order and national security. This approach produced a crisis in the sense of national unity throughout the country because it did not relate to those common elements of participation and belief which were politically important. Ideological commitment is a positive factor in national development, both politically and economically, because it maximizes commitment to national goals. Development could be defined as the measure to which a people work in common activity for common purpose. The task in Pakistan, therefore, is to attempt to align the religious loyalties of the people and the public policy needs of the country as seen by its leaders.

The problem posed by utilizing a religious ideology is that it has held historic and too often static norms, difficult to alter without a total change in the religious leadership. The atrophy of institutions of religious learning under colonial rule, and the nature of the urban elite in control of the government at present, produces a maximum amount of dissension when the religion becomes "policy prescriptive." President Ayub Khan has had no more notable success in manipulating religious symbols than his predecessors had, and hence has veered toward interpreting Islam in the Indian context, as the product of a unique Muslim people in history.

For the foreseeable future, Pakistan's governments will have to face the problems of reconciling a particular form of social organization with a historic faith. If the faith breaks down, in disillusionment and frustration, the basis of a continuing loyalty to the state will collapse unless the new society arising out of modernization offers a substitute *weltanschauung*. It is possible, of course, for a house divided to continue as a state, but for future national development a higher measure of common effort will surely be required. The meaning of ideology must then be squarely faced.

CHAPTER 16

PAKISTAN AND THE
SECULAR STATE

FREELAND ABBOTT

By ALMOST any standards one chooses to adopt, Pakistan is not a secular state. By the terms of its Constitution, effected in 1962, an Islamic Research Institute has been established in Karachi to assist "in the reconstruction of Muslim society on a truly Islamic basis."[1] The customary basic rights of western society are applicable in Pakistan only "as enunciated by Islam," and the state itself is "based on Islamic principles of social justice."[2] The Constitution stipulates as a basic principle that "no law should be repugnant to Islam."[3] The President is charged with appointing an Advisory Council of Islamic Ideology to give advisory opinions, when asked, to the national or provincial assemblies, or to the president or any provincial governor, as to whether any proposed law is or is not repugnant to Islam,[4] or whether it violates any of the sixteen Principles of Law-making, or fundamental rights, enumerated as part of chapter one of the Constitution. The first amendment to the Constitution, in effect since January 15, 1964, besides changing the name of the state to "the Islamic Republic of Pakistan," made it obligatory on the part of the Advisory Council to review all laws, existing as well as future, with the object of bringing them into "conformity with the Holy Qur'an and the Sunnah" (rather than the more general term, "Islam"); the amendment also gave judicial weight to the Principles of Law-making, by making them enforceable in the courts—except for thirty-one laws specifically exempted from such scrutiny.[5] The Advisory Council can also recommend to the central and provincial governments means by which the Muslims of Pakistan can be better Muslims.[6] It is possible that the law upon which an advisory opinion is sought may be passed before the advice is furnished, and remains valid regardless of the nature of the advice.[7] However, this latter point may be affected by

Freeland Abbott is professor of history at Tufts University.

[1] Art. 207 (2).   [2] Preamble.
[3] Art. 6 (Principles of Law-making 1).   [4] Art. 204 (1 b).
[5] *New York Times*, December 26, 1963. The change in name of the state was reported to have been a move designed by the government to help it "tide over the agitation against the present Constitution by religious extremists." See *ibid.*, February 5, 1963.
[6] Art. 204 (1 a).   [7] Art. 204 (3).

the decision to consider the Principles of Law-making as enforceable in the courts, inasmuch as the first principle relates to repugnancy to Islam.

The capital of the Republic is stipulated as being Islamabad,[8] and it is significant that a large mosque is to occupy the center of the city. The president must always be a Muslim.[9] A set of twenty-four Policy Principles, which each "organ and authority of the State, and . . . each person performing functions on behalf of an organ or authority of the State" is expected to observe, is expressly spelled out (although a law not in keeping with these principles is not open to question).[10] The first Policy Principle asserts that the Muslims of Pakistan should be enabled to live "in accordance with the fundamental principles and basic concepts of Islam." The only other Policy Principle that specifically mentions Islam announces that "the bonds of unity among Muslim countries should be preserved and strengthened"; while others relate to the elimination of usury (*riba*), and discouragement of the consumption of alcohol.

This is quite impressive evidence of the religious character of the Islamic Republic of Pakistan. There is no attempt to separate the state and religion. The state, by the first Policy Principle, is definitely instructed to support the Islamic faith, to make compulsory the teaching of the Qur'an and Islamic studies to the Muslims of Pakistan, to promote Muslim moral standards, and to insure the proper organization of Muslim taxes, religious endowments, and mosques. For the Muslim, the Islamic Republic of Pakistan is very definitely a religious state; for the non-Muslim, there can be little doubt that he must live as a member of a social minority if only because he is a part of a religious minority.

But if the Constitution contains such obviously religious articles, it also contains many articles usually associated with a secular state— that is, a state in which an apparent separation of the state and organized religion is maintained. Every citizen, regardless of religion, is equal before the law,[11] and every citizen is eligible for any public service, and any public office except that of president.[12] It is expressly stated, as one of the now legally enforceable Principles of Law-making, that freedom of religion should be maintained.[13] In at least one respect the Republic of Pakistan may go farther than does the Republic of

---

[8] Art. 211 (1).   [9] Art. 10 (a).   [10] Art. 7.
[11] Art. 2; Art. 6 (Principles of Law-making 2).
[12] Art. 8 (Principles of Policy 14). At the present writing the chief justice of Pakistan is a Christian.
[13] Art. 6 (Principles of Law-making 7).

India, for the former constitution makes it illegal to spend "public moneys for the benefit of a particular religious community or denomination except moneys raised for that purpose."[14] India has, as some Pakistanis are proud to relate, spent far more on the construction and restoration of Hindu temples than Pakistan has spent on Muslim mosques. So far as the author knows, the mosque scheduled to be built in the center of Islamabad, unless it is to be built by subscription, will be the first money the central government of Pakistan has spent in this manner, although it has contributed to the restoration of some Sikh temples on the ground that the Sikh community in Pakistan was too small to afford the work, and that the temples were traditional sites of pilgrimage for the Sikh community. An Islamic Arabic university is to be set up in Dacca, the capital of East Pakistan, however, by the government of East Pakistan—the result, it is reported, of a demonstration by forty thousand madrassah students.[15]

The Constitution further stipulates that no law should be effected in Pakistan that would authorize the compulsory acquisition of property for other than a "public purpose," and by the terms of the Constitution public purpose is thought of as "any industrial, commercial or other undertaking which is of benefit to the public."[16] The compulsory taking of private property for religious purposes does not seem to have been in the minds of the authors of the Constitution.

The Principles of Law-making (now enforceable in the courts) also state that "No law should deny to any person access to a public place (other than a place intended solely for religious purposes) on the ground of race, religion, caste or place of birth."[17] The introduction of slavery into Pakistan in any form is to be forbidden,[18] as is the practice of untouchability.[19]

It is obvious that the molders of the Constitution had no intention of creating a religious state in the sense in which such states have existed in Europe—or in the sense in which Europe has customarily thought of an Islamic state. The Constitution of Pakistan, instead, seems designed to insure the widest latitude, consistent with social order, among all religions; by its terms Muslims will receive encourage-

14 Art. 6 (Principles of Law-making 7 [e]).
15 *Asian Recorder* (March 12-18, 1963) vol. 9, p. 5090.
16 Art. 6 (Principles of Law-making 10 [4]).
17 Art. 6 (Principles of Law-making 13).
18 Art. 6 (Principles of Law-making 15).
19 Art. 6 (Principles of Law-making 14).

354

ment—although not distinct civil benefits—in the practice of their faith.

DEFINITION OF THE SECULAR STATE

Perhaps we will receive a clearer picture of the nature of Pakistan if we apply to it the graphical concept of the secular state devised by the editor of this volume. Dr. Donald E. Smith, in his *India as a Secular State*, has diagrammed the secular state as a triangle: the base represents the separation of state and religion, one side represents the relationship between religion and the individual, and the other side the relationship between the state and the individual.[20] In the case of Pakistan, freedom of religion is guaranteed by the Constitution; every citizen has the right to adopt, or reject, whatever faith he chooses—although one must emphasize that social pressures favoring the dominant belief undoubtedly exist, as they exist in many other countries. We can, accordingly, draw in the side of our triangle showing the relationship between religion and the individual. The basis of citizenship in Pakistan is the individual, not membership in a particular religious community; under the law every citizen is equal, and the Muslim has no more rights, and no more duties, than the non-Muslim; no religious tax, for instance, may be extracted from one religious group for the benefit of another, and any person who feels aggrieved has full recourse to the courts. Accordingly, we can draw the second side of our triangle, that showing the relationship between the state and the individual. Except for the base line, Pakistan fulfils the requirements of a secular state. But it is the nature of the base line that is essential, and it is because of this that Pakistan is so frequently adjudged a religious state.

The nature of this base line, however, requires consideration, for the character of a religious state may be affected by the manner in which it unites religion and the state just as the character of a secular state may be affected by the nature of its separation. In western Europe there are almost as many forms of church-state relationships as there are states, and each professes to be secular. (Part of our problem, perhaps, is that we are trying to measure the twentieth-century world with a nineteenth-century liberal-democratic yardstick.) England, for example, although unquestionably a secular state, maintains a national church, and requires that the sovereign be an adherent of that church. Would it be possible for another state to maintain a different kind of union between religion and state which would still permit it

[20] Donald Eugene Smith, *India as a Secular State*, Princeton University Press, Princeton, 1963, p. 4.

to be properly classified, in western terms, as a secular state? This is the question we must ask about the Islamic Republic of Pakistan.

It would be proper to ask another question, too. So long as we express ourselves only in terms of the secular state we need not pay too much attention to the nature of a religious state. But the question should be asked: Just what *is* a religious state? Are there any truly religious states in the world today? Is a religious state merely one that doesn't conform to our diagrammatic triangle? Or is it merely a state in which a common morality is expounded—and enforced? Is it a state in which there is a common sense of right and wrong? A definition of this sort seems uncommonly loose, for isn't a sense of morality essential to any society? We may push this point further and assert that what the secular state avoids is a *particular* morality as propounded by a definite faith, whether Buddhist, Christian, Hebrew, Muslim, or whatever; it may be that the real distinction of a secular state is that it admits that even in the realm of morality there is room for disagreement. Yet this, too, is an uncertain position, for if we apply it logically then Pakistan, a state in which a dogmatic interpretation of the faith has been consistently and vigorously attacked, emerges as Islamic but not religious.

Actually, the term "religious state" is not very meaningful for today's world, and it is questionable whether the term "secular state" has much more value. The western mind seems to be constructed along the lines of Newton's third law of motion: for every action there must be an equal and opposite reaction. For every positive there must be a negative; for every black there must be a white. If there are secular states there must be religious states. It is also true that for every century there is also a later century, and that the meaning of words, and the ideas they carry, changes with the centuries. Just as the term "Islamic state" connotes a different meaning to different people (Pakistan, officially, is an Islamic *Republic*), so does the word "religion" have its own differing connotations. This is an element, in fact, of some importance in any discussion of Pakistan—or in any consideration of the secular state. It is an element, incidentally, which also works both ways. If, as many Muslims insist, the West does not understand such a religion as Islam because at one and the same time it encompasses both the secular and the religious, then it is also true that many Muslims do not understand the concept of the secular state as it has developed in the not irreligious West, and they tend to divorce it completely from all religious and ethical values.

The nature of our diagrammatic base line, however, still remains to

'secular' does not mean irreligious, in Western usage, while 'Islam' does not mean unsecular, in Pakistani usage.

be considered. It is obviously closely related to the Pakistan Constitution and its application. This is a strangely nebulous document, incorporating elements of the presidential and parliamentary, and the federal and unitary, systems of government. The net result is a very strong president, a rather weak one-house National Assembly, a Supreme Court whose power has been severely curtailed, and a government that is neither federal nor unitary. It is, in short, uniquely Pakistan's Constitution, obviously designed to meet situations peculiar to Pakistan. So vast are the president's powers that in a very real sense the religious character of the country must be a reflection of the attitude of the president. Mawlana Abul 'Ala Mawdudi, the leader of the Jama'at-i-Islami, a Pakistan religious party, and the most articulate of the more conservative Muslims of Pakistan, would, were he president, undoubtedly use the Constitution in a manner far different from that in which Mohammad Ayub Khan presently uses it.

One of the significant questions that must be asked is how likely is it that an advocate of the more conservative, or traditional, wing of Islamic thought in Pakistan can achieve control of the government? If it is likely, then there can be no doubt that the religious future of Pakistan has little to do with the secular state as envisioned by the West. This is a point we will take up later.[21] The Constitution has determined the nature of political activity in Pakistan, and the opposition to the government has rallied around the cry of "Parliamentarianism and Democracy!" The first amendment represents an effort to curtail the extensive powers of the president, and at the same time enhance the rule of the courts and the national assembly.

In a very real sense Pakistan represents a state balanced between two great cultural traditions, and the Constitution of Pakistan reflects this. Mr. J. W. Syed, a Pakistani scholar, has noted that out of its particular European context the word "secular" loses all of its meaning and import.[22] This is a position that ignores the fact that western tradition is now part of the intellectual tradition of many Pakistanis—including Mr. Syed and almost every responsible official in the government. The secular state is not an intellectual idea completely foreign to the rulers of Pakistan—this is one of the main things that disturbs orthodox Muslims, but the western concept of the secular state must compete with the Muslim idea that the state is a kind of adjunct of the religion, and that the various religious groups should be

21 See Syed Abul 'Ala Maudoodi (Khurshid Ahmad, ed.), *Islamic Law and Constitution*, Jama'at-i-Islami Publications, Karachi, 1955, for an exposition of an Islamic state as envisaged by Mawdudi.

22 J. W. Syed, "Islam and Secular Democracy," *The Islamic Literature*, May 1954, vol. 6, no. 5, p. 5.

divided into their respective communities *(ummah* or *millat).*

The idea of the secular state developed out of the experience of western Europe as a strongly organized church struggled for political power with strongly organized governments, a struggle that first ended with compromise as the medieval Christian Church agreed to let bishops be named by the state provided that they were invested in office by the church. The Protestant Reformation, in turn, breaking the unity of the medieval church, forced a new statement, that the citizen should follow the faith of the prince. This decision, too, failed, and in France led to the *politiques* who preferred to let people follow their respective faiths so long as they did not disturb the body politic.

In England, Elizabeth, the leader of a new national church, expressed her own interpretation of this position by remarking that men should not be forced to make windows of their souls; accordingly, she refrained from overt persecution of those who did not welcome her national church, so long as they attended. Almost a century after the death of Elizabeth a new decision was on its way to achievement: that it would be better, both for religion and for government, if the church and its interests were completely separated from the state and its interests. This development reflected a wide variety of influences, not least of which was a new philosophical-psychological estimate of man—that he was not born with set instincts and ideas, somehow instilled by God before birth, but that he was a creature responsible for his own ideas and traditions, and these he developed more as a result of his own experiences than as a result of his inheritance.

On this basis, constructed by John Locke and David Hume in England, by Descartes, Diderot, and Voltaire on the continent, and by Roger Williams in America, the basis of the idea of the secular state was laid.

THE MUSLIM HISTORICAL EXPERIENCE

The Muslim experience has not echoed that of the Christians. No great organized church, in the western sense, developed. The Qur'an opposes a priesthood, and insists that no man needs an intermediary with God. To Muhammad religious life was not a part-time thing; he believed that if man's religion means anything it must be practiced continually. Honor, accuracy, fair play, a kept promise, the fear of God, respect for man—all these things were part of religion in Muhammad's view. Consequently, the Qur'an gives no injunction to render unto Caesar that which is Caesar's, and unto God that which is God's. "There is no such thing as a profane world," wrote Sir Muhammad Iqbal, the Indian Muslim poet who is generally considered to have first expressed the idea of a separate state on the subcontinent for Muslims. "All this immensity of matter constitutes a scope for the self-realization of spirit. All is holy ground. As the Prophet so beautifully puts it, the whole of this earth is a mosque."[23]

Islam began, then, by emphasizing that the function of the state is to reflect the highest religious qualities; its purpose is to provide protection for the faith and a suitable environment in which it can prosper. Arab tribal law was considerably modified, and often replaced, by the Islamic law, but there was no tradition of a strong, well-developed pagan law, such as that of Rome, on which to build directly. Islam developed its own law out of the Qur'an and the actions of Muhammad, the exemplar, as interpreted by, and agreed to by, the religious scholars. The struggle between religion and state that marked western development did not appear in the Islamic world, partly because no church in the western sense developed, and partly because so much of the law that was applied was religious law.

The Muslim heritage, then, is not to think in terms of two competing entities—the church and the state, each struggling to gain the upper hand. The ideal becomes not the separation of religion and state, but the unification of religion and state. In actual fact, of course, Muslim rulers have found it expedient to practice a division that did not exist in theory. The Abbasid caliphs, ostensibly the protectors of the faith, were for the most part treated like pawns by the actual political power of the day. Some of the Sultans of Delhi in fourteenth-century India, such as 'Ala-ud-din Khilji and Muhammad ibn Tughluq, practiced a division of civil and religious law. The former at one time remarked, "To prevent rebellion, in which thousands perish, I issue such orders as I conceive to be good for the state, and the benefit of the people. Men are heedless, disrespectful, and disobey my commands; I am then compelled to be severe to bring them into obedience. I do not know whether this is lawful or unlawful; whatever I think to be for the good of the state, or suitable for the emergency, I decree."[24] Such an attitude was far from unique, and the term 'urf ('ada) was used to identify those actions that reflect

[23] Quoted by J. W. Syed, above, pp. 11-12. Actually the idea of a separate Muslim State in India was broached several times before Sir Muhammad Iqbal, in his presidential speech at the 1930 session of the Muslim League in Lahore, made his forcible presentation of the case for such a state.

[24] Quoted in R. C. Majumdar, H. C. Raychaudhuri, and Kalikinkar Datta, *An Advanced History of India*, Macmillan Co., London, 1961, pp. 306-307. For a comment on Muhammad ibn Tughluq, see p. 318.

general usages as distinct from the religious law. The Ottoman Empire, in addition to *'urf,* established *kanuns,* or civil law, along with the religious law *(shari'ah).* In fact, the fundamental law of the empire in respect to dignitaries, customs and ceremonies, the administration of military fiefs, and the status of non-Muslims, among other things, was of this nature.[25] Nevertheless, no tradition of the separation of church and state developed because the *kanuns* only supplemented the religious law; that law remained essential to the community.

The attempts of Pakistan to draw up a constitution are particularly interesting because these two strains—that of the secular state and that of the religious state—are intertwined in the minds of the authors of the two Constitutions Pakistan has effected. The Pakistan Constitution is not just a compromise between federal and unitary, or parliamentary and presidential forms; it is also a compromise between differing concepts of Islam, even while calling for the unity of Islam. This is a struggle that has been going on since the independence of Pakistan.

Mohammad Ali Jinnah, the founder of Pakistan, seems to have thought of Islam primarily in social terms—his definitions of the Islamic state were vague, but they were never couched in what the West would consider religious terms. His battle-cry before partition, that there were "two nations" in India, the Hindu and the Muslim, and that they could never get together, was predicated in social rather than religious terms. A typical utterance is to be found in his Presidential Address before the Lahore Session of the All-India Muslim League in March 1940: "It is extremely difficult to appreciate why our Hindu friends fail to understand the real nature of Islam and Hinduism. They are not religions in the strict sense of the word, but are, in fact, different and distinct social orders, and it is a dream that the Hindus and Muslims can ever evolve a common nationality, and this misconception of one Indian nation has gone far beyond the limits and is the cause of most of your troubles and will lead India to destruction if we fail to revise our notions in time. The Hindus and Muslims belong to two different religious philosophies, social customs, literatures. They neither intermarry nor interdine together and, indeed, they belong to two different civilizations which are based mainly on conflicting ideas and conceptions. Their aspects on life and of life are different. It is quite clear that Hindus and Musalmans derive their inspiration from different sources of history. They have different

[25] See the entries in the *Encyclopedia of Islam* under *'ada, kanun,* and *'urf.*

epics, different heroes, and different episodes. Very often the hero of one is a foe of the other and, likewise, their victories and defeats overlap. To yoke together two such nations under a single state, one as a numerical minority and the other as a majority, must lead to growing discontent and final destruction of any fabric that may be so built up for the government of such a state."[26]

A former chief justice of Pakistan, Muhammad Munir, recalling his experiences on the 1947 Boundary Commission to establish a line between India and Pakistan, recently wrote: "The wealth of the non-Muslims in Lahore represented the sweat and labor of the Muslims and it was with a view to doing away with this inequitable position that the Muslims had demanded a state where undominated by the Hindu he could improve his lot and enjoy a position of economic independence. The present argument that Pakistan was demanded in order to enable or compel the Muslims to lead their lives in accordance with the injunctions of Islam was then in nobody's mind. The transcendental had not yet been lowered into a commonplace and the Holy Book and Tradition had not been converted into a potent weapon of the politician, though implicit in the demand had been the hope that Pakistan would provide a favorable ground for experimentation in Muslim social and political doctrines."[27] And, indeed, the early remarks of Mr. Jinnah (as in his opening address to the Pakistan Constituent Assembly) and Ghulam Muhammed would seem to support this view. It was a view only partially to prevail, largely, perhaps, because the non-Muslim population, as fearful of being a minority in Pakistan as the Muslims had been in India, fled. The complexion of the new state was changed overnight, and in a country now predominantly Muslim, the role of the religiously conservative was greatly enhanced.

The Muslim religious leaders, most of whom had had little contact with the West, and that often extremely superficial, entertained quite a different picture of Islam—and their influence among the rural population (approximately 90 per cent of all Pakistanis) was great. The fear of a government controlled by the religious leaders (which would certainly mean the loss of power by most of the hundred leading families of Pakistan) helped insure that the path of the Pakistan government would not be smooth. There could be no doubt that the kind of government envisaged by the religious leaders would be not only a misfit, but a liability, in the modern world. Modern

[26] Jamil-ud-din Ahmad, ed., *Speeches and Writings of Mr. Jinnah*, Muhammad Ashraf, Lahore, 1952, vol. 1, pp. 177-178.
[27] M. Munir, "Days to Remember," *Pakistan Times*, June 23, 1964.

banking practices would be unacceptable, as the payment of interest (*riba*) is forbidden in the Qur'an; minorities, while receiving protection, would be forced to pay a special tax (the application of which had in Mughal times provoked rebellion among the Hindus); and any Muslim who adopted a different faith would be executed as a traitor.

The attempt to insure that the *kind* of religious state Pakistan was to become was not based on medieval applications required that the government move slowly. It was necessary to educate the country, to persuade people that an Islamic state could be something more than the narrow institution described by the mullahs. It is significant that when, on January 6, 1964, the Jama'at-i-Islami was declared illegal and its leaders (including Mawlana Mawdudi) arrested, the government alleged that they had indulged "in subversive activities against the state" and constituted "a danger to the public peace."[28] President Ayub Khan is reported to have told a Muslim gathering two months before that he deplored religious groups taking part in politics, and warned Muslims against being trapped by people who, in the garb of religion, were trying to achieve political power.[29]

Some years earlier Governor General Iskander Mirza had brashly announced that religion and politics don't mix; Ayub Khan is forced to try, at least, to make them flow together. Nevertheless, these are actions a westerner might more readily associate with a secular, rather than a religious, state. The westerner might also be surprised at the consistency with which certain interpretations espoused by the more conservative religious elements in Pakistan have been replaced by the government with interpretations we can only call "modern." One cannot, it must be emphasized, call them "secular," except in a western sense, for in Islam theoretically all things are religious. Let us cite three widely varying areas of conflicting interpretation.

RELIGION AND PUBLIC ORDER

The first area concerns religion and problems of law and order. There was, for example, the case of Juma, a peasant of Sind who became enamored of his neighbor's wife. When the latter prevented him from seeing her, Juma secretly entered his neighbor's house, killed the seventy-year-old mother with a hatchet, and wounded two others

---

[28] *Pakistan Times*, June 18, 1964. These quotations are from the notification appearing in the *Gazette of West Pakistan*, January 6, 1964, as quoted in the high court judgment dismissing a writ petition which challenged the government's action in declaring the Jama'at-i-Islami an unlawful association.

[29] *Muslimnews International* (Karachi), November 1963, p. 8.

(including the wife of whom he was enamored). He was tried in the sessions court and on December 9, 1952, was sentenced to death. The sentence was confirmed by the Chief Court of Sind and a petition to the Federal Court was dismissed. Juma, through his advocate, then appealed for mercy to the governor general (Ghulam Muhammed at the time), on the ground that his sentence under the prevailing law, based on the British Indian penal system, was repugnant to the Holy Qur'an.[30]

The mercy petition was supported by a *fatwah* from Mufti Fazal Muhammad, and four affidavits by near relatives of the murdered woman, pardoning his guilt, each of which read, "I hereby forgive him and pardon his guilt per rights invested in me by the Holy Qur'an and *shari'ah* and I demand that the said Juma, son of Gulsher, condemned prisoner, be released forthwith. Neither should he be hanged nor punished for the same."[31]

The Mufti's legal opinion (requested by Juma's advocate) said that Islam, as interpreted by the Qur'an and the Sunnah, sets a murderer free if he is excused and pardoned by the relatives of the deceased. But the Mufti's opinion ignored other passages. The Qur'an also stipulates that "whosoever saves a life, it is as though he had saved the lives of all men" and conversely, "whoever kills a person . . . it is as though he had killed all men."[32] This passage would seem to indicate that the punishment or pardon of a murderer rightfully belonged to the state and not to the aggrieved individuals. But this particular passage specifically refers to the Israelites; how broadly should it be interpreted?

Thus, considerable leeway existed—and does exist—for differing interpretations. Juma's appeal, it might be noted, failed to convince the authorities, and he was hanged. The practical effect of this decision was to support one reading of the Qur'an over another. The decision regarding Juma was based, fundamentally, less on religious grounds than on the practical question of maintaining social order within the state. On these grounds, too, the Jama'at-i-Islami, with their direct appeal to many religiously-minded Pakistanis based upon a particular interpretation of the Holy Qur'an and Sunnah, was declared illegal.[33] While these actions involved the state with religious issues, the decision

[30] The story of Juma may be found in the *Pakistan Times* in the issues of January 3, 6, 10, 18, 1954, and in the Sunday *Statesman* (India), January 17, 1954.

[31] *Pakistan Times*, January 3, 1954. A *fatwah* is a legal opinion given by a mufti, or canon lawyer, of standing. See *Encyclopedia of Islam, fatwa*.

[32] The Quranic passages primarily involved here are 2:178-179 and 5:32.

[33] It should also be stressed that one of the strong attractions of the Jama'at-i-Islami was the free dispensaries and other welfare projects it supported.

in each case was to curtail an interpretation of Islam seemingly in-consistent with the demands of a modern state.

It was this same practical problem that lay behind the decisions of the judges who participated in the inquiry into the causes of the 1953 riots in the Punjab. Directed against the Ahmadiyah sect, and encouraged by the *ulama*, these rioters asserted that the Ahmadis were not Muslims at all but heretics because the sect's founder, Mirza Ghulam Ahmad (c. 1835-1908), testified that he was a prophet, and the members of the sect believed that he was. Anyone who maintained that Muhammad was not the last prophet, the rioters urged, should not have the status of Muslims in an Islamic state. The inquiry ques-tioned the religious leaders as to what it was that made a man a Muslim. Naturally enough, there was a wide range of disagreement in their answers, although they all agreed that the Ahmadis were not Muslims. The obvious lesson seemed to be that a religious de-finition alone was not sufficient to determine whether or not a man was a Muslim, else Islam would prove to be a far more divisive than unifying force. Pakistan has not yet, in fact, discovered a simple, objec-tive definition of a Muslim. A Muslim is someone who says he is a Muslim, however he might interpret Islam, or however many of the "five pillars of Islam" he might, or might not, observe. One of the purposes, indeed, of the Islamic Research Institute established by the Constitution, is to find some modern basis around which Muslims can identify.

MUSLIM FAMILY LAWS

A second area in which traditional interpretations are being re-placed by others concerns the controversy over the Muslim Family Laws Ordinance, promulgated by President Ayub Khan on March 2, 1961. This law was based upon the report of a seven-member com-mission created in August 1955 to consider whether the existing laws relating to marriage, divorce, and family maintenance were in keeping with Islamic injunctions concerning the status of women. The com-mission was composed of six individuals of definitely modernist views, and one religious scholar who published a lengthy dissent.[34] In brief, the commission recommended that polygamy be thoroughly dis-couraged, that divorce procedures be tightened up and that the wife's right of divorce also be acknowledged; that all marriages and divorces

[34] Marriage Commission Report, *Gazette of Pakistan Extraordinary*, June 20, 1956; the note of dissent was published separately on August 30, 1956. See Free-land Abbott, "Pakistan's New Marriage Law: A Reflection of Qur'anic Interpre-tation," *Asian Survey*, January 1962, vol. 1, no. 11, pp. 26-32.

should be registered; that adequate maintenance be assured for all wives; and that the legal age at which girls could be married be raised to sixteen years.

These recommendations were urged, according to the commission's majority, because they were in the true spirit of Islam; most of them were incorporated in the Muslim Family Laws Ordinance. That law has, of course, been attacked by many of the *ulama* as thoroughly un-Islamic. The Qur'an, they say, specifically permits the marriage of girls of less than sixteen,[35] and Muhammad's favorite wife (after Khadijah) was far younger than this at the time of her marriage to him.

The *ulama* objected, too, to the provision relating to divorce, arguing that the law made an absolute right of divorce to the husband, as it was granted in the Qur'an, into an action dependent on a third party—the Arbitration Council created by the ordinance. The Qur'an, the *ulama* argued, nowhere makes the husband's right of divorce conditional on taking the matter to any council or having to obtain a verdict from a court of law; instead, the Qur'an specifically charges that men are in charge of women.[36]

The idea of placing restrictions on polygamy (beyond the four wives sanctioned by the Qur'an), or even of regarding polygamy as objectionable, is considered by the *ulama* as totally foreign to Islam. Muhammad, after the death of Khadijah to whom he was happily married for a quarter of a century, did have several wives, and so did most of his Companions. In short, to the learned *ulama* of Pakistan, everything concerned with the Muslim Family Laws Ordinance was anathema. The government, on the other hand, maintained that the laws were more truly Islamic than the preceding practice had been, for that practice virtually denied individuality to women.

Even the registration of marriages was objected to, not because the *ulama* failed to see the advantages of registration, for they did; what they objected to was making the registration of every marriage compulsory because the religious law of Islam did not institute any such office as that of marriage registrar, nor did it require that there be a Muslim present who would officiate at the ceremony (in general, only two witnesses to the marriage were required).[37] In the case of this law there was a clear dispute as to the meaning of the Qur'an. Nevertheless, the government prohibited the distribution of a pamphlet containing the *ulama*'s views, and slowly began to enforce the law.

---

[35] Qur'an 65:4.   [36] Qur'an 4:34-35.
[37] *Muslim Family Laws Ordinance as Commentted* [sic] *by Ulama in the Light of Qur'an and Sunnah*, Hyderabad, n.d., 36 pp.

Under the steady hand of the martial law regime, the *ulama* could do little except to nurse their wounds bitterly. After martial law was lifted early in 1963, a bill to repeal the Muslim Family Laws Ordinance was introduced in the national assembly—the orthodox elements had chosen this measure as one with which they could fight Field Marshal Ayub Khan. A standing committee of the national assembly considered the bill to repeal the Family Laws and recommended that it not be passed. President Ayub Khan referred the matter to the Islamic Advisory Council.[38] In the West Pakistan provincial assembly a resolution in favor of the repeal of the Muslim Family Laws Ordinance was easily passed; it was easier to vote for the resolution and please one's rural constituents, than to vote against it and risk one's political position, regardless of personal conviction, especially as it was only a resolution. The bill to repeal came to a vote in the national assembly on November 26, 1963, and, after twenty hours of debate, was defeated 56-28—an emphatic declaration that whoever was controlling opinion in the legislature, it was not the *ulama*. A month later the Fundamental Rights Bill, the first amendment to the 1962 Constitution, extending somewhat the role of the courts by making all of the Constitution's Principles of Law-making defendable in court, specifically excluded the Muslim Family Laws Ordinance from review—it thus remains the law of the land and cannot be challenged in any court. This act is one of the more important achievements of Ayub Khan's regime, and should be ranked along with land reform in West Pakistan.

Whatever the nature of the Islamic state envisaged by the present leaders, it is far removed from the picture of Pakistan still sometimes presented by the foreign press as a "theocratic state."[39] The speeches of President Ayub Khan have been very forceful in this matter, emphasizing the need "to promote a true and correct study and understanding of Islam in the context of modern science and knowledge."[40] Islam, the president asserted in a speech at Cairo University, has moved farther and farther away from the spirit of religion and has drifted into mere conformity—originality has given way to superficiality, reason has given way to superstition, and the courage to inquire freely has "succumbed to blindfolded subservience to tradition." He continued: "The kingdom of crowns, which the Muslims have lost in the course of their history are far less important than the kingdom

---

[38] London *Times*, July 3, 1963; July 16, 1963.
[39] For a recent example, see the *Illustrated News of India*, April 26, 1964, p. 9.
[40] November 9, 1960; Press Information Department, Government of Pakistan, E. No. 6741.

of free and searching mind which they have lost in the process of intellectual stagnation. The result was that while life kept moving onwards, knowledge and practice of Islam continued to lag centuries behind. Instead of remaining a complete and dynamic code of life, as it was intended to be, Islam thus became an object of external adoration to worship which one had to constantly look backward in a world which is constantly moving forward. To liberate the spirit of religion from the cobwebs of superstition and stagnation which surround it and move it forward is, therefore, one of the major demands on our system of education."

Under conditions in which the vast majority of the people believe in the faith as portrayed by the rural religious leaders (the *imams* and the *ulama*, who have at best only a superficial grasp of western ideas, and that often selected to belittle the West), it is naive to expect a purely secular state—even in western terms. Somehow the popular attitude towards Islam has to be made forward looking, has to be interpreted, in the words of many modernist Muslims, "positively and not negatively."

A third area which illustrates the Pakistan government's approach to religious questions is the handling of the problem of interest. The payment of *riba* (that is, increase—or more specifically, any unjustifiable increase of capital for which no compensation is given)[41] is expressly forbidden in the Qur'an as a practice of unbelievers, and its abandonment is made a test of one's belief.[42] "No amount of sophistry or verbal hairsplitting," an orthodox Muslim has written, "can obscure the fact that Islam is strictly against all forms of usury and interest."[43]

So intractable a position as this, of course, threatens the financial foundation of a modern state, and particularly so when the state is as dependent on foreign credits as is Pakistan. The Pakistan government has, in fact, charged interest to borrowers from the very first; nevertheless, it has always had to face some undercurrent of feeling that this, in an Islamic state, is not quite right. Individuals have tried to explain away interest by calling it some other name—such as "service charge," or have tried to identify *riba* with usury only (or sometimes with compound rather than simple interest), but none of these efforts has successfully resolved the problem. The government has continued its practice, has invited discussion of the problem (perhaps hoping to further education in modern economic thought), and has

[41] See the entry *riba* in the *Encyclopedia of Islam* for a detailed discussion of the difficulties of interpretation this Quranic injunction has entailed.
[42] Qur'an 2:275-280; 3:120; 4:161.
[43] Qaisan Afzal in *Muslimnews International*, December 1963, p. 38.

referred it to the Islamic Advisory Council. But the problem is not one, as Dr. Fazlur Rahman, director of the Central Institute of Islamic Research has pointed out, that can be easily solved—nor solved at all without "careful thought and judgment."[44] The fact is that the meaning of the term *riba* in the Qur'an is not clear, and because of this the problem of interest has been a perennial problem among Muslims almost from the time the revelation was received. Many modernists, such as the late Khalifa Abdul Hakim, tend to dismiss it with the simple, although historically questionable, argument that because it was one of Muhammad's last revelations, it was never fully explained by him before his death. Consequently, they argue, one can only follow one's best judgment on the matter.

A MODERNIST ISLAMIC STATE

Each of these illustrations indicates that while Pakistan may not be a secular state, neither is it a religious state in the sense in which that term is usually understood in the West. One of the distinctive marks of John Calvin's Geneva, to cite a definitely religious state, was that the Genevans had formulated their concepts of Protestant Christianity: they were building a government to apply that which they already understood. But Pakistan is in the process of finding out what an Islamic state is. Geneva merely applied a different set of religious concepts to the world in which it lived. Pakistan lives in a world different from that in which many Islamic interpretations were formulated; consequently, it must also deduce modern connotations for the ideas and attitudes expressed in the past. This movement is not peculiar to Pakistan alone, for it has been evident in the Muslim world since before the middle of the last century. What is peculiar to Pakistan is the extent to which the Pakistanis feel it necessary to rationalize their position, reflecting, perhaps, the fact that the Muslims of the subcontinent have always formed a religious minority.

Looking at the matter clinically, the government of Pakistan has three groups in particular among its educated class to whom it must appeal: those who, in the western sense, wish an outright separation of all religious organizations and institutions from the state—many of whom are the *politiques* of a new century, and all of whom must be considered as secularists; a second group is made up of those who

---

44 For a summary of the *ulama* reaction to this, from which the quotation has been taken, see *The Muslim World*, July 1964, vol. 54, pp. 220-223. It is only fair to say that the Mawlana's account of the opinion of Dr. Fazlur Rahman is at best over-simplified. See Fazlur Rahman, "*Riba* and Interest," *Islamic Studies*, March 1964, vol. 5, no. 1, pp. 1-43.

believe that Islamic principles should be made applicable to modern conditions—the "modernists"; and a third group—broadly conceived—consists of those who believe in the reapplication of Muslim practice as it existed sometime in the past, or who emphasize that it is not interpretations of Islam, but concepts of the contemporary world, that must change. Of these three groups, the one whose ideas most nearly approximate the religious state as pictured by the West is the last, and one of its most active representatives has been Mawlana Mawdudi. The government has, in fact, chosen the second course, and Dr. Fazlur Rahman, as well as the majority of the members of the Islamic Advisory Council, are its leading representatives. The first group has not been ignored—that the government let the bill for the repeal of the Muslim Family Laws Ordinance come to an open vote may be interpreted as reassurance to the secularists that the more conservative religious forces possessed more voice than vote.

The monthly journal *Ummah* (The Muslim Community), a publication of the Central Institute of Islamic Research, published in its first issue an article which serves to indicate something of the character of the religious state envisaged by modernist religious leaders in Pakistan. Dr. Rafiq Ahmed wrote: "There is a sense in which it is true to say that, in Islam, the political life of the Community cannot be divorced from its religious faith. But that does not mean either that politics forms a necessary part of Islam or that Islam has given us a definite system of political organization. What it does mean is that the political life of the Community, regardless of a system, should be guided by the Islamic ideals of justice and morality. And the very fact that the Faith can exist, and indeed has existed, without political autonomy shows that the relation between the faith and politics is not one of absolute dependence. *But they do nevertheless need and complement each other for a healthy growth of the Community.*"[45] To the western ear this may sound like strange language from a religious source in a religious state; it comes close to describing how many westerners look upon their own secular state in terms of their own ideals of justice and morality. But the westerner, in thinking of Pakistan, has often been guilty of looking backward, of approaching Islam from a negative position; he has failed to realize the difference—or perhaps one could say the similarities—between the Muslim concept of religion in practice and his own past, and the experiences of his own society, with that of the Islamic world. There is

[45] Dr. Rafiq Ahmed, "On the Need for Islamic Research," *Ummah*, May 1964, vol. 1, no. 1, p. 23.

some element of truth, of course, in each of these attitudes, but there is a considerable element of error as well.

"The Muslim liberal," wrote Fazlur Rahman, "on whose shoulders fell the main burden of framing an Islamic Constitution, rightly felt that Islam possessed an inherent ability to express itself in fresh forms consonant with the needs of the age." The search of the Muslim liberal is for modern applications of Islamic principles—and we have sketched three such applications. "Islam, thus," Fazlur Rahman continued, "possesses inherently the capacity to reformulate its ideals in new forms."[46] Historically, in a religious state ideals have become set; they do not seem to have been in the process—certainly not the active process—of reformulation. It is just another way in which Pakistan does not fit the customary western picture of a religious state.

It is highly unlikely that the country will ever become a religious state in the western meaning of that term, for in the last analysis, in Pakistan as in many other states, the source of power remains the army—and a modern army requires a degree of training and skill impossible to maintain in a medievally-based religious state. Islamic principles will be seen in that which will make the country strong and secure the best social order. Yet we are nearer one world than we have ever been, and more and more man's problems become mutual and his defenses interdependent. It is true that Pakistan is not really a secular state, but neither is it truly a religious state; its division between two cultures cuts deep, and its role may well be to evolve a conformity, or at least a harmonization, one with the other. "Pakistan is an Islamic Republic," declared a member of the opposition in the national assembly. "Nothing should be done which militates against either Islam or democracy."[47] The future of Pakistan, and the future of Islam in Pakistan, lies in the significance of those words.

[46] Fazlur Rahman, "An Islamic State," London *Times*, August 14, 1963.

[47] Allama Rehmatullah Arshad (Muslim League—Councillor, Bahawalpur), June 19, 1964. See *Pakistan Times*, June 20, 1964.

CHAPTER 17

THE IDEOLOGY OF
MAWLANA MAWDUDI

CHARLES J. ADAMS

THE PURPOSE of this study is to present and analyze the views of the well-known Indo-Pakistanti Muslim thinker, pamphleteer, and later politician, Abu-l-A'la Mawdudi. There are many reasons for focusing attention upon Mawdudi. He has been one of the influential figures of the Muslim community in the Indian subcontinent since the middle 1930's and more especially since the creation of Pakistan in 1947. Before the partition of the subcontinent he was engaged in serious and bitter literary debate with the several parties seeking to shape the future of an independent India according to their diverse ideals.[1] Later, his views and those of his party were an important element in the constitutional discussions that preoccupied Pakistanis for the first years of their national existence,[2] and he has commanded the loyalty of a sufficient number of his fellow countrymen for the possibility of his actually coming to political power and putting his ideas into effect to haunt Pakistan's successive governments. More important, however, is the fact that Mawdudi, in building his vision of the ideal society and the place of the true Muslim within it, has had to face all the important issues that modernity poses for Muslim faith. But it is not the questions only that are of importance; the solutions he has posed have also proven to have an enormous attraction for ordinary Muslims whose religious heritage has disposed them to think much as Mawdudi does. Mawdudi, or rather the point of view he typifies, is one choice in the Muslim's quest for an orientation to the modern world. In looking at him we shall be considering one of

Charles J. Adams is director of the Institute of Islamic Studies, McGill University.

[1] The most convenient summary of Mawdudi's attitudes toward the contending groups in pre-partition India is the collection of essays and papers in three volumes known as *Musulman awr Mawjudah Siyasi Kashmakash*. Each of these volumes contains essays written at a certain period. The three volumes reflect, therefore, the changes in emphasis in the political and ideological struggle of the ten years prior to partition and Mawdudi's reactions to them. These essays, most of which appeared originally in Mawdudi's journal, have been published a number of times in collected form both in India and in Pakistan and are readily available. Some of them have also been published separately.

[2] The best and most detailed work on Mawdudi's role in the constitutional debates is Leonard Binder, *Religion and Politics in Pakistan*, University of California Press, Berkeley, 1961.

the typical religious stances to be seen among our Muslim contemporaries, and that not in India and Pakistan alone but in the rest of the Muslim world as well.[3]

THE MAN AND THE MOVEMENT

It is necessary first of all to give a short biographical sketch of Mawdudi in order to place his ideology in proper perspective.[4] Such a sketch will serve also to illuminate his ideas, since they were worked out in response to the problems posed for Muslims by the changing Indian scene from 1920 onwards. Then we shall consider some of the principal emphases of Mawdudi's thought as they illustrate his analysis of and response to the great problems of a Muslim in the twentieth century.

Mawdudi was born in 1903 into a family with a long religious tradition; he was the son of a practicing mystic who in his early days had flirted with the innovations and new ideas coming to India from the West. His father's piety was the dominating childhood influence and accounts for Mawdudi's education having been in the traditional pattern of Islamic religious studies. The father seems to have taken particular care that neither of his sons be exposed to the English language, the subject matter of modern sciences, or the social customs of the West. The boys were educated at home and kept in isolation from others of their own age. In later life Mawdudi made an effort to fill the gap in his education. With a private tutor he succeeded in teaching himself English, and he employed this new skill to launch upon a program of reading in modern western thought. In an autobiographical note he speaks of having mastered the essential content of such sciences as sociology and psychology in a relatively short time.

Mawdudi began to take a part in public affairs at a tender age. The years of his boyhood had corresponded with the birth of political

[3] The foremost examples elsewhere are the Daru-l-Islam movement of Indonesia and al-Ikhwan al-Muslimun of Egypt and the Near East.

[4] The best sources for Mawdudi's earlier history are several Urdu works containing writings by and about him. Chief among them are: *Mawlana Mawdudi apni awr dusron ki Nazar Men*, ed. by Muhammad Yusuf, Maktabah al-Habib, Lahore, 1955; Muhammad Sarwar, *Mawlana Mawdudi ki Islami Tahrik*, Sindh Sagar Akadimi, Lahore, 1956; and Ali Sufyan Afaqi, *Abu-l A'la Mawdudi*, Sindh Sagar Akadimi, Lahore, 1955. The books by Yusuf and Afaqi are favorable to Mawdudi while Sarwar is hostile. There is a brief discussion of Mawdudi's political ideology in Khalid Bin Sayeed, "The Jama'at-i-Islami Movement in Pakistan," *Pacific Affairs*, 1957, vol. 30, pp. 59-68. For the history of Mawdudi's political evolution and that of his party there is a clear statement in the pamphlet by Mawdudi, *Jama'at-i-Islami us ka Maqsad, Ta'rikh, awr La'ih-i-'Amal*, Markazi Maktabah-i-Jama'at-i-Islami, Lahore, 4th printing, 1953.

consciousness among Indian Muslims, and he was sixteen years old
when the great nationalist struggle for Home Rule led by Gandhi
burst over India in 1919. Gandhi's movement was quickly merged
with the Khilafat movement, a specifically Muslim agitation for the
protection of Turkey from dismemberment by the Allies of World
War I and the protection of the Muslim holy places in Arabia. During the succeeding years Mawdudi was caught up in the fervor and
enthusiasm of the nationalist struggle, as was almost every other Indian. There was but little to distinguish him from others of his
countrymen. His analysis of the problems of India on the one hand
and of the Muslim world apart from India on the other led him to
see one fundamental evil at the root of both, namely, the tyrannical
power of British imperialism which he hated and wished to see destroyed. In view of his later aloofness from the struggle for independence in India, it is interesting to note the ardor and the radical
character of his views in the early 1920's. He was among those who
opposed Gandhi's counsel of moderation and agitated for complete
independence for India. When Gandhi called off the non-cooperation
movement in 1921, Mawdudi, who was then editor of a fairly important Urdu newspaper, criticized him bitterly for betraying Indian independence. By 1925, however, his thinking had begun to take a new
turn. Non-cooperation was finished; the Turkish Khilafat was also
a lost cause, and the Indian National Congress under Gandhi's leadership had begun to manifest an increasingly Hindu character. Mawdudi came to see that the interests of India's Muslims no longer lay
in cooperating with the Hindus to throw off British rule, and, more
important, a religious orientation toward the situation of India's
Muslims began to take shape in his mind.[5] As time passed Mawdudi
became increasingly aware that the fact of being Muslims laid him
and his co-religionists under the obligation to strive toward the
achievement of a peculiar pattern for human society, ultimately
based upon the divine revelation in the Qur'an.

Through most of the 1920's Mawdudi was employed as a journalist,
as editor, in fact, of the organ of India's well-known organization of
Muslim divines, the Jami'at Ulama-i-Hind. The time came toward
the end of the decade when journalism no longer satisfied him, and
he left the profession for more serious pursuits. Dissatisfaction with
the increasingly nationalist orientation of the Jami'at Ulama also

[5] The important factor in creating the new religious orientation was the work
that went into the writing of Mawdudi's first important book, *al-Jihad fi-l-Islam*.
The book was written to defend Muslims against Hindu charges after the murder
of a prominent Hindu leader by a Muslim fanatic in 1926.

affected his decision. The important work of his life began in 1933 with his assumption of the editorship of a journal called *Tarjumanu-l-Qur'an*, published from Hyderabad, Deccan. This magazine has appeared with only occasional interruptions from 1933 to the present time and has been the principal vehicle of Mawdudi's thought. Mawdudi's explanation for taking up this work makes it clear that he conceived of his new responsibilities as in the nature of a religious mission with a desperate urgency behind it. He professed to fear that a gigantic flood was about to break over the Muslims of India, far worse in its effects than the depredations of the British—this flood he identified as the stream of ideas and customs of western origin which were leading the young men of the community away from true Islam. In the 1920's the enemy, the British, had been external and relatively easily dealt with; this new enemy was more powerful and more insidious because it was internal, threatening to sap the very foundations of Islamic commitment. His writings were, therefore, directed to stem the flood of western influences, to instruct the Indian Muslims in true Islam, and to show by rational argument the superiority of the Islamic system to the foreign and non-Islamic ideas that were challenging it. He thought of himself as the rallying-point of a vigorous new Islamic movement about to come into being, and it was his hope—a disappointed one, it may be added—that the religious men of the Muslim community would marshal themselves behind him.

In 1937 the direction of Mawdudi's interest took yet another turn. As the result of the first elections under the 1935 Government of India Act, the Muslim League, which up to this point had not been truly representative of the Muslims of the subcontinent, suddenly took on enormous importance. With the majority of Muslim opinion now behind it the Muslim League began vigorously to urge its fundamental conviction, that the Muslims of India constituted a separate and distinct nation with a claim to all a nation's rights. As this proposition met with ever-increasing enthusiasm from Muslims, Mawdudi saw in it another disaster about to engulf his people, the danger that they would be seduced from Islam by nationalism. Consequently, during the years from 1937 to 1941 most of his efforts went to analysis and refutation of the ideas basic to the major political contestants in India, the Indian National Congress and the Muslim League. He endeavored to show that both were nationalist, that nationalism is a western phenomenon resting on the false philosophy of western civilization, and that the Muslim's loyalty, which is religious, can never be given to an entity such as the nation. His blows fell upon Muslims as well as Hindus, upon Muslim nationalists as well as nationalist Muslims. In the previous years his attack upon foreign ideas and his defense of Islam had been along a broad front of concepts, institutions and practices; now it became rather sharply focused upon the political struggle in India where he saw the danger taking its acutest form. His method, however, remained the same, to appeal by intellectual argument to the classes enjoying leadership. At no point does he seem to have contemplated political action, not to speak of revolutionary methods.

Mawdudi's move to action came in August of 1941, in direct response to the Lahore Resolution of the Muslim League which for the first time set the achievement of Pakistan as that party's objective. The situation had now become so critical for the Muslim community, as Mawdudi saw it, that he could no longer be content with writing essays and fighting purely at the ideological level. With a small number of supporters he formed an organization which he called the Jama'at-i-Islami (literally, the Islamic Society or group) with himself at its head. After an initial period of organization and consolidation, the organization was intended to enter actively into the social and political life of India to effect a transformation there on an Islamic pattern. The explanation given for founding an organization was essentially one of strategy. Mawdudi came to believe that the best way to transform a society is by the creation of a small, informed, dedicated and disciplined group who might work to capture social and political leadership. He cited the Fascists in Italy and Germany and the Communists in Russia as examples of groups which, though tiny minorities in a total population, were able to exercise effective control. It was not the ideals of the Fascists and Communists but their method which attracted him; his goal was rather the restructuring of Indian society in an Islamic pattern. It was a requirement, therefore, that his group should be thoroughly Islamic both in ideas and conduct, and to this end he built a program of instruction and training. He expressed the ideal at which he aimed as the creation of a *salih jama'at*, a righteous group, a saving element, or a holy minority, which should leaven the whole lump of society.

Mawdudi found it necessary to embark on active work with his group before he was really ready to do so; the precipitating event was the partition of India in the summer of 1947. At the time Mawdudi was living with his closest followers in a small separate community in East Punjab. All through the previous ten years his stand toward the aspirations of the Muslim League had been hostile, but the atmosphere in India during the disturbances of partition was such that he was compelled to go to Pakistan. For a time the Jama'at-i-Islami was inactive, but suffered the suspicion of government because of its previous opposition to the creation of Pakistan; soon, however, it came into its own and plunged into the task of helping to build the new nation in systematic fashion. At first it gave its efforts to helping refugees and solving other immediate social problems of partition, but it soon turned to more political concerns. The Jama'at-i-Islami with Mawdudi as its chief spokesman began to mount a campaign for the creation of a truly Islamic state in Pakistan. The argument put forward was that Pakistan had been fought for and won in the name of the Muslims and their Islamic aspirations;[6] it was now the duty of the leadership to create a state and a society based upon Islamic ideology, following Islamic policies, and actively striving toward an Islamic ideal.

For the first time, also, Mawdudi began to make an appeal to the masses as well as to the educated classes, sending preachers and spreading literature in the villages of the West Pakistan countryside. This campaign was very effective; the group consisted of earnest and dedicated men, was well organized, and possessed an articulate ideology expressed in an abundant literature. There was no other group in Pakistan at the time so unified, disciplined, or so sure of what it wanted, certainly not the Muslim League. To the Jama'at-i-Islami's advantage also was the great appeal of a religious cause to ordinary Pakistani citizens. The government soon found itself bombarded with demands for the creation of an Islamic state, and the Jama'at-i-Islami emerged as a genuine political party in opposition to the Muslim League government, and with the Islamic state as its platform. All of Pakistan was swept with enthusiasm for an Islamic order of things; and the western-educated, modernist-inclined group actually in control of the government began to be fearful of seeing its liberal, democratic vision of Pakistan frustrated. It is not surprising, therefore, that the government acted swiftly to put Mawdudi and two of his

---

6 This argument was only partially true. Pakistan had been won in the name of the Muslims, but the pre-partition political struggle had evidenced but little of the conscious awareness of Islamic ideals for the life of the state that Mawdudi was now ascribing to it. In fact, it had been precisely the failure of the Muslim League to espouse and follow such ideals that had aroused Mawdudi's determined opposition. His chief argument against the Muslim League had been the accusation that the League was nationalist and irreligious in its outlook. Mawdudi's opponents quickly took advantage of the weapon offered by his pre-partition opposition to the Pakistan movement and were able with some justice to accuse him of a *volte face*. See Shaykh Muhammad Iqbal, *Jama'at-i-Islami par, ek Nazar*, Malik Din Muhammad and Sons Booksellers, Karachi (1952?).

lieutenants in jail when some careless remarks about the war in Kashmir gave them a pretext. Mawdudi was arrested on October 4, 1948, on grounds of activities prejudicial to the security of the state.

The Jama'at-i-Islami continued its struggle for the Islamic state all the time its leader was in the Multan prison. When he was released (May 1950), he was, if anything, more powerful and more popular than ever before. His organization had grown to cover Pakistan;[7] there were branches and reading rooms in every administrative district of the country save one, an extensive program of relief work, mobile medical clinics dispensing free medical care, and an extensive program of publication. In the major cities a network of cell groups was created, each holding weekly meetings for discussion of Islamic ideology and enforcing discipline upon its members. The Jama'at-i-Islami had not yet begun to contest elections, but that was soon to follow according to the party's program. Mawdudi reached what was probably the peak of his power in early 1953, when he served as the spokesman of the *ulama* of Pakistan in connection with the anti-Ahmadiyah movement then causing unrest in the country. He did not approve of the violent turn taken by the movement and tried hard but unsuccessfully to keep the Jama'at-i-Islami from becoming involved in any "direct action."[8] After the riots in Lahore he was arrested (March 1953), and condemned to death (May 1953) by a court-martial on the thinnest of legal grounds.[9] The sentence was a trans-

[7] The strength of the Jama'at-i-Islami has never been great in East Pakistan. Though it established branches in Bengal and built an organization there, it has been essentially a West Pakistani group with its principal support deriving from the lower middle classes, lower and middle grades of civil servants, and students.

[8] Mawdudi's role in the Khatm-i-Nubuwat or anti-Ahmadiyah movement is discussed in detail in the so-called Munir Report: *Report of the Court of Enquiry constituted under Punjab Act II of 1954 to enquire into the Punjab Disturbances of 1953*, Superintendent, Government Printing, Punjab, Lahore, 1954. The report absolves Mawdudi personally of any responsibility for Jama'at-i-Islami support to advocates of "direct action." At the same time it demonstrates Mawdudi's inability to control his lieutenants in the organization, many of whom have always been more radical than he. In spite of Mawdudi's disapproval and explicit instructions it is clear that the Karachi branch of the Jama'at-i-Islami did actively advocate and encourage "direct action."

[9] There is no question that Mawdudi approved and supported the objectives of the Khatm-i-Nubuwat movement, at least so far as the specifically religious issue and the status of the Ahmadiyah minority were concerned. He made a number of speeches and wrote articles repeating the common arguments against the Ahmadis and urging that they be declared a minority. He was also the leader and spokesman of the convention of *ulama* that met to consider the matter. The demand that the Ahmadis be declared a minority was also incorporated into the list of Jama'at-i-Islami demands relative to an Islamic constitution. On the whole, however, his was a voice of moderation. To the extent that his participation in the movement brought attention to the problem and excited public opinion

parent effort by high ranking military officials to rid the country of a man whose ideas and influence they deplored. The reaction was an immediate public outcry, gravely embarrassing to the government which had not been consulted and seemingly did not approve the drastic step taken. Under this pressure the sentence was eventually commuted,[10] but Mawdudi again found himself in jail, with some of his followers, for a considerable period. He took up his work of propaganda for the Islamic state after being released for the second time, but public support for the cause had waned and a chill of disillusion had replaced the former ebullient enthusiasm of Pakistanis for their experiment in nationhood. Mawdudi himself appeared to become less sure of the absoluteness of his views and to find more that was worthy of approval in the life of Pakistan. Somewhat surprisingly, Mawdudi and the Jamaʻat-i-Islami accepted the 1956 Constitution of Pakistan with only minor suggestions for changes. The Constitution envisaged a parliamentary democracy, pledged to observe a series of non-justiciable guiding principles of an Islamic character, and bound by a provision to pass no laws contrary to the Qur'an and the Sunnah. Mawdudi seemed to feel that the majority of his demands had been met in the Constitution, and his intention appears to have been to work henceforward as leader of a political party within the democratic framework.

The Jamaʻat-i-Islami fell under the general ban on political parties imposed by the leaders of the military coup of 1958; its properties were confiscated, and it was forbidden to indulge in political activities of any kind. It is somewhat ironic that the coup should have come when it did, since the Jamaʻat-i-Islami had just made its first full-scale contest of an election and had emerged with a resounding victory (in the Karachi municipal elections). After 1958 Mawdudi lived quietly in Lahore, where he was permitted to speak or write on politically innocuous subjects but was closely watched to prevent his reemergence as a factor in the political situation. At first the rev-

---

against the Ahmadis, Mawdudi may be accused of a degree of guilt for the violence and destruction that followed. Clearly, he had contributed to the growth of a movement that snowballed beyond the ability of anyone to control it. Equally clearly, however, he was not guilty of the charge brought against him in the military court. The essay for which he was condemned was written and published before the edict of the military authorities forbidding further discussion of the Ahmadiyah question in the press. Mawdudi was charged, tried, and condemned on the basis of an *ex post facto* ruling. The relative innocuousness of the essay in question, entitled *Masʻalah-i-Qadiyani*, is shown by the fact that it has never been withdrawn from circulation and is still readily available.

10 First to fourteen years rigorous imprisonment and then to two years.

olutionary government was severe in controlling political activities, and Mawdudi along with everyone else was effectively muzzled. There cannot be much doubt, however, of his disapproval of many elements in the ideology and policy of the revolutionary regime. Even during the period of strictest control Pakistanis felt relatively free to voice their disapproval of the government's policy and action on a private basis, and a certain amount of criticism of the government came to be tolerated even in the press.

After the first election of Provincial and National Assemblies under the Basic Democracies scheme (1962), a much greater latitude was allowed for criticism of the government. An opposition quickly formed in the assemblies, and its views were disseminated in the press. In July of 1962 the ban against political parties was lifted, and shortly afterwards President Ayub himself became a member of one of the parties. Although the Jama'at-i-Islami had been unable to function during the long period of interdiction against political parties, it had preserved its organization and leadership intact. No more than an announcement from Mawdudi was required to bring the Jama'at-i-Islami back into the political field with a full panel of charges and demands to register against the government. It was the first of the political parties to resume full activity in an effective manner.

The arguments which Mawdudi and his followers urged against the Ayub regime ranged from such minor points as elimination of the world "Islamic" from the official name of the country to criticism of the land reform program. The detailed criticisms can be presented under three major headings: (1) that the regime had acted un-Islamically and was undermining the Islamic basis of Pakistan, (2) that it had frustrated democracy in the country, and (3) that its administration was poor, and was responsible for the confusion in the country. In 1963 the Jama'at-i-Islami began a new attack on the government's increasingly friendly policy toward Red China. Public opinion, however, was against the party's stand on this shift in foreign policy, and Mawdudi with his followers came under strong condemnation. In January of 1964 Mawdudi and forty-three other leaders of the Jama'at-i-Islami were arrested and imprisoned on the charge of activities disturbing to public order. For the third time in his active political life Mawdudi found himself behind bars because of his political views. At the same time the Jama'at-i-Islami was again placed under interdiction by the authority of an old amendment to the Criminal Act dating from 1908.

This proved to be the shortest of Mawdudi's imprisonments. On

September 25, 1964, the Supreme Court ruled the ban on the Jama'at-i-Islami to be illegal, since the act on which it was based was contrary to the Constitution of Pakistan in denying freedom of association. On October 9, 1964, the High Court of West Pakistan handed down a similar verdict on the imprisonment of Mawdudi and his forty-three followers, and they were released immediately. Almost the first act of Mawdudi was to make a long public speech in which he aligned himself and his party with the coalition supporting Miss Fatimah Jinnah (against Ayub Khan) as candidate for the presidency of Pakistan. The election campaign, which Ayub Khan eventually won, had been in progress for about a month at the time. Politically, Mawdudi's support for the opposition coalition was consistent and logical, but it must have posed something of a difficulty for him to reconcile his new political associations and his advocacy of a woman candidate with his Islamic principles. His disapproval and fear of a government which he felt to be tyrannical and un-Islamic was evidently strong enough to leave him no choice but to join the opposition.

Before concluding this historical sketch we may ask, "What have been the bases of Mawdudi's appeal to Pakistanis?" The principal one, it seems clear, is the very fact of his having approached the problems of his fellow Muslims in religious terms. Mawdudi speaks a language that the majority of Muslims understand and offers analyses and solutions to problems by appeal to the values that have been formative in the Islamic heritage. His thinking is continuous with the Islamic past as that of the western educated leadership is not. Thus, he has the advantage of an initial predisposition in his favor. I also believe that for him personally the vision of society he has upheld reflects a genuine religious experience, and this fact—that is, his own sincerity—cannot but communicate itself to those who witness his concern and his moral outrage when Muslims are derelict in their religious duty and bring ruin on their own heads.

The second basis of appeal is closely related to this. Perhaps nowhere else in Pakistan could one find a group of men with the dedication and moral excellence of the Jama'at-i-Islami. In a country where cynicism and corruption have been growing problems, these men have quietly and conscientiously lived up to the principles they profess. The moral appeal of this body of upright men has been incalculable among those classes of Pakistani society who are excluded from wealth and power and who feel themselves victimized by the corruption of persons who do possess them. Third, some credit must be given to Mawdudi's logical turn of mind and his ability to construct a connected argument. Behind the exaggerations and over-simplifications necessitated by political polemics, there has been a set of logically structured ideas. One may question that Mawdudi rightly deserves to be called a thinker or an intellectual, in a strict sense, but he has appeared as such to many Pakistanis. They find in him a certainty of his own convictions, the capacity to state these convictions persuasively and to elicit their relevance for the pressing problems of social life. He has thus been able to persuade many persons of the intellectual, as well as the religious, validity of his position. Lastly, consideration should be given to Mawdudi's ability as an Urdu stylist. Although Mawdudi cannot be said to have grace and beauty of expression, he has learned to put down his ideas in a flowing and direct fashion that is perhaps unique among present-day Urdu authors. This has been important, since he has depended principally on his writings to win the sympathies of the educated classes. The largest item in the budget of the Jama'at-i-Islami has always been for publications and their distribution, so that his writings have penetrated every corner of Pakistan and many other parts of the world.

THE IDEOLOGY OF ISLAM

We may turn now to some of the main emphases of Mawdudi's thought. The proposition from which all else follows is the sovereignty of God. The first clause of the Muslim creed, which reads *La Ilaha illa Allah*, Mawdudi interprets to mean "there is none other to be obeyed but God." On the basis of Quranic exegesis he argues that the message of the prophet to his contemporaries was not the declaration of the existence of God; that was unnecessary. It was rather a summons to give exclusive obedience to a God who was already recognized and well known among them. The substance of Muhammad's preaching was that the Arabs should forsake their lesser loyalties in favor of the one important loyalty. Similarly, in the modern world, the task of an Islamicizing movement is not so much to proclaim the importance of a point of view that makes place for a divine being, for the existence of God and his governance of the world are knowable by unaided reason. Its purpose is practical, to create in the lives of individuals and the conduct of society generally the relationship to God that is called obedience, or Islam. Assent to the reality of God, intellectually and otherwise, is a necessity, but the implications of divine sovereignty go far beyond mere assent. A man or a society has acknowledged God's sovereignty when deliberately and humbly it has set out to do what God commands, and only then.

Mawdudi conceives God principally as will or demand or imperative, and his view of Islam is, in consequence, moral through and through.

It is necessary to lay some emphasis upon God's exclusive possession of sovereignty, for this is the operative consideration in much of Mawdudi's criticism of the world around him, particularly of modernism and nationalism among the Muslims of the subcontinent. The right to give commands and exact loyalty belongs *only* to God and to none other. Acceptance of any other principle of authority is a sin against divine majesty and equivalent to the worst offense known to the Muslim vocabulary—idolatry or associating partners with God (*shirk*) in his exclusive prerogatives. The negative implications of this insistence upon a single center of authority in human affairs are quite clear; neither the nineteenth-century conviction of the right of the individual to determine his own stand in the world in freedom nor the democratic doctrine that government and law flow from the consent of the people are reconcilable with it. Mawdudi considers the moral evil of the age to consist in having accepted sovereigns other than God—the will of the people, the law of rulers, the nation-state, custom, personal preference, or whatever—and holds, furthermore, that the sufferings of the age in their entirety are to be traced to this error. By nature God is *ma'bud*, that which is served, and man in relation to him is *'abd*, slave or servant; any different relation is religiously wrong and historically disastrous.

Mawdudi has no difficulty in supporting his controlling assumption of exclusive divine sovereignty by rational argument. It may be noted in passing that one of the predominant aims of his work has been to demonstrate the complete rationality of the "Islamic system" that he presents as the norm for men, and this apologetic purpose is something which he shares with virtually every other modern Muslim thinker. Mawdudi builds his argument by observing that all the non-human or sub-human world acknowledges the sovereignty of God in quite unmistakable fashion. The heavenly bodies, the seasons, all aspects of the world about us are governed by principles ordained by their creator. They obey none but his decrees and, indeed, cannot do otherwise. Their obedience to the law of nature renders them Muslims or submitters to the authority of the one who has created them; and their sustained obedience is the necessary condition for the very continued existence of the universe itself. Were they ever to defy the will of the creator that has set their appointed rounds, the result could only be chaos.

Why should it be otherwise with the affairs of men? All that separates man from the rest of creation in his relation to God is his having been endowed with free will, which allows him to choose whether or not he will submit. In its entirety the physical world demonstrates the necessity of a law that is the principle of its order and its smooth functioning, and the basis of its very existence. It is inconceivable that the universe could exist lacking such a principle of order. Logically and inevitably, or so Mawdudi feels, it follows that there must also be such a law for human society, neglect of which produces chaos and suffering for men. He is, thus, affirming not only the obligation of men to submit to God's commands, the eternal existence in the will of God of a normative pattern for human life, but also expressing a confidence that life determined by God's *shari'ah* is effective and successful life—necessarily so, because such life is natural and in accord with the creative force of the universe.

Mawdudi's <u>second proposition</u> is that the law of human conduct is clearly known and readily accessible. It is a demand of reason that this, too, should be the case, for men cannot follow the order that guarantees their well-being here and hereafter if they do not understand what it is. Specifically, the sources from which knowledge of the law may be obtained are two: (1) the Holy Book of God that has been sent down in a number of "editions" as it were, through a series of prophets, and (2) the guidance derived from the lives of the messengers who came with the book. These two, the Qur'an and the tradition of the prophet, lay down a number of specific things, both prescriptions and proscriptions, and recommend or disapprove others. If these sources are understood in the depths of their divine wisdom, they will be seen to have met and solved all the great problems of life in the principles they put forward. Their guidance is both sufficient and comprehensive. Subordinate aspects of Islamic life, where detailed directives are lacking, are to be worked out in the spirit of the specific commands of God.

Mawdudi's stance in judging the world about him is thus quite simple and also, I would insist, thoroughly religious. <u>There is a divinely ordained law, and we know what its content is.</u> All life that observes the plain commandments of the law is Islam or submission to God, and all that does not is something else. Mawdudi prefers the term *Jahiliyat* for the something else, a word classically used for pagan times in Arabia before the coming of the prophet. Every man and every society must make the choice between Islam and *Jahiliyat*, and the evidence of the choice made will be seen in the willingness or refusal to observe the plainly stated commands of God's Book and

His prophet. The attitude toward the plain commands is a kind of touchstone that Mawdudi has employed to judge the major trends in Islam. We may see, for example, how it has determined his verdict upon both the modernist and conservative elements of the community.

First, the modernists. India has had a strong Muslim modernist movement since the last quarter of the nineteenth century when her Muslims first began to feel the attraction and the threat of modern thought. As in other regions of the Muslim world, a group of men appeared who recognized the radical changes modernity has introduced to the world, who saw the inevitability of accepting the new situation and who began seriously to examine the question of how one can live Islamically in the modern world. Such men are modern because they have no choice in the matter, and they want also to be Islamic. Their keen sense of the Muslim's depressed state has led them to reexamine and reformulate the significance of much that is basic in the Qur'an and the tradition of the prophet, but their reasons for doing so have, at least with the serious ones, been religious.

One might think that Mawdudi would look upon men with real religious interests as his natural allies, but this is far from being the case. His own deep sense of God's awesome sovereignty will not allow him to rest easy with the fact that these men, for whatever reasons, compromise some of the clear commands of the basic Islamic sources or criticize others in the name of progress, individual liberty or rationality. They have, he feels, been more concerned to advance with the times and to protect the material interests of the Muslims than to observe the commands of God. They have allowed themselves to be seduced by the values of an alien system of life, and though they may consider themselves to be offering an understanding of Islam that will enable the Muslims to meet the problems of the modern age, they are, in fact, leading the community away from its greatest spiritual resource. In principle there is no difference between them and irreligious atheists, for neither obeys the commands so clearly stated by God's Book and His prophet. In fact, Mawdudi prefers the atheists, for they at least are honest. The others call themselves Muslims but all the while act and think un-Islamically, playing the role of saboteurs who destroy the power of the Muslim community from within.

Mawdudi is much more charitably inclined toward the conservatives of the community, but they still fall under the judgment of having

384

failed to be truly Islamic. The modernists he excoriates and damns, intellectually and personally, with the strongest language at his disposal. The criticisms of the conservatives are also biting, but they are in the nature of reproof offered to those one loves and from whom one has expected better things. The sin of the conservatives has been that they have added a great number of rules of their own devising to the clear commands of the Qur'an and prophetic tradition. Beginning with the basic sources, as they rightly should, they have gone on to deduce subsidiary rules which they then insist have the same importance as the clear commandments of the basic sources themselves. This process has gone so far, Mawdudi believes, that the majority of the *ulama* can no longer distinguish the fundamentals of Islam from the details of its application, and so they identify Islam with the elaborate structure of the medieval legal schools. This is a gross error, no less *Jahiliyat* than the substitution of anything else for God's sovereignty.

The *ulama's* erection of their own deductions into fundamental principles of the Islamic system has brought about the evil of sectarianism and provided the opening for the intrusion of western ideas into the minds of the youth of the community. The *ulama*, who ought to have been the effective defense of the Islamic way, by their own confusion and rigidity have precipitated the greatest spiritual danger of the community's history. Mawdudi calls, therefore, for a return to the real and original fountains of the Islamic ideal, and would dispose of all the excess intellectual and religious baggage accumulated by the community in its journey through the centuries. Disencumbered of these accretions the Islamic ideal would immediately demonstrate its vitality and relevance to the problems of modern life—it would be the key to successful living. This proposal to return to the original source and discard all else is more radical than may be recognized, for it means that Mawdudi sets his face against both the *muqallad* legal schools and the mystics, one of which has been the moral custodian and the other the spiritual custodian of the heritage of the community for a thousand years. In effect, he is asking for an intellectual short-circuit of the entire course of Islamic history from the death of the prophet's fourth successor to the present. He rejects that history and denies that it is Islamic or in any way normative for the Muslim of today. Now, it must be pointed out that just such a criticism of the *ulama* and just such an attitude to the past in almost precisely the same terms is advanced by the modernists. Mawdudi shows himself in this particular much closer to the methods and spirit of modernism than his broadside blasts against them would cause one to think, a point to which we shall return shortly.

In this matter of Mawdudi's attitudes toward modernists and conservatives, we are talking about what theologians like to call "the problem of religious authority." At first glance Mawdudi would seem to have resolved the problem quite simply by in effect denying that it exists. If there is a divine law clearly enunciated in the two basic Islamic sources, a Muslim has only to accept what he finds there. It should be realized, however, that this simple position is enunciated only to serve the ends of polemics. Actually, the matter is much more complicated even in Mawdudi's understanding. There are three factors that make it so: (1) the fact that the basic sources are silent on many matters of concern to the Muslims and must be supplemented by some other principle of authority; (2) the fact that in addition to their clear commands the basic sources have a number of others, the exact meaning of which is doubtful and require interpretation; and (3) the fact that even the clear commands must be understood in the light of whatever historical circumstances may prevail.

In view of these considerations Mawdudi found it necessary to resort to personal judgment for working out the detailed significance of God's commands. Against the *ulama* and in the line with the thrust of modernism generally, he asserts the right to exercise reason or one's own personal *taffaquh* (legal deduction) in deciding what even the clear commands of God shall mean. What a Muslim should think or do and what it means to be a Muslim cannot become clear without the help of reason. Although Mawdudi restricts this element of personal judgment by saying that it must be conducted in subjection to the spirit of the clear commands and never against them, it is clear that he has departed very far from the simple insistence that one must do what the Book and the prophet say—as he has also departed from the position of the *ulama*. Most of the conservatives consider themselves to be bound to one of the four accepted legal schools, in India and Pakistan normally the Hanafi school, and insist that the opinions of the doctors of the schools must be followed in all particulars. Accordingly, one of their dogmas has been that the right of personal interpretation no longer exists, all necessary interpretation having already been done by great men of the past. Unanimously, the modernists have seen this dogma of the legal schools as an obstruction to progress and a denial of the true genius of the Qur'an and the prophet. Mawdudi agrees with the modernists on both scores, insisting alike on the necessity of a personal appropriation of the Islamic truth and on the justification of personal judgment by the basic Islamic sources.

Personal judgment provides Mawdudi, as it does the modernists, with an instrument for discriminating between the essentials of the prophet's teaching and the form in which they had to be cast if they were to be understood by the seventh-century Arabs. Personal judgment releases him from both literalism and slavish bondage to the legal schools, and positively, offers the means for adapting Islam's eternal truth to changed circumstances. Discrimination between the essence or spirit and the form of Islamic commandments, be it noted in passing, is admission of an element of historical conditioning in the Qur'an, something that has the most radical theological consequences from the standpoint of a traditional Muslim, but to which Mawdudi seems insensitive.

Reason, it is apparent, plays a quite important role in his understanding of religious authority. The case is similar with the modernists, whom, however, Mawdudi has condemned for their appeal to reason. Where exactly then does the issue between these opponents join? In three basic propositions they are clearly in agreement: (1) in holding that Islam encourages, even commands, the exercise of reason by the community to understand God's decrees; (2) in the belief that nothing in the content of Islamic principles is contrary to or in defiance of reason; and (3) in the conviction of the superiority in purely rational terms of the system outlined in the Book and the Sunnah. There is no quarrel between Mawdudi and the modernists respecting the right to employ reason; the issue arises rather over the exact role and authority of the reason in the life of a religious man. The modernists have erred because they judge even the Book of God and the Sunnah of the prophet by the standard of reason. First of all they ask: "Is it reasonable to believe such and so?" They ought to ask: "Is it Islamic?" In Albert Hourani's neat formulation the modernist creed holds that "Islam is truly reasonable," but this is putting things upside down, in Mawdudi's eyes. The religiously valid position must be expressed by an exact reversal of the terms; "True reason is Islamic." For him the final authority is always the Book and the Sunnah.

In its legitimate use Mawdudi considers reason to have only an instrumental function: it can decide which is the better of two things being compared, but it cannot independently establish the truth. Its work is like that of a judge in a law court, who decides on the merits of two cases presented to him but who has neither the responsibility nor even the power to find out the real truth of matters. If both cases are false, he can decide which of them is more plausible, but he is powerless to discover what has really transpired. Reason, therefore, can lead one to see the superiority of the Islamic system to any other compared with it, but once one has decided rationally to become a Muslim, reason no longer has any function of judgment. Its legitimate employment is then found in spelling out the implications of the clear commands of the original Islamic sources the eminent rationality of which is already established. Mawdudi finds the modernists to be involved in a self-contradiction in their resort to reason. Having chosen to be Muslims, which involves a judgment of reason, they proceed on the grounds of reason to produce ideas and urge courses of action that are non-Muslim. They first signify their intention to follow the divine law and in the next breath proclaim their freedom from all restriction. Although the most effective appeal of the modernists to young Muslims has been their claim of rationality, Mawdudi feels that probing examination will prove them inconsistent and anything but reasonable.

So far we have spoken of two aspects of Mawdudi's thought, the fundamental conception of divine sovereignty, and his assurance of knowing the divine law with its attendant problems. We may now turn to a third by calling attention to the preponderant role that society as a whole, as opposed to individuals, has played in Mawdudi's thinking. One of his most often reiterated points is that the Islamic system is comprehensive, taking within its purview the entirety of human activity. To mark out certain areas of life as belonging to God and others as belonging to Caesar would be to deny divine sovereignty over the whole. As he said at one point: "The *shari'ah* is a complete scheme of life and an all-embracing social order— nothing superfluous and nothing lacking." Mawdudi has always been interested in the cultivation of individual virtues and, though this fact is often obscured by his concern with argument on public issues, in fostering a depth of personal faith in his followers as well. Nevertheless, he cannot be satisfied with the rectification of the lives of individuals; his ultimate objective must be transformation of the social order. The overarching social concern is the clear implication of his notion of divine sovereignty.

In turn, the transformation of society demands political power. So much may be seen from the example of the prophet in Medina, but there is a rational basis for the view as well. For Mawdudi holds to the belief that societies are built, structured, and controlled from the top down by the conscious manipulation of those in power. Nothing, absolutely nothing, is more important for the realization of the Islamic ideal on earth than that the right people, holding the right ideas, should occupy the posts of governors in society. In his words: "A man who has devoted any thought to the matter knows that in human affairs the most important thing is, 'who holds the bridle reins?' Human society is like a carriage. Just as a carriage goes where the driver wishes, so a human civilization goes where the leaders desire. It is obvious that common people must act according to the pattern ordained by those who possess power, who control the means of forming public opinion, who form the systems for individual and social life, who determine the standards of morality, etc. If these are in the hands of righteous people, worshippers of God, then it is inevitable that the whole of social life be God-worshipping. . . . None of the purposes of religion can be accomplished so long as control of affairs is in the hands of *kafirs*."[11] Mawdudi's judgment on western civilization and its ill-begotten spawn, nationalism, takes its departure from this theory of social dynamics. Everything about western civilization is wrong, has to be so, because its leaders have constructed it and are trying to conduct it on false beliefs. When the roots are rotten, no tree produces a worthwhile fruit. His criticism of the modernist, liberally inclined, wielders of power in Pakistan exhibits the same analysis. They must be replaced because they hold ideas that are a denial of God's sovereignty. No matter how experienced, expert, wise or capable they may be, they lack the fundamental of fundamentals, the conception of the proper aim for society. Since society will always pursue the path marked by its leaders, the task of solving Pakistan's many problems is one of finding the right people and installing them in the controlling posts.

Mawdudi's criticism of Pakistan's government did not rest on evaluation of specific policies or actions, and, indeed, for all his interest in the political scene, he could not be brought to talk about such things in specific terms. Political analysis, based on Mawdudi's premises, must always be moral and religious judgment upon persons. This is true even when he speaks of a technical problem such as flood control; he explained to me in a conversation in 1956 that Pakistan would suffer no more devastation from the overflow of the Indus when he had succeeded in establishing people in government who care enough to do something about the matter. No amount of argu-

11 Mawdudi, *Tahrik-i-Islami ki Akhlaqi Bunyaden*, Markazi Maktabah Jama'at-i-Islami, Karachi, 5th printing, 1954, pp. 5-6.

ment could bring him to admit that there are enormous, perhaps insuperable, technical problems in so major a project of flood control or that the resources to carry through the project might be difficult to find. In this light, it is easy to understand why Mawdudi placed so much faith in the Jama'at-i-Islami as his tool for achieving the Islamic revolution in Pakistan. The Jama'at-i-Islami was intended to create a corps of disciplined, morally upright, ideologically sound persons who might occupy the crucial positions in the future Islamic state Mawdudi hoped to bring into being. His program for the future of the nation was the expansion of the Jama'at-i-Islami until it had absorbed the state, had, to all practical intents and purposes, become the state.

THE ISLAMIC STATE

It should be clear by this point that Mawdudi's conviction of the fundamental importance of the divine law requires him to believe in an all-powerful, monolithic state, upholding a definite religious ideology and using the full weight of police and judicial powers to ensure that all aspects of its life will reflect the character of its Islamic ideology.[12] The absolute authority of the state is incontestable—being nothing less than the social expression of God's sovereignty over all. Totalitarianism, however, need cause one no concern, in this unique instance, because God's commands working in the life of the state are just and benevolent.

The first requirement of a genuinely Islamic state is that the *shari'ah* should be observed and recognized as the basic law of the land. Mawdudi considers the *shari'ah* to imply, even demand, the existence of a state, and to provide a complete blueprint for its constitution in addition to rules governing the lives of individuals. Each aspect of the organization and functioning of the state he derives from directives of the Qur'an, the tradition of the prophet, or the example of the first four caliphs. The source and sanction of all law in a state based upon *shari'ah* is divine ordinance, and there remains no function of true law-making to be exercised by the people, their representatives, or even by the ruler.

The state may be, in fact should be, ruled by a single man whose tenure of office and power are limited only by his faithfulness to the ideology which the state reflects in its constitution. Mawdudi is here acknowledgedly inspired by his interpretation of the early caliphate.

[12] The best single source in English for the study of Mawdudi's views on this subject is *The Islamic Law and Constitution*, tr. and ed. by Khurshid Ahmad, Islamic Publications Ltd., Lahore, 1960.

The man to occupy this highest and most responsible of posts should be the "best man" of his society, one whose wisdom, ability, learning and conduct commend him without reservation to his fellow Muslims. Active candidacy for any post of power in the Islamic state, but above all the post of ruler, would be a disqualification since it is a form of self-seeking. Those charged with the responsibility of leadership are to be elected, but must somehow be chosen by the people without their having themselves coveted or striven for power and honor.

The ruler of the Islamic state is to be assisted by a legislative council,[13] composed of men with the educational qualifications to make valid applications of the fundamental law of the Qur'an and the Sunnah. Specifically, they must be well grounded in Arabic, have studied the sciences of Quranic interpretation, know the corpus of prophetic tradition with the auxiliary disciplines developed historically in criticism of it; but before all else, they must be men of unimpeachable personal conduct and with a sound intention of doing God's will as they see it. To put it in plain English, they will be learned men of the type of Mawdudi himself.

Mention of a legislative council has allowed Mawdudi to argue that Islamic government as he conceives it is not dictatorial but fundamentally democratic. This argument is of dubious merit, for the legislative council is clearly a law-finding as opposed to a law-making body, and it is not a fundamental requirement that it should be representative. The scope of the legislative council's function is confined to extrapolation from the clear commands of the basic Islamic sources and various forms of advice to the ruler. The clear commands themselves cannot be abolished, changed or tampered with by the council. They constitute rather a deposit of divine wisdom from which the legislative council is to take guidance, in considering situations where the clear commands do not obviously and immediately apply. Mawdudi has a vast confidence in the ability of reasonable and God-fearing men to agree upon the implications of divine guidance and to arrive at adequate solutions to problems. There is a further limitation upon the legislative council in that its opinions are not binding upon the ruler. In normal circumstances the two would work together in cooperative harmony; but should a situation arise where there is a difference between the ruler and his legislative council and where the opinion of the ruler is Islamically right, then the

[13] The principle to which appeal is made in justifying this aspect of Islamic government is that of "consultation" (*shura*). Mawdudi finds his authority in the Quranic phrase "consultation among them in their affairs" (Surah 42:38) and in the example of the caliph 'Umar who allegedly appointed a council of advisers to assist him.

ruler is to prevail. In his discussions of the matter, however, Mawdudi does not consider the mechanics of resolving such a conflict.

There will be no political parties in the Islamic state and no provision for a loyal opposition. As the state is ideological in character with its government dedicated to upholding the clearly known will of Almighty God, an opposition party or parties could only represent rejections of the divine pattern for the society. No ideological state, argues Mawdudi, will tolerate an opposition that seeks to overthrow and destroy the state itself. Democracies do not allow Communists to exist in their midst any more than Communists tolerate those who attack their socialist order. The Islamic state has both the right and the duty to suppress ideas or activities that frustrate its effort to make Islamic ideology permeate the life of society.

Although Islamic ideology must be the fundamental concern of the state, it is still possible for non-Muslims to live within its boundaries in peace and stability. As *dhimmis*, persons protected by the state, the non-Muslims may enjoy security of life and property and the right to practice their own religion as they see fit. They may even act as servants of the state in some minor capacity. On the negative side, however, they may not propagate their religious ideas among the Muslims nor may they exercise any real political power. It has been a demand of the Jama'at-i-Islami that "minorities," as the non-Muslims are to be designated in an Islamic constitution, should be excluded from all policy-making posts. It can hardly be expected that one who does not understand or accept the Islamic ideology should be an effective agent of a society endeavoring to realize its implications.

In a similar vein the Jama'at-i-Islami has insisted that minorities must vote as separate electorates. The device of separate electorates, which was introduced to India by the British as a means of guaranteeing a voice in government to minority groups, would be employed in the Islamic state to insure that no elements of non-Muslim influence might erode or affect the Muslim community's direction of the state. Though a minority might never expect to win an election outright, under a unified electorate situations are conceivable in individual constituencies in which the minority might hold the balance of power and be able to cast the decisive votes. From being a means of protecting the minority, the separate electorate would be transformed into an instrument for preserving political control in the hands of the Muslim majority.

The previous paragraphs have sketched some of the features of the Islamic state as they are developed theoretically in Mawdudi's many speeches or writings. It should be remembered, however, that Mawdudi has been not only a pamphleteer and theorist but also an active, practical politician. In practice he has often shown willingness to compromise with ideas and positions that are more or less contrary to his ideal theories. As he has gained in experience, he has exhibited a definite trend toward less rigidity in his views. The Jama'at-i-Islami's approval of the 1956 Constitution, which provided for a genuine parliamentary government, is an outstanding example of flexible adaptation to the changing political siutation. Our descriptions of Mawdudi's ideology and his concept of the Islamic state, therefore, should not be understood as fixed for all time in their details, but rather as guides to certain central themes in Mawdudi's thinking and to his general manner of approach.

The major point we have endeavored to make is that Mawdudi and the considerable numbers who agree with him have understood the purpose and destiny of human life in terms of a divine law. With all seriousness they affirm that men should live in accord with the divine pattern and have actually put themselves to the task of realizing God's Kingdom, which is nothing other than the rule of divine law, on earth. When men as individuals and in society have submitted themselves to the law, they have done all that is required of them. Among our contemporaries, there is perhaps no more massive or serious effort to proclaim the continuing relevance of divine guidance as the norm for life.

MAWDUDI THE INNOVATOR

In this concluding section an effort will be made to place Mawdudi and his movement in the historical context of recent Islamic development. On first encountering Mawdudi, one is likely to classify him with those whose purpose is to preserve the inviolable integrity of received Muslim tradition, that is, to look upon him as a kind of reactionary or traditionalist, albeit with some peculiarities of his own. Much in his thought would give support to such an interpretation. We have seen, for example, that he appeals to a law embodying eternal truth, which he contends is unchangeable and all-sufficient, and which he upholds as the only norm for Muslims. Likewise, we have noted the depth and passion of his reaction to what he considers the innovations of modernism and the foibles of people who are swept along by the currents of the time. At no point in his writings known to me does Mawdudi ever explicitly grant the inadequacy of the principles of the law laid down in the basic Islamic sources, or admit to seeing a need for modification in them. The challenge to genuine Muslim faith as he analyzes it is rather to preserve and utilize fully what has been given.

Mawdudi's own self-interpretation also provides evidence for ranking him with the conservatives. If asked what he is doing to meet the problems of the modern world, Mawdudi would reply that he is expounding the original message of the Qur'an and the prophet, upholding the law which from the beginning has embodied the divine will for the universe. In no way does he think of himself as offering something new or personal; nothing could be further from his intention. Distressed as he was by the divisive effects of sectarianism, he has always emphasized heavily that the doctrine he expounds is not a new interpretation of Islam, indeed, not an interpretation at all, but on the contrary only a reiteration of pure, original Islam without embellishment or change. The religious mission he conceived for himself was one of preserving and reviving a law he thought in danger of being lost.

Despite all these considerations, a more critical analysis of Mawdudi will show him, I believe, to be an innovator of a fairly radical type and to be no less responsive, even in his notions about fundamental Islamic matters, to the peculiar historical conditions of the Muslim community in his lifetime than are his modernist opponents. Mawdudi, I would argue, is a product of recent Muslim history, and his presentation of Islam is not a photographic duplication of the faith of the prophet, but, like modernism, a reaction to questions posed by the unique situation of Muslims in the modern world. Furthermore, it is possible to establish that even the content of Mawdudi's understanding of Islam reveals ideas deriving from the alien civilization and age that he wishes to ward off.

One of the principal evidences to support these assertions is the peculiar sense of Mawdudi's view that Islam is a law, or a "system" of truths and principles forming an integrated and comprehensive whole, in other words, an ideology. The tendency to conceive Islam as a "system" of ideas or an ideology emerged strongly in the late nineteenth century and is by no means unique to Mawdudi. One will look in vain to find a systematic and comprehensive body of law or anything resembling one in the Qur'an, the *hadith*, or the early days of the Muslim community. Affairs in the first years were conducted in a very free fashion, with the Muslims adopting much from people around them. If there was a principle limiting the freedom of action of rulers and individuals, that principle was traditional, the practice of the city of Medina where the companions of Muhammad were concentrated. The systematic view of the sources of law is a product of the third Islamic century, not of the prophet's time, and when it did emerge after long controversy included sources other than those which Mawdudi recognizes as authoritative.

It is no easier to satisfy the quest for a comprehensive all-embracing system of which Mawdudi speaks in late medieval Islam. Muslim jurists in that period had almost nothing to say, for example, about the conduct of state, not to speak of describing institutions of government and the manner of their functioning. With the passage of time the province of the jurists became so restricted that even today *shari'ah* or Islamic law is normally understood to be a body of legal rules that relate only to personal status, such things as marriage, divorce, inheritance, etc. What lies behind Mawdudi's desire to find a system where none existed is, I believe, the unconscious influence of the type of nineteenth-century philosophy that has brought about the emergence of "ideologies" in the twentieth century. As evidence, attention may be called to the great emphasis that Mawdudi lays upon reason, logical consistency, establishment of truth by deduction, etc. The approach to problems of social life which appeals to such principles is of a piece with the German idealism that has fathered the great ideologies of our time. It is possible also to discern behind this quest for a system a profound, though again perhaps not a conscious, perception of the threat to every religious orientation posed by modern thought. Mawdudi talks of a "system" that his ancestors felt no need of because it is reassuring to do so; the system is a kind of fortress whose intellectual walls will turn aside the arrows of doubt and skepticism.

Another important piece of evidence in our case is the resemblance that Mawdudi bears to the modernists in spirit, method and content of thought. If the modernists are what their name implies in respect to these things, it is difficult to avoid the conclusion that Mawdudi also is profoundly determined by his historical circumstances. In spite of a deep hostility to modernism, we have noted several points where he exhibits a fundamental kinship with it. Consider, for example, the purpose of apologetics that permeates Mawdudi and the modernists alike. Both have been driven to take up the defense of Islam, and both apprehend the enemy to be the same. It is true that Mawdudi thinks of the modernists as a fifth column within the Islamic fold, but, formally put, his objective is identical with theirs. Both want to prove the superiority of the Islamic spiritual heritage to the values and ideas born in the modern West. Of perhaps greater significance is that in each case the defense is effected by demonstrating that the Islamic heritage realizes the values and ideas of the modern West in their perfect or most valid form.

Though both are, perhaps, mistaken in their understanding, Mawdudi and the modernists alike have judged rationality to be the ultimate criterion for the western world. In unison they have asserted the rationality of Islam, examining a host of its separate doctrines in this light, and claiming always to find a greater realization of true rationality in Islamic viewpoints than can be seen elsewhere. The telling point is that the argument is conducted on the ground and by the standards which are conceded to have been set by the modern world. How important and great a change is involved in this orientatation can be appreciated if one reflects on al-Ghazali's vigorous attacks on reason, or on the manner in which Ibn Taymiyah would have handled many of the issues discussed.

Parallelism between Mawdudi and modernism is apparent also in the appeal to a principle of discrimination that distinguishes between the spirit or essentials of Islam and the forms of their embodiment. Both have claimed the ability to disengage the spirit or essentials of God's guidance, and in spite of some differences in the content of the principles they discern, the method is the same. In each case the principle of discrimination has been employed to liberate themselves from the authority of the cumulative Muslim past and to undercut the position of the *ulama* who represent that authority. The same principle also allows each to affirm the flexibility of Islamic law and its continuing relevance to all new problems that may arise. Reliance on the principle of discrimination is an indirect but, nevertheless, powerful way of proclaiming the place within the Islamic scheme of things of such liberal values as progress and the right of the individual to exercise his own judgment. Mawdudi is not aware of these implications of his stand, and he would doubtless repudiate the suggestion of his being a fellow-traveler with the modernists. But were there no other evidence on the matter, Mawdudi's sharing of modernist attitudes toward the Islamic past would be enough to establish his subjection to the same historical forces that have formed those attitudes.

It is our conclusion, therefore, that Mawdudi is best understood as a representative of one important Muslim reaction to the challenges of the modern world. His efforts, like those of numerous others, have been inspired by the need to mount a vigorous defense against destructive inroads from the outside. The method adopted has been to revive what Mawdudi looks upon as the pure and static ideal pattern of the basic sources of Islamic wisdom. In reclaiming that ideal pattern Mawdudi understands himself to be rejecting what is modern, but without his realizing it, much that is modern has worked to form his grasp of the ideal and his method of expounding it.

CHAPTER 18

ISLAM AND NATIONAL
INTEGRATION IN PAKISTAN

KHALID BIN SAYEED

IT IS COMMON knowledge that both negative and positive factors brought about the establishment of Pakistan.[1] It was not merely the fear of the Hindu numerical majority in the subcontinent that brought together the Muslims of the two physically separate territories now known as West and East Pakistan. Muslims of these areas feared that the Hindu majority would not allow the Muslims to establish their unique cultural and political identity. The Qur'an claims that its message of Islam is a vast improvement on what Judaism or Christianity had offered to the world. So the Muslim leaders of India, while trying to persuade their fellow believers about the validity of their demands for a separate state, posed the formidable question: What similarity can there be between Islam and Hinduism, which, to quote Jinnah, "challenged each other at every point of the compass?"

Two of the trenchant contrasts between the two faiths that were stressed were the Islamic oneness of God as opposed to Hindu idolatry, and the Islamic egalitarian brotherhood of believers as opposed to the Hindu caste system. When their opponents pointed out that great numbers of Muslims were descendants of converts from Hinduism such pleas fell on deaf ears, because converts do not like to be reminded of their origins and would do everything to dispel the impression that in religious ardor they lag behind their fellow believers. How Islamic were the Muslim masses? Even in the heart of predominantly Muslim-majority areas in West Pakistan, "the peasantry," wrote Sir Malcolm Darling, "almost to a man confess themselves the servants of the one true God and of Muhammad, his Prophet, but in actual fact they are the servants of landlord, moneylender and pir."[2] And as one moved away from the Indus basin, whatever vigor there was in the Islamic cultural stream was lost in the Hindu sea. Arguments that Muslim peasants differed very little from

Khalid Bin Sayeed is professor of political studies at Queen's University, Kingston, Ontario.

[1] This chapter, in a slightly different form, was published originally in *The Middle East Journal*, Summer 1963.

[2] Malcolm Lyle Darling, *Rusticus Loquitur*, Oxford University Press, London, 1933, p. 214.

the customs and manners of their Hindu neighbors were silenced by
the claim that the Islamic state of Pakistan would enable Muslims to
purify their culture and pursue their beliefs in an Islamic environment.

What are the basic characteristics of the Islamic state? These are to
be found in the concept of Islamic law and how it can be amended.
According to one of the famous Muslim definitions of law: "The
science of law is the knowledge of the rights and duties whereby man
is enabled to observe right conduct in his life, and to prepare himself
for the world to come," as opposed to the conception of Roman or
modern law, which is largely molded by the historical experience of
a people. The fundamental principles of Islamic law have already
been laid down for all time by God in the Qur'an. These include
matters like conduct of war against non-Muslims, treatment of non-
Muslims, regulations regarding inheritance and marriage, *zakat* (charity under state or community auspices), penalties and punishment
for criminal offenses, etc. Another source of Islamic law is the authoritative tradition of the Prophet. The Prophet himself had put some
of these Islamic principles into effect during his lifetime, as a law-
giver and head of the state, and had also made authoritative pronouncements as to how they should be interpreted and applied. These
are called the Sunnah or Traditions of the Prophet.

A third source is the *ijma* or the consensus of the community. There
has been some dispute as to whose consensus the *ijma* represents. Is it
the consensus of the learned doctors and divines or the consensus of
the entire community of believers? The counterpart of *ijma* or consensus is *ijtihad* which means "exercise of judgment." Modernists
would claim that *ijtihad* made Islam a dynamic religion in the sense
that Muslims were free to mold their legal and political doctrines
according to changing circumstances. The orthodox *ulama* took a
stand against this, and pointed out that exercise of judgment did not
imply that an individual Muslim or the legislature could stretch the
meaning of the Quranic principles in such a way that their spirit
was lost or distorted. Some of them would assert that since the gaps
in the Muslim legal system had all been filled by the *ijtihad* of successive generations of doctors, supported by the consensus of the community, the "gate of *ijtihad* was closed."[3]

THE POLITICIANS AND MODERNIST ISLAM

What was the state of affairs when Pakistan came into being? It was

[3] H. A. R. Gibb, *Modern Trends in Islam*, University of Chicago Press, Chicago,
1945, p. 13.

true that the *ulama* had played a vital role in enlisting the support of the rural masses for the Pakistan movement. But the leadership was largely in the hands of upper middle-class lawyers and merchants and the big landowners of the Punjab and the United Provinces. The most powerful among these were the lawyers and the intellectuals, who had been brought up on the writings of Amir Ali and Iqbal.[4] Both of these writers had said that Islam was a dynamic religion, and that all that was best in modern science and democracy was reflected in the principles of Islam. Practices like polygamy, the right of divorce being available only to men, and the so-called inferiority of women in Islam were distortions or misguided interpretations of the original principles. The Prophet had married widows in order to save them from poverty and social disgrace. Polygamy had been allowed because of the excess of women over men, a result of the death toll in tribal wars. But the Qur'an had explicitly recommended that monogamy was better than polygamy.[5] Similarly, Islam was perfectly democratic because it insisted on the equality of all believers irrespective of their national or racial origins. The first four Caliphs had been chosen in a democratic fashion. The later institutions of monarchy and feudalism which had crept into Islam were a result of the moral and spiritual lapses that Muslims had suffered and therefore they could not be said to have been derived from Islamic principles.

The Muslim League government of Pakistan, dominated by lawyers and university-educated landowners, believed that the parliamentary government that had been established in Pakistan under the adapted Government of India Act, 1935, was by no means at variance with the principles of Islam. The new State Bank of Pakistan, the National Bank of Pakistan and the Industrial Development Corporation were institutions which were necessary for the existence of a modern state. Muslims had lagged behind in banking and other commercial enterprises. They should be encouraged to take to such professions with eagerness and speed. Islam had frowned upon the taking and giving of interest, but this was because interest had originally encouraged usury. It was suggested that Islam was not against interest charged for the services and risks taken by the banking institution.

On the other hand, the rural masses of Punjab and Bengal had been told time and again that Pakistan would mean the establishment of an Islamic state. Their *mullahs* had preached to them during Friday sermons that the modern cinema encouraged sexual laxity

4 See particularly Amir Ali, *The Spirit of Islam*, 2nd ed., Christophers, London, 1922, and Muhammad Iqbal, *Reconstruction of Religious Thought in Islam*, Oxford University Press, London, 1934.
5 Qur'an 4:3.

and that the current evils of gambling, drinking and free mixing of men and women to be found among Muslim urban classes were reprehensible. They thought that now that Pakistan had come into being, all these evil practices would be prohibited. Nothing demonstrates more graphically the contrast in expectations between the illiterate rural masses and the urbanized and westernized elites, on the question of the Islamic state, than the story of Qaid-i-Azam Jinnah being cheered by the peasants of a Sindhi village as "Long live Mawlana Muhammad Ali Jinnah." It is reported that Jinnah stopped his car and told the peasants not to call him Mawlana as he was not their religious leader but a political leader.[6] The peasants perhaps thought that the founder of the new state would become one of their pious Caliphs.

In March 1949 the famous Objectives Resolution was moved in the Constituent Assembly by the prime minister, Liaquat Ali Khan. It declared that "sovereignty over the entire universe belongs to God Almighty alone," but He had delegated this authority to the state of Pakistan and that this was to be exercised through its people "within the limits prescribed by Him." The resolution also stated that (a) "the state shall exercise its power and authority through the chosen representatives of the people" and that (b) "the principles of democracy, freedom, equality, tolerance and social justice, as enunciated by Islam, shall be fully observed." (c) "The Muslims shall be enabled to order their lives in accordance with the teachings and requirements of Islam as set out in the Holy Qur'an and the Sunnah."[7]

All this suggested that the resolution could be interpreted in different ways. Modernists could say that the resolution guaranteed a democratic constitution and the sovereignty of the people. The orthodox could point out that democracy did not imply, by any means, absolute popular sovereignty because the resolution clearly stated that the people of Pakistan on whom God had conferred His authority were to exercise their power "within the limits prescribed by Him." Further, the fact that the resolution clearly stated that Muslims would be enabled to order their lives in accordance with the teachings and requirements of Islam as set out in the Holy Qur'an and the Sunnah meant that the legislature could not repeal or modify Islamic provisions like the prohibition of alcoholic drinks, interest and gambling, and the severe punishments such as cutting off of hands for theft and stoning to death for adultery.

6 Hector Bolitho, *Jinnah Creator of Pakistan*, Murray, London, 1954, p. 213.
7 *The Constituent Assembly of Pakistan Debates*, 1949, vol. 5, pp. 1-2.

These, according to a fundamentalist like Mawlana Mawdudi, the head of the Jama'at-i-Islami movement, constituted mandatory legislation which was beyond the purview of any legislature in a Muslim country.[8] Then came the recommendatory provisions. But, according to Mawdudi, there was also the sphere of permissible legislation under which the Muslim society could legislate, keeping in view the ever-increasing requirements of every age. However, he was quite emphatic that the present western-educated Muslim leaders of Pakistan were not competent to initiate legislation even within the permissible field, because they were neither well versed in Islamic doctrine nor good Muslims. On the other hand, there were others like Mawlana Abul Hasanat, president of the Jami'at-al-Ulama-i-Pakistan, who were of the opinion that Islamic law was complete and merely required interpretation by well-qualified experts. This meant that there was hardly any room for further legislation.[9]

One cannot help feeling that leaders like Liaquat were probably temporizing with a difficult situation. They had assured the Muslims that an Islamic state based on the Qur'an and the Sunnah would be established, and the Muslim masses had supported the demand for Pakistan because of these assurances. The leaders still needed the support of the masses and particularly that of the influential *ulama*. In the Constituent Assembly Mawlana Shabbir Ahmad Usmani supported the Objectives Resolution. It is inconceivable that Liaquat and his cabinet would have allowed the incorporation of primitive law into the Pakistan penal code. But the Objectives Resolution had created the impression that Pakistan would move in the direction of an orthodox Islamic state.

NATIONAL UNITY AND SECTARIAN CONFLICT

On the question of rights of minorities, the Objectives Resolution did suggest that minorities would be entitled to the same fundamental rights "including equality of status, of opportunity, and before law" as Muslims. But Mawlana Shabbir Ahmad Usmani in his speech during the debate was of the opinion that, since an Islamic state was an ideological state, "people who do not subscribe to those ideas may have a place in the administrative machinery of the state but they cannot be entrusted with the responsibility of framing the

[8] Syed Abul 'Ala Mawdudi, *Islamic Law and Constitution*, Jama'at-i-Islami Publications, Karachi, 1955, p. 34.
[9] *Report of the Court of Inquiry Constituted Under Punjab Act II of 1954 to Inquire Into the Punjab Disturbances of 1953*, Government Printing, Lahore, 1954, p. 102.

general policy of the state or dealing with matters vital to its safety and integrity."[10]

It is obvious that Islam has set up a wall between believer and unbelievers. The word *kafir* (infidel) is repeatedly used in the Qur'an. Similarly, *jihad* (holy struggle for the spread of Islam) is recommended, though there are several other verses which stress tolerance and generous treatment of minorities. Then there are other verses which suggest that Islam should be preached by peaceful means and, if unbelievers persist in their beliefs, they should be left unmolested. But the over-all impression is that a community of believers is surrounded by a hostile world, and that the latter will not leave Muslims alone unless they are converted or overcome.

The treatment of certain sects within the fold of Islam who did not accept the beliefs and practices of the Sunni majority became a matter of immediate concern in Pakistan. The community which provoked intense hostility among the orthodox *ulama* was that of the Ahmadis. They number about 200,000, and believe that their prophet, Mirza Ghulam Ahmad (1835-1908), appeared in order to reform and renovate the original religion of Islam. Ever since Mirza Ghulam Ahmad proclaimed his faith towards the end of the nineteenth century, Muslims have felt outraged that one of the cardinal doctrines of Islam, namely, the finality of the Prophethood under Muhammad, who had brought the best and the most perfect faith, was being challenged. Mawlana Shabbir Ahmad Usmani, in a pamphlet called *Ash-shahab*, alleged that the Ahmadis were apostates and showed that in Islam the appropriate penalty for apostasy was death. It was well known that a few Ahmadis had been stoned to death in Afghanistan. Intense feelings of hostility toward them existed even before partition. But after Pakistan came into being and Sir Muhammad Zafrullah Khan, an Ahmadi, became its foreign minister, it was felt that he and others were not only propagating their faith but also establishing themselves in positions of importance in the administrative and political structure of Pakistan.

The campaign against the Ahmadis started soon after the establishment of Pakistan. According to the *Report of the Court of Inquiry Set up to Inquire into the Punjab Disturbances of 1953*, commonly known as the Munir Report, the campaign against them had assumed a clear pattern from 1948 on. Religious leaders would publicly describe Zafrullah as an apostate and a traitor and often justify the killing of Ahmadis. In a number of cases described in the report,

[10] *The Constituent Assembly of Pakistan Debates*, 1949, vol. 5, p. 45.

enraged individuals would leave these meetings in such a state of fury that they would search out Ahmadis and kill them. This campaign gained steady momentum and several religious leaders combined to demand that Ahmadis should be declared a minority and Sir Zafrullah and other Ahmadis should be dismissed from office. It was significant that both the central and provincial Muslim League governments were aware that this campaign was gathering momentum and watched it with mounting alarm, but until the very end took no clear and firm action against it.

It has been estimated that about 377 Muslim League leaders from all over West Punjab actually supported the movement. The chief minister of West Punjab, Mumtaz Daultana, was most reluctant to take any vigorous stand against it because he felt that it would be politically dangerous. Instead of suppressing it, he tried to direct its main course towards Karachi so that the central government might bear the responsibility. The result was that Muslims in several districts of Punjab, excited by the speeches of the *ulama* and the *imams* in general meetings and mosques, and probably encouraged by the weakness of the government, resorted to lawlessness. In February 1953 martial law had to be imposed and the chief minister, Daultana, was replaced by the central government.

The way Prime Minister Nazimuddin and Daultana reacted to the demands of the *ulama* that Ahmadis should be declared a minority community provides a revealing commentary on the conflict between their moral or religious convictions and their political interests. Daultana, who is reported to have impressed his dons with his brilliance at Oxford, must have felt that it was not proper on the part of the *ulama* and other agitators to display such intolerance towards a religious sect but, guided by his political interests, he thought that he could not suppress such an agitation without incurring unpopularity among the great majority of Muslims in his province. Nazimuddin, on the other hand, though educated in Cambridge, was an intensely religious man. He was probably in sympathy with the demands of the *ulama*, whom he also respected, but thought that it would be politically unwise to accede to them: Pakistan would earn a bad name in foreign countries because the foreign minister, Sir Zafrullah, enjoyed an international reputation. Such actions by the prime minister would have created the impression abroad that Pakistan was acting in a medieval fashion.

Another conclusion which emerges from the religious disturbances and the Munir Report is that Islam, instead of uniting the different sections of the country, could work as a divisive factor. In the case of religious disturbances, one could see that there was not only a conflict between the great majority of Muslims and Ahmadis, but also between the orthodox *ulama* and the western-educated ruling classes. If such controversies were allowed to be raised, there could also be a conflict between Sunni Muslims, who are greatly in the majority, and the small but influential minority of Shi'i Muslims.

We have already referred to the liberal interpretations of Islam by Amir Ali and Iqbal. These two could have been good starting-points for Pakistan's intellectual and political elite, in formulating a liberal and progressive Islamic ideology. Why did not the leaders think along these lines? Perhaps there are two answers. First, there was an acute shortage of talent. The result was that both political and intellectual leaders became absorbed in building and operating the administrative apparatus of the country. Second, perhaps political leaders did not feel that there was any dire need for a political ideology. Merely by mouthing religious slogans and catch phrases, they had been able to mobilize Muslim support for Pakistan, and they thought they could continue to operate in the same way. Such a method of operation, however, was bound to attract political opportunists. Thus, the Muslim League in 1946 appointed a *Masha'ikh* Committee consisting of twelve members, some of whom were well-known religious leaders, to campaign for the Muslim League in the general elections. Others on the committee were highly westernized landowners, who were given fictitious titles of *pir* and *masha'ikh* so that the Muslim masses might be persuaded to vote for the Muslim League. Those who have seen these men either in the Lahore Gymkhana Club or in their luxurious drawing-rooms would find the situation highly amusing; indeed it was of such men that Philip Mason wrote: "It is no doubt a chance association, but if you speak of the ruling class in Pakistan today, I think of men watching the polo in Lahore, the kind of people you'd see at point-to-point races in England, with check caps pulled down over their eyes and horsey coats with slanting pockets."[11]

EDUCATION AND ISLAMIC VALUES

When martial law was imposed in October 1958 and the former activities of politicians and civil servants were investigated, astonishing disclosures were made regarding corruption and maladministration. It was ironical that in a state which had been established to demon-

[11] Philip Mason, "India and Pakistan After Ten Years," *The Listener*, September 5, 1957, p. 336.

strate an Islamic way of life, two of its seven prime ministers were accused of corruption and asked by the martial law regime to return their ill-gotten wealth to the state. Nearly all the educational and political leaders would blame the British system of education for this state of affairs. It had been designed to produce, as Macaulay said in his *Minute*, "a class of persons, Indian in blood and color, but English in taste, in opinion, in morals, and in intellect." Cynics would perhaps further add that these leaders resorted to corruption because they could not maintain their English or American tastes on Pakistani salaries. However, one should not condemn this education out of hand because Indians imbibed Europe's liberal nationalism from it, as indeed the two Nehrus and Jinnah and Liaquat did. But the fact remained that by itself this education had not created a national consciousness among Pakistan's leaders and for a great majority of people it was only a passport to a clerical job.

The Qur'an stresses repeatedly the concept of the *ummah*. It constantly differentiates this *ummah* from the infidels. But how is it, one may ask, that a conference of psychologists in Pakistan held in 1959 declared "that the average Pakistani tends to be selfish rather than cooperative?" "The average Pakistani is preoccupied with his own petty desires and megalomaniac whims because no all-absorbing national interest is within sight."[12] Similarly, Edward C. Banfield, basing his observations on the study of an Italian village, has observed: "That the Montegranesi are prisoners of their family-centered ethos— that because of it they cannot act concertedly or in the common good —is a fundamental impediment to their economic and other progress."[13] These findings apply to a people whose faith, Roman Catholicism, like Islam, offers a total view of the world. All this goes to suggest that abstract ideas are not enough, that they must have an underpinning of group activity reaching down to the lowest unit of society. Obviously this has been missing in Pakistan.

It can be said to the credit of the new regime that at least it has initiated a discussion of these fundamental problems. The *Report of the Committee on National Education* is interspersed with recommendations like these: "That religious instruction be made compulsory throughout the primary and middle stages. . . . Emphasis on activities requiring the subordination of the individual to the team or group. There should be a persistent effort to make the student community-

12 Q. M. Aslam and M. A. Ansari, eds., *Observations and Recommendations Made by a Conference of Psychologists*, Bureau of National Reconstruction, Karachi, n.d., p. 8. Held on September 21-26, 1959.

13 Edward C. Banfield, *The Moral Basis of a Backward Society*, The Free Press, Glencoe, Ill., 1958, p. 163.

conscious. We want to produce men and women who will work hard because they believe that idleness and slackness are morally wrong, and because they see in hard work a means to their own personal salvation and the salvation of their country."[14] Social studies have been made compulsory from grades VI-X and Islamic studies from grades VI-VIII.[15] It may also be pertinent to point out that emphasis is being laid in schools on Islam in a Pakistani environment. The *Report of the Curriculum Committee for Secondary Education* points out: "Students of Islamic History, as now presented, will develop confidence in themselves and instead of looking for leadership to other Muslim countries, will try to lead others in the presentation of Islam."[16]

What is missing in these recommendations is the role that mosques and religious schools attached to mosques can play in developing group activity and civic consciousness. Children in the villages go to small schools attached to mosques, where the teaching of the Qur'an and elementary religious education are imparted. Village mosques and even those in cities can play a vital role in promoting group activities of various sorts in the way that churches in western countries have done. The Constitution Commission has recommended that the *imams* should be trained, not only in religious studies but also in modern sciences, so that they may explain Islam in the context of modern conditions to both the uneducated and "those who are of the western way of thinking."[17]

When outsiders wonder whether the two physically separated units will remain together Pakistanis proudly state that the cementing force of Islam will overcome the geographical distance and cultural diversities. But obviously this cementing force has not been strong enough to persuade Pakistanis to arrive at a political settlement, and the economic battle has continued unabated both under the martial law regime and the present constitutional autocracy. Many observers have suggested that the elite in both wings are becoming increasingly secularized, and that the impact of modernity and secular forces seem to be different in West and East Pakistan.[18]

[14] *Report of the Commission on National Education*, Manager of Publications, Karachi, 1959, pp. 238-240.

[15] *Report of the Curriculum Committee for Secondary Education* (Classes VI-XII), Ministry of Education, Rawalpindi, 1960, pp. 41 and 44.

[16] *Ibid.*, p. 43.

[17] *Report on the Constitution Commission, Pakistan,* Manager of Publications, Karachi, 1962, pp. 125-126.

[18] See also Khalid Bin Sayeed, *Pakistan The Formative Phase*, Pakistan Publishing House, Karachi, 1960, p. 452.

RELIGIOUS ATTITUDES AND MODERNIZATION

I am undertaking a survey of religious attitudes and their impact on nation building and modernization in Pakistan. To begin with, a preliminary survey of 103 university students from both East and West Pakistan has been completed. These students were selected by their instructors; they were considered not only above average but were also expected to be cooperative in filling out a fairly long questionnaire of twenty-six questions. Some questions were designed to elicit the educational background of both the students and their parents; others sought information regarding how and at what age a student came under the influence of political and social ideas. Finally, the questionnaire probed into the religious background of the student and his views regarding the degree of compatibility between religion and modern science, his views concerning Islam's attitude to non-Muslims, and the effectiveness of Islam as a bond of unity between East and West Pakistan. The results may be tabulated as follows:

Islam As an Effective Bond of Unity between East and West Pakistan

	Yes	*No*	*Not Answered*	*Total*
East Pakistan	14[a]	14	2	30
West Pakistan	59[b]	5	9	73

[a] Out of the 14 in East Pakistan who said that Islam was an effective bond, 2 were of the opinion that it was not the only bond and both mentioned fear of India as an additional bond.

[b] Out of the 59 in West Pakistan who said that Islam was an effective bond, 17 were of the opinion that Islam was not the only bond. Nine said fear of India was an additional bond and other bonds cited were economic advantages, common history, and nationalism.

It is apparent that the West Pakistanis who think that Islam is an effective bond of unity constitute a far greater proportion of the total than do East Pakistanis who hold the same view. Fifty-nine out of 73 West Pakistanis, or 80.8 per cent, think that Islam is an effective bound whereas only fourteen out of thirty East Pakistanis, or 46.6 per cent, regard Islam as an effective bond of unity between East and West Pakistan. It is true that the number of East Pakistanis who have answered the questionnaire is much smaller, but this defect is partially corrected by the interviews in depth of another forty East Pakistanis.

These forty East Pakistanis included students, teachers, civil servants, other professional men and housewives. It is significant that they have all had religious instruction during their childhood, which included the reading of the Qur'an in Arabic, which they do not understand. Some of them have read the Qur'an in Bengali or English translations. Most of them are frank enough to admit that the Qur'an does not exercise much influence on their day-to-day activities, but nevertheless they all have deep reverence for the Qur'an as a sacred book. A great majority also are of the view that Islam as a unifying force between the two regions is gradually losing its strength. In these interviews, East Pakistanis displayed a sense of loneliness and isolation and pointed out that East Pakistanis would like to continue their union with West Pakistan for economic and geographical reasons. Thus, again, the binding force is the fear of India. Resentment towards West Pakistan may be considerable, but fear and suspicion of India is much greater.

A number of Muslim leaders during the pre-partition period put forward the view that in Islam there was no separation between religion and politics. Therefore, it was argued that Muslims demanded a separate territory to establish an Islamic state. This view is still shared by the majority of students who were interviewed. But it is significant that 37.9 per cent of the students who answered the questionnaire think that there can be a separation between religion and politics. When asked whether Islam and modern sciences are compatible, 70.8 per cent answered that there is no conflict between the two.

However, those who still believe that Pakistan can never abandon its *raison d'être*, namely, the establishment of an Islamic state, point out that the Muslim masses in both East and West Pakistan gave their full support to the westernized elite only when they were warned that Islam was in danger, and when later assured that an Islamic state would be established. The questions which have not yet been answered satisfactorily are: what kind of Muslim is a rural East Bengali? How strictly or sincerely does he practice his faith? The same sort of question may be asked about the state of Muslim consciousness in the rural areas of West Pakistan.

There is an excellent study on East Pakistan by A. F. A. Husain entitled *Human and Social Impact of Technological Change in Pakistan*. Unfortunately, the number of persons interviewed is very small when one considers the nature of the conclusions the author has drawn from the interviews he conducted. The study suggests that

Muslims from the districts of Noakhali, Chittagong, Tipperah and Sylhet are more religious than Muslims from other districts;[19] the influence of the *pirs* and the mawlanas is strong here. From 50 to 60 per cent say their daily prayers regularly and perhaps a larger number keep the fast during the month of Ramadan.[20] But Muslims who leave their villages and start working in the cities do not adhere to the rituals as rigorously.[21] What is equally significant is that not as many Muslims in other districts like Bogra, Khulna, Mymensingh and Dinajpur practice their faith strictly.[22] The findings of my own survey, though based so far only on interviews of students at Dacca University, suggest that the educated groups when separated from their rural homes become either indifferent or lax in the observance of the rituals.

The Qur'an is in Arabic and the sermons are also recited in Arabic. It has been estimated that out of the total population of 32.2 million Muslims in East Pakistan in 1951, only 1.1 million could read the Qur'an or Urdu.[23] It is well known that a very small number can understand Arabic. Since religion controls so many activities, a people who takes religion itself on trust without even understanding the meaning of words uttered in prayers, cannot develop very inquiring or creative minds. It may be disputed whether Islam has influenced them to adopt a fatalistic attitude towards their environment and living conditions, but nearly all those interviewed from the various districts pointed out that people were strongly fatalistic, that concerted action for building dams, embankments or roads was rare, that nothing could be done to check their growing numbers because religion stood against birth control, and that calamities were often sent by God to punish people for their sins.[24]

When one looks at West Pakistan, the picture is the same. The studies that one has to rely on are dated, namely, the *District Gazetteers*. But the excellent works of Sir Malcolm Darling, like *Rusticus Loquitur*, and *At Freedom's Door*, offer us penetrating insights into religious attitudes and the influence of the *pirs* and *mullahs*. According to Darling, "Only one per cent (of the *mullahs*)—probably a liberal estimate—can explain what they read."[25] In Attock he notes that the *pir* in influence "rivals the landlord and surpasses

[19] A. F. A. Husain, *Human & Social Impact of Technological Change in Pakistan*, Oxford University Press, Dacca, 1956, vol. 2, pp. 14-15, 23-24, 41-42, 51-52.
[20] *Ibid.*
[21] *Ibid.*, pp. 148, 184, 268, 305, 311.
[22] *Ibid.*, pp. 27-28, 32, 37, 46.   [23] *Ibid.*, vol. 1, p. 91.
[24] *Ibid.*, vol. 2, pp. 10, 15, 24, 28-29, 33, 36-37, 42, 51-52, 149, 184, 270.
[25] Darling, p. 302.

the money-lender."[26] In Muzaffargarh and the Indus riverain, "with the large majority he has taken the place of Allah."[27] In Jhang, a *pir* with a B.A. returned after six weeks with his booty collected after giving forty or fifty charms daily to his followers. "They were mostly given to those who wanted *aulad* or *daulet*—off-spring or wealth; but they were also given to young men to compass their amorous desires, to the less beloved of two wives to oust the favorite, to those who wished to marry but had been repulsed, to men smarting for revenge (*dushman marne ke liye*), to litigants anxious for the success of their suits, to those troubled with sick bodies or whose cattle were ill, and even to those who wished to divide lovers. Seventy-five per cent of his clients were women."[28] The influence of the *pirs* of West Pakistan is reflected in both the national assembly and the assembly of West Pakistan. In an interview with the author, Makh-doom Mohammad Zaman, a member of the national assembly, and the famous Sajjada Nashin of Hala in Sind, said that he had 900,000 followers in Pakistan and India, most of whom were concentrated in lower Sind. His rival, the Pir of Pagaro, told the author that he controlled eighteen out of thirty-three Sind members in the West Pakistan assembly.

Can one infer from the fatalistic attitude that exists among the rural people both in East and West Pakistan that such an attitude may be ascribed to the influence of Islam? If so, one can go on to argue that Islam stands in the way of modernization. Such an interpretation perhaps would not be fair either to Islam or to the facts. Sir Malcolm Darling himself, though struck by the enormous influence of the *pirs* and the fatalistic attitude of the peasants in the Punjab in 1930, was more hopeful of the impact of changes, such as better agricultural facilities and education in 1946-1947.[29]

Similarly, one can argue that Islam has not stood in the way of the phenomenal industrial expansion that has taken place in Pakistan, largely as the result of government encouragement to private enterprise. Papanek in his pioneering study has demonstrated that five small "communities"—Halai Memon, Chinioti, Dawoodi Bohra, Khoja Ismaili, and Khoja Isnashari—have been very largely instrumental in industrializing Pakistan. He points out that the government and the civil service provided the favorable framework within which this

26 *Ibid.*, p. 301.   27 *Ibid.*, p. 276.
28 *Ibid.*, p. 245.
29 Malcolm Lyle Darling, *At Freedom's Door*, Oxford University Press, London, 1949, p. 347.

expansion could take place, and suggests that the value system of Pakistan was not hostile to entrepreneurial activity.[30]

One can argue that the people of these communities were originally trading castes before their conversion to Islam, and they did not develop the industrial potential of Pakistan because they were Muslims. Those who have interviewed these new entrepreneurs would also suggest that some of them are not very religious, and most of them take the view that religion and commerce cannot be mixed up and that the first concern of a businessman or an industrialist is to make money. Even those who are quite religious in their attitudes, like certain Memon industrialists who were interviewed by the author, take the view that Islam has never been hostile to industry and commerce. On matters such as interest they put forward the views of writers like Amir Ali, who suggest that Islam is against usury and not against the interest charged by modern banks for risk bearing. Thus, one may point out that as the result of the British impact and the emergence of the market economy, the industrial and commercial elite have been modernized to such an extent that they genuinely believe that Islam and modern commerce and industry can coexist.

ISLAM AND NATION BUILDING

How can one sum up the role that Islam has played in nation building in Pakistan? There is considerable evidence to show that Jinnah, with all his brilliance and forensic ability, could not have achieved Pakistan had not the two cries, "Islam in Danger!" and "Pakistan an Islamic State!" been raised. But we have seen that attempts to Islamicize the constitution have often divided the people of Pakistan. Sunnis versus Shi'as is an old conflict, and in 1953 the *mullahs* and mawlanas instigated riots against the Ahmadis. It has also been suggested that East Pakistani Muslims have often been influenced by Hindu culture, that their intellectuals still relish Tagore more than Iqbal and that the rural masses still take part in Hindu Jatras.[31] In this case, one can see that Islam rallied the Bengalis and the Punjabis under the same banner for the achievement of Pakistan, but an insistence on a pure Islamic culture can further worsen the relationship between East and West Pakistan.

We have seen that when Pakistan came into being the political institutions the new state had to establish were western in character, and that traditional Islam had nothing to contribute. The new in-

[30] Gustav F. Papanek, "The Development of Entrepreneurship," *The American Economic Review Papers and Proceedings*, 1962, vol. 52.
[31] A. F. A. Husain, vol. 2, pp. 14, 28, 32, 37, 42, 148.

stitution of Basic Democracies is not Islamic in origin but dates back to the days of Lord Ripon. Ayub, however, can take credit for the change that he has brought about in the Muslim personal law, in the form of the Muslim Family Laws Ordinance, 1961. The Ordinance places several obstacles to a Muslim male's right to divorce his wife or wives and makes polygamy a difficult proposition. The new regime has also made efforts to educate and modernize the outlook of *imams* of mosques, and in East Pakistan the Bureau of National Reconstruction has organized regular classes for the training of the *imams*. The matter of rewriting sermons to suit modern conditions has also been discussed, and the necessity of Bengali translations of sermons has been stressed.[32]

It is noteworthy that former politicians very largely kept the masses in their apathetic state and attempted to set up parliamentary institutions at the top. Ayub, perhaps for both intellectual and personal reasons, is not in favor of a restoration of full-fledged democracy at the top, but is deliberately disturbing "the placid, pathetic contentment of the masses."

Ayub has made it clear that he is not in favor of traditional Islam. He is acutely aware that in order to defeat the traditionalists he must suggest that Islam is in favor of scientific progress, rationalism and birth control. A clear indication of how his mind is working is provided by the new Central Institute of Islamic Research that has been created under Article 207 of the new Constitution. Its purpose is not merely to undertake research and instruction in Islam but also to assist in "the reconstruction of Muslim society." An article by its director, Dr. Fazlur Rahman, points out that: ". . . to insist that to-day's commercial bank—with an overall controlled economy—comes under the Quranic prohibition and is banned by the Prophetic Sunnah is not so much historical or religious honesty but an acute crisis of human confidence and uncompromising cynicism. The Qur'an and the Sunnah were given for intelligent moral understanding and implementation, not for rigid formalism."[33] Thus one can see which way the wind of change is blowing. The *ulama* and orthodox people find this wind very chilly indeed.

[32] *Report of the Activities of the Bureau of National Reconstruction*, East Pakistan Government Press, Dacca, 1962, pp. 3-4.

[33] Fazlur Rahman, "Sunnah and Hadith," *Islamic Studies*, 1962, vol. 1, p. 33.

CHAPTER 19

THE CONTROVERSY OVER THE MUSLIM FAMILY LAWS

FAZLUR RAHMAN

FROM THE time when the *ulama* began to record the details of their laboriously worked out legal system of Islamic *fiqh* (jurisprudence), Sultans and Caliphs in power took it into their hands to issue ordinances. Having ceased to permit any appreciable amount of fresh thinking on Islamic law, the custodians of the *shari'ah* had to find room for this extra-*shari'ah* legislation enacted by the rulers. This activity of legislation, although present in various regions of the Muslim world, was most systematically pursued by the Sultans in the Ottoman Empire where a body of law came into existence known as *kanun*, as distinguished from *fiqh*.

With the impact of modern western learning, modernist movements arose throughout the Muslim world, first of all in Turkey which had been in the closest contact with Europe, and subsequently in Egypt, India and elsewhere. All these movements laid a fresh emphasis on the doctrine of *ijtihad*, i.e., original thinking and judgment. The principle of *ijtihad* had been accepted in classical Muslim law but, in actual practice, its operation had come to an end by the time the *ulama* had perfected their legal systems during the first three centuries of Islam. Subsequently, powerful individual voices had arisen to restore the efficacy of *ijtihad*, the most important of these voices being that of Ibn Taymiyya during the fourteenth century. Immediately before the dawn of modernism, autonomous reform movements had swept over almost the entire Muslim world, beginning with the Wahhabi movement in Arabia in the eighteenth century and its contemporary, the school of Shah Waliy Allah (d. 1762) in India. But although all these movements had emphasized the right of the individual to perform *ijtihad*, i.e., independent thinking, their content remained fundamentally within the orbit of the classical schools of Muslim law within which a certain amount of flexibility was introduced.

But when the modernist took the lead in the Muslim countries from the latter half of the nineteenth century onward, although his emphasis on *ijtihad* was in principle a continuation of these

Fazlur Rahman is director of the Central Institute of Islamic Research, Karachi.

earlier movements, the program that he envisaged was much more radical and sought to introduce basic changes into the content of the classical body of Islamic law. The first modernist attempt at a reformulation of the family laws of classical Islam was the introduction of the Ottoman Family Laws in 1917 which, although subsequently abrogated in Turkey, remained as a legacy in certain parts of the dismembered Ottoman Empire. In Egypt a series of legislative enactments took place from 1920 onward, and in India the Dissolution of Muslim Marriages Act was passed in 1939, granting the right of divorce to women under certain circumstances and prohibiting child marriage. In 1935 the Syrian government passed a law restricting polygamy, and permitting the marriage of a second wife only if the husband could show himself to be financially capable of maintaining both wives. The most radical law passed for the first time, however, was that of Tunisia which prohibited polygamy altogether. In certain Muslim countries, Jordan for example, the modernist family laws enacted were subsequently abrogated under pressure from the conservatives.

We shall examine the Muslim Family Laws Ordinance in Pakistan in some detail and also the reactions that it has produced. While doing so, we shall also make a few remarks on the nature and reasoning involved in legal modernism in general in Pakistan. There are four important provisions of this ordinance: succession, compulsory registration of marriages, restriction on polygamy, and regulation of divorce. We shall first deal with the question of the restriction on polygamy because, of all the provisions, this one has aroused the most vigorous protests on the part of the conservatives and, in a fundamental sense, most affects the general status of women in society.

RESTRICTIONS ON POLYGAMY

The ordinance lays down a procedure for a second polygamous marriage. A man wishing to marry a second wife must submit an application to that effect to the chairman of the Arbitration Council in which he must state the reasons justifying his second marriage and also state whether or not the consent of the existing wife or wives has been obtained. On the receipt of the application, the chairman shall ask the existing wife or each of the existing wives to nominate their representatives, and also the applicant to nominate his representative. These representatives, together with the chairman, shall constitute the Arbitration Council and shall decide whether the proposed marriage is necessary and just. The Arbitration Council must record the reasons for arriving at its decision—which can be appealed against, but only once. The reasons which the Arbitration Council may consider as valid grounds for granting permission for a second marriage include sterility, physical infirmity, physical unfitness for conjugal relations, willful avoidance of a decree for restitution of conjugal rights or insanity on the part of the existing wife.

It should be noted first that the ordinance does not say that if a second marriage is contracted without the previous permission of the Arbitration Council, the marriage would be invalid. It lays down that if a marriage is contracted without such previous permission, the husband shall be liable to pay forthwith the entire dower due to the existing wife or wives and, secondly, he may be imprisoned for a maximum period of one year or fined a maximum of 5,000 rupees or both. Despite these penalties, the marriage itself remains valid.

This provision has been opposed by conservatives of all shades of opinion, who have said that it violates the Quranic injunction, "If you fear that you cannot do justice to orphans, then marry from among women who please you, two, three or four" (4:3). Now it must be admitted, to start with, that the practice of all Muslims from the beginning of Islam has been to regard this verse as a permission for a man to take up to four wives, although there have been some bright spirits in the past who, by various ingenious interpretations, have even raised the number to twenty-four. The entire classical *fiqh*-law of the Muslims permits this and assumes this. But the modernist thinking of various shades on this question has been, since the second half of the nineteenth century, that the Qur'an really meant to legislate monogamy but that polygamy was permitted under certain special circumstances. Among these modernists of various shades were non-*ulama* westernized intellectuals like Sir Syed Ahmad Khan and Syed Amir Ali, as well as Shaikh Muhammad Abduh of Egypt, who belonged to the ranks of the *ulama*, and is regarded as one of the greatest *ulama* of modern times.

The modernists contend that if we study this whole Quranic verse of which part has been quoted, their stand becomes clear. The verse says: "Marry what please you from among women, two, three or four; but if you cannot do justice, then marry only one." It is then argued that since no man can really do justice among several wives, the Qur'an, in fact, prohibits polygamy as a general rule. In 4:128, the Qur'an further tells us "and you shall never be able to do justice among women no matter how desirous of this you may be. So do not incline completely [away from one wife] leaving her suspended in the air." The modernist finds categorical support for his thesis in the first part of these verses which says in no unclear terms that it is impossible for a man to do justice among more than one wife. The conservative, on the other hand, seeks support in the latter half of the same verse and says that since the Qur'an asks us not to "incline away completely" from one wife, it seems to presuppose the coexistence of several wives. The conservative then challenges the modernist interpretation of the term "justice" and says that "justice" here means equality in external dealings and parity of treatment, i.e., that if a husband gives a certain amount of allowance to one wife, he must give the same to the other, etc.

What are we to say about the relative merits of these contentions? I think that the conservative interpretation of "justice" cannot stand examination; otherwise the Qur'an would not have stated categorically that it is *impossible* for a man to do justice among several wives because equality of external treatment, however difficult it may be in certain circumstances, is not impossible of achievement. Justice, therefore, must include and, indeed, primarily imply the inner inclination of the husband towards the wife. There are certain other weighty statements of the Qur'an also to be taken into consideration in this connection. While characterizing the relationship of husband and wife in family life, the Qur'an makes certain statements which reveal its deeper assumptions: "And among the signs of God is that He has created for you from among yourselves spouses and He has created between you a relationship of love and mercy. Verily, in this there are signs for people to think" (30:21). The Qur'an repeats the same thing while speaking of the relationship of the first couple, Adam and Eve. Again, "your wives are garments unto you and you are garments unto them" (2:187). This clearly shows that the proper relationship that the Qur'an envisages between the husband and the wife is that of love and mercy and that the marital bond cannot be defined basically in terms of external treatment. It assumes that the external treatment will follow this inner relationship of love. When, therefore, the Qur'an says that it is impossible to do justice among women, it is clearly saying that it is impossible to love more than one woman in the same way. The conservative contention on this point is undoubtedly weak.

There is other evidence in the Qur'an to show that the concept of the normal family life according to it must be monogamous. The fundamental concept of the "pair" which occurs in the Qur'an in various contexts, more than a score of times, when studied closely, clearly leads to this conclusion. In 51:49, the Qur'an states as a general law of creation that "everything We have created in pairs." But there are numerous passages where this concept occurs about human relationship in family life. "We have made you pairs" (35:11); and, "We have created you in pairs" (88: 8). In 4:19, the Qur'an says, "if you intend to replace one spouse with another . . ."; this verse clearly assumes that if one wants to have another wife the normal method is to bring her *in the place* of the first wife rather than add her to the latter.

But the formidable question arises, how does one explain the continuous unbroken practice of the Muslim tradition? The conservative has a point when he says, first, that there has been this continuous practice of polygamy and, second, that the Qur'an itself, in some of its statements noted above, tacitly assumes polygamy and even, in fact, explicitly permits four polygamous marriages. The honest reply of modernist scholarship would be to admit this fact and to say that although the ideal of Islam is to produce a monogamous society, it nevertheless permitted polygamy because polygamy had become endemic to the social structure of Arabian life. The Qur'an, therefore, while accepting the status quo and making improvements upon it as best it could on the legal plane, went further morally in the hope that society would slowly move toward a monogamous pattern.

In fact, this is not the case only with the Quranic stand on the question of monogamy and polygamy but is equally true of the Quranic stand on the question of slavery. Whoever studies the Qur'an with any care, cannot but be impressed by its insistent moral exhortations to free slaves. So far as the *legal* position goes, the Qur'an accepted the status quo because slavery was an integral part of the social structure of those days, and it produced great improvements in the general treatment of slaves. It was therefore hoped that, under the influence of the Qur'an's moral teaching, society would gradually move toward the total emancipation of slaves.

This brings us to the general character of the process of prophetic reform. The Prophet was not an impractical visionary who simply made high-sounding moral pronouncements. It was a central function of the Prophet and his mission, after having made these moral pronouncements, to be effective in society and to move it in a certain direction. In other words, the Prophet was a seer-cum-reformer. But at any given time a reformer, however zealous, cannot change society beyond a certain point. The Prophet, therefore, had to act both on the moral plane and the legal plane.

It must be recognized that the legislative part of the Qur'an, which according to us Muslims is the revealed Word of God, nevertheless presupposes the flesh and blood of the society to which it was immediately applied. So far as its legal enactments, therefore, are concerned, the eternal value therein must be distinguished from the social context in order to be applicable to changing conditions. But instead of this direct approach, which not only does not threaten but even strengthens the evidence for the revealed character of the Qur'an, the modernists in general, and particularly in Pakistan, rely on artificial arguments based on forced interpretations of the verses of the Qur'an. They thus unnecessarily weaken their case against the conservatives and hinder the modernization of law.

Before we go any further, it should be pointed out that the Family Laws Ordinance essentially seeks to make a compromise between the modernist and the conservative positions. We have already seen that it really does not declare the second marriage illegal even if it is enacted without the permission of the Arbitration Council; it merely penalizes the offender. Second, and more important, if our line of reasoning and the reasoning of the modernists in general has been correct, the law *logically* falls short of it. For the law makes the second polygamous marriage dependent on the permission of the Arbitration Council which, in turn, is dependent on the permission of the first wife. If we are right in concluding that the Qur'an categorically declares that one cannot do justice among several women, then to say that one may marry a second wife if the first wife permits this, is tantamount to saying that if the first wife *permits* injustice to be done her then that injustice may be legally allowed. That is to say, if the modernist contention is correct, then the Qur'an seems to prohibit polygamy. However, if the Prophet himself, with his unique charismatic authority, could effect only a certain measure of social change at a given time, a Muslim government of the present day cannot go beyond certain limits. To ignore these limits would be socially disruptive and, in fact, would lead to the creation of two different societies within one country. In view of the ultra-traditionalism of the conservatives of Pakistan, who, as we shall see, are in general much more conservative than the conservative *ulama* of the Middle East, this law is a reasonable compromise. It has already produced good results in several ways and has been appreciably effective in diminishing the incidence of polygamy since it came into operation.

Even as it is, the law has been subjected to very severe criticism. Among the arguments advanced by the conservatives there is one point which may appear to have some moral weight, and this should be considered. It has been alleged that restrictions on polygamy would tend to increase the incidence of extra-marital sexual relationships and attendant social problems. In this connection, the conservative has not been slow to point out that there is, relatively speaking, a high incidence of extra-marital relationships in western societies, which he attributes to the existence of monogamy. A little reflection, however, would show that this argument is quite mistaken. It is admitted that in certain sectors of present-day western society a loose sexual morality does exist, but this phenomenon has little to do with monogamy and is explained primarily by the impact of industrialization and its effects on the family structure. The developing societies of Asia must also prepare to deal with the rapid social changes that are taking place and will take place as a result of industrialization. But these facts cannot be construed as an argument for polygamy.

THE REGULATION OF DIVORCE

The second important point on which the ordinance seeks to regulate and reform Muslim family life is the question of divorce. The right of divorce for the wife, under certain circumstances, had already been recognized in the Muslim Marriages Dissolution Act referred to above. Traditionally this right had been given only to the man, who exercised it unilaterally. Certain schools of classical law, like Hanafi, allowed the woman to exercise this right provided she inserted such a condition in her initial marriage contract. The wife could, for example, get written into the marriage contract a proviso that should the husband decide to marry another wife then she, the first wife, could ask the court to free her of this marriage contract and grant her a divorce. This was known technically as *tafwid* or delegation of right. Section 8 of the Muslim Family Laws Ordinance extends this right: "Where the right to divorce has been duly delegated to the wife and she wishes to exercise that right or whether any of the parties to a marriage wishes to dissolve the marriage otherwise than by *Talaq* (i.e. the pronouncement of the divorce-formula by the husband), the provisions of section 7 shall, *mutatis mutandis* and, as far as possible, apply."

The right of women to divorce, which now exists in almost all the Muslim countries, has, nevertheless, been made the object of great controversy by the conservatives. In the Middle East their position has been undermined and weakened but in Pakistan and India it is quite strong. The conservatives put forward the argument that the husband is the wiser of the two spouses, and therefore exercises his privileges and rights more prudently. When the debate is based on this assertion, the conservative quotes the two following verses of the Qur'an: "Men are managers over women" (4:32), and "To women are rights equal to their duties according to good customs but men are a degree higher" (2:28). The Qur'an is not, of course, speaking of divorce in either of the two verses, but simply asserts a general superiority of man over woman. It is interesting to note that the modernist has usually tended to argue from the first half of the second verse ("and to women are rights equal to their duties") that men and women, with regard to their mutual rights and duties, are exactly on a parity. This in itself would be plausible but it would be difficult to shut one's eyes to the words "and men are a degree higher." The question, however, is whether the Qur'an really wishes to give the husband the exclusive right to divorce, and this is certainly neither stated nor implied in the two verses.

The principle of interpretation that we employed earlier, that in interpreting legal and socio-economic statements of the Qur'an, one must pay due regard to the actual conditions of the immediate society to which they were addressed, seems the only satisfactory way of answering this question. If we adopt this line of reasoning, we must simply note the historical fact that society at that time was dominated by men, and women were relegated to a markedly inferior position. But it would be difficult to argue from these verses that society must always remain like seventh-century Arabian society, or, for that matter, like medieval society in general. In any case, the conservative contention that man must monopolize the right of divorce is not borne out by any statement of the Qur'an. But as we noted before, the modernist in general, and particularly in this subcontinent, does not usually have recourse to this straightforward approach but concocts novel interpretations of the Qur'an which often conflict with both history and Arabic grammar.

Rejecting the traditional procedure under which an emphatic thrice-uttered pronouncement of divorce by the husband took immediate effect, the Family Laws Ordinance has laid down that the divorce must take place in three instalments, and further, that the divorce cannot be effective until the Arbitration Council has considered it. The law states: "Any man who wishes to divorce his wife shall, as soon as may be after the pronouncement of *Talaq* in any form whatsoever, give the chairman notice in writing of his having done so and shall supply a copy thereof to the wife. Whoever contravenes this provision shall be punishable with simple imprisonment for a term which may extend to one year or with fine which may extend to 5,000 rupees or with both." The law further provides that the divorce thus pronounced shall not be effective until the expiration of ninety days from the day on which notice is delivered to the chairman. Within thirty days of the receipt of notice, the chairman is to constitute an Arbitration Council for the purpose of bringing about a reconciliation between the parties, and the Arbitration Council shall take all steps to bring about such a reconciliation. The Arbitration Council is composed of the chairman, a representative of the wife and a representative of the husband.

In most Middle Eastern countries, similar arrangements have existed and have been accepted. But in Pakistan strong objections have been raised, chiefly on the ground that an "emphatic divorce" (when a man says to his wife "I divorce thee" three times) becomes immediately effective and that only in the case of a non-emphatic divorce can the husband retract his divorce. This question was also a subject of controversy among the medieval doctors of Islamic law. Historical evidence shows that, during the Prophet's time, graduated divorce was the general rule. It is said, however, that when, during the caliphate of the second caliph 'Umar, this practice was misused, 'Umar decreed that if a man uttered an emphatic divorce to his wife, the wife would be immediately divorced and freed from the marital bond. The abuse of the graduated divorce, we are told, arose from the abundance of foreign women present in Mecca and Medina after the rapid conquests during 'Umar's time. Many men began to torture their wives by pronouncing a divorce, keeping them in suspense for a year or so, then retracting the divorce—only to repeat the whole procedure a number of times. 'Umar's decree was a remedial measure to deal with this state of affairs; but it was taken over particularly by the Hanafi school of law and in time superseded the earlier practice of the Prophet's time. Indeed, on closer examination, the Hanafi law of divorce in general shows a certain inner consistency and gives the strong impression of having been devised to keep the moral bond as strong as possible. The adoption of 'Umar's decree was regarded as a deterrent to the irresponsible utterances of divorce. Unfortunately, in practice it defeated its purpose, because a man in a fit of temper does not seriously consider the consequences of the severance of the marital bond. This fact, incidentally, is a grave comment on the conservative contention that man in general is more prudent and considerate, and will exercise his right with moderation. In fact, unilateral hasty divorce on the part of the husband has been one of the major social ills of Muslim society.

The conservatives have also taken exception to the bringing of divorce cases before a tribunal. They say that bringing such personal affairs before an open tribunal, instead of settling differences in private, is a blind following of western practices which will have a demoralizing effect on family life. It must be admitted that nobody has yet found the panacea for the ills that beset this most frail and sensitive area of human relationships. It is undoubtedly true that the publicity connected with such cases is not a good thing, and, if one could prevent it, it would save both embarrassment and a certain amount of sensationalism and demoralization that undoubtedly occurs. For one thing, however, the tribunal envisaged is not exactly a public body; the only person who does not belong to the two families is the chairman. It may also be argued that the fear of going before a tribunal may act as a potent deterrent to the couple from acting irresponsibly. The conservative may also be asked whether the publicity that is bound to accrue in such cases is really worse than the tyranny to which women have been subjected in private in traditional Muslim society. Finally, if grave injustices are committed, is it not better to bring them to the public eye?

Turning to the third area of family law reform, the ordinance provides for the compulsory registration of marriages; the penalty for failure to comply with this provision is fine or imprisonment or both. Even this provision, which is essential in order to reduce the chaos which has arisen from non-registration of marriages, has been criticized almost universally by the conservatives. The critics agree that the registration of marriages is desirable, but they have generally urged that, instead of penalizing non-compliance, it would be sufficient not to recognize unregistered marriages for the purpose of certain judicial procedures. The inadequacy of this kind of provision is obvious, although we do not deny its effectiveness in the very long run. However, if a large number of marriages do remain unregistered and many such cases subsequently appear before the courts, it would be very difficult for the courts to deny them recognition. The criticism of this innocuous provision reveals the intensity of the conservative opposition to the ordinance, without any reference to the criterion of reasonableness.

THE RIGHT OF INHERITANCE

The next major problem to which the ordinance addresses itself is that of providing a share for orphan grandchildren from the inheritance of their grandfather, equivalent to the share the father would have received had he been alive. This question has exercised the minds and spirits of legal modernists for a long time. According to the classical Muslim *fiqh*, if a grandfather dies, the inheritance is divided among his living sons and daughters; the children of any already deceased son or daughter are deprived of inheritance. The principle on which the classical law is based states: "A nearer in kinship excludes the remoter from the inheritance." It is most probably the case that this was the practice in pre-Islamic Arabia; but in a tribal society the elders of the tribe, or the tribe as a whole, are duty bound to look after the interests of the less privileged. In the medieval patriarchal system the uncles took upon themselves the care and upbringing of the child thus excluded from the inheritance of his grandfather. In modern times, however, the situation is quite different and becomes more acute every day, because of the increasing disinclination on the part of uncles to assume responsibility for their deprived nephews.

The Egyptian law, in order to solve this problem, provides that the grandfather must make a will in favor of the children of his deceased sons or daughters comparable to the shares these would have received if they had been alive. In case of non-execution of such a will by the grandfather, the Egyptian law presumes the existence of such a will and assigns shares to the children of the deceased sons and daughters. The Egyptian law had recourse to this particular solution because of a general principle of wills in the Qur'an which says: "It is incumbent upon you—when death visits any one of you and he leaves property—to make a will in favor of your parents and other relations according to good custom; this is due upon those who fear God" (2:180). The Egyptians thought that in this way they would produce an "Islamic" solution to the difficulty without having recourse to the introduction of a new element into the inheritance principles of classical Muslim *fiqh*. The main difficulty with such a law, however, is that if a grandfather, knowing full well the plight of his grandchildren if he does not provide for them through a will, still does not do so, how can one establish the presumption of a will?

The Family Laws Ordinance of Pakistan simply states: "In the event of the death of any son or daughter of the *propositus* before the opening of succession, the children of such son or daughter, if any, living at the time the succession opens, shall *per stirpes* receive a share equivalent to the share each such son or daughter, as the case may be, would have received if alive." This clause does not deny the principle of the classical Muslim law that "the nearer excludes the remoter." But it should be pointed out that this clause does introduce a new element (which supervenes on the old principle), namely, the principle of inheritance by representation or *per stirpes*. If this principle is accepted it will entail further necessary adjustments in the classical Islamic law of inheritance, even though the ordinance itself only envisages the welfare of the orphan grandchildren. Suppose there are two brothers, each having children, and that one brother dies before the other. Now, when the second brother also dies, according to the new principle, his nephews who are children of his predeceased brother, would also be entitled to their share of inheritance equivalent to the share their father would have got, as a brother, if he were alive. In the classical Muslim law, however, such nephews are debarred from inheritance. This is only one example; a host of changes will be necessitated by the acceptance of the principle of *per stirpes*.

The exponents of the ordinance, however, bring forward another argument which, if accepted, might limit the change only to the orphan grandchildren. This argument is based on the contention that just as the Quranic term "father" includes not only the immediate father but the grandfather and all the predecessors in the ascending series, so does the term "children" or "sons" include not only the immediate children but also the grandchildren. Therefore, what a deceased son would have received from the share of his father is now due to his immediate children. This would certainly limit the inheritance share to the orphan grandchildren, although it is not unlikely that other, still unforeseen, problems will arise in the operation of the law. Secondly, it should be pointed out that, if this interpretation is accepted, the principle of representation or *per stirpes* cannot be invoked.

Some exponents of the ordinance have recourse to an additional argument which, however, is more dubious. They say that the ordinance does not really accept any new principle and that it works wholly within the framework of the classical principle of the exclusion of the remoter by the nearer. According to this contention, a son excludes *his own* children from the inheritance of his father because he is nearer to his father than are his children. But the moment he is removed by death, there is no longer anyone to exclude the grandchildren from the inheritance of the grandfather. It is obvious, however, that the classical law does not only say that a son is nearer to his father than are his own children, but that he is nearer to his father than all the grandchildren from all sons and daughters of his father. It should further be pointed out that this contention is opposed to the argument that the term "children" includes not only the immediate sons and daughters but equally the grandchildren in the descending order, and both arguments cannot be invoked at the same time.

Some of the criticisms advanced against this measure by the conservatives constitute one of the greatest moral absurdities in the ethical history of man. It has been said, for example, that if the grandfather does not look after the interests of his own grandchildren, the orphans should be considered like those suffering from a natural affliction just like any other orphans whose father died *in poverty*. The fact of the matter is that there are few themes more emphasized in the Qur'an than the welfare of orphans and the poor in general. The Qur'an says, for example: ". . . and give to the orphans their properties and do not replace their good property by a bad one and do not mix their wealth and property with your own; this is, indeed, a grave sin." (4:2). What is more, the Qur'an says that if, on the opening of a succession, relatives come who are not entitled to a share in the inheritance but are orphans or poor people in general they must be given some substantial help. The Qur'an goes on *to* say: "Let people consider that if they were to leave behind themselves weak and unprotected children, how they would fear for them; let them, then, fear God and speak well" (4:8-9). Would it not then be a grave anomaly if a religion which has bestowed so much attention upon the welfare of orphans in general were to leave the orphan grandchildren of a rich grandfather in poverty while their uncles and cousins enjoyed the very same property?

Another criticism, while conceding the necessity of making some arrangements for orphan grandchildren, says that Pakistan should follow the Egyptian law in this respect and resort to compulsory will. We have already pointed out one difficulty with regard to this solution, but a more fundamental problem, from the Quranic point of view, may be noted. The Quranic verse asks people to make wills in favor of "their relatives," and has, therefore, a general application if it is to be enforced by law. Its application, therefore, cannot be restricted to the grandfather vis-à-vis a grandchild. All relatives must make compulsory wills in favor of all relatives, unless some principle of specification can be introduced. The Pakistani law is against no provision of the Qur'an and the Sunnah and, in fact, fulfils a very fundamental socio-moral requirement of Islam in a forthright and direct manner.

OBSTACLES TO ISLAMIC RENEWAL

As the foregoing exposition has indicated, the conservatives in Pakistan are generally uncompromisingly conservative. The debates which have long ceased in the Middle East and the questions which are taken to have been settled in favor of some kind of modernist interpretation there are still heatedly pursued in Pakistan. There are several reasons for this. First, the fact that the Muslims have always been a minority in the subcontinent compelled them to emphasize and cling tenaciously to relatively external expressions of the faith, expressions which are more or less formal, at the expense of inner growth. The inner growth has no doubt also occurred, and it is, after all, this subcontinent which has produced a thinker like Dr. Muhammad Iqbal. Yet the importance of this fact in our history cannot be minimized.

Second, the academic life of our religious seminaries, which are run on traditional lines, has been rather inferior as compared to certain centers in the Middle East such as al-Azhar and even the Zaytunah in Tunis. The quality of our *ulama* in general, despite certain exceptional men who have arisen now and again, is generally poorer than that of the Middle Eastern *ulama* in point of scholarship. In Pakistan, academic life was still further impoverished after partition, because whatever worthwhile institutions of Islamic learning there were in the subcontinent are now located in India, and we had to start from scratch, particularly in West Pakistan. Third, the Middle Eastern countries are in more direct and frequent contact with Europe, and this influence has naturally had some effect on the development of the *ulama* also. Lastly, and as a major consequence of the preceding factor, in Egypt a man like Shaikh Muhammad Abduh (d. 1905) arose from the ranks of the *ulama* and exerted a powerful influence, despite initial opposition, on subsequent orthodox developments in the Middle East. In this subcontinent, however, people who have played a prominent role in introducing modernist thinking to Islam have been outside the ranks of the *ulama* and, although they have left a tremendous legacy to the Muslim community as a whole, have not been able to influence the custodians of the *shari‘ah* to any large extent.

CHAPTER 20

ISLAM AS A FACTOR IN PAKISTAN'S FOREIGN POLICY

SISIR GUPTA

PAKISTAN ACQUIRED her international personality in August 1947 with relatively few emotional or intellectual international commitments.[1] Unlike the Indian National Congress, the Muslim League had remained largely silent and had never committed itself on such issues as Spain and China, Abyssinia and Czechoslovakia, fascism and communism. Several reasons can be adduced for this relative absence of an international orientation within the Muslim League. In the first place, the period between the League's demand for a sovereign state and its coming into being was extremely brief and was a time of rather simplified world politics, namely, war. Second, even during these years there was little certainty about the nature and form in which the Muslim demand would be fulfilled in the future constitutional setup in India. Third, the Muslim League's internal task was in a sense more difficult and absorbing than that of the Congress. In a period of growing cynicism about religion in the world as a whole, the chances of the League's success depended precisely on keeping up such loyalties. Fourth, there was no internationally oriented personality in the higher echelons of the Muslim League. Fifth, articulate left-wing opinion which might have related internal and international developments was either non-existent or silent in the League. Lastly, the League had a somewhat unique role within the general pattern of developments in Asia—to emphasize the internal problems of the region rather than the external problems that the Asian countries faced in common. It is interesting to note that when the Indian Council of World Affairs organized the first Asian Relations Conference in New Delhi in 1947, the League declined to attend it on the ground that it was "a thinly disguised attempt on the part of the Hindu Congress to boost itself politically as the prospective leader of Asian peoples."[2]

Sisir Gupta is research secretary at the Indian Council of World Affairs, New Delhi.

[1] This chapter, in a slightly different form, was published originally in *India Quarterly*, July-September, 1962.

[2] Quoted in Werner Levi, *Free India in Asia*, University of Minnesota Press, Minneapolis, 1952, p. 38.

Against this general lack of a foreign affairs orientation, however, must be noted the fact of the historical sympathy and interest of the Muslims of India for other Muslim countries of West Asia and North Africa. In the decades following the Indian Mutiny which ended in the smashing of the archaic symbols of India's freedom and of the prospects of a return to the *ancien regime*, there was a search among the Indian elites for past glory and greatness. In this, the immediate past was overlooked; the Hindus looked back for psychological sustenance to Sanskrit and ancient Indian culture and the Muslims to the early Islamic period of West Asian history.[3] It is interesting to note the comment of a Muslim historian: "While we have historical literature by Bengali Muslims on Islam, Arabia, Egypt, Turkey, Afghanistan, etc. we have very few works from Muslims on Bengal or India."[4]

Like many other aspects of Muslim life this reflected the unique social structure that the Indian Muslims had evolved at the time. The old aristocratic and conservative attitudes persisted in isolation from the new trends which the western impact on India had created.[5] Sir Syed Ahmad Khan attempted to correct this outward orientation of the Muslims; he was openly opposed to any allegiance to the Turkish Khilafat,[6] and stated that Indian Muslims had little reason to get excited if the British government attacked Afghanistan.[7] However, once the grip of this Aligarh outlook loosened and the Indian Muslims discovered the need and possibility of participating in Indian politics, the pan-Islamic attitude reasserted itself. Muslim leaders within the Indian National Congress often expressed their emotional attachment to other Muslim peoples of West Asia. In 1923, Abul Kalam Azad in his presidential address to the Congress declared: "India must make common cause with the universal struggles of Eastern nations to shake off the fetters of slavery 'and should assure Egypt, Syria, Palestine and Morocco of her sympathy with their struggle."[8] Mohammed Ali, presiding over the Congress in 1926, commended the idea of an Eastern Federation.[9] The Khilafat Movement was the organized expression of such sentiments.

Interestingly, there was a difference between these typical Muslim

---

[3] Jawaharlal Nehru, *The Discovery of India*, Signet Press, Calcutta, 1946, p. 364.
[4] A. R. Mallick, "Modern Historical Writing in Bengali," *Historians of India, Pakistan and Ceylon*, ed. C. H. Philips, Oxford University Press, London, 1961, pp. 446-460.
[5] Nehru, pp. 363-367.   [6] *Ibid.*, p. 367.
[7] Nehru, *Autobiography*, Bodley Head, London, 1936, p. 462.
[8] Quoted in Levi, p. 22.
[9] Bimla Prasad, *The Origins of Indian Foreign Policy*, Bookland, Calcutta, 1960, p. 72.

sentiments and the over-all Congress outlook; this was dramatically illustrated by the Congress decision to alter the terms of its support to West Asian countries between 1922 and 1923. In 1922 the Congress had asked not only for the restoration of Turkey's sovereign rights but also for her guardianship of the world of Islam; in 1923, it dropped all reference to Islam and congratulated the Turkish people on their success, which was "a presage of the freedom of all nations of the East." Again in 1922, the Congress had wanted all mandated territories to be freed from non-Muslim control; in 1923, it asked for removal of all alien control.[10] While the Muslim leaders in the Congress stressed the need for an Eastern Federation, with India as its easternmost unit, the non-Muslim Congressmen pleaded for a large Asian Federation. It was only Dr. Ansari, among the Congress Muslim leaders, who envisaged an Asian Federation, adding that India was fortunately placed in that a part of its population had affinities with the West Asian countries and another part with the East Asian ones.[11]

The Muslim League itself had little to do with such ideas at this stage and, with the exception of Iqbal, none of its leaders expressed an open preference for any pan-Islamic grouping. The League, however, did develop a broad sympathy for Muslim causes in the world. In December 1924, the League condemned British actions in Egypt; in January 1926, it protested against the mandate system; in 1929, sympathy was expressed for King Amanullah of Afghanistan; in 1931, Italy was condemned for her atrocities in Tripoli; in 1933, it urged the scrapping of the Balfour Declaration and protested against British policy in Palestine. In 1937 Jinnah said: "May I point out to the British government that this question of Palestine, if not fairly and squarely met, boldy and courageously decided, is going to be the turning point in the history of the British Empire."[12] In 1938, the League expressed its confidence in the Grand Mufti; in 1939, the League was represented in the Palestine Conference at Cairo by Choudhury Khaliquzzaman. In 1941, the League adopted the following resolution after Allied troops had moved into Iran and Iraq to depose pro-Nazi governments: "The Mussalmans of India are greatly perturbed at and view with alarm the military occupation of certain Muslim states in the Near East by Great Britain and her allies. The Working Committee, therefore, urge upon the British government and her allies to declare unequivocally that the sovereignty and inde-

10 *Ibid.*, p. 69.   11 *Ibid.*, p. 76.
12 M. Ahmad, *Pakistan and the Middle East*, Kitabi Markaz, Karachi, 1948, p. 162.

pendence of those Muslim states will be immediately restored as soon as circumstances permit and that the pernicious system of mandates and the creation of zones of influence for European powers will not be resorted to." A later resolution on Iran was more strongly worded: "The Working Committee learnt with dismay the news of the unprovoked aggression against Iran by Great Britain and Russia and warn the Allies that this action will still more complicate the Near Eastern situation and alienate the sympathies of Muslim India and create bitterness in their hearts, which will result in the withdrawal of every help by them to the Allied cause."[13] In 1943 the League adopted three other resolutions: one urging the freedom of Muslim colonies of Italy; the second, asking for the abolition of mandates; and the third, condemning the French action in Lebanon.[14]

An event in the Muslim League session of 1941, however, illustrated, more than did these resolutions, the intensity of Indian Muslim feeling for the peoples of West Asia. The loyalist premier of the Punjab, Sir Sikander Hayat Khan, attempted to stop the League from adopting a resolution on Iran; he stated that Reza Shah was pro-Nazi and disliked by the people of Iran. He was hooted in the meeting and prolonged shouts applauded the cause of Reza Shah.[15]

In the Muslim League's emphasis on Muslim causes in the world, two elements may be noted: one, the broad anti-imperialist urge of all the colonial peoples at this stage; and two, the need and urgency of cultivating a "Muslim" sense of belonging among the adherents of the organization. There was a degree of contradiction in this dual posture, and the attitude of other Muslim countries toward the Muslim League was not one of great enthusiasm. In the 1941 session of the League, the Raja of Mahmudabad complained that no Muslim outside India had expressed any sympathy with Indian Muslims and yet they were pouring money and blood into support of the non-Indian Muslims.[16] A Pakistani author complained in 1948: "When Indian Muslims under severe handicaps were striving to establish Pakistan, they received no encouragement from the Middle Eastern Powers. Some of the Arab dignitaries, led away by the false mischievous propaganda of the enemies of Islam, even condemned the creation of Pakistan. The isolationist stand taken by Kemalist Turkey, to which Indian Muslims had pinned great hopes, made their disappointment all the more acute."[17] Keith Callard has referred to the same phenomenon in different terms: "For many Muslims outside it

13 *Ibid.*, pp. 165-166.   14 *Ibid.*, p. 167.
15 *Indian Annual Register*, 1941, II.
16 *Ibid.*   17 Ahmad, p. 207.

has been more important to align Asians and Africans against the colonial powers than to defend Muslim causes against non-Muslims. The Congress argument that specifically Muslim demands hampered national independence found wide acceptance in other Asian and Middle Eastern countries."[18]

Note must also be taken of the unique nature of the provinciality of the Indian Muslims, inasmuch as it reflected no existing inferiority of theirs but a situation of the distant past. In the Muslim world the Indian Muslim was among the most advanced; but his provinciality in relation to highly romanticized but archaic societies like Saudi Arabia impeded the much-needed exposure to the impact of the West and an understanding of the modern realities of world politics.

PAKISTAN, INDIA, AND THE WORLD

It was with this commitment of support for Muslim causes that Pakistan was born. In conducting her foreign policy, however, the one single factor of overriding consequence has been her relations with India.[19] Recent Pakistani publications on foreign policy have frankly accepted this. In *Pakistan and the United Nations*, written on behalf of a high-level study group, Sarwar Hasan says: "Robert Schuman, former prime minister of France, once observed that since 1871 the foreign policy of his country had been continuously dominated by one main preoccupation, that of ensuring her security and independence from her neighbor, Germany. Unfortunately, the foreign policy of Pakistan has in a similar manner been dominated by considerations of security and independence from its neighbor, India."[20] It is of some significance that, since 1956, the military alignments of Pakistan have been officially explained in terms of threats from India, not from any other source. Suhrawardy, when prime minister, defended Pakistan's alliances in these terms: "Now if there are some among you who hold that it is better for us to remain friendless and alone, or who think that there is no danger, or if the danger comes it will be a good thing to be absorbed by India, then they should not accept the policy which I am now laying down."[21] Explaining his policy of alignment to an Indonesian audience at Bandung in December 1960, President Ayub said: "Please remember that

[18] Keith Callard, *Pakistan: A Political Study*, Allen and Unwin, London, 1957, p. 314.

[19] *Ibid.*, p. 313.

[20] K. Sarwar Hasan, *Pakistan and the United Nations*, Manhattan, New York, 1960, p. 50.

[21] *Prime Minister's Statement on Foreign Policy*, December 9, 1956, Government of Pakistan, Karachi, 1957.

it is an Asian country which has been oppressing us and continues to oppress us."[22] Russia and China were not the possible enemies that Pakistan feared; Suhrawardy said in 1957: "I seek the friendship of China. I am not isolated. I feel perfectly certain that when the crucial time comes, China will come to our assistance. It has already done so. . . . When I have nothing against Russia and against China, and have no desire to be against them, why should they be against us."[23] In 1963, agreements were signed regarding the border between China and Pakistan.

That India is the major factor in Pakistan's foreign policy is not due merely to the disputes which bedevil their mutual relations, but also to the more basic factors involved in the making of attitudes. Keith Callard pointed out that problems of relations with India have "dominated foreign affairs, defense and economic policy and have lain behind many of the moves of internal politics." He went on to state: "In large measure Pakistani feeling toward India has been a continuation of the political struggle before partition. . . . The idea that a country has a foreign enemy is easy for the mass of the people to understand, and it also provides a powerful stimulus to unity. For Pakistan, India has filled this role."[24]

This internal aspect apart, issues of prestige have also been important. "Mr. Jinnah had never agreed to any constitutional formula which would have denoted a lesser status for the Muslim League. India contained two nations: one sovereign nation is the equal of any other sovereign nation. . . . Many political leaders and most of the articulate section of the population have reacted with emotional intensity to any suggestion of Indian superiority in any field. . . . The degree of passion has been heightened by the feeling, largely justified, that on every matter on which the real interests of the two nations have come into conflict, India has contrived to emerge victorious."[25]

It is against this background of Pakistan's foreign policy and attitudes that developments in relation to the Muslim world have to be viewed. On the morrow of its freedom, Pakistan felt the pressing need of attracting sympathy and attention from other peoples of the world. It was symbolic of Pakistan's difficulties that the United Nations legal department decided that while independent India continued as a member state, Pakistan had to apply for membership in the United Nations. What heightened this sense of helplessness was the fact that

---

[22] *Asian Recorder*, 1960, p. 3748.
[23] *Winding up of Foreign Policy Debates*, Government of Pakistan, Karachi, 1957.
[24] Callard, p. 17.   [25] *Ibid.*, p. 304.

the Commonwealth failed to give any help to Pakistan in the Kashmir dispute. In 1949, Liaquat Ali said in London: "Pakistan must not be taken for granted; Pakistan is not a camp-follower of the Commonwealth."[26] *Dawn* demanded in an editorial at this time: "British elements should be eliminated from civilian positions and from those positions in the armed forces for which Pakistani substitutes can be found. Even for those positions in which foreigners must be appointed, because suitable Pakistani personnel are lacking, search should first be made outside the British Isles."[27] As for others, "Russia was an enemy of the empires of Western Europe, but had shown no enthusiasm for Pakistan as a separate unit";[28] "China was still under Chiang Kai-shek—a personal friend of Nehru and an admirer of the Congress"; the United States "knew and sympathized much more with the land of Gandhi and Nehru than with that of Jinnah."[29]

Suggestive of Pakistan's plight was the incident of the Moscow invitation. The Truman administration invited Nehru to visit the United States in 1949, and the Pakistan prime minister secured an invitation from Moscow soon afterwards. However, the visit never came off because, it is said, the Soviet government did not reply to the Pakistani prime minister's communication asking for a date. *Newsweek* reported on December 21, 1949: "After several weeks of unsuccessful attempts, Liaquat Ali Khan gave up in disgust and announced that it would not be possible for him to make a trip. No one in Karachi has any idea why Moscow failed to carry through its invitation."

As Callard noted: "In the first appraisal of her position among the community of self-governing nations, Pakistan could find no single country which could be counted as an unfailing friend and ally willing to lend aid and comfort in time of need."[30] In this bleak situation, Islam appeared to Pakistan to offer the only bond in the name of which she could appeal for other nations' support.

Apart from this inevitable search for friends was the continued need to cultivate a distinctive sense of belonging in a country which was cut out of a natural historical, geographical and cultural unit. Also important was the urgency of stressing the continued difference with India. Maintaining that Pakistan had no other security against the natural tendency of one government to absorb another in a topographical basin, Aslam Siddiqui says: "To escape the consequences of this axiomatic development Pakistan has to put up some shield.

26 *Dawn*, May 14, 1949. 27 *Ibid.*, May 8, 1949.
28 Callard, p. 303. 29 *Loc.cit.* 30 *Loc.cit.*

That shield obviously is religion, on the basis of which partition of the Indo-Pakistani subcontinent took place."[31]

THE SEARCH FOR MUSLIM UNITY

There was a large measure of confidence in Pakistan, immediately after partition, that the Muslim countries of the world would draw closer and, indeed, might move toward a pan-Islamic grouping of nations. Muslim unity, according to this view, was the natural corollary of a renewed sense of Islamic identity; the creation of Pakistan was itself a symbol of this postwar phenomenon. A. B. Rajput wrote in his book on the Muslim League: "Thus with the birth of Pakistan the hope of pan-Islamic unity and brotherhood brightened afresh among the Islamic states of Asia."[32] Another author, M. Ahmad, wrote in the same year: "The younger generation of the Arab leaders consider the Arab League as the authentic answer to their long-held and mounting desire for the unification of Muslim states which possess the common bond of the Muslim religion and the urge for complete freedom. The fact is that even without the Caliphate, a more powerful idea of Islamic solidarity has originated."[33] It is interesting to note the terms in which this solidarity was sought by Pakistani intellectuals. To quote Ahmad: "A real agreement among these potential allies can alone ward off the menace of Hindu, Russian, American and British imperialisms. The Muslim state or states which may be inhibited from making a common cause in the fatuous hope that these menacing imperialisms will attack others and leave them in peace, will be left in isolation and condemned to annihilation."[34]

While such ideas were germinating in some minds even in 1948, concerted attempts for Muslim unity were made only during 1949 after the prime minister's statement in London that Muslim nations between Cairo and Karachi could play an important role between the two Power blocs. On his way home from London in May 1949, he stopped in Cairo, Baghdad and Teheran, and in his speeches stressed the Islamic ideals of Pakistan: "In the laboratory of Pakistan we are experimenting with the principles and ideals of Islam and hope to put before the world a progressive code of life."[35] In Teheran he said: "My hope for the future is that Iran and Pakistan will be like one soul in two bodies."[36] Earlier, an organization called the Motamar-e-Alam-e-Islam (Muslim World Conference) had started func-

---

[31] Aslam Siddiqui, *Pakistan Seeks Security*, Longmans, Lahore, 1960, p. 17.
[32] A. B. Rajput, *The Muslim League*, Lahore, 1948, p. 204.
[33] Ahmad, pp. 205-206.   [34] *Ibid.*, p. 213.
[35] Siddiqui, p. 88.   [36] *Loc.cit.*

tioning in Karachi; in February 1949 its first session was attended by delegates from nineteen Muslim countries. On his return from London, Liaquat Ali made moves for a conference at the governmental level, but the Arab and non-Arab countries did not show much interest.[37]

Their lack of interest became more evident when an exploratory mission by Choudhury Khaliquzzaman, the then president of the Muslim League, ended in a fiasco. The Pakistan leader had earlier propagated his ideas of an "Islamistan" in a pamphlet on the subject,[38] and in 1949 had visited the West Asian countries and London in order to promote the idea. Although ostensibly concerned only with a people-to-people campaign for an Islamic bloc, the League leader exceeded his brief and canvassed for a security pact with British support. The reactions in Arab countries to his mission were unfavorable, if not hostile. *Dawn*, in an editorial, "Caution Islamistan," wrote: "His approach was to have been on a people-to-people basis, but within a few days of his tour he seems to have directed attention to the governments of the countries that he visited rather than to their peoples. . . . He set out to sell the idea to Muslims alone, but if we are not mistaken he went to London to discuss the issue with the Commonwealth Relations Office and the Foreign Office of the British government. . . . Furthermore, the idea of getting together of the peoples of the various countries, it appears, has developed into the suggestion of a security pact on the enlarged pattern of the pact agreed upon by the Arab League countries . . . even if such a security pact were practicable, apart from the question of being desirable in the present world context, it will have to be underwritten militarily as well as politically by certain non-Muslim foreign powers. . . . In fact . . . he has been attempting . . . to enlist the active support of those foreign powers . . . [this] naturally prompts some quarters to ask: Security against whom?"[39]

While the overtly political attempts at pan-Islamic integration failed, an International Islamic Economic Conference was held in Karachi in November 1949 under non-official auspices. At the conference, the prime minister of Pakistan said in his inaugural address: "Pakistan has one and only one ambition—to serve Islam and humanity. . . . We all belong to the great brotherhood of Islam. Islam alone can solve some of the problems facing the world today."[40] Finance Minister Ghulam Muhammed envisaged Islamic unity and coopera-

[37] *Loc.cit.*
[38] W. C. Smith, *Islam in Modern History*, Mentor, New York, 1959, p. 88 n.
[39] *Dawn*, November 15, 1949.   [40] *Ibid.*, November 26, 1949.

tion leading to the creation of a third bloc of nations. He held: "Besides being united in a common faith, a common outlook and a common way of life, we form also a geographic unity." More interesting than this stereotyped appeal for unity was the ideological basis on which coming together was sought at this time: "We are now under pressure from two different ideologies, both striving to gain our allegiance. We are told that there are only two ideologies; you must accept one and repudiate the other. . . . One purpose of convening this conference is to grapple with this dilemma and determine objectively and frankly whether we are constrained to subscribe to the one or the other." Ghulam Muhammed continued and gave his answer: "We cannot put implicit faith in the western democratic system nor can we subscribe to communism, although there are some aspects of this vast and comprehensive experiment which we must appreciate. . . . Islamic society has never been subjected to the stress and strains of class war and morbid hatred of the rich has never been one of its characteristics. . . . Islam is the golden mean between these two extremes; it is a non-violent method of rectifying unsocial and detrimental inequalities."[41] The conference ended with high hopes of regional economic cooperation among Muslim nations as a prelude to political integration.

The second Motamar Conference in Karachi held in February 1951 also raised high hopes of Muslim unity. Delegates came from all countries containing Muslims, including the People's Republic of China but excluding the USSR and India; the Grand Mufti of Jerusalem presided over the conference. In the Muslim Women's Session, Begum Liaquat Ali stressed the need for bringing up children on Islamic principles. In the general conference the prime minister of Pakistan set the political tone: "The underlying idea of the movement for the achievement of Pakistan was . . . to secure a territory, however limited, where the Islamic ideology and way of life could be practiced and demonstrated to the world. A cardinal feature of this ideology is to make Muslim brotherhood a living reality. It is therefore part of the mission which Pakistan has set before itself to do everything in its power to promote closer fellowship and cooperation between Muslim countries. . . . The world is in sore need of light. I have no doubt that light can be provided by Islam."[42] The Grand Mufti endorsed this call for unity and asked for the creation of a Muslim bloc, cooperating in matters of culture, economics, politics and defense. Another organization, the Muslim Peoples' Organization,

[41] *Loc.cit.*
[42] *Dawn*, February 10, 1951.

held a conference in early 1952, again attended by delegates from a number of Muslim countries.

All three organizations—the International Islamic Economic Conference, the Motamar-e-Alam-e-Islam and the Muslim Peoples' Organization—had their headquarters in Karachi and maintained permanent secretariats there. These pan-Islamic organizations reflected the internal political groupings within Pakistan: "One member of the Pakistan cabinet is the founder-president of the International Islamic Economic Conference; another member of the same cabinet is, we believe less officially, closely associated with the Motamar, and the former head of Pakistan's national political organization is bestowing his foster care on the embryonic Muslim Peoples' Organization."[43] The references are to Ghulam Muhammed, Fazlur Rahman and Khaliquzzaman—a Punjabi, a Bengali and a Hindustani—and the involvement of internal politics with this aspect of foreign policy becomes obvious. A certain degree of pan-Islamism had become at this stage the *sine qua non* for furthering political ambitions.

It should be noted that none of the conferences held in Pakistan was official or inter-governmental. Attempts made in 1949 and 1952 to hold official Islamic conferences failed. In a press conference on May 2, 1952, Foreign Minister Zafrullah tried to remove some of the fears and apprehensions in the minds of other governments. The points he made, noted below, illustrate the nature of the criticism heard elsewhere of Pakistan's efforts for Islamic solidarity. Zafrullah said: "In some quarters it has been said that this is an attempt by Pakistan to destroy their League. This is an attempt by Pakistan to lead the Muslim world. This is to restrict cooperation among the Asian and African states. Every one of these and similar other assertions, if they are not due to misunderstanding and misconception, are deliberate falsehoods by mischievous people. . . . It is also said that there is some game Pakistan wants to play; that it desires the states whom it wants to invite to participate in this system so that they should pull Pakistani chestnuts out of the fire. If such an idea exists I wish to completely refute it." A third plank of the criticism was not refuted by the foreign minister but only referred to: "It has become a fashion to charge Pakistan of being a theocratic state. But why is it that the Muslims, at least a greater part of them, claim that the world can be led back to human happiness and prosperity through Islam? Why do we make that claim? Why is it that the claim is not made by other communities on behalf of their faiths? . . . There must be something in that." Finally, the foreign minister made one more

43 *Ibid.*, February 9, 1951.

438

appeal to the Islamic antipathy to the West: "Our emotions are today held in greater bondage to the West than before independence. . . . We are sinking deeper and deeper into intellectual slavery."[44]

Despite the foreign minister's earnest explanation that Pakistan had no motive in calling the conference except to serve humanity and Islam, the other Muslim countries still held back and the government conference failed to materialize.

Subsequently Islamic conferences did take place in Pakistan, but they evoked less and less enthusiasm. In April 1954 Karachi was the venue for a third session of the International Islamic Economic Conference. It confined itself to purely economic affairs;[45] "after this it became dormant and its activities have remained confined to Pakistan."[46] In 1957, Lahore was the venue for an Islamic Colloquium; there was little political significance attached to it and many of the participants were western scholars on Islam. An International Assembly of Muslim Youth was started in Karachi in 1955; the chief organizer of the association was the secretary of the Motamar. But the high pitch of Islamic enthusiasm of the 1949-1952 period was not reached again. This was the period of Muslim League rule, beginning after the death of Jinnah in September 1948—Jinnah had little enthusiasm for pan-Islam—and ending in 1953 with the dismissal of Nazimuddin, when the civil servants virtually took over the government.

DISILLUSIONMENT WITH THE ARABS

It became clear at this time that the realities of the Muslim world were different from those expected by Pakistan, and the enthusiasm for pan-Islamism began to decline. Two days after the foreign minister's press conference in May 1952, *Dawn* wrote: "The time has come for Pakistan's intelligentsia to realize that Pakistan is not adding to its prestige in the international field by running after certain other countries which are economically and otherwise in a far less stable position than Pakistan itself and which can really be of little help to us. If we concentrate on building up our resources and our strength . . . the day will come when many will be candidates for our friendship without our chasing them. Let us not forget that we in Pakistan constitute a Muslim world in ourselves. We say to our nation: give up sloganism and be realists."[47]

More important in this connection was the political transformation that was now under way in Western Asia. The Egyptian Revolution of 1952 opened up entirely new dimensions of Arab aspiration and

44 *Ibid.*, May 3, 1952.   45 *Ibid.*, April 26, 1954.
46 Siddiqui, p. 90.   47 *Dawn*, May 4, 1952.

paved the way for further secularization of Arab politics. It brought to the fore the dormant contradictions between the interests of West Asian and Western European countries, of which Mossadeq's nationalization of the Anglo-Iranian Oil Company in 1951 was a forerunner.

What prevented Pakistan's fuller participation in this new milieu was her alliance with the western powers, which began to take shape about this time. There are two views of the development of this alignment. The one held by most Pakistanis is that after trying to maintain a neutralist position for five years, Pakistan discovered the need for strong allies against India, and joined the United States in defense pacts. The other view is the one held by some American observers (e.g. Selig Harrison) and by some Indians, that Pakistan was always anxious to do so and it was the United States which now had an administration which welcomed Pakistan. In fact, Harrison traces the story further back.[48] In any event, 1952-1953 marked the turning point in Pakistan's foreign policy: "In 1953 two changes took place. In the United States, Eisenhower was installed as president with John Foster Dulles as secretary of state; in Pakistan, Ghulam Muhammed dismissed Nazimuddin and replaced him by Prime Minister Mohammed Ali, formerly ambassador to Washington. Mr. Dulles wanted pacts; Mohammed Ali liked the Americans. Pakistan wanted money and arms."[49]

Developments followed in quick succession. In February 1954, Pakistan accepted military aid from the United States, in September 1954 she joined the Southeast Asia Treaty Organization and in September 1955 the Baghdad Pact.

The latter pact projected Pakistan in West Asia into a role entirely different from that envisaged earlier by the various Islamic conferences, namely a third force, a golden mean between capitalism and communism. India vigorously criticized the pact, as did Egypt, Syria, Jordan and Saudi Arabia. It was interpreted in these countries as an anti-Arab move, an extension of western domination and one designed to divide the Arabs. Typical of the criticism is the following broadcast from Radio Mecca: "Is it, therefore, possible for any person to believe that an Islamic state, such as that of Pakistan, should accede to those who have joined hands with Zionist Jews. . . . Whatever may be the case, Pakistan, a country so dear to us and to other Arab countries, cannot be expected to put her hand in the hands of those who have bad intention towards the Arabs."[50] Official apologists of Pakistan, on the other hand, have maintained that it was to help the

[48] Selig S. Harrison, "Case History of a Mistake," *New Republic*, August 10, 1959.
[49] Callard, p. 321.   [50] Quoted by Hasan, p. 76.

Muslim countries and to unite them that the Baghdad Pact was created. In 1956 *Dawn* advised other Muslim countries: "Let them shake off their illusions, their vanities, and jealousies—*and join the Baghdad Pact*. If they do so that body can immediately be transformed as to become a Muslim NATO with plenty of teeth in it. Nehru does not want it because he wants a Hindu hegemony; Moscow does not want it because it wants a Red hegemony. And the Arabs foolishly rise to the bait. Our suggestion may sound fantastic in Cairo and Riyadh in their present moods, but if their hearts and minds could be freed from the mesmeric influence of Islam's enemies masquerading as friends they might wake up with a shudder of guilt to discover that theirs today is the fantastic and suicidal policy."[51] Suhrawardy claimed in 1957 that Pakistan belonged to the pact which had 125 million Muslims in it and that those who stayed out had only 25 million.[52] Ayub Khan said in April 1961 that it was Pakistan's desire to forge a united front with the Muslim countries, to strengthen them and ensure their progress and prosperity, which had led her to join the Baghdad Pact.[53]

There may be merit in this claim that Pakistan joined the Baghdad Pact to promote Muslim interests. However, students of foreign affairs in Pakistan have not failed to note that the Baghdad Pact has tarnished the image of Pakistan in the Muslim world. Sarwar Hasan noted the following disadvantages of the pact: (1) It led to a setback for Pakistan among the African and Asian nations; (2) instead of helping, the pact worsened the position of Pakistan in her disputes with India; and (3) "Pakistan has fallen in the estimation of the Arabs." Elaborating the third point, Hasan says: "The Baghdad Pact undoubtedly divided the Arab world. Pakistan by its membership of the pact was held responsible for contributing to that division. By destroying Arab unity and by making the Arabs more suspicious of western intentions, the Baghdad Pact increased instability in the region."[54]

Pakistan's relations with the Arab world in general entered their most critical phase a year after the signing of the Baghdad Pact. Following the U.S. decision to withdraw aid for the Aswan Dam, Nasser nationalized the Suez Canal in July 1956. Pakistan upheld Egypt's sovereign rights over the Suez Canal and her right to nationalize it. But at the London conferences on Suez shortly after this, Pakistan's role was different from that of Ceylon, Indonesia, India and the USSR, and Pakistan was publicly criticized in Egypt for her

[51] *Dawn*, October 6, 1956.
[52] *Winding up of Foreign Policy Debates.*
[53] *Pakistan Times*, April 5, 1961.   [54] Hasan, p. 76.

failure to disassociate herself from the Dulles Plan which was totally unacceptable to Egypt.[55] In the first London conference on Suez, the countries which supported the Dulles Plan included the Baghdad Pact countries of Turkey, Iran and Pakistan; those who opposed it included India and Indonesia.

Eight days before the invasion of Suez, the foreign minister of Pakistan deprecated unthinking enthusiasm for pan-Islamism. The days of pan-Islamism, he said, were over and Pakistanis should first guard the interests of their own Muslims and then of other Muslims of the world. He said: "Pak-Islamism and not pan-Islamism should now be the new slogan. You have no future if you indiscriminately fight or die for Muslims outside Pakistan even though they be the dearest friends of your enemy."[56]

Yet when Suez was invaded, protests came not only from left-oriented groups in East Pakistan—the British consulate in Dacca was burned down[57]—but also from conservative Islamic groups in West Pakistan. An editorial comment in *Dawn* said: "They [the people of Pakistan] are asking and we are giving voice to their questions: Is this not the rise once again of bigoted and perverted Christendom against the world of Islam in alliance with the Jews! Is this not a threat poised against the Muslims from the Atlantic to the Pacific?"[58] The government's role was, however, less spectacular. Along with other Baghdad Pact members, Pakistan did protest against the invasion, but her protest was not among the strongest. When the Colombo powers met in New Delhi to discuss the Suez issue, the Pakistan prime minister excused himself from the meeting.[59] Although Prime Minister Suhrawardy later maintained that it was "partly as a result of our efforts that the Anglo-French forces were withdrawn from the Egyptian territory,"[60] Pakistan lost many friends among the Arab peoples.

The Egyptians, particularly, were unimpressed and showed their dislike for Pakistan when they refused to accept a Pakistani contingent in the UN troops in the Gaza strip. When Prime Minister Suhrawardy proposed a visit to President Nasser in November, the Egyptian government regretted its inability to receive the Pakistani leader.[61]

Smarting under this rebuff, Suhrawardy said at Lahore that the Anglo-French action in Suez was merely "an attempt on the part of these powers to see that the Suez Canal remained free for interna-

[55] *Ibid.*, p. 183.
[57] *Ibid.*, p. 1153.
[59] *Indian Affairs Record*, December 1956.
[60] Suhrawardy, *Statement on Foreign Relations and Defence*, Government of Pakistan, Karachi, 1957.
[61] *Asian Recorder*, 1956, p. 1174.
[56] *Asian Recorder*, 1956, p. 1116.
[58] *Dawn*, November 1, 1956.

tional navigation. The invasion aimed at restricting the sovereignty of one country for the benefit of the world."[62] He also derided the concept of a Muslim bloc as against the Baghdad Pact: "The question is asked, why don't we get together rather than be tied to a big power like the UK or America? My answer to that is that zero plus zero plus zero is after all equal to zero."[63] He also said: "The fact is that the Muslim countries today are so divided among themselves that it is difficult for them to sit together." Again: "We find that whereas we go out in sympathy for them, there is hardly any reciprocity on the other side for us. We find that Egypt, for instance, has declared that it is on the side of India on the Kashmir issue."[64]

The intense conflict between Pakistani and Arab opinion was reflected in newspaper comments even before the Suez invasion. King Saud, on an earlier visit to India, had expressed satisfaction that in India Muslims were well treated. Again, when Nehru paid a return visit to Riyadh, in September 1956, he was greeted there as "Rasul-ul-Salam" (messenger of peace). In Pakistan the word "Rasul" is used only for the Prophet, and Pakistani papers launched a severe attack on the Saudi Arabian government. *Dawn* ended an editorial thus: "However disappointing may be the policies of the governments in most of the Muslim countries, the Muslim people are sound at heart and share the broader Islamic outlook. Some day they will assert themselves and the Muslim world will re-discover its soul which selfish rulers and juntas are now foolishly mortgaging to the enemies of Islam."[65] In another article in early October, *Dawn* complained: "When it is the cause of some other Muslim country, the Egyptians and most other Arabs pooh-pooh the Islamic appeal. Our own Kashmir issue is the most striking example. They do not realize how thin is such hypocrisy."[66] In an editorial, "So this is Nasser," *Dawn* wrote: "Nasser's hatred of Pakistan, and love of Bharat and its Nehru, is an attitude of mind not warranted by facts but conditioned by insensate bias and blind prejudice the source of which may well be examined by psychiatrists. It is nevertheless a matter of deep regret that in the veins of this turbulent egotist not the blood of Islam should seem to flow but the turbid waters of the Nile. Nasser will never be our friend; he will never think in terms of Islam. . . ."[67]

RELATIONS WITH AFGHANISTAN

Pakistan's appeal as an upholder of the idea of Islamic integration

[62] *Ibid.*, p. 1179.
[63] *Prime Minister's Statement on Foreign Policy*, December 9, 1956.
[64] *Loc.cit.*
[65] *Dawn*, September 27, 1956.
[66] *Ibid.*, October 6, 1956.
[67] *Ibid.*, December 1, 1956.

was greatly curtailed by the unhappy state of her relations with Afghanistan, which were often strained to the breaking point. The Afghan government never accepted the boundaries between the two countries and had challenged the Durand Line on the ground that it was signed under duress. Even in 1942 the Afghans had attempted to raise the question, when Sir Stafford Cripps was discussing his plan for India's freedom. When Pakistan became independent, Afghanistan was the only country to voice its protest and its inability to vote for her admission to the United Nations. Shortly afterwards, Jinnah entered into negotiations with Afghanistan but the negotiations broke down and the status of the tribes along the border remained unsettled.

By 1949, relations between Pakistan and Afghanistan had further deteriorated. While Pakistan claimed that the Pakhtoonistan movement was an Afghan "stunt," Afghanistan charged Pakistan with having violently suppressed their people's urge for freedom in the tribal areas. On June 12, 1949, Pakistan planes bombed a village within Afghan territory; although Pakistan apologized soon afterward, relations from this time onward have remained intensely strained. In the following years clashes were often reported. The integration of West Pakistan into one federal unit, which forced the Pushto-speaking areas into an unwilling marriage with West Pakistan, dominated by the Punjabis, led to a fresh outburst of propaganda war in 1955. On March 30, the Pakistan embassy building in Kabul was attacked by rioters; on April 1, mobs in Peshawar attacked the Afghan consulate and tore down the Afghan flag.[68] On May 6, 1955, *Dawn* demanded: "Our embassy in Afghanistan is, according to international law, a part of Pakistan territory, and the sanctity and security of that territory has been violated. After having given the Kabuli junta, in vain, sufficient time to make honorable amends for the aggression, it should now be perfectly legitimate for us to resort to police action to chastise the aggressor."[69]

This friction with Afghanistan has continued. In March 1961, Afghanistan complained of a major offensive by Pakistani troops in the tribal areas. Pakistan admitted bombing the Pathan areas but said that it was done to blow up the ammunition dumps of Afghan agents.[70] Relations deteriorated in the following months: on August 22, Pakistan closed down its consulates in Afghanistan and demanded the closing down of Afghan consulates in Pakistan. On August 30, Afghanistan said that diplomatic relations with Pakistan would be

[68] For a further discussion of the issues involved, see Sisir Gupta, "Pakistan's Relations With Afghanistan," *Foreign Affairs Reports*, July 1955.
[69] *Dawn*, May 6, 1955.   [70] *Asian Recorder*, 1961, p. 3935.

severed if they did not withdraw their demand for closing down the consulates. On September 3, the border between Pakistan and Afghanistan was closed and on September 6 diplomatic relations between the two countries were severed.[71] Diplomatic relations were reestablished in 1963, but the dispute over Pakhtoonistan continues.

PROBLEMS AND PROSPECTS

Notwithstanding these grave problems and the occasional statements deriding Muslim unity, the urge for such solidarity has characterized the policies of the Pakistani governments. Even when the Egyptian-Pakistani relations were at their nadir, the Muslim League—the major opposition party—revived the demand for a united Muslim world bloc for their "security and survival."[72] Feroz Khan Noon, the then prime minister, talked in 1958 of a Pakistan-Iran-Afghanistan federation—a slogan which League leader Qayum Khan had promulgated earlier. In 1960 a Pakistani author made this the main theme of his book on Pakistan's security: "In this struggle for survival, these three nations must come close together and resist attempts by the Soviet Union or the West to impose allegiance on them. The danger is very real. Already Central Asia is lost; Bokhara and Merv are no longer Muslim; part of the Islamic homeland is lost to the Jews."[73] The Arabs were regarded as lost, and the lament continued: "At present nationalism is strongest in the Arab world, which is unfortunate in two respects. Modernism has been introduced with little regard for Islam and its intellectual revival is considerably indebted to Christian writers. The recent cordiality with communism may prove a third complicating factor. All this might lead to an unbridgeable gulf between the Arabs and the non-Arabs in the Islamic civilization and finally to its disintegration. Pakistanis believe that Islam itself is a nationality."[74] It may be noted here that in Pakistan many regarded the Arab League as a retrograde development.[75]

Even Ayub Khan, who functioned in a relative political vacuum, found it necessary to strive for Muslim solidarity or at least to pay lip service to it. Speaking at Layalpur on April 4, 1961, the president said that he favored the idea of a Muslim Commonwealth, to which the Malayan prime minister had made a reference earlier in London.[76] In June 1961 the prime minister of Northern Nigeria, Sir Ahmadu Bello, discussed the idea with Ayub Khan.[77] Pakistan has not made any progress in this direction, however; on the other hand,

71 *Ibid.*, p. 4211.　　　　　　72 Callard, p. 315.
73 Siddiqui, p. 159; see also pp. 33, 132 and 162.
74 *Ibid.*, p. 160.　　　　　　75 *Dawn*, May 4, 1952.
76 *Pakistan Times*, April 5, 1961.　　77 *Dawn*, June 28, 1961.

it has drifted farther apart from most other Muslim countries. The Belgrade Conference of September 1961, attended by most of the Muslim countries, illustrated the increasing isolation of Pakistan: by and large her foreign policy still remains different from that of the large majority of Muslim states.

In fact, one obstacle standing in the way of Pakistan's ties with other Muslim countries is the striking similarity between the outlook of most Muslim states and India in regard to many international issues. There is also a deliberate attempt on the part of India to cultivate cultural and political ties with Muslim countries. And so long as it is an "either India or Pakistan" proposition, it is unlikely that Pakistan will be able to claim the larger share of the Muslim world's sympathy, just as even her allies are finding it increasingly difficult to choose Pakistan and ignore India. It is important to point out that India has as many treaties of friendship with the Muslim countries as Pakistan has, excluding the military pacts with the CENTO countries. Callard has noted: "Once partition was accomplished, many of the other Muslim states were reluctant to make a choice between friendship for India or Pakistan. If a choice had to be made, India, as more powerful, more stable, and more influential, was likely to have the advantage."[78] The problem for Pakistan is precisely this: it is only in terms of her difficulties with India that she has invoked the cause of Muslim unity.

Another impediment for Pakistan has been that while she is engaged in building up an Islamic state, in many Muslim countries leaders like Sukarno and Nasser are engaged in internal struggles against groups which share the Pakistani view of Islam's potentialities in the modern world. The Masjumi in Indonesia and the Muslim Brotherhood in the UAR are banned, and their activities regarded as anti-state.[79]

There are other difficulties in moving towards closer cooperation with other Muslim countries on the basis of a common faith. In the first place, any attempt at a West Asian regional integration into a Muslim bloc presupposes a similar urge for Islamic belonging in other Muslim peoples. In other words, it projects into the Muslim world an assumed Muslimness which is unique in the case of Pakistan, and reflects its continued problems in the South Asian context. Second, it assumes that there are non-religious factors in their com-

[78] Callard, p. 314.
[79] In 1958 a Pakistani writer, after a visit to Indonesia, reported that while some political parties there admired Pakistan, the ruling circles were enamored of India and were reluctant to take any stand on Kashmir. Rais Ahmad Khan, "Pakistan in South-East Asia," *Pakistan Horizon*, December 1958.

monness; third, that other Muslim countries will see the threat of "Hindu imperialism" which Pakistan allegedly faces; fourth, it involves problems of defining the region of Muslim cooperation. The Muslim world extends from Indonesia to Nigeria and its politics differs from one country to another. Even in Pakistan itself, on the major problems of national integration and the role of religion in politics, there is no unanimity or even a consensus. Lastly, in the politics of the Muslim world, Pakistan is somewhat on the periphery. To say the least, it is very doubtful whether a peripheral state can become the cornerstone of Islamic unity.

As Callard says: "The political upsurge elsewhere was based largely on territorial and racial nationalism, anti-western, anti-white. Religion played a part in this, but it was a lesser part than color, language and political theory of violent opposition to colonialism and exploitation. For many Muslims, elsewhere, it has been more important to align Asians and Africans against the colonial powers than to defend Muslim causes against non-Muslims."[80] John S. Badeau describes the same obstacle to Muslim unity in more abstract terms: "Pan-Islam is difficult to conceive as the basis for a modern empire, because it is almost impossible for any group of states to become integrated into the international structure when they are based upon a political and ideological pattern at variance with the rest of the world. So long as Islamdom contained the center of its gravity and was self-sustaining politically and economically, it could afford to maintain its distinctive political organization. But, today, it is difficult to perpetuate such isolated political monads and to assume that they will move together with the rest of the world in a pre-established harmony. . . . No group of states can set up a bloc built upon radically different political concepts without being in continuous tension with the rest of the world. Islamdom cannot insulate itself against the seepage of the most universally accepted political concept of our times—nationalism."[81]

Some Pakistani intellectuals, however, regard this as a temporary phenomenon and feel convinced of the inevitability of the ultimate assertion of Islam. Samin Khan blames the Christian Arabs for deliberately infusing secularism in the Arab world and for reviving the pre-Islamic past of the Arabs; but regarding the future he has no doubt: "Arab nationalism does not rest either on ethnographic or territorial chauvinism. It is based first on the Arabic language and, secondly,

---

[80] Callard, p. 314.

[81] John S. Badeau, "Islam in the Modern Middle East," *Foreign Affairs*, October 1959.

though indirectly, on Islam. . . . The history of the Arabs is the history of Islam. . . . Once nationalism has taken its normal course and achieved its objective . . . it then looks for an ideal—permanent and sublime ideal. Since Arab nationalism will not serve the purpose, the forces of history which are much stronger than the temporary transient factors of nationalism shall assert themselves."[82] While only the future can reveal the validity of these two views, there is no doubt that Pakistan is often poised not only as a detractor of Afro-Asian solidarity but, what is more, as one of the parties in the most serious dispute in the Muslim world—the dispute over Pakhtoonistan.

It is possible that behind Pakistan's policy to seek Muslim solidarity lie more basic factors of history. Says Dr. Brown: "Pakistan as a Muslim nation looks westward to the lands where Islam was born and became great. Western Pakistan, especially, illustrates the same phenomenon of association with western regions, which it has exhibited in the past. It feels itself culturally akin to those areas outside the subcontinent, rather than to the areas east of it, though they are geographically close to it and economically its natural partners."[83]

A significant aspect of this observation is the difference implied in it between East and West Pakistan. Indeed, this difference cannot be exaggerated. Cultural difference apart, the East Pakistanis may well prefer closer relations with Malaya and Indonesia, to those with Afghanistan and Iran. An Iran-Pakistan federation, for example, would completely alter the political power structure in Pakistan and reduce the advantage of the larger population, which East Pakistan enjoys, to nothing. Moreover, East Pakistani politics centers around many secular issues which were thrown up in 1954.[84] It is unlikely that any sudden Islamic resurgence can push them into the background.

Yet, in this age of super-powers, Pakistan must belong to a larger group. In a sense, it is correct that the age of nationalism is becoming outdated. The trend is everywhere towards the evolution of higher loyalties—Arab unity, West European Community, the free and the Communist worlds, the Alliance for Progress in the Western Hemisphere, the African personality and Malaysia in Southeast Asia—these are all indications of the growing tempo of regionalism. Muslims of the world, like other peoples, have fallen into step and are becoming integrated regionally.

[82] Samin Khan, "Arab Nationalism," *Pakistan Horizon*, December 1958.

[83] W. N. Brown, "Pakistan and West Asia," *Pakistan Miscellany*, Pakistan Publications, Karachi, vol. 22, 1958, p. 30.

[84] This election resulted in the most spectacular upset in Pakistan's political life.

Sisir Gupta

Where does Pakistan stand in this emerging pattern? It is here that inevitably South Asia becomes more than a mere cartographic expression. Whatever be the approach that Pakistan brings to bear on the question of her future association with other nations or her future partnership in a regional organization, the rest of South Asia will remain a strong contender for her supra-national loyalty. In fact, the continued emphasis on Islam in Pakistan, even after being constituted as a Muslim-majority state, may well be regarded as a measure of her inability to run away from her minority status in the complex of South Asian realities.

PART IV
CEYLON: THE POLITICS OF
BUDDHIST RESURGENCE

CHAPTER 21

THE SINHALESE BUDDHIST REVOLUTION

DONALD E. SMITH

THE INDEPENDENT Ceylon which emerged in 1948 gave little or no indication of the linguistic and religious conflicts and social revolution which were to overtake it within a decade. Outwardly, all was calm. The transition from colonial status to political freedom was a smooth one. Indeed, independence was attained by Ceylon quite painlessly, largely as a by-product of India's freedom struggle. The United National Party which came to power drew its strength from the highly westernized middle class and largely represented its interests, although adult suffrage since 1931 had forced the UNP politicians to court the Sinhalese masses. These politicians were steeped in the tradition of British liberalism and were in many cases outspoken admirers of British institutions. Some of these politicians were Christians, many of the Buddhists among them had Christian relatives, and many had received part of their education in Christian schools in Ceylon or had studied in England. The British principles of liberalism, democracy and the religious neutrality of the state were committed to a class which understood and appreciated these values. With a standard of living considerably higher than that of India, Pakistan and Burma, all indications in 1948 were that Ceylon would continue to develop peacefully along familiar lines.

Just beneath the placid surface, however, were powerful forces which could not be accommodated within the existing social and political setup, for this had been developed over the decades without reference to certain basic realities. Buddhism was a vital component of traditional Sinhalese nationalism, but the central concern of the nationalist movement in the twentieth century was the succession of constitutional reforms which had little or nothing to do with popular sentiments and required no mass movements. Buddhism was relegated to the background, and the *bhikkhus* (monks) were replaced by lawyers, politicians and civil servants as the leaders of national

Donald E. Smith is associate professor of political science at the University of Pennsylvania.

life—but continued to be influential with the rural Sinhalese Buddhist masses.

Christian, and especially Roman Catholic, influence was strong in the ruling United National Party, but the Buddhists represented 64 per cent of the total population of Ceylon and the Christians only 9 per cent. The best educational institutions in the country were managed by the Catholic and Protestant churches, but largely maintained by government grants. The English language and western culture dominated the social life of the middle and upper classes to a far greater extent than in India or Burma. The Sinhalese language was neglected, for an English education was the door to well-paid jobs in the professions and government service. While there was open competition for such positions, both the Christians as a group and the industrious Ceylon Tamils (11 per cent of the population, the majority of whom are Hindus) achieved success far out of proportion to their numbers, and dominated a number of departments in the services.

These are the essential facts of the situation which obtained in 1948, and there is little room for disagreement about them. The facts, when added up, could produce only one conclusion: the Sinhalese Buddhist majority was in a markedly inferior position vis-à-vis other communities, and its language, religion and culture had been relegated to a secondary place. In the context of a democratic political structure it was inevitable that drastic adjustments would be made, simply because elections are decided by majorities. The deep-seated resentments of the Sinhalese Buddhists, their gradual realization that independence under a UNP government had not substantially altered their situation, and S. W. R. D. Bandaranaike's skill in using these communal grievances and in appealing to religion and language as prime political loyalties, led to the dramatic revolution at the polls in 1956. Communal loyalties and antipathies have provided much of the motive force of Ceylon politics down to the present day.

The essential facts of the Sinhalese Buddhist situation, as noted above, were hardly open to question. But the deep sense of grievance was not derived primarily from these facts themselves, but from an historical interpretation which claimed to explain them. The sense of outrage, of righteous indignation, derived from the Sinhalese Buddhist's conviction that his community had been the victim of great historic injustices deliberately perpetrated by the British and the minorities. It was not enough to state that Buddhist schools were few and poor as compared with those of other denominations; it was necessary to assert that the British had "destroyed" the indigenous Buddhist system of schools, that with the most sinister motives they had handed the education of the island over to the Christian missionaries and had discouraged later Buddhist enterprise in founding state-aided schools. Roman Catholic education had made rapid strides not because of superior organization and greater effort, but because it had been favored by the British government. The history of the period of foreign rule is a matter of very lively popular interest in Ceylon today; in India, Pakistan and Burma it is of interest only to scholars.

After 1956 the Buddhist-oriented government sought to meet some of the communal demands it had helped to stimulate. Sinhalese was made the one official language; the denominational schools were nationalized, thus striking a solid blow at one source of Roman Catholic power. But the redress of certain communal grievances alone did not make Buddhism strong. The internal problems of Buddhism—the reform of the Sangha, and the building of a coherent organization of laity and clergy—these remained. With the British gone and the minorities being rapidly put in their place, a Sinhalese Buddhist government had to come to grips with these problems with no convenient scapegoats in sight.

THE UNP AND BUDDHA JAYANTI

Shortly after independence it became evident that the principle of the religious neutrality of the state would be increasingly difficult to implement. Mr. D. S. Senanayake, the first prime minister, proclaimed the ideal of a united Ceylonese nation, and the Constitution of Ceylon provided the framework of equal citizenship in a secular state. Section 29 of the Constitution includes the following:

(1) Subject to the provisions of this Order, Parliament shall have power to make laws for the peace, order and good government of the Island.
(2) No such law shall
    (a) prohibit or restrict the free exercise of any religion; or
    (b) make persons of any community or religion liable to disabilities or restrictions to which persons of other communities or religions are not made liable; or
    (c) confer on persons of any community or religion any privilege or advantage which is not conferred on persons of other communities or religions; or
    (d) alter the constitution of any religious body except with the

consent of the governing authority of that body:
Provided that, in any case where a religious body is incorporated by law, no such alteration shall be made except at the request of the governing authority of that body.
(3) Any law made in contravention of subsection (2) of this Section shall, to the extent of such contravention, be void.

However, the same Constitution provides for free elections, and the politicians had long known the usefulness of religion in election campaigns.

S. W. R. D. Bandaranaike was the son of a prominent Anglican layman who had been knighted by the British sovereign. He was educated at St. Thomas College (near Colombo) and at Oxford. Along with other politically ambitious young men, he became a convert to Buddhism after the 1931 Donoughmore constitutional reforms granted universal franchise.[1] Bandaranaike started a political party, the Sinhala Maha Sabha, which became the largest single element in the United National Party formed in 1946. He became a member of the UNP cabinet under Prime Minister D. S. Senanayake and was for some time regarded as his heir-apparent. However, it soon became evident that Senanayake favored his nephew, Major John Kotelawala, as successor to the top post.[2] Bandaranaike sought to strengthen his personal political following by reviving the Sinhala Maha Sabha and by giving leadership to the Buddhist revival movement. In 1950 he made a number of speeches urging that Buddhism be given special constitutional recognition. On one occasion he declared: "The adoption of Buddhism as the state religion will usher in an era of religio-democratic socialism. More than two-thirds of the population of Ceylon are Buddhists, and it is therefore inevitable that Buddhism should be the state religion."[3] Prime Minister D. S. Senanayake, whose wife was a Christian, disagreed sharply with this emphasis. In 1951 Bandaranaike resigned from the cabinet and joined the opposition.

The prime minister, whose outlook had been molded by nineteenth-century British liberalism, was resolutely opposed to governmental intervention in matters of religion. When a delegation of high-ranking Buddhist monks from Kandy met him to request state protection

[1] The term "Donoughmore Buddhist" is well known in Ceylon politics.
[2] W. Howard Wriggins, *Ceylon: Dilemmas of a New Nation*, Princeton University Press, Princeton, 1960, pp. 110-111. This is an excellent comprehensive study of politics in independent Ceylon. See especially chapter 6, "Religious Revival and Cultural Nationalism." See also Robert N. Kearney, "Sinhalese Nationalism and Social Conflicts in Ceylon," *Pacific Affairs*, summer 1964, vol. 37, pp. 125-136.
[3] Winburn T. Thomas, "Ceylon Christians Faced by Crisis," *Christian Century*, 1951, vol. 68, pp. 58-60.

and support for Buddhism, he replied that spiritual development was entirely up to the individual, and that government was inherently incapable of promoting spirituality. "The Buddha has pointed out the path of development, and no state aid can take man there."[4] In 1951 D. S. Senanayake met an All-Ceylon Buddhist Congress deputation of venerable elders of the Sangha and prominent laymen led by Dr. G. P. Malalasekera. The deputation specifically requested the appointment of an official commission to inquire into the grievances of the Buddhists. The prime minister pointedly asked the group whether, in addition to the Three Refuges of Buddha, Dhamma and Sangha, they wanted to add a Fourth Refuge—Government. A commission of inquiry was not appointed.[5] D. S. Senanayake died in 1952, and neither of the UNP prime ministers who followed him (his son Dudley Senanayake, and then Sir John Kotelawala) were of the same stature as the "Father of the Nation," and neither found it possible to resist the temptation to mix religion and politics.

During this crucial period the whole Buddhist world became caught up in a powerful wave of enthusiasm over the Buddha Jayanti—the celebrations which were to mark the 2,500th anniversary of the passing away of the Buddha. The full-moon day of May 1956 was set as the exact date, but Buddha Jayanti activities were begun more than two years before this date. In Rangoon the Sixth Great Buddhist Council brought together learned monks from all five Theravada Buddhist countries to embark on the monumental task of editing the Pali canon and producing an authoritative version of the Tripitaka. According to Buddhist tradition, the teaching of the Buddha would last 5,000 years, and the 2,500th year would mark a great turning point in the history of Buddhism. At this time the Dhamma would be spread throughout the world and would produce an unprecedented spiritual awakening.[6]

In Ceylon the Buddha Jayanti had a special national significance, for according to the Mahavamsa (the Great Chronicle) Prince Vijaya, the founder of the Sinhalese race, landed on the Island just as the Buddha on his deathbed prepared to enter *nibbana*. Addressing the god Sakka, the Buddha declared that in Lanka (Ceylon) would his religion be established, and that Vijaya, his followers, and Ceylon

[4] *Ceylon Daily News*, December 6, 1950.
[5] *Catholic Action: A Menace to Peace and Goodwill*, Bauddha Jatika Balavegaya, Colombo, 1963, p. 126.
[6] Sir John Kotelawala, "The Significance of the Buddha Jayanti," in Ananda W. P. Guruge and K. G. Amaradasa, eds., *2500 Buddha Jayanti Souvenir*, Lanka Bauddha Mandalaya, Ministry of Local Government and Cultural Affairs, Colombo, 1956, p. 1.

were therefore to be carefully protected.[7] The year 1956 marked "the unique three-fold event—the completion of 2,500 years of Buddhism, of the life of the Sinhalese race, and of Ceylon's history."[8] The land, the race and the faith were intimately associated in the nationalist mystique which the Buddha Jayanti helped to elaborate. The Sinhalese nation came into being with the blessing of the Buddha, is a "chosen race" with a divine mission to fulfil, and now stands on the threshold of a new era leading to its "great destiny."[9]

The Buddha Jayanti, an event of unique religious and national significance, could not be celebrated on a sufficiently grand scale without the active participation of the government of Ceylon. In the absence of a well-knit Buddhist organization (Sangha and laity) with considerable financial resources, the celebrations could be successful only if directed by an agency of the state. On the initiative of Mr. Dudley Senanayake, the proposal was made to the prime minister that the Buddha Jayanti be celebrated on a national scale with the active cooperation of the government. Following cabinet approval, Prime Minister Kotelawala in October 1954 appointed the Lanka Bauddha Mandalaya (Buddhist Council of Ceylon) to organize and direct the Buddha Jayanti activities. The inauguration of the council was itself an impressive event. Over 2,500 Buddhist monks assembled at the Independence Memorial Hall to recite the religious verses which would ensure an auspicious start to the council's labors. The prime minister's inaugural address and the other speeches were delivered to an assembly of almost 10,000 people.[10]

Several of the eminent speakers dealt with the controversy which had arisen over the propriety of the government's religious involvement. A venerable thero (elder) of the Malwatte chapter of the Siam sect (the largest of the Ceylonese Sangha's three sects) asserted emphatically that all of the obligations which the British sovereign had assumed under the Kandyan Convention of 1815 had accrued to the present government. Under article 5 of this convention the British had agreed to protect and maintain the rites, ministers and places of

[7] Wilhelm Geiger, trans., *The Mahavamsa or the Great Chronicle of Ceylon*, Ceylon Government Information Department, Colombo, 1950, pp. 54-55.

[8] D. C. Vijayavardhana, *Dharma-Vijaya or The Revolt in the Temple*, Sinha Publications, Colombo, 1953, p. 3. This important book was written on the eve of the Buddha Jayanti, and attempted among other things to set forth a Sinhalese Buddhist ideology.

[9] *Ibid.*, p. 438.

[10] *Jayanti*, vol. 1, May 1955, p. 3. This was the monthly magazine of the Lanka Bauddha Mandalaya, edited by the general secretary, Dr. Ananda W. P. Guruge, a high-ranking official in the department of education and a devout Buddhist layman.

worship of the Buddhist religion. He quoted the late prime minister, D. S. Senanayake, as having stated clearly that the Constitution itself was "governed and circumstanced" by the Kandyan Convention.[11] The venerable monk concluded: "There can therefore be nothing irregular if the present government accords a special regard to the Buddhist religion and its affairs. On the contrary, to fail to show a special regard for the welfare of the Buddha Sasana is provenly to do a great wrong."[12]

The Buddha Jayanti program drawn up by the Buddhist Council was an elaborate one involving heavy outlays of state funds—over 5,000,000 rupees ($1,060,000). In an impressive ceremony the prime minister invited the members of the Sangha to translate the Pali Tripitaka into Sinhalese, a project sponsored by the council.[13] A very ambitious and costly undertaking was the preparation of an encyclopedia of Buddhism, which would be an authoritative reference work. Dr. G. P. Malalasekera, a well-known Pali scholar and at that time Ceylon's ambassador to the USSR, was appointed editor-in-chief, and a large number of foreign scholars were associated with the project.[14] Work was also begun on a general encyclopedia in Sinhalese to commemorate the 2,500th anniversary of the landing of Vijaya on the Island.

The Dalada Maligawa (Temple of the Tooth) in Kandy houses the most venerated object of worship in the Buddhist world—the tooth relic of the Buddha. One of the most meaningful aspects of the Buddha Jayanti program was the restoration of this great religious and national monument.[15] Pamphlets, magazines and books on the Buddha Jayanti were published, preaching missions equipped with amplifiers and film projectors toured the country and innumerable public meet-

11 The important question of the Kandyan Convention is considered in some detail below.

12 *Jayanti*, vol. 1, May 1955, pp. 8-10. The leading elder of the Ramanya sect took the same position. Senator A. M. A. Azeez of the Muslim community, speaking on "The State and Religious Neutrality," saw no particular problem, since "in the context of current affairs any efforts that help towards the spiritual reawakening of a section of our country whether large or small would invariably promote the regeneration of the country as a whole." *Ibid.*, p. 14. But Mr. R. Singleton-Salmon warned against mixing Buddhism with politics, and noted that "already there are signs that pressure is being brought to bear in the so-called interests of Buddhists." *Ibid.*, p. 15.

13 Following the traditions of the ancient kings of Ceylon, the prime minister presented to each of the scholar monks a leaf manuscript of the section of the scriptures entrusted to him for translation. *Ibid.*, p. 18.

14 G. P. Malalasekera, "Encyclopedia of Buddhism—Its Plan and Scope," *The Buddhist*, vol. 29, May 1958, pp. 60-62.

15 *Jayanti*, vol. 1, July 1955, pp. 14-15, and December 1955, p. 27.

ings were organized by local government officials. Memorials were erected in many places to honor the great figures of the Buddhist revival and Sinhalese Buddhist nationalism. The question of establishing a Buddhist University was also considered by the council, although nothing materialized immediately as a result of this proposal.[16]

The Buddha Jayanti was an important landmark in the development of religion-state relations in Ceylon. The 2,500th anniversary of the death of the Buddha was obviously a unique event. Given the immense popular enthusiasm which was generated by the occasion, given the strongly nationalistic overtones of the event coming just a few years after independence, it was inevitable that the religious neutrality of the state should be largely forgotten. The identification of Buddhism with the state on this occasion was all but complete, and a precedent was established for massive intervention by the government in religious affairs. The important political result was that the UNP politicians who had hoped to benefit from their association with the Buddha Jayanti found that more communally-oriented opposition groups were in a far better position to exploit the revivalist enthusiasm than they were.

THE BUDDHIST COMMITTEE OF INQUIRY

The All-Ceylon Buddhist Congress has been a powerful force in the resurgence of Buddhism. Its direct and indirect role in the elections of 1956 was of very great importance, and it continues to be an influential pressure group which no government can afford to ignore. The organization was founded in 1918 as the result of the efforts of a group of well-known Buddhist leaders including C. A. Hewavitarne, F. R. Senanayake and D. B. Jayatillake. The organization had its origin in the Young Men's Buddhist Association movement, and was first known as the All-Ceylon Congress of YMBA's. Around 1924 the name was altered to All-Ceylon Congress of Buddhist Associations, and in 1940 it was changed to its present name.[17] The Congress was incorporated by an act of Parliament in 1955. Among the general objects of the corporation listed in the act are: "to promote, foster and protect the interests of Buddhism and of the Buddhists and to safeguard the rights and privileges of the Buddhists," and "to represent the Buddhists and act on their behalf in public matters affecting their interests."[18]

[16] "Lanka Bauddha Mandalaya Annual Report," *Jayanti*, vol. 1, October 1955, pp. 27-32.

[17] *Presidential Address of Sir Lalita Rajapakse*, All-Ceylon Buddhist Congress, December 30, 1961, Colombo, 1962, pp. 2-3.

[18] All-Ceylon Buddhist Congress Act, No. 24 of 1955, section 3 (a) and (c).

The dominant figure in the congress for the past two decades has been Dr. G. P. Malalasekera, who served as president from 1939 to 1957. A man of great energy and determination, Dr. Malalasekera has provided the leadership in a number of important Buddhist enterprises. In 1947 a resolution was adopted by the congress calling for an international conference of Buddhists, and in June 1950 the World Fellowship of Buddhists was inaugurated at a meeting presided over by the two mahanayake theros (chief abbots) of the Siamese sect at the Temple of the Tooth in Kandy. Dr. Malalasekera was elected the first president of the World Fellowship of Buddhists.[19] Regular sessions of the organization have since then been held in Japan, Burma, Nepal and Cambodia.

As has already been mentioned, Dr. Malalasekera and his deputation from the All-Ceylon Buddhist Congress were unsuccessful in their 1951 attempt to get the government to appoint a commission to inquire into the state of Buddhism in the country. The memorandum presented to the prime minister at that time, titled *Buddhism and the State*, was a 26-page indictment of the British government with respect to its religious policies, and a call for immediate action on the part of the government to restore Buddhism to its rightful place.[20] This interesting document did not receive much attention at the time, but was in fact a concise statement of the argument later elaborated in great detail by the Buddhist Committee of Inquiry. Since the request for the appointment of an official commission was not granted, a Buddhist Committee of Inquiry was set up in April 1954 by the All-Ceylon Buddhist Congress itself.

The committee of inquiry was composed of seven high-ranking members of the Sangha and seven Buddhist laymen. The committee became popularly known as the "Buddhist Commission," adopted procedures usually associated with official commissions, and was erroneously regarded by many people as a body vested with governmental authority. Over a period of eleven months the committee toured the length and breadth of the Island, traveling approximately 6,300 miles, hearing evidence from organizations and individuals representing all sections and points of view within the Buddhist community, both laity and Sangha. Over 1,800 laymen and 700 monks gave evidence before the committee. The report of the committee was submitted to the All-Ceylon Buddhist Congress at a mass meeting held

---

[19] *World Fellowship of Buddhists: Report of the Inaugural Conference*, Colombo, n.d., pp. 1-17, 98-100.

[20] *Buddhism and the State: Resolutions and Memorandum of the All-Ceylon Buddhist Congress*, Colombo, 1951.

at Ananda College on February 4, 1956. Over 3,000 monks and a vast gathering of Buddhist laymen hailed the completion of the report as an epochal event. The full report of the committee was in Sinhalese, and came to 189 printed pages. The abridged English version of 124 pages was titled *The Betrayal of Buddhism*.

The importance of the report may be gauged by the judgment of a distinguished Christian scholar that it is one of the most remarkable documents of modern Ceylon's history. While critical of its historical analysis and recommendations, Dr. G. C. Mendis pointed out that it had clearly captured the imagination of a large section of the Buddhists and had had an immediate political impact. Regardless of its scholarly merits or lack thereof, "no one can ignore a report which contributed to the defeat of a government which had some continuity for about twenty-five years and put in its place another which was expected to support its recommendations."[21]

The report began by recounting the story of Buddha's three visits to Ceylon. Seated on a rock at Uruvela, in India, the Buddha surveyed the world and saw Lanka as the place most suited for preserving the purity of his Doctrine. "Then he rose to the sky and traveling along the pathway of space, in the manner of a heroic lion, radiant with the infinite grace of a Supremely Enlightened One, arrived in Lanka for the first time, freed it of the uncivilized impure elements that infested it, blessed it with the Great Protective Chant of Amity, taught the Law to a vast concourse [of spiritual beings] . . . bestowed a handful of locks of his hair to Sumanadeva, and returned to Uruvela."[22] This tradition of the Buddha's visits to Ceylon, like that which synchronizes his death with the founding of the Sinhalese race, is an important emotional element in Sinhalese Buddhist nationalism.

The report was revolutionary in its assumptions and recommendations, revolutionary in terms of Buddhist thought and traditional practices. It ignored the doctrine of *kamma* as the Buddhist explanation of the present condition of an individual or a society. Previous Buddhist writings attributed the Dutch invasion of the Kandyan Kingdom and the consequent decline of Buddhism to the bad *kamma* accumulated by the people of Ceylon in previous existences. But the committee of inquiry found it unnecessary to look beyond historical cause-and-effect relationships. The orthodox Buddhist cyclical view of history, which assigned only 2,500 years more to Buddhism itself before its extinction, was superseded by a modern view of life which

21 G. C. Mendis, *Ceylon Today and Yesterday*, Associated Newspapers of Ceylon Ltd., Colombo, 1957, p. 108.
22 *The Betrayal of Buddhism*, Dharmavijaya Press, Balagoda, 1956, p. i.

emphasized historical development and progress. The Buddhist emphasis on the individual's withdrawal from the world in order to extricate himself from the cycle of rebirth was replaced by the conviction that the political, economic and social system of modern Ceylon must be transformed.[23]

These revolutionary assumptions were paralleled by equally revolutionary recommendations. While British rule was held largely responsible for the decline of Buddhism, there was no proposal to revert to the system of relationships which linked religion and the state under the Sinhalese kings. The British were bitterly charged with having betrayed the Buddhists by their failure to implement the religious obligations assumed under the Kandyan Convention (hence the title *The Betrayal of Buddhism*), but there was to be no return to the pre-British past. The report urged the abolition of the whole educational system, but recommended replacing it not with the traditional Buddhist *pansalas* (monastery schools) but with a modern system of state schools. The grievances of the past provided the emotional thrust of the report, but the solutions proposed looked to the future, not to the pre-colonial past. In both its assumptions and its recommendations the report reflected the modern outlook of the English-educated Buddhist laymen who wrote it.

Article 5 of the Kandyan Convention of 1815 stated: "The Religion of the Buddhoo professed by the Chiefs and inhabitants of these Provinces is declared inviolable and its Rites and Ministers and Places of Worship are to be maintained and protected." The customary religious prerogatives of the Sinhalese kings were assumed by the crown and exercised until 1853. Among these powers were the appointment and dismissal of ecclesiastical officials, the custody and protection of the tooth relic, the organization of religious ceremonies at Kandy, and the supervision of the administration of Buddhist temple lands. The British government ceased to exercise these functions in 1853, as the result of an agitation led by the missionaries and certain officials who objected strenuously to this intimate connection between a Christian government and the Buddhist religion.[24]

---

[23] Mendis, pp. 110-111.

[24] Many officials without strong religious motives, in Ceylon as in India, were convinced that a strict policy of religious neutrality was the only sound approach for a western imperial power in Asia, that governmental involvement in the affairs of Asian religions was bound to produce unhappy results. The Buddhist Commission Report, however, reduced the complex problems of policy to very simple terms. "Missionary and official alike desired the end of the traditional social order. The government wanted to dispossess the people and the temples of their land and break down the system of landholding. . . . Traditional institu-

The committee's most serious charge against the British government was that it had refused to establish a centralized governing authority for the Buddhists by which they could manage their own affairs, especially in the administration of Buddhist temporalities (temple lands). An ordinance was passed in 1846 to create a Central Buddhist Committee consisting of laity and clergy which would perform these functions, but the measure was disallowed by the crown. One of the reasons for its rejection was that, in the words of a legal adviser to the crown, it would give "a dangerous organization to the Buddhist hierarchy." The government promised in 1853 to give the Buddhists "an honest working constitution," but this promise, the report emphasized, was never fulfilled.[25]

After 1853 the administration of the temple lands deteriorated swiftly. The important point which the committee of inquiry largely ignored was that this deterioration took place at the hands of the Sangha, which became a powerful vested interest. Buddhist monks and local headmen were responsible for gross abuses in the management of the temple land. The Buddhist Temporalities Ordinance of 1889 transferred the control of Buddhist properties in each district to a committee of laymen elected by the monks and laity of the area. In 1904 the presiding monks of the Siamese sect and other leading dignitaries of the Sangha addressed a petition to King Edward VII in which they protested this ordinance, and asserted their own prerogatives in the most unequivocal language. The three inseparable components of the Buddhist religion, they argued, are the Buddha, the Dhamma and the Sangha. The Sangha, unlike all other religious orders in the world, forms an integral part of the religion itself, and is entitled to equal adoration with the Buddha and the Dhamma. As to the laity, they form no part of the religion, and can have no proprietary rights in religious endowments. "When a temple is built and dedicated and lands are gifted to the Buddhist religion they become the absolute property of the Sangha, who are the only living rep-

---

tions like our family system, local government institutions and the religious institutions which cemented the social life of the people had to be destroyed." *The Betrayal of Buddhism*, p. 5.

25 *Ibid.*, p. 6. For some of the other factors involved in the decisions of the British government, see *Companion to the Buddhist Commission Report: A Commentary on the Report*, Catholic Union of Ceylon, Colombo, 1957, pp. 107-110. Much of the historical material contained in the original Sinhalese version of the report was deleted in the English version. A considerable part of this material was later published separately by the member of the commission who wrote it. See Tennakoon Vimalananda, *Buddhism in Ceylon under the Christian Powers*, M. D. Gunasena and Co., Ltd., Colombo, 1963.

resentatives of Buddhism on earth."[26] [6]The organizational problem of Buddhism, especially the relationship between the Sangha and the laity, was certainly not created by colonial rule, as charged in the report.

Buddhism did indeed suffer in some respects during the period of British rule. But the committee presented a distorted view by suggesting that this was mainly due to an imperialist conspiracy against Buddhism, and by ignoring the internal organizational problems of Buddhist religion which foreign rule exposed. Most of the difficulties which Buddhism now faces are the unfortunate by-products of policies aimed in quite a different direction: the governmental, legal, economic, social and educational modernization of Ceylon. In the transition from a feudal traditional society to a modern society, Buddhism has undoubtedly suffered. However, the process has also been one of shock and renewal in which, in the long view, Buddhism has gained. Buddhism is now taking the offensive and confidently confronts the western world with its universal message. In the new era of world Buddhism the leadership has been provided not by Thailand, which escaped western domination, but by two countries which were formerly a part of the British Empire, Burma and Ceylon.

One of the principal themes of the report, substantiated and elaborated from many different angles, was the pressing need for the creation of a coherent Buddhist organization which would link together the Sangha and the laity in an organic relationship. What was needed, in short, was a Buddhist *church*. The commission saw this as the only suitable modern alternative to the traditional pattern in which the king organized and regulated the various manifestations of Buddhist religion. The report rejected the traditional pattern as of no relevance in the present day.

Starting with the proposition that in modern Ceylon the nation is composed of various religious groups, the proposal of a state religion was rejected and the principle of the secular state was emphatically affirmed. There were non-Buddhists in the elected legislature as well as Buddhists, and even the latter were not elected on the basis of their religion but on other considerations. "We therefore do not think it desirable that Buddhism should have any official connection with a secular state governed by a legislature not consisting of Buddhists."[27] It would be incompatible for a secular government to attempt to use its powers to purify the Sangha. The commission recom-

---

[26] *Correspondence Relating to the Buddhist Temporalities Ordinance*, Sessional Paper No. IV of 1907, Government Printer, Colombo, 1907, p. 7.
[27] *The Betrayal of Buddhism*, p. 32.

mended the creation of a suitable body, similar to the Buddha Sasana
Council in Burma, in which the principal religious prerogatives of the
Buddhist kings would be vested. This body would be created by
legislation, as in Burma. "When this has been done and the government has taken other steps necessary to rehabilitate the Buddhist religion, it must in our view sever all connections with Buddhism."[28]

The committee of inquiry was acutely aware of the handicaps imposed by Buddhism's lack of centralized organization. Since each
temple was administered separately, there could be no pooling of
financial resources to establish educational and social welfare institutions where most needed. Since the Sangha had no organic connection
with the laity, the Buddhist educational movement which was started
by Colonel Henry Steele Olcott in 1880 remained a lay movement.
As a consequence, the religious influence of the Sangha was denied
to Buddhist children, and the Sangha lost "the opportunity of modern education which would enable them to minister to the needs
of the Buddhist laity in the new society that was created."[29]

The commission's deep sense of frustration over the organizational
deficiencies of Buddhism derived in large measure from the competitive disadvantages of their religion vis-à-vis well-organized Christian
bodies, especially the Roman Catholic Church. The report made a
strenuous effort to show that governmental discrimination against
Buddhism was still operative in the legal device of incorporation
which was utilized by the Christian churches. Incorporation, it was
held, conveyed extraordinary legal and financial advantages to the
churches which could not be had by the Buddhist religion.[30] Section
29 (2) (d) of the Constitution of Ceylon protects the internal constitution of an incorporated religious body from alteration by acts of
Parliament. The net result of such discriminatory provisions? According to the report: "Over Ceylon, Christianity sits enthroned, and
Ceylon bound hand and foot has been delivered at the foot of the
Cross."[31]

The committee bitterly attacked the Roman Catholic Church. The
power of this church in independent Ceylon was regarded as a continuation of western imperialism in religious garb. The archbishop

[28] *Ibid.*, p. 33.

[29] *Ibid.*, p. 8. The commission's ambivalent attitudes toward Ceylon's colonial
experience were revealed in many parts of the report. British rule was a calamity,
yet modern education and democracy were important values somehow dissociated
completely from their source.

[30] *Ibid.*, pp. 15-20, 27-31. For the Roman Catholic reply to these arguments, see
Companion to the Buddhist Commission Report, pp. 129-132.

[31] *The Betrayal of Buddhism*, p. 31.

of Colombo was represented as having immense wealth derived from commercial enterprises. This financial power was used for political purposes, and Catholic Action groups in government offices attempted to guide policies along lines dictated by the Catholic hierarchy. "Democracy in Ceylon is faced today with the gravest danger it can know from religious bodies corrupted with wealth and power. The colonial government in 1846 saw a Central Buddhist Committee even under government supervision capable of 'mischievous influence.' How much greater is the danger of centralized religious organizations, incorporated by law with no checks on their power in a democratic state yet in its infancy?"[32] The committee was highly critical of the Catholic centralized organization, but at the same time it fervently wished that Buddhism would develop at least some of the characteristics of this effective hierarchy.

In addition to the proposal for the creation of a Buddha Sasana Council, some of the main recommendations of the report were: the revision of Ceylon's status to that of a republic within the Commonwealth, the amendment of Section 29 of the Constitution, the appointment of a minister for religious affairs, the nationalization of all assisted schools and training colleges,[33] the declaring of Poya days (Buddhist sabbath days) as public holidays, the banning of horse-racing, the prohibition of the sale of intoxicating beverages, the termination of the services of nuns working in hospitals, and the establishment of training centers for those seeking admission to the Sangha.

THE 1956 ELECTIONS: PARTIES AND ISSUES

Prime Minister Sir John Kotelawala stirred up a hornets' nest when in September 1954 he declared that the Constitution would be amended to give parity of status to Sinhalese and Tamil as the official languages of the country. The language problem of Ceylon after independence involved two distinct but interrelated questions. English versus Swabasha ("self-language") concerned the extent to which the languages of Ceylon, Sinhalese and Tamil, would replace English in government administration, the courts, educational institutions, etc. Parity versus Sinhala Only concerned the relative status to be accorded to Sinhalese and Tamil. While many points connected with the former question were still unresolved, Sir John's statement of September 1954 provoked a heated controversy, in which the pro-

---

[32] *Ibid.,* p. 24.
[33] This important recommendation had a profound and almost immediate political effect. It is considered below in the section on education.

ponents of Sinhala Only organized the mass support of the majority community. Under powerful public pressure the UNP abandoned its stand on parity and embraced Sinhala Only. To enable the UNP government to seek a mandate from the electorate to implement its new language policy, a proclamation from Queen's House dissolved the Parliament of Ceylon on February 18, 1956.[34]

The Sri Lanka Freedom Party had been formed by S. W. R. D. Bandaranaike in 1951 after his resignation from the cabinet. Having won only nine seats in the 1952 elections, the SLFP clearly needed allies, but the other non-Tamil opposition parties were Marxist groups: the Communist Party, the Lanka Sama Samaja Party (LSSP) and its offshoot, the Viplavakari Lanka Sama Samaja Party (VLSSP). A few days after the dissolution of Parliament, four distinct political groups announced the formation of the Mahajana Eksath Peramuna (MEP, People's United Front), based on a common program of opposition to the UNP and commitment to Sinhalese as the sole official language. Mr. Bandaranaike's SLFP was joined by the Marxist VLSSP led by Mr. Philip Gunawardena, the Basha Peramuna (Language Front), and a group of Independents. With this curious coalition formed, and having reached no-contest agreements with the other Marxist parties, S. W. R. D. Bandaranaike was ready to do battle with a somewhat complacent UNP. Having espoused Sinhala Only, the party in power considered the elections already won.

The timing of the dissolution and new elections immediately became the subject of a heated controversy. Parliament was not due to be dissolved until May 1957. The government's decision to hold elections in early 1956 meant, according to the critics, the inevitable disruption of the spiritual atmosphere which was being generated in the country by preparations for the Buddha Jayanti celebrations. Elections would spread political discord, bring divisions among the Buddhists, and frustrate hopes for a Buddhist revival in Ceylon. A large meeting of monks at the Town Hall in Colombo urged the government to postpone the election until after the Buddha Jayanti year (May 1956 to May 1957). The venerable Mapitigama Buddharakkhita Thero, whose political career is discussed in detail in a later chapter, declared on that occasion that they had learned by experience that they might not be able to make the government change its decision.

34 For a detailed discussion of the 1956 elections see I. D. S. Weerawardana, *Ceylon General Election 1956*, M. D. Gunasena and Co., Ltd., Colombo, 1960. See also chapter 9 in Wriggins.

Therefore, they should forthwith organize themselves to work for the defeat of the UNP at the polls.[35]

"No election before the Buddha Jayanti" quickly became a popular slogan with the monks. About 250 *bhikkhus* fasted on the steps of the House of Representatives, then marched to Victoria Park to dramatize their protest against the government. Monks staged *satyagraha* demonstrations in many towns throughout the country, denouncing the elections as Mara (Satan) from whom Buddhism had to be protected.[36] While the prime minister gave several unconvincing reasons for the decision to hold the elections at that seemingly inappropriate time, one probable consideration was that anti-UNP Sangha organizations were already beginning to make their influence felt, and lay Buddhist groups such as the All-Ceylon Buddhist Congress were growing in strength. Much of the evidence given before the Buddhist Committee of Inquiry was highly critical of the UNP regime. These unfavorable developments and trends could only be strengthened by the fervor of the Buddha Jayanti.[37] The government held fast to its announced decision. The elections were held on April 5, 7 and 10; the Buddha Jayanti celebrations began on May 23.

Language, religion and culture were the issues which dominated the election campaign, yet the differences in party platforms between the UNP and the MEP were not great. Since both were committed to Sinhala Only, the Sinhalese voter had to decide which party was more sincere in its commitment and would be more likely to fulfil its promises. S. W. R. D. Bandaranaike rightly judged that the question of Buddhism would be an important issue generally in his favor, but he also labored under handicaps. The joint program of the MEP reflected the limitations of a coalition which included Marxists in an election campaign dominated by religious issues. The MEP manifesto included the following colorless and undramatic statement on religion: "While realizing the position of Buddhism in this country as the faith of a large majority of the people we guarantee the fullest freedom of worship and conscience to all, and accept the position that there shall be no discrimination on religious grounds. We generally approve the recommendations of the report of the Buddhist Committee of Inquiry."[38] It was significant that in the Sinhalese ver-

---

[35] *Ceylon Daily News*, February 16, 1956. For a detailed treatment of the monks' activities in the 1956 election campaign see chapter 22, "The Political Monks and Monastic Reform."

[36] *Ceylon Observer*, February 25-26, 1956.

[37] Wriggins, p. 330; "Sangha Campaigns," *Ceylon Observer*, July 17, 1962.

[38] *Ceylon Daily News*, March 8, 1956.

sion of the manifesto the qualifying word "generally" in the last sentence did not appear.

Bandaranaike's own party in the MEP coalition, the SLFP, naturally dealt with the question of Buddhism in more specific terms. Following the analysis of the Buddhist report, the SLFP manifesto argued that over a period of four hundred years western imperial masters had pursued policies calculated to destroy the influence of Buddhism. Still, Buddhism was inextricably woven into the fabric of the national life and culture of Ceylon. "So that in rebuilding our people in this new era of freedom, it is very essential to remedy the injustices done to Buddhism and to enable the Buddhists to take the fullest advantage of their religion and culture."[39] But the manifesto made it clear that the rehabilitation of Buddhism did not require that it be made the state religion.

Mr. Philip Gunawardena's VLSSP, the Marxist group in the MEP coalition, could reconcile the emphasis on Buddhism with its own ideology at several levels. With some justification it was argued that Buddhism was a philosophy, not a religion, and that some of its tenets (atheism, rejection of priestcraft, scientific approach to problems) had much in common with Marxism. The Buddhist revivalist and the Marxist shared a deep-seated hostility toward the Roman Catholic Church, which both regarded as a creature of western imperialism and the enemy of nationalism. In the social structure of present-day Ceylon it was not difficult to identify "the masses" with the Sinhalese Buddhist majority struggling against the entrenched power of the upper classes in which Christians were disproportionately well represented. Philip Gunawardena spoke of the need for a program of action which would be in consonance with national culture.[40] It would indeed be difficult for anyone to define national culture without reference to the Sinhalese language and Buddhism.

The UNP election manifesto pointed out that the party had always recognized Buddhism as the religion professed by the vast majority of the people and had acted accordingly, although without compromising the constitutional principle of non-discrimination on religious grounds. The UNP government had assumed active leadership in the national celebration of the Buddha Jayanti. The translation of the Tripitaka into Sinhalese, the restoration of the Temple of the Tooth and all the other projects were the result of the government's initiative in promoting Buddhism. The government would also give its careful attention to the recommendations of the Buddhist committee's re-

[39] Weerawardana, p. 58.   [40] *Tribune*, March 15, 1956.

Donald E. Smith

port.[41] During the campaign UNP candidates frequently cited the government's record in the Buddha Jayanti to refute opposition charges that it had neglected Buddhism.

The UNP had received considerable support from the Roman Catholic Church in previous elections, and in the context of increasingly aggressive Buddhist communalism the Catholic-UNP identification was to prove a serious disadvantage to the government party. The archbishop of Colombo issued a pastoral letter in 1952, just before the elections of that year, warning Catholic voters against supporting certain candidates. The position was stated strongly: "No Catholic with even an atom of Christian conscience can vote for a candidate who belongs to a political creed banned by the Church—let it be Communism or any other—or has pledged himself directly or indirectly to an electoral program inimical to God and His Church, or who is in sympathy with those who are hostile to the Church."[42] While the Marxist parties were clearly the chief target of this directive, it was worded in such a way that it could be interpreted to include even Bandaranaike's SLFP. The militant Buddhist emphasis, if examined, was almost always found to contain some measure of anti-Catholicism.

The UNP was obviously the chief beneficiary of the church's 1952 electioneering. In 1956 the archbishop issued no pastoral letter on the subject, perhaps because of the severe criticisms of the church's political role publicized by the Buddhist committee's report. However, warnings were given to the faithful from pulpits all over the Island. Catholics were forbidden to vote for Marxists, and those who disobeyed would be committing a grievous sin and would be liable to excommunication.[43] And, of course, Marxists were included in the MEP coalition. The story was circulated that the Catholic Church had contributed 1,000,000 rupees to the UNP election campaign fund.[44] The story was false, but effective. In an election campaign fought in the midst of a Buddhist resurgence, the UNP was identified in many minds with the interests of an alien religion professed by a small privileged minority.

The MEP made its strongest appeal to the rural Sinhalese masses who were responsive to the Buddhist symbols so skillfully employed, and to the Sinhalese-educated lower middle class which found its

[41] Weerawardana, pp. 53-54.
[42] Lakshman Wickremesinghe, "The Catholic Perspective and the Political Situation: A Criticism," *The Pilgrim*, 1960, vol. 4, no. 1, pp. 20-23.
[43] *Ceylon Observer*, March 12, 1956.
[44] *Ceylon Daily News*, March 3, 1956.

influence small in a society dominated by the English-educated. The Buddhist monk, the Ayurvedic physician and the vernacular school teacher, the traditional leaders in village life, threw their support to a party which promised them an important role in a new society built on Sinhalese Buddhist culture. The MEP was the party of the common man who was still rooted in this culture; the UNP was the party of the westernized elite, of the privileged classes, of the big landlords and capitalists. The UNP politicians, it was charged, had abandoned Sinhalese Buddhist culture for the ways of the West. They felt most at home in European dress at a cocktail party or dance; they despised all the customs and traditions which were part of Ceylon's national culture. While there was some exaggeration and distortion in this image of the UNP projected by MEP propaganda, it undoubtedly contained a large measure of truth.

The election campaign proceeded in an intensely communal atmosphere. Before it started a newspaper editorial correctly predicted that, since the main issues would be language and religion, "every candidate will be trying to win the plaudits of his electorate by declaring himself to be more extremist than his opponent."[45] The communal orientation of the election was taken for granted by all, and the press did very little to encourage secular politics. For example, one newspaper published a full-page analysis of the 89 constituencies in the country. The constituencies were described in the following manner: "*Panadura*. There are 62,273 voters. 90 per cent are Sinhalese and 5 per cent Moors. 88 per cent are Buddhists, 4 per cent Christians and 5 per cent Muslims. Prospective candidates are . . ."[46]

The 1956 elections resulted in an overwhelming victory for the MEP which won 51 seats. Bandaranaike's own party in the coalition, the SLFP, won 41 of these. The UNP was shattered in a disastrous defeat, and emerged with only 8 seats. 1956 was a crucial year for Buddhism in Ceylon. It marked the Buddha Jayanti, the Buddhist Committee of Inquiry Report, the electoral victory of a party pledged to restore Buddhism to its rightful place, and the emergence of the Sangha as an important political force.

BANDARANAIKE AND BUDDHISM

In partial fulfilment of his election promises to restore Buddhism to its "rightful place," Prime Minister S. W. R. D. Bandaranaike took two steps which met with relatively little opposition. He created a ministry of cultural affairs, and established two Buddhist universities.

[45] "First Things First," *Ceylon Observer*, January 16, 1956.
[46] *Morning Times*, February 25, 1956.

Donald E. Smith

It will be convenient to discuss these here, although some important aspects of their development came after Bandaranaike's death in 1959.

From its inception the ministry of cultural affairs was deeply involved in religion. N. Q. Dias, a senior civil servant and prominent Buddhist militant, became the first director. The philosophy which its program reflected was later succinctly stated by a minister of cultural affairs who wrote an article titled "Our Religion is the Basis of Our Culture."[47] Religion, of course, meant only Buddhism, and there was no recognition given to the very considerable cultural contributions made by Hinduism, to say nothing of Christianity and western civilization. "Since the day Arahat Mahinda introduced Buddhism into Ceylon the life and thought of the people of this country have been molded by this message. Throughout our history we find that all aspects of our culture have had Buddhism as their background."

It will be recalled that the UNP government had appointed the Lanka Bauddha Mandalaya (Buddhist Council of Ceylon) in 1954 to organize and direct the Buddha Jayanti activities. Several of these were long-term projects which after 1956 became the responsibility of the department of cultural affairs.[48] Among them were the construction of memorial buildings, the restoration of the Temple of the Tooth, and the compilation and publication of the encyclopedia of Buddhism, the Sinhalese encyclopedia and the Sinhalese-Pali Tripitaka. Despite the strong Buddhist orientation and philosophy, support was also given to Hindu and Muslim religious programs. Buddhist, Hindu and Islamic religious affairs advisory committees were set up to help select suitable programs which would then be aided by the department. An important difference was that Buddhist programs were frequently administered directly by the department, while Hinduism and Islam were usually aided by grants made to the institutions of these religions. The 1960 report stated that the Roman Catholic archbishop of Colombo had been granted 10,000 rupees for religious publications and an additional 10,000 rupees for religious instruction.

The promotion of Buddhism took many forms. Dhamma schools patterned after the Christian Sunday schools were supplied with books free of charge. The All-Ceylon Buddhist Congress was given an annual subsidy for the publication of a monthly paper called *Bauddhalokaya*, and grants for other Buddhist religious activities. A

[47] Maitripala Senanayake (minister of industries, home and cultural affairs), "Our Religion is the Basis of Our Culture," *The Buddhist*, vol. 31, January-April 1961, pp. 5-6.
[48] The department of cultural affairs is the administrative agency of the ministry.

sizable annual grant was made to the YMBA (Young Men's Buddhist Association) for conducting Dhamma examinations. A film produced in India, "Gautama the Buddha," was purchased by the government of Ceylon, and two cinema vans of the department showed it in rural areas all over the Island. The Buddhist Publications Society, Kandy, received grants for its program of worldwide distribution of Buddhist literature. Building grants were given to Buddhist religious institutions such as temples, monasteries and *pirivenas*. Buddhist missionary work in New Delhi, London and West Berlin received department support.[49]

In terms of the future development of Buddhist religion, the most far-reaching activity of the department of cultural affairs was its intensive effort to develop a strong organizational link between itself and the Buddhist temples found in all parts of Ceylon. The problem of Buddhist organization was one of the major concerns of the Buddhist Committee of Inquiry, as has been noted. On the recommendation of the Buddhist religious affairs advisory committee, the department established or recognized almost 4,000 Vihara Sasanarakshaka Societies, temple associations for the promotion of Buddhism. A model constitution for these societies was drawn up by the department. Membership was to be limited to the resident monks and lay devotees of the respective temples. The objects of the organization were to improve the connection between the laity and the Sangha, to promote knowledge and the observance of *sil*,[50] to establish and improve Sunday Dhamma schools, to promote temperance activities, and to work for the prevention of crime. Article 9 of the model constitution stated: "This society should comply with the circulars issued by the department of cultural affairs on the advice of the Buddhist advisory board."[51] Each temple society would send four representatives as members of the regional Sasanarakshaka board, which would also include the member of Parliament for the area, if a Buddhist. One such board was established in each of the 88 revenue districts of Ceylon. The department of cultural affairs thus stood at the apex of a hierarchy, over 88 regional boards which represented nearly 4,000 temple societies. The functions of the hierarchy were purely religious, and there was no involvement in the administration of Buddhist

[49] *Administration Report of the Director of Cultural Affairs*, reports for 1958, 1959 and 1960.

[50] *Pancha sil* are the Five Precepts of basic morality. To observe *sil* on Poya (sabbath days) the layman must follow eight precepts, including fasting after noon.

[51] "Introduction to the Sasanarakshaka Societies in Temples and Regional Sasanarakshaka Boards," typescript, Department of Cultural Affairs.

temporalities (temple lands).[52] However, the organization, under close governmental supervision, could obviously be developed along different lines at a later date.

Another step in S. W. R. D. Bandaranaike's program of restoring Buddhism to its "rightful place" was the establishment of two Buddhist universities, or rather, the elevation to university status of two famous monastic institutions of higher learning (*pirivenas*). The tradition of the *pirivena* in Ceylon is almost as old as Buddhism itself, but was all but lost in modern times until revived in 1873 by an eminent monk-scholar, the venerable Hikkaduwe Sri Sumangala Nayaka Thero.[53] In that year he and a group of thirteen Buddhist laymen founded the Vidyodaya Pirivena of Maligakanda, Colombo. Later another important seat of monastic learning, the Vidyalankara Pirivena, developed along similar lines. Both institutions belonged to the Malwatte chapter of the Siam sect. From 1875 onward the British government made annual grants to recognized *pirivenas* for the advancement of oriental scholarship.[54] Pali and Buddhist studies made up almost the entire curriculum.

In 1956 Mr. Wijayananda Dahanayake, minister of education, proposed that the Vidyodaya Pirivena and the Vidyalankara Pirivena be granted university status, a proposal which met with the prime minister's approval. In the bill which was then drafted, the objects and reasons stated that the two institutions enjoyed an international reputation as seats of advanced oriental learning and lacked only the legal status of universities. The bill sought to remedy this defect, and the two universities thus created would also produce Sinhalese qualified graduates in accordance with the government's language policy.[55] The bill was enacted by Parliament in 1958.

The universities were empowered to make provision "for the advancement and dissemination of knowledge and for the promotion of Sinhala and Buddhist culture."[56] The universities were to be open to all persons of the male sex regardless of race, creed or class, and

[52] Even so, leaders of the Siam sect of the Sangha objected to what they feared would be the government's "nationalization" of the temples. Based on interviews with officers of the department.

[53] Ven. Akuratiye Amarawansa Thero, "The Role of the Pirivena in the Revival of Buddhist Learning," *The Buddhist*, vol. 29, May 1958, pp. 75-76.

[54] There are now about 200 *pirivenas* which are recognized and aided financially by the government. For the regulations concerning them, see *Ceylon Government Gazette*, August 7, 1959.

[55] Weliwitiye Sorata Nayaka Thera, "This University," *Journal of the Vidyodaya University of Ceylon*, vol. 1, August 1960, pp. 14-17; *Second Anniversary Souvenir of the Inauguration of the Vidyodaya University of Ceylon*, 1961, pp. 1-6.

[56] Vidyodaya University and Vidyalankara University Act, No. 45 of 1958, section 5 (a).

no test of religious belief or profession would be imposed. Religious instruction, however, could be prescribed for *bhikkhus*. Because of the universities' monastic background, women would be permitted to study as external students only.[57] The elaborate administrative structure of the universities was patterned after that of the University of Ceylon, which has been developed on the lines of London University. The governor general of Ceylon was to be the chancellor and the minister of education the pro-chancellor ex-officio. The act required that the vice-chancellors of the two universities be *bhikkhus*. The court of each university could make statutes provided these were not repugnant to the Vinayapitaka. In accordance with the Vinaya, *bhikkhu* professors were to be paid certain allowances in lieu of salary.[58]

A very extensive building program was begun on the two campuses. At the Vidyodaya University the new buildings were large concrete structures of modern design, and many observers wondered whether the atmosphere of scholarly piety which permeated the traditional *pirivena* could flourish or even survive in such a setting. Efforts were made, however, to maintain some of these traditions. At the Vidyodaya University all students were required to take Sinhala Buddhist culture as one of their subjects, and all monk students had to study Buddhadhamma. In 1963 about 40 of the 100 members of the teaching staff, and 400 of the 1,500 students, were *bhikkhus*.[59]

Both in the parliamentary debate and in later discussion, however, fears were expressed that in these Buddhist universities both education and Buddhism would suffer. Critics declared that in the modern world there could be no full-fledged university from which women were excluded, or in which there were no courses in anatomy, biology and zoology because of religious objections to the dissection of bodies. How could the Vidyodaya University offer a B.Sc. course without teaching these subjects?[60] Other critics deplored the secularizing ef-

---

[57] *Ibid.*, section 6.

[58] *Ibid.*, sections 11 (1), 16 (a), 35.

[59] Based on interviews with university officials in April 1963.

[60] These points were emphasized in a draft report of the Universities Commission, which suggested that one of the *pirivena* institutions be made a full-fledged university for laymen, while the other be developed to meet the needs of the Buddhist monks exclusively. *Ceylon Daily News*, April 24, 1963. This proposed segregation of the monks and laymen was strongly opposed by the vice-chancellor of the Vidyalankara University. *Ibid.*, April 12, 1963. The final report was a caustic indictment of virtually every aspect of the operation of these institutions. The major recommendation was: "That, as the higher education of the *Bhikkhu* and the higher education of the laity cannot be brought under one organization, the two Pirivena Universities should cease to exist at the earliest possible moment." *Report of the Universities Commission 1962*, sessional paper 16 of 1963, p. 168.

fect of the present system on the *bhikkhu* students.[61] Monks who study political science and economics at these universities will naturally want to play a more active role in the politics of the country. It was argued that monks who are graduated with a B.A. or M.A. degree will be sorely tempted to forsake the yellow robe and seek secular employment. This has indeed happened already to an alarming extent.[62] Buddhism's encounter with modernity in the person of a *bhikkhu* university student opens up new possibilities for creative Buddhist thought and broadened influence for the Sangha. But there are also serious problems created or at least intensified by this encounter.

The creation of a ministry of cultural affairs met with no opposition, and the establishment of the two Buddhist universities with relatively little. A third step in S. W. R. D. Bandaranaike's religious program was the appointment of a Buddha Sasana Commission to inquire into the state of Buddhism in Ceylon and recommend steps to restore it to its rightful place in national life. This was the official commission which D. S. Senanayake had refused to appoint in 1951, and in the absence of which the non-official Buddhist Committee of Inquiry had been set up in 1954. The Buddha Sasana Commission was appointed in 1957, but in the face of the most intense opposition of the Siam sect of the Sangha.

The Buddhist monks were among the most vociferous advocates of Sinhala Only. Bandaranaike found their unyielding stand on this issue helpful in the 1956 election but thereafter embarrassing and obstructive. In accordance with his election promises, a Sinhala Only bill was enacted by Parliament two months after the new government took over, setting off widespread Sinhalese-Tamil communal disturbances in which 150 people were killed. In the face of a threatened Tamil civil disobedience campaign in August 1957, Bandaranaike signed a pact with the Federal Party leader, S. J. V. Chelvanayakam, which recognized Tamil as the "language of a national minority in Ceylon." On April 9, 1958, a group of about 200 *bhikkhus* and 300

[61] The *bhikkhu* "is a person who has devoted his life to an effort to reach *Nibbana*. Whatever helps him in his effort is of value to him. Judged by this standard, it is doubtful if a university pirivena education will be of much value." Sinha Basnayake, "The Value of University Pirivena Education," *The Buddhist*, vol. 33, July 1962, p. 25.

[62] The Vidyodaya University regulations state: "Students who enter the university availing themselves of the privileges accorded to *bhikkhus* will be expelled if they disrobe themselves." *Vidyodaya University of Ceylon: Entrance Regulations 1963-1965*, chapter 11, rule 10. According to officials in the department of education, however, many monks cast off the yellow robe after graduation and seek jobs as teachers in the state schools.

others camped in front of the prime minister's house, vehemently denounced the pact and demanded its abrogation. Bandaranaike, who had fought off opposition within his own cabinet, gave in to the monks. Mrs. Vimala Wijewardene, the health minister, announced the prime minister's capitulation and, on the monks' insistence, got Bandaranaike's written pledge that the pact was no more. In the wake of its abrogation came an unprecedented outburst of communal violence in which 300-400 lives were lost.[63] The Sangha's relations with the Bandaranaike government form a fascinating chapter in the recent political history of Ceylon, and merit detailed separate treatment below.[64]

EDUCATION AND THE BUDDHIST REVOLUTION

Almost half of *The Betrayal of Buddhism*, the English version of the 1956 report of the Buddhist Committee of Inquiry, was devoted to the subject of education in Ceylon. The nationalization of state-aided denominational schools in 1960-1961 was the direct outcome of its recommendations.

As in other parts of the report, most of the discussion was concerned with the historical background of the problem. The major thesis advanced was that British educational policy was strongly influenced by the desire to promote the conversion of Ceylon to Christianity, and that the system of state-aided denominational schools was designed to serve this end behind a false façade of official religious neutrality.

Without a doubt, British policies during the first few decades of their rule were openly pro-Christian. In 1796 the British won control of the maritime areas of Ceylon, succeeding the Dutch empire builders who had unhesitatingly suppressed Catholicism (brought by the Portuguese), and had used education and the promise of government jobs to win converts to their Protestant faith. In 1799 an important proclamation was issued by the British governor: "We, Frederick North, governor of Ceylon, do inform all native headmen, school masters and inhabitants within the jurisdiction of Colombo that it is our earnest desire that the Christian religion should be continued and propagated as much as possible and therefore do order all the afore-mentioned persons to assist everyone in their offices and situations in order that the Christian religion which has been planted with so much labor on this Island may be cultivated to the glory of

---

[63] Tarzie Vittachi, *Emergency '58: The Story of the Ceylon Race Riots*, Andre Deutsch, London, 1958, pp. 20, 28-29.
[64] See chapter 22.

God and for the salvation of the immortal soul."[65] The British continued the Dutch system of state schools, but placed them under the management of the highest dignitary of the established Church of England. In 1821 this was the Archdeacon of Colombo, who also received the title of Principal of Schools and King's Visitor.

In 1812 Protestant missionary societies began their work in Ceylon, and established schools which later received government grants. The Buddhist report made much of the discriminatory policies pursued by the government up to 1869, but neglected to point out that the Catholics (a large majority of the Christian population) were in as disadvantageous a position as the Buddhists, Hindus and Muslims.[66] In 1869 the grant-in-aid system was established by which all religious bodies could manage their own schools with government grants based solely on the secular instruction imparted in them. It was a stated policy of equality of opportunity, of free competition. Along with these private schools which received aid were state schools managed directly by the government. Essentially, this was the system which lasted right up to 1960.

The basic fact is that the various religious bodies were very unequally prepared to avail themselves of these equal opportunities. Protestant bodies had a long headstart, and were in a good position to expand their educational work. The Catholic Church had to overcome a certain degree of official antagonism toward it, but had a highly efficient organization and good leadership, and energetically set about building a strong network of schools. The Buddhists, depite the inspired leadership of Colonel Olcott, did not do as well. Here again, their fundamental problem was the lack of a centralized Buddhist organization which could pool all resources and coordinate educational efforts. Olcott's Buddhist Theosophical Society was a lay organization which had to function without the cooperation of the Sangha, and without the financial support which could have been provided from the income of temple lands. Still, considerable progress was made in the field of Buddhist education. In 1884 there were only 8 state-aided Buddhist schools; in 1924 the number was 406. During the same period the number of Protestant schools increased from 575 to 742, and Catholic schools from 203 to 528.

But these figures do not tell the whole story. The large majority of the schools of all three religious groups were vernacular schools (Sinhalese or Tamil medium of instruction), but both Protestants and Catho-

---

[65] Cited in *The Betrayal of Buddhism*, p. 43.

[66] This valid criticism of the report is made repeatedly in the Catholic Union's *Companion to the Buddhist Commission Report*.

lics devoted much of their resources to building a number of select English-medium higher-grade schools (called colleges in Ceylon) which came to dominate the educational scene. These institutions became known for their high academic standards, good discipline, strong emphasis on English, westernized cultural atmosphere, and middle- and upper-class values. These were the prestige institutions which led to the university, either in Ceylon or England, and the B.A. degree in turn led to coveted posts in the civil service. The Buddhists were able to develop very few such institutions; the most famous was Ananda College in Colombo. Christian educational superiority was thus the basis of Christian influence in government circles. Many of the high-ranking civil servants were Christians, and many of the prominent Buddhist politicians were "old boys" of Christian schools.

The Buddhist committee report ignored or minimized the inherent weaknesses of the Buddhist community in the educational competition with well-organized Christian bodies, and attributed the latter's success to the support of a government which deliberately discriminated against the Buddhists. The report sought to give the impression that the same religious motives stated so bluntly in Governor North's proclamation of 1799 continued to determine British educational policy right up to independence. It was not so much the analysis of the Buddhist situation in 1956 as the charge that a great historic injustice had been perpetrated over a century and a half which gave the report its emotional power. Any dispassionate scholarly account would have to concede that there was far more substance to the British policy of religious neutrality, certainly by 1880, than that suggested by the report.

Whatever the limitations of the report from the historian's point of view, it dramatized the very real anomalies of the situation which prevailed in independent Ceylon. The terms of the educational partnership between the state and private bodies changed gradually until almost the entire financial burden was being borne by the state. The Education Act of 1947 introduced the free education scheme, under which the government paid the teachers and forbade the levying of fees by those state-aided schools which opted to join the scheme. The Education (Amendment) Act of 1951 gave state-aided schools the choice of either (1) becoming entirely private without state aid but with the right to levy fees, or (2) joining the free education scheme, in which case the government would not only pay the teachers' salaries but make grants for school laboratories, workshops and libraries. Most of the denominational schools elected the second course, partly because it seemed more democratic to offer free education than to serve only the classes which could afford to pay fees, but mostly because of the financial security provided by such extensive state assistance.

The system of state schools, of course, continued side by side with that of state-aided schools, and the differences between the two systems were rapidly narrowed as the state's financial responsibility increased. In 1955 there were 4,044 state schools and 2,273 state-aided denominational schools. The majority of the denominational schools were managed by Catholic and Protestant bodies. Of the state-aided colleges included in this figure, the Christians had 35, the Buddhists only 9. In the Catholic schools 40 per cent of the pupils were non-Catholics (mostly Buddhists), and in the Protestant schools the overwhelming majority were Buddhists or Hindus.

While the Buddhist committee report was at some places quite misleading in its use of statistics, the basic facts which it emphasized were undisputable. The Christians, 9 per cent of the population, controlled a large segment of the education of the country and most of the prestige institutions which led to the university. Most of the cost of Christian educational dominance was being borne not by the Christians but by the Buddhist taxpayers, for the Buddhists were 64 per cent of the population.

The report recommended that by January 1, 1958, "all assisted schools should be taken over by the state."[67] It recommended that the right of setting up new schools be vested exclusively in the state, and that if over 51 per cent of the pupils in a state school were of one particular religion, the head of the school should be of that faith. The attempt to convert any person under twenty-one years of age from one religion to another in an educational institution should be made a punishable offense. A religious body should have liberty to establish and maintain schools, but entirely at its own expense with no state aid whatsoever. Furthermore, it should be illegal to admit to such a school a child of a different religion from that of the management. The report also recommended the nationalization of teacher training colleges.

The 1959 report of the Buddha Sasana Commission reinforced these recommendations. This official commission asserted: "The full educational rights of Buddhist children can be obtained only through state schools."[68] The system of denominational schools emphasized

[67] *The Betrayal of Buddhism*, p. 97.
[68] *Buddha Sasana Commission Report*, p. 280.

divisions and hindered national unity, was a heavy financial burden on the state, did not allow the creation of a national system of education, and should therefore be abolished. However, an interesting interim plan was proposed. "Until such time as the state accepts the above recommendations and starts implementing them, the following should be done by the state immediately: The state should create immediately an organization of Buddhist representatives to establish in suitable places schools for Buddhist children. This should be done as it is not possible at present for Buddhists to establish new schools."[69] These Buddhist schools were to be financed entirely by the state from funds which would be saved by cutting off all aid to the assisted schools!

It was clear that the fundamental objection was not to denominational schools as such but to denominational schools controlled by a minority community. In the debate which preceded nationalization the Buddhist position was frequently represented as the demand for a modern national system of state schools. However, the driving emotional force behind the movement was largely the resentment felt toward a minority which had won a disproportionately large share of the educational pie, whatever the terms of the competition.

THE NATIONALIZATION OF SCHOOLS

In March 1958 Mr. S. W. R. D. Bandaranaike, in an address to the All-Ceylon United Bhikkhu Congress, urged great caution in the matter of taking over the assisted schools. "While I try to safeguard the rights of Buddhism I cannot aim a death-blow at others. It is not only the Catholics but also some Buddhists who are opposed. . . ." If schools like Ananda College or St. Joseph's College were taken over, he argued, vast sums would have to be paid in compensation for their lands and buildings.[70]

S. W. R. D. Bandaranaike was assassinated by a monk on September 25, 1959. The political situation which led to the elections of March and July 1960 is described in detail in other chapters.[71] The widow of the slain prime minister, Mrs. Sirimavo Bandaranaike, became the leader of the SLFP.

Even by the time of the March 1960 elections the SLFP was not committed to a policy of nationalization. The party manifesto recognized the useful educational service provided by the existing denominational schools, and simply stated: "It will be our policy to establish

[69] *Ibid.*, p. 281.
[70] *Ceylon Daily News*, March 17, 1958.
[71] See below, chapters 22 and 23.

government schools providing a system of education with religious instruction acceptable to all in areas at present catered for by such denominational schools and thereafter to withdraw state grants to denominational schools."

On the eve of the July 1960 elections an SLFP spokesman, Mr. Felix R. Dias Bandaranaike, later minister of finance, stated the party position on education: "We shall appoint as soon as we form the government two special committees, one for the revision of the scheme of studies to give a national outlook to education imparted in schools and the other to prepare the way to bring the entire system of education under a central authority."[72] After the SLFP victory Mrs. Bandaranaike reiterated this position. The throne speech of August 12, 1960, however, announced the policy of the new government in the following words: "My government proposes, without discrimination on religious grounds, to introduce legislation to take over assisted grade III schools, including primary, post-primary and rural schools. Grade I and grade II assisted schools will be taken over subject to the privilege which will be allowed to such schools to remain without state aid as private schools in conformity with the Education Code."[73]

While SLFP government spokesmen and MP's held that there was some kind of mandate from the electorate to nationalize the schools based, among other things, on S. W. R. D. Bandaranaike's general approval of the Buddhist committee's report in 1956, there was very little to substantiate this claim. Whatever the reasons behind it, there was a radical change in declared party policy between the July 1960 elections and the throne speech a month later. The most plausible explanation is simply that the SLFP was afraid to contest the election on such a controversial issue, but decided to push ahead with the nationalization after its resounding victory.[74] The nationalization measure was supported by the majority of the population (most of the Sinhalese Buddhists favored it), but this support was never sought at the polls.

In the parliamentary debate and public discussion of the proposed legislation, the Roman Catholics argued that the issue of religious liberty was very much involved. It was a matter of conscience with Catholics that they have their own schools so that their children could be educated in a religious atmosphere, and it was a requirement of

---

[72] *Ibid.*, June 9, 1960. [73] *Ibid.*, August 13, 1960.
[74] See the parliamentary debate in *House of Representatives*, 1960, vol. 40, no. 9, cols. 1573-2444. The discrepancies in SLFP policy statements were pointed up effectively by the speeches of W. Dahanayake and J. R. Jayewardene, cols. 1635-1654, 1670-1684, 2166-2176.

canon law that parents send their children to such schools.[75] Supporters of the bill pointedly asked how this religious atmosphere was divided so that it would not affect the 40 per cent non-Catholic pupils. It was charged that Christian schools were engaged in proselytization at state expense, although there was very little evidence that this had been a real problem in recent decades. Although Protestant bodies deplored the haste with which the nationalization bill was introduced, their opposition was far less intense than that of the Catholics, and many Protestant leaders accepted it as the only solution to the anomalies of the existing system.

Defenders of the denominational schools pointed to their high standards and generally recognized superiority over state schools, largely the result of private sacrifice and hard work. The Marxist parties, the LSSP, CP and Philip Gunawardena's group now called the MEP, which had had a no-contest agreement with the SLFP in the July 1960 elections, vigorously supported the nationalization measure. They attacked the "privileged class atmosphere" of the denominational colleges, the "obscurantist and reactionary role" of the Catholic Church, and pressed for a "truly national" system of state schools. Here again, Buddhist and Marxist interests seemed to coincide.

The Assisted Schools and Training Colleges (Special Provisions) Bill was passed by the House of Representatives by a vote of 101 to 44, then by the Senate, and received the governor general's assent on November 17, 1960. The act provided for the appointment of the director of education as manager of all assisted schools other than schools which the proprietors elected to administer as unaided schools. The choice, however, could hardly be called a free one, for the restrictions placed on unaided schools were calculated to make their existence impossible. Under the act, an unaided school was not permitted to admit a pupil whose parent did not profess the religion of the proprietor of the school. It had to maintain all the facilities and accommodation for pupils as before, but could levy no fees.[76] Thus, without government grants and without fees, the unaided school would be dependent solely on the resources of the religious body. The only way to secure the right to levy fees was by a poll administered by the director of education in which 75 *per cent* of the teachers and parents

[75] For the Catholic position see: D. J. B. Kuruppu, *Probe into an Education System*, Catholic Book Depot, Colombo, 1958; Edmund Peiris, *The New Educational Policy*, Colombo Catholic Press, n.d. [1960]; *Companion to the Buddhist Commission Report*; many articles in *The Messenger*, Colombo.

[76] Assisted Schools and Training Colleges (Special Provisions) Act, No. 5 of 1960, section 6.

of children in the school voted for fees. *Pirivenas*, educational institutions operated by Buddhist monks with government grants, were
excluded from the operation of the act.[77]

On December 1, 1960, the director of education became the manager
of 2,554 schools. Under the provisions of the act, 55 schools (42 of
them Roman Catholic) elected to become private non-fee levying
schools. The proprietors of several schools took the initial steps to
have polls held on the question of fees, but later abandoned the idea.
The Roman Catholics fought the nationalization measure to the
bitter end. Mass demonstrations protested the take-over as the result
of Communist influence on the government. With the tacit approval or
possibly at the instigation of the church hierarchy, Catholic parents
physically occupied hundreds of Catholic schools, threw up barricades
around them and refused to allow education department officials to
enter. Through the month of December 1960 the crisis became increasingly acute. The government did not want to use force for this
would surely result in bloodshed, and martyrdom would only serve the
Catholic cause.

The prime minister met Roman Catholic and National Christian
Council deputations in an effort to find a way out of the school dead-
lock. Fearing some kind of compromise, a strong delegation from the
All-Ceylon Buddhist Congress met the prime minister to remind her
that the Buddhists of the country demanded firm action.[78] Cardinal
Gracias came from Bombay to consult with the Ceylon hierarchy, and
after a marathon meeting with members of the cabinet, the archbishop
of Colombo announced that the Catholics were being asked to withdraw their occupation of the schools.[79] A few days later the last of
the squatters moved out.

The Catholic opposition was not only unsuccessful; it proved to be
of inestimable benefit to the SLFP government in pushing through the
next piece of legislation. The House of Representatives was summoned
to meet on January 18, 1961, and quickly enacted a measure which
vested in the crown, without compensation, all the property of the

[77] Mr. W. Dahanayake, who, as minister of education, had played the leading
role in the creation of the two *pirivena* universities and in the drafting of the
Pirivena Code of 1959, stated that the 200 state-aided *pirivenas* were post-primary
assisted schools not different in any way from those affected by the legislation. The
reason for the exclusion of the *pirivenas*, he declared, could only be that the
government was afraid of treading on the religious rights of the Buddhists. Opposing the bill, he called on the government to mete out the same treatment to
other religionists. *House of Representatives*, 1960, vol. 40, no. 9, cols. 1700-1718.

[78] *Ceylon Daily News*, January 10-13, 1961.

[79] *Ibid.*, January 19-20, 1961.

schools managed by the director of education under the previous act.[80] In one of his speeches in Parliament, the education minister declared that the bill was "designed to transfer the ownership of school property to its real owners—the children of this country." He went on to state that to demand compensation for school property was highly immoral.[81] S. W. R. D. Bandaranaike's statement on the necessity of paying compensation for nationalized school property was quoted repeatedly by opposition MPs, but to no avail. The Constitution of Ceylon, unlike that of India, required no compensation for property compulsorily acquired by the state, and none was paid.

Christian dominance in education was destroyed by the legislation of 1960 and 1961. Although some Buddhists were quite sincere in their demand for a national system of education, the most important motives behind the take-over of denominational schools were communal, not educational. There was indeed injustice in the system under which a religious minority of 9 per cent ran the best schools at state expense, even if it ran them well and even if other communities also benefited from them. But many observers feel that there was injustice in the means chosen to correct this anomalous situation, and the solution has left an embittered Catholic minority. Had the state withdrawn all grants to denominational schools but allowed them to levy fees, while devoting all of its financial resources to building up a first-class system of state schools, there would have been no room for complaint, and the educational result would have been maximized. But it is considerably easier to nationalize a working system than to build one.

The National Education Commission was appointed in March 1961 to survey the whole problem and to make recommendations for the establishment of a unified national system of education. But there was little evidence of a *national* outlook in the commission itself. It was almost obsessed with the idea of redressing communal imbalances. Noting that there was a preponderance of teachers belonging to certain minority religions, the commission recommended: "It is desirable that the teachers employed in national schools should bear some relation to the proportion in which school children are distributed according to religion. We, therefore, recommend that the recruitment of teachers should be done for some time to come with an eye to achieving this object. In the interests of the children it is

[80] Assisted Schools and Training Colleges (Supplementary Provisions) Act, No. 8 of 1961.
[81] *House of Representatives*, 1961, vol. 42, no. 4, cols. 396, 398.

also desirable that the head of the school should be of the religion of the majority of the children in the school."[82]

In 1962 there were 63 private schools in Ceylon, 15 of which had become fee-levying under the 1951 act and 48 of which had become non-fee-levying under the 1960 act. The commission condemned all these private schools as "citadels of privilege" and "pockets of religious separatism." "They are completely incongruous in a national system of education inasmuch as they are restrictive in their admissions and are not open to all the children who live in an area."[83] The commission deliberately ignored the glaring fact that under the 1960 legislation a private school was not allowed to admit pupils of a different religion. It rejected the view that unaided private schools had a right to exist in a democratic country, claimed that the state could bear the expense of running these 63 schools without difficulty, and recommended that they be taken over immediately.[84]

The commission held that the Sinhalese Buddhists, 64 per cent of the population, were still being systematically discriminated against in all areas at the University of Ceylon, and recommended a system of quotas based on religious communities in admission, scholarships and appointments to the public service.[85] Elsewhere in South and Southeast Asia, quotas were designed to safeguard minority interests, but here the object was to protect the majority.

BUDDHIST ASCENDENCY

On January 27, 1962 the government arrested twenty-five persons, including a number of high-ranking army and police officers, on a charge of having conspired to overthrow the government. All but a few of the accused were Christians, mostly Roman Catholics. The trial of those involved in the abortive coup d'état was postponed several times because of procedural objections raised by the defense.

[82] *Interim Report of the National Education Commission, 1961*, Sessional Paper 1 of 1962, p. 38. See the notes of dissent and rejoinder by the majority of the commission, pp. 81-84, 92-93. Several Buddhist laymen who served on the Buddhist Committee of Inquiry were also members of this commission—T. Vimalananda, L. H. Mettananda, and C. D. S. Siriwardane.

[83] *Final Report of the National Education Commission, 1961*, Sessional Paper 17 of 1962, p. 139. See the notes of dissent and rejoinder, pp. 176-196.

[84] *Ibid.*, p. 141.

[85] *Ibid.*, pp. 144-153. See the notes of dissent, pp. 201-211. The commission was divided 10 to 9 on this recommendation. The ministry of education later expressed its disapproval of it. *Times of Ceylon*, April 11, 1963. For discussions of the many issues dealt with by the commission see: *Some Reflections on National Education*, Colombo Catholic Press, Colombo, n.d. [1962]; *Religious and Social Issues*, 1962, vol. 1, no. 1; *Community*, 1962, vol. 4, no. 2; *Journal of the National Education Society of Ceylon*, 1963, vol. 12, no. 1.

But an almost immediate result of the alleged coup attempt was the pressure put on the government to replace Governor General Sir Oliver Goonetilleke, an Anglican Christian, with a Sinhalese Buddhist. Sir Oliver, who was the first Ceylonese governor general (appointed in 1954), resigned and left the country.

Mr. William Gopallawa, Ceylon's ambassador to the United States and a staunch Buddhist, was chosen to succeed him. On March 2, 1962, Gopallawa assumed office in a ceremony of great symbolic significance for Sinhalese Buddhists. Rejecting the traditional uniform with scarlet sash, plumed helmet, sword and scabbard, he wore the simple white cloth and banian of the common man. His Excellency placed a tray of jasmine flowers before an image of the Buddha, installed for the first time at Queen's House, while members of the Sangha chanted verses from the Buddhist scriptures. This was also the first time monks were freely welcomed there.

The lighting of the traditional oil lamp and the blowing of conch shells signified the installation of the new governor general. Then, in a ceremony reminiscent of the ancient days of the Sinhalese kings, the governor general sat at the feet of a learned *bhikkhu* who reminded him that though he was now highest in the land he must himself be governed by the law of the Buddha.[86] In many ways this ceremony expressed the psychological fulfilment of Buddhist aspirations thoroughly blended with nationalist sentiment.

The Sinhalese Buddhist revolution, carried out within the framework of parliamentary democracy, achieved its most important objectives between 1956 and 1962. Certain injustices have been rectified, valid communal grievances have been redressed. But the cost has been high, paid in the coin of national integration. The communalization of politics during this period has set in motion forces which will not be easy to reverse. The progressive identification of Ceylonese nationality with the Buddhist religion and the Sinhalese language is a trend which can only be divisive and disruptive of national unity, whatever the short-run political advantages. Attention must now be turned to the much more difficult task of national integration.

[86] Editorial, *The Buddhist*, vol. 32, February-March 1962, pp. 67-68.

CHAPTER 22

THE POLITICAL MONKS AND MONASTIC REFORM

DONALD E. SMITH

A BRITISH CIVIL servant who had spent many years in Burma wrote at the turn of the century: "No one can imagine even in the far future any monk of the Buddha desiring temporal power, or interfering in any way with the government of the people."[1] Like many others, the writer started with the formal tenets of Buddhism and drew logical inferences from them. The monk is engaged in the quest for Nirvana, he reasoned, and political power can be of no possible assistance, but on the contrary is likely to prove a snare to spiritual progress. The Vinaya, the code of regulations governing the Sangha (order of monks), prohibits the monk's involvement in all worldly affairs. Twenty years later, however, British rule in Burma was shaken by the first important nationalist leader—the Buddhist monk U Ottama.

In Ceylon the Sangha had exercised certain traditional political prerogatives from earliest times. It is recorded in the ancient chronicles that on the death of King Saddha Tissa (second century B.C.), his younger brother was elected sovereign with the *consent* of the Sangha. There were many such instances in which the approval of the Sangha was deemed essential to legitimate the exercise of political power.[2] During the British period the Sangha remained an important center of nationalist sentiment which on occasion found political expression in acts of resistance.

Many factors combined to maximize the political potential of the Sangha. The monk's high prestige could be judged from the Buddhist layman's intonation of the formula: "I take refuge in the Buddha, I take refuge in the Doctrine, I take refuge in the Sangha." This high prestige could easily be translated into political influence. The monks also had organization, that essential ingredient of political

Donald E. Smith is associate professor of political science at the University of Pennsylvania.

[1] Harold Fielding-Hall, *The Soul of a People*, Richard Bentley and Son, London, 1898, pp. 104-105. For a detailed discussion of the role of the political monks in Burma both before and after independence see Donald E. Smith, *Religion and Politics in Burma*, Princeton University Press, Princeton, 1965.

[2] Venerable Pahamune Sri Sumangala, "Foreword," in *The Revolt in the Temple*, pp. 18-19; Walpola Rahula, *History of Buddhism in Ceylon*, M. D. Gunasena and Co., Ltd., Colombo, 1956, pp. 69-77.

effectiveness, in a network of monasteries which reached virtually every village in the island. And having no jobs, families or material possessions, the monks had little to lose through political extremism.

Most important of all, there were powerful motives which impelled the monks to political activism. The Sangha in pre-1956 Ceylon was an alienated elite, for of all sectors of society it had lost most under the impact of foreign rule. From a place of honor under the Sinhalese kings, the monks had become an anachronism in the modern western-ized society developing around them. Their traditional educational functions had been usurped by government and missionary schools, and their ignorance of the English language kept them from effective communication with those who wielded power. To the monks, the idea of radical political change had a powerful appeal.

THE MAKING OF A POLITICAL MONK

It will be useful at this point to describe the background of the most political monk of them all, the Venerable Mapitigama Bud-dharakkhita, who was largely responsible for organizing the Sangha campaign in the 1956 elections. Buddharakkhita was born in 1921, entered the Sangha in 1936 at the age of 15, and received the higher ordination in 1947. He resided in the precincts of the famous Kelaniya temple which, according to Buddhist tradition, marks a place visited by the Lord Buddha himself. In recent decades the history of this important shrine, the Raja Maha Vihare, has been closely connected with that of a leading family of Kelaniya, the Wijewardenes. In 1927 a new era in the history of the temple was inaugurated when Mrs. Helena Wijewardene laid the foundation stone for its restoration, a project on which she spent large sums of money. Mr. Walter Wije-wardene, her son, became the first president of the Kelaniya Dayaka Sabha (Laymen's Council) which supervised the administration of the temple. On his death his brother, Mr. D. C. Wijewardene, was elected president of the council.[3]

The presiding monk of the temple (the term "chief priest" is frequently used, despite its inaccuracy) died just before the 1947 gen-eral elections. Buddharakkhita, then the junior pupil of the Thero (elder), claimed the incumbency in opposition to the senior pupil. Mr. D. C. Wijewardene, president of the laymen's council (and his wife, Mrs. Vimala Wijewardene) supported Buddharakkhita. However, Mr. J. R. Jayewardene and the other members of the council sup-ported the senior pupil. Prolonged and bitter litigation was begun

[3] Ven. Mapitigama Buddharakkhita, "Kelaniya—City of Piety," *Ceylon Daily News*, January 15, 1957.

between Buddharakkhita and the senior pupil over succession to the position of chief incumbent. J. R. Jayewardene was D. C. Wijewardene's nephew and an important political figure, at that time representing the Kelaniya constituency in the State Council. In the 1947 elections to the first Parliament, Buddharakkhita campaigned against him, but the monk was not secure in his own position and hence still not too influential. J. R. Jayewardene won the Kelaniya seat on the UNP ticket.[4]

Buddharakkhita was a founder member and patron of S. W. R. D. Bandaranaike's SLFP formed in 1951. As the 1952 elections approached, circumstances seemed more favorable to Buddharakkhita. By now he had won his court case and was secure in his incumbency. The family breach (Wijewardene-Jayewardene) had widened. Under Buddharakkhita's influence, Mrs. Vimala Wijewardene became the SLFP candidate to oppose her husband's nephew, the UNP cabinet minister J. R. Jayewardene, for the Kelaniya seat. But Jayewardene won again.

In 1956, Mr. R. G. Senanayake, an Independent who had been forced out of the UNP and a political rival of J. R. Jayewardene, was invited by Buddharakkhita to contest the Kelaniya seat. Senanayake had a secure seat near Kurunegala which he had held since 1944. The object clearly was not to win a seat but to defeat Jayewardene. In the election campaign no political party supported Senanayake. Buddharakkhita managed the entire local campaign from his headquarters in the temple, and Senanayake won. Buddharakkhita also directed Mrs. Vimala Wijewardene's campaign in the Mirigama constituency and she too was successful.

Buddharakkhita's involvement in politics thus began with a dispute over ecclesiastical office in which he was opposed by the local member of Parliament. Once his incumbency in that influential office was secure, he could and did build a political machine of his own. But his power became nationwide in 1956 through an organization of Buddhist monks for political action.

Sangha Sabhas (monks' associations) were being organized in various parts of Ceylon as early as 1953, partly through the efforts of Buddhist laymen, and with the chief object of making preparations for the Buddha Jayanti. A number of these associations, drawn from all three sects, combined to form the Sri Lanka Maha Sangha Sabha. Early in 1955 Mr. L. H. Mettananda, a former principal of Ananda

---

[4] The information in this and the following two paragraphs is largely based on interviews with Mr. J. R. Jayewardene in April 1963.

College, started a public campaign to denounce the UNP government for its "stepmotherly" treatment of Buddhism. He accused
the government of discrimination against the Buddhists and favoring
the Catholics in educational policy and appointments. Mettananda
was an influential member of the Buddhist Committee of Inquiry
and well known for his anti-Catholic views.[5] He clearly perceived the
enormous political potential of the Sangha, and bent his efforts toward enlisting and organizing the monks of the Sri Lanka Maha Sangha
Sabha in his anti-government campaign.

Meanwhile, another monks' association was formed, the All-Ceylon
Congress of Bhikkhu Societies, with Mapitigama Buddharakkhita
Thero and Talpawila Seelawansa Thero as joint secretaries. Partly on
the initiative of L. H. Mettananda, these two Sangha organizations
came together shortly before the 1956 elections to form the Eksath
Bhikkhu Peramuna (United Monks Front). Most of its members were
drawn from the Amarapura and Ramanya sects, although Buddha-
rakkhita himself came from a low-country temple of the Siam sect.
The EBP became the powerful and indispensable political ally of
Bandaranaike's electoral coalition, the MEP.[6]

ROLE OF THE MONKS IN 1956

Early in the campaign the monks' task was clearly set forth in a
Sinhalese newspaper published by pro-MEP Buddhists. "The *bhikkhus*
should be present in every polling booth. They should explain to the
people how to use the vote correctly. A keen interest should be taken
because the Buddha Jayanti celebration is close by. A government
that will work for the country, religion and its culture should be
elected. The end of the Sasana will not be very long if we remain
in silence. . . . We appeal to *bhikkhus* to visit every Buddhist home
and to direct them on the right path. You may have to confront
many difficulties. But be ready to sacrifice your life to restore a
Buddhist Ceylon."[7] There were over seventy-five regional monks'
associations affiliated with the Eksath Bhikkhu Peramuna, and each
of these units undertook to campaign actively for the local MEP
candidate. In the constituencies in which there was no MEP candidate in accordance with the no-contest agreement, the EBP supported
the anti-UNP candidate. Thus, Buddharakkhita declared publicly that

---

[5] See the articles "Monks at Hustings" and "Sangha Campaigns," numbers 6
and 7 in the series "Background to Politics," *Ceylon Observer*, July 16 and 17, 1962.
  [6] See L. H. Mettananda's letter to the *Ceylon Daily News*, September 4, 1956.
  [7] *Rodaya*, February 25, 1956, quoted in W. Howard Wriggins, *Ceylon: Dilemmas
of a New Nation*, Princeton University Press, Princeton, 1960, p. 345.

the EBP would give every assistance to the Marxist LSSP candidate at Kotte.[8]

The monks campaigned from house to house, addressed meetings, prepared and published campaign literature. Excerpts from the Buddhist Commission Report were read in the temples on Buddhist sabbath days, and the anti-UNP implications of the report expounded. Some EBP pamphlets dealt with economic questions such as the rice issue in addition to the heavy emphasis on religion and language. It published a slashing attack on the Lake House press (one of Ceylon's two major newspaper combines, and strongly pro-UNP) written by L. H. Mettananda. The pamphlet denounced this press as Christian-dominated and anti-Buddhist, and accused it of seeking to westernize the people and corrupt their morals.[9]

An extremely effective EBP poster depicted the hordes of Mara (Satan) attacking a Buddha statue. Sir John Kotelawala, as Mara, sat on an elephant (symbol of the UNP) along with one of his reputedly numerous girl friends. Behind him were a crowd of his westernized (dancing, drinking, meat-eating) followers, Lake House capitalists, Uncle Sams carrying dollars, Catholic priests and members of the Catholic-dominated armed forces.[10] The whole gamut of Sinhalese Buddhist criticism of the UNP was epitomized in a striking allusion which also implied a prophecy. For in the temple paintings, Mara who attacks the Buddha is thrown down from his elephant and defeated.

On March 3, 1956, the EBP held a meeting to publicize the *Dasa Panatha*, ten principles drawn up by the organization to indicate the proper objectives and policies for the future government of the country. Over 3,000 monks from all parts of Ceylon attended the meeting. S. W. R. D. Bandaranaike, Philip Gunawardena and A. E. Goonesinghe were also present and accepted the ten principles on behalf of the MEP.[11] Kneeling before the assembled monks, the politicians received these ten campaign principles much as the individual layman receives the Five Precepts from a *bhikkhu*. The meeting dramatized the fact that here was a political party which respected traditional Buddhist ways, which showed proper deference to the Sangha and was desirous of following its guidance.

[8] I. D. S. Weerawardana, *Ceylon General Election 1956*, M. D. Gunasena and Co. Ltd., Colombo, 1960, p. 106.
[9] *Ibid.*, pp. 116, 132-133.
[10] This poster is reproduced in *ibid.*, p. 174 and Wriggins, p. 357.
[11] "Sangha Campaigns," *Ceylon Observer*, July 17, 1962.

The ten principles themselves contained nothing new. Apart from the commitments to make Sinhalese the one official language and to implement the Buddhist Commission Report, the principles were vague—to follow the rule of non-violence, to oppose injustice, to protect democracy, to promote the national heritage (including Ayurvedic medicine), to guarantee freedom of religion, to promote the general welfare, to bring about a fairer distribution of wealth, and to refuse government assistance to institutions which promoted communal disharmony. The last point was directed principally against the Catholic Church.

S. W. R. D. Bandaranaike claimed that 12,000 Buddhist monks were actively supporting the MEP campaign. This was an obvious exaggeration, but the UNP was nevertheless alarmed at the general trend. The EBP monks, although a small minority of the Ceylon Sangha, were relatively well organized and extremely vocal. Prime Minister Kotelawala attempted to deny the obvious, declaring that the story that the Sangha was pro-MEP was a "baseless falsehood." He said that some individuals were masquerading as monks as a cloak for their Communist activities,[12] and on another occasion he condemned the EBP monks as "rogues in yellow robes."

High-ranking elders of the Sangha presided at UNP campaign meetings (even when the UNP candidate was a Catholic), and made speeches condemning Bandaranaike as a Donoughmore Buddhist and praising the government's role in the promotion of Buddhism.[13] There was considerable support from the presiding monks in some of the leading temples. But the pro-UNP monks were no match for the EBP. Kotelawala therefore persuaded the heads (Mahanayake Theros) of the Malwatte and Asgiriya chapters of the Siam sect to issue a joint edict: "*Bhikkhus* of our sects, whoever they may be, who are engaged in canvassing votes for any party, should completely abandon such campaigning, remain impartial and behave in such manner as to secure peace and unity among the people, and prepare the way for the proper celebration of the Buddha Jayanti."[14] But the Mahanayake Theros in Kandy could exercise very little control over the activities of monks in other parts of the Island.

Buddharakkhita played an influential role in the 1956 elections, both as a leader of the Eksath Bhikkhu Peramuna and in his personal capacity. He toured almost all the constituencies contested by the MEP, addressed many public meetings and directed the monks'

---

12 *Ceylon Daily News*, March 16, 1956.
13 *Ibid.*, March 3, 14, 22, 1956.
14 *Ceylon Observer*, March 24, 1956.

political work.[15] He had access to the considerable wealth of the Kelaniya temple and was accustomed to a relatively luxurious way of life (he always traveled in his own car driven by a chauffeur). Buddharakkhita later claimed that he had spent 100,000 rupees (about $21,000) on the campaign.[16]

The MEP, for its part, showed no reluctance to recognize its indebtedness to the monks when the resounding victory was won. S. W. R. D. Bandaranaike publicly thanked the Sangha for its support, and immediately after the formation of the new cabinet he and his ministers visited the Kelaniya temple to pay homage to Buddha—and to Buddharakkhita.

BANDARANAIKE AND BUDDHARAKKHITA

Some of Bandaranaike's most acute religio-political problems arose from his indebtedness to Buddharakkhita and the Eksath Bhikkhu Peramuna for their powerful and effective support in the 1956 elections. Political debts had to be paid, but how much and in what coin?

Buddharakkhita emerged as one of the most influential and powerful personalities in the country. His good friend, the widow Mrs. Vimala Wijewardene, whose political campaigns he had managed in 1952 and 1956, was made the minister of health. She in turn appointed Buddharakkhita to the Board of Indigenous Medicine, a board with considerable powers of patronage. The politically active Ayurvedic physicians in the country were closely allied with the Eksath Bhikkhu Peramuna, so this board was a useful tool with which Buddharakkhita could extend his political influence. In view of his lack of medical qualifications, however, the appointment was very unpopular, and he soon resigned.[17]

Buddharakkhita's real power was completely independent of official position. He exercised it through his personal contacts with the prime minister and other cabinet members, through the EBP's pressure on the government, and through his position on the Sri Lanka Freedom Party executive committee. The comparison of Buddharakkhita with Richelieu and Rasputin would not be far-fetched. Much of his political work was done from his elegant air-conditioned flat behind the

[15] "The Big Shot," *Ceylon Observer*, May 12, 1961.

[16] From the judgment of the Court of Criminal Appeal, *Ceylon Daily News*, January 16, 1962.

[17] One newspaper, either naively or with tongue in cheek, referred to Buddharakkhita's "inexplicable appointment" to the board by Mrs. Vimala Wijewardene, the protest against the appointment and his resignation in May 1957. *Ceylon Observer*, May 26, 1957.

Kelaniya temple, where every morning dozens would gather—teachers, MPs, village headmen, party officials—seeking favors, jobs, transfers and advice. "And there, in Kelaniya Raja Maha Vihare, Buddharakkhita held his court. Often, a telephone call to a minister would suffice, and a grateful government had given the privilege of a direct telephone link with Colombo! And why not? He was the power behind the throne or, at least, he felt so and was made to feel so. It is a fact that he had entree to the highest in the land."[18]

The Eksath Bhikkhu Peramuna did not give up its political activities with the victory of 1956, but became a center of power quite independent of the MEP government it had helped to elect, a pressure group which could support or criticize government policies and personnel. At first its criticism was guardedly expressed or only implied. The EBP became convinced, however, that the government was not moving fast enough, especially on the language question. EBP press releases and statements sought to enlist public support and intensify the demand that government act in accordance with the will of the people (defined by the EBP). Direct pressure was kept on the cabinet, and there was no major issue on which the EBP position was not forcefully presented. One commentator concluded: "All the reports add up to the fact that the EBP has assumed . . . the role of a supra cabinet. . . . Stalwarts of the EBP claim that ministers and even high government officials are at their beck and call; that they promptly reply to any summons from the EBP headquarters; that they are often put on 'trial' at EBP headquarters where they explain their actions and attitudes toward national problems."[19]

Tensions within the MEP coalition government soon gave way to open conflicts. Mr. Philip Gunawardena, minister of agriculture and food, and the two other Marxists in the cabinet began to apply pressure on Bandaranaike for the immediate nationalization of foreign-owned tea estates, insurance companies and banks. Gunawardena used his following among organized labor to foment strikes in an effort to demonstrate his power. By early 1958 a fierce struggle between Buddharakkhita and Gunawardena was being openly waged.

Philip Gunawardena in a speech in the House of Representatives accused Buddharakkhita, whom he renamed "Buddy Racketeer," of organizing an unlawful procession and carrying a gun. He also alluded to the monk's "sexy appearance."[20] Buddharakkhita replied with a long open letter to the prime minister in which he stated

[18] "The Big Shot," *Ceylon Observer*, May 12, 1961.
[19] *Times of Ceylon*, March 24, 1957. Cited in Wriggins, p. 207.
[20] House of Representatives, March 6, 1958.

that during the last two years Bandaranaike had inspired the people's confidence. "But I have great doubts how long that confidence will remain unshaken in the hearts of the people if you continue to keep within your cabinet such reactionary totalitarians who are making use of Marxism for their personal gain."[21] In a second open letter to the prime minister a week later, Buddharakkhita attacked Gunawardena's competence as food minister, asserting that his five-point plan was not a practicable solution to the problem of the high cost of living.[22] In another public statement the monk recalled that at the EBP meeting held at the Town Hall, Colombo, in 1956, Mr. Philip Gunawardena had "accepted the *Dasa Panatha* on his knees like a frenzied toothless cat," but had unfortunately forgotten virtuous conduct all too soon.[23]

When the country faced a serious economic crisis due to "the fanatical strikes started by power-seeking politicians" in late 1958, an EBP executive committee resolution in a strident tone called on the prime minister either to stop the strikes immediately or get the government to resign. The resolution was passed unanimously by the committee which included two members of the SLFP central executive committee, Buddharakkhita Thero and Talpawila Seelawansa Nayaka Thero.[24] By this time there was strong personal opposition to the Marxist ministers among their cabinet colleagues, but disinclination to run the political risks involved in breaking up the coalition. The Marxists were, however, finally forced out of the cabinet.

As the Colombo municipal elections approached in early 1959 the left and right within the SLFP became polarized, and an important victory was won by the right wing. Mr. Nimal Karunatilleke, general secretary of the party and regarded as Bandaranaike's mouthpiece, proposed to the SLFP executive committee a no-contest agreement with the LSSP and CP in the Colombo elections. His proposal was obviously inspired by the prime minister. Mr. W. Dahanayake and the two EBP monks spearheaded the opposition. The bulk of the SLFP leadership was right-wing, but in the past Bandaranaike had always been able to intimidate them and bring them into line. On this occasion, however, and for the first time, he failed to carry his viewpoint and the slogan "No truck with Marxist parties" won the day. According to one commentator: "It is no secret that the organizer who put fighting spirit into the right wing was none other than the Venerable Buddharakkhita Thero. Under the inspiration of the

21 *Ceylon Daily News*, March 12, 1958.   22 *Ibid.*, March 19, 1958.
23 *Ibid.*, August 25, 1958.   24 *Ibid.*, December 31, 1958.

reverend gentleman speaker after speaker repudiated the proposal of an alliance with the left."[25]

At the same stormy session of the executive committee it was necessary to elect a successor to Karunatilleke as general secretary of the SLFP. Buddharakkhita stressed the need to have party officials who would not "bow down" to the Marxist parties, and nominated Mr. J. C. W. Munasinha, a Roman Catholic. Here again Bandaranaike found it difficult to direct developments as he was accustomed to doing. He suggested that Munasinha would perhaps be overburdened if he had to take on this responsibility in addition to his jobs of junior minister and chief whip. But Munasinha replied that he was prepared to accept the party post, and even hinted that he might resign the other jobs if the work became too great. The prime minister could not press his point and Munasinha was unanimously elected. Buddharakkhita outwitted and outmaneuvered Bandaranaike at every turn.[26]

The serious breach between the two men was widened further by the failure of an ambitious business venture in which Buddharakkhita had an interest. The failure was primarily due to the government's unwillingness to "cooperate." In May 1958 a company was formed called The Associated Colombo Shipping Lines Limited. The directors were Buddharakkhita's brother, Dr. K. K. U. Perera, Mr. H. P. Jayawardene and a third person, Dr. Perera's brother-in-law. Two of the directors went to London to arrange the financing of the company; their air tickets were paid for with Buddharakkhita's personal check. Mr. Stanley de Zoysa, then minister of finance, assured the new company that it could compete for the transport of government cargoes, and invited it to make tenders for the transport of 200,000 tons of rice from Burma to Ceylon. In February 1959, at about the same time the power struggle within the SLFP executive committee resulted in Buddharakkhita's victory, the chairman of the company wrote to the prime minister requesting the contract for the rice lift for the 1959, 1960 and 1961 options. The request was refused.[27]

Buddharakkhita continued to be treated with the utmost deference in public, as illustrated by a dramatic incident which took place at the plenary session of the SLFP in May 1959. Bandaranaike was in the midst of his presidential address to the party. "Our policy is our belief that cultural and religious values must be preserved and fostered," he declared. He then paused and all eyes followed his to

[25] *Ibid.*, February 7, 1959.
[26] *Ibid.*, February 2, 4, 7, 1959; *Ceylon Observer*, February 6, 1959.
[27] From the judgment of the Court of Criminal Appeal, *Ceylon Daily News*, January 16, 1962.

the entrance of the hall to see the Venerable Buddharakkhita Thero enter and walk slowly toward the platform. All of the ministers and party officials on the platform rose as a man as he approached Bandaranaike. The prime minister paid him obeisance, the ministers bowed, and Buddharakkhita took his place on the platform with the other members of the Sangha. Bandaranaike resumed his speech only after the monk sat down.[28]

But Buddharakkhita's inward alienation from the Bandaranaike regime was by this time complete. Early in June 1959 the executive committee of the Eksath Bhikkhu Peramuna decided to appoint a three-man committee to investigate whether, in the light of recent political developments, it might be necessary to start a new political party in Ceylon.[29] The EBP's break with the SLFP was now openly acknowledged. Buddharakkhita had contributed greatly to Bandaranaike's political success, and now felt himself betrayed. He had spent 100,000 rupees (over $21,000) to get Bandaranaike elected, but his investment had paid very meager dividends.

On September 25, 1959, Talduwe Somarama Thero, a monk and also an Ayurvedic physician, appeared on the veranda of the prime minister's house with a group of petitioners. Bandaranaike bowed respectfully before the *bhikkhu*, who then took out a revolver and shot him four times. The prime minister died the next day. In the course of the police investigation eight persons were arrested including Buddharakkhita, H. P. Jayawardene (one of the directors of the shipping company) and Mrs. Vimala Wijewardene. Buddharakkhita and Jayawardene were charged with conspiracy to murder Bandaranaike. According to the prosecution case, they were the two "arch-conspirators" behind Somarama who fired the fatal shots. On May 12, 1961, Buddharakkhita, Jayawardene and Somarama were convicted and sentenced to hang. Eight months later, however, the Court of Criminal Appeal reduced Buddharakkhita's and Jayawardene's sentence to life imprisonment.[30]

Thus ended the life of S. W. R. D. Bandaranaike, who fell victim to the extremist forces of resurgent Buddhism which he himself had helped to set in motion. He had erred in assuming that, simply because he could at first use these forces to serve his own ends, he would be able to control them indefinitely. This error proved fatal. And thus ended the career of the most remarkable political monk of modern times.

[28] *Ceylon Observer,* May 17, 1959.
[29] *Ibid.,* June 8, 1959.
[30] *Ceylon Daily News,* May 13, 1961 and January 16, 1962.

Political Monks and Monastic Reform

The Buddha Sasana Commission was appointed on March 4, 1957, to inquire into and report on: (1) the proposals of the Buddhist Committee of Inquiry concerning a Buddha Sasana Council and a system of ecclesiastical courts, (2) measures which should be adopted to improve the management of Buddhist temporalities and the training of *bhikkhus*, and to prevent unordained persons from putting on the yellow robes of the Sangha, (3) the registration and control of Buddhist places of worship, and (4) any other matter which is necessary "for the purpose of according Buddhism its rightful place in Ceylon."[31] Fifteen persons were appointed to the commission, ten monks and five laymen. There were two monks from the Ramanya sect, two from the Amarapura sect, and six from the Siam sect (three from the Malwatte chapter and three from the Asgiriya chapter). These six, however, had no representative status and served on the commission only as individuals. Five members of the commission (three monks and two laymen) had served on the Buddhist Committee of Inquiry.[32]

The Siam sect opposed the appointment of a commission from the beginning. In October 1956 the Bandaranaike government announced its intention of setting up this commission, but the reaction of the Siam sect was so hostile that the president of the All-Ceylon Buddhist Congress himself urged the minister of cultural affairs to defer taking this step for which the Congress had agitated so long. The heads of the Siam sect refused to send their representatives to the commission, and when it was finally constituted over their protests, appealed to the governor general of Ceylon to prohibit its making any inquiry into the internal affairs of their sect.[33]

The Siam sect was established in the middle of the eighteenth century as a monopoly of the highest caste, the Goyigamas.[34] It is the largest of the three sects, constituting about 65 per cent of the Sangha, and by far the wealthiest. It is centered in the up-country districts around Kandy, and controls extensive tracts of valuable land granted to the Sangha by the Sinhalese kings. The temple lands in the Kandyan area today total about 376,000 acres.[35] The Siam sect is extremely

---

[31] *Interim Report of the Buddha Sasana Commission*, sessional paper 25 of 1957, Government Press, Colombo, 1957, p. 3.

[32] It is worth noting that the Eksath Bhikkhu Peramuna was not consulted on the personnel of the Buddha Sasana Commission. *Ceylon Daily News*, March 4, 1957.

[33] *Ibid.*, January 9 and March 12, 1957.

[34] Bryce Ryan, *Caste in Modern Ceylon*, Rutgers University Press, New Brunswick, N.J., 1953, pp. 39-41; Wriggins, pp. 191-192.

[35] *Commission on Tenure of Lands of Viharagam, Dewalagam and Nindagam*, sessional paper 1 of 1956, Government Press, Colombo, 1956, p. 98.

Donald E. Smith

conservative, partly because its center is far from the coastal cities where foreign influence has been greatest, and partly because its vested interests are threatened by change. The Siam sect has consistently manifested a fundamental distrust of government, and an official commission charged with making recommendations on Buddhist temporalities and Sangha reform could only meet with its most resolute opposition. The Amarapura and the Ramanya sects are of more recent origin, centered in the low country, without much wealth, composed chiefly of non-Goyigama monks, and relatively more receptive to modern influences.[36]

Despite intense opposition from the heads of the Siam sect, the Buddha Sasana Commission went about its work. It issued a questionnaire, considered the 500 replies or memoranda, held public meetings and recorded evidence. In order to gain relevant information, members of the commission visited Burma, Thailand, Cambodia and Laos. After over two years of work, the commission submitted its report to Prime Minister S. W. R. D. Bandaranaike.

The report made four major recommendations. First, it proposed the creation of a Buddha Sasana Council consisting of two chambers, a chamber of the Sangha composed exclusively of monks to deal only with matters concerning the monastic order, and a chamber of clergy and laity to deal with broader problems of concern to the entire Buddhist community. This council would be in charge of the construction of new monasteries and temples, Buddhist social welfare work, the celebration of festivals, and all religious activities. Second, the commission recommended the establishment of ecclesiastical tribunals to deal with cases in which monks are involved. All major offenses would be tried in the ordinary law courts, but in the case of minor offenses and in civil suits if both parties were monks, the *Maha Sanghadhikarana* (Chief Ecclesiastical Court) would have jurisdiction. This court would hear cases involving disputes over succession to the position of chief priest of a temple, cases involving removal from such posts, and cases in which a man's claim to be a *bhikkhu* is disputed.

Third, the report recommended the establishment of a new government department under a Commissioner of Temple Lands. Monks would no longer control the management of such properties, and instead of having a separate trustee for each temple, the trusteeship of all *vihara* land would be placed in the hands of the one commis-

[36] The Amarapura sect was established in 1800 to break the Goyigama monopoly of the Sangha, but its caste-consciousness is hardly less, membership being limited to the Karava, Salagama and Durava castes. The Ramanya sect contains *bhikkhus* of practically all castes. The caste basis of the Sangha sects is frequently condemned by lay Buddhist reformers. See D. C. Vijayavardhana, p. 585.

sioner. Fourth, regulations would be imposed to prevent indiscipline within the Sangha. A more efficient system for the registration of *bhikkhus* would be instituted, and each monk would be required to have an identification card issued by the Buddha Sasana Council. Restrictions were to be imposed on the *future* appointment of monks to salaried positions, and the report carried the admonition: "Monks should keep away from party politics."[37]

The report was submitted to Prime Minister Bandaranaike a few months before his assassination by a monk. The government withheld publication of the report for some time after the assassination. During this period a massive revulsion of public opinion against monks in general swept the Island. Laymen refused to give their seats to *bhikkhus* in buses and trains, and the traditional pattern of deference to and veneration of the Sangha was temporarily forgotten. A shaky government headed by the former education minister, Mr. W. Dahanayake, imposed a rigid press censorship, and the Competent Authority ordered the newspapers not to discuss questions relating to the Sangha. It was feared that such articles might further inflame public opinion and lead to violence.[38]

In November 1959 this restriction was lifted, and a large number of articles and editorials demanded that the government take immediate and vigorous steps to "cleanse the Sangha." The pro-UNP English-language press pointed out that the problem was in large measure one created by the ruling party itself. "The last few weeks have only brought to a head a revulsion which had long been gathering against those men who have put on the yellow robe only as a shield for their anti-social and vicious activities. This revulsion was the result of the immense growth in the influence, power and wealth of the *duseela* monks during the last few years. It is the ruling party today which

[37] *Buddha Sasana Commission Report* (in Sinhalese), Government Press, Colombo, 1959, p. 278. The author wishes to express his deep gratitude to Mr. L. S. Perera for translating the summary of recommendations (pp. 276-287) into English for him. The Buddhist Temporalities Ordinance of 1931, still in force, provides for the registration of monks, both novices *(samaneras)* and those who have received the higher ordination *(upasampadas)*. These records are kept by the registrar general of the government of Ceylon. The ordinance makes it an offense (punishable by a fine of fifty rupees) for anyone to put on the yellow robe and assume the position of a *bhikkhu* without being registered. *Buddhist Temporalities Ordinance*, 1956 revision, sections 41 and 42. Officials in the registrar general's office informed the author that there are relatively few unregistered monks in Ceylon. The register is inaccurate, however, because the Mahanayake Theros of the sects of the Sangha frequently fail to report the disrobing or death of a monk. In many cases they themselves have not been informed.

[38] "Duseela Monks," *Ceylon Observer*, November 12, 1959. "Duseela" means unprincipled, the opposite of *sil*, virtuous conduct.

bears the fundamental responsibility for this corruption. There were bad monks (as there are bad men in any religious order) in the Sangha even before 1956, monks who had broken the discipline of their order to meddle in politics and worldly affairs. But it was the MEP which brought the *duseela* monks to the forefront of national life. The MEP no doubt hoped to utilize them merely as an instrument by which they could come to political power. But having summoned up these forces they were unable to control them. The *duseela* monks began to demand and to obtain the price of their participation in the political victory of 1956. They began to dictate policy to the government, to wrest places and positions for themselves and above all to make money by the most devious means."[39] Another editorial gave expression to the powerful public demand: "Bring to book the assassins of Mr. Bandaranaike, and cleanse the Sangha."[40]

The Buddha Sasana Commission report became the symbol of Sangha reform, despite the fact that many of its recommendations regarding the monks were quite cautious. Ten of the fifteen members of the commission were *bhikkhus,* and they wanted to bring about needed reforms without harsh condemnation, which would tend to undermine the laity's reverence for the Sangha as a whole. The opposition of the Siam sect, the fact that the commission did its work during the heyday of the Eksath Bhikkhu Peramuna's power, and the compromised position of several *bhikkhu* members of the commission itself with respect to Vinaya regulations, were other factors which helped to produce the tone of moderation in the report.

Led by the All-Ceylon Buddhist Congress, a number of lay groups committed to far-reaching changes in the organization and functions of Buddhist religion seized their unprecedented opportunity and pressed for immediate implementation of the report.[41] However, it was felt by many that the report did not go far enough. One Buddhist laymen's group, the Sasanarakshaka Bauddha Mandalaya, criticized the commission for failing to recommend effective means to purify the Sangha, the most immediate prerequisite for the revival of Buddhism in Ceylon. The report failed to recommend the immediate removal of monks who were earning salaries or engaged in business, and left room for monks to engage in politics provided they did not join

---

39 "Cleansing the Sangha," *Ceylon Daily News,* November 12, 1959.
40 "Only Buddhist Opinion Can Ensure Reform of Sangha," *ibid.,* November 14, 1959. See also Sirisoma Jayasinghe, "Let Us Cleanse the Sangha," *Ceylon Observer,* November 16, 1959.
41 *Ceylon Daily News,* November 12 and December 2, 1959; *Times of Ceylon,* November 27, 1959.

political parties.[42] Other critics pointed out that, with respect to the delicate question of salaries, the report carefully safeguarded the interests of the *bhikkhu* members of the commission itself, for several of them were drawing government salaries as principals of *pirivenas*.[43]

The presiding elder of the Ramanya sect immediately announced his approval of all the recommendations of the commission, and the central council of the Amarapura sect unanimously decided to accept the report "with certain modifications."[44] A joint meeting of the Malwatte and Asgiriya chapters of the Siam sect was held to discuss the Buddha Sasana Commission report. It was pointed out that many present had not read the report, but the secretary of the Asgiriya chapter stated that it was not necessary to do so since they had already made up their minds to oppose it! With reference to the proposed Buddha Sasana Council, the assembled monks asserted that these two monastic chapters with their ancient and unbroken traditions already constituted two Buddha Sasana councils, which required only legal sanction for the successful enforcement of Sangha regulations.[45]

The minister for cultural affairs, Mr. P. B. G. Kalugalla, met with the Mahanayake Theros (presiding monks) of the two chapters to try to secure their cooperation, but this meeting only led to more controversy. The monks claimed that the minister had assured them that there would be no implementation of the report without their consent. Mr. Kalugalla's version was that he had promised nothing, but had simply invited their views on various subjects mentioned in the report. The minister declared that the public was anxiously awaiting the implementation of the report "to retrieve the Sangha from the depths to which it has sunk."[46] Three weeks later, however, Prime Minister W. Dahanayake, after a visit to the Malwatte and Asgiriya temples in Kandy, weakly declared that reforms should come from within the Sangha, and that he would never be party to any legislation against the wishes of the Sangha, particularly against the wishes of the two leading chapters.[47]

IMPLEMENTING THE REPORT

The year 1960 was dominated by two general elections, and little was heard of the Buddha Sasana Commission report. W. Dahanayake

---

42 *Ceylon Daily News*, November 27, 1959.

43 *Ibid.*, January 5, 1960.

44 *Ibid.*, November 14, 1959 and December 18, 1959.

45 *Ceylon Observer*, November 16, 1959. One venerable elder of the Malwatte chapter later declared that the politicians wanted to control the *bhikkhus* and have the right to expel them from the Buddha Sasana so that they could propagate their own political ideologies. *Ceylon Daily News*, December 4, 1959.

46 *Ibid.*, November 18-19, 21, 1959.   47 *Ibid.*, December 17, 1959.

could not hold his cabinet together, and was forced to dissolve parliament and call for general elections. In the March 1960 elections Dudley Senanayake led the UNP to victory (50 seats to the SLFP's 46), but without a majority in Parliament was unable to secure a vote of confidence a month later. In the July 1960 general elections the SLFP, led by Mrs. Sirimavo Bandaranaike, widow of S. W. R. D. Bandaranaike, won a resounding victory, taking 75 seats to the UNP's 30. The new government nationalized state-aided private schools in late 1960 and early 1961, and this legislation provided the substance of religious controversy for several months. It was not until the middle of 1961 that the new Bandaranaike government turned its attention to the report.

Time—almost two years since the completion of the report—had solved nothing. The problems were as knotty as ever, and it was therefore not surprising that the minister for cultural affairs recommended the creation of a new department of religious affairs to handle the Buddha Sasana Commission recommendations.[48] This proposal was not accepted. The prime minister announced that as the first step in implementing the report no government jobs would be given to *bhikkhus*. In accordance with this decision a large number of monk applicants for appointment as S. S. C. certified teachers were turned down.[49] The decision was immediately attacked by certain high-ranking monks as a sinister move to wipe out the Sangha, since qualified *bhikkhus* would thereby be encouraged to leave the order and obtain the teaching jobs as laymen.[50]

In July 1961 the minister for cultural affairs appointed a Buddhist advisory committee to advise him in implementing the report. The committee consisted of four members of the Buddha Sasana Commission, the chairman, the Venerable Kalukondayawe Pannasekera Mahanayake Thero, and three laymen. In view of the considerable controversy which by this time had been stirred up, the advisory committee decided to give the public the opportunity to express its views on the subject through representations to the director of cultural affairs.[51]

In a broadcast talk to the nation the prime minister, Mrs. Bandaranaike, expressed surprise that there was opposition to Sasana reforms. She traced the recent history of the Buddhist movement, referred to the monks' support of her late husband in the 1956 elec-

48 *Ceylon Observer*, June 25, 1961.
49 *Ceylon Daily News*, June 16, 1961; *Ceylon Observer*, July 5, 1961.
50 *Ceylon Daily News*, July 6, 1961. Some UNP politicians also professed to see such motives behind the government's decision.
51 *Ceylon Observer*, July 19, 1961; *Ceylon Daily News*, August 29, 1961, January 16, 1962.

tions, and recalled his steps to promote Buddhism after he became prime minister. The appointment of the Buddha Sasana Commission was one such step. Mrs. Bandaranaike refuted the wild charges made against the government, and condemned the politicians who were exploiting the issue. "It is wrong to say that the government is seeking to destroy the freedom of the Sangha by legislation. The government does not intend to interfere in any way with the rules of the Vinaya or in matters relating to the different nikayas [sects]. All that we propose is to implement the recommendations of the Sasana Report in consultation with the Sangha for the preservation of the Sasana in the same manner as was done by the Buddhist kings of old."[52] Although early in the address she had spoken appreciatively of the *bhikkhus'* support in the 1956 elections, she defended the recommendation that monks should keep out of party politics. Since in every temple there were laymen belonging to all political parties, it would create disharmony if the monks were to take sides. Mrs. Bandaranaike concluded by appealing to the Sangha to cooperate in the implementation of the report.

The All-Ceylon Buddhist Congress, the Young Men's Buddhist Association and other lay organizations, along with a number of prominent monks, gave strong support to the government. Many articles were published and speeches delivered which diagnosed the ills of the Sangha and prescribed vigorous reform by the state as the only effective remedy, and one completely in accord with Sinhalese Buddhist traditions.[53] To counteract the "mischievous propaganda conducted by certain politicians," the ministry of cultural affairs distributed 50,000 copies of the lengthy report (351 pages) throughout the country.[54]

But the forces of reform, even with the leadership of the government, were no match for the defenders of the status quo. The dean of the faculty of Buddhism at the Vidyalankara University boldly attacked the fundamental assumptions and recommendations of the

[52] *Ceylon Observer*, July 27, 1961.

[53] According to the Ven. Pandit Hempitigedara Gnanaseeha Thero: "When the recommendations of the Sasana Commission are implemented hundreds of errant *bhikkhus* will be forced to discard the yellow robe and leave the ranks of the Sangha. A purified order, free of undesirable elements, would come into being." *Ceylon Observer*, June 25, 1961. See especially the following articles: G. P. Malalasekera, "Why I Want Sasana Reforms," *ibid.*, July 14, 1961; Ven. Kalukondayave Pannasekara Thero, "Sangha Reforms," *ibid.*, July 17, 1961; "Cleanse the Sangha: Now or Never," *Ceylon Daily News*, May 13, 1961; C. D. S. Siriwardane, "An Intelligent Buddhist's Guide to the Buddhist Problem," *The Buddhist*, vol. 32, October 1961, pp. 38-40, 43.

[54] *Ceylon Daily News*, October 3, 1961.

report. No government of laymen could tell the Sangha what to do. "On religion we are the sole authorities. We monks have got the training and we are the custodians of our religion." He rejected all governmental regulation regarding monastic discipline, the administration of Sangha property, the monks' remunerative employment, and their political rights.[55] He later stated that the *bhikkhus* had kept away from politics during the last two elections (March and July 1960), but were now prepared to enter the political field again to protect Buddhism and the nation from the threat posed by the Buddha Sasana Commission report.[56] The militant Talpawila Seelawansa Thero, formerly Buddharakkhita's close associate in the Eksath Bhikkhu Peramuna and the SLFP executive committee, announced that he was coming back to politics to fight the cultural affairs minister's proposal to implement the report. The monk, over sixty years old, declared that the former UNP government was 10,000 times better than the present regime.[57]

The Mahanayake Theros of the Siam sect proposed a united front of the three sects to oppose implementation of the report. In 1959 the other two sects had expressed their general approval of the document. The Amarapura sect was partly won over, and in secret conclave passed a resolution rejecting the report, although chiefly on procedural grounds, the objection being that it had not been placed before the Sangha for approval before submission to the government. The Ramanya sect, however, remained steadfast in its position.[58] In another move calculated to stave off governmental intervention, the Siam sect set about drawing up a constitution to reform itself.[59]

One opposition MP, Mr. R. G. Senanayake, declared that Buddhism was faced with the greatest threat of extermination that had ever confronted it in the history of Ceylon, as the government was maneuvering to disintegrate the Sangha through the Sasana Commission report. Another MP took the position that mere mortals had no right to interfere in the code of conduct for monks, as the Vinaya had been ordained by the Lord Buddha himself.[60] A Buddhist layman writing on the subject deprecated the excessive criticism of the Sangha by the laity, and pointed out that according to the law of *kamma* the

55 Bambarande Sri Seevali Thero, "Government 'Vinaya' not for Monks," *Ceylon Observer*, July 15, 1961.
56 *Ceylon Daily News*, September 6, 1961.
57 *Ibid.*, July 6, 1961.
58 *Ceylon Observer*, July 15, 1961; *Times of Ceylon*, July 20, 1961; *Ceylon Daily News*, July 27, 1961, January 29, 1962.
59 *Ibid.*, December 20, 1961.
60 *Ibid.*, December 18, 1961; *Ceylon Observer*, July 6, 1961.

consequences of a monk's moral lapses will be reaped by him alone. Why, then, should laymen try to regulate his life?[61]

The government slowly backed down. The cultural affairs minister announced that the commission's recommendations would be modified so as not to harm in any way the honor and dignity of the Sangha. In March 1962 the ban on the employment of monks was lifted by the government on the recommendation of the minister of education.[62] In February 1963 it was disclosed that the *majority* of the teachers selected by the education department that year were monks (300 out of 402 appointees), most of them graduates of the Vidyodaya and Vidyalankara Universities.[63] The one positive step taken by the government to implement the report was thus reversed, and no further steps appeared to be contemplated. It was reported in early 1963 that the public representations and memoranda which had been solicited were lying unattended in the offices of the department of cultural affairs, and that the four-man advisory committee on the implementation of the report had held no meetings recently.[64]

The years of frustration have gradually produced a new realism among the proponents of Buddhist reforms. By 1966 it was no longer possible to assert that the fundamental problems of Buddhism in Ceylon were caused by the discriminatory policies of British rule, the negligence of westernized UNP politicians, or the machinations of the Catholic Church. The problems stem from the nature of Buddhism itself as a basically monastic religion in which Sangha-laity ties are tenuous at best, from a system of Buddhist temporalities which is a vestige of Sinhalese feudalism, and from the limitations of government as an agency of religious reform when it is subject to the innumerable forces operative in democratic politics. Above all, the problems stem from the natural conservatism of a venerated institution, the Sangha, which is itself the chief object of reformist efforts but which is sufficiently well organized to resist change with great effectiveness. The Sangha has never reformed itself. It has been reformed by autocratic Buddhist kings, but not by democratically elected parliaments. Nor is it likely to be.

Buddhism in Ceylon is today in the throes of revolutionary change, but this change is not being directed by the reformers or by anyone.

[61] G. W. David DeSilva, "The Order of Brethren," *The Buddhist*, vol. 32, October 1961, pp. 41-43.

[62] *Ceylon Daily News*, November 6, 1961, March 23, 1962.

[63] *Ibid.*, February 6, 1963. However, according to education department officials who were interviewed, many of these monks became laymen as soon as they received their appointments.

[64] *Ibid.*, January 29, 1963.

Donald E. Smith

The change is being wrought through the impact of impersonal forces as the old order yields to the new. Modern society has deprived the monk of his traditional functions (especially in the field of education), a capitalist economy undermines his adherence to the Vinaya rule against touching money, urban life allures him with its worldly temptations, and a university education provides him with secular alternatives to life in the Sangha. The tendency for monks to leave the order has reportedly increased alarmingly, and in 1962 the All-Ceylon Buddhist Congress appointed a committee to investigate the whole problem.[65]

It seems likely that the forces of modernization will continue to take a heavy toll on the ranks of the Sangha. It is difficult to see how the monastic order will fit into the modern society which is now emerging. This is an extremely serious situation because of the centrality of the Sangha in Buddhist doctrine, ritual and practice. It is quite possible for Hinduism to flourish without priests or for Islam to prosper without *ulama*, but in Buddhism the believer venerates the Three Jewels: Buddha, Dhamma and Sangha.

While thoughtful Buddhist laymen would like to see the Sangha strengthened, they are at the same time aware that the orthodox Buddhist emphasis on the monastic life has severely limited the relevance of Buddhism as it faces the problems of a dynamic society. "If Buddhism is to survive it must take its place in society and its principles must influence the changes that are going on. Yet it is clear that within the last century or two Buddhism has contributed little to the social changes that have gone on around us. . . . Buddhism . . . must cease to be purely a monastic religion, and it must provide the solutions for the questions that interest people today. . . ."[66]

The development of a Buddhist social ethic, and the organizational means to apply it to contemporary problems, are the pressing requirements of the times. But it is still not clear how this social gospel is to be reconciled with the ideal of renunciation, nor what place is to be accorded the Sangha within the framework of a modern Buddhist organization.

[65] *Ibid.*, October 3, 1962.
[66] Siriwardane, pp. 39-40. See also Bhikkhu Sangharakshita, "An Intelligent Buddhist's Guide to the Buddhist Problem—II," *The Buddhist*, vol. 32, January 1962, pp. 53-54; editorial, "Buddhism at Cross-Roads," *ibid.*, vol. 32, September 1961, pp. 25-26; editorial, "The Reform of the Sangha," *ibid.*, vol. 33, January-February 1963, pp. 83-84.

CHAPTER 23

BUDDHISM IN CEYLON POLITICS
1960-1965

A. JEYARATNAM WILSON

BEFORE HIS WORK was done, S. W. R. D. Bandaranaike was laid low by the bullet of a monk assassin. He was succeeded by his minister of education, W. Dahanayake. The new prime minister was an abject failure in the management of his parliamentary majority and, faced with the possibility of defeat on the floor of the House, he had Parliament dissolved in December 1959.

MARCH 1960 ELECTION: RELIGION AND LANGUAGE

At the general election which followed, the main contenders were the United National Party, the Sri Lanka Freedom Party, the Lanka Sama Samaja Party and the Mahajana Eksath Peramuna (the People's United Front), a Buddhist Socialist force which was an amalgam of Philip Gunawardena's party and L. H. Mettananda's Dharma Samaja (Social Justice) Party.

Due to the disrepute into which the Buddhist clergy had fallen after Mr. Bandaranaike's assassination, the monks did not enter the fray in the same forthright manner as in the general election of 1956. But nevertheless the parties were mindful of their obligations to the Sinhalese Buddhists and their manifestos were drawn up with this fact evidently very much in mind.

The Mahajana Eksath Peramuna's program provided the clearest evidence of this trend.[1] In regard to religion it promised to implement the recommendations of the Buddhist Committee of Inquiry, to reform the Buddhist clergy by establishing appropriate institutions which would relieve it of "inheritance, possession or management of income-earning property,"[2] and ensure that as in the times

A. Jeyaratnam Wilson is a lecturer in political science at the University of Ceylon.

[1] The program is reproduced in fair detail in *Ceylon Daily News Parliaments of Ceylon 1960*, Colombo, n.d., pp. 204-209.

[2] Mr. Philip Gunawardena, who during the election campaign became noted for his impolitic and uninhibited pronouncements, stated a fortnight before the elections that there were large tracts of land which belonged to the Malwatte and Asgiriya chapters (the principal chapters of the Siamese sect) and to the Roman Catholic Church, and that none of the income of these lands was spent on the poor. He declared that he would teach these people a lesson if he obtained power and that he would distribute their land to the landless. *Ibid.*, p. 16.

of the Sinhalese kings the state would undertake the responsibility for the education of the Buddhist clergy. The Front would also take steps to give recognition to Buddhist temples as cultural centers, in addition to their being used as places of worship. Further, the entry of foreign missionaries would be controlled, legislation would be enacted to prohibit the conversion of a person by "force, fraud or other undue means," and a commission would be appointed to investigate the "non-religious activities of religious bodies and other charities" in Ceylon.

In the sphere of education, the Front pledged itself to do away with the "existing colonial system of education" and to replace it by "a national and unified system." Education would become the monopoly of the state and this would ensure the end of Christian missionary enterprise in the educational sphere. The religion of the parent would be taught to children in all schools. This had been demanded by Buddhist parents even before independence, but the Christian managers (especially the Roman Catholics), in keeping with their policy of utilizing the schools as vehicles for conversion, were opposed to non-Christian religious instruction being given in their schools.

On language, the Front insisted that Sinhalese should enjoy primacy and fully replace English as the official language. Tamil would be given its "due place," but as a medium of education it would be confined to the primary and secondary stages. At the university level, Sinhalese would be the sole medium of education.

The problem of the Indian estate Tamils would be dealt with in a more practical and vigorous manner. All those eligible for citizenship would be compelled to study the official language. Estates in areas where there was unemployment among Ceylonese would be compelled to employ a quota of Ceylonese labor or, as an alternative, pay a tax to the local authority concerned which would use the proceeds to provide employment for such Ceylonese. The Front would provide all possible inducements to Indians to leave the country and would ensure that all Indians of whatever class would be compulsorily retired at the age of fifty.

In foreign policy, the Front would ensure that Ceylon would remain a neutral country and have her neutrality guaranteed by other nations. This policy, it stated, would be "the most fitting for a Buddhist country like Ceylon."

The Sri Lanka Freedom Party followed close on the heels of the Mahajana Eksath Peramuna in regard to the exploitation of Buddhist grievances.[3] But it had, unlike the MEP, a record to present and sought to trade on it. It did not go to the same lengths as the MEP.

In the religious sphere, it declared that it would take note of the fact that Buddhism in Ceylon was the religion of a large majority of the people. At the same time it would guarantee "the fullest freedom of worship and conscience to all" and added that it accepted the position that "there shall be no discrimination on religious grounds." What this would have meant in practice it is difficult to envisage. In all probability it meant that the Sinhalese Buddhists would get their due share in the public sector, but this could not have been achieved without some form of discrimination. The party further pledged that it would take steps to implement the recommendations of the Buddha Sasana Commission that Mr. Bandaranaike's government had appointed. These recommendations sought to effect a reform of the Buddhist priesthood in accordance with Buddhist principles.

In education, the SLFP held that it recognized the fact that "education is primarily the responsibility of the state." But at the same time it stated very significantly its awareness that "a useful educational service is provided by existing denominational schools which conform to the standards of the Education Code." The party would however take steps to establish state schools in areas at present served by denominational schools, and thereafter would withdraw the financial assistance provided to the latter by the state. Religious instruction to children of all religions without any discrimination would be given in these state schools.

On language, the party held that it would continue to implement the Official Language Act so as "to make Sinhalese in reality the official language of the country." No hardship would be caused to the minority communities. Indeed the Tamil language had, it said, been accorded "a degree of reasonable use" by the legislation of Mr. Bandaranaike.

With regard to the problem of the Indian estate Tamil population, the SLFP stated that steps would be taken to progressively Ceylonize estate labor and to persuade non-citizen Indian labor to adopt Indian citizenship and leave the country. Stringent legislation would be enacted to deal with "illicit entry into the country by persons from the Indian coast," and measures would be taken to regulate the purchase of land by non-nationals, which in this case meant Indian nationals. The party's position here was hardly different from that of the Mahajana Eksath Peramuna.

[3] See *ibid.*, pp. 190-195, for fairly detailed extracts from the Sri Lanka Freedom Party's Manifesto.

A. Jeyaratnam Wilson

The SLFP's campaign in the beginning was led and managed by C. P. de Silva, who had been the late Mr. Bandaranaike's deputy and closest lieutenant. Toward the latter stages, the widow of the late prime minister, Mrs. Sirimavo Bandaranaike, threw herself into the campaign wholeheartedly and it is believed that her personality and appeal played a major role in effecting a shift of votes from the Mahajana Eksath Peramuna of Philip Gunawardena and L. H. Mettananda to the Sri Lanka Freedom Party.

Compared to these two Buddhist parties, the United National Party which could be categorized as standing to the right of center and the left-wing Lanka Sama Samaja Party adopted a comparatively noncommunal approach to the problems of the day. But even they were to some extent affected by the climate of Buddhist opinion in the Sinhalese areas. The president of the UNP, Dudley Senanayake, asserted in a message to the party that national unity had received "severe reverses" and that during the recent past "the forces of disruption represented by the extremists" had exploited "race, religion, poverty, and the most susceptible and inflammable passions of the people to confuse and destroy the national structure."[4]

On Buddhism, the party preferred to adopt a policy of friendly intervention. The Nikayas (sects of the Sangha) would, with their consent, be accorded corporate status by law. An organization comprising representatives of the Buddhist clergy and laity would be established to work for the welfare of both sections. But this would be done without infringing the autonomy of the Nikayas.[5] Freedom of religion would be guaranteed to everyone resident in Ceylon.

On language the UNP adopted an attitude which was in some respects similar to that of the SLFP, but in others much more liberal and more specifically defined. Sinhalese would be the official language but it would replace English gradually in the administration of the country. It would therefore not be an overnight switch causing hardship to public servants not proficient in Sinhalese, especially the Tamils. All citizens who were not proficient in the official language

[4] *Ibid.*, p. 195.

[5] *Ibid.*, p. 198. It is significant that in the party's policy statement approved at its sessions on March 29, 1958, there was not a single reference to what it proposed to do in regard to the Buddhist clergy or even Buddhist grievances, other than such vague pronouncements as the need for "religious education and upbringing" and for "the spread of spiritual values." This policy statement which was in fact declared to be the party's manifesto was slightly revised just before the general elections to ensure that there were some references at least to the pressing problems of the Sinhalese Buddhists. All the same, there was not a word in the policy statement on the Buddhist Committee of Inquiry. See *Progress through Stability: United National Party Manifesto*, approved by the party sessions on March 29, 1958.

would have the right to transact business with the state "without any inconvenience," which in effect meant the right to transact business with the state in their own language. All government publications and notifications would be in both languages. Public servants after gaining admission to the service would have to obtain a working knowledge of the language in which they were not proficient. This implied that public servants would have to obtain a knowledge of both Sinhalese and Tamil. The medium of examination would be that in which the candidate had obtained his education.[6]

The UNP, however, was emphatic on its stand regarding the Bandaranaike-Chelvanayakam Pact. It was not a language solution alone, it insisted, but a method of dividing the Island on racial lines. The Tamil language should be given a status on an all-Island basis without infringing the principle of Sinhalese being the only official language. But it should not be given any regional status for this would divide the country.[7] In regard to judicial proceedings, judgments could be delivered at the discretion of the court in Sinhalese, Tamil or English. Decisions on a point of law would have to be given in English but, after the Statutes of Ceylon have been translated into Sinhalese, such decisions would have to be given in Sinhalese. Witnesses could give evidence in any court in Sinhalese, Tamil or English, and adequate provision would be made to have such evidence translated into the appropriate language.[8]

On the subject of education, the party was quite out of step with the demands of the Buddhist militants, and it was definite about its policy.[9] It accepted the principle that "a religious environment is an essential part of a child's education." But for this purpose it would organize a system of "state denominational schools," while at the same time providing assistance to the existing state-aided denominational schools. The only difference would be that the existing denominational schools would be given grants in respect of children of their denominations in the school, not in respect of the others.[10] Again this change would be introduced only after a sufficient number of state denominational schools had been built. When this would happen could be anybody's guess but at any rate the Roman Catholic Church seemed fairly assured that it would not be for a long time. The party declared that, in pursuance of this policy, denominational

---

[6] *Ibid.*, pp. 21-24.   [7] *Ibid.*, pp. 23-24.

[8] *Ibid.*, p. 22.

[9] *Ibid.*, pp. 17-18 and p. 27, and *Ceylon Daily News Parliaments of Ceylon 1960*, p. 197.

[10] It should be noted that over 90 per cent of the Christian state-aided schools had a majority of non-Christian children in their schools.

schools would not be taken over by the state, adding, however, that it would utilize the services of the Sangha in the cause of education.

On the Indian question, the ground covered was familiar, only varying in its degree of rigidity as compared with the Sri Lanka Freedom Party and the Mahajana Eksath Peramuna. The UNP claimed the credit for first taking the necessary legislative measures to control the problem. It however insisted that the SLFP had not taken adequate steps to offer inducements to Indian citizens to leave Ceylon. The party would, if called on to form a government, control illegal immigration, repatriate those who were Indian citizens when necessary, and offer suitable inducements to the stateless Indian Tamils to leave Ceylon.[11]

From the Buddhists' point of view, however, the policies and program of the United National Party were not dynamic enough to persuade them to vote for it in sufficient numbers to give the party an over-all majority. To the rural masses the UNP still bore its pre-1956 record of being a party of oppression, a party of the rich and privileged. To the Buddhist militants and the Sinhalese Buddhist pressure groups, it had still not established its bona fides as a party pledged to redress their religious and economic grievances. The UNP therefore failed in the general election of March 1960 to win the support necessary to form a stable government, and in the succeeding general election of July 1960 it was convincingly defeated by the economic and communal dynamism of the forces led by Mrs. Bandaranaike. The inadequacies of the UNP's economic policies and its lack of fervor and seeming dedication to the "national" religion and the "national" language were exposed to the world by its national-minded adversary, the Sri Lanka Freedom Party.

The Trotskyist Lanka Sama Samaja Party made a bid for power for the first time in its twenty-five years of existence.[12] It claimed that it was the only party contending in the general election on a non-communal program putting forward candidates from the three major communities, Sinhalese, Tamil and Muslim, and fighting for seats in every part of the country.

Its economic policy was basically Marxist. But it was the party's attitude to language and its secular approach to religion that incurred the hatred of the Buddhist militants and lost the support of the Sinhalese rural masses. On religion the LSSP had hardly anything attractive to offer. It merely stated that it would guarantee freedom

[11] *Progress through Stability*, p. 24.
[12] *A Short History of the Lanka Sama Samaja Party*, Colombo, pp. 62-64 and *Ceylon Daily News Parliaments of Ceylon 1960*, pp. 202-204.

of religious belief, worship and organization. It would ensure that in all state schools, religious instruction would be provided to children according to the wishes of their parents.

On the related question of ayurveda, it declared that it would institute a National Ayurvedic Medical Service alongside the western medical system. This interest in the indigenous medical system did not impress the native physicians who were almost wholly Buddhists. The national cultures too were given some attention in the party's manifesto. The party declared that every assistance would be given to the development of national art, music and drama.

On education, there was an apparent change of policy. The LSSP was willing to permit denominations and other institutions and individuals to run their own educational institutions provided they conformed to the requirements laid down by the state. They would however have to run as private schools and would receive no assistance from the state. There was therefore no question of education becoming the sole monopoly of the state. The party would however take steps to provide facilities for everyone to have an adequate education through state schools. This modification of policy was evidently intended to appeal to the urban middle class, especially the lower income salariat. But from the Buddhist point of view, it was further evidence of the party's alienation from the mainstream of Buddhist nationalist opinion.

The LSSP reaffirmed its policy on language which was already widely known. It did not however speak of parity of status for Tamil with Sinhalese, as in the general election of 1956. This time the party declared that it stood for Tamil being recognized as an official language and for the right of the Tamil people to be governed in their own language; at the same time note must be taken of the fact that Sinhalese was the language of the majority of the people. What such a formula would have involved in practice was not adequately explained. When the LSSP was pressed to define its stand as the election campaign gathered momentum, the party leader, Dr. N. M. Perera, issued a statement (the accuracy of which it is difficult to guarantee, since it was reported by an unsympathetic press) that their language policy was hardly different from that of the late S. W. R. D. Bandaranaike. This created further confusion in the public mind, and doubts among the Tamil minority, as to what the LSSP actually stood for. On the problem of the Indian estate Tamil population, the party stated that this would have to be settled by negotiation with the government of India. Those persons who had made Ceylon their permanent home should be granted citizenship rights while the others would have to be regarded as Indian citizens.

The LSSP enjoyed a high reputation among the urban population as the guardian of the rights of the opposition in Parliament, and Dr. N. M. Perera had acquired tremendous personal prestige for his part in bringing to book most of the conspirators in the assassination of the late S. W. R. D. Bandaranaike. Nevertheless, the party fared disastrously at the election. To rural people it was a highly urbanized party, to the Buddhist-conscious elements it was anti-religious, to the middle classes it was a Marxist organization identified with revolutionary-type politics. There was also much truth in the explanation proffered by the party's general secretary. "It was clear," he wrote, "that the wave of Sinhalese communalism represented by the cry of 'Sinhalese Only,' though not as powerful as in 1956, was still an important factor and prevented large numbers of anti-capitalist minded people who would otherwise have voted for the LSSP from voting for the LSSP which took the position of making Tamil also an official language. The Indian question was also a question which adversely affected the party in up-country areas."[13]

The results of the general election of March 1960 were inconclusive. The United National Party, as the largest single group in the House of Representatives with 50 seats out of 151 (excluding the 6 appointed members who would vote with the government), was called upon to form the government.

DISSOLUTION AND NEW ELECTIONS

The deciding factor in the House was the Tamil Federal Party. If the latter had thrown in its lot with the government, there would have been some assurance of stable government for at least a reasonable length of time. Perhaps this was uppermost in the mind of the prime minister, Mr. Dudley Senanayake, when he made a statement to the nation after he was sworn in.[14] He declared that the most significant lesson of the election results was the overwhelming verdict against those who had tried "to inflame racial and communal passions to gain political power." He went on to add that from "the complexity of this situation we may yet be able to bring about the reunification of the people of Ceylon," without which no government could hope to carry out the urgent tasks of national development.

There was not a word in this statement concerning the grievances of the Sinhalese Buddhists or the need to proceed with the imple-

13 *A Short History of the Lanka Sama Samaja Party*, p. 63.
14 *Ceylon Daily News Parliaments of Ceylon 1960*, pp. 17-18.

mentation of the Official Language Act. Not even the Throne Speech of the new government contained any promises to look into these delicate problems. On the contrary, the Throne Speech referred to the need to provide for an educational system with a religious background through state denominational schools as well as state-aided denominational schools. This was the last thing that the Sinhalese Buddhist pressure groups wanted. It was of course a most welcome policy pronouncement as far as the Roman Catholic Church was concerned.

Either the United National Party was sure of its sources of support and therefore heedless of the demands of the dissatisfied Buddhist sections of the electorate or it was making an all-out effort to win the favors of the Tamil Federal Party. One possibility was that the party was sure of a constant factor in the Sinhalese electoral areas, which could be depended on to back it in any circumstances. It was therefore calculating on getting the extra support it needed so desperately to win an over-all majority by appeasing the Tamil minority. There was the other possibility that the party was playing for time, hoping to maneuver itself into a position of strength with the assistance of the Tamils and then, having gained stability, to proceed with the more important task of looking into the grievances of the dissatisfied Sinhalese Buddhist elements. There was however no doubt that the UNP had turned its face against any plan for a state monopoly of education, against a privileged position for Buddhism and against a ruthless implementation of Sinhalese as the only official language throughout the country. Whatever the political calculations may have been, these strands of opinion could easily be discerned.

But the price that the Tamil Federal Party wanted for its cooperation was too high. The implementation of the Bandaranaike-Chelvanayakam Pact was one of the minimum demands that the Federal Party Leader, S. J. V. Chelvanayakam, placed before the prime minister, but this was the very thing against which Senanayake had so violently campaigned, and it was therefore evident that there could be no basis for cooperation between the two parties. Mr. Senanayake tried to impress on the Federal Party leaders the bold aspects of his language policy. But it was in vain. For there was the prospect that if Senanayake's minority government were defeated, the governor general would call on the Sri Lanka Freedom Party, the next largest group in the House with only four seats less than the UNP, to form the government. And the leaders of the SLFP had promised the Tamil Federal Party that they would implement the policies of the late S. W. R.

D. Bandaranaike, one of which they said was the pact that he had signed with Chelvanayakam.[15]

During the period of Senanayake's brief premiership, tremendous pressure was brought to bear on the Tamil Federal Party to support the new government. This pressure, it was interesting to note, came from the professional men, the top-grade administrators, the merchant princes, and not least from the leaders of the Roman Catholic Church, all of whom were without a doubt the prime sources of strength of the United National Party.[16] But it was an attempt to fuse two irreconcilables. Their efforts were therefore doomed to failure from the outset.

On April 22, 1960, the debate on the Throne Speech ended and the voting took place: the opposition amendment was carried by 86 votes to 61. Mr. Senanayake then advised the governor general to dissolve Parliament. The latter invited the leaders of the opposition parties for consultations, to explore the possibilities of forming a stable alternate government. He was evidently convinced that this was not possible, though the opposition leaders thought otherwise. He therefore granted the prime minister's request and Parliament was dissolved.[17]

The resulting general election was mainly a clash between the two major parties. The most important issues were education and the Tamil Federal Party. The two left-wing groups, the Lanka Sama Samaja Party and the Communist Party, entered into a no-contest electoral pact with the Sri Lanka Freedom Party in order to defeat the United National Party, which the general secretary of the LSSP characterized as the party of "the big capitalists of Ceylon and an agency of imperialism."[18]

The UNP went to the country on its existing program. But it alleged that its rival had a secret understanding with the Tamil Federal Party, the main items of which were the granting of regional autonomy to the Tamil areas, an official status for the Tamil language, and revision of the rigorous citizenship laws against the Indian

[15] The writer has personal and firsthand knowledge of the negotiations that the Tamil Federal Party was involved in with the United National Party and the Sri Lanka Freedom Party.

[16] Personal information.

[17] For a detailed account of the events before the dissolution of Parliament and an analysis of the constitutional implications of the governor general's decision, see my "The Governor-General and the Two Dissolutions of Parliament, December 5, 1959 and April 23, 1960," *The Ceylon Journal of Historical and Social Studies*, 1960, vol. 3, no. 2, pp. 194-207.

[18] For the full text of the statement, see *Ceylon Daily News Parliaments of Ceylon 1960*, p. 215.

estate Tamil population. Mr. Senanayake said that the same demands had been made of him, but not even for the sake of the premiership was he willing to betray his country to the Tamil Federal Party. The other members of his party were more open in their propaganda. They declared from campaign platforms that if the SLFP was returned, the country would be betrayed to the Tamils, and it would be the end of the Sinhalese race.[19]

Nearly every Sinhalese electorate was provided with huge maps on which were marked the areas of north, east and central Ceylon which the SLFP would hand over to the Tamils if it was returned to power. This one fact was the dominating theme of the UNP's campaign. It was perhaps calculated that propaganda on these lines would scare the average Sinhalese voter into casting his vote against the Sri Lanka Freedom Party.

The SLFP at this election was ably led by a dynamic personality, Mrs. Sirimavo Bandaranaike. She asked the electorate for the opportunity to carry out the policies that her late husband had been deprived of implementing because of his untimely death. She had a powerful emotional appeal for the electorate, but this was not the only factor which swept her into power. She had at the same time successfully marshalled behind her all the forces of economic deprivation, Buddhist dissatisfaction and urban radicalism. She denied that she had any secret pact with the Tamil Federal Party. As if to prove her bona fides, there was Mr. K. M. P. Rajaratne and his extremist National Liberation Front on the sidelines, campaigning on her behalf in most of the up-country Kandyan Sinhalese electorates.

The Sri Lanka Freedom Party had made one vital change in its election manifesto which was indeed a substantial concession to the Sinhalese Buddhist pressure groups. This was on the question of education. The party general secretary, in a statement clarifying the position, described the existing system of education as outmoded, antinational and not conducive to religious or racial harmony. The key sentence was: "it will readily be granted that education paid for by the state should be given by the state." After pointing out that "in advanced countries like America this is the principle followed," the statement went on to say that this was the principle on which the SLFP proposed to work. They would therefore provide for education by the state based on "a system of non-sectarian schools." There would

[19] The *Ceylon Daily News* and *Times of Ceylon* of this period are replete with accounts of this type of speech made by United National Party leaders and candidates, as well as the contradictions issued by the Sri Lanka Freedom Party leaders.

be no objection to denominational schools continuing, but they would receive no assistance from the state. Such schools would have to conform to the rules laid down by the government.[20]

The verdict of the electorate on July 20, 1960, was a vote of overwhelming confidence in the Sri Lanka Freedom Party. It won an absolute majority of seats in the House of Representatives and was therefore able to form a government in its own right. On July 21, Mrs. Sirimavo Bandaranaike, the leader of the party, was sworn in as prime minister.

SCHOOLS, LANGUAGE, PRESS

The new premier, in a message to the nation[21] shortly after she assumed office, affirmed that she and her party would do all they could to ensure that people of all communities, of whatever race or religion, would receive from the new government "equality of treatment and a fair deal." There need be no fears, she added, of "maltreatment of the minorities." The Sinhalese Buddhist militants, however, felt that in the new government they had finally obtained an instrument which they could utilize to achieve their own ends. But the government did not prove as flexible as they would have liked it to be.

The first step was the legislation to take over all state-aided denominational schools. These could if they so desired become private schools, but they could not levy fees from those pupils who had already entered the institutions on a non-fee basis. This would have imposed severe hardships on the management but the Roman Catholic Church, in particular, was determined to brave them.

The Roman Catholics decided to resist the plan to nationalize their schools. They occupied the schools and refused to hand them over to the government. This resistance went on for several weeks, while the government did nothing and hoped that the Roman Catholics would wear themselves out. An impasse had been reached with neither side willing to concede any ground. For a time it seemed as if the situation would never change unless drastic action was taken by the government. The head of the Roman Catholic Church in Ceylon, Archbishop T. B. Cooray, in a pronouncement said that the Roman Catholics were determined to resist the takeover "even unto blood." Then suddenly the protest was called off as a result of the intervention of Cardinal Gracias, a high Roman Catholic dignitary from India.

The Lanka Sama Samaja Party and the Communist Party gave their

[20] For the full text see *Ceylon Daily News Parliaments of Ceylon 1960*, pp. 214-215.

[21] *Ibid.*, pp. 25-26.

wholehearted support to the government for the Schools Bill in the House of Representatives, some of their leaders in fact acting as spokesmen for the government during the debate. The United National Party, significantly enough, opposed the bill despite the welcome that the measure received from the Buddhist public. The Tamil Federal Party also cast its votes against the bill. The government's success in effecting the nationalization of aided schools unquestionably gave a great measure of satisfaction to a majority of the Sinhalese Buddhists.

Once the education issue was settled, the government next proceeded to deal with the language question. The courts, Parliament and the administration were the main subjects to be dealt with. Legislation was framed to provide for Sinhalese as the language of all courts in every part of Ceylon, including the Tamil areas. Despite the bitter protests of the Tamil Federal Party and the threat that it would resort to extra-parliamentary methods of obstruction, the government persisted in going through with the legislation. On the question of the language of parliamentary proceedings, the government proved to be more conciliatory. Legislation was originally framed to provide for Sinhalese as the only language for transacting business in Parliament. Then a compromise was accepted. The language of business would be Sinhalese but every facility would be provided to have simultaneous translations in Tamil and English.

There was, finally, the question of implementing in full the provisions of the Official Language Act once the deadline of its postponement was reached on December 31, 1960. The Federal Party reminded the prime minister that her late husband had assured the Tamil minority, especially the Tamil public servants, that the act would be worked in such a way as to cause no hardship to those who were not proficient in the official language. But the government was evidently in no mood to compromise here, and besides, it was under pressure from its own ranks and especially from the Sinhalese Buddhist militants. On January 1, 1961, the announcement was made that Sinhalese had in fact and in reality become the official language throughout the length and breadth of the Island.

Here again the Sinhalese extremists argued that the government was practicing a deception on the public, that much of the work in government departments was still being done in English and that little effort had been made to enforce the use of Sinhalese as the language of administration in the Tamil areas. In the forefront of this protest movement was K. M. P. Rajaratne and his National Liberation Front. There was some truth in these allegations. But the government for various reasons, administrative and political, was not willing to force the pace.

The Tamil Federal Party next decided on a course of non-violent direct action. On February 20, 1961, it launched a campaign of civil resistance based on Gandhian methods of non-violence.[22] The administration in Jaffna (the chief Tamil city in northern Ceylon) was brought to a standstill when Federal Party volunteers blocked the entrances to all government offices. In a couple of weeks the campaign spread to all the Tamil-speaking areas of north and east Ceylon and the administration in these areas was totally paralyzed. On April 17, a state of emergency was declared and the army was deployed to remove the non-violent obstructionists from the entrances to all government offices in the northern and eastern provinces.

It was several months before the emergency was called off. During the interim period, some halfhearted attempts were made to find a solution to the problem but no headway was made. Thereafter, in successive Throne Speeches, the government announced its intention of presenting legislation for the introduction of regional councils. A committee of public servants was appointed to gather evidence and frame proposals, but despite much work on the subject no bill was presented to Parliament.[23] During the latter stages, a militant Sinhalese Buddhist organization, the Bauddha Jatika Balavegaya (National Front for the Protection of Buddhism) loudly denounced the scheme for regional councils as a step toward the division of the country.[24] K. M. P. Rajaratne was also vociferous in his condemnation of the proposals. The government was evidently not willing to incur the displeasure of these elements especially at a time when its popularity was on the wane.

In late January 1962 there was an alleged attempt to overthrow the government by a coup d'état organized by some of the important officers in the armed forces and the police. The attempt was foiled. The majority of those who were involved and thereafter charged for conspiracy to overthrow the government belonged to the Roman Catholic faith. The spokesman for the government alleged that the attempt was made because those in power were the true guardians of Buddhism and that, had the coup succeeded, it would have spelled the end of Buddhism in Ceylon. Attempts were made to implicate the

[22] S. Ponniah, *The Freedom Movement of the Tamils in Ceylon,* Jaffna, 1963, provides the full story.
[23] See *Ceylon Daily News,* July 17, 1964, for the details of the District Councils Bill.
[24] *Times of Ceylon,* July 13, 1964.

United National Party. Special legislation was enacted to deal with the coup suspects, which was opposed by the United National Party, the Federal Party and the Lanka Sama Samaja Party. The last mentioned, however, withdrew its opposition when the government agreed to a compromise—to limit the application of the provisions of the bill to the particular case in question.

Thereafter a complete reorganization of the armed forces and the police was undertaken, the main purpose of which was to place trusted men in positions of responsibility. The permanent secretary to the ministry of defense, Mr. N. Q. Dias, was reported to have been largely responsible for the changes. He was an active Buddhist worker and allegedly one of the principal targets of the accused conspirators.

The government next interested itself in the problem of the press. Several abortive attempts to frame legislation had been made earlier. These had been rejected by the government parliamentary group for one reason or another, in particular because their provisions did not go as far as the members of the group would have liked. Now a Press Commission was appointed under the chairmanship of a retired Supreme Court judge, Mr. K. D. de Silva, to examine the whole problem and to make recommendations. When the commission commenced its public sittings, almost every important Buddhist organization which came before it was critical of the workings of the Ceylon press. It was Christian-dominated, westernized, anti-national, spiteful of Sinhalese culture, contemptuous of Buddhism. This was the burden of their evidence. They therefore wanted the present ownership disbanded and the press to be placed in the charge of a broad-based corporation which would have adequate Buddhist representation. Most of these witnesses, however, were opposed to control of the press by the state. The commission in its interim findings issued in August 1964 endorsed the criticisms, and recommended that an independent Press Council should be established and thereafter the newspapers should be placed in the hands of a state corporation.

THE BUDDHIST-MARXIST COALITION

Meanwhile a new factor had appeared on the political scene, causing serious apprehension among those Buddhist organizations which had earlier demanded the takeover of the press. In June 1964 a new government was sworn in, a coalition between the Sri Lanka Freedom Party and the Lanka Sama Samaja Party. The latter was given three portfolios in the cabinet and its leader Dr. N. M. Perera was appointed minister of finance. It was now said that if the press were taken over with these Marxists in the government, it would spell the end of Sinhalese culture, Buddhist civilization and the Sangha. It would pave the way to dictatorship and destroy human freedom.

Prior to the presentation of the press bill in Parliament the Trotskyist minister of finance presented his first budget for the financial year 1964-1965; in it there was a controversial proposal to permit the free tapping of toddy (a kind of liquor) from coconut trees. The minister explained that the purpose of this proposal was to put an end to the traffic in illicit liquor, which caused serious loss of revenue to the government and was also proving a menace to the health of the people. Buddhist monks, Buddhist pressure groups and the Sinhalese extremists, however, seized on this proposal to embarrass the Trotskyists. It was alleged that this was a subtle move on their part to wean the people away from religion.[25] There would be a "toddy torrent" in the country, it was said.

Political capital was made of the fact that in a country where temperance had always been advocated as a Buddhist virtue, the Marxists in keeping with their policy of undermining religion were seeking to corrupt the people through the toddy proposal. The prime minister, sensing the Buddhist anxiety, at first postponed consideration of the issue and finally decided to drop it. In the letter to the Mahanayake Thero of the Malwatte chapter explaining her stand on the press issue, she recalled that in regard to the toddy proposal, "in deference to the wishes of the Maha Sangha my government decided not to proceed with the proposal to permit the tapping of coconut trees."[26] This was an instance where the Trotskyists would have liked to stand their ground. Their spokesmen had defended the proposal in a forthright manner. But the government in the end was forced to submit to the pressure of Buddhist opinion.

When the Trotskyists now wanted to push through the proposal to take over the press, it was alleged that all these actions were part of a conspiracy to overthrow the Sinhalese Buddhist civilization. The campaign against the press takeover was evidently well organized. Efforts of the opposition groups to involve the Buddhist clergy proved highly successful—some influential sections of the Sangha appeared on government platforms but many others spoke on behalf of the opposition.

On November 3, 1964, a deputation of senior members of the Sangha including the Mahanayake Thero of the Malwatte chapter

[25] For the details of the charges, see the text of the prime minister's letter to the Mahanayake Thero (high priest) of the Malwatte chapter reproduced in the *Ceylon Daily News*, November 27, 1964.
[26] *Loc.cit.*

met the prime minister and expressed their opposition to the move to nationalize the press.[27] They stated, however, that they were in favor of some measure of control, including the setting up of an independent Press Council. The prime minister remained obdurate, and subsequently in a letter to the Mahanayake Thero of Malwatte explained the reasons for persisting in her stand.

Buddhist monks and Buddhist organizations all over the country led a vigorous agitation against the proposal. On November 6, 1964, nine important Buddhist associations formed a Joint Action Committee and issued a statement requesting the government to appoint an independent Press Council before introducing any measure to nationalize any section of the press.[28] This Joint Action Committee included, among others, representatives of the All-Ceylon Buddhist Congress, the Young Men's Buddhist Association, the Buddhist Theosophical Society, the Bauddha Jatika Balavegaya, the Mahabodhi Society and the Buddhist Student's Federation.

On November 10, the Mahanayake Theros of Malwatte and Asgiriya (the two principal chapters of the Siamese sect) issued a proclamation calling upon all members of the Buddhist clergy to attend a meeting scheduled for November 28 in Colombo, to protest against "the toddy proposal and the proposed takeover of the press."[29] At this meeting, which was also addressed by the leaders of the United National Party, the Jatika Vimukthi Peramuna and the Mahajana Eksath Peramuna, Mr. Dudley Senanayake, president of the UNP and the leader of the opposition, was reported to have said that in the past the Maha Sangha had come to the rescue of the nation, advising the people on every national issue. The Maha Sangha was playing the same role at the present juncture. He concluded with the solemn words: "We will here and now pledge before the Maha Sangha that we will not betray them but will follow their valuable advice and act accordingly.[30] In a statement to the press on November 27 Mr. L. H. Mettananda, president of the Bauddha Jatika Balavegaya, condemned the moves on the part of the Trotskyists and their allies to take over the Lake House Press.[31]

The government for its part organized meetings to explain why it

[27] *Ibid.*, November 4, 1964.
[28] *Ibid.*, November 7, 1964.
[29] *Ibid.*, November 17, 1964.
[30] For a fairly full report of the meeting, see *ibid.*, November 30, 1964.
[31] The text of the statement appears in *Ceylon Daily News*, November 28, 1964. The Lake House Press controls over 70 per cent of the newspaper undertakings in Ceylon. The government proposal was to take over only the Lake House Press. Other newspapers would not have been affected.

wanted to take over the Lake House newspapers. At these meetings too, Buddhist monks were in a prominent role. Government spokesmen said that they were only following the recommendations of the Press Commission, before which numerous Buddhist associations had demanded that ownership of the press should be diffused. At a mass rally in Colombo on November 5, the venerable vice chancellors of the two Buddhist Universities, Vidyalankara and Vidyodaya, leading Buddhist monks, declared their support for the government's proposal to take over the Lake House Press.[32] The retired chief justice, H. H. Basnayake, a leading Buddhist worker, countered this with the argument that as the vice chancellors were paid *bhikkhus* (monks), they supported the "Press Grab" proposals.[33] On November 8, the government organized a mass rally in Colombo at which the prime minister said that they were only following the recommendations of the Press

In the face of mounting opposition (it is difficult to say how much of it was artificial and how much of it was organized for reasons other than pure concern for Buddhism) the government decided on another course of action which it hoped might reassure the Buddhists. The fifth session of Parliament was abruptly prorogued on November 12, when it was found that the press bills that had been presented had certain procedural shortcomings which would have invalidated them. Now when Parliament met on November 20 for its sixth session, the Throne Speech, in addition to containing the previous proposals for the takeover of the Lake House Press, also envisaged legislation to guarantee Buddhism its proper place as the religion of the majority.[35] It was also mentioned that freedom of worship would at the same time be guaranteed to all other religions. The significance of this pronouncement lay in the fact that it had the support of the Trotskyists, who had up to that time refused to involve themselves in Buddhist communalism or to utilize Buddhism for political purposes.

The Buddhist militants scoffed at this proposal. They alleged that it was part of a Marxist maneuver to lull the Sinhalese Buddhists into a false sense of security. The Maha Sangha Peramuna (the Sangha Front, one of the many organizations which sprang up overnight during this period) in a statement issued on November 19, described the proposal as "an insidious device to stall the present agitation by the Maha Sangha and the Buddhist public."[36] It said that this was "fraudulent cunning" on the part of the government and its Trotsky-

32 *Ibid.*, November 6, 1964.   33 *Ibid.*, November 11, 1964.
34 *Ibid.*, November 9, 1964.
35 *Ceylon Daily News*, November 21, 1964.
36 *Ibid.*, November 20, 1964.

ist allies. The Mahajana Eksath Peramuna and the Jatika Vimukthi Peramuna, in sponsoring a joint amendment to the Address of Thanks on the Throne Speech, stated that this was "a shameless and cynical attempt" to deceive the Buddhist clergy and the Buddhist public.[37] They demanded in the joint amendment that legislation should be enacted to declare Buddhism the state religion and to provide that the governor general, prime minister, cabinet ministers, heads of departments, staff officers, officers of the armed forces and heads of schools should be Buddhists.

None of the groups that had been campaigning against the proposal to take over the Lake House Press seemed to be impressed by this new move on the part of the government. On the contrary the campaign was stepped up, and matters came to a head on the crucial day (December 3) when the voting on the joint opposition amendment to the Address of Thanks took place.

The opposition amendment stated that the government had "miserably failed to solve the pressing problems of the people, such as unemployment, the high cost of living and housing."[38] It was passed by 74 votes to 73. The deputy leader of the government, Mr. C. P. de Silva,[39] along with thirteen other members of the government parliamentary group voted with the opposition. What C. P. de Silva had to say about his reasons was interesting, for it was indicative of the extent to which Buddhism had become involved in the national politics of the country. In his speech in the House of Representatives on December 3, he said that "the coalition government accepting the anti-religious principles of totalitarianism has discarded the advice of the Maha Sangha of the three Nikayas thereby leading the country to chaos."[40] The prime minister's response was to dissolve Parliament and take the issue to the country.

One of the most important achievements of any Ceylonese prime minister in the sphere of relations with India was the agreement that Mrs. Bandaranaike reached with Prime Minister Lal Bahadur Shastri, on the disputed question of the stateless Indian population in Ceylon, some five weeks before her government was defeated in the House of Representatives. The main terms of the agreement signed on October 29, 1964, were that India would take back 525,000 of the

[37] For the full text of the amendment, see *Ceylon Daily News*, November 25, 1964.

[38] See *ibid.*, December 4, 1964, for a detailed account of the events which led to the downfall of the government.

[39] C. P. de Silva was leader of the House of Representatives and held the portfolio of minister of land, irrigation and power. He had acted for the prime minister on every occasion on which she was out of the country.

[40] *Ceylon Daily News*, December 4, 1964.

Indian estate Tamils over a period of fifteen years, while Ceylon would admit 300,000 of them to citizenship. The question of the remaining 150,000 would have to be decided sometime in the future, as there were vital differences of opinion between the two governments about them.[41] The agreement was of the utmost significance to the Sinhalese people in general and to the Kandyan Sinhalese in particular. Again, the Buddhist clergy showed interest in the politics of this agreement. The delegation of high-ranking Theros which met the prime minister on November 3 congratulated her on resolving the dispute with India. The venerable vice chancellors of the Vidyalankara and Vidyodaya Universities, at the mass rally in Colombo on November 5, also offered their felicitations. On the other hand a number of organizations of Buddhist monks in a statement issued on December 2 announced that they would, among other things, campaign against "the Indo-Ceylon Agreement where Ceylon was sold to India."[42]

The reactions of the political parties were intriguing. The United National Party maintained silence, although the prime minister insisted[43] she had consulted its leader, Mr. Dudley Senanayake, at every stage during the negotiations. The Lanka Sama Samaja Party leaders, who had long campaigned for citizenship rights for the Indian estate Tamil population, gave their support to the prime minister's solution of the problem. The Mahajana Eksath Peramuna and the Jatika Vimukthi Peramuna expressed the narrow nationalism of the Sinhalese Buddhist extremists when, in the joint amendment they moved to the Address of Thanks on the last Throne Speech, they demanded that the agreement be abrogated and that steps be taken to repatriate every one of about 1,600,000 of Indians resident in Ceylon. They insisted that the prime minister was ignorant of the actual figures of Indians in Ceylon. The Tamil Federal Party condemned the agreement. Mr. Chelvanayakam, the Federal Party leader described it as "a pact between racialists."[44]

This record of Mrs. Sirimavo Bandaranaike's premiership is one of many contradictions. On one hand the policies that her government pursued during its earlier phase were weighted considerably in favor of the Sinhalese Buddhists. On the other hand, toward the end of her ministry she entered into a coalition with the Trotskyists who had long been known for their liberal attitude to communal prob-

[41] See *ibid.*, October 29-30, 1964, for the full details of the agreement.
[42] *Ibid.*, December 3, 1964.
[43] See the text of the prime minister's statement in the Senate on November 10 in *Ceylon Daily News*, November 17, 1964.
[44] *Ibid.*, November 17, 1964.

lems. She insisted that the Trotskyists had accepted her policies, while the Trotskyists did not hesitate to declare on every occasion that they were still Marxists. Mrs. Bandaranaike's government came very close to involvement in hard alliances with the Sangha and Buddhist pressure groups. But on the other hand, there were many occasions when she was not slow to declare that she strongly disagreed with clergy as well as laity. On balance, it will not be an exaggeration to say that Mrs. Bandaranaike made use of the Buddhist forces in the country more than she permitted them to use her government for their own purposes. Her legislative record did not satisfy the extremists but it gave immense satisfaction to the vast majority of the Sinhalese Buddhists. It was only the minorities who remained alienated.

In the March 1965 general elections, the SLFP with its Marxist coalition partners faced the UNP and its allies, including C. P. de Silva's splinter group. In the election campaign the UNP stressed the dangers that democracy and Buddhism would face from the Marxists, and alleged that it was only a matter of time before the Marxists would infiltrate and capture the SLFP. The UNP had considerable success in mobilizing the monks, and a number of pro-UNP *bhikkhu* organizations sprang up.[45] The Mahanayake Thero of the Malwatte chapter denounced the Marxists in strong language.[46] The SLFP-Marxist coalition, on the other hand, attacked the UNP as a tool of the Catholic Church, western capitalism and American imperialism, and accused it of having sold out to the Tamils.

The UNP won a plurality, but its leader Dudley Senanayake was able to form a government only with the support of the Federal Party. A Tamil (the Federal Party's nominee) was appointed to the cabinet for the first time since 1956. Anxious to assert its fundamental Sinhalese Buddhist identity, however, the new government in the Throne Speech declared that Buddhism would be restored to "the place it occupied when Lanka was free," that Buddhist sabbath days would be made public holidays, and that in consultation with the Sangha it would "promulgate such measures as are necessary for the Maha Sangha to fulfil its noble mission."[47]

45 *Ibid.*, January 22 and March 16, 1965.
46 *Ibid.*, February 2, 1965.
47 *Sun*, April 10, 1965.

CHAPTER 24

BUDDHIST REORGANIZATION
IN CEYLON

C. D. S. SIRIWARDANE

THE WINDS OF change swept over Ceylon a hundred and fifty years ago, carrying away with them much that belonged to the old social and economic order that had existed in the island from almost the beginning of her history. The changes were intended to bring about a complete revolution embracing almost every aspect of the nation's life, the form of government, the economy, the language, the religion, the customs and social institutions of the people. Much that belonged to the old order was swept away and much that was left behind was so impaired and enfeebled that it had little influence on the new society.

And now the winds are blowing once again. This time the social and economic order built during the colonial regime is being gradually assailed in order to provide a place for those who stood submerged under colonial rule. The process has brought about so many conflicts between affected interests that it is difficult to forecast the future and say what forces will, in the end, determine the shape of things. How far will the traditional values which prevailed before the country passed under colonial rule influence her future?

Throughout Ceylon's recorded history Buddhism has been the chief cultural influence in the country. But Buddhism lost the place it held in society when Ceylon lost her independence, and has emerged seriously impaired after the period of colonial rule. Can Buddhism make its contribution to the building up of a new society in the disorganized state in which it finds itself today? Can its doctrines influence society through the acts of individual Buddhists or small groups in the face of opposition from its traditional opponents, the organized Christian churches, and still more from its new enemy of secularism? Must Buddhism not purge itself of the disruptive elements within its own ranks if it is to make a useful contribution to society? To answer these questions it is necessary to analyze the forces which have lent Buddhism strength throughout its long life

C. D. S. Siriwardane is an advocate of the Supreme Court of Ceylon and a lecturer at the Ceylon Law College.

of twenty-five centuries, and see whether the same forces are capable of supporting it in the years to come.

ROYAL PATRONS OF BUDDHISM

Buddhism and Jainism both arose in India in the sixth century B.C., and had much in common. Both rejected the elaborate ceremonies which perpetuated the laity's dependence on the Brahmin priesthood. The founders of both religions came from Kshatriya familes and preached against the domination of the Brahmins. Both renounced wealth and high position and devoted themselves to a life of asceticism. Both formed religious orders of followers, male and female, and also established lay orders of persons who, while they did not become ascetics, followed the faith in their daily lives. Both preached the ideal of *ahimsa*, denied the existence of a supreme deity, and preached salvation through man's own efforts without external support.

Yet Jainism remained a small sectarian movement within India, while Buddhism spread and flourished throughout most of Asia. Perhaps the extreme length to which Jainism pushed its doctrine of *ahimsa* was partly responsible for its limited popularity. Its theory of self-mortification as a means of obtaining deliverance could not have appealed to any but the most ascetic minds. Very few rulers embraced Jainism, and those who did, like Chandragupta, were overcome by the ascetic ideal and renounced the world. He did not continue in his royal functions to give Jainism a position of power, but took to the monastic life and starved himself to death.

Buddhism succeeded where Jainism failed, namely, in attracting the patronage of rulers. Even in his own lifetime the Buddha was able to draw on the support of kings. He himself was of royal stock, his father having been the head of a small clan called the Sakya clan whose state was situated among the foothills of the Himalayas. His royal upbringing and his vast intellectual capacity attracted the attention of many kings of the day whose names figure in the Suttas. They became his devoted supporters and their patronage undoubtedly helped nascent Buddhism to establish itself in the area where the Buddha lived and preached. Royal patronage thus had an important influence on early Buddhism which learned to adjust itself to harmonize with the requirements of the state. The Buddha advised the *bhikkhus* (monks) to see that their conduct conformed to the royal wish unless the latter came into conflict with Buddhist principles.[1] The rules regarding admission to the Sangha were so framed as

---

[1] *Mahavagga* III, 4, 3.

to avoid inconvenience to royal officials.[2] For example, no member of the armed forces could be enrolled in the Sangha until he had obtained release from military service. In fact, Buddhism has preserved this tradition of harmony with the state. During the 2,500 years of its existence, history has no record of a violent clash between Buddhism and the state.

It is also significant that the Buddha established no organization of the laity. The only organization he left behind was that of the Sangha, the order of monks, to whom he entrusted the duty of preserving and propagating the doctrine. "Go ye forth, my brethren," he said to them, "for the gain of many, for the welfare of many, out of compassion for the world, preach ye this doctrine, which is glorious in the beginning, in the middle and in the end. Preach ye a life of holiness, perfect and pure." In the days when books were little known, the Dhamma reached the people through the words of the monks.

The Sangha consisted of those who had, like the Buddha, renounced the world and devoted their whole life to the spiritual development which led to the supreme goal of Nibbana. A person entering the order gave up worldly belongings; the only property he could have were two sets of clothing, a tool for cutting firewood, a needle, a water strainer, and a begging-bowl for his food. On entering the order, he appears to have, in theory, died to the world of laymen and been born in the community of the monks. He lost his right of inheritance from his family, he lost his caste distinctions, and was released from all liabilities which he owed to the state. He derived his rights from the community of monks of which he became a member. He was bound by the Vinaya, or rules of monastic discipline, which he bound himself to observe when he entered the Sangha.

While the monks were prohibited from owning private property with the exception of the eight articles needed in their daily life, the Buddha came near the idea of a corporation when he permitted them to accept gifts to the entire Sangha, or the whole fraternity. Lands and buildings were bestowed on the Sangha in the Buddha's own day, for example, the magnificent abode of Jetavanarama given by the great philanthropist Anathapindika. This must have been the Buddha's favorite abode for it figures very often in the Suttas. The rule permitting the acceptance of gifts on behalf of the Sangha was much abused in later times, as monks relaxed the austere rules of the Vinaya in favor of worldly comforts. But in the Buddha's day

---

[2] *Ibid.*, I, 40, 4.

there were without doubt checks to prevent these gifts being misused by the Sangha or weakening the discipline within the order.

The Sangha lived outside the habitations of ordinary men, though not too far away. Twice a month the monks in each community had to meet for the recital of the Patimokka, a formulary for obtaining release from offenses by confession and penance. The list was recited from memory by an elder and confession was made by anyone who had fallen into guilt by the violation of any rule. If silence followed the recital, the senior monk would declare *patimokka* or absolution with the words *parisuddha 'ti vedissami*—I shall understand they are pure.

The fortnightly meeting of monks was the way in which the Buddha intended that the purity of the Sangha should be maintained. Two occasions are mentioned in the Suttas when the Buddha was asked whether he would not appoint a successor to take his place as head of the Sangha. The first occasion was when Devadatta made the inquiry with evil motive, and the second time when Ananda, the Buddha's favorite disciple, knew that the Master was nearing the end of his life. In each case the Buddha's answer was the same—the Sangha needed no head, the Dhamma and the Vinaya were adequate to preserve the Sasana. What the Buddha meant, of course, was that so long as the monks observed the Vinaya rules the purity and strength of the Sangha would be maintained.

When there was a confession of guilt at the fortnightly meeting, the assembly decided in what form atonement should be made. There were the more serious types of offenses which could not be expiated. A monk guilty of an act which involved *parajika* suffered ecclesiastical death. Each monk in a community bound himself to it by his undertaking to observe the Vinaya. If he broke one of the lesser rules he could purge himself of the guilt. If, on the other hand, he did not admit his fault it became a matter of concern for others within the community. Anyone in the assembly could bring such a fact to the notice of the assembly. A charge would be framed and the person suspected called upon to plead. A formal inquiry would follow and there would be a decision from the assembly. The aim of the trial was to get the guilty party to accept his fault. If he did not accept the decision of the assembly, he was free to depart from the community; the rest could not have him in their community as long as he could not accept the majority decision. The monks, of course, could not forcibly disrobe a member of the Sangha. The worst punishment they could administer was to ostracize a wrongdoer, who would then find life impossible within the community. The rules of procedure for these trials were carefully laid down to ensure fair play and justice, even going beyond the requirements of natural justice as understood in modern law.

The rules of the Vinaya were laid down so as to permit each community of monks to regulate the conduct of its own members. Yet there was sufficient freedom given to the individual who felt that the majority decision was unacceptable so that he could maintain his own independence. While the Vinaya rules and the Patimokka recitals, properly observed, could have preserved the purity of a small community of monks, they could not by themselves prevent the emergence of heretical or indisciplined monks or even of bands of people who masqueraded in the garb of monks and received the homage and bounty of laymen. Against such persons, who were an even greater source of danger to the Sangha than were a few members of a community who occasionally violated a rule, the institutions of the Sangha provided no remedy. Nor could these institutions effectively deal with the monk who lived a corrupt life away from the community to which he belonged and did not attend the fortnightly recitals. Against these evils the Sangha had to depend on the assistance of external forces.

Two centuries after the passing away of the Buddha the Maurya Emperor Ashoka was converted to Buddhism. His conversion was an event as important for Buddhism as was the conversion of Constantine for Christianity. Buddhism became elevated to the position of the state religion of the Maurya Empire and entered on an era of expansion. The Rock and Pillar Edicts left by the great emperor are evidence of the change that came over Buddhism through Ashoka's influence.[3] A conscious effort was made to influence society through the principles of the Buddha's doctrines; Buddhism was rescued from social irrelevance, from being solely a set of monastic ideals. We see for the first time Buddhism in action as a practical faith helping to mold society.

Ashoka set the example of what a Buddhist monarch should be. He sent missionaries abroad, and held councils of the Sangha to promote the purity of the monastic order. He gave freely to the Sangha, putting up buildings for their use and shrines where the people could worship, and in this way harnessed the arts, architecture, painting and sculpture, to the service of religion. Many Buddhist kings in India and elsewhere took him for a model, though none ever equalled his moral stature.

[3] J. C. Powell-Price, *A History of India*, Nelson, London, 1955, p. 48.

The decline of Buddhism in India started about 182 B.C., not fifty years after the death of Ashoka. His dynasty was overthrown by Pushyamitra, a Brahminist, and once royal patronage was withdrawn the decline was rapid. Hinduism had the assistance of a privileged priestly caste to perpetuate the religion. Buddhism, rejecting ritual and the worship of gods and without a hereditary priesthood, was vulnerable. Buddhism had relied solely on the support of kings, and wherever such support was found Buddhism was able to assert itself, only to decline and die when it was no longer available. The final blow to Buddhism in India was given by the Muslim invaders. Can a doctrinal system hope to maintain its influence without either its own organization or the support of some external power? The lesson that one may draw from the history of Buddhism in India is that it may not.

Elsewhere in South and Southeast Asia the expansion of Buddhism followed the same pattern as that in India. A king accepted Buddhism, his subjects followed his example, and Buddhism became the state religion. But unlike India, in the Theravada countries of Ceylon, Burma, Thailand, Cambodia and Laos, there have been long unbroken lines of Buddhist kings. In all these lands there has been a strong king-Sangha partnership which undoubtedly accounts for the long life that Buddhism has had in Asian countries outside India. In Ceylon the connection between Buddhism and the state was long and uninterrupted, and the union between the state and the Sangha became closer than in any other country.

The king-Sangha partnership is perhaps best seen today in Thailand, which has preserved its Buddhist monarchy up to the present day. The king of Thailand is the head of the order and appoints the Patriarch or Sangharaja and other high officers of the Sangha. The Sangharaja administers the affairs of the order with the assistance of a cabinet of ten ministers drawn from the Sangha. A state department headed by a civil servant carries out the decisions of the Sangharaja and undertakes the management of Sangha property. An ecclesiastical tribunal presided over by a monk tries *bhikkhus* accused of violating rules of the Vinaya. The king maintains religious buildings and constructs new ones as the need arises; Buddhism plays an important role in all affairs of the state and Buddhist festivals are observed as state occasions. There is more organization of the Sangha in Thailand than in other Theravada lands although the king-Sangha partnership is still the basis of such organization.

In Thailand the administration of the temples and the Sangha has been made effective by modeling it on the pattern of the civil administration. Functions which cannot be carried out by monks because of Vinaya prohibitions, such as the administration of funds, are taken over by the religious affairs department under the minister of cultural affairs. State assistance in the administration of the Sangha has provided the conditions necessary for the monks to live up to the austere rules of the Vinaya, with no contradiction between precept and practice. In the Buddhist monarchies Buddhism will continue in the traditional manner in harmony with the state as long as this basic relationship remains unchanged.

Buddhism came to Ceylon in the days of Ashoka and has remained ever since as the religion of the majority. The king-Sangha partnership that started with Devanampiyatissa in 315 B.C. was carried on without interruption until 1815, when the last king of Kandy was compelled to abdicate and the country was ceded to the British. Throughout this long period Buddhism leaned on the support of the kings, the majority of whom attempted to conform to the traditional pattern originated by the Buddhist kings in India.

The kings established monasteries and gave them large endowments of lands for their upkeep. They also decreed that the *rajakariya*, or compulsory services due to the state from tenants of certain lands, should be remitted in favor of temples and monastic establishments. In this manner a class of hereditary tenants was created, which performed services for these religious institutions in return for the lands they held. The kings also built *dagabas* and *viharas* for the worship of the people, and established monastic colleges for the use of both the clergy and the laity. Often a king tried to surpass his predecessors in the size and magnificence of the buildings erected in the service of religion. Various arts and crafts were employed for beautifying these buildings, and religion influenced every aspect of life in the country.

The king-Sangha tradition was maintained unbroken in Ceylon for a longer period than in any other country. Ceylon's insularity and its freedom from large-scale invasions ensured the continuity of Buddhist kings through twenty-two centuries of her history. Unlike the situation in India, there was no other powerful religion to challenge the position of Buddhism in Ceylon until Christianity came on the scene. During this long period Buddhism became closely intertwined with the affairs of the state. The Sangha became an important and influential group within society; the *bhikkhus* became the teachers of kings and men. In the monasteries were fostered all branches of learning which were needed to advance the welfare of the people, including the arts of medicine and astrology. The larger monasteries had hospitals attached to them, in which the art of healing was prac-ticed and taught. The village temple ministered likewise to the needs of the village people. Each village had two important institutions which helped to knit the people together into an organic unit. One was the village council or *gamsabhawa,* the council of elders which met and decided all important issues within the village and settled local disputes. Often the monks participated in these proceedings. The other was the village temple where the monks made their con-tribution to the welfare of the village in many ways. The village was a close-knit community, enjoying a large measure of autonomy and held together by these institutions.

The king as the head of the state became the protector of religion. Buddhism was the state religion and the important festivals became public occasions. As head of the Sangha he made appointments to important offices of the Sangha, and appointed and exercised super-vision over lay trustees of the temple property. He became the cus-todian of the two important relics of the Buddha, the bowl and tooth relics which, in course of time, came to be regarded as palladiums. As protector of the faith he performed an important function, namely, that of keeping the order pure, free from schisms and heresies. The chronicles are full of instances of kings who from time to time had heretics tried by public tribunals and punished. In many cases they were disrobed and sometimes whipped in public. The king also from time to time summoned councils of the Sangha, to frame monastic regulations which were then promulgated by the king.

BUDDHISM UNDER BRITISH RULE

The king-Sangha tradition, unbroken through twenty-two centuries, came to an abrupt end in 1815 when the Kandyan provinces were ceded to the British. There is evidence that the chiefs and monks responsible for the cession gave much thought to the problem that presented itself—of providing for the functions of the king in regard to Buddhism. But the incompatibility of a Christian governor under-taking the functions of an absolute Buddhist monarch must have been apparent. The chiefs and the monks were anxious about the safety of Buddhism and wanted a guarantee against hostile action by the gov-ernment. A compromise was finally found and was agreed to by the Governor, Sir Robert Brownrigg, and an article safeguarding the po-sition of Buddhism was included in the Convention that was signed. It read as follows: "The religion of the Buddhoo professed by the chiefs and inhabitants of these provinces is declared inviolable and its rites and places of worship are to be maintained and protected." Brownrigg confessed to the Earl of Bathurst, in a bulletin dated the day after the signing of the Convention, that he included the article only because it was a *sine qua non* of the cession. It was distasteful to Brownrigg, an ardent Christian who considered the spreading of Christianity in Ceylon to be part of his official duties. To the chiefs, on the other hand, it was not conceivable that Buddhism could exist separate from the state. The formula helped both parties to overcome the difficulty for the moment.

In the years 1815-1853 the government gradually withdrew from the undertakings of 1815. Anything more than mere tolerance and freedom of worship for the Buddhists was considered not in keeping with the principles of a Christian government. Besides, the government suspected the monks of political intrigue. The rebellion of 1818 only proved their suspicions. "The priests," reported the governor, "appear to be the grand movers of these plots by their influence over the chiefs."[4] British policy was directed thereafter toward gradually undermining the power of the monks, who were always viewed as potential troublemakers.

There were, however, other changes not anticipated in 1815. Within two decades of the Convention a far-reaching revolution was to commence both in state and in society. On the recommendations of Colonel Colebrooke important reforms were brought about which mark a turning point in the history of this country. The most important change was undoubtedly the abolishing of *rajakariya* or compulsory service to the king. Colebrooke condemned the *rajakariya* system because it had the effect of keeping people bound to certain vocations and because its burden fell unequally on different people. The removal of the system allowed freedom of movement on the part of labor and released people from restrictions imposed on them by their birth; it became possible for them to seek whatever employment they liked.

But an exception was made in the case of certain types of tenants. Of this class the larger part consisted of tenants of temple and *dewale* lands. These tenants were to continue to perform the traditional services to the temple trustees. The exception was undoubtedly created in the interests of the temples and in order not to upset the *bhikkhus*. But its effect was in the long run to be disadvantageous to the temples and consequently to the interests of Buddhism. The temples and their tenants became a relic of the past, cut off from the

[4] Lennox Mills, *Ceylon under British Rule*, Oxford University Press, London, 1933, p. 160.

currents of social change flowing through the country. The monks of the Kandyan provinces who had an exalted position in the old feudal order became a class increasingly hostile, as time went on, to social changes in the rest of society. Temple tenants bound to the customs and institutions of a social order that was no more gradually came to regard the monks and trustees as reactionaries who upheld serfdom. The monks, who had traditionally worked in harmony with state and society, gradually became transformed into a discontented class, cut off from progress and conscious of the fact that they had fallen from the lofty place they had once held.

In 1870 the temple and *dewale* tenants of Sabaragamuwa petitioned the governor for legislation to release them from the serfdom of the temples. The agitation resulted in the Service Tenures Ordinance, which introduced a system of commutation in lieu of personal services. Present-day socialist legislation is making further inroads into rights of temples which derive their incomes largely from lands worked by peasant cultivators. For example, the Paddy Lands Act of 1958 granted security of tenure to tenant cultivators and a division of the crops more advantageous to the tenant. The Kandyan temples, deriving their revenues largely from paddy lands, have had their incomes greatly curtailed by the act. The act itself is a great boon to the tenants; the *bhikkhus* who are protesting against the act appear in the unenviable role of reactionaries against a very beneficial measure.

There were other changes of a far-reaching nature, as the country began to pass from an economy based on the cultivation of paddy to one based on plantations. The village units began to be neglected and their organization to break up. After the rebellion of 1818 the legal recognation given to the decisions of village councils was withdrawn and they became powerless to administer the affairs of the villages. Thus the only institution existing at the time competent to maintain law and order was clipped of its powers, and the villages gradually began to lapse into crime. Moreover, with the neglect of village irrigation systems the villages became impoverished. The introduction of taverns, licensed by the government as a revenue-earning measure, added to the deterioration of village life. With this deterioration the temples gradually began to lose their influence over the village, a process that has gone on up to the present day.

In 1840 the leading Christian missionaries and some of the public officers began an agitation against the support given to the Buddhist religion by the government. Since the Kandyan Convention the government had carried on some of the functions of the Sinhalese kings toward Buddhism. The government had custody of the tooth relic, made the customary appointments to Sangha eccleciastical offices, maintained Buddhist shrines and administered temple lands. Objection was taken to a Christian government's participation in "heathen idolatry" and it was urged that the government should transfer these functions to a central committee of Buddhists. The Buddhists protested against the violation of the Convention and declared their inability to manage their affairs.

The motives that actuated the suggestion of a central committee were probably not altogether altruistic. The missionaries regarded the support of the government as the one factor which upheld the prestige of Buddhism and protected it from disintegration. It was expected that, with its withdrawal, the religion would collapse and the ground would be cleared for mass conversions to Christianity. An ordinance was passed in 1846 to create this central committee, but it was disallowed by the Queen on the advice that it would give a "dangerous organization" to the Buddhists. Six years later, a despatch from the secretary of state instructed the governor to cease to exercise the functions hitherto performed in regard to the Buddhist religion. The last vestige of the royal protection of Buddhism was destroyed in 1853, and Buddhism was left without any organization to take its place.

Had Buddhism remained long in the position into which it fell in 1853 its decay would have been rapid. The spoliation anticipated by the agitators in 1843 would have left Buddhist temporalities badly reduced, and the irresponsible control of property by *viharadhipathis* who had taken the vow of poverty would have brought the Sangha into great disrepute. In fact, within two decades "scandalous abuses" of temple property were reported which even shocked the higher public officials. But the Christian missionaries who were impatient for results had by then begun a campaign of religious controversy which aroused the Buddhists, and a great Buddhist revival was the result. The Buddhist revival of the latter half of the last century had far-reaching results. It stimulated interest in Buddhism in foreign countries and was responsible for bringing Colonel Olcott, the American lawyer who became the leader of the Buddhist movement in Ceylon. Under his leadership the Buddhists began to enter the field of social activity.

The Buddhist awakening coincided with changes in the relationship between the state and the Christian church. In 1886 the government disestablished the official church, which had up to then been a state department, and granted it the status of an incorporated body. The Church of England became a central authority for the Christians of that communion. It was vested with unlimited powers over property and with all the churches, schools and other institutions managed by the ecclesiastical department. The government in 1886 ceased to have official connections with any religion. Under this ordinance the Anglican Church became a corporation with no control by the government. It became capable of acquiring property and making investments; its accumulations of wealth centrally controlled would enable it to go on perpetually. The propagation of Christianity thereafter was carried on through churches, schools, orphanages, homes for the aged and other charitable and philanthropic activities organized and financed by the central authority.

In 1889 the government agreed to give the Buddhists a minimum of legal organization to enable them to manage their temporalities, and the first Buddhist Temporalities Ordinance was passed. The governor, who sponsored the bill, in his opening address explained in some detail the policy of the government toward Buddhism. His remarks are helpful in understanding the underlying weakness of Buddhist organization as compared with that granted to the Christian churches. "What is intended is simply to give to the Buddhists as has been given to the Church of England, the means of managing their own affairs, with however this important difference, that instead of one governing body there will be several independent governing bodies in the different districts."[5] The ordinance provided for separate lay trustees for each temple, controlled by district committees and subject to strict audit under the direction of judicial authority. The governor explained further that "by adopting this plan the danger of creating a new and formidable power such as was created by the Ordinance of 1846 was escaped." The measure was opposed vigorously by the leading members of the Christian community even in the form in which it was ultimately passed. They were against any kind of organization being granted to the Buddhists.

The Buddhist Temporalities Ordinance now in force is only a modification of the Ordinance of 1889. The district committees have been replaced by the Public Trustee, who exercises supervisory powers over temple trustees. In the case of smaller temples a *bhikkhu* is trustee, while in the larger temples the *viharadhipathi* or senior *bhikkhu* nominates a trustee, it being permissible for him to nominate himself. The nomination of a lay trustee is very exceptional. The Ordinance of 1931 also introduced for the first time a system of registration for *bhikkhus*, and passing as a *bhikkhu* was made a punishable offense. There is no case, however, of the enforcement of this rule.

[5] Address of the governor on October 31, 1888, Ceylon Legislative Council.

C. D. S. Siriwardane

The present problem of Buddhist organization can now be examined. Buddhism has hitherto been mainly a doctrinal system, not an organization, and the contribution it has made to the country has been through its association with the state and state organization. The only organization that Buddhism has hitherto had is that of the Sangha, and it is doubtful whether the strength and purity of the Sangha can be maintained without the assistance of some external authority. That authority has hitherto been the state. Can the state, as it has come to be in Ceylon today, fulfil that function? This is unthinkable under the present system, with a government elected on party lines by a population consisting of persons of different religions. There is nothing that Buddhism would gain by being involved in the dust and strife of party politics. Moreover, history has shown that even under absolute kings the strength of Buddhism waxed or waned with the strength of the ruler. With an elected government the future is precarious. There appear to be only two solutions to the problem: either Buddhism remains without a central organization, or it establishes a central authority with little or no connection with the state.

Is Buddhism in need of an organization? The Buddha Sasana Commission appointed by the government, consisting of representatives of both the Sangha and the laity, answered with a most emphatic affirmative.[6] Various societies and associations have been formed which have as their aim "the upholding of Buddhist rights," by which is meant no more than giving back to Buddhism the strength it has lost. But none of these enthusiastic bodies can suggest anything more than that the government should legislate prohibiting *bhikkhus* from doing this or owning that. That something must be done is universally accepted, but there is no agreement on what the particular solution should be. The majority of Buddhists cannot tear themselves away from the idea of state association with religion.

The lack of organization is revealed in many ways. The first to suffer has been the Sangha. The unfortunate policy of the Malwatte and Asgiriya chapters of the Siam sect not to admit any but persons of one favored caste to higher ordination has perpetuated disunity in the Sangha. The other sects are themselves subdivided into minor divisions, mainly also on the basis of caste. There are, at present, no doctrinal differences; those that exist are purely of a formal nature. But how long such divisions will be based on formal differences one

[6] *Buddha Sasana Commission Report* (in Sinhalese), Government Press, Colombo, 1959. For a discussion of reactions to this report, see also chapter 22.

cannot predict. Large numbers of young *bhikkhus* are receiving higher education at the universities and it is not unlikely that, in their desire to break away from traditional ways of thinking, they may introduce doctrinal differences. If they do, the Sangha organization is not strong enough to deal with them.

The Buddha Sasana Commission recommended that the government enact legislation to create a central authority for the Buddhists to be called the Buddha Sasana Mandalaya, a deliberative body consisting of two councils. One council would be composed of *bhikkhus* representing the three sects. The Council of the Sangha, as it would be called, would meet to discuss matters relating to the Sangha and would bring about common understanding among the sects. It would draw up and promulgate regulations relating to the conduct of *bhikkhus* which would apply to monks of all sects and thus bring about uniformity of practice. This would be the first step toward the abolition of sectarian divisions. The proposal was vehemently opposed by the Malwatte and Asgiriya chapter of the Siam sect, which feared any disruption of the ecclesiastical status quo.

The second problem concerning the Sangha is the question of discipline. The recommendation of the Buddha Sasana Commission was that the state should grant legal recognition to the status of *bhikkhu* and that an ecclesiastical court should be established which would have the power to annul a *bhikkhu's* status after inquiry. Such courts have already been established in Thailand, Cambodia and Laos, and appear to have provided a satisfactory solution.

But there is need also for organization to deal with the material needs of the Sangha. In the old village units the support and maintenance of the monks was a duty readily undertaken by all Buddhists. The interests of the monks were so closely linked with those of the laity that each had to support the other. However, the village no longer depends on the temple as it did in the past, and the bonds of interdependence have almost disappeared. The problem of maintenance of the modern *bhikkhu* is therefore a most difficult one. Without effective organization, it is not possible to harness the support that is available. *Bhikkhus* have, in consequence, to resort to various methods to earn their living. Many are led to accept teaching and other posts and even to engage in minor trades that can be carried on without too much publicity. Unless the laity are able to ensure conditions that will enable the *bhikkhus* to live strict lives, it is useless to expect purity in the Sangha, and it is foolish to blame the monks for these violations of the Vinaya.

The management of temple lands has been a difficult problem since British times. The present system of management by the senior *bhikkhus* of each temple is incompatible with their vow of poverty and inefficient from the administrative standpoint. Trustees can only lease out the lands and collect the proceeds, and too often the temptation is to obtain more from the leases than is shown on statements of accounts and other documents. Such a state of affairs brings discredit on the entire Sangha and is one of the chief reasons for its internal weakness and declining prestige today. The lessees, whose tenure is usually for a short period, do not find it profitable to develop the lands but merely scrape whatever they can get out of them during the lease period. The Buddha Sasana Commission recommended the vesting of all these lands in a special officer, with their management entrusted to a committee of the proposed Sasana Mandalaya. This body would pay the special officer in trust for the temples the same annual income hitherto derived by the temples, and utilize any surplus for the furtherance of Buddhism. It was recommended that the law should be amended to enable the Mandalaya to invest its own funds for the development of these lands and recover its investment over a long period. It was hoped that the scheme would pave the way for the ultimate consolidation of these land holdings, with the consent of the *bhikkhus* of the respective temples, so that they might be used for the general welfare of Buddhism.

Lastly, the Buddha Sasana Commission recommended that the proposed Buddha Sasana Mandalaya should also have a council composed of both the Sangha and the laity, which would be concerned with all such matters relating to Buddhism as were not specially reserved for the Council of the Sangha. It was to be the more important of the two councils, which would undertake to promote the general welfare of the Buddhists, meet the challenge to Buddhism from opposing forces, and deal with the state in regard to the rights of the Buddhists. It was to undertake the traditional functions of the Buddhist king in promoting the general welfare of Buddhism and also take upon itself the functions appropriate to a religious organization in modern society.

The Buddhist concept of the state comes close to the western theory of social contract. When such a theory is accepted there is an underlying assumption that the state as the other party to the contract needs constant watching. This is all the more necessary today when the state is not represented by a single head whose personal integrity would serve as a guarantee of good government. It is the duty of religious organizations to see that the state does not break its covenant with the people, especially with regard to the moral values that the state must uphold. At the present time the existing Buddhist organizations are too much swayed by the financial support they receive from the state, and none of these organizations is prepared to relinquish such assistance to preserve its independence of thought and action. It is only a strong central organization, commanding all the financial and other resources of the Buddhist community, which will be powerful enough to ensure that the state fulfil its obligations to the Buddhists, and will stand firm in its opposition to the forces of materialism.

INDEX

Abbasids, 359
Abbot, Freeland, 364
Abduh, Muhammad, 416, 427
Abdul Kadir v. Dharma, 282, 289
Abdullah, Sheikh, 86-87
Abraham v. Abraham, 296, 300
Adams, C. C., 141
Adi-Dravida, 224
Adi Granth, 156-57
Adorno, T. W., 252, 262, 266
Advani, L. K., 93
Advisory Council of Islamic Ideology, 45, 352, 366, 368-69
Afaqi, Ali Sufyan, 372
Afghanistan, 429-30, 443-45, 448
Afzal, Qaisan, 367
Agamas, 284
ahimsa, 532
Ahir, 57, 59, 284
Ahmad, Jamil-ud-din, 361
Ahmad Khan, Syed, 350, 416, 429
Ahmad, Khurshid, 43, 357, 390
Ahmad, M., 430-31, 435
Ahmad, Mirza Ghulam, 364, 403
Ahmadis, 364, 377-78, 403-04, 412
Ahmadiyah sect, *see* Ahmadis
Ahmed, Fakhruddin Ali, 129
Ahmed, Rafiq, 369
Ahmed, Shahabuddin, 124, 132
Aiyangar, V. K. Rangaswami, 317
Akali Dal, 86, 88; and Punjabi Suba movement, 25, 90, 150-54, 174-75; opposed by Jana Sangh, 85, 90, 96, 98; origin of, 160-61, 169-70; interpretation of Sikhism, 161-64; fear of absorption by Hinduism, 164-67; charges of anti-Sikh discrimination, 167-69; organization and resources, 170-71; political methods, 172-73
Akbar, 156
Akbarabadi, Saeed Ahmad, 146-48
Akram Khan, 344
al-Azhar, 427
al-Ghazali, 396
al-Ikhwan al-Muslimun, 372
Al-jamiyat, 140
'Ala-ud-din Khilji, 359
Alam, Manzoor, 144
Ali Abdur-Raziq, 141
Ali Khan, Liaquat, *see* Liaquat Ali Khan
Ali Khan, Mir Ahmed, 116, 122, 130
Ali, Mohammed, 429, 440

Ali, Sadiq, 133
Aligarh Muslim University, 107, 146-47
All-Ceylon Buddhist Congress, 14, 473; founding of, 460-61; as political pressure group, 14, 460, 469, 475, 485; and Buddhist Committee of Inquiry, 461-62, 469; and Buddha Sasana Commission, 500, 503, 506; committee on Sangha, 509; and press nationalization, 526
Amanullah, King, 430
Amaradasa, K. G., 13, 457
Amarapura sect, 492, 500-01, 504, 507
Amarawansa, Akuratiye, 475
Ambalvi, Amar Singh, 150
Ambedkar, B. R., 135, 300; on relation of caste to Hinduism, 37-38; conversion to Buddhism, 37-38, 191-92, 195, 203-05, 211-12, 300; and Republican Party, 135, 207-08, 211-12; and Scheduled Castes Federation, 135, 192, 201, 204, 207; biographical sketch, 193, 195-96, 203; and separate electorates, 197-99, 202; and Independent Labor Party, 200-01; drafting of Constitution, 202; views on Marxism, 204, 209-10
Ames, Michael M., 37
Amir Ali, 34, 400, 405, 412
Anandrav Bhikaji Phadke v. Shankar Daji Charya, 282-83
Anglican Church, *see* Church of England
Angurbala v. Debabrata, 329
Anjuman-i-Taraqqi-Urdu, 106, 115-16
Anjuman Tahafuz-i-Urdu, 115
Annadurai, C. N., 222; founder of DMK, 223, 268; political methods of, 223-24, 226, 228; and dissension within DMK, 231-32
Ansari, Ghaus, 264
Ansari, M. A., 406, 430
Anthony, Frank, 110
Anwar, N. Mohammed, 119
Appadorai, A., 151
Appaya v. Padappa, 287
Arab League, 435-36, 445
Arabia, 348, 414, 421, 424, 429, 432
Arabs, 439-41, 443, 445, 447-48
Aramugha Konar v. Narayana Asari, 291
Arshad, Rehmatullah, 370

Index

artha, 5
Arunachellam v. Venkatachalapathi, 331
Arya Pratinidhi Sabha v. State of Bihar, 307
Arya Samaj, 7, 93-94, 127, 157-59, 296
Asgiriya chapter, 494, 500, 504, 510, 526, 543-44
Ashoka, 11, 535-37
Ashraf, 264
aslaf, 141
Aslam, Q. M., 406
Ataturk, 341
atma, 5, 300
Atmaram v. King-Emperor, 283, 292
Atre, P. K., 207
Aurangzeb, 54
Austin, G. A., 202
authoritarianism, 249-55, 261-62, 266-67, 269, 274-75; and education, 265-66, 271; and fatalism, 269-70
Awami League, 27
Ayodhya, 54, 61-62, 64, 72
Ayub Khan, Mohammad, 27, 339; interpretation of Islam, 32-33, 44-45, 342, 349-51, 362; and Muslim Family Laws Ordinance, 43, 364, 366, 413; and Pakistani nationalism, 44-45, 347; and 1962 Constitution, 27, 357; joins political party, 379; elected president, 380; on foreign policy, 432-33, 441, 445
Ayyar, A. S. Nataraja, 320
Azad, Abul Kalam, 94, 128, 138, 342, 429
Azad Hind, 140
Azeez, A. M. A., 459

Babar, 54, 62
Backward Classes, 115, 193, 207, 298, 301, 310. *See also* Scheduled Castes
Badeau, John S., 447
Badrudduja, Syed, 110
Baga Reddy, M., 115
Bagchi, S. C., 320
Baghdad Pact, 440-43
Bagyidaw, 14
Bahadur, Hafiz Ali, 105
Baig, Mirza Shukur, 109, 124
Baj, S. R., 332
Bakshi Ghulam Mohammed, 87
Balaji v. State of Mysore, 298, 302
Balakrishnan, P. K., 182
Balfour Declaration, 430
Baliga, B. S., 218
Bameswar v. Anath, 325

Bandaranaike - Chelvanayakam Pact, 514, 518
Bandaranaike, Felix R. D., 483
Bandaranaike, Sirimavo, 482; on nationalization of schools, 483; and 1960 elections, 505, 513, 520-21; on Buddhist reforms, 505-06; and Indo-Ceylon agreement, 528-29; and Buddhist resurgence, 529-30
Bandaranaike, S. W. R. D., 28; 1956 election, 39, 454, 470-72, 493-95; on non-alignment, 45; conversion to Buddhism, 456; formation of SLFP, 468, 491; relations with Buddharakkhita, 472-73, 491, 495, 497-99; promotion of Buddhism, 475, 477, 483, 500-01, 512; on language issue, 477-78, 516, 518; on school issue, 482, 486; assassination, 482, 499, 503, 505, 510, 517
Banerji, D. C., 85, 91
Banfield, Edward C., 406
Banias, 59, 229
Bansode, Kisan Fagoji, 194
Baradaeus, Jacob, 185
Barelwi school, 147
Barhai, 57
Baseer Khan, Abdul, 135
Basnayake, H. H., 527
Basnayake, Sinha, 477
Basu, Durga Das, 145, 311
Bauddha Jatika Balavegaya, 523, 526
Bauddhalokaya, 473
Bava, T. O., 111
Bawaria Sikh, 301, 303
Bello, Ahmadu, 445
Bhagaban v. Narayana, 325
Bhagavad Gita, 240-41, 258, 318
Bhagwan Koer v. Bose, 299
Bhaichand Tarachand Gandhi v. State of Bombay, 326
Bhairon Singh, 98
Bhaktavatsalam, 132
bhakti, 317
Bhalla, Balraj, 79-80
Bhandari, Sundar Singh, 93
Bharwad Kama v. Bai Mina, 304
Bhat, S. C., 331
Bhatia, Prem, 166
Bhau Ram v. Baij Nath, 304
Bhave, Vinoba, 34, 246
bhikkhus, see Sangha
Bhoodan, 242
Bhopal Singh v. State, 291
Bhupati Nath Smrititirtha v. Ram Lal Maitra, 316

Bihar Hindu Religious Trusts Act, 312
Binder, Leonard, 40, 371
Birdwood, Lord, 175
Board of Ta'limat-i-Islamia, 40
Bodhisatva, 212
Bohras, 120, 411
Bolitho, Hector, 401
Bombay Devadasis Protection Act, 324
Bombay Harijan Temple Entry Act, 326
Bombay Public Trusts Act, 312-13
Bondurant, Joan V., 237, 246
Bose, N. S., 340
Brahmins, 127, 136; as priests, 7, 38, 220, 257-58; relations with king, 8-9; anti-Brahmin movement in Madras, 37, 128, 213-25, 227-33, 267-68; anti-Brahmin movement in Maharashtra, 194; in U.P. politics, 56, 59; and RSS, 81; in Kerala politics, 177, 179, 187-88; superiority rejected by Buddhism, 204, 532; in Communist Party, 209, 225; legal caste rights, 283-84, 290, 292, 296; and religious endowments, 316-17, 320-21
Brass, Paul, 56
British rule, 22, 54, 339, 342; religious neutrality, 30, 144, 478; policy toward Sikhs, 158-61; and Syrian Christians, 187; and untouchables, 193-95, 197-99; and non-Brahmin movement, 214-16, 218-19, 223, 268; and legal system, 279-80, 282, 309; and Muslims, 373-74; decline of Buddhism, 453-54, 458, 461, 463-64, 470, 489-90, 508, 538-42; educational policy, 478-80
Brown, W. N., 448
Brownrigg, Robert, 538-39
Buddha, 203, 212, 457, 460, 474, 488, 538; doctrinal teachings, 10-12, 45, 464, 489, 507; and democracy, 35; blesses Ceylon, 457-58; legendary visits to Ceylon, 462, 490; in SLFP poster, 493; relations with kings, 532-33. *See also* Buddha Jayanti, Buddhism
Buddha Jayanti, 44, 457-60, 468-73, 491-92, 494
Buddha Sasana Commission: and reform of Buddhism, 31, 501-02, 512, 543, 545; appointment of, 477, 500; monks' opposition to, 477, 500-01, 503-07; and nationalization of schools, 481-82
Buddha Sasana Council, 466-67, 500, 502, 504

Buddharakkhita, Mapitigama, 29-30, 39, 468, 490-99, 507
Buddhism, 3, 9; Theravada, 7, 10, 12-15; Mahayana, 10, 12, 15; theory of history, 10-11, 462-63; tolerance, 11-12; ecclesiastical organization, 12-15, 29-30, 464-67, 474; ethics, 15; religious and political functions, 14-15; regulation of society, 15; reform of, 31, 500-09, 531-46; and democracy, 35; and socialism, 35-36; and Marxism, 35-36, 470, 524-28, 530; and politics in Ceylon, 43-44, 453-530; in Maharashtra, 191-212; in Burma, 10, 13-14, 453-55, 465-66, 501, 536; in Thailand, 10, 13-14, 465, 501, 536, 544; conversion to, 191-95, 200, 203-07, 209, 300-03, 310; as state religion, 456; decline under British, 463-67, 470; decline in India, 536. *See also* Sangha
Buddhist Committee of Inquiry, 469, 472, 477, 487; appointment of, 460-61; political significance of, 462, 510, 513; historical interpretations of, 462-64; and Buddhist reorganization, 464-66, 474, 500; and Catholicism, 466-67, 492; and nationalization of schools, 478
Buddhist Temporalities Ordinance, 464, 502, 542
Buddhist Theosophical Society, 479, 526
Buddhist Universities, 472, 475-77, 485
Bureau of National Reconstruction, 33, 413
Burhan, 143, 147
Burma, 10, 13-14, 453-55, 465-66, 501, 536

Cady, John F., 13
Caldwell, Robert, 221
caliph, 17-18, 34, 390, 435
Callard, Keith, 26, 431-34, 440, 445-47
Cambodia, 10, 501, 536, 544
Campbell-Johnson, Alan, 152-53
capitalism, 440
Carvaka, 238, 356
caste, relation to Hindu religion, 6, 9-10, 15, 34, 37-38, 196-200, 217, 219-22, 277-310; and politics, 36-38, 57-59, 61, 63, 65-66, 69, 71-73, 92, 128, 191-93, 195-210, 213-34; and Hindu law, 41, 277-310; and personal aspirations, 272-73; in Sangha, 543. *See also* Brahmins, Scheduled Castes, untouchability

Index

Caste Disabilities Removal Act, 286
Catholic Action, 467
Catholics, 29, 479, 481-85, 487, 493, 498, 511, 521, 523. *See also* Roman Catholic Church
Central Institute of Islamic Research, 32-33, 368-69, 413
Chacko, P. T., 182, 189
Chagla, M. C., 128, 147
Chamars, 57, 59, 285
Chanda Singh, 167
Chandragupta, 532
Chandran, J. R., 219, 225
Chandrasekhara Mudaliar v. Kulandaivelu Mudaliar, 299-300
Chathunni v. Appukuttan, 282
Chatterji, N. C., 74, 83, 85-88
Chatturbhuj Vithaldas Jasani v. Moreshwar Pareshram, 295
Chaudhuri, Nirad, 341-42
Chelvanayakam, S. J. V., 477, 518-19, 529
Chettiar, A. C., 221
Chetty, P. T., 214
China, 14, 141, 379, 433-34, 437
Chitpawan Brahmins, 81, 283
Chitralekha v. State of Mysore, 310
Christianity, 16-18; and ideology, 21; and fatalism, 256-60; conversion to, 300-03; influence on Hinduism, 317-18, 322-23, 326; influence in Ceylon. 453-54. *See also* Catholics, Christians, Protestants, Roman Catholic Church, Syrian Catholics, Syrian Christians
Christians, 16, 22, 25-26, 28-29, 60, 66, 480-81, 487-88
Christie, R., 262
Chungu Manjhi v. Bhabani Majhan, 299
Church of England, 185-86, 479, 541-42
Civil Procedure Code, 304, 328
Cohn, Bernard S., 59, 324
Colebrooke, 539
Comm. Hindu Rel. End., Madras v. Narasimham, 313
Comm. H.R.E. v. Sri Lakshmindra Thirtha Swamiar, Shirur, 331
Commonweal Party, 86, 225
communism, 21, 89-90, 120, 204, 209-10, 437, 440, 445, 471
Communist Party, 91, 101, 115, 171, 375, 392; in Faizabad constituency, 66-70; in Kerala, 114, 128, 180-81, 183-84, 187-89; and Muslims, 116, 120, 122-23, 127-28; opposed by Ambedkar, 209-10; and DMK, 225, 231; in Ceylon, 468, 497, 519, 521

Congress Party (Indian National Congress), 55, 58-61, 67-70, 237, 333, 434; and secularism, 24, 51-53; factionalism, 63, 65, 110-11, 134; and Jana Sangh, 78, 80, 84, 91, 95, 98, 101; and Muslim minority, 104, 109-10, 115-19, 122-26, 128, 130-32, 134, 138, 340-42, 373-74; and Sikh minority, 151, 163, 169, 172, 175; in Kerala politics, 178-84, 187, 189-90; and Buddhist minority, 192, 210; and untouchables, 195, 200, 293; and Dravidian movement, 213, 215-17, 225-29, 231-33, 267-68; and foreign policy, 428, 430, 432
Constitution of Ceylon, 455-56, 459, 466-67, 486
Constitution of India: uniform civil code, 145-46, 290; on untouchability, 289-92, 295, 298, 304, 309; on position of castes, 277-78, 280, 289-92, 295, 297-98, 301-02, 304-07, 309-10; on religious endowments, 311-12, 328, 332; on compensation, 486
Constitution of Pakistan, 352; Islamic Republic, 352, 360; repugnancy clause, 352, 378; and unity of Muslim countries, 353; and secular state, 352-54, 357; and governmental structure, 357, 360, 393; and Central Institute of Islamic Research, 364, 413; and Muslim Family Laws, 366; and freedom of association, 380
Coomaraswamy, Ananda K., 240
Cooray, T. B., 521
cow slaughter, 106, 121
Cripps, Stafford, 151, 444
Crooke, W., 8
Curran, J. A., 75
Curzon, Lord, 341

Dahanayake, Wijayananda: proposed Buddhist universities, 475, 485; opposed school nationalization, 483, 485; opposed no-contest agreement with Marxists, 497; as prime minister, 502, 510; and Sangha reforms, 504
Dandekar, R. N., 5
Darling, Malcolm L., 398, 410-11
Dar-ul Harb, 341
Dar-ul Islam, 341
Das Gupta, Surendranath, 238, 243
Das, Pitamber, 95
Datar, B. N., 302
Datta, Kalikinkar, 359

Index

Daultana, Mian Mumtaz, 347, 404
Davis, Kingsley, 166
Dawoodi Bohras, 411
Deepika, 186-87
De Lubac, Henri, 245
democracy, 139, 149, 236; and Christianity, 21, 33, 467; and Hinduism, 33-34, 236, 267; and Buddhism, 33, 35, 488; and Islam, 33-34, 139-41, 149, 400; and casteism, 92, 199; and one-party rule, 134; Ambedkar's ideas on, 199, 209; in Pakistan, 357, 413; in Ceylon, 453, 466-67, 488
Deo, P. K., 99
Deoki Nandan v. Murlidhar, 313, 326
Depressed Classes, 196-200, 214, 293. *See also* Backward Classes, Scheduled Castes
Derrett, J. D. M., 281, 290, 318-19, 323, 329-31, 334-35
Desai, A. R., 340
de Silva, C. P., 513, 528, 530
DeSilva, G. W. D., 508
de Silva, K. D., 524
devadasis, 324
Devanampiyatissa, 537
Devanandan, P. D., 216-18, 221-22
Devarajiah v. Padmanna, 292, 301
Devchand Totaram v. Ghaneshyam, 288
de Zoysa, Stanley, 498
Dhamma, 11, 204, 457, 464, 473-74, 533
Dhari, Alakh, 158
dharma, 5, 76, 242, 247, 317
Dharma Samaja Party, 510
dharmakarta, 321
dharmasastra, 280. *See also* Shastras
dhimmis, 392
Dias, N. Q., 473, 524
din, 148
Dini Ta 'limi Kaunsil, 143
Dipendra Nath v. State of Bihar, 307
divorce, 41, 130, 280, 364-65, 400, 413, 415, 420-23
Dogra, P. N., 79, 87, 89
Donoughmore reforms, 456
Dravida Kazagham (DK), founding of, 218, 267-68; rejection of Hinduism, 219-22, 227; and Hindi question, 222, 227; relations with Congress, 226-29, 231-33
Dravida Munnetra Kazhagam (DMK), 96, 110, 135; formation of, 222-23, 268; party organization, 223-24; political program and methods, 224-26, 268; in 1957 elections, 229, 231-32; in 1962 elections, 213, 232-33

Dravidasthan, 213, 218, 220, 222, 225, 228-29, 231-33
Dube, Yaduvendra Dutta, 98
Dulles, John Foster, 440, 442
Durand Line, 444
Durgah Committee Ajmer v. Syed Hussain Ali, 314, 330
Durgaprasada Rao v. Irulappa Konar, 299
Durgaprasda Rao v. Sundarsauaswaram, 303
Durlab Singh, 152
Dushkin, Lelah, 293

ecclesiastical courts, 500-01, 536, 544
education: and traditional attitudes, 256, 260-61, 265-66, 271-75; nationalization in Kerala, 187-89; and national integration, 406-07; nationalization in Ceylon, 454-55, 478-87, 511-12, 514-16, 520-22; Buddhist universities, 475-77
Egypt, 141, 149, 414-15, 424, 426-27, 429-30, 435, 439-43, 445
Eksath Bhikkhu Peramuna (EBP), 29, 500; formation of, 492; as political pressure group, 29, 39, 496, 499, 507; in 1956 elections, 39, 492-95; break with SLFP, 499; and Buddha Sasana Commission, 500, 503
elections (Ceylon): of 1947, 490-91; of 1956, 460, 467-72, 491; of 1960, 482-84, 504-05, 507, 510-17, 519-21; of 1965, 530
elections (India): of 1937, 201, 342-43, 374; of 1951-52, 55, 81-85, 225, 468, 491; of 1957, 61, 67-72, 90-95; of 1962, 25, 51, 57, 59-61, 68-72, 96-100, 109, 172, 212, 233, 268
Elenjimittam, Anthony, 75
Eliot, Charles, 155, 158
Erdman, Howard L., 110
excommunication, 120, 292, 304, 306, 324
Ezhavas, 37, 176, 178, 181-84, 190

Faizabad constituency, 25, 51-73
Faridi, A. J., 105
Farookhi, Abdul Latif, 114
Faruqi, Ziya-ul-Hasan, 35, 117, 147, 340
fatalism, 250-55, 274-75, 410-11; and religion, 256-60; and education, 260-61; and authoritarianism, 269-70; and occupation, 271-73
Fateh Singh, Sant, 170, 174-75
fatwahs, 32, 363

551

Index

Fazal Muhammad, 363
Fazul Haq, 74
Federal Party, 477, 517-19, 522-24, 529-30
Fielding-Hall, Harold, 489
fiqh, 414, 416, 424
Fisher, Margaret W., 237
Five Precepts, 15, 474, 493
Franda, Marcus F., 130
Freedom of Religion Act, 286
Frenkel-Brunswik, Else, 262

Gadipalli Paroyya v. Goyina Rajaryya, 303
Gaffar, H. R. Abdul, 131
Gaikwad of Baroda, 195-96
Gaikwad, Bhaurao, 196, 211
Gajanan Maharaj Sansthan v. Ramrao, 316
Gajendragadkar, J., 314
Galanter, Marc, 37
Ganatantra Parishad, 86, 99
Ganatantri Dal, 27
Gandhi, M. K., 53, 55, 202, 215, 225, 340, 434; uplift of untouchables, 37, 191, 198-99; assassination, 76; technique of action, 117, 236-40, 242, 523; religious nationalism, 344, 373; and Sarvodaya, 236-40, 242, 246-47
Gandhi, Phoolchand, 127
Gautama Dharmasutra, 9
Gavai, G. A., 195
Geiger, Wilhelm, 458
Ghalib, Shaikh, 112
Ghani Khan, Abdul, 109
Ghosh, Atulya, 130
Ghosh, D. P., 85, 91, 93
Ghulam Muhammed, 361, 363, 436-38, 440
Gibb, H. A. R., 16, 18, 399
Girijanund v. Sailajanund, 326
Gnanaseeha, Hempitigedara, 506
Gobind Singh, 156, 162
Godse, Nathuram, 76
Gokalp, Ziya, 141
Gokhale, B. G., 11
Golwalkar, M. S., 75; view on minorities, 75-76, 82; relations with Jana Sangh, 78, 80, 97
Goonesinghe, A. E., 493
Gonetilleke, Oliver, 488
Gopal v. Hanmant, 281
Gopal v. Subramania, 284
Gopallawa, William, 488
Gossamee v. Rumanlolljee, 319
Gould, Harold A., 59

Gour, Raj Bahadur, 127
Govinda Amrita v. Emperor, 286
Govinda Menon, Panambilli, 180, 187-88, 190
Govinda v. Shyama, 329
Gowda Saraswat Brahmins, 294, 305
Goyigamas, 500-01
Gracias, Cardinal, 485, 521
gramdan, 242
Gunawardena, Philip, leader of VLSSP, 468, 470; in Bandaranaike's coalition, 493; minister of agriculture, 496-97; on Marxism and Buddhism, 470; leader of the MEP, 484, 510, 513
Gupta, C. B., 63, 94
Gupta, H. R., 78
Gupta, Sisir K., 102-03, 444
Gurcharan Singh, 154
gurdwaras, 169-70, 173
Gurmukh Singh v. Union of India, 301, 303
Gurnam Singh, 163, 170
Guru Datt Singh, 51, 61-70, 72-73
Guru Estate v. Comm., I.T., Bihar and Orissa, 325-26
Guruge, Ananda W. P., 13, 457-58
Gurusami Nadar v. Krulappa Knoar, 303
Gwyer, Maurice, 151

Habib-ur-Rahman, 116
Hadibandhu v. Banamali, 292
hadith, 394
Hagen, Everett E., 249-50, 253, 266, 269, 274-75
Haja Sheriff, K. G. S., 113
Hakim, Khalifa Abdul, 35, 368
Halim Khan, Mohammed, 112
Hanafi law, 149, 386, 420, 422
Hansraj, Mahatma, 79
Harbans Singh, 161
Hardgrave, Robert L., 213
Hargovind Singh, 98
Harijans, 131, 135, 154, 168, 216, 300, 302. See also Scheduled Castes
Haroon v. Haji Adam, 288
Harrison, Selig S., 209, 216, 218, 223-25, 268, 440
Hasan, K. Sarwar, 432, 440-41
Hasan, Syed, 115, 121-22
Hasan, Syed Akhtar, 121-22
Hasanat, Abul, 402
Hashim, M. M., 113, 123-24
Hastings, James, 8, 17
Hayat Khan, Sikander, 431
Hedgewar, K. B., 75

Index

Hermanta K. Mukherjee v. Prafulla K. Bhattacharjee, 325
Hewavitarne, C. A., 460
Hindi, 82, 111, 154, 217-18, 222, 225, 227, 230, 268, 341
Hindi Raksha Samiti, 90, 93
Hindu Adoptions and Maintenance Act, 42, 290
Hindu Code Bill, 212, 290
Hindu Maha Mandal, 179, 183
Hindu Mahasabha, 7, 24, 41, 52, 68, 79; relations with Jana Sangh, 25, 74, 78, 83, 85-88, 91, 93, 96, 99; and Hindu Nation theory, 75, 100-01; and RSS, 76, 80
Hindu Marriage Act, 41, 290
Hindu Minority and Guardianship Act, 290
Hindu Rashtra theory, 24-25, 75
Hindu Religious Endowments Commission, 31, 38, 319, 327, 331
Hindu Succession Act, 42, 290, 314, 333-34
Hinduism, 3, 4, 61; theory of history, 4-6, 15-16, 238-43, 246-47; religious tolerance, 6, 12; sectarian divisions, 7, 230-31, 305-10; religious and political functions, 8-9, 14-15; social regulation, 9-10, 15; ecclesiastical organization, 15; reform of, 30-31, 311-36; and democracy, 34; and socialism, 34, 236-48; and caste, 6, 9-10, 15, 34, 37-38, 196-200, 217, 219-22, 277-310; mythology, 105, 144, 220-21; social ethics, 235-36; and Sikhism, 155-60, 164-69; and Sarvodaya, 236-48; and fatalism, 256-60; legal definition of, 299-303; concept of merit, 317-18; Hindu temples, 31, 105, 180, 182-83, 196-97, 283, 291, 294, 301, 306, 322, 324, 328, 332, 334-35, 354
Hoare, S., 198
Hourani, Albert, 387
Hukam Singh, 86, 159
Hume, David, 358
Husain, A. F. A., 409-10, 412
Husain, Nasir, 66, 69-70
Hussain, Mohammed Dawar, 109, 124
Hussain, Zakir, 132, 146

Ibn-i-Khaldun, 142
Ibn-i-Rushd, 141
Ibn-i-Sina, 142
Ibn Taymiyah, 396, 414
Ibn Tughluq, Muhammad, 359
Ibrahim, C. A. Mohammed, 131

Ibrahim, Hafiz Mohammed, 109-10, 128
Ihtisham-ul-Haq, 42
ijma, 399
ijtihad, 148, 399, 414
Imaduddin, 123
imams, 17, 33, 404, 407, 413
In re Kerala Education Bill, 307
In re Thomas, 302
Independent Labor Party, 192, 200-01
Inder Singh v. Sadhan Singh, 282
Indian National Congress, *see* Congress Party
Indonesia, 18, 441-42, 446, 448
Ingersoll, Robert, 217
Iqbal, Javid, 45, 342, 350
Iqbal, Muhammad, 350, 412, 427; and modernism, 400, 405; and Islamic socialism, 35; and Islamic state, 139, 358-59; and pan-Islamism, 430
Iqbal, Shaykh Muhammad, 376
Iran, 430-31, 435, 442, 445, 448
Irschick, Eugene F., 214-15
Isaacs, Harold R., 211
Islam, 3, 6; theory of history, 15-16; religious tolerance, 16-17; ecclesiastical organization, 17-18, 29-30; regulation of society, 17-20; reform of, 32; and democracy, 34; and socialism, 34-35; and fatalism, 256-60; in India, 102-49; and national integration in Pakistan, 339-51, 398-413; and state in Pakistan, 352-70; as interpreted by Mawdudi, 371-97; and Pakistan's foreign policy, 428-49. *See also* Islamic law
Islamabad, 350, 353-54
Islamic law, 15, 30, 300; nature of, 20; Family Laws Ordinance, 33, 42-43, 364-66, 369, 414-27; law of marriage, 43, 364-65, 415-20; law of divorce, 43, 364-65, 420-23; law of inheritance, 423-27; efforts to reform in India, 105, 116-17, 123, 130, 145-49; law of wakf, 132, 144-45. *See also shari'ah*
Islamic state, 40, 44, 409, 412, 446
Ismail, M. Mohammed, 108
Ismail, S. Mohammed, 108, 112

Jackson, J. Hampden, 245
Jacobites, 184-86, 188-89
Jaferbhay, Abid Ali, 128
Jagdev Singh v. Pratap Singh, 307
Jahiliyat, 383, 385
Jahoda, M., 262
Jainism, 6, 9, 157, 294, 300-01, 532

Jama'at-i-Islami, 106, 114, 357; in pre-partition India, 375; in independent India, 106, 114, 116-17, 120, 139; in Pakistan, 357, 362-63, 372, 375-81; organization of, 375-76, 390; on Islamic law, 116, 402; on non-Muslims, 392; and Communism, 120, 375; on 1956 Constitution, 378, 393; on separate electorates, 392; on secular state, 139; on Islamic state, 376-79; declared illegal, 362-63, 378-79; opposition to Ayub Khan, 379-80
Jami'at-al-Ulama-i-Hind, 116-17, 140, 146, 373
Jami'at-al-Ulama-i-Islam, 30, 40
Jami'at-al-Ulama-i-Pakistan, 40, 402
Jamshedji C. Tarachand v. Soonabai, 315
Jana Sangh, 7, 38, 51, 63, 110, 236; origins of, 59-61, 74-80; relations with RSS, 60-61, 75-78, 80-82, 85, 87-89, 93, 100; 1951-52 elections, 81-85; consolidation 1952-57, 85-90; merger efforts, 87-88; 1957 elections, 66-72, 90-95; relations with Swatantra Party, 95-96; 1962 elections, 25, 59-61, 66-72, 96-100, 268; relations with Republican Party, 210; prospects, 100-01
Jang, Safdar, 54
Janki v. Koshalvanandan, 329
Jasnani v. Emperor, 286
Jatika Vimukthi Peramuna, 520, 522, 528-29
Javitz, Senator, 108
Jayasinghe, Sirisoma, 503
Jayatillake, D. B., 460
Jayawardene, H. P., 498-99
Jayewardene, J. R., 483, 490-91
Jethabhai Narsey v. Chapsey Kooverji, 288
jihad, 403
Jinnah, Fatimah, 380
Jinnah, M. A., 40, 201; two-nation theory, 24, 26, 360-61, 398, 433; and partition, 222-23, 343-45, 412; death of, 346, 439; and modernist Islam, 349, 401; and liberalism, 26, 401, 406; on Palestine question, 430; and Afghanistan, 444
Jogendra Nath Das v. Charan Das, 321
Jogesh v. Sree Sree Dhakeswari, 325, 329
John, A. J., 187
Joint Political Congress, 178, 182, 187
Joshi, Jagannathanrao, 93

Joshi, S. M., 207
Judaism, 6, 16
Juma, 362-63
Jung, Mehdi Nawaz, 130
Justice Party, 211, 214-19, 222, 267

Kabir, Humayun, 128
Kabir, Jehangir, 115, 130
Kachochyi, Muzaffar Hussain, 135
Kadar, Salebhoy Abdul, 106, 131
Kahan Singh, Bhai, 158
Kalacherry, Mar James, 188
Kalugalla, P. B. G., 504
Kamaraj Nadar, K., 127, 213, 226-29, 232-33
kamma, 10, 462, 507
Kandyan Convention, 458-59, 463, 538-41
Kane, P. V., 317, 320
Kanji Gagji v. Ghikha Ganda, 304
kanuns, 360, 414
Kapur, J. L., 297
Kapur Singh, 155-56, 162
Karava, 501
karma, 5, 243, 259, 297
Kartar Singh, 164
Karunatilleke, Nimal, 497-98
Karve, Irawati, 262-64, 308
Karwadi v. Shambharkar, 300
Kashmir, 22, 45, 82, 86-89, 210, 346, 377, 434, 443, 446
Kashmiri, Shorish, 138
Katju, K. N., 98
Katyayana, 320
Kautilya, 323
Kayasthas, 59, 63, 127
Kazan Chand v. Emperor, 285-86
Kearny, Robert N., 456
Keer, Dhananjay, 199, 201-02
Kelaniya temple, 39, 490, 495-96
Keluskar, K. A., 203
Kerala Bhushanam, 186
Kerala Congress, 182, 189-90
Kerala Dhwani, 186
Kerala Prakasam, 186-87
Kerala Times, 187
Kesavan, C., 178, 182
Keshadhari Sikhs, 157, 161
Khadijah, 365
Khairmode, Cangdeo Bhavanrao, 196
Khaliquzzaman, Choudhury, 342, 430, 436, 438
Khalsa, 156, 162-63
Khan of Mamdot, 344
Kharat, Shankarrao, 200
Khatris, 59, 63

Khilafat movement, 340, 373, 429
Khizr Hyat Khan, 344
Khojas, 411
Khundmeri, Khatija Alam, 122
Khushwant Singh, 155-56, 158-60, 164-65, 167, 170
khutbas, 33
Kidwai, Rafi Ahmed, 128
Kikani, L. T., 286
Kisan Mazdoor Praja Party, 80, 86
Kotelawala, John, 456-58, 467, 493-94
Koya, Ummer, 120
Kripalani, J. B., 79-80, 96, 100
Kripalani, Sucheta, 94
Krishna Menon, V. K., 95-96
Krishna Pillai, N. K., 177
Krishnapal Singh, 80
Kshatriyas, 8, 155, 296-98, 532
Kudiarasu, 217
Kulkarni, M. G., 205
Kumaraswami v. Lakshamana, 329
Kunju, P. K., 178
Kuruppu, D. J. B., 484
Kutti Chami Moothan v. Rama Pattar, 284

Lambert, Richard D., 52, 212
Landau, Jacob M., 134
Lane-Poole, Stanley, 54
Lanka Bauddha Mandalaya, 458, 473
Lanka Sama Samaja Party (LSSP), 468, 484, 510; no-contest agreement with SLFP, 493, 497, 519; coalition with SLFP, 524; non-communal approach, 513, 515; platform in 1960 elections, 515-17; and school nationalization, 521-22; on Indo-Ceylon agreement, 529
Laos, 10, 501, 536, 544
La Ponce, J. A., 103
Latifi, Danial, 136
Laxmi Narasingha Swami Mahaprabhu v. Patta Sahuani, 331
Lebanon, 134, 431
Lenin, 244
Lerner, Daniel, 265
Levi, Werncr, 428-29
Levinson, Daniel J., 266
Levy, Reuben, 264
Lewis, Bernard, 140-41
Lewis, Oscar, 263
Liaquat Ali Khan, 40; leadership after Jinnah's death, 346; moved Objectives Resolution, 401-02; liberal nationalism, 406; on foreign policy, 434, 436

Lingayats, 7, 283
Lipset, Seymour M., 262
Livingston, Gordon, 200
Locke, John, 358
Lohia, Rammanohar, 96, 100, 207, 245, 268
Lubell, Samuel, 109

Ma'arif, 143
Macaulay, Thomas B., 406
Macauliffe, M., 159-60
MacDonald, Duncan B., 17
Madhok, Balraj, 74-75, 77, 79-80, 87, 93-95, 98-99
Madhavan, P. K., 182
Madhavrao Raghavendra v. Raghavendrarao, 324
Madina, 140
Madras Devadasis (Prevention of Dedication) Act, 324
Madras Hindu Religious Endowments Act, 312, 328
Madras Temple Entry Act, 305, 326
madrassahs, 40, 105, 354
Mahabodhi Society, 526
Mahagujarat Janata Parishad, 90
Mahajana Eksath Peramuna (MEP), 468-69; formed by Bandaranaike, 468, 470; in 1956 elections, 469, 471-72, 492, 495, 503; role of Marxists in coalition, 470-71; new group led by Gunawardena, 484, 510; in 1960 elections, 510-12, 515; opposition to press nationalization, 526; on state religion, 528; on Indo-Ceylon agreement, 529
mahants, 311, 323-24, 327, 329-32, 334
Mahant Ganeshgir Gosai v. Fatehchand Bania, 324
Mahant Kesho Das v. Amar Dasji, 330
Mahant Moti Das v. S. P. Sahi, 331
Mahant Narayan Dessjivaru v. State of Andhra, 312
Mahant Ram Saroop Dassji v. S. P. Sahi, 333
Maharajah of Kolhapur v. Sandaram Ayyar, 281, 293
Mahars, 191-95, 200-01, 203-09, 211, 283, 295
Mahavamsa, 457-58
Mahavir, Bhai, 79-80, 86
Maheshkar, D. R., 196
Mahmud, Syed, 128-29, 140
Maitra, Sushil Kumar, 235

Majeed, M. S. A., 113
Majid, S. M. Abdul, 110, 131-32
Majid, T. A., 128
Majlis-i-Tahqiqat-i-shara'iyah, 148
Majlis Ittihad-ul-Muslimin, 122-23
Majlis Tamir-i-Millat, 117
Majumdar, R. C., 359
Malabar Mail, 186-87
Malalasekera, G. P., 457, 459, 461, 506
Malayala Manorama, 177, 180, 186, 190
Malik, Hafeez, 340
Malkani, K. R., 77, 93
Mallick, A. R., 429
Malwatte chapter, 458, 475, 494, 500,
    504, 510, 525-26, 530, 543-44
Mangudkar, M. P., 203
Manjooran, Mathai, 187
Manohar Ganesh v. Lakhmiram, 326
Manu, 41, 217
Maqsood Ali Khan, 130
Mar Thoma Church, 184-86, 188-89
Maravars, 224, 283
Margoliouth, D. S., 17
Marriappa v. Vaithilinga, 285
Marriott, McKim, 309
Marthamma v. Munuswami, 299
Marwaris, 229-30
Marxism, 141, 468; and Islam, 16, 35,
    104-05, 120, 122; and Sarvodaya, 34,
    236-38, 241, 244-45, 247; and Bud-
    dhism, 35-36, 204, 470, 496-97, 515,
    517, 524-28, 530; and Catholicism,
    471, 484
Masani, M. R., 99-100
Mason, Philip, 405
Masuma Begum, 111, 130
maths, see mutts
Mathislagan, 226
Mathur, Jagdish Prasad, 93
matrilineal system, 176-77
Mawdudi, Abul 'Ala, 357, 369, 371;
    biographical sketch, 362, 372-81;
    ideology, 381-90; on Islamic state,
    390-93, 402; analysis of, 393-97
McCormack, William, 277
Mecca, 422, 440
Medina, 388, 394, 422
Mehta, Ashok, 208
Mehta, Satya, 153
Mendis, G. C., 462-63
Menzies, Archbishop, 185
Meshram, D. P., 207
Mettananda, L. H., 487, 491-93, 510,
    513, 526
Meynaud, Jean, 104
Michael v. Venkataswaran, 300, 302

Michael Pillai v. Barthe, 284
millat, 347, 358
Mills, Lennox, 539
mimamsa, 320
Mirza, Iskander, 362
missionaries, 479, 511, 535, 540-41
Mohanlal v. Habibullah, 316
Mohiuddin, Ahmed, 128
Mohiuddin, Maqdum, 122
Moinuddin, Khwaja M., 116
Moka Dora, 296-98
moksha, 5, 240, 243, 317
Momin Brotherhood, 115
monks, *see* Sangha
Montagu-Chelmsford Reforms, 195, 215
Mookerjee, Ashutosh, 74
Mookerjee, S. P., 74-75, 77-81, 83, 85-
    88, 91
Mooknayak, 196
Moon, Penderel, 152
Moplahs, 111, 136
morcha, 118, 173
Morgan, Kenneth W., 5, 11-12
Mossadeq, 440
Motamar Conference, 437
Moula Sahib, 112
mu'ahadah, 140
Mudaliar, A. Krishnaswamy, 86
Mughal Empire, 54, 142, 156, 341, 362
Muhammad, 16-17, 22, 105, 358-59, 364-
    65, 368, 381, 394-95, 398, 403
Mujeeb, M., 142-43
Mukherjea, B. K., 312, 314, 316, 318-
    19, 326, 329-30, 333
Mulla, Anand Narain, 116
Munasinha, J. C. W., 498
Mundassery, Joseph, 189
Munir, Muhammad, 361, 404
Munshi, K. M., 99
muqallad, 385
Muslim Brotherhood, 446
Muslim Family Laws Ordinance, 33,
    42-43, 366, 369; law of marriage, 43,
    364-65, 415-20; law of divorce, 43,
    364-65, 420-23; law of inheritance,
    423-27. *See also* Islamic law, *shari'ah*
Muslim law, *see* Islamic law
Muslim League, 40, 45, 52, 370; and
    Pakistan demand, 24, 35, 56, 138, 151-
    52, 218, 342-44, 359, 360, 374-75; in
    independent India, 25, 96, 105, 108,
    114, 119, 124, 128, 132, 135, 181, 184,
    201; and separate electorates, 26-27;
    and Islamic integration, 347-49; op-
    posed by Mawdudi, 374-76; and mod-
    ernist Islam, 400; and Ahmadis, 404-

05; and foreign policy, 428, 430-31, 433, 435-36, 439, 445
Muthuswami v. Masilamani, 288, 293, 303
mutts, 305, 316, 323-24, 328, 331, 334

N. D. Vaidya v. B. R. Ambedkar, 285
N. Ramaswami Mudaliar v. S. A. Aiyasami Chettiar, 316
Nadvi, Abul Hasan Ali, 106, 144
Naicker, E. V. Ramaswamy, 37, 215-16, 218-22, 226-28, 232-33, 267
Naidu, T. Varadarajulu, 214
Nain Sukh Das v. State of U. P., 291, 298
Nair, K. K. K., 62
Nair Service Society (NSS, 176-84, 189-90
Nairs, 37, 176-84, 186-87, 189-90, 283
Nakamura, Hajime, 12
Nanak, Guru, 155, 157, 162
Nanduri Yogananda v. Sri Agetheswaraswamivaru, 321
Nar Hari Shastri v. Shri Badrinath Temple Committee, 325
Narang, Gokul Chand, 155-56
Narasu, Laksman, 203
Narayan Bhagwantrao v. Gopal Vinayak, 313
Narayan, Jayaprakash, 37
Narayan, Shriman, 308
Narayana Pillai, T. K., 179-80, 187
Narayanan Seshacharyulu v. N. Venkatacharyulu, 325
Nasser, Jamal Abdul, 48, 441-43, 446
Natarajan, 226
Nathan, T. A. V., 215
National Christian Council, 485
National Democratic Party, 86, 88
National Education Commission, 29, 486-87
National Liberation Front, *see* Jatika Vimukthi Peramuna
nationalism: and Hinduism, 6, 24, 33, 340; and Sikhism, 163; and Buddhism, 33, 453, 458, 460, 462, 470, 473; and Islam, 33, 35, 340-42, 347, 374-75, 389, 408, 445; territorial nationalism, 26, 347, 447-48
Navalkar, H. N., 194
Nazimuddin, Khwaja, 344, 404, 439-40
Nedunchezhian, 226
Nehru, Jawaharlal, 24, 42, 48, 55-56, 74, 87, 89, 96, 141, 151, 202, 212, 340, 406, 429, 434, 441, 443
Neuberger, Senator, 108

neutralism, 440, 511
nibbana, 457, 477, 533
Nirvana, 489
Noon, Feroz Khan, 445
North, Frederick, 478, 480
Nuri, Mohammed Yasin, 128

Objectives Resolution, 402
Oke, V. R., 77-78
Olcott, Henry Steele, 466, 479, 541
Ottama, 489
Ottoman Empirc, 18, 142, 360, 414-15
Overstreet, Gene D., 209
Owaisi, Abdul Wahid, 123
Owaisi, Salahuddin, 122, 124, 130

Paddy Lands Act, 540
Padmanabhan, Mannath, 177; leader of NSS, 177-78; in nationalist struggle, 179; in struggle against Communist government, 181, 183, 189; and fall of Sankar government, 182
Pakhtoonistan movement, 444-45, 448
Pakistan National Congress, 27
Pakutharivu, 217
Pali, 206-07, 459, 475
pandas, 322, 325-26, 333
Panduram v. Biswambar, 304
Panikkar, K. M., 9, 277
pan-Islamism, 45, 48, 435, 438-39, 442, 446-47
Pannasekera, Kalukondayawe, 505-06
pansalas, 463
Pant, Pandit, 301
Panth, 153, 157, 161-64, 170-71
Papanek, Gustav F., 411-12
Park, Richard L., 52, 64
Parmanand, Bhai, 79
Parmeshwaran, C., 77
Parameswaran Nair, P. K., 178
Patel, Sardar, 169
Patimokka, 534-35
Patnaik, N., 325
Peiris, Edmund, 484
People's Democratic Front, 120-22
Perera, K. K. U., 498
Perera, L. S., 502
Perera, N. M., 516-17, 524
Philips, C. H., 37, 429
Pillai, Pattom Thanu, 179-82, 184, 187
pir, 410-11
pirivenas, 474-76, 485, 504
Political Parties Act, 27
polygamy, 41, 43, 106, 146, 148, 364-65, 400, 413, 415-20
Ponniah, S., 523

Index

Poona Pact, 199
Poplai, S. L., 96, 236
Powell-Price, J. C., 535
Poya days, 467, 474
Praja Parishad, 79, 87, 89
Praja Socialist Party, 66, 68, 86, 91, 96-97, 124, 178-79, 181, 187, 189, 233, 268
Prakash, Indra, 75, 88
Prasad, Bimla, 429
Prasad, Brij Nandan, 55, 71
Prasad, Rajendra, 212
Prayag v. Govindacharlu, 325
Press Commission, 524, 527
Preventive Detention Act, 108
Priyadatt Ram, 63, 65-67, 69-70, 72-73
proselytism, 6, 484
Protestant Reformation, 358
Protestants, 478-79, 481, 484
Proudhon, 245
Punjabi Suba movement, 90, 150-75
Punjabrao v. D. P. Mershram, 310
Puranas, 217, 222, 257, 281
purdah, 106, 130
purohita, 8-9
Pye, Lucian, 266

qaum, 347
Qayum Khan, 445
Qur'an, 16, 18, 20, 40, 256, 348, 353, 361, 394, 398, 409-10; laws repugnant to, 41, 352, 378; and family laws, 42-43, 145-49, 364-65, 400, 416-19, 421, 424-26; divine sovereignty, 358-59, 373, 381, 383-85, 387, 399, 401; and interest, 362, 367-68, 413; and criminal law, 363; concept of Islamic state, 390-91, 402; on unbelievers, 16-17, 403; concept of *ummah*, 406; teaching of, 407

Radhakrishma v. Radharamana, 325
Radhakrishnan, S., 5, 34
Radhaswami sect, 7
Radiance, 114, 136
Raghunath v. Javardhan, 288
Raghu Vira, 95, 99
Rahim, A. A., 111, 131
Rahman, Fazlur, 368-70, 413, 438
Rahman, Mohammed Abdur, 114, 121-22
Rahman, Mohammed Ataur, 125
Rahman, S. M. Fazlur, 118
Rahmatullah, S. M., 109, 112
Rahula, Walpola, 489
Rais Ahmad Khan, 446

Raja Bira Kishore Deb v. State of Orissa, 326
Rajagopalachari, C., chief minister of Madras, 215, 228; education policy, 217, 226; founder of Swatantra Party, 94; attitude toward Muslims, 127; relations with Jana Sangh, 99; relations with DMK, 232
rajakariya, 537, 539
Rajan, P. T., 218
Rajapakse, Lalita, 460
Rajaratne, K. M. P., 520, 522-23
Rajput, A. B., 435
Rajputs, 56, 58-59, 61, 69
Raju v. Adv.-Gen., 313
Raju, P. V. G., 127
Ram Brahma v. Kedar, 318
Ram Rajya Parishad, 68, 83, 85, 87-88, 91, 96, 99
Rama, 11, 54, 62, 220, 227
Rama Rao v. Board of Commissioners, H. R. E., 326
Ramadan, 132, 410
Ramakrishna Singh v. State of Mysore, 298
Ramakrishna Mission, 7
Raman, V. P., 226-27, 232
Ramanujacharyulu v. Panduranghacharyulu, 329
Ramanujan, S. G. Manavala, 221
Ramanya sect, 459, 492, 500-01, 504, 507
Ramaswamy Iyer, C. P., 188
Ramayana, 54, 220-21
Rameshwaranand, Swami, 38
Ramprapanna Ramanuj Das v. Sudarsan, 323
Ranadive, B. T., 209
Ranga, N. G., 99
Rangrao v. Gopal, 315
Ranjit Singh, 157
Rao, A. Rama, 95
Rao, D. N., 117
Rao, Narsing, 127
Rasheed, A. A., 118
Rasheeduddin Khan, 120, 127
Rashtriya Swayamsevak Sangh (RSS), 61-62; formation of, 52, 60, 75; ideology of, 75-76, 82, 101; constitution of, 76-77; link with Jana Sangh, 25, 60, 74, 78, 80-81, 87-89, 93, 100
Ratan Singh, 164
Ratansi D. Moraji v. Admr. General of Madras, 282, 299
Ratilal Panachand Gandhi v. State of Bombay, 328, 330

Index

Rattan Singh v. Devinder Singh, 300-01
Rattu, Nanak Chand, 200
Rau, P. Kameswara, 331-32
Ravanna Koovanna v. Vana Pana, 315
Ray, Verne, F., 309
Raychaudhuri, H. C., 359
Raza Khan, Mohammed, 103, 123
Reddi, Gopala, 127
Reddi, Subba, 127
religious neutrality, 160, 453, 455, 459-60, 463, 478, 480
Religious Trusts Bill, 312
Representation of the People Act, 109, 304-05
Republican Party, 68; founding of, 203, 207; and Buddhists of Maharashtra, 38, 192, 207-12; and Muslims of U.P., 135, 210; in 1962 election, 208; demand for Scheduled Caste privileges, 193
repugnancy clause, 352, 378
Revolutionary Socialist Party, 181
Reza Shah, 431
riba, 358, 362, 367-68
Ripon, Lord, 413
Rizvi, Syed Kasim, 123
Roman Catholic Church, 284, 406, 473; effective organization, 4, 466, 479; interaction with modern ideologies, 21, 33; and Marxism, 21, 470-71, 484, 510; political influence in Kerala, 185-87; and Communist government in Kerala, 180, 187-89; and Kerala Congress, 190; political influence in Ceylon, 28, 455, 471, 508, 519, 530; and school nationalization in Ceylon, 455, 479, 481-86, 514, 518, 521-22; criticized by Buddhist report, 466-67, 494
Round Table Conference, 198-99
Rudolph, Lloyd, 220, 228
Runchordas v. Parvatibai, 316
Ruskin, John, 238
Ryan, Bryce, 500

S. K. Wodeyar v. Ganapati, 283
Saddha Tissa, 489
sadhus, 7, 38. See also *sannyasis*
Sadogopachariar v. Rama Rao, 285
Sahajdhari Sikhs, 157, 161, 165
Saifuddin Saheb v. State of Bombay, 292, 306
St. Thomas, 184-86
Salagama caste, 501
Samadani (MLA), 146
Samartha, S. J., 5

Samin Khan, 447-48
Sampath, E. V. K., 217, 223, 225-26, 229-32
Sampurnanand, S. M., 63
Samyukta Dal, 89
Samyukta Maharashtra Samiti, 90, 92, 207-09
Samyukta Socialist Party, 208
Sanford, R. Nevitt, 262, 266
Sangannagonda v. Kallangonda, 290
Sangha: organization of, 11-13, 29-30, 35, 455, 513, 532-38, 543-45; political role, 7, 14-15, 29-30, 39-40, 468-69, 472, 477-78, 489-99, 525-30; reform of, 31-32, 455, 467, 500-10, 540-46; under British rule, 453-54, 538-42; and D. S. Senanayake, 456-57; and Buddha Jayanti, 458-59; and Buddhist Committee, 460-62; and Buddhist temporalities, 464-66, 540, 542; and Buddhist universities, 476-77; and schools, 479, 485, 515; and installation of governor general, 488
Sangha Sabhas, 491
Sanghar Umar v. State, 291, 305
Sangharaja, 13, 536
Sangharakshita, Bhikkhu, 509
Sanjiva Reddi, N., 108, 112, 122
Sanjivayya, D., 111
Sankar, R., 179, 181-84, 190
Sankaralinga Nadan v. Raja Rajeswara Dorai, 282, 292
sannyasis, 38-39, 216-17, 226, 243, 290, 315, 318, 323, 331
sanskaras, 41
Sanskrit, 257, 281, 315, 429
Sanskriti, 76, 79, 81
Sapta Koteshwar . . . Trust v. Ramchandra, 319
Saran, Shankar, 333
Saraswathi Ammal v. Rajagopal Ammal, 315
Sarkar, R. N., 332
Sarup Singh, 162-63
Sarvodaya, 34, 237, 240-42, 246-47
Sarwar, Muhammad, 372
sati, 30
satyagraha, 87-88, 90, 117, 193, 196-97, 202, 216, 469
Saudi Arabia. 440, 443
Savarkar, V. D., 24, 75
Sayeed, Khalid Bin, 340, 372, 407
Sayyads, 264
Scheduled Castes; in Pakistan, 26, 345; special benefits for, 59, 69, 295, 298; and Congress Party, 69-70; and Jana

Index

Sangh, 72-73; reservation of seats, 102, 295; in Maharashtra, 191-93, 206; Ambedkar's leadership, 196, 200-01, 211-12; conversion to Buddhism, 203-04; and Republican Party, 207-09, 211-12; and Hinduism, 298-302, 310

Scheduled Castes Federation, 135, 192, 201, 204, 207-09

Schuman, Robert, 342

secular state, 69; and religious reform, 31, 329; and national integration, 43; ideological commitment to, 52-53, 60; and Muslim minority, 102, 138-45, 147, 149; and recognition of caste, 310-11; in context of Pakistan, 352-53, 368-69; definition of, 355-58; in Ceylon, 455, 465

Seelawansa, Talpawila, 497, 507

Seethi Saheb, K. M., 105

Self-Respect Movement, 215, 217, 219

Sen, Asoke K., 118, 146

Senanayake, D. S., 455-57, 459, 477

Senanayake, Dudley, 457; and Buddha Jayanti, 458; in 1960 elections, 505, 513; as prime minister, 505, 517, 519, 530; relations with Federal Party, 517-18 520; opposed press nationalization, 526; on Indo-Ceylon agreement, 529; in 1965 elections, 530

Senanayake, F. R., 460

Senanayake, Maitripala, 473

Senanayake, R. G., 491, 507

separate electorates, and communalism, 23-24, 340; in Pakistan, 26-27, 392; abolished in India, 24, 108, 119, 134, 202, 291; demanded by Ambedkar, 197-99

Seshadri, G. S., 218

Shah Jehan Begum, 111

Shah Nawaz Khan, 128

Shamsuddin, Jukaku, 130, 132

Shanars, 283, 285

Shankaracarya, 320, 324

shari'ah, 130; scope of, 20, 142-43, 360, 388, 390, 395; opposition to reform of, 116, 130, 132-33, 146-48, 427; law of marriage, 148; criminal law, 363; interpretation of Akbarabadi, 146-48; interpretation of Mawdudi, 388, 390, 395. *See also* Islamic law, Muslim Family Laws Ordinance

Sharma, M. C., 78-80, 82, 88-89, 94

Shastras, 315. *See also dharmasastra*

Shastri, Lal Bahadur, 193, 528

Shastri, Prakash Vir, 94

shebait, 318-23, 325-27, 329-34

Sheo Shankar v. Emperor, 284

Sherwani, Haroon Khan, 125-26

Shi'as, 130, 132, 149, 264, 405, 412

Shils, Edward, 343

Shinde, V. R., 199, 203

Shiromani Gurdwara Parbandhak Committee, 170

Shivraj, N., 192

Short, Billy, 152

Shri Badrinath Temple Act, 312

Shri Jagannath Temple Act, 333

shura, 391

Shyamsunder v. Shankar Deo, 296

Siam sect, 30, 458, 461, 464, 475, 477, 492, 494, 500-01, 503-04, 507, 510, 526, 543-44

Siddiqui, Aslam, 434-35, 439, 445

Sidhrajbhai Sabbaj v. State of Gujerat, 307

Sikhism, 150, 154; origins and evolution, 155-64; unorthodoxy, 164-67; alleged discrimination against, 167-69; and Akali Dal, 169-75; and fatalism, 256-60; conversion to, 300-03

Singer, Milton, 230

Singh, Rana Jung Bahadur, 94

Singh Sabha movement, 158-60

Singleton-Salmon, R., 459

Sinhala Maha Sabha, 456

Siraat, 114, 136

Siriwardane, C. D. S., 487, 506, 509

Sixth Great Buddhist Council, 457

Sm. Raikishori Dassi v. Off. Trustee of W. Bengal, 334

Smith, Donald E., 14, 24, 53, 75, 102, 105, 134, 154, 193, 329, 355

Smith, Wilfred Cantwell, 15-16, 34, 104, 140, 143, 345, 436

Sobel, Irving, 53, 61

social contract theory, 545-46

socialism, 141; and Christianity, 21, 33; and Hinduism, 33-34, 236; and Buddhism, 33, 35-36; and Islam, 33-35, 141; and Independent Labor Party, 200; and DMK, 231; and Sarvodaya, 236-42, 246-47; concept of change, 236-42, 245-47. *See also* Marxism

Socialist Party, 79, 86, 96, 100, 207-208

Sohoni, Bapu Saheb, 89

Somar Puri v. Shyam Narain Gir, 323

Somarama, Talduwe, 499

Sontheimer, G. D., 319

Sorata, Weliwitiye, 475

Southborough Committee, 194-96

Index

Southeast Asia Treaty Organization (SEATO), 440
Soviet Union, 141, 217, 433-34, 441, 445, 459
Special Marriage Act, 299
Sree Kalimata Thakurani v. Jibandhan, 329
Sree Narayana Dharma Paripalana Yogam (SNDP), 176, 179, 182-84, 186-87, 190
Sree Narayana Guru, 182
Sree Sree Iswar Lakshi Durga v. Surendra, 325
Sri Jagannath Ramanuj Das v. State of Orissa, 331
Sri Lanka Freedom Party (SLFP): and Sinhalese Buddhist resurgence, 28; 1956 elections, 39, 468, 470-72; nationalization of schools, 482-86; role of Buddharakkhita, 491, 495, 497-99, 507; 1960 elections, 505, 510-13, 515, 518-21; coalition with LSSP, 524; 1965 elections, 530
Sri Lanka Maha Sangha Sabha, 491
Sri Sadasib Prakash Brahmacari v. State of Orissa, 331
Sri Seevali, Bambarande, 507
Sri Sumangala, Hikkaduwe, 475
Sri Sumangala, Pahamune, 489
Sri Venkataramana Devaru v. State of Mysore, 305, 326
Srinivas, M. N., 205
Srinivasan, Rao Bahadur R., 198
State of Bombay v. Narasu Appa Mali, 290
State of Jammu and Kashmir v. Jagar Nath, 298
State of Kerala v. Venkiteswara Prabhu, 294
State of Madras v. Champakam Dorairjan, 291
State v. Puranchand, 294, 301
State of Rajasthan v. Pratap Singh, 298, 305
subhavana, 297
Subrao v. Radha, 281
Sudhindra Thirtha Swamiar v. Comm., H. R. C. E., 331
Sudras, 41, 155, 281, 283-84, 290, 292-93
Suez Canal, 441-43
Suhrawardy, H. S., 27, 344, 348, 432, 441-42
Sukarno, 446
Sukumar Bose v. Abani Kumar Haldar, 334
Sunder, B. Sham, 116

Sunder Devi v. Jheboo Lal, 282
Sunnah, 41-43, 145, 147-49, 352, 363, 378, 387, 391, 399, 401-02, 413, 426
Sunnis, 130, 132, 149, 264, 403, 405, 412
Surendra v. Dandiswami, 324
Suri, Surinder, 98, 129
Suryabongse, Luang, 13
Swatantra Party, 80, 122; relations with Jana Sangh, 94-95, 99; in 1957 elections, 67-68; in 1962 elections, 96-99, 236; in by-elections, 100; and Muslims, 110, 122, 135; and Dravidian parties, 228, 232; and socialism, 236
Syed, J. W., 357, 359
Syria, 415, 429, 440
Syrian Catholics, 184-87, 189-90
Syrian Christians, 6, 176-78, 180-81, 183-90

taffaquh, 386
tafwid, 420
Tagore, Rabindranath, 412
Tahseel, Mohammed, 112, 122
Talaq, 420-21
Talbot, Phillips, 224
taluqdars, 55-56
Tamilnad Toilers Party, 86, 225
Tara Chand, 158
Tara Singh, 152-54, 161-63, 165-67, 170-71, 174-75
Tarjuman, 114
Tarjumanul-Qur'an, 374
Teja Singh, 158, 160-61
temple lands, 464, 479, 501, 510, 537, 539-42, 545
Temple of the Tooth, 459, 461, 470, 473, 538
Thailand, 10, 13-14, 465, 501, 536, 544
Thakur Mukundji Maharaj v. Goswami Persotam, 318
Thaliath, Joseph, 188
Thengadi, D. B., 93
theocracy, 9, 18, 339, 366, 438
Thiruvengadam, T. S., 219
Thittila, 11
Thomas, M. M., 219, 225
Thomas, Winburn T., 456
Three Refuges, 457, 489
Tilak, B. G., 340
Tilkayat Shri Govindlalji v. State of Rajasthan, 325
Tinker, Irene, 52, 64
totalitarianism, 390, 528
Travancore Legislative Reforms Act, 178
Tripitaka, 457, 459, 470, 473

Index

Trivedi, R. K., 117
Trivedi, Umashankar M., 85, 92, 98-99
Trotskyists, 525, 527, 529-30
Tulasiram Das v. Ramprasanna Das, 323
Tunisia, 415
Turkey, 18, 140-41, 341, 373, 414-15, 429-31, 442
two-nation theory, 24, 26-27, 360
Tyabji, Badruddin, 107

ulama: political influence, 7, 30, 40-41; as leaders of Islam, 18, 141-42, 396, 410, 414, 416, 427; and separate electorates, 26; opposition to reform, 33, 42-43, 132, 141-43, 147-48, 365-68, 399, 413, 419, 427; and Pakistani nationalism, 35, 400; in India, 117, 132, 141-43, 147-48; and Ahmadis, 364, 377, 403-04, 412; and Mawdudi, 385-86
Umar, 422
ummah, 358, 369, 406
Ummayyids, 142
Ummer Koya, P. P., 131
United Arab Republic, 446
United Monks Front, *see* Eksath Bhikkhu Peramuna
United National Party (UNP), 39, 453-54, 460, 473, 502, 508; under leadership of D. S. Senanayake, 456-57; and 1956 elections, 468-72, 491-94; and 1960 elections, 505, 507, 510, 513-15, 517-20; and school nationalization, 522; and attempted coup, 524; and press nationalization, 526; and Indo-Ceylon Agreement, 529; and 1965 elections, 530
United Nations, 433
United States, 434, 440-41, 443, 488, 520
Universities Commission, 476
untouchability, 72, 191-200, 203-04, 206, 212, 224, 283, 285, 290-95, 298, 304, 308-09
Untouchability Offenses Act, 291, 293-95, 304
Upadhyaya, Dindayal, 60, 80, 86, 90, 93, 96, 100
Upanishads, 9
Upoma Kuchain v. Bholaram, 282
Urdu, 106-07, 111-13, 115-16, 118, 121, 123, 125-27, 133, 136, 341, 373, 381, 410
Usmani, Shabbir Ahmad, 40-41, 402-03

V. Mahadeva v. Comm., H. R. E. Board, 335
V. Mariyappa v. B. K. Puttaramayya, 316
V. V. Giri v. D. Suri Dora, 296
Vaishnava sects, 7
Vajpayee, A. B., 89, 92-94, 98
Van Nieuwenhuijze, C. A. O., 18
Vanniyar, 225
Varma, Madan Mohan, 55, 63, 65-67, 69-71
varnas, 41, 281-83, 289-90, 292, 297, 308-09
Varnashrama Dharma, 214, 235, 242
Vedanta, 34
Vedas, 6, 8-9, 41, 194, 281, 288, 315, 319
Vellalas, 224, 283
Venkateswara Sarma v. S. N. Venkatesa Ayyar, 332
Venkatramayya v. Seshayya, 303
Venu, A. S., 220, 230
Verghese, T. M., 178
Verma, Vasdev, 161
Vidyalankara University, 475-76, 506, 508, 527, 529
Vidyarthi Parishad, 93
Vidyavaruthi v. Balusami, 330
Vidyodaya University, 475-77, 508, 527, 529
viharas, 13, 501, 537
Vihara Sasanarakshaka Societies, 474
viharadhipathis, 541-42
Vijaya, 459
Vijayavardhana, D. C., 35, 458, 501
Vikrama Das Mahant v. Daulat Ram Asthana, 329
Vimalananda, Tennakoon, 464, 487
Vinaya, 13, 476, 489, 503, 506-07, 509, 533-37, 544
Viplavakari Lanka Sama Samaja Party (VLSSP), 468, 470
Virendra, 167
Vittachi, Tarzie, 478
Voltaire, 358
von Furer-Haimendorf, C., 37
Vyas, Ram Kishore, 98

Wach, Joachim, 18
Wahhabi movement, 414
wakf, 106, 131-32, 144, 334
Wakf Act, 144
Walangkar, Gopal Baba, 194
Waliy Allah, Shah, 414
Weerawardana, I. D. S., 468, 470-71, 493

Weiner, Myron, 64, 74, 76, 88, 114, 136, 308
Wickremesinghe, Lakshman, 471
Wijewardene, D. C., 490-91
Wijewardene, Helena, 490
Wijewardene, Vimala, 478, 490-91, 495, 499
Wijewardene, Walter, 490
Williams, Roger, 358
Wilson, David, 281
Windmiller, Marshall, 209
World Fellowship of Buddhists, 204, 461
Wriggins, W. Howard, 28, 456, 468-69, 492-93, 496, 500
Wright, Theodore P., 103, 122, 125

Yagavkar, Gopal Swami, 193
Young Men's Buddhist Association, 460, 474, 506, 526
Yusuf, Abu, 148
Yusuf, Muhammad, 372

Zafrullah Khan, Muhammad, 403-04, 438
Zakaria, Rafiq, 131
zakat, 34, 106, 399
Zaman, Makhdoom Mohammad, 411
Zamindari Abolition and Land Reforms Bill, 58
zamindars, 55-56, 58, 108
Zaytunah, 427
Zelliot, Eleanor, 38
Zoroastrians, 6

ulama
imams
mawlanas
mullahs
pirs